Canadian Corporate Law

Cases, Notes & Materials

Third Edition

Canadian Corporate Law

Cases, Notes & Materials

Third Edition

Bruce Welling, B.Sc., LL.B., LL.M., Ph.D.
Professor of Law
University of Western Ontario

**Lionel Smith, B.Sc., LL.B., LL.M. (Cantab.),
D.Phil., M.A. (Oxon.) of the Alberta Bar**
James McGill Professor of Law
McGill University

**Leonard I. Rotman, B.A., LL.B., LL.M.,
S.J.D. of the Ontario Bar**
Professor of Law
University of Windsor

LexisNexis®
Butterworths

Canadian Corporate Law: Cases, Notes & Materials, 3rd edition
© LexisNexis Canada Inc. 2006
June 2006

Members of the LexisNexis Group Worldwide

Canada	LexisNexis Canada Inc., 123 Commerce Valley Drive East, Suite 700, MARKHAM, Ontario
Argentina	Abeledo Perrot, Jurisprudencia Argentina and Depalma, BUENOS AIRES
Australia	Butterworths, a Division of Reed International Books Australia Pty Ltd, CHATSWOOD, New South Wales
Austria	ARD Betriebsdienst and Verlag Orac, VIENNA
Chile	Publitecsa and Conosur Ltda, SANTIAGO DE CHILE
Czech Republic	Orac sro, PRAGUE
France	Éditions du Juris-Classeur SA, PARIS
Hong Kong	Butterworths Asia (Hong Kong), HONG KONG
Hungary	Hvg Orac, BUDAPEST
India	Butterworths India, NEW DELHI
Ireland	Butterworths (Ireland) Ltd, DUBLIN
Italy	Giuffré, MILAN
Malaysia	Malayan Law Journal Sdn Bhd, KUALA LUMPUR
New Zealand	Butterworths of New Zealand, WELLINGTON
Poland	Wydawnictwa Prawnicze PWN, WARSAW
Singapore	Butterworths Asia, SINGAPORE
South Africa	Butterworth Publishers (Pty) Ltd, DURBAN
Switzerland	Stämpfli Verlag AG, BERNE
United Kingdom	Butterworths Tolley, a Division of Reed Elsevier (UK), LONDON, WC2A
USA	LexisNexis, DAYTON, Ohio

Library and Archives Canada Cataloguing in Publication

Welling, Bruce, 1949-
      Canadian corporate law : cases, notes & materials / Bruce Welling,
Lionel Smith, Leonard I. Rotman. — 3rd ed.

Includes index.
ISBN 0-433-44591-2

      1. Corporation law — Canada — Cases. I. Smith, Lionel D.
II. Rotman, Leonard Ian III. Title.

KE1389.W45 2006   346.71'066   C2006-902628-9
KF1415.ZA2W45 2006

Printed and bound in Canada.

PREFACE

Our new edition continues the philosophy of the preceding ones, which is to provide a book that can be used in any Canadian jurisdiction for an English-language first course in corporate law.

One of the biggest changes in this edition is a new chapter on partnership law, courtesy of Len Rotman. We hope that this will make the book more useful for those who teach "Business Associations" rather than "Corporate Law" or "Company Law". Len has also added a new section at the end of Chapter 4, on Corporate Purpose, which presents different perspectives on the vocation of the business corporation.

Since our previous edition, probably the most important development from the courts was the Supreme Court of Canada's decision in *Peoples Department Stores Inc. v. Wise*. The Court disappointed many scholars by holding that corporate managers do not owe duties of loyalty to creditors of a corporation, whether it is in the vicinity of insolvency or not. This reaffirmation of basic principle was combined with a surprising holding, probably however confined to the civil law of Quebec, that those managers do owe their duties of care, diligence and skill directly to creditors. Just as did the fiduciary debate, this opens up potentially intractable questions as to how managers' liability would be apportioned as between creditor claimants and the corporation.

The resolution of the fiduciary debate seems set to allow us to move on to looking at the issues in ways that are more consistent with corporate law principles, and probably more productive of helpful solutions. For example, the "shareholder/stakeholder" debate is not necessarily one that should be fought out on the issue of to whom managers owe fiduciary duties. One of the main functions of the principle of corporate personality is to give a clear answer to the question of to whom such duties are owed; but the next question becomes, what factors may (or must) managers consider when they are deciding what is in the best interests of the corporation? And a further question, on which Canadian statutes invite debate and discretionary intervention: who should be allowed to take over the controls of a corporation for the purpose of enforcing duties that are owed to it? In most Canadian jurisdictions, these issues are overlaid by the amorphous oppression remedy, which potentially dispenses with traditional legal analysis in terms of rights and duties, and instead invites a discretionary curial supervision of the conduct of corporate affairs. This is an invitation that not all judges find easy to accept. The courts are bound to engage with these issues in the years to come, whether in the context of defensive tactics, under the rubric of corporate social responsibility, or simply where aggrieved creditors seek to hold managers accountable.

Len Rotman would like to thank his research student, Sheila O'Toole (Windsor Law '05) for her help, as well as the Law Foundation of Ontario for its financial assistance. Lionel Smith thanks Jayson Laplante for research assistance, funded by the James McGill Chair.

Lionel Smith
Montreal
May 2006

ACKNOWLEDGMENTS

A casebook on such a wide subject necessarily contains a great deal of reference to the work of others in the field, in the cases, the notes, the text, and especially in the selected readings. The authors and publishers of the following articles and textbooks have been most generous in giving permission for the reproduction in this text of work already in print. References, of course, appear where necessary and possible in the text. It is convenient for us to list below, for the assistance of the reader, the publishers and authors for whose courtesy we are most grateful. The following list is organized by publisher in alphabetical order:

Alberta Law Review and R.W. Ewasiuk
Ewasiuk, "The Business Corporations Act — the Distinction Between Bylaws and Articles of Association", Alberta Law Review, 21 Alta. L.R. 381, 1983. Reprinted with permission.

Cambridge Law Journal and L.S. Sealy
Sealy, "Fiduciary Relationships", [1962] Camb. L.J. 69. Reprinted with permission.

Carswell, a division of Thomson Canada Ltd.
Gillen, Mark R., *Securities Regulation in Canada* (Toronto: Carswell, 1992). Reprinted by permission of Carswell, a division of Thomson Canada Ltd.

Rotman, Leonard I., *Fiduciary Law* (Toronto: Carswell, 2005). Reprinted by permission of Carswell, a division of Thomson Canada Ltd.

Harvard Business School Publishing
Mace, Myles L., *Directors: Myth and Reality* (Boston: Division of Research, Harvard Business School, 1971), pp. 184 ff. Reproduced with permission.

Sweet & Maxwell Limited and D.D. Prentice and J. Payne
D.D. Prentice and J. Payne, "The Corporate Opportunity Doctrine" (2004), 120 Law Q. Rev. 198-202. Reproduced with permission.

Welling, Bruce
Corporate Law in Canada: The Governing Principles, 3rd edition (Scribblers Publishing, 2006). Reproduced with permission.

ABOUT THE AUTHORS

Bruce Welling, B.Sc. (R.M.C.), LL.B. (Western), LL.M. (London), Ph.D. (Bond). Professor Welling conducts classes in Corporate Law and Property at Western Law School, serves as Counsel to Anissimoff Professional Corporation, a London Patent Firm, and is a member of the National Academy of Arbitrators. He is the author of *Corporate Law in Canada: The Governing Principles*, 3rd ed. (Scribblers Publishing, 2006) and *Property in Things in the Common Law System* (Scribblers Publishing, 1996).

Lionel D. Smith, B.Sc., LL.B., LL.M. (Cantab.), D. Phil., M.A. (Oxon.), James McGill Professor of Law, McGill University, of the Bar of Alberta. Professor Smith taught law at the University of Alberta and Oxford University before joining McGill University in 2000. He was appointed James McGill Professor of Law in 2004. His research interests are in trusts, unjust enrichment, comparative law, and company and commercial law. He is the author of *The Law of Tracing* (Oxford University Press, 1997) and a contributor to *English Private Law* (Oxford University Press, 2000), *Waters' Law of Trusts in Canada*, 3rd ed. (Thomson/ Carswell, 2005) and *Commercial Trusts in European Private Law* (Cambridge University Press, 2005).

Leonard I. Rotman, B.A. (Toronto) ("With Distinction"), LL.B. (Queen's), LL.M. (Osgoode), S.J.D. (Toronto) of the Ontario Bar, formerly of the Faculty of Law, University of Alberta. In addition to his work in Corporate Law, Dr. Rotman teaches and writes in the areas of Aboriginal Law, Constitutional Law, Fiduciary Law and Trusts. He is the author of *Fiduciary Law* (Thomson/Carswell, 2005), *Aboriginal Legal Issues: Cases, Materials & Commentary*, 2nd ed. (LexisNexis/ Butterworths, 2003), *Parallel Paths: Fiduciary Doctrine and the Crown-Native Relationship in Canada* (University of Toronto Press, 1996), a contributor to M.R. Gillen and F. Woodman, eds., *The Law of Trusts: A Contextual Approach* (Emond Montgomery, 2000), and the author of numerous law review articles. His work has been cited by domestic and international commissions and courts.

TABLE OF CONTENTS

TABLE OF CASES

[A page number in boldface type indicates that a case has been excerpted in the text]

TABLE OF ABBREVIATIONS

Abbreviations for the federal and provincial company legislation are frequent and are listed as follows:

A.B.C.A.	Alberta Business Corporations Act, R.S.A. 2000, c. B-9
B.C.B.C.A.	British Columbia Business Corporations Act, S.B.C. 2002, c. 57
C.B.C.A.	Canada Business Corporations Act, R.S.C. 1985, c. C-44
M.C.A.	Manitoba Corporations Act, R.S.M. 1987, c. C225
N.L.C.A.	Newfoundland and Labrador Corporations Act, R.S.N. 1990, c. C-36
N.B.B.C.A.	New Brunswick Business Corporations Act, S.N.B. 1981, c. B-9.1
N.S.C.A.	Nova Scotia Companies Act, R.S.N.S. 1989, c. 81
O.B.C.A.	Ontario Business Corporations Act, R.S.O. 1990, c. B.16
P.E.I.C.A.	Prince Edward Island Companies Act, R.S.P.E.I. 1988, c. C-14
Q.C.A.	Quebec Companies Act, R.S.Q. 1977, c. C-38
S.B.C.A.	Saskatchewan Business Corporations Act, R.S.S. 1978, c. B-10
Y.B.C.A.	Yukon Business Corporations Act, R.S.Y. 2002, c. 20

CHAPTER 1

PARTNERSHIPS

A. INTRODUCTION

Partnerships are regulated by statute in all provincial and territorial jurisdictions in Canada (there is no such thing as a federal partnership). An organized partnership is usually governed by a written agreement, which establishes how the partners will manage the business and resolve disputes, how new partners can join, how income will be divided, and how a partner's share of partnership property is calculated if that partner wants to leave. Partnerships legislation serves as a default set of rules for many of these considerations where a partnership agreement does not exist or where such an agreement exists, but is silent on the matter in question.

This chapter aims to provide an overview of some of the fundamental issues pertaining to partnerships. More detailed considerations may be found in provincial partnerships legislation.

B. WHEN DOES A PARTNERSHIP EXIST?

As stated in the introduction to the casebook, a partnership is a legal institution which arises where two or more persons carry on a business together with a view to a profit. Under the civil law of Quebec, however, this definition is somewhat different: see *Civil Code of Quebec*, S.Q. 1991, c. 64, art. 2186.

Each of the phrases "carrying on a business", "in common" and "with a view to a profit" have particular meanings when used in the context of partnerships.

A "business", as defined in section 1(1) of the Ontario *Partnerships Act*, R.S.O. 1990, c. P.5, includes "every trade, occupation and profession".

"With a view to a profit" does not require that a profit must be made by the partnership business, but, rather, that reasonable attempts are made to have the partnership business be profitable. In *Continental Bank Leasing Corp. v. Canada*, [1998] S.C.J. No. 63, [1998] 2 S.C.R. 298, subsequently affirmed in *Backman v. The Queen*, [2001] S.C.J. No. 12, [2001] 1 S.C.R. 367 and *Spire Freezers Ltd. v. Canada*, [2001] S.C.J. No. 11, [2001] 1 S.C.R. 391, the Supreme Court of Canada affirmed that investors must have a "view to a profit" for a partnership to come into being. The idea of a "view to a profit" is to be contrasted with undertakings designed for charitable, social, or cultural purposes, which are not carried on with a view to a profit.

The phrase "in common" is the most difficult of these terms to define with any degree of precision. It contemplates that the parties are acting in concert based on some agreement between them (whether express, implied, or otherwise presumed from their conduct). The majority of cases involving the determination of whether a partnership exists revolve around the interpretation of this latter phrase, as, for example, in the following case.

A.E. LePAGE LTD. v. KAMEX DEVELOPMENTS LTD.

(1977), 78 D.L.R. (3d) 223, 16 O.R. (2d) 193 (C.A.), aff'd [1979] 2 S.C.R. 155

The judgment of the Court was delivered orally by

Blair J.A.: — This is an appeal from a judgment of Madam Justice Van Camp in which she allowed the claim of the respondent, a real estate agent, for commission under an exclusive listing agreement. During the term of the exclusive listing agreement the property, a large apartment building, was sold through another agent and the amount of the commission claimed was $45,000. Judgment was given against the appellants but not against the corporate defendant, Kamex Developments Limited. The question in this case is whether the appellants constituted a partnership and, if so, whether the defendant March signed the listing agreement as a partner binding the partnership.

The appellants purchased the property in question in 1970, under the name of one of them, "M. Kalmykow in trust". The defendant corporation was then incorporated to hold the property in trust for the appellants. It executed a declaration of trust and concurrently entered into a written agreement with them.

The agreement specified that the property was to be held by the defendant corporation in trust for the appellants in proportion to their interests as set forth therein. It provided that revenues and profits from the property should be paid to them in proportion to their interests and that they should be liable to pay any deficiency to the corporation in the same proportions. It provided for the sale or transfer of the interests of the appellants in the property to third parties after the other appellants named in the agreement had been given a first opportunity of refusal. The agreement also provided that any decision "regarding the sale or other dealings with the said apartment building" was to be made by a majority vote defined as the majority of the interests in the property of the appellants. The evidence disclosed that the appellants met monthly in order to discuss the operation of the property and also the possibility of its sale.

At some stage the property was listed for sale by what is called an open listing. A decision was taken by the appellants as a group that there should be no exclusive listing. Employees of the respondent approached March, one of the appellants, and as a result he executed the exclusive listing agreement. The learned trial Judge found that he signed this agreement on behalf of all the other appellants, and that he was understood to have done so by the employees of the respondent. She also found that he was not authorized by the appellants to sign the exclusive listing agreement and his act had not been approved by them.

Many issues were raised in the course of this argument but because of the nature of the pleadings it is unnecessary to refer to all of them. The respondent's statement of claim alleged:

> On October 6, 1972, the Plaintiff entered into a written agreement (hereinafter referred to as "The Listing Agreement") with the Defendant, March. At the time of execution of the Listing Agreement, the Plaintiff was advised by March that he was a member of the partnership and had authority to enter into the Listing Agreement on behalf of the partnership. It was a term of the Listing Agreement that such Exclusive Authority was to be irrevocable until one minute before midnight on November 30, 1972.

This pleading confines the respondent to an assertion that it dealt with the appellant March as a representative of a partnership. Hence, the prime issue in this appeal is whether or not the appellants were a partnership. This involves an answer to the elementary question of whether the appellants as co- owners of the property thereby became partners.

A partnership is defined in the *Partnerships Act*, R.S.O. 1970, c. 339, s. 2, as follows:

> 2. Partnership is the relation that subsists between persons carrying on a business in common with a view to profit, but the relation between the members of a company or association that is incorporated by or under the authority of any special or general Act in force in Ontario or elsewhere, or registered as a corporation under any such Act, is not a partnership within the meaning of this Act.

The key words of the definition refer to "persons carrying on a business in common with a view to profit". The mere fact that property is owned in common and that profits are derived therefrom does not of itself constitute the co- owners as partners. Section 3, para. 1 of the *Partnerships Act* reads as follows:

> 3. In determining whether a partnership does or does not exist, regard shall be had to the following rules:
>
> 1. Joint tenancy, tenancy in common, joint property, common property, or part ownership does not of itself create a partnership as to anything so held or owned, whether the tenants or owners do or do not share any profits made by the use thereof.

Whether or not the position of co-owners becomes that of partners depends on their intention as disclosed by all the facts of the case. It is necessary to determine whether the intention of the co-owners was to "carry on a business" or simply to provide by an agreement for the regulation of their rights and obligations as co-owners of a property. The test was stated by Roach, J.A., in *Thrush v. Read*, [1950] O.R. 276 at p. 279, [1950] 2 D.L.R. 392 at p. 396, as whether:

> ... on a true construction of the agreement, and having regard to all the circumstances, it should be held that the parties to that agreement intended to become, and thereby became, partners in a joint venture and that therefore they were not merely co-owners of the common property.

At p. 280 O.R., p. 396 D.L.R., he said:

> In addition to the joint ownership created by the agreement, it becomes necessary therefore to find within that agreement an intention on the part of the parties thereto to carry on a business in common with a view of profit.

In that case it was clear that the purpose of a mining syndicate was not simply to hold claims as co-owners but to carry on the business of dealing in mining claims, rights and privileges and turn the same to account. There is no such intention to carry on a business in this case.

This case is comparable to *Robert Porter & Sons Ltd. v. Armstrong et al.*, [1926] S.C.R. 328, [1926] 2 D.L.R. 340, where on facts not too dissimilar from the present case, it was held that the co-owners of property were not partners. There Duff, J., dealt with the fundamental distinction between partnership and co-ownership at p. 330 S.C.R., p. 342 D.L.R.:

> The real question is whether, from the evidence before us, one ought to infer an agreement in the juridical sense that the property these two persons intended dealing with was to be held jointly as partnership property, and sold as such. Is this what they contemplated? Had they in their minds a binding agreement which would

disable either of them from dealing with his share — that is to say, with his share in the land itself — as his own separate property? A common intention that each should be at liberty to deal with his undivided interest in the land as his own would obviously be incompatible with an intention that both should be bound to treat the corpus as the joint property, the property of a partnership. English law does not regard a partnership as a persona in the legal sense. Nevertheless, the property of the partnership is not divisible among the partners in specie. The partner's right is a right to a division of profits according to the special arrangement, and as regards the corpus, to a sale and division of the proceeds on dissolution after the discharge of liabilities. This right, a partner may assign, but he cannot transfer to another an undivided interest in the partnership property in specie.

The learned trial Judge considered that the intention of the co-owners to purchase the building, hold it as an investment and sell it for profit constituted them as partners in a business carried on for profit. With respect, I am of the opinion that the mere fact that co-owners intend to acquire, hold and sell a building for profit does not make them partners. As Duff, J., said in *Porter v. Armstrong*, at p. 329 S.C.R., p. 341 D.L.R.:

> Foster and Miller unquestionably intended to buy the property, to sell it again at an enhanced price, and thereby to make profit. Indeed, the sole object of purchasing the land was to dispose of it profitably. No doubt they intended to share the outlay equally between them. As regards the purchase money, the law would, of course, give to either of them a right of contribution against the other for any payment on the joint debt in excess of his own proper share, and on a sale, each would be entitled to share in the price according to his interest. The inevitable result, if the property was held in common and sold, would be that, as between Foster and Miller themselves, the right to share in the profits and the legal responsibility for losses would be equally distributed. But these consequences all flow from the fact that these two persons were jointly responsible for the purchase money, and that each was entitled to an undivided moiety in the equitable estate vested in them, as the result of the contract of purchase.

In this case the intention of the parties to maintain their rights as co-owners of the property is clear beyond doubt from the documents. In addition, it should be noted that the appellants wished to identify and keep separate their respective beneficial interests in the property for income tax purposes. Their intention would have been defeated if they were regarded as a partnership and the apartment building had become the property of the partnership. The fact that they are obliged by their agreement to offer a right of first refusal to the other co-owners in the event of sale is not inconsistent with their basic right to deal with their respective interests in the property.

The claim against the appellants as partners must fail because no partnership existed and the subsidiary question whether March's signature bound them as partners does not arise. The question remains whether the defendant March, one of the co-owners, who signed a listing agreement incurred personal liability thereby. Since he signed as an agent to the knowledge of the employees of the respondent with whom he dealt, he is not personally liable: *Bowstead On Agency*, 12th ed. p. 258. The question whether any claim might be made against him for breach of warranty of authority did not arise because it had not been pleaded.

The appeal will be allowed with costs and the judgment below varied to dismiss the action against the appellants with costs. The cross-appeal will be dismissed without costs.

Appeal allowed.

NOTES

1. The problem in *Kamex* was not with the manner in which the appellants had organized their business activity, which was a legitimate exercise, but the way the respondent agent framed his claim. By resting his claim exclusively upon the existence of a partnership and March's ability to bind it, the agent ignored the fact that not all cooperative business ventures where profits are shared are partnerships. As expressly indicated in the Court of Appeal's judgment, the agent could have also claimed against March personally, such as by claiming breach of warranty of authority, but did not do so.

2. In *Lansing Building Supply (Ontario) Ltd. v. Ierullo* (1989), 71 O.R. (2d) 173 (Dist. Ct.), a case with similar facts to *Kamex*, three individuals and three corporations controlled by them held a property in common (through the three corporate vehicles) which they intended to develop and sell as condominiums. The co-ownership agreement between the individuals and the corporations indicated an absence of intention to enter into a partnership regarding the venture in question. However, one of the defendants ordered building supplies from the plaintiff and characterized the venture as a partnership between himself and the other two individual defendants. The plaintiff sued all of the individual defendants for money owed for the building supplies, alleging that they were partners in a partnership. In distinguishing *Kamex* and finding that a partnership did exist, Murphy D.C.J. held that the terms of the co-ownership agreement contained many of the attributes of a partnership and that the parties' conduct was consistent with those of partners in a partnership.

Another case that considered the relationship between entities that were engaged cooperatively in the ownership of real property with a view to a profit, but whose result differed from that in *Kamex*, is *Volzke Construction Ltd. v. Westlock Foods Ltd.*

VOLZKE CONSTRUCTION LTD. v. WESTLOCK FOODS LTD.

[1986] A.J. No. 424, 45 Alta. L.R. (2d) 97 (C.A.)

Moir J.A. (for the Court, allowing the appeal): — The appellant is a general contractor doing business in Northern Alberta with its headquarters in the Town of Westlock. As general contractor it undertook to build in two phases an addition to the Westlock Shopping Centre. It was not paid its final billing. It accordingly sued the respondent company alleging that the respondent was in partnership with another limited company Bonel Properties Ltd. and was liable for the debt.

...

The respondent had the I.G.A. franchise in the Town of Westlock. Bonel Properties Ltd. approached Horne & Pitfield, the franchisee, to take space in the expanded Westlock Shopping Centre which was to be built on to an existing mall. They were told to get in touch with David Shefsky, who was the main shareholder in the respondent Company.

Mr. Shefsky was not content to be a tenant. He wanted to be an owner. As a result he made an offer to Bonel Properties Ltd. for a 20 per cent interest in the Westlock Shopping Centre. He agreed and did pay $32,000.00 for this interest. This is clearly shown in Exhibit 10. The opening paragraph is:

> "This will confirm that Dave Shefsky is prepared to purchase an undivided twenty (20%) per cent interest of the Westlock Shopping Centre at and for a consideration of thirty two thousand ($32,000.00) dollars."

The letter closed as follows:

> "Dave Shefsky is signing this agreement as an indication of his intent to complete the purchase of an undivided twenty (20%) per cent interest in the property as at June 15, 1977."

This offer was dated June 7, 1977 and was accepted on the same letter agreement on June 8, 1977.

The plans for the expansion of the Westlock Shopping Centre had been prepared. Tenders were called for. However, Volzke went to Dave Shefsky and asked about obtaining the construction job. He was told by Shefsky that the contract would go out for tender but that Shefsky would introduce Volzke to his partners. He did so. When the tenders came in they were too high. Bonel Properties Ltd. discharged the architect. Volzke made certain suggestions to save costs. The contract was awarded to him on the basis of cost plus $30,000.00 on each of the two phases of the new construction. This led to the finding that the amount owing was $76,928.88. That finding is not challenged in this appeal.

A bank account, with printed cheques, was opened in the name of Bonel Properties Ltd. and Westlock Foods Ltd. Only the principals of Bonel Properties Ltd. had signing authority. All accounts were submitted to Bonel Properties Ltd. Each of Volzke's accounts was paid as rendered up to December 22, 1978. On that date Dave Shefsky died. The final account rendered after that date remained unpaid.

After Dave Shefsky's death Mrs. Shefsky carried on. She was refused signing authority on the bank account. She sent prospective tenants to Bonel Properties Ltd. Bonel Properties Ltd. negotiated all leases. Tenants made complaints re repairs etc. to the manager of Westlock Foods Ltd. store. Bonel Properties Ltd. arranged to complete the repairs and maintenance and paid the bills on the printed cheques of Bonel Properties Ltd. and Westlock Foods Ltd.

The interim financing of the additions to the Westlock Shopping Centre were arranged through the Treasury Branch. Both Bonel Properties Ltd. and Westlock Foods Ltd. executed the debenture in March of 1978. They were jointly and severally liable. Later a mortgage was placed with Investor's Syndicate which was signed by both companies, Bonel Properties Ltd. as to 80 per cent and the respondent as to 20 per cent.

Unhappy differences soon arose between Bonel Properties Ltd. and Westlock Foods Ltd. Apparently Westlock Foods Ltd. as a tenant wanted things that Bonel Properties Ltd. as landlord did not want to give them. Disputes arose. Also the bank account did not provide for Westlock Foods Ltd. management as signing authorities. The title to the land on which the I.G.A. Store sat was transferred to show 80-20 ownership but title to the original Westlock Shopping Centre and the parking lot and the land on which phase 2 of the shopping centre was built remained in the name of Bonel Properties Ltd. only.

Westlock Foods Ltd. started an action against Bonel Properties Ltd. They filed affidavits. The learned chambers judge held that there was either a partnership or joint venture between the parties. He gave to Westlock Foods Ltd. an interest in the entire operation, including the parking lot. He acted upon the affidavit of Mrs. Shefsky. When the matter went before the master to do an accounting Mrs. Shefsky filed a further affidavit outlining her activities in aiding the business in its operation. This affidavit was put to Mrs. Shefsky in cross-examination and entered as an exhibit. It showed activities entirely consistent with the partnership.

In this case the learned trial judge examined the cases submitted by the appellant's counsel and extracts from *Lindlay, on Partnership* presented by respondent's counsel. He reached the conclusion he did by finding that there was no intention to enter into a partnership and that as Westlock Foods Ltd. had no control over the business it could not be a partnership. In this we are of the view that he erred in law.

In our respectful opinion we think the learned trial judge should have proceeded by looking at the *Partnership Act*, R.S.A. 1980, c. P.2. Partnership is defined in that Act as follows:

"1. In this Act,

...

(d) 'partnership' means the relationship that subsists between persons carrying on a business in common with a view to profit;"

Nothing is said in the definition about control. We know that you can have silent partners or managing partners. Control has nothing whatever to do with the existence or non-existence of a partnership.

Secondly, there is no doubt that everyone agrees that the parties agreed that they would share the costs of developing the business of Westlock Shopping Centre on an 80-20 basis. Further, it was common ground that they would share the profits, if any, on an 80-20 basis. This is entirely clear.

Thirdly, we know that they spoke of each other as partners. Westlock Foods Ltd. or Mr. and Mrs. Shefsky sent tenants to Bonel Properties Ltd. They received complaints and arranged for rectification of the complaints. They were to share both the cost of expanding the mall and the profits it would make as a business.

The *Partnership Act* deals with this question in s.4(c) which reads:

"4. In determining whether a partnership does or does not exist, regard shall be had to the following rules:

...

(c) the receipt by a person of a share of the profits of a business is prima facie proof that that person is a partner in the business, ... "

Counsel for the respondent argues that there are two phases of the arrangements between the parties. The first is the construction of the shopping centre. The second is the running of the business of the shopping centre. We can find no authority for such a proposition nor is there anything in the actions of the parties or their words which leads to this highly unusual and very unfair result. This argument was not advanced before the learned trial judge and was first mentioned in oral argument before us.

On all of the facts: the letter, Exhibit 10, which says he is buying a 20 per cent interest in Westlock Shopping Centre; the introduction of the principals of Bonel Properties Ltd. as his partners; the bank account and the printed cheques; the Treasury Branch and Investors Syndicate financing; the right to be consulted about new tenants; the sending of prospective tenants; the "on the spot" looking after the construction faults and repairs; the bank account and the admission that they were to share the costs on an 80-20 basis as well as the profits being divided on that same basis; and, finally, the previous action between the parties; drives us to the conclusion that Bonel Properties Ltd. and Westlock Foods Ltd. were partners in the business of operating the Westlock Shopping Centre. ...

NOTES AND QUESTIONS

1. The *Volzke* case indicates that control is not determinative of the existence of a partnership. What was significant to the court was that: (i) a joint chequing account was established; (ii) the two companies agreed to share the costs of developing the mall; (iii) the companies agreed to share profits and losses; (iv) the companies spoke of each other as partners and sent clients to each other, and; (v) the companies jointly managed the property in question.

2. In *Volzke*, the parties engaged in ongoing and active management of the property in question. Could the same be said of the situation in *Kamex*?

3. The *Kamex* case illustrates but one situation where two or more parties are cooperating in a business venture with a view to a profit but where the nature of their cooperation does not result in a judicial determination that a partnership exists. What about a scenario where one party loans money to a partnership and is repaid out of partnership profits? Is the lender, by virtue of deriving benefit from the profits made by a partnership, a partner in that partnership? An early case considering this issue is reproduced below.

POOLEY v. DRIVER

(1876), 5 Ch. D. 458 (Eng. M.R.)

[In 1868, Messrs. Borrett and Hagen signed a partnership agreement to conduct a grease, pitch, and manure manufacturing concern. The partnership capital had been divided into 60 equal parts, with Borrett holding 17 parts and Hagen 23 parts. The remaining 20 parts were to be owned by people advancing loans to the partnership according to the measure of their contributions.

The defendants had entered into an agreement with Borrett and Hagen, advancing the latter £2,500 upon the terms of a draft deed that was never executed. The deed described the Drivers as co-partners and made various provisions for the repayment of the money advanced by the Drivers to the partnership. Until the Drivers were repaid, they held 5 parts of the partnership and were to share in the partnership profits accordingly.

The plaintiff held several bills of exchange from the partnership worth approximately £5,000. In 1873, the partnership went into liquidation and the plaintiff sought payment of the money owing on the bills from the defendants, alleging that they were partners in the partnership. The defendants denied that they were partners and maintained that they were merely lenders of money to the partnership under a contract in writing as contemplated by the *Partnership (Bovill's) Act, 1865*, 28 & 29 Vict. c. 86.)]

Jessel M.R.: — The real question I have to decide in this case is, whether certain contracts, which are admitted to have been entered into, made the Defendants partners in the firm of *Charles Borrett & Co.* If they did, then the Plaintiff, the holder of certain bills of exchange drawn or indorsed by that firm — whether he gave value for them or not is admittedly immaterial — is entitled to the relief which he asks: if not, the action must be dismissed.

The partnership was for the term of fourteen years; the loan also was for the same term. If the partnership comes to an end sooner, the loan must come to an end sooner; so that, in fact, if you were to describe the contributors as dormant partners in the concern, liable to a limited extent to loss, and with a guarantee of their capital from the active partners, you would exactly describe their position; and I do not know of any other shorter mode of describing the position of these contributors.

Well, if that is so, is not that exactly the thing which it was intended should not take place — that a man should not put forward another to carry on the business ostensibly and himself take the profits? It is the very object and meaning of the transaction, as I understand it, to give these contributors that very position which dormant partners usually occupy, with certain collateral advantage — exceptional, perhaps, but not altogether unusual; unusual, no doubt, in the sense that I have seldom seen — I was going to say so barefaced, but, when you come to see the reason of it, I will say so palpable — an intention exhibited on the face of the documents to give the contributors all the benefits of the partnership, and if possible, to secure them from suffering from the liabilities. The reason of it was this: The framers of the instrument thought that *Bovill's Act* would protect them, and that comes again to a question of law, as to whether the Defendants who executed the deeds are in a better position than the Defendants who did not.

First of all, as to the Defendants who did not. I decided yesterday, and I merely repeat it, that Messrs. Driver, not being parties to any instrument in writing signed by them, were not parties to a "contract in writing" within *Bovill's Act*, and therefore could not have the benefit or protection afforded by that Act. But, with regard to the Defendant, who did execute the deeds, of course they would be entitled to the benefit of the Act, and then the mere question I have to try is whether they have rightly construed the Act.

It was said, and said with considerable force, by Mr. Chitty and Mr. Mathew, that they never intended to be partners. What they did not intend to do was to incur the liabilities of partner. If intending to be a partner is intending to take the profits, then they did intend to be partners. If intending to take the profits and have the business carried on for their benefit was intending to be partners, they did intend to be partners. If intending to see that the money was applied for that purpose and for no other, and to exercise an efficient control over it, so that they might have brought an action to restrain it from being otherwise applied, and so forth, was intending to be partners, then they did intend to be partners. But if it is tried by the other test, whether they intended to be protected under *Bovill's Act* from liability to third persons, then I think they did intend to be protected from liability.

But it comes back again to the same point, namely, what is the true construction of the Act? Is what they did within the provisions of the Act, or without?

I must say the Act is not so easy to construe as some Acts are, and not so difficult as some Acts are; but it seems to have been framed on an impression that the law of partnership was in a different state from what it actually was. I should be sorry to say that on my own authority, but I find it stated in pretty plain terms by the Privy Council in the case of *Mollwo, March, & Co. v. Court of Wards*, and something of the same kind was stated by other Judges, but being Judges of Courts of first instance, I do not refer to them. The Privy Council said (1): "Some reliance was placed on the statute 28 & 29 Vict. c. 86, s.1, which enacts that the advance of money to a firm upon a contract that the lender shall receive a rate of interest varying with the profits, or a share of the profits, shall not, of itself, constitute the lender a partner, or render him responsible as such. It was argued that this raised an implication that the lender was so responsible by the law existing before the passing of the Act. The enactment is no doubt entitled to great weight as evidence of the law, but it is by no means conclusive; and when the existing law is shown to be different from that which the Legislature supposed it to be, the implication arising from the statute cannot operate as a negation of its existence."

Now, I am afraid that that criticism is by no means ill-founded. The first section of the Act is this: "The advance of money by way of loan to a person engaged, or about to engage, in any trade or undertaking upon a contract in writing with such person, that the lender shall receive a rate of interest varying with the profits, or shall receive a share of the profits arising from carrying on such trade or undertaking, shall not, of itself, constitute the lender a partner with the person or the persons carrying on such trade or undertaking, or render him responsible as such.

The law was decided before the Act, by a long train of decisions before the time of Lord Eldon, who found it established. He says in *Ex parte Hamper* that the lending of a sum of money on a *bona fide* contract to receive a rate of interest varying with the profits, did not make a man a partner; although, I suppose, I may take it to be the equally well-established rule, though perhaps not so conclusively established, that the receiving of a share of the profits did: the two were lumped together by the statute, and therefore it was said, and rightly said, that there being, so to say, a misapprehension of the law which was supposed to be affected by the Act, you cannot look upon the Act itself as declaratory one way or the other.

That being so, what is the effect of the Act? The Act is this that the advance of money must be "by way of loan." Now what does that mean? It is not the "advance of money", but "the advance of money by way of loan". I take it to mean this, that the person advancing must be a real lender; that the advance must not only profess to be by way of loan, but must be a real loan; and consequently you come back to the question whether the persons who enter into the contract of association are really in the position of creditor and debtor, or in the position of partners, or in the only third position which I think could be suggested, that of master and servant. But the Act does not decide that for you. You must decide that without the Act; and when you have decided that the relation is that of creditor and debtor, then all the Act does is this: it says that the creditor may take a share of the profits, but, as I understand the law as laid down by the higher authorities to which I have referred, if you have once decided that the parties are in the position of creditor and debtor you do not want the Act at all, because the inference of partnership derived from the mere taking a share of profit, not being irrebuttable, is rebutted by your having come to the conclusion that they are in the position of debtor and creditor. That, in fact, was the decision in the case of *Mollwo, March, & Co. v. Court of Wards*, and in the case of *Cox v. Hickman*. Therefore you have already decided that for yourself, and the Act does not seem to me, as far as regards the first section, to do you any good at all.

Then the only other point is as to the meaning of "shall not, of itself, constitute," &c. Now there is a possible meaning to be given to the word "itself". It may mean this — though I am not sure that it does — that in construing a contract which, before the Act, by the mere circumstance of there being a share in the profits, would have raised a cogent, though not an irrebuttable inference that the so-called lender was a partner, though he professed to be a lender, the mere fact of his taking profits shall not alone raise that inference. Well, if that is the meaning — and I think Mr. Lindley attributes that meaning to it — it does not assist me very much in coming to a decision, for of course in this case there are many other circumstances besides participation in profits ... I must decide for myself whether the parties are really in the position of creditor and debtor before I can apply the Act at all.

The words are, "advance of money by way of loan," and Mr. Lindley's note is this: "Observe these very important words. Agreements are constantly framed with all sorts of clauses, which together probably expose the lender to the risks he is desirous of avoiding" — that is, to the risk of being a partner. I do not know why those words, "of itself", were put into the Act, unless it was supposed by the framer … that sharing profits would otherwise have created a partnership of itself. If you take that meaning, then it is an alteration of the law; but *Cox v. Hickman* decided that that was not so, and never had been so …

That disposes of the law of the case as far as I am concerned. I now come to the consideration of the details of the documents, which are certainly framed in a very singular way. They seem to me to have been purposely framed with a view of giving the whole benefit which partnership could give to the contributors, and, if possible, something more than they could have obtained as partners.

···

… [T]he moment the contributors became parties to this deed, as I shall show they were or did become afterwards, they became entitled to shares in the capital absolutely. Then it goes on, "The capital of the said business shall be used and employed in the regular course of trade for the benefit of the partnership, and shall not be drawn out during the continuance of such partnership."

This is a very important clause, when you consider that the contributors get the benefit — as I shall show presently they do — of every covenant in the deed of partnership. The result, therefore, is this, that they became not only entitled to the shares of the capital, but entitled to compel the ostensible partners to employ that capital in the regular course of trade, and might have obtained an injunction to prevent their diverting it to any other purpose. They had therefore, to that extent, a control over the capital, namely, a control over its employment; thus they were not at all in the ordinary position of lenders.

The lender does not become entitled to any part of the assets of his debtor in specie. He has only a contract which entitles him to claim payment from the debtor as a personal demand, but this supposed creditor becomes entitled to a portion of the capital in specie, and gets the right besides to prevent the legal owners of the property from applying it to any other than a particular purpose, whether they desire to do so or not. He acquires two rights, the right to an aliquot portion of the capital itself, and a right to control the disposal of the rest of the capital.

Then there is a covenant that the partners shall conduct the business during the partnership to the best of their ability. Let us test the case by that covenant. The lender can compel these people against their will to carry on the business — I do not mean to say he can actually make them carry on the business, because that is a covenant which a Court of Equity always declines to enforce, but he could have an action for damages against them for breach of the covenant, and at all events he gets the benefit of that contract. They must carry on the business, as I shall presently, for his benefit because they have contracted to do so.

Then the 7th clause is that proper books of account and other books shall be kept in the usual way. Then there is a provision that the partners shall not sell, lend, or borrow without mutual consent; then that they shall not allow the assets to be taken in execution; and then that neither partner shall take any servants without the consent of the other. Then there is a provision as to outgoings; then a provision for one of the ostensible partners drawing out certain sums for maintenance. Then, that on the last of July in every year a general account shall be taken, and a general valuation made in the usual way, and put into a book. Then the 14th clause is this, which is very important: — [His Lordship read it.]

The moment the contributors got the benefit of this they were clearly entitled to a share of the profits as profits. Nothing can be plainer than the terms of the provision, and it shows the intention of the parties.

Then the 15th clause is this: — [His Lordship read it.] Then there is a provision to this effect, that if either of the partners becomes bankrupt the other shall have liberty to dissolve, and then the property shall become the property of the non-bankrupt partner upon his paying the value of the bankrupt partner's share to his assignees.

Then there is a provision for the widow or children of the partners; then a provision in the event of the death of either partner, which I do not think it necessary to read, and some other provisions as regards death, which precede the last clause, which is the usual arbitration clause. That is the partnership deed.

Now we come to the other deeds, which for this purpose I treat as deeds of even date. They are not exactly of even date, but they are nearly contemporaneous The partnership dates from the 10th of October, 1868. The arrangement made with Messrs. Driver was made somewhere about the same time, and was made by a document which was never executed. It was a draft of an indenture dated the day of October 1868. I may say, in passing, that the other deeds, those executed by Bannatyne & Pye, are about the same date — one being dated the 28th of October, 1868, and the other the 7th of November, 1868 — and are in the same terms, and I will take them as having been executed shortly after the partnership.

Messrs. Driver's document recites the partnership deed; it recites some of the provisions that I have read; and then it goes on: "Whereas the said Rolles Driver and Samuel Neale Driver have agreed to advance by way of loan to the said C. Borrett and E. Hagen, under the provisions of an Act of Parliament passed in the 28th and 29th years of Her present Majesty, c. 86, entitled, "An Act to Amend the Law of Partnership", the sum of £2,500 to enable them the said C. Borrett and E. Hagen to carry on the said trade or business for the term and under and subject to the stipulations and conditions hereinafter mentioned, expressed, and declared concerning the same." Then it is witnessed, "That in consideration of the sum of £2,500," &c., the said Borrett and Hagen first of all covenant that they Borrett and Hagen, "will within six calendar months after the 1st of July, 1882, or within six calendar months after the sooner determination of the said partnership, pay unto the said Rolles Driver and Samuel Neale Driver, their executors, administrators, or assigns, the sum of £2,500."

That is a very remarkable thing for a loan. It is a loan during the continuance of the partnership. It is to be paid within six calendar months after its natural expiration, or within six months after any other expiration of the partnership. Therefore, although they call it a "loan", and although I agree that, standing alone, the fact of the duration of the loan being the duration of the partnership might not of itself be conclusive, it all tends in the same way to show that this was really intended as an advance of capital to the partnership business, made for the purpose of carrying it on, and not as an ordinary loan.

The next clause — and this is very important — is: "That the said C. Borrett and E. Hagen, their respective executors and administrators, shall in all things conform to, fulfil, and observe the covenants, clauses and agreements contained in the said recited deed of partnership of the 10th day of October, 1868, and such deed of partnership shall at all times be open to the inspection of the said Bolles

Driver and Samuel Neale Driver, their executors or administrators, at the office where the said business shall be carried on." That imports the whole of the provisions of the prior deed into this deed, and makes Borrett and Hagen covenant to observe them, thus giving to the Drivers those rights both with respect to capital and profits, which I have already adverted to.

Then the next clause provides that Borrett and Hagen will, during the continuance of the loan — that is, during the maintenance of the partnership — make out accounts, and once a year, on the 1st of October, pay Messrs. Driver, on account of profits, a sum equivalent to five sixtieth parts of the profits for the year preceding the 18th of July then last past. Some argument was rested upon that, but nothing turns upon it, for this covenant never actually came into existence. If it had, I should have held that it did not vary the case in the least; that the prior clause gave them a share of proceeds as profits under the partnership, and this only makes Borrett and Hagen pay on account of the profits a sum equivalent to five sixtieth parts, showing that what they had to pay really was still profits. But that clause never came into force, because there was a proviso at the end of it to this effect, that if the sum of £10,000 was not advanced — and it was not — then Borrett and Hagen, or one of them, would "on the 1st day of October in every year during the continuance of the said loan pay to the said Rolles Driver and Samuel Neale Driver, their executors, administrators, or assigns, in lieu of the said five equal sixtieth parts of the said clear gains and profits as last aforesaid, such a proportion of the said clear gains and profits as last aforesaid as the said sum of £2,500 bears to the whole capital for the time being employed in the same business, such capital being estimated in the manner provided by the said indenture of partnership."

So that we have the interest of the loan not varying merely with the profits of the business, but varying in the proportion which the loan, which was part of the capital, bore to the whole capital, a circumstance which I think by no means immaterial in showing that it was not a genuine loan in the sense of creating the relation of debtor and creditor, but that it was indeed an advance of part of the capital.

Then the deed goes on with a very remarkable provision, "That if either the said Rolles Driver or Samuel Neale Driver shall become bankrupt or shall compound with his creditors, or in case any difference or dispute shall at anytime during the said term of fourteen years arise between the said parties hereto, or their representatives, and which differences or disputes shall be considered by arbitration, as hereinafter mentioned, to justify the determination of the arrangement hereby agreed upon, it shall be lawful for the said C. Borrett and E. Hagen, or the survivor of them, or their or his executors and administrators at any time hereafter to pay the said sum of £2,500, less any sum they shall have been overpaid on account of the said business, to the said Rolles Driver and Samuel Neale Driver, their executors, administrators, or assigns, together with the share of the said profits (if any) to which the said Rolles Driver and Samuel Neale Driver, their executors, administrators, or assigns, shall then have become entitled"; and thereupon the agreement is to be at an end.

Now that certainly is a very astonishing provision in an ordinary contract of loan. What has the bankruptcy of the creditor got to do with it? You pay the assignee, or trustee, as he is now called. It is a very remarkable thing that the bankruptcy of the creditor should put an end to the agreement, but you find it by no means remarkable if it was intended that they should really be partners. You find a similar provision in the actual partnership deed. Without attaching too much weight to this, I think it is very material.

Then there is another remarkable clause: "Within six calendar months after the expiration or sooner determination of the partnership, a final settlement of the accounts of the partnership shall be forthwith made in writing by the said C. Borrett and E. Hagen, their executors or administrators, concerning all the stock-in-trade, plant, moneys, credits, and effects then due or belonging to the said partnership estate, and also of all debts and sums of money (if any) due or owing from, and of all liabilities of the same, and a just valuation shall be made of all the particulars included in such account which shall require and are capable of valuation, and immediately after such last-mentioned account shall have been so taken and settled, the said C. Borrett and E. Hagen shall forthwith pay thereout to the said Rolles Driver and Samuel Neale Driver, their executors, administrators, or assigns, the sum of £2,500." So that the covenant is in accordance with the partnership deed to pay the £2,500 out of the assets and debts due to the partnership. I know there is another covenant to pay Messrs. Driver, which is personal, but there stands a covenant to pay out of the assets.

Then there is a provision for payment to the Drivers of "five equal sixtieth parts or shares of all the net profits of the said business." That gives them all the surplus profits that they have not yet received, including the proportion of the capital they are entitled to.

Then there is the proviso that they shall refund. It is very oddly worded, but it is agreed on all hands that it means this, that if, at the end of the partnership period, the amount already paid to the Drivers for profits shall exceed the total profits made in the business, they shall refund the excess not exceeding the £2,500. I have rather given the effect than the words, because the words are somewhat ambiguous; but it is admitted that that must be the meaning, or, in other words, that the lender, having received profit for interest, if the business afterwards makes a loss, would have to pay back, subject to the limit that he is never to be called upon to pay more than he has received, and, subject also to this, that he is never to be called upon to pay more than the total amount of his so-called loan. It is certainly a wonderful provision, if it is a *bona fide* loan, and not a mere colourable transaction to get a share of the profits without being liable to losses. Did ever any one hear of anybody lending his money on such terms, or of the notion that, after having received the profits in lieu of interest, he is to pay back the whole of them, it may be, because subsequently the business, conducted not for him, but for other people, who are really his debtors, shall have given rise to losses? It appears to me that if you want to prove that the business was conducted for him, this is cogent evidence of it. It was not conducted entirely for the benefit of the persons who were merely debtors and who stood in that relation to the supposed creditor.

Then there is an arbitration clause, which is very usual in partnership articles, but not a very usual one in a mere loan deed.

These are the documents on which I am called upon to decide, and I must say that I have come to a clear conclusion that this is not a transaction of loan within the meaning of the Act of Parliament; that the true relation of the parties towards one another was that of dormant and active partners, and not of mere creditors and debtors; that in this case I need not rely on one provision or on two provisions, but on the whole character of the transaction from beginning to end. It is an elaborate device, an ingenious contrivance, for giving these contributors the whole of the advantages of the partnership, without subjecting them, as they thought, to any of the liabilities. I think the device fails; and that, looking at the law as it stands, I must hold that they are partners, and liable to the consequences of being partners, and to the whole of the engagements of the partnership, and consequently liable for the whole of its debts.

The Plaintiff is, therefore, entitled to a judgment on these bills.

Judgment accordingly.

NOTES

The circumstances that caused concern in *Pooley v. Driver* are still relevant today. For that reason, the pertinent sections in *Bovill's Act* that provided the basis for Jessel M.R.'s determination in *Pooley v. Driver* may still be observed in modern Canadian partnerships legislation. For example, s. 3(3)(*d*) of the Ontario *Partnerships Act*, R.S.O. 1990, c. P.5, states:

3. In determining whether a partnership does or does not exist, regard shall be had to the following rules: ...

(3) The receipt by a person of a share of the profits of a business is proof, in the absence of evidence to the contrary, that the person is a partner in the business, but the receipt of such a share or payment, contingent on or varying with the profits of a business, does not of itself make him or her a partner in the business, and in particular,

...

(d) the advance of money by way of loan to a person engaged or about to engage in a business on a contract with that person that the lender is to receive a rate of interest varying with the profits, or is to receive a share of the profits arising from carrying on the business, does not of itself make the lender a partner with the person or persons carrying on the business or liable as such, provide that the contract is in writing and signed by or on behalf of all parties thereto;

Partnerships may be created as a result of intention or they may arise in its absence, such as through the conduct of parties in circumstances where the parties never thought about entering into such a business vehicle. Either way, a partnership is a matter of contract between the partners, as reflected in the principle of consensualism, which is discussed in Part D.1(e) below.

C. THE LEGAL NATURE AND CHARACTERISTICS OF PARTNERSHIPS

Although, as indicated above, partnerships involve the carrying on of business in common with a view to a profit, to what extent is a partnership distinct from the individuals or entities that have joined together to create it? This issue is considered in the case below.

THORNE v. NEW BRUNSWICK (WORKMEN'S COMPENSATION BOARD)

(1962), 33 D.L.R. (2d) 167 (N.B.S.C., App. Div.)

The judgment of the Court was delivered by

McNair C.J.N.B.: — This is a special case stated by the Workmen's Compensation Board under s. 34(8) of the *Workmen's Compensation Act,* R.S.N.B. 1952, c. 255, in which our opinion is sought on a question of law which arose on an application for compensation made to the Board by one Osborne Thorne.

The Act provides for an Accident Fund established and maintained by assessments made against employers in the industries within its scope out of which compensation may be paid by the Board to a workman and his dependants when personal injury or death is caused to him by accident arising out of and in the course of his employment in any such industry.

The facts as stated by the Board may be summarized as follows: In February 1961 Thorne and one Jules Robichaud, both residents of New Brunswick, entered into an oral agreement to carry on in partnership within the Province a combined lumbering and sawmill business. It was agreed Robichaud would have charge of the woods operations, Thorne of the milling operations, and that each partner would personally work in his branch of the undertaking at a remuneration, termed wages, of $75 per week. They commenced business in early February 1961 and, in accordance with the requirements of the Act, duly notified the Board of the new undertaking, filed with it an estimate of wages for the current year and paid to the Board the provisional assessment applicable to the estimated payroll.

On April 3, 1961 Thorne suffered personal injuries by accident arising out of and in the course of the duties performed by him pursuant to the partnership agreement. He applied to the Board for payment of compensation, alleging he was a workman within the meaning of the Act and entitled thereunder to benefits. Clearly the business carried on by the partners constituted an industry within the scope of the Act and workmen in their employ would be eligible for compensation thereunder.

The question submitted for the opinion of the Court reads:

> Based on the foregoing facts was Osborne Thorne, on April 3, 1961, a workman employed by the said partnership within the meaning of the Workmen's Compensation Act so as to entitle him to compensation thereunder?

Partnerships are an emanation of the common law, the term "firm" to describe the relationship having been borrowed from mercantile law. The *Partnership Act, 1890* (U.K.), c. 39, is essentially a codification of the rules of common law and equity. Admittedly under such pre-existing rules no person could enter into a contract with himself or be his own employer and, as a partnership was regarded as having no legal existence distinct from the individuals composing it, no person could be an employee of a firm of which he was a member. We were informed by counsel that from its inception the Workmen's Compensation Board has followed that principle.

It is now however contended by the claimant that by virtue of statute law in force in the United Kingdom and in New Brunswick partnerships should be regarded as legal entities or persons distinct from their component members and that, in consequence, the firm of which he is a member was capable of entering into a contract of employment with him. Reliance is placed on principles enunciated in relation to trade unions in *Taff Vale R. Co. v. Amalgamated Soc. of Ry. Servants*, [1901] A.C. 426, H.L., which were adopted and applied in *Internat'l Brotherhood of Teamsters, etc. v. Therien*, 22 D.L.R. (2d) 1, [1960] S.C.R. 265.

The *Taff Vale* case decided a trade union registered under the *Trade Union Acts* 1871 and 1876 of the United Kingdom, being a legal entity, can be sued in its registered name, In the *Therien* case it was held a trade union certified as a bargaining agent under the *Labour Relations Act* of British Columbia is likewise a legal entity suable in tort. The ratio of the decisions is that the granting by the Legislature of rights, powers and immunities to such bodies is quite inconsistent with the notion it was not intended they should be constituted legal entities or persons exercising such powers and enjoying such immunities.

...

There is a fundamental distinction between the legislation involved in the *Taff Vale* and *Therien* cases and the *Partnership Act* of New Brunswick, as the latter does not purport to legalize or validate partnership firms, a status or condition already enjoyed by them under the common law. It is contended, however, that by its enactments relating to partnerships the Legislature has given them rights, powers and attributes not previously possessed and imposed on them duties and liabilities not previously existing which has resulted in their establishment under the law as legal entities. Support for the new concept is sought not only in the *Partnership Act* but also in O. 48a of our Rules of Court and certain dicta of Farwell, J. ... in the *Taff Vale* case ...

O. 48a was in 1891 incorporated as such into the existing English Rules of Court made under the authority of the *Supreme Court of Judicature Acts* 1873 and 1875. Counsel's suggestion is the provisions of O. 48a were necessitated to meet procedural problems resulting from the new concept of a partnership firm as a legal entity, distinct from its members, allegedly resulting from the enactment of the *Partnership Act, 1890* (U.K.), c. 39.

O. 48a is for the most part a compilation of earlier English Rules. In notes thereto in Annual Practice 1961 at p. 1151 it is stated:

> This Order repeals O. 7, r. 2; O. 9, rr. 6, 7; O. 12, rr. 15, 16; O. 16, rr. 14, 15; O. 42, r. 10; and O. 45, r. 10, of the R.S.C., 1883, and stands in lieu thereof. Rules 1-10 of the order form a code relating to partnership firms and must be construed together.

An examination of the former Rules reveals that prior to the enactment in 1890 of the *Partnership Act* of the United Kingdom a partnership firm was in English jurisprudence recognized as an entity in the sense partners could sue or be sued in the firm name and execution issue against property of the partnership on a judgment against the firm. The earlier procedural provisions can have no greater significance or effect than they possessed before the *Partnership Act* of 1890 was enacted and, in our view, their incorporation into O. 48a in 1891 lends no support to the contention that Act created for partnership firms a new status.

The nature and purpose of such provisions of O. 48a as were new were discussed in *Worcester City and County Bank Co. v. Firbank, Pauling & Co.*, [1894] 1 Q.B. 784, C.A. At pp. 787-8 Lord Esher, M.R., says:

> The first question in this case is whether the writ was properly issued. The writ, which is in form for service within the jurisdiction, was issued against a firm in the firm name. The foundation of the decisions on this subject which have been cited to us is, that, although under the rules a writ may be issued against a firm in the firm name, it is really in effect a writ against all and each of the members of the firm, just as if the writ had been issued against them in their individual names; and it was therefore held under the former rules that, where a writ against partners in their individual names could not be served without leave, they or some of them being resident out of the jurisdiction, neither could a writ be issued without leave against them under the firm name. In the present case the facts are these. I think that it has

been made out that this is a Natal firm, i.e., a colonial firm. ... For the present purpose I think that a colonial firm is in the same position as a foreign firm. ... The rules as they existed prior to the making of Order XLVIII.A have been construed to the effect that a writ such as this could not be issued without leave against a foreign firm, the members, or some of the members, of which were resident abroad. That has appeared to those conversant with the matter to involve a hardship, and it was for the purpose of getting rid of that hardship I believe that Order XLVIII.A was framed. In rule I of that order the words "and carrying on business within the jurisdiction" are used in addition to those which had been used in the former rules. In conjunction with that rule we have rules 3 and 8 of the same order. ... Reading rule I of Order XLVIII.A with rules 3 and 8, it seems to me that it is now immaterial whether the writ is against an English firm or against a foreign or colonial firm. ... If the firm carries on business within the jurisdiction, then whether it is an English or a foreign firm, and whether it also carries on business in a colony or abroad or not, a writ may be issued against the partners in the firm name without leave under Order XLVIII.A, r. 1.

See also by Lopes, L.J., at p. 789 and Davey, L.J., at pp. 790-1.

The reasons so given for the adoption in 1891 of the new provisions contained in O. 48a lend no countenance to the submission the Order constitutes a recognition of a new concept, resulting from the *Partnership Act* of 1890, of a partnership firm as a legal entity distinct from the individuals composing it. As respects New Brunswick law the proposition appears entirely fanciful in light of the fact our first *Partnership Act*, passed in 1921, post-dated by twelve years our adoption of the English O. 48a being found in toto in our original Rules of Court of 1909.

Support for the theory advanced by the claimant is also sought in the language of Farwell, J., in his judgment in the *Taff Vale* case particularly where he says: "Now it is undoubtedly true that a trade union is neither a corporation, nor an individual nor a partnership between a number of individuals" (p. 427) and again "it is competent to the Legislature to give to an association of individuals which is neither a corporation nor a partnership ... a capacity ..." (p. 429). From such collocation of words and phrases we are asked to infer judicial recognition by this learned jurist of the new concept.

That such language was never intended by its author to denote such recognition is made clear by his later observations in *Sadler v. Whiteman*, [1910] 1 K.B. 868, C.A. At p. 889 Farwell, L.J., (as he then was) says:

> In English law a firm as such has no existence; partners carry on business both as principals and as agents for each other within the scope of the partnership business; the firm name is a mere expression, not a legal entity, although for convenience under Order XLVIII.A it may be used for the sake of suing and being sued. ... It is not correct to say that a firm carries on business; the members of a firm carry on business in partnership under the name or style of the firm.

See also *Von Hellfeld v. Rechnitzer & Mayer Freres & Co.*, [1914] 1 Ch. 748, C.A.; *Odegarde v. Lynch et al., Erickson v. Lynch et al.*, [1935] 2 D.L.R. 493, 9 M.P.R. 127 (N.S.C.A.); and *Noble Lowndes & Partners v. Hadfields, Ltd.*, [1939] 1 Ch. 569.

Our *Partnership Act*, now R.S.N.B. 1952, c. 167, is modelled on the Act of the United Kingdom. Its s. 5 reads:

> 5. Persons who have entered into partnership with one another are for the purposes of this Act called collectively a firm, and the name under which their business is carried on is called the firm name.

Such enactment is identical with s-s. (1) of s. 4 of the Act of the United Kingdom. Its s. 4 contains however, as s-s. (2), this further enactment:

> (2) In Scotland a firm is a legal person distinct from the partners of whom it is composed. ...

The inclusion of those provisions in the parent Act deprives of all force the suggestion that by other provisions in the Act the Legislature intended to make of partnership firms generally legal entities or persons.

The true principles are, we feel, correctly formulated in *Pollock on Partnership*, 15th ed., p. 24, where it is said:

> The law of England knows nothing of the firm ... as an artificial person distinct from the members composing it, though the firm is so treated by the universal practice of merchants and by the law of Scotland. In England the firm-name may be used in legal instruments both by the partners themselves and by other persons as a collective description of the persons who are partners in the firm at the time to which the description refers: and under the Rules of the Supreme Court actions may now be brought by and against partners in the firm name. An action between a partner and the firm, or between two firms having a common partner, was impossible at common law, and until 1891 it remained open to doubt whether such actions were possible since the *Judicature Acts*; but they are now expressly authorised by the Rules of Court. (Note 80 here follows reading: "Order XLVIIIA, r. 10. But not so as to enable a partner to be in substance both plaintiff and defendant: *Meyer & Co. v. Faber*, [1923] 2 Ch. 421, C.A.).

See also *Lindley on Partnership*, 11th ed., p. 154; *Palmer's Company Law*, 20th ed., p. 770; and *Modern Company Law* by Gower, 2nd ed., p. 214.

Ellis v. Joseph Ellis & Co., [1905] 1 K.B. 324, C.A., lends support to the views we entertain. The action, brought under the *Workmen's Compensation Act 1897* of the United Kingdom which contains a definition of "workman" corresponding closely to that found in the New Brunswick Act, was against the surviving members of a firm by the dependants of a deceased partner who under a mutual agreement worked in the colliery for wages and had, up to the time of his injury, been paid at the stipulated rate out of the proceeds of the business. It was held the Act contemplated the case of a workman employed by some other person or persons and that the deceased, having been himself one of the partners in the firm for which he was working, could not be said to have been employed by them. At p. 329 Collins, M.R., says:

> It seems to me obvious ... that a person cannot for the purposes of the Act occupy the position of being both employer and employee.

And Mathew, L.J., says, *ibid.*:

> The argument on behalf of the applicant ... appears to involve a legal impossibility, namely, that the same person can occupy the position of being both master and servant, employer and employed. The deceased man in this case was a partner; and the arrangement made between him and his co-partners as to the payment of wages to him was really an agreement with regard to the mode in which accounts were to be taken between the partners, and to the share of profits to be received by him in excess of that received by the other partners in consideration of the work done by him.

Since the argument in the case at bar our attention has been drawn to two recent decisions of the English Court of Appeal in which the word "entity" was used as descriptive of a partnership firm. They are *Davies v. Elsby Brothers Ltd.*, [1960] 3 All E.R. 672 and *Whittam v. W. J. Daniel & Co.*, [1961] 3 All E.R. 796. In our view their language falls far short of a recognition in English jurisprudence of the doctrine that as a matter of substantive law a partnership is a legal entity or *persona juridica* separate and distinct from the individuals composing it.

It is in our view regrettable that the claimant failed to seek the benefit of s-s. (2) of s. 4 of *the Workmen's Compensation Act* which provides:

> (2) An employer in an industry within the scope of this Part may be admitted, on such terms and conditions and for such period and from time to time as the Board may prescribe, as being entitled for himself and his dependents, as the case may be, to the same compensation as if such employer were a workman within the scope of this Part.

For the reasons stated the question presented for our opinion must be answered in the negative.

NOTES

1. The *Thorne* case illustrates that partners cannot be employees of a partnership. The rationale for this ruling is that unincorporated associations do not enjoy the attributes of separate legal personality that would enable a partner to be an employee of a partnership. In this sense, the partnership is no different than a sole proprietorship, where the proprietor may not serve as an employee of the proprietorship business because the proprietorship has no legal personality separate from that of the proprietor. Compare these situations with that in *Lee v. Lee's Air Farming Ltd.*, [1961] A.C. 12, [1960] 3 All E.R. 420, [1960] 3 W.L.R. 758, 104 Sol. Jo. 869 (N.Z. J.C.P.C.), which is reproduced in Chapter 4. That case considers whether a person who was the governing director and controlling shareholder of a corporation, as well as its chief pilot, could be an employee of the corporation for the purposes of workers' compensation legislation.

2. What is more important, for present purposes, about the *Thorne* case is that it demonstrates that the partnership is not a legal entity separate and distinct from the identities of its partners. Since a partnership is not a legal entity, when we talk about the partnership, or use the partnership's name, what we mean is "all of the partners". Just as in a sole proprietorship, where the business is carried on by the proprietor and the business assets belong to him or her, in a partnership the business is carried on by all of the partners and the business property is held by all of the partners as tenants in common. This is indicated by Duff J. in *Boyd v. British Columbia (Attorney General)* (1917), 54 S.C.R. 532 at 555-56:

> When it is said therefore that property held in the names of the partners as partnership property is held "in trust for the partnership" it should be understood that what is meant is not that the partners are not the beneficial as well as the legal owners of the property but that as between the partners themselves and those claiming under them the property is dedicated to the purposes of the partnership, and that each partner holds his interest in trust for such purposes. The partners are owners in the fullest sense both at law and in equity.
>
> It is true nevertheless that as between the partners themselves and those claiming under them and generally speaking as between the creditors of the

partnership and the creditors of an individual partner the share of an individual partner in the partnership assets is merely the share to which he may prove to be entitled in the clear surplus of the assets after the partnership affairs have been wound up, the property sold and the debts and liabilities paid.

See also, for example, s. 21(1) of the Ontario *Partnerships Act*, R.S.O. 1990, c. P.5, which states:

> 21(1) All property and rights and interests in property originally brought into the partnership stock or acquired, whether by purchase or otherwise, on account of the firm, or for the purposes and in the course of the partnership business, are called in this Act "partnership property", and must be held and applied by the partners exclusively for the purposes of the partnership and in accordance with the partnership agreement.

3. Since the partnership is merely an aggregate of the partners, partnership profits and liabilities flow directly to the partners according to the terms of any partnership agreement (or, absent such an agreement, according to the default provisions of the relevant partnerships legislation). Accordingly, the liability of partners in a partnership is the same as the liability of a sole proprietor, namely unlimited personal liability.

4. In spite of what is discussed above, in some circumstances the partnership appears to possess a separate identity. Thus, in section 5 of the Ontario *Partnerships Act*, it is said that "Persons who have entered into partnership with one another are, for the purposes of this Act, called collectively a firm, and the name under which their business is carried on is called the firm name". This provision does not change the legal understanding of the partnership as an aggregate of its partners, though, but is merely a term of convenience for the purposes of the legislation.

Consider also Rule 8.01(1) of the Ontario *Rules of Civil Procedure*, R.R.O. 1990, Reg. 194, which states:

> 8.01(1) A proceeding by or against two or more persons as partners may be commenced using the firm name of the partnership.

This rule pertains to all forms of partnerships, including limited partnerships: see *Kucor Construction & Developments & Associates v. Canada Life Assurance Co.*, [1988] O.J. No. 4733, 167 D.L.R. (4th) 272 at 289 (C.A.). It should be noted, however, that this provision does not change the legal understanding of the partnership as an aggregate of the partners and being without a separate legal personality. The reason for this provision is indicated in *Kucor* at 290:

> To overcome the practical problems of litigation involving partnerships whose membership is large, or when some partners live outside the jurisdiction, rule 8.01(1), and its predecessors, was introduced to recognize a partnership as a legal entity for the procedural purpose of suing or being sued in the firm name of the partnership. ...

5. Section 96(1)(*a*) of the federal *Income Tax Act*, R.S.C. 1985, c. 1 (5th Supp.) contemplates the partnership as a separate person that is deemed to be resident in Canada for the purpose of calculating a partner's percentage of partnership income. However, the partnership is not taxed as an entity unto itself, but taxation is assessed against the partners at a personal level, thereby indicating that the partnership's legal status is not changed by the *Income Tax Act*.

All in all, the understanding of the partnership as merely the aggregate of its partners remains a basic proposition that is altered in some circumstances, such as those described immediately above, but only for procedural and not substantive purposes.

D. HOW PARTNERSHIPS CONDUCT BUSINESS

In the majority of instances, partnerships conduct business on the basis of partnership agreements. Partnership agreements may take virtually any form so long as it may be demonstrated that the partners have agreed to their terms. In the absence of a partnership agreement, or where an agreement exists, but is silent on a particular matter, provincial partnerships legislation provides a set of default rules that govern the partners' relations.

More conceptually, partnerships are all about relationships, specifically the relationships of partners to each other and the relations of partners, through the partnership vehicle, to third parties dealing with the partnership.

1. The Relationship of Partners to Each Other

The relationship of partners to each other is characterized by its personal nature, its fiduciary character, reciprocal agency, the principle of presumptive equality and the ability of the partners to consensually alter certain elements of partnership affairs.

(a) The Personal Nature of Partnerships

Insofar as partnerships come into existence by the (express or implied) agreement or conduct of the parties, the partnership is considered to be personal to the parties agreeing to conduct business in this manner. For this reason, partnerships legislation does not allow for third parties to gain the full rights of partners on the assignment of one partner's rights to a third party. The personal nature of the interaction between partners is illustrated, for example, in s. 31 of the Ontario *Partnerships Act*, R.S.O. 1990, c. P.5. Section 31 holds that an assignment of a partner's share in an active partnership does not entitle the assignee to engage in the management or administration of the partnership business or affairs, to require accounts of partnership transactions, or to inspect partnership books, but merely allows the assignee to receive the share of profits that the assigning partner would have been entitled to. The assignee is also bound to accept the account of profits agreed to by the partners.

Since the partnership is considered to be personal to the partners entering into this type of arrangement, a partnership is dissolved upon the death or insolvency of a partner: see s. 33 of the Ontario *Partnerships Act*. The personal nature of the partnership is also illustrated by the fact that this default provision may be altered by the partners through the terms of a partnership agreement.

(b) Fiduciary Character

The relationship between partners is fundamentally one of high trust and confidence. The nature of partners' relations requires them to implicitly trust each other since, in the absence of agreements to the contrary, any partner may bind the partnership without having to obtain the consent of the other partners. This ability also leads to the characterization of partners' relations as one of reciprocal agency. The agency element of partners' relations is discussed in Part (c) below.

Since partners must necessarily trust in and rely upon their partners, the partnership may be appropriately characterized as one of reciprocal fiduciary duties among its partners. The fiduciary character of partnerships is described in W.A. Gregory, *The Law of Agency and Partnership*, 3rd ed. (St. Paul, Minn.: West, 2001) at 298, as "[o]ne of the most significant aspects of the partnership relation". The fiduciary character of partnerships is foundational; it may not be contracted out of because it is intricately tied to the very fabric of partnerships.

To ensure that the interests of the partnership — and, therefore the partners — are not detrimentally affected by the improper exercise of power by any one partner, fiduciary principles are imposed upon all partners regarding their conduct within the partnership vehicle. These principles ensure that partners do not abuse the powers they have with respect to the partnership business. Partners' fiduciary duties govern each partner's exercise of power over the partnership business.

The fiduciary character of partnerships requires that partners subordinate their personal interests to those of the partnership collective, that is, the collective interests of the partners in the partnership (since the partnership has no legal status independent of its partners). Partners must also subordinate the interests of third parties to those of their partners. In short, fiduciaries must discard all considerations other than single-mindedly acting in the best interests of the partnership collective regarding that collective's interests relating to the partnership venture. Fiduciaries are not required to completely abnegate self-interest or the interests of non-partners; they must only do so regarding their partners' interests that are related to the activities of the partnership. This is one reason why it is necessary to properly define the scope of partnership activity.

That fiduciaries, including partners, are entitled to pursue self-interest outside of the confines of their fiduciary interactions is reflected in the notion of fiduciary "particularity," which holds that not all aspects of a relationship characterized as fiduciary are, themselves, fiduciary: see the discussion in L.I. Rotman, *Fiduciary Law* (Toronto: Thomson/Carswell, 2005), especially at pp. 286-93; see also *Lac Minerals Ltd. v. International Corona Resources Ltd.*, [1989] S.C.J. No. 83, 61 D.L.R. (4th) 14 at 61 [1989] 2 S.C.R. 574. As Bryson J. explains in *Noranda Australia Ltd. v. Lachlan Resources NL* (1988), 14 N.S.W.L.R. 1 at 15 (S.C.), it is ordinarily the case that "a person under a fiduciary obligation to another should be under that obligation in relation to a defined area of conduct, and exempt from the obligation in all other respects". Thus, outside of the area in which fiduciary obligations are owed by a fiduciary, the fiduciary retains personal economic liberty: *ibid.*

The rationale for the fiduciary nature of partnerships was elegantly stated by Chief Justice Cardozo in his judgment in *Meinhard v. Salmon*, 249 N.Y. 458 at 463-64, 164 N.E. 545 at 546 (N.Y.C.A. 1928):

> Joint adventurers, like copartners, owe to one another, while the enterprise continues, the duty of the finest loyalty. Many forms of conduct permissible in a workaday world for those acting at arm's length, are forbidden to those bound by fiduciary ties. A trustee is held to something stricter than the morals of the marketplace. Not honesty alone, but the punctilio of an honour the most sensitive, is then the standard of behavior. As to this there has developed a condition that is unbending and inveterate. Uncompromising rigidity had been the attitude of courts of equity when petitioned to undermine the rule of undivided loyalty by the "disintegrating erosion" of particular exceptions. ... Only thus has the level of

conduct for fiduciaries been kept at a level higher than that trodden by the crowd. It will not consciously be lowered by any judgment of this court.

Although *Meinhard v. Salmon* did not concern a partnership, but the relation between joint venturers, its pronouncement on joint venturers' reciprocal fiduciary duties was derived from the law pertaining to partnerships.

The fiduciary duties of partners require partners to act with honesty, loyalty, integrity, and in the utmost good faith regarding their partnership activities. Although the term "fiduciary" is not used in partnerships legislation, the fiduciary duties of partners illustrated in ss. 28 to 30 of the Ontario *Partnerships Act*, R.S.O. 1990, c. P.5 are representative of the duties contained in other provincial partnerships legislation:

> 28. *Duty as to rendering accounts* — Partners are bound to render true accounts and full information of all things affecting the partnership to any partner or the partner's legal representatives.
>
> 29(1) *Accountability for private profits* — Every partner must account to the firm for any benefit derived by the partner without the consent of the other partners from any transaction concerning the partnership or from any use by the partner of the partnership property, name or business connection.
>
> (2) *Extends to survivors and representatives of deceased* — This section applies also to transactions undertaken after a partnership has been dissolved by the death of a partner and before its affairs have been completely wound up, either by a surviving partner or by the representatives of the deceased partner.
>
> 30. *Duty of partner not to compete with firm* — If a partner, without the consent of the other partners, carries on a business of the same nature as and competing with that of the firm, the partner must account for and pay over to the firm all profits made by the partner in that business.

Although the above sections of the Ontario Act are representative of the fiduciary duties of partners enumerated in provincial partnerships legislation, some other partnerships statutes are more explicit in their use of fiduciary-type terminology. For example, s. 22(1) of the British Columbia *Partnership Act*, R.S.B.C. 1996, c. 348 states that "A partner must act with the utmost fairness and good faith towards the other members of the firm in the business of the firm".

Some of the implications of partners' fiduciary duties may be seen in *Olson v. Gullo*, reproduced immediately below.

OLSON v. GULLO

[1994] O.J. No. 587, 17 O.R. (3d) 790 (C.A.)

Morden A.C.J.O.: —

... Antonio Gullo, Sr., and the plaintiff were equal partners in a partnership formed to develop a 1,000-acre tract of land in the Town of Georgina. Mr. Gullo, through Gullo Enterprises Limited, bought and sold, for his own account and not for the partnership, a 90-acre parcel of land in this tract and made a $2,486,940 profit on this transaction. Relying upon the reasons for judgment of MacKinnon A.C.J.O. for this court in *Lavigne v. Robern* (1984), 51 O.R. (2d) 60, 18 D.L.R. (4th) 759, the trial judge awarded the whole of this profit to the plaintiff. The appellants submit that she erred in concluding that the plaintiff was entitled to anything more than one-half of the amount of the profit on the transaction.

Before dealing directly with the legal issue respecting the extent of the plaintiff's right of recovery, I shall set forth a more complete statement of the facts. Mr. Gullo met the plaintiff in Florida in the fall of 1987. The plaintiff began working as a marketing consultant for Mr. Gullo's family company, Glacier Clear Marketing, Inc., in January 1988. In February of 1988 Mr. Gullo shared a room in the hospital in Newmarket with a member of the council of the Town of Georgina, who told him that the council was looking for a developer to create an industrial park in the town.

Mr. Gullo obtained information and decided that a particular tract of land of 1,000 acres in the town on the west side of Woodbine Avenue close to the Town of Keswick would be suitable. He discussed the project with the plaintiff and showed him the lands.

The first issue which the trial judge was obliged to determine was whether the plaintiff and Mr. Gullo had made a partnership agreement respecting the purchase and development of the land in question. The trial judge's statement of the evidence and her findings on this issue are as follows [pp. 149-50]:

> It is the plaintiff's position that during the month of February 1988, he and Gullo entered into an oral partnership agreement for the purpose of acquiring, developing and eventually disposing of the 1,000 acres situate on the west side of Woodbine Avenue. Gullo was to contribute his expertise as a real estate speculator and developer, and Olson was to provide his skills in marketing, promotion, public relations and financing. Olson further contends that it was also agreed that he and Gullo would contribute equal amounts of capital as required to purchase the various farms and they would share equally in the profits.

> The defendants, on the other hand, flatly deny that there ever was any partnership agreement. They contend that at no time was there any relationship of trust, confidence and dependence created between the parties. It is their position that Gullo was interested in developing an industrial park and devoted a great deal of time attempting to purchase lands within the 1,000-acre tract. His offers were turned down by the farmers and he abandoned the project because of the high price of agricultural land. He decided to purchase the Walshe farm [the 90-acre parcel in question in this proceeding] as a long-term investment. Assuming the land assembly went ahead, Olson's sole function was to find investors interested in developing the project and for this service he would receive a finder's fee or commission.

> According to the evidence, in March 1988, Gullo retained real estate agents at Family Trust Corporation. Over the next few months, these agents submitted agreements of purchase and sale in the name of Gullo Enterprises Limited in Trust to a number of farmers owning land within the 1,000-acre parcel. During this period Olson arranged for funds to purchase his share of the various parcels and discussed the project with prospective investors.

> The evidence also established that during this period the price of farmland in the area increased dramatically and, consequently, Gullo led Olson to believe that the project was no longer feasible as it would be virtually impossible to purchase any farms in the 1,000-acre tract because of rising prices. Nevertheless, unknown to Olson, in May of 1988, Gullo Enterprises Limited in trust, entered into an agreement to purchase a 90-acre farm, known as the Walshe property, for approximately $20,000 an acre and, prior to closing, assigned the purchase agreement to Wesrow Estates Inc. at a profit of approximately $2,500,000. The Walshe farm was part of the 1,000 acres located on the west side of Woodbine Avenue in the Township of Georgina and is shown as parcel 7 on the preliminary study, dated March 1988. In

September 1988, Olson discovered that Gullo had secretly entered into agreements to purchase and sell the Walshe property at a considerable profit. He expressed his disappointment and anger to Gullo and his employment with Glacier Clear Marketing Inc. terminated the end of that month. This action was commenced November 4, 1988.

The trial judge concluded on this issue that [p. 150]:

The evidence is overwhelming that in February 1988, Norman Olson and Antonio Gullo orally agreed that they would be equal partners in purchases of parcels of land in a defined 1,000 acres located on the west side of Woodbine Avenue in the Township of Georgina. It was agreed that the parties would each provide half the moneys required to purchase the various farms and the land would be registered in both their names in due course. It was also agreed that Gullo would negotiate the purchases because of his experience in land assembly and that Olson would find interested investors and prepare promotional material related to the property and the project. Their respective roles were in keeping with their background and expertise.

She further found that [p. 152]:

... The evidence establishes that at no time did Gullo advise Olson of the purchase and sale of the Walshe farm and he never asked Olson to pay his share of the purchase money. He surreptitiously planned to pocket the entire profit of approximately $2,500,000.

With respect to Mr. Gullo's evidence, the trial judge said that "I cannot find him to be a credible witness".

It was, possibly, open, on the evidence, to find that whatever the agreement was between the parties, Mr. Gullo thought that it was confined to developing the whole of the 1,000 acres and that, when it became clear in April of 1988 that this was not possible because of rising prices, the agreement was at an end. There was also evidence on which it could be found that Mr. Gullo did not attempt to hide the Walshe transaction from the plaintiff and, in this respect, it was not a secret transaction.

Mr. Gullo gave evidence on cross-examination that he realized in April of 1988 that the proposed land assembly could not be put together and that it was "dead". This might have been the basis for his thinking that the partnership was no longer in existence. There was also evidence of a faxed copy of the assignment of the agreement of purchase and sale respecting the transaction in question arriving in the office at Glacier Clear Marketing, Inc. where the plaintiff was working on September 27, 1988, from which the inference could be drawn that it was not intended by Mr. Gullo that the matter be kept secret from the plaintiff. Mr. Hately submitted, on behalf of the appellants, that this was consistent with Gullo's view that there was no partnership at the time.

I am not persuaded, notwithstanding these possibly favourable pieces of evidence on the question of Mr. Gullo's state of mind, that the trial judge, who was obliged to consider all of the evidence, erred in concluding that Mr. Gullo "surreptitiously planned to pocket the entire profit of approximately $2,500,000".

I now turn to the scope of the remedy. As I have said, the trial judge relied upon the judgment of this court in *Lavigne v. Robern*, *supra*, in ordering that the plaintiff recover the whole of the profit on the transaction and not just one-half of it, that is, the plaintiff's partnership interest in it. In *Lavigne* the plaintiff, the defendant, and a Dr. Quastel owned all of the shares in a corporation. The plaintiff owned 40 per cent of the shares, the defendant 50 per cent and Dr. Quastel 10 per cent. The defendant undertook to sell the company as agent for the plaintiff and Dr. Quastel. He negotiated a sale at a price of $17,300.

At the time of the sale the defendant secretly arranged for a private "consulting" contract for himself for $50,000 to be paid over a period of two years. It was conditioned on the completion of the sale of the company. The defendant, in fact, did not do any consulting work.

The trial judge held that the defendant had breached his fiduciary duty to the plaintiff. He held that the defendant should pay to the plaintiff 40 per cent of the $50,000, the plaintiff's share in the company. The defendant was left with 60 per cent, his 50 per cent interest and Dr. Quastel's 10 per cent interest.

This court dismissed the defendant's appeal against the finding of liability and reserved its decision on the plaintiff's cross-appeal on the scope of the remedy. The plaintiff submitted that the defendant should not benefit in any way from his breach of duty. At pp. 62-63 MacKinnon A.C.J.O. said:

> It is clear on the authorities that the agent who breaches his trust and secures for himself a secret profit by way of bribe, commission or payment must disgorge that secret profit. There is, in such cases, a presumption that the payment of the secret profit was a bribe in payment for the fiduciary's use or misuse of his powers. That was the conclusion in the instant case.

> There was evidence that the company was worth $100,000. It was sold by the defendant for $17,300. The defendant then received $50,000 by way of a secret profit. Although it is irrelevant whether the beneficiary or principal suffers loss from the corrupt bargaining, having regard to the above facts I am persuaded that the plaintiff did suffer a loss and that the company was sold at a gross undervalue to the benefit of the defendant. This might be a consideration in determining just what amount the defendant should disgorge and renders it less a "windfall" in the hands of the plaintiff. However, it must be remembered that the issue of "windfall" profit to a principal has been considered by the courts and in *Regal (Hastings) Ltd. v. Gulliver et al.*, [1942] 1 All E.R. 378 at p. 394, it was rejected as an "immaterial consideration".

> Counsel were unable to refer us to any authorities which dealt with the question whether the wrongdoer could benefit indirectly from his wrongful act. If he is a partner in a firm or a substantial shareholder in a company and he is forced to disgorge his secret profit to the firm or company does he take his share of that profit as partner or shareholder?

> ...

> In dealing with this problem I start from the simple basis that the defendant under the recited circumstances must not be allowed to profit from his own wrongdoing. This may be an adoption of a penal rule of equity but it is warranted in this case: *Peso Silver Mines Ltd. v. Cropper* (1965), 56 D.L.R. (2d) 117 at p. 154, 54 W.W.R. 329; Jones, "Unjust Enrichment and the Fiduciary's Duty of Loyalty", 84 L.Q.R. 472 (1968). One can assume that a minimum sale price for the company was $67,300. The partners received $17,300 which was divided in accordance with their shareholding agreement. If the defendant had openly and honestly negotiated a sale for $67,300 he would have received 50% of the $67,300. This is precisely the amount he receives under the judgment now appealed.

> In my view this is an inappropriate disposition of the counter-claim. If it is accepted that the defendant should not profit by his wrongdoing, there is no penal aspect to the present result. As the matter now stands he receives precisely what he would have received if he had acted honestly and brought his associates into the

picture to share in the genuine sale price. The result provides no disincentive. In such cases, if the judgment were to stand, the fiduciary could breach his trust hoping to hide the breach and retain the secret profit, and if he failed to do so, he could still retain his 50% (or whatever his percentage interest in the company was) of the secret profit.

In the result, the court allowed the cross-appeal and directed that the plaintiff recover $40,000 from the defendant. Because Dr. Quastel was not a party to the proceeding the defendant was allowed to retain his $10,000 share of the secret profit.

Although *Lavigne v. Robern* was not a partnership case, it clearly had partnership features and I can appreciate the relevance of its reasoning to the issue in the present case. For the reasons which I shall give, I have concluded, however, that it was contrary to principle and authority in the present case to deprive the defendants of their one-half share in the transaction in question.

The relevant fiduciary principle with which to begin the analysis is expressed in s. 29(1) of the *Partnerships Act*, R.S.O. 1990, c. P.5, which reads:

> 29(1) Every partner *must account to the firm* for any benefit derived by the partner without the consent of the other partners from any transaction concerning the partnership or from any use by the partner of the partnership property, name or business connection.

(Emphasis added)

The same principle is expressed in s. 30 of the Act which reads:

> 30. If a partner, without the consent of the other partners, carries on a business of the same nature as and competing with that of the firm, the partner *must account for and pay over to the firm* all profits made by the partner in that business.

(Emphasis added)

As I have emphasized, s. 29(1) provides that the obligation is to pay the benefit from the transaction "to the firm" and s. 30 contains the same term. These provisions are an accurate reflection of the common law at the time they (as ss. 29 and 30 of the *Partnership Act, 1890 (U.K.)*, c. 39) were enacted. The obligation is to account for the benefit to the partnership, not to the other partner or partners to the exclusion of the defaulting partner. The cases are conveniently collected in *Lindley on Partnership*, 6th ed. (1893), the first edition after the enactment of the *Partnership Act, 1890*, at pp. 316-25. An illustrative case is *Dunne v. English* (1874), L.R. 18 Eq. 524, 31 L.T. 75, which is described in Lindley at pp. 317-18 as follows:

> In *Dunne v. English*, the plaintiff and the defendant had agreed to buy a mine for 50,000l., with a view to re-sell it at a profit. It was ultimately arranged that the defendant should sell it to certain persons for 60,000l., and that the profit of 10,000l. should be equally divided between the plaintiff and the defendant. The defendant, however, in fact sold the mine for much more than 60,000l. to a company in which he himself had a large interest. The plaintiff was held entitled to one-half of the whole profit made by the re-sale.

> There was in this case some evidence that the plaintiff knew that the defendant had some interest in the purchase beyond his share of the known profit of 10,000l.; but the plaintiff did not know what that interest was, and the real truth was concealed from him. It was held that the defendant being the plaintiff's partner, and

expressly entrusted with the conduct of the sale, was bound fully to disclose the real facts to the plaintiff, and not having done so, could not exclude him from his share of the profits which the defendant realised by the sale.

(Emphasis added)

The measure of recovery was the plaintiff's share in the profit, as required by the terms of the partnership, not the whole of it.

Most of the decisions which have applied this fiduciary principle have involved clandestine dealings by a partner for his own advantage and not for the benefit of the partnership, but the principle also applies where the advantage is obtained openly, but without the consent of the partnership: see *Clegg v. Edmondson* (1857), 8 De G.M. & G. 787, 26 L.J. Ch. 673 (L.J.J.).

I appreciate that s. 29(1), which reflects the settled principle respecting the duty of a partner and the remedy for breach of that duty (accounting for the secret profit to the firm), may not exclusively cover the matter before us. By its terms, s. 29(1) does not preclude depriving the partner who acted wrongly of his or her share of the benefit. Further, s. 45 of the *Partnerships Act* provides that: "[t]he rules of equity and of common law applicable to partnership continue in force, except so far as they are inconsistent with the express provisions of this Act" and there can be considerable flexibility in the granting of equitable remedies.

We must, however, begin our consideration with the basic premise that the profit in question is the property of the partnership, not of all the partners except the defaulting partner. To exclude the wrongdoer would be to effect a forfeiture of his or her interest in this partnership property. The point may be understood by considering a starker form of wrongdoing — a case where a partner misappropriates partnership funds for his own benefit. In such a case I am not aware of any principle or decision to the effect that not only must the partner account to the partnership for the money but must also suffer a forfeiture of his or her interest in it. In fact, the case law of which I am aware is to the contrary.

The appellants rely upon the reasons of Middleton J.A. for the Appellate Division in *Sutton v. Forst* (1924), 55 O.L.R. 281, affirmed, apparently without reasons, by the Supreme Court of Canada on June 6, 1924. One of the issues in this case was whether the relationship between the parties was that of simple agency (Forst's contention) or that of partnership or joint venture (Sutton's contention). The plaintiff Sutton had made a secret profit of at least $500 on the acquisition of certain property. The trial judge had directed that (at p. 281):

… an account to be taken of the amount due to the plaintiff on the basis of an agreement in writing entered into between the plaintiff and defendant on the 5th February, 1921, under which the defendant was to pay to the plaintiff one-half of the profits that might be made on the purchase and sale of a certain property, over and above the money put into the purchase by the defendant and 10 per cent. interest thereon.

Middleton J.A. agreed with the trial judge that the relationship was not one of agency but, rather, "a joint undertaking by these two men in which the net profits were to be divided" (p. 284).

On the appeal, Forst contended that Sutton was liable not only to account for all of the secret profits he received but also that he should be deprived of the profits derived from the joint venture. Middleton J.A. dealt with this issue as follows at p. 284:

The law in relation to agency in many respects is a safe guide to the law applicable to partnership, but to say that because one partner proved false to his duty towards the partnership, and sought to make a secret profit for himself, he loses all his share in the common assets, is going far beyond anything which has yet been decided. Such misconduct, according to the law laid down in cases cited in *Halsbury's Laws of England*, vol. 22, p. 69, would give a right to dissolution of the partnership, as well as render the partner liable for the money received, but there is no hint of the forfeiture of the delinquent's share in the partnership.

While it would seem that Forst was attempting to have Sutton deprived of all of the profits in the joint venture, going substantially beyond anything related to what happened when the property was acquired and Sutton made his secret profit, I think that this statement of Middleton J.A. is nevertheless applicable to the case before us. Further, I do not interpret the description of the trial judgment, approved on appeal, as providing that the $500, or more, was to be paid to Forst, but rather that Sutton was to account for it under the terms of his agreement with Forst.

Sutton v. Forst, supra, was referred to, and its principle appears to have been applied, in *Triplex Gold Mines Ltd. v. Harrison* (1924), 26 O.W.N. 470 (H.C.J.), affirmed (1926), 31 O.W.N. 319 (C.A.), a case in which there were competing contentions of simple agency and joint venture.

I would observe that in other contexts it has been held that the principle that a wrongdoer should not profit from his wrong does not entail his forfeiture of existing rights. In *Sanderson v. Saville* (1912), 26 O.L.R. 616 at p. 622, 6 D.L.R. 319, Riddell J. said for a Divisional Court:

> So, too, while rights cannot be acquired by a wrong-doer from his wrong, "the rule only applies to the extent of undoing the advantage gained where that can be done and not to the extent of taking away a right previously possessed...:" per Bramwell, B., *Hooper v. Lane* (1857), 6 H.L.C. 443, at p. 461.

The point before us is squarely raised and decided by the Supreme Judicial Court of Massachusetts in *Shulkin v. Shulkin* (1938), 16 N.E. 2d 644. In this case the plaintiff, Irving Shulkin, sought the dissolution of a partnership and an accounting of the partnership affairs. He submitted that "the active partners, to the extent that both or either acted with infidelity toward the partnership, should, as already stated, be required to return the salaries drawn by them and should not be permitted to share in any of the profits made as a result of any wrongdoing, or in the value of the goodwill of the partnership" (p. 651).

Cox J. said for the court at p. 651:

> It is settled that, where a partner has wrongfully appropriated partnership property, or has made secret profits either in his dealings with the partnership funds or in transactions which properly come within the scope of the partnership business, or has acquired a share in fraud of his partner, he must account for the results to the partnership in order that his co-partners may share therein. *Leach v. Leach*, 18 Pick. 68; *Jones v. Dexter*, 130 Mass. 380, 39 Am. Rep. 459; *Holmes v. Darling*, 213 Mass. 303, 100 N.E. 611; *Shelley v. Smith*, 271 Mass. 106, 170 N.E. 826; G.L. (Ter. Ed.) c. 108A, s. 21. Irving Shulkin's contention, if followed, would deprive the wrong-doing partner of any participation in the fruits of his wrongful actions. The cases which he cites, however, in the main deal with the situation where a trustee, as distinguished from a partner, has made a profit by dealing with the trust property. Clearly in such a case the whole of such profit belongs to the principal of the trust. See *Ball v. Hopkins*, 268 Mass. 260, 167 N.E. 338. The same is true in the case of an agent who makes a secret profit as a result of a purchase by him on behalf of his

principal. See *Raymond v. Davies*, Mass., 199 N.E. 321, 102 A.L.R. 1112. But we do not understand that this is the rule in the case where a partner is a wrongdoer. The principle deduced from the cases which deal with such a situation seems to be that the innocent partner is to be put as nearly as possible in the same position which he would have occupied if there had been no wrongdoing, and that this result is accomplished by giving to him that portion of the property converted, or of the secret profit to which he would have been entitled, had the property converted been allowed to remain with the partnership until its dissolution or distribution, or had the secret profit been earned by the partnership in the usual course of its business.

Shulkin v. Shulkin is cited as stating the law on this point in 68 *Corpus Juris Secundum, Partnership* (1950), s. 437, p. 986. I have not found any United States decisions to the contrary. On the other hand, the following (all Massachusetts decisions) all cite Shulkin with approval on point: *Walsh v. Atlantic Research Associates Inc.*, 71 N.E. 2d 580 (Sup. Jud. Ct., 1947); *Flynn v. Haddad*, 520 N.E. 2d 169 (App. Ct., 1988); *Zimmerman v. Bogoff*, 524 N.E.2d 849 (Sup. Jud. Ct., 1988); and *Meehan v. Shaughnessy*, 535 N.E. 2d 1255 (Sup. Jud. Ct., 1989).

The respondent, in support of his submission that he is entitled to the whole of the profit, has referred to the remedy of the constructive trust of the whole of the mining property in question granted to the plaintiff in *International Corona Resources Ltd. v. Lac Minerals Ltd.*, [1989] 2 S.C.R. 574, 61 D.L.R. (4th) 14. I appreciate the relevance, by analogy, of the decision in *Lac Minerals* to the case before us but I do not think that that decision is of sufficient relevance to supplant the application of what I consider to be the well-established partnership precedents and principles relevant to the present case. I think that Lac Minerals' expectation of obtaining an interest in the property in question was a less firm foundation for reducing the plaintiff's recovery than the defendant Gullo's interest in the partnership asset in the present case. It is only with difficulty that it could be said that Lac Minerals suffered a forfeiture of an interest in the property.

There is a sensitive and evenly balanced discussion of this issue in Ellis, *Fiduciary Duties in Canada* (1993) at pp. 12-4.2 to 12-4.3, 18-5 to 18-6, and 20-11 to 20-13. The discussion includes reference to *Sutton v. Forst*, *Lavigne v. Robern*, and *International Corona Resources Ltd. v. Lac Minerals Ltd.*

The author comments on *Sutton v. Forst* at pp. 12-4.2 to 12-4.3:

Effectively the Court differentiates agency, where the agent acts under a condition of exclusivity for another's best interest, with the partnership, where the partners act with fiduciary responsibility to one another. The difference is key: the former requires selfless disinterest in the agent's own pursuits; the latter requires a concurrent mix of self-interest with loyalty to the partnership. This in itself creates a dilemma not extant under the agency relationship because enforcement against self-interest is premised on the absence of gain by the agent. In the case of the partner, the very relationship is premised upon mutual gain and therefore complete forfeiture is, in the circumstances, not envisaged by the premise upon which the relationship is built and therefore unduly penal.

However, the dilemma is not easily solved. The fiduciary concept requires an absolute prohibition against self-interest ahead of obligation. Such prohibition is the premise for rather penal forfeiture invoked elsewhere: see *Lavigne v. Robern* (1984), 51 O.R. (2d) 60 (C.A.) (Shareholders) and *International Corona Resources Ltd. v. Lac Minerals Ltd.* (1986), 53 O.R. (2d) 737 (H.C.); affirmed (1987), 62 O.R. (2d) 1 (C.A.); affirmed [1989] 2 S.C.R.; 574 (Joint Ventures), reviewed in Remedies.

In reality, it may be preferable to analyze the need for forfeiture in keeping with the facts of the case: in *Lavigne* the sanction is acceptable given the truly repugnant behaviour whereas in *Lac Minerals* the sanction contains no reflections that the benefit was envisaged to have been mutually beneficial.

The point made in *Sutton v. Forst* (1924), 55 O.L.R. 281 is significant: the sanction of forfeiture would be destructive of the very reltionship which established the fiduciary concern. However, the counterpoint is equally valid: the fiduciary duty of loyalty is strictly and severely enforced on the basis of public policy. The severity of the remedy is thus considered insignificant vis-à-vis enforcement of loyalty.

At p. 20-13 he says:

Conceptually, however, the inconsistency remains: if the court is, in reality, enforcing the fiduciary loyalty by implementing that bargain that pre-existed the breach, the virtual ignoring of that pre-existing relationship which gave rise to the fiduciary obligation itself (the examples used here are Lavigne as shareholder, Lac Minerals as joint venturer) is inconsistent with the court order effectively citing the relationship as the premise for recovery. Simply put, it is arguable that the exclusion of the defaulting party from its lawful participation in the relationship sought to be enforced is untenable even where supported by the simple maxim that the fiduciary cannot benefit through its wrongdoing. That maxim is easily used to remove from a trustee or agent gain not envisaged by the pre-breach relationship but is more problematic in the context of a relationship whereunder gain was envisaged despite the fiduciary relationship.

Certainly the public policy premise for the penal nature of the remedy is beneficial to those seeking to enforce a vehicle like the joint venture, partnership, etc., but extremely deleterious to that party breaching the mutual duty underlying it.

I have no doubt that stripping the wrongdoing partner of the whole of the profit, including his or her own share in it, is a strong disincentive to conduct which breaches the fiduciary obligation. Further, as a host of equity decisions have shown for at least two centuries, the fact that this would result in a windfall gain to the plaintiff cannot, in itself, be a valid objection to it.

I do not, however, think that it can accurately be said that the defaulting partner does profit from his wrong when he receives his pre-ordained share of the profit. With respect to this share, the partner's conduct in the impugned transaction does not involve any breach of duty. Under the terms of the relationship, with respect to this share, it was expected that the partner would act in his own interest. To the extent that there is a dilemma, I resolve the issue, in accordance with what I consider to be the more appropriate principles and authorities, against the forfeiture of the wrongdoing partner's interest in the profit.

I mention, for the sake of completeness, that in awarding the penal remedy the trial judge appears to have taken into account very serious criminal conduct of Mr. Gullo related to this litigation. This conduct took place after the events giving rise to Mr. Olson's claim and Mr. Gullo was convicted and sentenced for it. In my view it is not relevant to the remedy and it is not submitted on Mr. Olson's behalf that it is.

I turn now to the cross-appeal respecting the basis on which the plaintiff's costs should be assessed. Had the judgment below, which awarded the plaintiff a substantial windfall profit, stood, I would not have been inclined to interfere with the trial judge's award of party-and-party costs. The court's disapproval of the defendants' conduct would be demonstrated and the plaintiff would not be out of pocket with respect to his costs. However, in the light of the variation of the judgment which I propose, I think that this is now an entirely proper case for the award of solicitor-and-client costs of the action. The plaintiff has been the victim of the breach of a fiduciary obligation and it is appropriate for the court to express its disapproval of the defendants' conduct: see *Maximilian v. M. Rash & Co.* (1987), 62 O.R. (2d) 206 at pp. 210-12 (Dist. Ct.). The criminal conduct referred to in the preceding paragraph, which involved counselling to have Mr. Olson killed, is also relevant to this issue.

For the foregoing reasons I would allow the appeal, with costs, and vary the trial judgment to provide that the plaintiff recover one-half of the profit in question.

Appeal and cross-appeal allowed.

NOTES AND QUESTIONS

1. The "criminal conduct" referred to in *Olson v. Gullo* relates to the fact that Gullo had contracted to have Olson killed after Olson commenced legal proceedings against him. Gullo pleaded guilty to attempted murder and was sentenced to three years in prison. Ultimately, Gullo died before the judgment in the case above was released.

2. It was unquestioned by the Ontario Court of Appeal in *Olson v. Gullo* that a fiduciary who accepts a secret profit must disgorge it. The question that remained was whether partners who must account for secret profits obtained in breach of fiduciary duty may take their normal share of profits in their roles as partners.

3. The court's judgment in *Olson v. Gullo* rests on the construction of ss. 29(1) and 30 of the Ontario *Partnerships Act*, which are reproduced above. Since these sections contemplate that profits from transactions such as that undertaken by Gullo are to be paid to "the firm" and the Act contains no provisions indicating the need to strip defaulting partners of their share of the firm's profits earned from such a transaction, the court finds that Olson's recovery is limited to his partnership share, or 50 per cent. As Morden A.C.J.O., for the court, said, *ibid.* at 791 "I do not, however, think that it can accurately be said that the defaulting partner does profit from his wrong when he receives his pre-ordained share of the profit".

4. The judgment in *Olson v. Gullo* suggests that a "profit" would require something more than what was agreed upon in the partnership agreement. This is inconsistent with the ordinary understanding of the term. Profit simply means the excess of yield over cost. Further, it ignores Gullo's surreptitious purchase and sale of the land in question in an attempt to circumvent his obligations under the terms of the partnership. If Gullo did not respect his obligations under the partnership, he ought not be entitled to reap the benefits of the partnership's existence.

5. The court in *Olson v. Gullo* expressly acknowledges the existence of section 45 of the Ontario *Partnerships Act*, R.S.O. 1990, c. P.5, which says that "[t]he rules of equity and of common law applicable to partnership continue in force, except so far as they are inconsistent with the express provisions of this Act". The provisions in sections 29(1) and 30 of the Act relied upon by the court to warrant limiting Olson's relief to 50 per cent of the profits earned by Gullo are inconsistent with the fundamental fiduciary principle forbidding fiduciaries from benefiting from their breaches of duty. Further, such a result is questionable when the very nature of a partnership, as reflected in provincial partnerships legislation, is properly characterized as fiduciary.

6. How do the results in *Olson v. Gullo* compare with those in *Lavigne v. Robern* (1984), 51 O.R. (2d) 60 (C.A.), which is expressly referred to in the reasons for judgment of Morden A.C.J.O.? Recall that in that case, the plaintiff (40 per cent), defendant (50

per cent), and one Dr. Quastel (10 per cent) were shareholders in a corporation, Robel Research Laboratories Ltd. ("Robel"). When Robel fell on hard times, Robern arranged for sale of its shares to the parent company of Kopp Laboratories for $17,300. However, Robern also surreptitiously arranged a $50,000 private "consulting" contract for himself with Kopp which was to be paid over two years and was conditional on the sale of the shares. Lavigne commenced proceedings against Robern for his actions; Quastel, who had left the country some time previously, did not take part in the lawsuit.

In *Lavigne*, the trial judge accepted evidence that the shares of Robel were worth $100,000 rather than the $17,300 that was obtained and that Robern did not do any consulting for Kopp, but merely attended their offices once a month to pick up his cheque (during which time he was employed full-time by the provincial Department of Health and Welfare). Robern was found to have breached his fiduciary duty to Lavigne by selling the shares of Robel at a gross undervalue and pocketing a secret profit of $50,000. In determining that Robern was not entitled to any of the secret profit, the Court of Appeal explained that to find otherwise would entail that "the fiduciary could breach his trust hoping to hide the breach and retain the secret profit, and if he failed to do so, he could still retain his 50 per cent (or whatever his percentage interest in the company was) of the secret profit": *Lavigne, ibid.* at 63. For this reason, the court concluded that:

> ... the beneficiaries, being the plaintiff and the third partner, share the secret profit in accordance with the percentage of their original shareholdings, which means that the plaintiff will receive 80% of the $50,000, which amounts to $40,000. As the third partner is not a party to the claim and has made no claim, the result is that the defendant retains the third partner's $10,000 share of the secret profit.

Although the Ontario Court of Appeal's objective in *Lavigne* was to ensure that Robern not benefit from his breach, he did benefit to the amount of the $10,000 that would have been paid to Quastel had he joined the lawsuit. While Lavigne did not deserve this money, neither did Robern. If the court was concerned about ensuring that Robern not benefit from his breach of duty, it ought to have awarded the remaining $10,000 (which was, effectively, a windfall profit) to Lavigne, who committed no wrong, rather than to Robern who acted in breach of duty.

The fiduciary duties owed by partners is closely related to the agency that necessarily results from the formation of partnership.

(c) Agency

Agency principles are fundamental to the partnership. In general, each partner is the agent of all the others in matters relating to the business of the partnership. An agency is a voluntary arrangement whereby a person, called the principal, may appoint another, called the agent, to engage in certain activities on the principal's behalf. The scope of an agent's authority is prescribed by the principal, who may limit the agent's authority to the extent desired. Thus, agency arrangements may be limited or unlimited. The agent is liable to discharge the authority granted in good faith and according to the terms established by the principal. By appointing an agent, the principal is liable to be bound to a contract by the agent, and is liable for the torts of the agent committed within the scope of the agency.

The partnership is a form of reciprocal agency, since each partner may both bind and be bound by the actions of other partners. It is possible to restrict the ability of partners to bind the partnership by agreement; such restrictions will be effective, however, only where a third party contracting with the firm has knowledge of the restrictions on a partner's ability to bind the firm: see, for example, Ontario *Partnerships Act*, R.S.O. 1990, c. P.5, s. 9. Further discussion of the liability of partnerships for the actions of partners is discussed in section D.2, "The Relationship of Partners to Third Parties" below.

Since partners can so easily be made liable by one another, partnerships require not only a high degree of trust among partners, but also that the partners be willing to take an interest in the management of the business. It is clearly in partners' self-interest to do so; if they choose to be passive investors, they take a substantial risk of not only losing their investment but of incurring further liabilities as well. Because partners must trust one another given the nature of the partnership vehicle, they will not usually allow a partner simply to transfer his or her share of the partnership to someone else; refer back to the restrictions on the assignment of partners' interests, discussed in section D.1(a), "The Personal Nature of Partnerships" above. Getting out of a partnership, while extracting the value of one's interest, may therefore be a complicated proposition. The risk is reduced somewhat in a "limited liability partnership," which is discussed in Part F, below.

(d) Presumptive Equality

As indicated earlier, partnerships legislation establishes default rules that govern partnerships where no partnership agreement exists or where an agreement is silent. One of these default presumptions is the presumption of equality among the partners in respect of their sharing of partnership profits and losses. In addition, partnerships legislation permits each partner to be entitled to participate in the management of the firm; this is reflected in the idea of reciprocal agency, discussed above. There is no express requirement in partnerships legislation that partners must engage in management should they desire not to do so; the ability to participate is permissive, not mandatory: see, for example, Ontario *Partnerships Act*, R.S.O. 1990, c. P.5, s. 24, which says: "5. Every partner *may* take part in the management of the partnership business". [Emphasis added] All partners also are entitled to have access to and inspect the partnership books.

In spite of the presumption of equality contained in provincial partnerships legislation, there is no requirement that all partners must have equal rights and obligations within the partnership vehicle. Indeed, the precise rights and duties of partners may be established by agreement that varies the default provisions of the applicable partnerships statute. Partners' ability to make alterations to the default rules of partnerships legislation by agreement is evidence of the consensual nature of the partnership vehicle.

(e) Consensual Nature

While there are several default provisions in partnerships legislation, particularly those instituting a presumptive equality among the partners, the ability to contract out of such default rules is also foundational to partnerships legislation. This is reflected, for example, in s. 20 of the Ontario *Partnerships Act*, R.S.O. 1990, c. P.5, which says:

> 20. *Variation by consent of terms of partnership* — The mutual rights and duties of partners, whether ascertained by agreement or defined by this Act, may be varied

by the consent of all the partners, and such consent may be either expressed or inferred from a course of dealing.

As this section indicates, the consensual nature of the partnership vehicle pertains also to rights and duties determined by a partnership agreement, not only those established by statute.

The ability to contract out of partners' rights and duties demonstrates the importance of consensualism to the partnership vehicle. Consensualism, however, requires unanimity among the partners in order to effect such changes; a simple majority of the partners is insufficient outside of "ordinary matters" connected with the partnership business: see Ontario *Partnerships Act*, s. 24, point 8. It should be noted, however, that this section expressly distinguishes such "ordinary matters" from changes to the nature of the partnership business, which require the consent of all existing partners. This suggests that in foundational matters or matters of fundamental importance to the partnership, unanimity will be required. Aside from fundamental changes to the character of the partnership business, other examples of the consensual nature of the partnership requiring unanimity of the partners are the admission of new partners, the expulsion of existing partners, and the ability to dissolve the partnership at the insistence of any partner.

2. The Relationship of Partners to Third Parties

The relationship of partners to third parties dealing with the partnership revolves around liability issues. The general rule is that each partner is liable for all partnership contracts, debts and torts during the ordinary course of the partnership business. In fact, it may also be possible for non-partners to bind the partnership, as indicated in s. 7 of the Ontario *Partnerships Act*, R.S.O. 1990, c. P.5:

> 7. *Partners bound by acts on behalf of firm* — An act or instrument relating to the business of the firm and done or executed in the firm name, or in any other manner showing an intention to bind the firm by a person thereto authorized, whether a partner or not, is binding on the firm and all the partners, but this section does not affect any general rule of law relating to the execution of deeds or negotiable instruments.

It is possible to restrict the ability of partners to bind the firm via a partnership agreement. However, as contemplated in section D.1(c) "Agency," above, such restrictions will be effective only where a third party contracting with the firm has knowledge of the restrictions on the partner's ability to bind the firm. The general rule for the liability of a partnership for actions of partners is illustrated in s. 6 of the Ontario *Partnerships Act*:

> 6. *Power of partner to bind firm* — Every partner is an agent of the firm and of the other partners for the purposes of the business of the partnership, and the acts of every partner who does any act for carrying on in the usual way business of the kind carried on by the firm of which he or she is a member, bind the firm and the other partners unless the partner so acting has in fact no authority to act for the firm in the particular matter and the person with whom the partner is dealing either knows that the partner has no authority, or does not know or believe him to be a partner.

Determining what constitutes the "usual way of business of the kind carried on by the firm" involves looking to the business activities that the partnership is habitually engaged in.

Where partners' liability exists, it may be joint or joint and several. There are five basic scenarios posited by partnerships legislation regarding partners' liability to third parties. These are: (a) liability incurred by a partnership before one becomes a partner; (b) liability incurred by a partnership while one is a partner; (c) liability incurred by a partnership while one holds himself or herself out as a partner or allows himself or herself to be held out as a partner ("holding out" liability); (d) liability incurred by a partnership after a partner withdraws from the partnership, and; (e) posthumous liability of a partner.

(a) Pre-Partnership Liability

The general rule in partnerships legislation is that partners are not liable for debts incurred by the partnership before becoming a partner of that partnership: Ontario *Partnerships Act*, R.S.O. 1990, c. P.5, s. 18(1). This fits with the concept of consensualism discussed above. An exception to this general rule can exist, however, where, following a person's admission to the partnership, assets are properly (*i.e.* legally) seized in satisfaction of debts incurred by the partnership before that person became a partner. Since partnership assets belong to the firm rather than to the individual partners, the new partner's contributions to the firm can be used in satisfaction of debts incurred by the partnership before the new partner became a partner in the situation contemplated above.

(b) Liability as a Partner

While logic may dictate that it is not generally acceptable to hold a person responsible for debts incurred by a partnership before that person becomes a partner, that same logic also dictates that a person who is a partner of a partnership ought to be liable for debts and obligations of the firm incurred while that person is a partner: see, for example, s. 7 of the Ontario *Partnerships Act*, R.S.O. 1990, c. P.5. This liability is jointly held with the other partners of the firm: *ibid.* s. 10. Liability of this sort is not shed once a partner leaves the partnership; that partner — and that partner's estate after the partner's death, *ibid.* s. 10(1) — remains responsible for liabilities incurred by the partnership during the time that the partner was a partner in the firm: *ibid.* s. 18(2).

Partnership liability is not always jointly held. Partners will be jointly and severally liable for (i) losses or injuries caused to third parties by wrongful acts or omissions of a partner acting in the ordinary course of business of the firm or with the authority of the co-partners, and (ii) the misapplication of money or property of a third party received for or in custody of the firm: see *ibid.* s. 13.

Potential defences to partnership liability of the sort contemplated herein include demonstrating that (i) a partner acting on behalf of the firm had no authority to engage in the impugned actions *and* the third party dealing with that partner either knew that the partner in question had no authority to engage in that activity *or* the third party did not know that the partner in question was a partner, or (ii) the third party did not believe that the partner in question was, in fact, a partner of the firm: *ibid.* s. 6. Where a partner's power to bind the partnership is restricted by agreement, no act done in contravention of that agreement can be binding on the firm where third parties have notice of the terms of the agreement and the restrictions contained therein: *ibid.* s. 9.

(c) Holding Out Liability

As indicated above, it is possible for non-partners, such as employees, to bind a partnership, as indicated in s. 7 of the Ontario *Partnerships Act*, R.S.O. 1990, c. P.5. One method by which non-partners may bind a partnership, which is known as "holding out liability," is contemplated in s. 15 of the Act:

> 15(1) *Persons liable by "holding out"* — Every person, who by words spoken or written or by conduct represents himself or herself or who knowingly suffers himself or herself to be represented as a partner in a particular firm, is liable as a partner to any person who has on the faith of any such representation given credit to the firm, whether the representation has or has not been made or communicated to the persons so giving credit by or with the knowledge of the apparent partner making the representation or suffering it to be made.

Holding out liability is akin to a form of estoppel; where a person represents or knowingly allows the representation that he or she is a partner in a firm, that person cannot later be heard to say that he or she is not a partner of that firm in the face of potential liability.

Where might representations of this type exist? One example might be where a person knowingly allows the use of his or her name in the name of the partnership even though that person is not a partner. The knowledge aspect here is key. If the person in question was merely negligent or careless about ensuring that there were no representations of that person's partnership status to third parties, then it may not be said that the person "knowingly suffered" such a representation to be made: see, for example, *Tower Cabinet Co. Ltd. v. Ingram*, [1949] 1 All E.R. 1033, [1949] 2 K.B. 397.

For holding out liability to be established, it is not sufficient for the third party who has incurred loss merely to be able to indicate that a person knowingly suffered a representation of his or her status as a partner to be made. The third party must also rely upon the representation *and* advance credit to the firm on faith of that representation as contemplated expressly in s. 15(1) above.

Holding out liability may also come into play in circumstances where a partner has retired from the partnership. This scenario is contemplated immediately below.

(d) Liability after Withdrawal from Partnership

Where a partner leaves a partnership, that partner will retain liability as if he or she continued to be a partner absent adequate notice to third parties. Indeed, s. 36 of the Ontario *Partnerships Act* expressly holds that "[w]here a person deals with a firm after a change in its constitution, the person is entitled to treat all apparent members of the old firm as still being members of the firm until the person has notice of the change". An early case that considered what constituted adequate notice is *Clarke v. Burton*, reproduced below.

CLARKE v. BURTON

(1958), 13 D.L.R. (2d) 715 (Ont. H.C.)

McRuer C.J.H.C.: — This action is brought to recover the sum of $8,071.93, a balance of an account said to be due to the plaintiff for goods supplied and services rendered to the defendants.

...

The plaintiff carries on business as a garage and service station proprietor and the defendants carried on business as a partnership under the firm name of Burton's Insulation & Roofing. The defendant William Thomas Burton, who is the father of his co-defendants commenced the business some time prior to February 21, 1947. On that date he registered a declaration of partnership showing a partnership to exist between himself and his co-defendants. At the time the declaration of partnership was signed by the parties the defendant Charles Burton was an infant but he subsequently attained his majority and, with knowledge of the partnership relationship, continued to carry on as a member of the partnership. The fact that he was an infant at the time he signed the partnership declaration is immaterial to the matter that I have to consider.

Late in December 1951 domestic trouble arose between William Thomas Burton and his wife with the result that he left home to live with another woman. At this time Charles Burton told Mr. Clarke that he had left his father and his father had left home. From that time on Charles Burton carried on his own shingling business in his own name.

After Charles severed his relations with his father and his brother they continued to carry on the roofing and insulation business under the name of Burton's Insulation and Roofing. This name appeared on their trucks but as time went on the name was changed to Burton's Building Enterprises but no declaration of dissolution of the partnership was filed nor was any declaration of partnership of Burton's Building Enterprises filed until July 28, 1954. The plaintiff at no time knew that Charles Burton was a partner in the firm known as Burton's Insulation and Roofing. In fact, Mr. Clarke said in evidence that he regarded the business as the business of William Thomas Burton and he thought the defendant Charles Burton was an employee.

Following the dissolution of the partnership the plaintiff continued to supply the goods and services, and invoices were made out in the name of Burton's Roofing and W. Burton.

Following the dispute with his father, Charles Burton consulted a solicitor and told him that he had been a partner with his father but no action was taken to formally notify the creditors of Burton's Insulation and Roofing, or the plaintiff in particular, nor was any declaration of dissolution of partnership filed.

The conclusion that I have come to on the facts is that late in December 1951 Mr. Clarke was informed by Charles Burton that he had dissociated himself from his father's business and that, in fact, the plaintiff did not thereafter supply any goods or services to Burton's Insulation and Roofing on any understanding that Charles Burton had any connection with that firm. I think the plaintiff well knew that Charles Burton was carrying on his own business in his own name and fully understood that he was in no way associated with Burton's Insulation and Roofing. On these facts what is the liability of Charles Burton? Mr. Hassard puts his case squarely on the provisions of the *Partnerships Registration Act*, R.S.O. 1950, c. 271. Section I requires registration of a declaration of partnership where persons are associated. "in partnership for trading, manufacturing or mining purposes". Section 4 provides:

> 4(1) A similar declaration shall in like manner be filed whenever any change takes place in the membership of the partnership or in the name under which it carries on business, and every such declaration shall state the change in the membership of the partnership or in its name.

Section 6:

> Upon the dissolution of a partnership any or all of the persons who composed the partnership may sign a declaration (Form 2) certifying the dissolution of the partnership.

Section 7(1):

> Until a new declaration is made and filed by him, or by his partners or any of them, no person who signed the declaration filed shall be deemed to have ceased to be a partner.

Section 36 of the *Partnerships Act*, R.S.O. 1950, c. 270 provides:

> 36(1) Where a person deals with a firm after a change in its constitution, he is entitled to treat all apparent members of the old firm as still being members of the firm until he has notice of the change.

Section 46 provides that the *Partnerships Act* "is to be read and construed as subject to ... The *Partnerships Registration Act*".

Mr. Hassard's argument is, notwithstanding the provisions of s. 36 of the *Partnerships Act*, s. 7(1) of the *Partnerships Registration Act* creates a statutory liability imposed on Charles Burton to pay for the goods supplied by the plaintiff to Burton's Insulation and Roofing, notwithstanding that the plaintiff had knowledge that he no longer was connected with the firm. Curiously enough, counsel have been unable to refer me to any case and I have been unable to find any where this precise argument has been the subject of judicial determination.

In the view that I have come to in this case it is convenient to postpone discussion of the question of whether or not the Burtons were associated in partnership for trading or manufacturing purposes.

The following ordinary principles of law to be applied may be stated thus:

1. The ordinary law is that while the retirement of a partner in no way affects his rights or obligations to strangers in respect of past transactions (*Lindley on Partnership*, 11th ed., p. 369), yet if one not known to be a partner retires, the authority of his late partner to bind him ceases on his retirement although no notice of it be given (*Lindley on Partnership*, 11th ed., p. 287).

2. A known partner who has retired from the partnership will be liable for debts of the partnership contracted after his retirement until notice is given even though the creditor has had no dealings with the firm prior to dissolution: *C. P. Reid & Co. v. Coleman Bros.* (1890), 19 O.R. 93.

3. When an apparent partner retires or when a partnership between several known partners is dissolved those who dealt with the firm before the change took place are entitled to assume that no change has occurred until they have notice to the contrary: Anglin C.J.C. in *Huffman v. Ross*, [1926] 1 D.L.R. 603, S.C.R. 5. In such case the onus is on the retired partner to prove direct notice or facts and circumstances from which knowledge of retirement might fairly be inferred.

4. If a creditor did not know that a particular partner was a partner and that partner retired then, as from the date of his retirement, he ceases to be liable for partnership debts contracted by the firm to such person: *Tower Cabinet Co. v. Ingram*, [1949] 2 K.B. 397; see also *Eagle Shoe Co. v. Thompson* (1956), 2 D.L.R. (2d) 755.

5. If notice can be established, no matter by what means, it is sufficient. No formality is required: *Lindley on Partnership*, 11th ed., p. 296.

It is therefore clear in this case that apart from the *Partnerships Registration Act* the plaintiff could not recover against the defendant. In the first place, the plaintiff at no time considered the defendant to be a partner and in the second place, he had full knowledge that the defendant had severed all connection with his father and was in business for himself. This would have constituted notice even if the plaintiff had known that the defendant was a partner.

This brings me to discuss the effect of s. 46 of the *Partnerships Act* and s. 7(1) of the *Partnerships Registration Act*.

I have been unable to find any judicial interpretation of s. 46 of the *Partnerships Act*. Just what is meant by "is to be read and construed as subject to" is not clear as will become apparent when I discuss s. 7(1) of the *Partnerships Registration Act*.

Not only is there great dearth of Canadian jurisprudence to help me in the precise difficulty that arises, but since there is no provision in the English *Registration of Business Names Act*, 1916, c. 58, similar to s. 7 of the *Partnerships Registration Act* there is no British jurisprudence of direct assistance. There are, however, some cases that are of limited assistance.

...

Of all the cases I think *Corp. of Town of Oakville v. Andrew* (1905), 10 O.L.R. 709, throws the most light on the problem that I have to solve. In this case a partnership in a private banking business which had existed between the defendant and one H. was dissolved, but the business continued to be carried on in the firm name and no notice of dissolution was given nor any certificate thereunder registered. After the dissolution H., who was also treasurer of the municipal corporation, received as such, moneys belonging to the corporation out of which, and other moneys, he made certain payments for the corporation and deposited the balance in a chartered bank where the firm kept its account, subsequently using it in the firm's business. On the death of H. the account was overdrawn and the municipality sought to hold the defendant liable on two grounds: (1) that he held himself out to be a partner or that the partner in fact continued to exist; and (2) if the partnership was dissolved no declaration of dissolution had been filed. At p. 715 Moss C.J.O., after stating that the Chief Justice of the King's Bench had given judgment for the plaintiffs, chiefly on the ground that the defendant in consequence of his failure to file a declaration of dissolution of partnership must be deemed to be a partner, said:

> It is not necessary to place a construction upon the provisions of the Act because the absence of any notice and the continued use of the defendant's name rendered him liable to be treated by all persons dealing with the firm as still a member of the firm. The filing of a declaration was one mode of giving notice to the public, and the defendant neglected this as well as the usual common law methods of freeing himself from future liability to persons dealing with the firm."

The appeal was allowed on the ground that the plaintiffs were not customers and did not deal with the partnership in the transaction in question. It was contended, however, that the former partner, as treasurer of the municipality, was their agent to deal with the partnership. At p. 716 the learned Chief Justice said:

> If he acted as the authorized agent of the plaintiffs he knew at the time that the defendant was not a partner, and his knowledge should be attributed to the plaintiffs.

These passages from the judgment of the learned Chief Justice appear to me to clearly indicate that in his opinion a creditor who continues to deal with the partnership with full notice of the dissolution cannot claim against a retired partner merely because a certificate of dissolution has not been registered.

If the liability imposed under the statute is in the nature of estoppel as Mr. Justice Middleton said in [*Re T.W. Merrick, Jamieson v. The Trustee,* [1933] O.W.N. 295, 14 C.B.R. 331], the principles of law applicable to estoppel ought to apply. These principles can be no more clearly stated than in the language of Lord Birkenhead in *Maclaine v. Gatty,* [1921] 1 A.C. 376 at p. 386 where he said:

> The learned counsel cited various authorities in which these doctrines have been discussed, but the rule of estoppel or bar, as I have always understood it, is capable of extremely simple statement. Where A has by his words or conduct justified B in believing that a certain state of facts exists, and B has acted upon such belief to his prejudice, A is not permitted to affirm against B that a different state of facts existed at the same time. Whether one reads the case of *Pickard v. Sears* (1837), 6 A. & E. 469, or the later classic authorities which have illustrated this topic, one will not, I think, greatly vary or extend this simple definition of the doctrine.

If this is the doctrine of estoppel to be applied, I cannot see how one who has specific notice of the dissolution of the partnership can take advantage of an estoppel created by statute. To come to any other conclusion would, in my opinion, reduce the law to an absurdity. Take, for example, in this case, if the solicitor that Charles Burton consulted had written to the plaintiff and told him that the partnership was dissolved, that Charles Burton was no longer connected with it, and that he was commencing business for himself and the plaintiff continued to supply goods to the partnership, could any Court in good conscience give him judgment against Charles Burton simply because the formality of the registration of a dissolution had not been gone through, a formality that in no way affected the plaintiff? My conclusion is that there is no merit in the action and it should be dismissed on this ground alone.

Having arrived at this conclusion, it is not necessary for me to consider whether the persons involved were "associated in partnership for trading or manufacturing … purposes". The action will therefore be dismissed with costs.

Action dismissed.

NOTES

1.   Following *Clarke v. Burton*, it is clear that actual notice of a partner departing a partnership trumps technical reliance on the provisions of partnerships legislation with regard to parties that had had dealings with the firm prior to the retirement of the partner in question. The reason for this conclusion is that a third party cannot reasonably claim to have relied upon a retired partner continuing to be a member of the partnership where it is demonstrated that the third party knew that the retired partner was no longer associated with the partnership.

2.   In considering what constitutes adequate notice regarding a partner's departure from a partnership, separate considerations apply to third parties who had had dealings with the firm prior to the change in its constitution versus third parties who had not had any dealings with the firm before such change.

3. Regarding the former scenario, a retiring partner will retain liability to third parties who had had dealings with the firm prior to the partner's retirement unless:

   (i) actual notice is given to the third party, as in *Clarke v. Burton*;

   (ii) the third party never knew that the retiring partner was a partner, or;

   (iii) the partner retired from the partnership because of insolvency or death.

   See s. 36 of the Ontario *Partnerships Act*, R.S.O. 1990, c. P.5.

   As for third parties who did not have dealings with the firm before a partner's retirement, they may treat any "apparent member" of the firm as a continuing member of the firm for liability purposes absent adequate notice of the partner's retirement from the firm under s. 36 of the Ontario *Partnerships Act*. Adequate notice in this situation is achieved by placing an advertisement in *The Ontario Gazette* — the official publication of the Ontario legislature — pursuant to s. 36(2) of the Ontario *Partnerships Act*. It should be noted, however, that s. 37 of that Act allows any partner to publicly give notice of the retirement of a partner or the dissolution of a partnership and may require other partners to concur for that purpose where necessary. Retired partners will also not be liable to third parties who did not have dealings with the firm before a partner's retirement where the third parties did not know that that partner was a partner.

(e) Posthumous Partner Liability

Partners — or, more specifically, their estates — are not liable for partnership liabilities incurred after death. This proposition holds true whether or not the firm name, as it existed prior to a partner's death, remains in use after the partner's death or whether the deceased partner's name remains part of the partnership name after death: see, for example, Ontario *Partnerships Act*, R.S.O. 1990, c. P.5, s. 15(2); see also *ibid.* s. 36(3), which also applies to the estates of insolvent partners or to retiring partners who were not known to be partners by third parties dealing with the partnership.

E. DISSOLUTION OF PARTNERSHIPS

Unless otherwise provided for, a partnership is automatically dissolved upon the happening of certain events. If the partnership is established for a fixed term, the partnership automatically dissolves upon the expiry of that term. If the partnership is for an undefined term, notice by one of the partners of the intention to dissolve the firm will have that effect. Where the partnership is formed for a single adventure or undertaking, the conclusion of that adventure or undertaking will terminate the partnership. Finally, the death or insolvency of a partner will also conclude the partnership absent agreement to the contrary.

In addition, where it becomes illegal for the partnership business to be continued at all or to be continued by the existing members of the partnership, the partnership will be dissolved. Additionally, a partnership may be dissolved by the court upon application by a partner in a variety of circumstances, including where a partner is found to be mentally incompetent or of permanently unsound mind; where a partner, other than the partner suing, becomes permanently incapable of performing his or her part of the partnership contract; where a partner, other than the partner suing, is guilty of conduct that, in the opinion of the court, is calculated to prejudicially affect the carrying on of the partnership business; where a partner, other than the partner suing, willfully or persistently commits a breach of the partnership agreement or otherwise engages in conduct in matters relating to the partnership business that it is not reasonably practicable for the other partner or partners to carry on the partnership business in partnership with the partner; where the partnership can only be carried on at a loss, or; when circumstances have arisen that, in the opinion of the court, render it just and equitable to dissolve the partnership: see Ontario *Partnerships Act*, R.S.O. 1990, c. P.5, s. 35.

Where a partnership is dissolved, the distribution of partnership assets is set out by legislation. Section 44 of the Ontario *Partnerships Act* establishes the following process:

> 44. *Rules for distribution of assets on final settlement of accounts* — In settling accounts between the partners after a dissolution of partnership, the following rules shall, subject to any agreement, be observed:
>
> 1. Losses, including losses and deficiencies of capital, are to be paid first out of profits, next out of capital, and lastly, if necessary, by the partners individually in the proportion in which they were entitled to share profits, but a partner is not required to pay any loss arising from a liability for which the partner is not liable under subsection 10(2). [which pertains to limited liability partnerships, which are discussed below]
>
> 2. The assets of the firm, including the sums, if any, contributed by the partners to make up losses or deficiencies of capital, are to be applied in the following manner and order,
>
>   (a) in paying the debts and liabilities of the firm to persons who are not partners therein;
>
>   (b) in paying to each partner rateably what is due from the firm to him or her for advances as distinguished from capital;
>
>   (c) in paying to each partner rateably what is due from the firm to him or her in respect of capital.
>
> 3. After making the payments required by paragraph 2, the ultimate residue, if any, is to be divided among the partners in the proportion in which profits are divisible.

F. WHAT IS A LIMITED LIABILITY PARTNERSHIP?

A relatively new incarnation of partnership in Canada is the "limited liability partnership". The limited liability partnership ("LLP"), is a modified form of ordinary partnership under Canadian law. Thus, like an ordinary partnership, it has no legal status separate from those of its partners. The status of the Canadian LLP vehicle differs from the status of LLPs in some other jurisdictions; for example, in Britain, limited liability partnerships, under the *Limited Liability Partnerships Act, 2000* (U.K.), 2000, c. 12 do not constitute partnerships under British partnership legislation, but have separate legal personalities. Section 1 of the statute indicates some of the key distinctions of the U.K. LLP:

1(1) There shall be a new form of legal entity to be known as a limited liability partnership.

(2) A limited liability partnership is a body corporate (with legal personality separate from that of its members) which is formed by being incorporated under this Act; and-

(a) in the following provisions of this Act (except in the phrase "oversea limited liability partnership"), and

(b) in any other enactment (except where provision is made to the contrary or the context otherwise requires),

(c) references to a limited liability partnership are to such a body corporate.

(3) A limited liability partnership has unlimited capacity.

(4) The members of a limited liability partnership have such liability to contribute to its assets in the event of its being wound up as is provided for by virtue of this Act.

(5) Accordingly, except as far as otherwise provided by this Act or any other enactment, the law relating to partnerships does not apply to a limited liability partnership.

(6) The Schedule (which makes provision about the names and registered offices of limited liability partnerships) has effect.

The LLP has taken on significance in jurisdictions where incorporation — complete with the limited liability that necessarily accompanies it — is not permitted for most professionals, such as lawyers or accountants. Under the LLP, individual partners are not liable for the negligent actions or omissions of persons not directly under their supervision and control. Instead, the firm as a whole is liable. Partners remain liable for their own negligent actions or omissions. Subsections 10(2) and (3) of the Ontario *Partnerships Act*, R.S.O. 1990, c. P.5 is illustrative:

10(2) *Limited liability partnerships* — Subject to section (3), a partner in a limited liability partnership is not liable, by means of indemnification, contribution, assessment or otherwise for debts, obligations and liabilities of the partnership or any partner arising from negligent acts or omissions that another partner or an employee, agent or representative of the partnership commits in the course of the partnership business while the partnership is a limited liability partnership.

(3) *Liability of negligent partner* — Subsection (2) does not affect the liability of a partner in a limited liability partnership for the partner's own negligence or the negligence of a person under the partner's direct supervision or control.

For liability other than negligence, ordinary partnership rules apply. The LLP has proven to be rather popular for qualifying professional firms seeking to reduce the liability of their partners for professional negligence. Indeed, many large law firms have adopted this structure; they may be identified by the suffix "LLP" in the firm name.

The limited liability partnership is not to be confused with the rather different limited partnership, which is described below.

G. WHEN DOES A LIMITED PARTNERSHIP EXIST?

A limited partnership is a form of partnership, but with key distinctions from ordinary partnerships. First, it must be created by express action, namely the filing of a declaration of limited partnership: see Ontario *Limited Partnerships Act*, R.S.O. 1990, c. L.16, s. 3(1). This declaration must be renewed periodically; under the Ontario Act, this must take place every five years: see *ibid*. s. 3(3).

The most important of the distinctions between ordinary and limited partnerships concerns the liability of partners. Unlike the circumstance in an ordinary partnership, where all partners have unlimited personal liability, not all of the partners of a limited partnership have unlimited personal liability. A limited partnership, in fact, requires only one partner to have unlimited personal liability. That partner is called the general partner. While there may be more than one general partner in a limited partnership, a minimum of one must exist. All other partners may be limited partners whose liability is limited to the amount of their investment in the partnership.

It is possible to be both a limited partner and a general partner in a limited partnership. Where a person is both a limited partner and a general partner, that person's liability is that of a general partner, but, in respect of that person's contribution as a limited partner, that person has the same rights against the other partners as a limited partner: see, for example, Ontario *Limited Partnerships Act*, s. 5(2).

In exchange for their limited liability, limited partners are not entitled to actively take part in the control or management of the limited partnership. That privilege belongs solely to the general partner. Should a limited partner engage in the active control or management of the limited partnership, that limited partner will be held liable as a general partner.

It is not always clear where a limited partner has engaged in active control or management of the limited partnership. Consider the results in the following two cases.

HAUGHTON GRAPHIC LTD. v. ZIVOT

[1986] O.J. No. 288, 33 B.L.R. 125 (H.C.J.)

Eberle J.: — In this case, the plaintiff claims for payment of a debt for printing services supplied by it to a limited partnership called Printcast Publishing Network (hereafter called "Printcast"). The existence of the debt and the amount claimed of $128,251.79 are not in dispute. The plaintiff earlier obtained a default judgment against Printcast but that judgment has remained unsatisfied.

The plaintiff sues the two named defendants as limited partners of Printcast on the ground that, in addition to exercising their rights and powers as limited partners, each took part in the control of the business of the limited partnership, within the meaning of s. 63 in Part 2 of the Alberta *Partnership Act*, R.S.A., 1980, c. P.2, as amended by R.S.A. 1980 (supp.), c. 2; S.A. 1981 c. 28. It is common ground that the Alberta law relating to limited partnerships applies in this case.

FACTS

In 1980 the defendant Gary S. Zivot (hereafter called "Zivot") promoted Printcast as a limited partnership under Alberta law, for the purpose of launching a magazine called "Goodlife" to be published in the United States. Zivot's concept was for a structure similar to a radio or television network. The limited partnership was to be the promoter of the concept. It would sign up local affiliates and supply them with common editorial material. Each affiliate would obtain local advertising and would be responsible for addition of local material to fill out the magazine.

At the same time, Zivot incorporated Lifestyle Magazine Inc., (hereafter called "Lifestyle") to be the sole general partner in Printcast. Lifestyle was controlled by Zivot, who was the sole limited partner in the company. During subsequent financing stages, other limited partners were added, including the defendant Herbert Marshall (hereafter called "Marshall").

Lifestyle obtained the concept and the necessary development expertise for Printcast from Century Media Incorporated. That too was a company controlled by Zivot, and used by him as a vehicle for his "media development business". Century Media in turn employed Zivot, its president, as the live body to perform these services. Century Media's role in the matter is not of particular importance, the principle players being: Printcast, (the limited partnership); Lifestyle (the general partner); and Zivot and Marshall (two of the limited partners).

. . .

It is clear on the evidence and admitted by Zivot that commencing in January 1982 Zivot was known to suppliers as the "president" of Printcast. He used this title to introduce himself; he used business cards showing his relationship to Printcast; and when the magazine was published, its masthead showed Zivot as president and Marshall as executive vice-president of Printcast. Although the specific date on which Marshall joined the enterprise is unclear, there is no doubt that he played the role of executive vice-president of, and was also a limited partner in, Printcast throughout all the relevant time period.

There is no dispute about any of the above matters and I accept them as facts.

The arrangements for printing the magazine in Toronto were made between Nash, the president of the plaintiff, and Zivot, Marshall and two other employees of Printcast. I accept Nash's evidence that Zivot was introduced to him as president of Printcast and Marshall as vice-president. Nash gained the impression that Zivot was the man at the top with complete and ultimate responsibility for putting the magazine together and getting it on to the market. He also gained the impression that Marshall was in charge of the administrative side of the business, including the sales and production aspects of the magazine. A deal was struck for the plaintiff to print the Toronto magazine and, in late 1982, it printed the first five issues. Then Printcast went into bankruptcy, leaving the plaintiff unpaid for the printing of three issues.

Before the plaintiff did any printing, it is clear that Nash knew that he was dealing with a limited partnership. This was part of the information obtained for him about the credit-worthiness of Printcast, and is recorded in Exhibit 3. This information verified that the publishing venture had a capital of somewhere between $2,000,000 and $3,000,000, of which a substantial portion was held in certificates of deposit due to mature on July 1st and November 1st, 1982.

Beyond this information, I am satisfied that Nash was neither given nor obtained further detail about the commercial nor the legal nature of Printcast. Nash admitted that he was not familiar with the structure of a limited partnership. He was not told of the existence or identity of the general partner, Lifestyle, nor of Zivot's ownership and control of it. He was not told that both Zivot and Marshall were limited partners in Lifestyle. Thus, the contract for printing services could have been made by the plaintiff only with Printcast itself, and not with the general partner Lifestyle.

TAKE PART IN CONTROL

It was faintly pressed that the defendants could not be personally liable for the debt because they did not take part in the control of the limited partnership Printcast within the meaning of s. 63 of the Alberta *Partnership Act.*

The evidence however is all to the contrary. Zivot admitted that he was the directing mind of Printcast, that he was responsible for it, and that he managed it. Whether or not he made all of the managerial decisions, he said that he was responsible for all of them. Marshall was one of those directly under Zivot who made many of the managerial decisions in the areas of sales and administration. Zivot signed cheques on behalf of Printcast; Marshall also had the authority to do so. In fact, Zivot and Marshall were in complete control of Printcast.

In my opinion, the fact that both defendants were or may have also been acting as employees or officers of Lifestyle, all unknown to Nash, does not take the defendants outside the ambit of s. 63. The defendants' submission to the contrary must be rejected on the basis of the evidence which I accept.

...

S. 63 ALBERTA PARTNERSHIP ACT

On that state of facts, and in view of the overwhelming evidence that both defendants took part in the control of the limited partnership, I come back to s. 63 of the Alberta *Partnership Act.* It reads as follows:

> 63. Liability to creditors. — A limited partner does not become liable as a general partner unless, in addition to exercising his rights and powers as a limited partner, he takes part in the control of the business.

Although elaborate arguments were made as to the meaning of the section, I take a simpler view of it. If a limited partner takes part in the control of the business, he becomes liable under the statute as a general partner, i.e. unlimited liability to the extent of his assets. That is what happened in this case, and it is, effectively speaking, the end of the matter.

The elaborate arguments made only come into play if it should be found that the plaintiff somehow disclaimed reliance on that section. ...

... Section 63 does not contain any requirement of reliance. If reliance was a necessary precondition to unlimited liability for a limited partner, appropriate words should be in the statute. To conclude that the words in the section require such a condition would not, in my view, be an interpretation of the words used in the section, but would be a clear addition of a second, distinct requirement to the only one currently found in the language of s. 63.

In any event, mere knowledge by the plaintiff that a magazine was being promoted and published by a limited partnership does not assist the defendants at all. What engages the liability of the limited partner is his taking part in the control of the business.

Accordingly in my view the defences must fail.

...

There is a surprising absence of authority in Canada on the issues raised in this case. The only recent case to which I was referred is *Elevated Construction Ltd. v. Nixon et al.*, [1970] 1 O.R. 650. In his decision, Osler J. really dealt with different aspects of the Ontario *Limited Partnerships Act*, but at p. 655, in obiter he touched upon the question of the degree of control of the business that must be exercised by a limited partner in order to make him liable as a general partner. He pointed out that the cases are far from exhaustive, referring only to three cases from 1857 and one from 1877, all of which refer to the same limited partnership. He concluded by saying:

> ... The cases are of little assistance in determining where the line is to be drawn beyond which a limited partner is deemed to be taking part in the control of the business and each case will presumably have to be decided upon its own facts.

In opposition, the defendants relied upon s. 59 of the Alberta Act under the heading "Business Dealings by Partner With Partnership" which commences "A limited partner may loan money to and transact other business with the limited partnership ..." Emphasis was placed upon the permission to "transact other business with the limited partnership". The short answer to this submission was, I think, correctly put by counsel for the plaintiff, i.e., that, while s. 59 permits the transaction of business with the limited partnership, it does not permit the transaction of business by a limited partner on behalf of the limited partnership.

Finally it was submitted on behalf of the defendants that to hold them liable in this case means that a person who is an officer or director (or I suppose a senior employee) of the corporate general partner in a limited partnership would always be fixed with unlimited liability for the debts of the limited partnership by virtue of s. 63 of the Alberta Act on the ground that he is the person who has control of the corporate general partner. This conclusion does not logically follow. The section only applies to a person who, in addition to being an officer, director, senior employee, or other directing mind of the corporate general partner, seeks also to take advantage of personal limited liability as a limited partner in the limited partnership. In other words, s. 63 applies only if two conditions are met. One is that the person be a limited partner and the second is that he take part in the control of the business of the limited partnership. The section does not apply to someone whose sole role in and connection with the limited partnership is that of an officer, director or other controlling mind of the general partner.

...

Action allowed.

NORDILE HOLDINGS LTD. v. BRECKENRIDGE

[1992] B.C.J. No. 322, 10 B.C.A.C. 290 (C.A.)

Gibbs J.A. (orally):— This appeal has its genesis in a purchase of land in 1981 pursuant to an agreement dated April 7, 1981, which I will refer to as the sale agreement. The appellant Nordile was the vendor and Arman Rental Properties Limited Partnership, a limited partnership, was the purchaser. The purchase price was payable in part by a first mortgage for $216,000 to CMHC, and in part by a second mortgage back to Nordile for $600,089.54.

Arman fell into default under the mortgages. CMHC foreclosed in 1985. Arman and Arbutus Management Ltd., the general partner of the limited partnership, were the mortgagors in the second mortgage to Nordile. On December 28, 1985 Nordile obtained judgment for $389,191 plus interest and costs against Arman and Arbutus pursuant to the terms of the second mortgage. The judgment has not been satisfied.

Nordile commenced these proceedings on March 16, 1987, claiming a right to recover the amount of the unpaid judgment and costs from John Breckenridge and Hubert Rebiffe pursuant to the Partnership Act, R.S.B.C. 1979, c. 312. ...

Nordile rests its case on s. 64 of the *Partnership Act* which provides:

> "64. A limited partner is not liable as a general partner unless he takes part in the management of the business."

Breckenridge and Rebiffe were limited partners in the Arman limited partnership. They were minority shareholders in the general partner, Arbutus. They were also officers and directors of Arbutus. Breckenridge, and to a lesser extent, Rebiffe, managed Arbutus, and Arbutus managed Arman. However, paragraph 29 of the agreed statement of facts states unequivocally that when Breckenridge and Rebiffe participated in the management as directors they did so "solely in their capacities as directors and officers of the general partner, Arbutus". That agreed fact alone is sufficient to exclude liability under the "unless" provision of s. 64 of the *Partnership Act*. Acting solely in one capacity necessarily negates acting in any other capacity.

...

Appeal dismissed; Cross-appeal allowed in part.

NOTES AND QUESTIONS

1. Another basis for excluding personal liability on the part of Messrs. Breckenridge and Rebiffe in *Nordile Holdings* was the existence of a clause in the sale agreement which said that:

    F.   The parties hereto acknowledge that Arman Rental Properties Limited Partnership (the "Limited Partnership") is a limited partnership formed under the laws of British Columbia. The parties hereto agree that the obligations of the Limited Partnership shall not personally be binding upon, nor shall resort hereunder by had to, the property of any of the limited partners of the Limited Partnership or assignees of their interest in the Limited Partnership as represented by Units of the Limited Partnership but shall only be binding upon and resort may only be had to the property of the Limited Partnership or the General Partner of the Limited Partnership.

2. In both *Haughton Graphic* and *Nordile Holdings*, the general partner of the limited partnership was a corporation and the directors of those corporations were accused of engaging in control over the limited partnership, thereby rendering them liable as general partners. Why do you think the directors were found to be liable as general partners in *Haughton Graphic*, but not in *Nordile Holdings*? What facts distinguish the two cases? How does the judgment in *Nordile Holdings* affect your understanding of *Haughton Graphic*?

H. THE LEGAL NATURE OF A LIMITED PARTNERSHIP

Since the liability of limited partners in a limited partnership differs fundamentally from the liability of partners in an ordinary partnership, one might think that the legal nature of limited partnerships also differs from that of ordinary partnerships. This issue is contemplated, *inter alia*, in *Kucor Construction & Developments & Associates v. Canada Life Assurance Co.*

KUCOR CONSTRUCTION & DEVELOPMENTS & ASSOCIATES v. CANADA LIFE ASSURANCE CO.

[1998] O.J. No. 4733, 167 D.L.R. (4th) 272 (Ont. C.A.)

The judgment of the court was delivered by

Borins J.A.: — The issue raised by this appeal is whether, or under what circumstances, a limited partnership is entitled to rely on the statutory right of prepayment provided by s. 18(1) of the *Mortgages Act*, R.S.O. 1990, c. M.40, to discharge a long-term closed commercial mortgage purported to have been given by the limited partnership.

...

DISCUSSION

In my view, the starting point in determining whether s. 18(1) of the *Mortgages Act* is available to permit prepayment of the mortgage ... is s. 18(2) of the Act. If, pursuant to s. 18(2), the mortgage was "given by a joint stock company or other corporation", prepayment is precluded. As I have indicated, the position of counsel for the limited partnership is that the mortgage was given by the partnership and that as a limited partnership is neither a joint stock company, nor a corporation, it was entitled to prepay the mortgage. Central to this position is the issue whether a limited partnership is a discrete legal entity capable of holding title to real property, and conveying title upon the mortgaging of the property. Counsel for the respondents and the intervenors are united in their submission that a limited partnership is not a legal entity. In my opinion, they are correct.

Well respected authorities are uniform in the view that a limited partnership is not a legal entity. In 35 *Halsbury's Laws of England*, 4th ed. (Butterworths, 1994) at 136 it is stated: "A limited partnership, like an ordinary partnership, is not a legal entity." In R.C.P. Banks, *Lindley & Banks on Partnership*, 17th ed., (Sweet & Maxwell, 1995) it is said at 864: "A limited partnership is not a legal entity like a limited company but a form of partnership with a number of special characteristics introduced by the Limited Partnerships Act 1907." See, also, *Sadler v. Whiteman*, [1910] 1 K.B. 868 (C.A.), per Farwell L.J. at 889; *Re Lehndorff General Partner Ltd.* (1993), 17 C.B.R. (3d) 24 at 39 (Ont. Ct. (Gen. Div.)). The concept that neither a general, nor a limited partnership, is a legal entity, has been long accepted by Canadian and English law and, no doubt, is why a limited partnership is required by law to have a general partner through which it normally acts: *Limited Partnerships Act*, ss. 2(2), 8 and 13. As for a general partnership, s. 6 of the *Partnerships Act* describes through whom it may act.

As Farley J. observed in the *Lehndorff* case at 38, a limited partnership is a creation of statute. As such, had the legislature intended to create a new legal entity it is reasonable to conclude that it would have done so in the *Limited*

Partnerships Act, as it did in s. 15 of the *Business Corporations Act*, R.S.O. 1990, c. B.16, which provides that a "corporation has the capacity and the rights, powers and privileges of a natural person". See, also, the Canada *Business Corporations Act*, R.S.C. 1985, c. C.44, s. 15(1). This conclusion finds support in an examination of the history of the limited partnership: Alison R. Manzer, *Canadian Partnership Law* (Canada Law Book Inc., 1995), 9-5 et seq. Legislation enacting corporations and limited partnerships occurred relatively contemporaneously in the 19th century in England, Canada and the United States. The enactment of separate and fundamentally, different structures for the corporation and the limited partnership indicates that legislatures did not intend to invest the limited partnership with legal status. Indeed, as I will discuss, a limited partnership is a special kind of general partnership.

It follows that Ground J. was correct in holding that a limited partnership is not a legal entity.

As a limited partnership is not a legal entity, it becomes necessary to determine how a limited partnership carries on its business, and, in particular, how it can acquire, and hold title to, real property.

In the *Lehndorff* case, at pp. 38-40, Farley J. has provided a very helpful explanation of the features of a limited partnership and how its business is conducted. His reference to "Ontario LPA" is to the *Limited Partnership Act*:

> A limited partnership is a creation of statute, consisting of one or more general partners and one or more limited partners. The limited partnership is an investment vehicle for passive investment by limited partners. It in essence combines the flow through concept of tax depreciation or credits available to "ordinary" partners under general partnership law with limited liability available to shareholders under corporate law. See Ontario LPA sections 2(2) and 3(1) and Lyle R. Hepburn, *Limited Partnerships*, (Toronto: De Boo, 1991), at p. 1-2 and p. 1-12 ... A general partner has all the rights and powers and is subject to all the restrictions and liabilities of a partner in a partnership. In particular a general partner is fully liable to each creditor of the business of the limited partnership. The general partner has sole control over the property and business of the limited partnership: See Ontario LPA ss. 8 and 13. Limited partners have no liability to the creditors of the limited partnership's business; the limited partners' financial exposure is limited to their contribution. The limited partners do not have any "independent" ownership rights in the property of the limited partnership. The entitlement of the limited partners is limited to their contribution plus any profits thereon, after satisfaction of claims of the creditors. See Ontario *LPA* sections 9, 11, 12(1), 13, 15(2) and 24. The process of debtor and creditor relationships associated with the limited partnership's business are between the general partner and the creditors of the business. In the event of the creditors collecting on debt and enforcing security, the creditors can only look to the assets of the limited partnership together with the assets of the general partner including the general partner's interest in the limited partnership. This relationship is recognized under the Bankruptcy Act (now the BIA) sections 85 and 142.

> ...

> It appears to me that the operations of a limited partnership in the ordinary course are that the limited partners take a completely passive role (they must or they will otherwise lose their limited liability protection which would have been their sole reason for choosing a limited partnership vehicle as opposed to an "ordinary" partnership vehicle) ... The limited partners leave the running of the business to the general partner and in that respect the care, custody and the maintenance of the property, assets and undertaking of the limited partnership in which the limited

partners and the general partner hold an interest. The ownership of this limited partnership property, assets and undertaking is an undivided interest which cannot be segregated for the purpose of legal process ... The limited partners have two courses of action to take if they are dissatisfied with the general partner or the operation of the limited partnership as carried on by the general partner — the limited partners can vote to (a) remove the general partner and replace it with another or (b) dissolve the limited partnership.

Although a limited partnership is a partnership, and the *Partnerships Act*, which governs general partnerships, would apply to it unless its provisions are inconsistent with those of the *Limited Partnerships Act*, there are at least two important distinctions between a general partnership and a limited partnership which are evident from the provisions of the two Acts quoted earlier. The first distinction is that in a general partnership all of the partners are liable for the obligations of the partnership, whereas in a limited partnership the general partner is fully liable for partnership obligations, with the financial exposure of limited partners being limited to their contributions to the partnership. The second distinction is that in a general partnership any partner can conduct the usual business of the partnership, whereas in a limited partnership the limited partners are passive and the general partner manages and controls the business of the partnership.

It is important to emphasize that unlike a general partnership, a limited partnership has a special category of partner, a limited partner, whose obligation to the partnership is restricted to the contribution of its capital. By s. 13(1) of the *Limited Partnerships Act*, a limited partner is restricted from active participation in the business affairs of the partnership, in return for which he or she is given limited liability, similar to a shareholder in a corporation. Involvement by a limited partner in the business of the partnership may result in the loss of limited liability by that partner.

It follows, therefore, from the statutory characteristics of a limited partnership that if its management and control are the exclusive responsibility of the general partner, who derives its powers from the *Limited Partnerships Act*, it is through the general partner that a limited partnership acquires and conveys title to real property. "Title [to real property] is normally registered with the name of a general partner": D.J. Donahue and P.D. Quinn, *Real Estate Practice in Ontario*, 5th ed. (Butterworths, 1995), 115. It is, in my view, most unlikely that limited partners, as partners in a general partnership are required to do, would exercise the option of taking title in their own names, and thereby risk exposing themselves to unlimited liability by virtue of s. 13 of the *Limited Partnerships Act*. That a limited partnership, not being a legal entity, is incapable of acquiring title to real property finds recognition in s. 48(2) of the *Registry Act*, R.S.O. 1990, c. R.20, which provides that the only entities known to law capable of acquiring title to real property are limited companies and individuals.

We were not provided with the decision of any Canadian court which specifically addressed the issue of how title to real property is to be taken by a limited partnership. However, it would appear that in *Elevated Construction Ltd. v. Nixon* (1969), 9 D.L.R. (3d) 232 (Ont. H.C.), which was a *Vendors & Purchasers Act* application, Osler J. was of the view that title is to be taken in the name of the general partner. In 68 *Corpus Juris Secundum*, "Partnership", 1024, the early case of *The Madison County Bank v. Gould*, 5 Hill 309 (Sup. Ct. N.Y. 1843), is cited as authority for the proposition that legal title to real property acquired by a limited partnership should be registered in the names of the general partners and not the limited partners. At 313 the court held:

> The title to the mill should have been taken in the names of the general partners alone. The legislature evidently intended that the legal title to all the partnership property should be vested in the general partners; that they should sue and be sued; and that the whole business should be conducted just as though there were no special partner in the case.

A "special" partner was the equivalent of a limited partner.

In summary, because a limited partnership is not a legal entity capable of holding and conveying title to real property, provision is made in the *Limited Partnerships Act* for a general partner to conduct and manage the business of the limited partnership, including acquiring and conveying real property on its behalf. On the facts of this appeal, this was recognized by the general partner and the limited partners.

The limited partnership agreement of March 12, 1976, which created the limited partnership, provided that Kucor Ltd., as general partner, was to be in charge of the management, conduct and operation of the business of the limited partnership, including the execution of all agreements related to the acquisition of the land and the construction on it of the apartment buildings. Although in the original mortgage of September 8, 1977 to Maritime, Kucor was described as the mortgagor, it was executed by Kucor Ltd. in its capacity as the sole general partner of Kucor. Similarly, when the final extension of the mortgage occurred on August 1, 1987, the amending agreement, which was between Kucor, as mortgagor, and Morguard, as mortgagee, was executed by Kucor Ltd. in its capacity as the sole general partner of Kucor. In each instance, each limited partner executed a guarantee of the mortgage debt, but did not join in the mortgage as a mortgagor. As of August 1, 1987, there were 23 limited partners, each of whom was an individual. In addition, the limited partners and the board of directors passed resolutions authorizing Kucor Ltd., as general partner, to execute the amending agreement extending the term of the mortgage by 15 years and reducing the rate of interest on the mortgage debt.

In my opinion, it is clear on the facts and the law, that the mortgage was given by Kucor Ltd., and as it is a corporation, it is precluded by s. 18(2) of the *Mortgages Act* from preparing the mortgage under s. 18(1). It follows that Ground J. was correct in dismissing the application.

A more troubling problem is presented by Ground J.'s finding that the deed of March 30, 1976 by which Kucor Ltd. conveyed the property to the limited partnership was a nullity because a limited partnership is incapable of holding title to land, with the result that title remained with Kucor Ltd. which continued to hold the property "for the benefit of all of the partners in the limited partnership". To hold that the deed was a nullity means that it lacked legal validity and the conveyance did not occur.

To resolve the problem, it is necessary to determine the intent and purpose of the conveyance. In my view, this does not cause this court any difficulty as the record, which contains no disputed evidence, points to only one conclusion. From the land transfer tax affidavit in the deed, it is learned that Kucor Ltd. had acquired the property in trust for a limited partnership to be formed and that the intent and purpose of the conveyance were to convey the land to the limited partnership which, as I have indicated, had been formed. The difficulty, of course, was that the grantee should not have been the limited partnership as such. It should have been either the general partner, or all of the partners.

In my view, the intent of the deed was to convey the property from Kucor Ltd., which had acquired it in trust for a limited partnership to be formed, to itself in its capacity as the general partner of the limited partnership. Any doubt that this was the intent of the deed is resolved by the mortgage and its extension. The mortgage and the extension agreements were executed by Kucor Ltd., in its capacity as general partner. If the deed had been intended to be a deed to each limited partner, then each of them would necessarily have executed these documents as mortgagors, whereas they executed them as guarantors. Thus, any doubt about the intended grantee is resolved by this subsequent conduct: *Canada Square Corp. v. VS Services Ltd.* (1981), 34 O.R. (2d) 250 at 260-1, 130 D.L.R. (3d) 205 (C.A.).

Although by the form of the conveyance the deed was not capable of fulfilling its intended purpose, taking a functional approach, based on the above analysis it is clear that in fact it did. Its purpose was to regularize the commercial reality that the land was no longer solely the property of Kucor Ltd., but was the property of the limited partnership, and that in its capacity as general partner, Kucor Ltd. held title to it on behalf of all the partners. In my view, it was unnecessary to treat the deed as a nullity. It should be regarded as an ill-conceived attempt to convey title to the limited partnership. As this could be accomplished either by a conveyance to the general partner, or to all partners, it should be considered as a deed by Kucor Ltd. to itself in its capacity as general partner. Support for this conclusion is found in 68 *Corpus Juris Secundum*, "Partnership", 506-507, where it is stated that a deed to a limited partnership should be, and ordinarily would be, treated as transferring legal title to the general partner.

                                        ...

As a result of my conclusion that the mortgage was given by a corporation and that, therefore s. 18(1) of the *Mortgages Act* has no application, it is unnecessary to consider whether a limited partnership is a joint stock company within the meaning of s. 18(2), or whether the mortgagor made an effective tender within the meaning of s. 18(1).

                                        ...

For all of the above reasons, the appeal is dismissed with costs to the respondents Canada Life and Hongkong. In the circumstances of this appeal, no costs are awarded to the intervenors.

Appeal dismissed.

NOTES

The *Kucor Construction* case demonstrates that, at least in terms of their legal personalities, partnerships and limited partnerships are the same. Where legal personality becomes a more complex issue is with the corporate entity. An examination of corporate legal personality can be found in Chapter 4.

CHAPTER 2

THE CANADIAN CONSTITUTION

A. THE CONSTITUTIONAL FRAMEWORK

Canada is a federal state. There are 10 provinces, each with its own sphere of legislative powers, three territories with limited self-government, and a central (federal) Parliament. Each provincial legislature is assigned certain, specific powers relating to the creation of corporations and other, general powers to regulate the activity of corporations, wherever incorporated. Similarly, the federal Parliament has power to incorporate and a broad range of legislative powers affecting corporate activity throughout the country. Territorial powers over corporate law operate in a manner similar to those powers belonging to the provinces. Both provincially and federally incorporated corporations commonly do business intra-provincially, inter-provincially and internationally.

Some interesting theoretical problems arise from the fact that several different jurisdictions have legislative power to create corporations whose business activities are not restricted to the incorporating jurisdiction.

How this came about is, like much of Canadian constitutional law, relatively simple to outline, yet somewhat difficult to justify on any rational principles of political planning. Canada is constitutionally set up under a statute of the Parliament of the United Kingdom of Great Britain and Northern Ireland, known in its current manifestation as the *Constitution Act, 1867*. It originated as the *British North America Act, 1867* (U.K.), 30 & 31 Vict., c. 3. The name was changed and the basic Canadian constitutional documents were "patriated" in 1982, or so they say; the fact remains that Canada's constitution is evolutionary and based on a foreign statute, not founded on some uniquely Canadian revolution or "Grundnorm". But these details tend to have little practical impact on the day-to-day analysis of corporate law in this country.

To set the framework within which Canadian corporate legislation and activity take place, one must have some understanding of the constitutional division of powers. These are primarily set out in ss. 91 (for federal powers) and 92 (for provincial powers) of the *Constitution Act, 1867*. For those unfamiliar with the jargon of Canadian constitutional law, one bit of terminology requires explanation: both the federal Parliament and the provincial legislatures are restricted to making laws *in relation to* the listed subject matters under s. 91 and s. 92 of the *Constitution Act, 1867*, respectively.

WELLING, CORPORATE LAW IN CANADA: THE GOVERNING PRINCIPLES

(3rd ed., 2006), pp. 3-4

Suppose one legislative body, say the Saskatchewan legislature, purports to pass a statute. A plaintiff or defendant may claim that it is *ultra vires* the provincial legislature. The argument would be that the province attempted to legislate "in relation to" some matter over which the federal Parliament has exclusive legislative jurisdiction. If the argument prevails, the conclusion will be that the legislature attempted the impossible, the attempt to legislate failed, and there is no such statute. Now any statute could be described as being "in relation to" any one of several matters, some provincial and some federal, but there is a wealth of Canadian constitutional material on that point. Fortunately, it is usually clear if a statute is directed primarily at the creation of corporations. The primary "aspect" of legislation is usually sufficient to establish legislative competence, even if the statute incidentally affects matters outside that legislature's competence.

It is traditional to survey federal and provincial legislative powers "in relation to" matters of corporate law under two separate headings. First, there is the matter of legislative power to create new corporations. Second, there is the matter of legislative power to regulate the activities of existing corporations. For historical reasons, it is useful to analyze the provincial power first and the federal power second under each heading. After this traditional breakdown, a brief overview of the *Canadian Charter of Rights and Freedoms*, Part I of the *Constitution Act, 1982*, being Schedule B to the *Canada Act 1982* (U.K.), 1982 c. 11 is set out.

B. LEGISLATIVE POWER TO CREATE CORPORATIONS

There is generally thought to be little practical difference between provincial and federal incorporation today, except to the extent that the structure of the statute in a particular province differs from the federal model. In working through the following constitutional material, try to maintain a healthy skepticism as to whether the casual, practical assumption that provincial and federal corporations are functionally identical can be legally justified.

1. The Provincial Power

The provincial power to create business corporations is generally conceded to evolve from s. 92, art. 11 of the *Constitution Act, 1867*.

> 92. In each Province the Legislature may exclusively make Laws in relation to Matters coming within the Classes of Subjects next hereinafter enumerated; that is to say ...
>
> ...
>
> 11. The Incorporation of Companies with Provincial Objects.

NOTES AND QUESTIONS

What does the word "Companies" mean? Does its definition differ from that of the word "corporation"? How? Is it broader? Narrower?

The term is not defined in the *Constitution Act, 1867*. Looking at the word's historical development, it now seems safe to say that there is little legal significance to the fact that the term "Companies" as opposed to "corporations" appears in s. 92, art. 11, though their definitions are quite different.

The meaning of the clause "with Provincial Objects" was judicially considered by the Supreme Court of Canada in *Reference in the Matter of the Incorporation of Companies in Canada* (1913), 48 S.C.R. 331. The following questions, amongst others, were submitted by the Governor General in Council under the authority of s. 60 of the *Supreme Court Act*, R.S.C. 1906, c. 139:

1. What limitation exists under the *British North America Act, 1867* upon the power of the provincial legislatures to incorporate companies?

   What is the meaning of the expression "with Provincial Objects" in s. 92, art. 11, of said act? Is the limitation thereby defined territorial, or does it have regard to the character of the powers which may be conferred upon companies locally incorporated, or what otherwise is the intention and effect of the said limitation?

2. Has a company incorporated by a provincial legislature under the powers conferred in that behalf by s. 92, art. 11, of the *British North America Act, 1867*, power or capacity to do business outside of the limits of the incorporating province? If so, to what extent and for what purpose?

   Has a company incorporated by a provincial legislature for the purpose, for example, of buying and selling or grinding grain, the power or capacity, by virtue of such provincial incorporation, to buy or sell or grind grain outside of the incorporating province?

What do you think was the intended distinction in Question 1 between a "territorial" limitation and a limitation on the character of the "powers"? What do you think was the intended distinction, if any, in Question 2 between the words "power" and "capacity"? Consider the meaning of each word in light of the obviously territorial right of any province to legislate in relation to "property and civil rights" within its own borders.

Read the following reasons for judgment of Duff J., Anglin J. and Davies J. in *Reference in the Matter of the Incorporation of Companies in Canada* (1913), 48 S.C.R. 331, and consider whether they clear up the above questions. [The reasons for judgment of Idington J., Brodeur J. and Fitzpatrick C.J.C. are omitted.]

Duff J.: ... I think only a very general answer can be given to this question. "Objects" means, I think, *le but organisé* of the company, the business which the company is authorized by its constitution to carry on with a view to the profit which is the ultimate purpose of its members. This business must be such, I think, that it falls within the description "provincial" — the adjective provincial having reference to the incorporating province. ... I think a province can confer upon its companies the capacity to acquire rights and exercise their powers (in respect of matters relating to the business of the company), outside the province, so long as the business when looked at as a whole as that of an incorporated company (in connection, that is to say, with the capacities and powers of the company so exercisable beyond the limits of the province) is still a "provincial" business. Whether in any particular case that is or is not so is a question to be determined according to the circumstances of that case. ...

Anglin J.: ... What then was the purpose and effect of the introduction of clause 11 amongst the enumerated exclusive legislative powers of the provincial legislatures? I think it was intended to preclude the contention that, if the power of incorporation should be regarded as a substantive and distinct head of legislative jurisdiction, it was wholly vested in the Dominion Parliament as part of the residuum under the "peace, order and good government" provision of section 91 (see *Citizens Ins. Co. v. Parsons*, at pages 116, 117) because not expressly mentioned in the enumeration of provincial powers; and to make it clear that this power, if so regarded, is divided between the federal and provincial jurisdictions as conferred in part on the latter by clause 11 of section 92, and in part on the former, in the case of banks by clause 15, and in the case of other Dominion corporations under the "peace, order and good government" provision of section 91.

When it was deemed advisable to introduce into the list of provincial legislative powers a reference to the incorporation of companies the delimiting or qualifying words "with provincial objects" were added in order to preclude the contention that the exclusive legislative power expressed in clause 11 comprises the whole field of incorporation, to assure to the Dominion its jurisdiction in regard to incorporation as a convenient means of effectively legislating in regard to the subjects assigned to it and to serve as an index of the line of demarcation between the two legislative jurisdictions. It was thus made clear that from provincial jurisdiction there was excluded the incorporation of companies with Dominion objects — companies for the carrying on of works and operations within the legislative jurisdiction of the Parliament of Canada — companies formed for the transaction of affairs "unquestionably of Canadian interest and importance". ...

It is argued, and with much force, that if a provincial legislature may not in express terms confer on its corporate creature power to operate outside the territorial limits of the province, and if a provincial charter purporting to confer such extra-territorial powers is *ultra vires*, it follows that in every provincial charter there must be implied the limitation that the exercise of the powers of the company (at least what have been called "functional" powers or objects, as distinguished from incidental powers) shall be confined to the territory of the province, and that a provincial corporation upon whose objects or powers no territorial restriction is expressly imposed is, nevertheless, subject to the same limitation as if its operations were by its charter expressly confined to the province. No doubt that is the case when the nature of the objects of the corporation indicates that they are to be carried out in a certain locality within the province, e.g., the establishment and maintenance of a hospital, or the building of a railway. But I find nothing in the language of clause 11 of section 92 of the "British North America Act" which compels us to hold that the ordinary mercantile trading or manufacturing company incorporated by a province to do business without territorial limitation is precluded from availing itself of the so-called comity of a foreign state, or of a province, which recognized the existence of foreign corporations and permits their operations in its territory. Of course such foreign operations must be of the class authorized by the constituting instrument of the company and not in contravention of the law or policy of the state in which they are carried on.

... [T]he exercise of its powers by a corporation extra-territorially depends not upon the legislative power of its country of origin but upon the express or tacit sanction of the state or province in which such powers are exercised and the absence of any prohibition on the part of the legislature which created it against its taking advantage of international comity. All that a company incorporated without territorial restriction upon the exercise of its powers carries abroad is its entity or corporate existence in the state of its origin coupled with a quasi-negative or passive capacity to accept the authorization of foreign states to enter into transactions and to exercise powers within their dominions similar to those which it is permitted to enter into and to exercise within its state of origin. Even its entity as a corporation is available to it in a foreign state only by virtue of the recognition of it by that state. It has no right whatever in a foreign state except such as that state confers.

... Had Parliament intended in the case of the provincial power of incorporation to depart from the ordinary rule by confining the activities of every provincial corporation within the territorial limits of the province creating it, it seems to me highly improbable that the words "with provincial objects" would have been employed to effect that purpose. Some such words as "with power to operate only in the province" would have expressed the idea much more clearly and unmistakably. Inapt to impose territorial restriction the words "with provincial objects" may be given an effect, which seems more likely to have been intended and which satisfies them, by excluding from the provincial power of incorporation such companies as have objects distinctly Dominion in character either because they fall under some one of the heads of legislative jurisdiction enumerated in section 91, or because, they "are unquestionably of Canadian interest and importance."

The granting of a charter which in terms purports to confer on a corporation the right to carry on its operations in portions of Canada beyond the limits of the province is *ultra vires* the provincial legislature and an invasion of the Dominion legislative field because it is an attempt to enable the corporation to exercise its powers as of right in parts of the Dominion not subject to the jurisdiction of the legislature which confers them.

...

Davies J.: ... If I am right that the limitation on the power of a province to incorporate companies is a territorial one and limited to the province as distinguished from the Dominion at large then it is plain that every charter granted by statute, or letters patent under the "Companies Act" by the province must have that constitutional limitation read into it. ... A provincial company incorporated for the manufacture and sale of any article while confined to the province creating it so far as the manufacture and sale of the article was concerned could doubtless purchase outside of the province the machinery and raw material necessary to enable it to carry out the purposes for which it was brought into existence and so while confined to the province in carrying on its business of selling its manufactured products could do so to any one willing to buy from any other province so long as it did not attempt to carry on its business in such other province. But I cannot see, unless my construction of our constitutional Act is entirely wrong, how a company incorporated for mining, or fishing, or lumbering, or milling, or manufacturing, say in Nova Scotia, could carry on the business of mining, fishing, lumbering, milling or manufacturing in, say the Province of British Columbia or in any other province than Nova Scotia. To say that with regard to trading companies it is almost impossible for them effectively to carry on their business within the limits of a province, except with great inconvenience and possibly loss is merely to say that they should get a Dominion and not a provincial charter.

The distinction between capacity and power was dealt with, though somewhat vaguely, in *Bonanza Creek Gold Mining Co. v. The King*, [1916] 1 A.C. 566 (Ont. J.C.P.C.). The case involved a contract concerning mining operations in Yukon. One of the parties was a corporation incorporated under Ontario legislation and the other party made a constitutional argument concerning the Ontario corporation's incapacity to conclude such a contract. It was determined that there was no capacity problem. Viscount Haldane set up the analysis as follows.

[The question] is whether a company incorporated by [a province] can have capacity to acquire and exercise powers and rights outside the territorial boundaries of the province. ... The limitations of the legislative powers of the province expressed in s. 92, and in particular the limitation of the power of legislation to such as relates to the incorporation of companies with provincial objects, confine the character of the actual powers and rights which the provincial government can bestow, either by legislation or through the executive, to powers and rights exercisable within the province. But actual powers and rights are one thing and capacity to accept extra-provincial powers and rights is quite another.

This quotation from Viscount Haldane's reasoning seems to suggest that each province may confer the "rights" of a corporation within the province, but outside of the province it can only confer upon the provincially incorporated corporation the capacity to acquire such rights. Thus if the legislature of Alberta creates a corporation, it can only give the corporation "actual powers and rights" which are exercisable in Alberta. Attempting to give the corporation "actual powers and rights" exercisable elsewhere would be *ultra vires*.

QUESTIONS

According to s. 92, art. 11 of the *Constitution Act, 1867*, the provincial power to create corporations does not extend to the creation of corporations which do not have provincial objects. The key is establishing what the adjective "provincial" means in this context and then investigating the objects of the proposed corporation to see if they are provincial in nature.

1.   From the excerpts from *Reference in the Matter of the Incorporation of Companies in Canada* (1913), 48 S.C.R. 331, above, what does the adjective "provincial" mean?

2.   From the same case, what does the word "objects" mean?

3.   What do the words "capacity" and "power" mean? Why do you think "objects" was used instead of "capacity" or "powers" in s. 92, art. 11?

4.   The test for whether a particular corporation could be created by a province seems to be whether the corporation's "objects" could be accurately described by the adjective "provincial." Section 17(2) of the A.B.C.A. and s. 17(2) of the O.B.C.A. say "A corporation shall not carry on any business or exercise any power that it is restricted by its articles from carrying on or exercising ...". Section 33(1) of the B.C.B.C.A. says " A company must not (a) carry on any business or exercise any power that it is restricted by its memorandum or articles from carrying on or exercising". All these Acts have sections similar to s. 15(1) of the C.B.C.A.: "A corporation has the capacity and, subject to this Act, the rights, powers and privileges of a natural person."

     A typical Articles of Incorporation or Memorandum of Association form will have a blank in which the corporation must fill in any restrictions on its corporate objects (*e.g.*, C.B.C.A., Form 1). A common response is "not applicable". Is "not applicable" a provincial object? Does it meet the tests set up in the cases? Are the provinces acting *ultra vires* their power to incorporate by allowing the creation of persons whose objects are stated to be "not applicable" but who have the capacity, rights, powers and privileges of a natural person?

     Does it matter that the Acts have sections like A.B.C.A., s. 16(2): "A corporation has the capacity to carry on its business, conduct its affairs and exercise its powers in any jurisdiction outside Alberta to the extent that the laws of that jurisdiction permit"? Is s. 16(2) inconsistent with s. 15(1)?

5.   In *Alberta Government Telephones v. Canadian Radio-television and Telecommunications Commission*, [1989] S.C.J. No. 84 [1989] 2 S.C.R. 225, 61 D.L.R. (4th) 193, a corporation was created by the province of Alberta with the power to carry on a telephone business providing local, long-distance, interprovincial and international services. The court held that this was a federal undertaking within s. 92, art. 10(a) of the *Constitution Act, 1867*; in conjunction with s. 91, art. 29, that section gives the federal Parliament jurisdiction over

> Lines of Steam or other Ships, Railways, Canals, Telegraphs, and other Works and Undertakings connecting the Province with any other or others of the Provinces, or extending beyond the Limits of the Province ...

Prima facie, therefore, the corporation was subject to federal regulation, but it was held that it was immune from this as an agent of the provincial Crown. (See section C, "Regulating Corporate Activity".) On the issue of the province's powers to create this corporation, Dickson C.J.C. said, at p. 292 (S.C.R.) for the majority:

> The respondents and the Attorney General of Canada did not take the position that the Alberta legislature lacked constitutional jurisdiction to create a corporation with powers the exercise of which might ultimately render the corporation subject to federal legislation. Nor was the constitutionality of the provisions in the AGT Act granting the corporation the powers to enter into interconnecting agreements questioned. A provincial Crown corporation, once validly established, can attract rights, including immunity status, from other legislatures, whether they be federal or provincial: *Bonanza Creek Gold Mining Co. v. The King*, [1916] 1 A.C. 566 [26 D.L.R. 273] (P.C.). Therefore, AGT can legitimately attract additional extra-provincial powers and rights (for instance by entering into interprovincial agreements, as in this case) without necessarily stepping outside its legislative mandate. ...

> It is unnecessary, for the purposes of this appeal, to consider whether there are limits on provincial authority to create Crown corporations operating from the outset within the federal regulatory sphere.

2. The Federal Power

The *Constitution Act, 1867* gives specific legislative jurisdiction to the federal Parliament in 31 subsections of s. 91, but only s. 91, art. 15, "Banking, Incorporation of Banks, and the Issue of Paper Money," deals specifically with the matter of creating corporations. It is, however, generally agreed that the power to incorporate is included in the general residual clause in the preamble to s. 91:

> 91. It shall be lawful for the Queen, by and with the Advice and Consent of the Senate and House of Commons, to make Laws for the Peace, Order, and good Government of Canada, in relation to all Matters not coming within the Classes of Subjects by this Act assigned exclusively to the Legislatures of the Provinces. ...

Just what the creation of business corporations has to do with such concepts as peace and order and government, whether good or bad, is somewhat obscure. Nevertheless, that it does is probably now irrefutable, *stare decisis* being as it is. The question remains: What is the scope of this power?

CITIZENS INSURANCE CO. OF CANADA v. PARSONS

(1881), 7 App. Cas. 96 (Ont. J.C.P.C.)

[This action consolidated two different legal disputes, both involving contracts of insurance with William Parsons. One of the insurers was originally incorporated under a pre-Confederation enactment of the "province of Canada" (now split into Ontario and Quebec), and thus could be treated as a federal creation. The other insurer was incorporated in England. Both carried on business in Ontario. Questions were raised both as to the power of a province to regulate corporate activity (covered later) and to the scope of the federal power to create corporations. Much that was said on the latter point was *obiter dicta*, but it has subsequently become regarded as the analytical starting point.]

Sir Montague Smith (for the Judicial Committee): — The most important question in both appeals is one of those, already numerous, which have arisen upon the provisions of the British North America Act, 1867, relating to the distribution of legislative powers between the parliament of Canada and the legislatures of the provinces, and, owing to the very general language in which some of these powers are described, the question is one of considerable difficulty. Their Lordships propose to deal with it before approaching the facts on which the particular questions in the actions depend.

...

The scheme of this legislation [the *B.N.A. Act*], as expressed in the first branch of sect. 91, is to give to the dominion parliament authority to make laws for the good government of Canada in all matters not coming within the classes of subjects assigned exclusively to the provincial legislature. If the 91st section had stopped here, and if the classes of subjects enumerated in sect. 92 had been altogether distinct and different from those in sect. 91, no conflict of legislative authority could have arisen. ... [However, with regard to certain classes of subjects] generally described in sect. 91, legislative power may reside as to some matters falling within the general description of these subjects in the legislatures of the provinces. In these cases it is the duty of the courts, however difficult it may be, to ascertain in what degree, and to what extent, authority to deal with matters falling within these classes of subjects exists in each legislature, and to define in the particular case before them the limits of their respective powers. It could not have been the intention that a conflict should exist; and, in order to prevent such a result, the two sections must be read together, and the language of one interpreted, and, where necessary, modified by that of the other. In this way it may, in most cases, be found possible to arrive at a reasonable and practical construction of the language of the sections, so as to reconcile the respective powers they contain, and give effect to all of them. In performing this difficult duty, it will be a wise course for those on whom it is thrown, to decide each case which arises as best they can, without entering more largely upon an interpretation of the statute than is necessary for the decision of the particular question in hand.

...

[As to the power to create corporations], it is not necessary to rest the authority of the dominion parliament on [s. 91, art. 2: "the Regulation of Trade and Commerce"]. The authority would belong to it by its general power over all matters not coming within the classes of subjects assigned exclusively to the legislatures of the provinces, and the only subject on this head assigned to the provincial legislature being "the incorporation of companies with provincial objects", it follows that the incorporation of companies for objects other than provincial falls within the general powers of the parliament of Canada.

QUESTIONS

Call the provincial power to create corporations "A"; according to the Judicial Committee, the federal power is defined as "not A".

1. Does this mean that a federal "company" is properly incorporated only if it engages in business activities in more than one province? Must there at least be some activity that goes beyond the borders of one province, whether inter-provincially or internationally?

2. Alternatively, need it only have "objects" that are not "provincial objects"? Or is it sufficient that it is incorporated with the (a) right, (b) power, (c) capacity, or (d) legislative permission to carry on business in more than one province? What is the effect in this regard of s. 15(2) of the C.B.C.A., which provides that "[a] corporation may carry on business throughout Canada"?

3. Is there a functional limitation on the federal incorporation power or only a territorial one? How does this compare with the provincial power to incorporate?

4. Given the different wording of the provincial and federal legislative powers, one would not expect that provincial and federal corporations would play similar roles in the Canadian economy. Yet they do — within a province, across Canada, and in international markets. Why do you suppose constitutional challenges to their ability to do so are never made?

5. Section 92, art. 13 of the *Constitution Act, 1867* gives each province the power to create laws in relation to property and civil rights. C.B.C.A., s. 15(1) says "[a] corporation has the capacity and, subject to this Act, the rights, powers and privileges of a natural person". Does Parliament have the power to enact such a section? Is your analysis affected by C.B.C.A., s. 15(2)?

6. Suppose a successful entrepreneuse whose business interests are so varied that they defy categorization registers the appropriate "articles of incorporation" under the C.B.C.A. The sole purpose (objects?) she has in mind are (a) to make lots of money and (b) to minimize the amount of income tax payable on profits from the business.

    (i) Is the corporation properly in existence if its business activities are confined to the province of British Columbia?

    (ii) Must there be some element of extra-provincial activity?

    (iii) What facts would be relevant, in the evidentiary sense of relevance, to those questions?

7. Which of the Nova Scotia legislature or the federal Parliament has legislative power to create a management corporation to operate a lighthouse on Sable Island? What facts, and what documentary evidence, are relevant to this question?

C. REGULATING CORPORATE ACTIVITY

The idea of creating a corporation is clear enough, even if the scope of the powers to do so are a little bit murky. This part of the chapter deals with regulating the activities of corporations which already exist. In other words, it addresses the power of legislatures to restrict or control the behaviour of corporations. Any legislature can restrict the behaviour of a corporation it has created (subject to arguments based on the *Canadian Charter of Rights and Freedoms*; see section D). The question here is the ability to regulate the corporate creations of another legislature. Regulation can mean anything from a legislative pronouncement directed at a single corporation to a general legislative scheme which affects all persons and therefore affects corporations.

Disputes about the division of powers are disputes about whether a particular attempt to legislate has succeeded. The enumerated heads of power in s. 91 or s. 92 of the *Constitution Act, 1867* set out the powers of the respective legislatures. Most disputes about the division of powers come down to the characterization of the legislative attempt, or its "pith and substance" — its dominant matter or feature. It must be characterized as "in relation to" some "matter". If a provincial legislative attempt is to succeed, the legislation must be classified as "in relation to" one of the "matters" in s. 92. If a federal attempt is to succeed, the legislation must be classified as "in relation to" one of the "matters" in s. 91 (including the federal residual power). Note that the same wording can be viewed as having more than one "pith and substance" or as dealing with more than one "matter"; one being federal and the other provincial under what is known as the "double aspect" doctrine: see *Hodge v. The Queen* (1883), 9 A.C. 117 (J.C.P.C.); *Multiple Access Ltd. v. McCutcheon*, [1982] 2 S.C.R. 161, 138 D.L.R. (3d) 1.

Note also the distinct concept of "paramountcy": "where ... a given field of legislation is within the competence both of the Parliament of Canada and of the provincial Legislature, and both have legislated, the enactment of the Dominion Parliament must prevail over that of the province if the two are in conflict ...". (*La Compagnie Hydraulique de St. Francois v. Continental Heat and Light Co.*, [1909] A.C. 194 at 198, 18 Que. K.B. 193 (Que. J.C.P.C.)). Paramountcy therefore applies where (a) both the federal Parliament and a provincial legislature enact statutes pertaining to a matter *and* (b) the two statutes conflict. The result is that the provincial legislation is rendered inoperative (not *ultra vires*) to the extent of the conflict.

The power to regulate corporate activity in general is nowhere expressly granted in the *Constitution Act, 1867*. Therefore, when one is trying to determine the success or otherwise of a legislative attempt to regulate corporate activity, it will be unhelpful to classify the legislation as "corporate regulation". It may be that the legislative attempt fits into one of the enumerated heads that are not particularly about corporations. For example, a law that regulates the activities of a courier service might be classified as a law in relation to postal service, which would place it under a federal head of power. On the other hand, most statutory, common law or equity rules which affect corporate activity, but which are not specifically directed at corporations, could just as accurately be described as relating to such "matters" as property and civil rights, which would place them under provincial control.

The other, more subtle, alternative is that the power to regulate the activities of corporations can be found in corporate law. That is, at least some forms of regulation affect corporations so seriously that they constitute rules of corporate law, and therefore belong to whichever legislature created the corporation in question. For example, the power to create federal corporations includes authority to legislate regarding their status and corporate structure. On that basis, federal legislation governing takeovers of dominion corporations has been upheld as legislation in relation to the incorporation of companies other than with provincial objects, which only incidentally affects property and civil rights: see *Esso Standard (Inter-America) Inc. v. J.W. Enterprises Inc.*, [1963] S.C.R. 144, 37 D.L.R. (2d) 598.

Assume that a province has attempted to pass legislation that would affect the way in which a federal corporation carries on its business. Anyone arguing that this legislation is *ultra vires* could claim that the provincial legislation in question was "in pith and substance" legislation in relation to the "incorporation of companies with objects other than provincial". The argument could be that the provincial legislature attempted to enact federal corporate law. If that argument succeeded, then the legislative attempt would fail. Anyone trying to support the legislative attempt might argue that the legislation was in relation to property and civil rights. Even if that view prevailed, the provincial legislation might be inoperative to the extent that it conflicted with a federal statute, under the doctrine of paramountcy.

It is useful to separate the regulation of the activities of corporations, wherever incorporated, into provincial and federal categories. Under each subheading, we will address the two possibilities discussed above: first, that the regulatory activity falls into a non-corporate head of power; second, that it is in fact corporate law. The relevance of paramountcy will also be explored.

1. The Provincial Powers

Virtually any activity that a corporation carries on in Canada will take place in one province or another, and as a result, will initially appear to fall within one of the enumerated heads of power assigned to one of the provinces. The following extract from the *Constitution Act, 1867*, indicates the most common areas of provincial regulatory control.

> 92. In each Province the Legislature may exclusively make Laws in relation to Matters coming within the Classes of Subjects next hereinafter enumerated; that is to say, —
>
> ...
>
> 2.   Direct Taxation within the Province in order to the raising of a Revenue for Provincial Purposes.
>
> ...
>
> 9.   Shop, Saloon, Tavern, Auctioneer, and other Licences in order to the raising of a Revenue for Provincial, Local, or Municipal Purposes.
>
> 10. Local Works and Undertakings other than [three excluded classes].
>
> 11. The Incorporation of Companies with Provincial Objects.
>
> ...
>
> 13. Property and Civil Rights in the Province.

14. The Administration of Justice in the Province ... including Procedure in Civil Matters in [Provincial] Courts.

15. The Imposition of Punishment by Fine, Penalty, or Imprisonment for enforcing any Law of the Province ...

16. Generally all Matters of a merely local or private Nature in the Province.

QUESTIONS

A corporation is formed under the C.B.C.A. for the sole purpose of selling legal advice to the general public. Assume that the legislature of a province in which it wants to do business precludes corporations from practising law in the province.

1. Has the provincial legislature attempted to regulate the activities of a corporation? If so, where does the province derive its power to regulate this federal corporation?

2. Would it make any difference if selling legal advice was not the only business the corporation wanted to do?

3. Would it make any difference whether all, or just some, provinces did the same?

4. Could the federal corporation claim that the second-last province to prohibit its activities was, by effectively restricting the corporation's activities to one province, purporting to make laws in relation to the incorporation of companies for objects other than provincial?

5. Would your answers be different if each province permitted the sale of legal services to the public only by corporations incorporated in that province?

JOHN DEERE PLOW CO. v. WHARTON

(1914), 18 D.L.R. 353, 7 W.W.R. 706, [1915] A.C.330 (B.C. J.C.P.C.)

[The province of British Columbia required extra-provincial corporations to acquire provincial licences for the privilege of carrying on business in British Columbia. The B.C. statute made it an offence for a non-B.C. corporation to do business without a licence and said that any contracts made by a non-licensed extra-provincial corporation were unenforceable in the B.C. courts. The lower court issued an injunction against the corporation's doing business in British Columbia. This decision was appealed.]

Haldane L.C.: — ... The appellant is a company incorporated in 1907 by Letters Patent issued by the Secretary of State for Canada under the Companies Act of the Dominion. The Letters Patent purported to authorize it to carry on throughout Canada the business of a dealer in agricultural implements. It has been held by the Court below that certain provisions of the B.C. Companies Act have been validly enacted by the provincial legislature. These provisions prohibit companies which have not been incorporated under the law of the province from taking proceedings in the Courts of the province in respect of contracts made within the province in the course of their business, unless licensed under the Provincial Companies Act. They also impose penalties on a company and its agents if, not having obtained a license, it or they carry on the company's business in the province. The appellant was refused a license by the registrar. It was said that there was already a company registered in the province under the same name, and sec. 16 of the provincial statute prohibits the grant of a license in such a case. The question which has to be determined is whether the legislation of the province which imposed these prohibitions was valid under the B.N.A. Act.

...

... The expression "civil rights in the province" is a very wide one, extending, if interpreted literally, to much of the field of the other heads of sec. 92, and also to much of the field of s. 91. But the expression cannot be so interpreted, and it must be regarded as excluding cases expressly dealt with elsewhere in the two sections, notwithstanding the generality of the words. If this be so, then the power of legislating with reference to the incorporation of companies with other than provincial objects must belong exclusively to the Dominion Parliament, for the matter is one "not coming within the classes of subjects assigned exclusively to the legislature of the provinces", within the meaning of the initial words of sec. 91, and may be properly regarded as a matter affecting the Dominion generally and covered by the expression "the peace, order and good government of Canada".

Their Lordships find themselves in agreement with the interpretation put by the Judicial Committee in *Citizens Insurance Co. v. Parsons* 7 A.C. at pp. 112, 113 on head 2 of sec. 91, which confers exclusive power on the Dominion Parliament to make laws regulating trade. This head must, like the expression, "property and civil rights in the province" in sec. 92, receive a limited interpretation. But they think that the power to regulate trade and commerce at all events enables the Parliament of Canada to prescribe to what extent the powers of companies the objects of which extend to the entire Dominion should be exercisable, and what limitations should be placed on such powers. For if it be established that the Dominion Parliament can create such companies, then it becomes a question of general interest throughout the Dominion in what fashion they should be permitted to trade. Their Lordships are, therefore, of opinion that the Parliament of Canada had power to enact the sections relied on in this case in the Dominion Companies Act and the Interpretation Act. They do not desire to be understood as suggesting, that because the status of the Dominion company enables it to trade in a province and thereby confers on it civil rights to some extent, the power to regulate trade and commerce can be exercised in such a way as to trench, in the case of such companies, on the exclusive jurisdiction of the provincial legislatures over civil rights in general. No doubt this jurisdiction would conflict with that of the province if civil rights were to be read as an expression of unlimited scope. But, as has already been pointed out, the expression must be construed consistently with various powers conferred by secs. 91 and 92, which restrict its literal scope. It is enough for present purposes to say that the province cannot legislate so as to deprive a Dominion company of its status and powers. This does not mean that these powers can be exercised in contravention of the laws of the province restricting the rights of the public in the province generally. What it does mean is that the status and powers of a Dominion company as such cannot be destroyed by provincial legislation. This conclusion appears to their Lordships to be in full harmony with what was laid down by the Board in *Citizens Insurance Co. v. Parsons*, 7 A.C. 96; *Colonial Building Association v. Attorney-General for Quebec*, 9 A.C. 157; and *Bank of Toronto v. Lambe*, 12 A.C. 575.

It follows from these premises that these provisions of the Companies Act of British Columbia which are relied on in the present case as compelling the appellant company to obtain a provincial license of the kind about which the controversy has arisen, or to be registered in the province as a condition of exercising its powers or of suing in the Courts, are inoperative for these purposes.

···

To attempt to define *a priori* the full extent to which Dominion companies may be restrained in the exercise of their powers by the operation of this principle is a task which their Lordships do not attempt. The duty which they have to discharge is to determine whether the provisions of the provincial Companies Act already referred to can be relied on as justifying the judgment in the Court below. In the opinion of their Lordships it was not within the power of the provincial legislature to enact these provisions in their present form. It might have been competent to that legislature to pass laws applying to companies without distinction, and requiring those that were not incorporated within the province to register for certain limited purposes, such as the furnishing of information. It might also have been competent to enact that any company which had not an office and assets within the province should, under a statute of general application regarding procedure, give security for costs. But their Lordships think that the provisions in question must be taken to be of quite a different character, and to have been directed to interfering with the status of Dominion companies, and to preventing them from exercising the powers conferred on them by the Parliament of Canada, dealing with a matter which was not entrusted under sec. 92 to the Provincial Legislature. … They think that the legislation in question really strikes at capacities which are the natural and logical consequences of the incorporation by the Dominion Government of companies with other than provincial objects.

Appeals allowed.

BONANZA CREEK GOLD MINING COMPANY v. THE KING

[1916] 1 A.C. 566, 26 D.L.R. 273 (Ont. J.C.P.C.)

[An Ontario corporation had been set up and the question arose whether it had the legal capacity to contract to mine gold in Yukon; it made no difference that it was Yukon rather than a province, say, Saskatchewan. The Judicial Committee saw the interplay between the constitutional powers of a home province and a host province as follows.]

Viscount Haldane [at p. 576 (A.C.)]: — … [The question] is whether a company incorporated by provincial letters patent, issued in conformity with legislation under s. 92 of the British North America Act, can have capacity to acquire and exercise powers and rights outside the territorial boundaries of the province. In the absence of such capacity the certificates, licences, and leases already referred to were wholly inoperative, for if the company had no legal existence or capacity for purposes outside the boundaries of the province conferred on it by the Government of Ontario, by whose grant exclusively it came into being, it is not apparent how any other Government could bestow on its rights and powers which enlarged that existence and capacity. The answer to this question must depend on the construction to be placed on s. 92 of the British North America Act and on the Ontario Companies Act.

Sect. 92 confers exclusive power upon the provincial Legislature to make laws in relation to the incorporation of companies with provincial objects. ... Such provincial objects would be of course the only objects in respect of which the province could confer actual rights. Rights outside the province would have to be derived from authorities outside the province. ...But actual powers and rights are one thing and capacity to accept extra-provincial powers and rights is quite another. ... The words "legislation in relation to the incorporation of companies with provincial objects" do not preclude the province from keeping alive the power of the Executive to incorporate by charter in a fashion which confers a general capacity analogous to that of a natural person. Nor do they appear to preclude the province from legislating so as to create, by or by virtue of statute, a corporation with this general capacity. What the words really do is to preclude the grant to such a corporation, whether by legislation or by executive act according with the distribution of legislative authority, of power and rights in respect of objects outside the province, while leaving untouched the ability of the corporation if otherwise adequately called into existence, to accept such powers and rights if granted ab extra. ...

NOTES

In *John Deere*, above, it was argued that federal legislation that allowed the creation of the corporation doing business in British Columbia came into conflict with provincial legislation prohibiting the activity of the corporation in the absence of a licence. The result in the case was that the federal corporation did not have to get a licence. Do you think this was because (a) provincial legislation was in conflict with federal legislation; the federal legislation was therefore paramount, and the provincial legislation inoperative; or (b) the provincial attempt at legislation was, in pith and substance, corporate law and therefore *ultra vires* to the extent that it applied to federal corporations? What difference would it make? Hint: paramountcy is a one-way street; division of powers is a divided highway. See C. Lavoie, "L'immunité constitutionelle des corporations provinciales" (1987), 28 Cahiers de Droit 223.

In *Bonanza Creek*, above, the conflict was between the legislative power of one province to create a corporation and that of a second province to determine what the corporation would be permitted to do within the second province's borders. Note again the importance of distinguishing among the concepts of capacity, powers and rights, and privileges. If an Ontario corporation, necessarily incorporated "with provincial objects," wishes to do business in Saskatchewan, but is prohibited from doing so by the Saskatchewan legislature, this prohibition can hardly be described as an attack on the "status and essential powers" of the Ontario corporation. The Ontario creation of the corporation and the Saskatchewan prohibition of its activities within Saskatchewan are provincial acts that can stand together. Note, however, the difference when a federal corporation runs up against the Saskatchewan prohibition. Created "for objects other than provincial" (*Citizens Insurance Co. of Canada v. Parsons* (1881), 7 App. Cas. 96 (Ont. J.C.P.C.), above), the federal corporation is entitled *to some extent greater than an Ontario corporation* to exercise powers in Saskatchewan and in every other province. Just how far this argument can be taken remains to be seen.

The difficult task of applying the "status and essential powers" test in corporate law has arisen most often as a result of securities legislation. Early provincial attempts to legislate in this area were held *ultra vires* by the courts. See *R. v. Henderson* (1924), 51 N.B.R. 346 (C.A.); *Manitoba (Attorney General) v. Canada (Attorney General)*, [1929] A.C. 260, [1929] 1 W.W.R. 136 (P.C.). However, since 1932, the trend has been to protect the provinces' rights in the area of securities legislation by not allowing federal powers to interfere with provincial securities legislation. See *Lymburn v. Mayland*, [1932] A.C. 318, [1932] 2 D.L.R 6, 57 C.C.C. 311, [1932] 1 W.W.R. 578 (P.C.); *Duplain v. Cameron*, [1961] S.C.R. 693, 30 D.L.R. (2d) 348, 36 W.W.R. 490.

Many of the leading cases were reviewed and the general approach taken by the courts towards provincial regulation of the business activities of federal corporations was set out in *Canadian Indemnity Co. v. British Columbia (Attorney General)* (1976), 73 D.L.R. (3d) 111, [1977] 2 S.C.R. 504, [1976] 5 W.W.R. 748, 30 C.P.R. (2d) 1. The plaintiff, a federal corporation, sought a declaration that the B.C. *Automobile Insurance Act* and the *Insurance Corporation of British Columbia Act* were *ultra vires* the B.C. legislature. These statutes essentially nationalized the automobile insurance business in British Columbia, requiring all motor vehicle owners to have insurance. Justice Martland surveyed the cases on point and then concluded with the following statement of law (at p. 122 [D.L.R.]):

> Parliament can create and maintain the legal existence of a corporate entity, with which a Province cannot interfere. But a provincial Legislature within its own field of legislative power can regulate, in the Province, a particular business or activity. The fact that a federally-incorporated company has, by federal legislation, derived existence as a legal person, with designated powers, does not mean that it is thereby exempted from the operation of such provincial regulation. It is subject to such regulation in the same way as a natural person or a provincially-incorporated company [citing *Morgan* v. *A.-G. P.E.I.* (1975), 55 D.L.R. (3d) 527, per Laskin, C.J.C.].

QUESTIONS

1. Could British Columbia now safely nationalize the rest of the insurance business? All business activities within the province?

2. What if nine of the ten provinces prohibited all business activities except those conducted by provincial Crown corporations? At what point does the federal trade and commerce power take over?

3. Why isn't a provincial monopoly on auto insurance a violation of the federal *Competition Act*, R.S.C. 1985, c. C-34?

In this area generally, see the excellent article by Professor J. Ziegel, "Constitutional Aspects of Canadian Companies," *Studies in Canadian Company Law*, 1st ed., Ziegel, ed., (Toronto: 1967) and N.W.C. Ross, "The Extra-Provincial Licensing Statutes: Their Scope, Validity and Consequences" (1979), 4 Can. Bus. L.J. 183.

We saw above how the "status and essential powers" test can be seen as based either on paramountcy or on the division of powers. The scope of the paramountcy doctrine has been substantially affected by the following decision.

MULTIPLE ACCESS LTD. v. McCUTCHEON

[1982] 2 S.C.R. 161, 138 D.L.R. (3d) 1, 18 B.L.R. 138

[Insider trading is the buying or selling of corporate securities by certain persons ("insiders") who know information about the corporation that has not yet been released to the general public. Both the *Canada Corporations Act*, R.S.C. 1970, c. C-32 and the *Ontario Securities Act*, R.S.O. 1970, c. 426 contained insider trading rules in functionally identical sections. The provincial legislation was conceded to be *intra vires*. The federal legislation was found to be *intra vires* by the majority. The remaining issue was whether both were applicable to a federal corporation.]

Dickson J. (for the majority): — Having found ss. 100.4 and 100.5 of the Canada Corporations Act to be intra vires the Parliament of Canada and ss. 113 and 114 of the Ontario Securities Act to be intra vires the Legislature of Ontario there remains but to respond to the third and final question. Are ss. 113 and 114 of the Ontario Act suspended and rendered inoperative in respect of corporations incorporated under the laws of Canada.

... Although the appellant argues, weakly, that there are minor differences in the legislation, Henry J. found an identity of purpose, conduct and remedy. Does mere duplication constitute "the conflict" required by the paramountcy doctrine in order to render a provincial statutory provision inoperative? This is the issue upon which Mr. Justice Henry at trial and Mr. Justice Morden in the Divisional Court parted ways. The same difference of opinion is reflected by the commentators.

Mr. Justice Henry chose a more narrow and if I may say so, more modern, test of conflict with the concomitant result of leaving to the provinces ample legislative room. He adopted the test propounded by Mr. Justice Martland in *Smith v. R.*, *supra*.

> It may happen that some acts might be punishable under both provisions and in this sense that these provisions overlap. However, even in such cases, there is no conflict in the sense that compliance with one law involves breach of the other. It would appear, therefore, that they can operate concurrently (at p. 800 [S.C.R.]).

On the basis of the "overwhelming weight of recent authority" Mr. Justice Henry found that the two sets of statutory provisions could "live together and operate concurrently". Any "diseconomies" resulting from the proliferation of laws and administration were inherent in the federal system. Double liability would be avoided by "cooperation between administrators and the ordinary supervision of the courts over duplication of proceedings before them".

Morden J. adopts the older and more prevalent view of the commentators that "The authorities establish one of the implications of Dominion paramountcy to be that provincial duplicative legislation is suspended and inoperative. Simple duplication by a province is not permitted".

The conflict between the reasons of Mr. Justice Henry and the reasons of Mr. Justice Morden lies in large measure upon the opinion of the latter that the paramountcy doctrine became applicable because a plaintiff could resort to one set of provisions only and, having done so, there would be no scope for the other to have operational effect. That is unquestionably an important consideration but it is not, in my view, conclusive. The provincial legislation merely duplicates the federal; it does not contradict it. The fact that a plaintiff may have a choice of remedies does not mean that the provisions of both levels of government cannot "live together" and operate concurrently.

...

With Mr. Justice Henry I would say that duplication is, to borrow Professor Lederman's phrase, "the ultimate in harmony". The resulting "untidiness" or "diseconomy" of duplication is the price we pay for a federal system in which economy "often has to be subordinate to ... provincial autonomy" (Hogg, at p. 110). Mere duplication without actual conflict or contradiction is not sufficient to invoke the doctrine of paramountcy and render otherwise valid provincial legislation inoperative.

In principle, there would seem to be no good reason to speak of paramountcy and preclusion except where there is actual conflict in operation as where one enactment says "yes" and the other says "no"; "the same citizens are being told to do inconsistent things"; compliance with one is defiance of the other. The Courts are well able to prevent double recovery in the theoretical and unlikely event of plaintiffs trying to obtain relief under both sets of provisions. The fact that a Court must authorize proceedings under the Ontario Act provides a safeguard against double recovery if the company has already proceeded under the federal Act. In addition the Court at the final stage of finding and quantifying liability could prevent double recovery if in fact compensation and an accounting had already been made by a defendant. No Court would permit double recovery.

I find that ss. 113 and 114 of the *Securities Act* of Ontario are not suspended or rendered inoperative in respect of corporations incorporated under the laws of Canada by ss. 100.4 and 100.5 of the *Canada Act*.

[The minority, having found the federal sections *ultra vires*, expressed no opinions on this issue.]

NOTES

1.   The cases on securities regulation, and the decision in *Canadian Indemnity Co. v. British Columbia (Attorney General)* (1976), 73 D.L.R. (3d) 111, [1977] 2 S.C.R. 504, [1976] 5 W.W.R. 748, 30 C.P.R. (2d) 1, represented a trend towards allowing more provincial regulation of federal corporations. To the extent that the "status and essential powers" test is based on paramountcy, *Multiple Access Ltd. v. McCutcheon* showed a judicial reluctance to find that federal and provincial legislation are in conflict unless the conclusion is inescapable. The decision in *Reference re ss. 91 and 92 of the Constitution Act, 1867*, [1991] M.J. No. 190, 73 Man. R. (2d) 81, [1991] 4 W.W.R. 193, 80 D.L.R. (4th) 431 (C.A.) suggested a turning of the tide. At issue was the applicability to federal corporations of provincial legislation which (a) required registration if a corporation used a "business name" which was different from its corporate name (that is, the name on the certificate of incorporation); (b) allowed a provincial official to order a corporation not to use a particular *business name* if the official thought that confusion would result; and (c) allowed a provincial official to order a corporation to change its *corporate name*, or at least not to use it (and to use a business name instead), if the official thought confusion would result from the use of the corporate name. There were also issues generated by federal trade marks, which are not addressed here. The reasons for judgment are somewhat confusing, but the majority held that (a) a federal corporation could be required to register if it used a business name in the province; and (b) a federal corporation could be ordered to use a different business name if it used its business name only in *intra-provincial* business in the province; if, however, the corporation used the name to carry on business *inter-provincially*, this engaged the federal "trade and commerce power" (*Constitution Act, 1867*, s. 91, art. 2), and ousted the provincial jurisdiction over the name. Justice Twaddle, for the majority of three judges, said (at p. 91 [Man. R. (2d)]):

> The divide between a federally incorporated company which does business in each of several provinces and one which conducts its business across provincial boundaries is sometimes hard to draw. Yet, I am convinced that it is on such a division that legislative jurisdiction depends.
>
> Although it will often be difficult to decide whether a particular business falls within the exclusive provincial jurisdiction over intra-provincial trade or within

the exclusive federal jurisdiction over interprovincial trade, I do not for myself have any doubt that the use of a business name by a company in the conduct of a business which necessarily straddles a provincial boundary falls within the latter. It must be determined in any particular case whether a company which does business in each of several provinces does so in such a fashion that each provincial operation can be looked upon as a separate local business or is so integrated in its operation that each component requires continuity of name if the whole is to succeed in its commerce. An in-store bakery might fall within the former class whilst a national distributor of goods might fall within the latter, at least with respect to the distribution aspect of its business.

Finally, the majority held (c) that a federal corporation could not be ordered to change its corporate name, or even to use a business name instead of its corporate name (at p. 92 [Man. R. (2d)]):

It was not argued, and I do not think it is in doubt, that the province may enact legislation which requires a company incorporated in Manitoba either to change its corporate name or to refrain from using it in the conduct of its business. Nor is there any reason to doubt that the provincial legislature can ban a company which is not federally incorporated from carrying on its business in the province. Such a ban can be imposed absolutely or on the conduct of business under the corporate name.

The controversial issue is whether the province may require a federally incorporated company to use a name other than its corporate one for business purposes in Manitoba.

...

Even if the legislature only intended to restrict a federally incorporated company in the use of its corporate name, as distinct from requiring a change of name, the legislation is of doubtful validity. The name of a corporation is more than a label by which it is known: it is also, to use the language of Blackstone, "the knot of the combination". The corporate name is thus entwined with the status of the corporation and must be used as required by corporate law. With respect to a federally incorporated company, the relevant corporate law is that enacted by Parliament: see *Re Upper Churchill Water Rights Reversion Act*, [1984] 1 S.C.R. 297 [at 325].

...

At the present time, the *Canada Business Corporations Act*, R.S.C. 1985, c. C-44, [s. 10(5)] requires a federally incorporated company to use its corporate name in the same commercial documents as those specified in s. 191(6) of the Manitoba statute [*Corporations Act*, R.S.M. 1987, c. C-225]. That happy coincidence is unimportant. What is important is that federally incorporated companies are regulated in the use of their corporate names by federal corporate law, just as provincially incorporated companies are similarly regulated by provincial corporate law. The use of the corporate name is thus within the field of corporate law and, in the case of federally incorporated companies, within the exclusive jurisdiction of Parliament. The province has no jurisdiction to regulate the use of the corporate name of a federally incorporated company.

Two judges dissented in the case. Justice O'Sullivan refused to answer the questions referred to the court. Justice Jewers (sitting *ad hoc*) dissented on substantive grounds, saying that the regulation in issue was of general application and did not destroy the status and essential powers of federal corporations, and that the distinction between intra-provincial and inter-provincial trade was irrelevant.

Does this case support the view that the "status and essential powers" test derives from paramountcy, or from the division of powers? Could it derive from both? See also *Bell Canada v. Quebec (Commission de la santé et de la sécurité du travail)*, [1988] S.C.J. No. 41, [1988] 1 S.C.R. 749, 51 D.L.R. (4th) 161, and *Irwin Toy Ltd. v. Quebec (Attorney General)*, [1986] S.C.J. No. 36, [1989] 1 S.C.R. 927, 58 D.L.R. (4th) 577, in which the Supreme Court discussed the provincial regulatory power in the light of its effects, not specifically on federal corporations, but more generally on federal undertakings.

2.   The upshot of all of this is that provinces can regulate the corporations of other provinces to an unlimited degree, but can regulate federal corporations to a limited and difficult-to-define degree. All provinces and territories have legislation which requires corporations created elsewhere to comply with certain formalities. The requirements and the penalties vary. The regulations are summarized in N.W.C. Ross, "The Extra-Provincial Licensing Statutes: Their Scope, Validity and Consequences" (1979), 4 Can. Bus. L.J. 183.

The effect of the constitutional issues discussed here is that some of these provisions may not apply to federal corporations. The practical outcome is that there is not much difference between a federal and a provincial corporation. A B.C. corporation can carry on business in any or all provinces, so long as it complies with the licensing regulations. A federal corporation might be exempt from some of them, but the cost of establishing this might not be worth the benefit.

2. The Federal Powers

The federal Parliament is given no specific power to regulate the activities of business corporations. Federal powers, like provincial powers, are described in the *Constitution Act, 1867* as being "in relation to [specified] matters". Corporations, wherever incorporated, will be affected by federal legislation. For example, the *Income Tax Act* applies to anyone resident or doing business in Canada. However, corporate activity in general, which for our purposes means business activity, is more often affected by provincial laws.

There are two reasons for this. One, as already set out, is the broad range of provincial control over local matters, including "property and civil rights in the province". The other is the judicial emasculation of what might otherwise have been a broad federal "regulation of trade and commerce" power under s. 91, art. 2. In *Canada (Attorney General) v. Alberta (Attorney General) (The Insurance Reference* [1916] 1 A.C. 588, the Judicial Committee said:

> [I]t must now be taken that the authority to legislate for the regulation of trade and commerce does not extend to the regulation by a licensing system of a particular trade in which Canadians would otherwise be free to engage in the provinces.

This view has been consistently upheld over the years. (See, *e.g.*, *Re Board of Commerce Act, 1919 and Combines and Fair Prices Act*, 1919, [1922] 1 A.C. 191 (J.C.P.C.); *Canadian Federation of Agriculture v. Quebec (Attorney General) (Margarine Case)* [1951] A.C. 179 (J.C.P.C.) and the Ontario case of *Labatt Breweries of Canada Ltd. v. Canada (Attorney General)*, [1980] 1 S.C.R. 914.)

There are particular heads of federal power giving Parliament exclusive jurisdiction over certain types of business activity. Most of these are well known to anyone who has studied Canadian constitutional law. Many of them tend to be monopolized by either federal Crown corporations or federally regulated industries. The postal service (s. 91, art. 5) and the whole area of banking and the issue of money (s. 91, arts. 14, 15, 16, 18, 19, 20) are thus under federal control. Constitutional issues which are as yet unresolved arise as a result of increasing competition from corporations offering courier services and operating chequing and deposit-taking businesses.

NOTE

In *Alberta Government Telephones v. Canadian Radio-television and Telecommunications Commission*, [1989] S.C.J. No. 84, [1989] 2 S.C.R. 225, 61 D.L.R. (4th) 193, a corporation was created by the province of Alberta with the power to carry on a telephone business providing local, long-distance, inter-provincial and international services. The court held that the business was a federal undertaking within s. 92, art. 10(a) of the *Constitution Act, 1867*. That means the corporation's business was subject to federal regulation, doesn't it? The majority held that, as an agent of the provincial Crown, the corporation was immune from federal regulation which did not specifically bind the Crown. How does that work?

The most difficult area of analysis remains the extent to which the federal power to create corporations includes the regulation of their ongoing activities. As noted earlier, this is based on the rather general wording of the preamble to s. 91, which gives the federal Parliament power to make:

> ... Laws for the Peace, Order and good Government of Canada, in relation to all Matters not coming within the Classes of Subjects by this Act assigned exclusively to the Legislatures of the Provinces ...

Reference re ss. 91 and 92 of the Constitution Act, 1867, [1991] M.J. No. 190, 73 Man. R. (2d) 81, [1991] 4 W.W.R. 193, 80 D.L.R. (4th) 431 (C.A.) suggests that the corporate name is one example of an area of regulation which is so tied up with the status of the corporation that it belongs solely to the jurisdiction which created the corporation. There is clear support for the extension of this idea to rules concerning intra-corporate relationships in federal corporations, that is, rules governing the relationships among shareholders and between shareholders and management.

MULTIPLE ACCESS LTD. v. McCUTCHEON

[1982] 2 S.C.R. 161, 138 D.L.R. (3d) 1, 18 B.L.R. 138

[Insider trading is the buying or selling of corporate securities, usually shares, by certain persons, usually corporate managers or influential shareholders, who know something about the corporation's prospects that has not yet been released to the general public. If the insider who trades is a buyer, the seller will already be involved in the corporate organization. Where, however, the insider sells, the buyer may be a complete stranger. It is therefore not obvious that insider trading is an intra-corporate matter included in the federal power to create corporations. The question arose whether insider trading rules, conceded to be a proper subject of provincial legislation, could be included in a federal incorporating statute and applied to federal corporations.]

Dickson J. (for the majority): — [T]he first constitutional question [is], are sections 100.4 and 100.5 of the Canada Corporations Act *ultra vires* the Parliament of Canada in whole or in part.

...

First, in the legislative scheme of things we find ss. 100.4 and 100.5 in a corporations act dealing with company law matters.

Parliament has not yet enacted any comprehensive scheme of securities legislation. To date the Canadian experience has been that the provinces have taken control of the marketing of securities, differing in this respect from the United States where the Securities and Exchange Commission has regulated trading and primary distribution of securities. I should not wish by anything said in this case to affect prejudicially the constitutional right of Parliament to enact a general scheme of securities legislation pursuant to its power to make laws in relation to interprovincial and export trade and commerce. ... The federal government, it may be noted, has already produced Proposals for a Securities Market Law for Canada (1979).

...

In one of its aspects, insider trading legislation, dealing as it does with fundamental corporate relationships, may certainly be characterized as company law. Some commentators such as Williamson go so far as to say that:

> The insider reporting requirements seem, in the light of the history of Canadian corporation and securities law, more properly part of a companies act than of a securities act. (Supplement to Securities Regulation in Canada at p. 358)

And Professor Ziegel has written (Studies in Canadian Company Law (1967), vol. 1, at p. 170):

> Prima facie the regulation of proxies and insider trading belong exclusively to the domain of company law because they affect the relationship between the directors and its shareholders and the solicitation of voting powers at meetings of the company.

... There may be a temptation to regard the insider trading provisions of the Canada Corporations Act as redundant having regard to the almost identical provisions found in the Ontario legislation applicable to federal companies as well as Ontario companies. Any such temptation should be resisted. The validity of the federal legislation must be determined without heed to the Ontario legislation. Further, a number of the provinces have not yet enacted insider trading legislation. Striking down the federal legislation would leave federal companies, having head offices in those provinces, and their shareholders, without the double protection, which Ontario shareholders now enjoy. A declaration of invalidity of the federal Act would create a potential gap in the present regulatory schemes that might be exploited by the unprincipled.

I turn now to the main question. Does the "matter" (or pith and substance) of the insider trading provisions of the federal Act fall within a "class of subject" (or head of power) allocated to Parliament. Counsel for the Company and for the Attorney General of Ontario contends that s. 100.4 applies to a very large class of persons who are involved in transactions relating to the securities of the company. These provisions, it is said, do not relate to the status of a federal company or to domestic or internal constitution of the company but rather create civil rights or obligations which can only be the subject-matter of provincial legislation in relation to property and civil rights in a province.

With respect, I do not agree. ... Viewed in isolation it can no doubt be argued that their matter is the trading in securities. Viewed in context, however, they are, in my opinion, company law.

...

Insider malfeasance affects, directly and adversely, corporate powers, organization, internal management. It affects also financing because shareholders and potential shareholders must be assured the company's affairs will be scrupulously and fairly conducted; otherwise the raising of capital, clearly an element of company law, will be inhibited.

...

I agree with the submission of counsel for the Attorney General of Canada that the impugned provisions of the Canada Corporations Act are directed at preserving the integrity of federal companies and protecting the shareholders of such companies; they aim at practices, injurious to a company or to shareholders at large of a company, by persons who because they hold positions of trust or otherwise are privy to information not available to all shareholders. ... [**Dickson J.** next set out some views on the "double aspect" doctrine in constitutional law, and concluded.] In my opinion, ss. 100.4 and 100.5 have a general corporate purpose and a "rational, functional connection" with company law. The sections in my view are *intra vires* the Parliament of Canada.

Estey J. (for the minority): — The appellants ... attack the constitutionality of ss. 100.4 and 100.5 of the Canada Corporations Act on the ground that these provisions are not to be properly classified in law as corporate regulation but rather are a usurpation of provincial power with reference to property and civil rights.

...

The basic corporate existence, that is the objects, corporate powers, its internal government, its rules for the raising of capital, and the classes of securities which it may issue for that purpose, its relationship to its creditors, the limitation of liability of shareholders, directors, and officers of the company for the actions of the company, are all matters clearly within the federal action when providing by legislation for the creation of legal entities with objects other than "provincial objects" as the expression is employed in s. 92(11).

[By contrast, the] provisions in the Securities Act of Ontario, are indeed provisions directed to the regulation of the holding and trading of securities in the province of Ontario. They may well have incidental impact upon corporations whose securities are involved in this regulation but the central thrust of the legislation is not the constitution of the corporation but the regulation of the trading of the corporation's securities in the province as an incident of general regulation of securities trading.

The common law has for two centuries before the advent of corporate securities trading statutes known remedies for persons injured in securities transactions and somewhat related subjects such as the abuse of corporate opportunities by company officials. The concept of fiduciary duty and the beneficiaries' rights arising on its breach has long been applied to the issuance, sale and purchase of company shares.

...

The net cast by these sections is by no means confined to gathering in directors, officers or shareholders of federal companies. [**Estey J.** considered all the persons that these sections embrace, then continued.] ... Obviously, to make the sections effective their reach must include all persons who might reasonably be expected to be in a position to improperly make use of confidential corporate information to the detriment of holders of securities of that company and to the company itself. But that is simply a recognition of the true purpose of these provisions. They are not to complete a constitution or to regulate the relationship of the company to its shareholders, or to empower its officers or organs of corporate government to function. The purpose is to protect the general public from suffering a loss on their investment and corporate securities due to defined improper conduct by a wide range of persons who may be in a position to affect the value of these securities in the hands of the public. This is made doubly clear by the provision in s. 100.4 for the compensation of loss suffered by another person by reason of the transaction in question whereas in the case of the company the recovery takes the form of an accounting by the wrongdoer for any direct benefit or advantage received by him.

[**Estey J.** examined ss. 100.4 and 100.5 in more detail, then concluded.] [W]e are not here dealing with sections of a provincial act which sterilize or impair the federally incorporated company's ability to conduct its affairs, nor in the case of the federal statute are we dealing with traditional corporate legislation required to fill out the constitutional and functional aspects of a federal incorporation. I conclude, therefore, that ss. 100.4 and 100.5 of the *Canada Corporations Act*, are ultra vires the Parliament of Canada.

...

I do not wish to leave this matter without observing that this case was argued and heard on the footing that the Attorney General for Canada supported these sections in the Canada Corporations Act, entirely on the basis as set out in *John Deere Plow, supra*; i.e., that the provisions in question are corporate in nature and are part of the exercise of a valid constitutional function by the Parliament of Canada under the peace, order and good government clause in s. 91 and/or the trade and commerce power under s. 91(2) whereby Parliament is authorized to prescribe the powers of companies whose objects extend to the entire Dominion. Counsel for the Attorney General for Canada did not wish to found the validity of these sections upon an independent claim that, by reason of the potential extraprovincial nature of securities trading, they could be sustained by the authority of s. 91(2) alone. I venture to say that there will be more and more challenges in the future to the dominant position now occupied by the securities exchange authorities of the province in which the major stock exchange of the country is located. As the magnitude and number of multi-provincial security transactions increase the strain on the present unbalanced regulatory system will mount. It remains to be seen whether this will precipitate a change in the national appreciation of constitutional requirements and federal legislative policy. Until such a development occurs the disposition of this appeal must be found in the light of the positions herein taken by the parties. These reasons therefore reflect only the record as advanced by the proponents and opponents of the traditional arguments on the constitutional nature of corporate and securities legislation.

WELLING, CORPORATE LAW IN CANADA: THE GOVERNING PRINCIPLES

(3rd ed., 2006), p. 31

The provincial and the federal powers to regulate business corporations aren't restricted to controlling the activities of their own corporate creations. Some aspects of corporate activity, such as the extent of a particular corporation's legal powers and the intra-corporate power structure created by its corporate constitution, are treated as extensions of the legislative jurisdiction to incorporate: in those matters, regulation is by the incorporating legislature. In most areas of endeavour, however, the regulation is of *business* activity, whether pursued by corporations or individuals. Here, the legislative power to regulate evolves from the assignment of "Matters" in s 91 and s 92 of the *Constitution Act 1867*.

D. THE CANADIAN CHARTER OF RIGHTS AND FREEDOMS

Part I of the *Constitution Act, 1982* (ss. 1-34), the *Canadian Charter of Rights and Freedoms*, has changed Canadian law in significant ways. For one, it has restricted the established "supremacy of Parliament" principle whereby it was assumed that absolutely any law could be passed by either the federal Parliament or one of the provincial legislatures. Many *Charter* sections apply to corporations.

As discussed further in Chapter 4, corporations are generally accorded the status of "persons" for the purposes of legal analysis. The *Interpretation Act* in any province will be found to contain a provision similar to s. 35 of the federal *Interpretation Act*, R.S.C. 1985, c. I-21, s. 35(1): "In every enactment, ... 'person', or any word or expression descriptive of a person, includes a corporation." On the other hand, it has been held that interpretation acts do not apply to the *Charter*, since it is a constitutional document: *Law Society of Upper Canada v. Skapinker*, [1984] 1 S.C.R. 357, 9 D.L.R. (4th) 161.

Let's look first at what the legislators probably had in mind when they enacted the *Canadian Charter of Rights and Freedoms*. The word "individual" is used in s. 15. It seems safe to say that this section was not intended to apply to corporations, since "individual" is one of the expressions traditionally used where one wishes to exclude corporations. Indeed there is evidence that in this context, the word was specifically chosen for this purpose. In ss. 3, 6 and 23 we find the word "citizen": since citizenship is a statutory concept which is inapplicable to corporations, it would appear that these rights were not intended to be available to them. (See P.W. Hogg, *Constitutional Law of Canada*, 4th ed. (Toronto: Carswell, 1997), pp. 837-41.)

Elsewhere, one finds the words "everyone" (ss. 2, 7, 8, 9, 10, 12 and 17), "any person" (ss. 11 and 19), "any member of the public" (s. 20) and "anyone" (s. 24). The French version uses *chacun* in most of these cases, but *tout inculpé* in s. 11, *le public* in s. 20 and *toute personne* in s. 24. The implication is that not only individual persons are protected.

The following sections have arisen frequently in legal disputes involving corporations:

2.   Everyone has the following fundamental freedoms:

(*a*) freedom of conscience and religion;

(*b*) freedom of thought, belief, opinion and expression, including freedom of the press and other media of communication;

(*c*) freedom of peaceful assembly; and

(*d*) freedom of association.

...

7. Everyone has the right to life, liberty and security of the person and the right not to be deprived thereof except in accordance with the principles of fundamental justice.

8. Everyone has the right to be secure against unreasonable search or seizure.

...

11. Any person charged with an offence has the right

...

(*b*) to be tried within a reasonable time;

(*c*) not to be compelled to be a witness in proceedings against that person in respect of the offence;

(*d*) to be presumed innocent until proven guilty according to law in a fair and public hearing by an independent and impartial tribunal;

...

(*f*) except in the case of an offence under military law tried before a military tribunal, to the benefit of trial by jury where the maximum punishment for the offence is imprisonment for five years or a more severe punishment ...

Despite the wording, judges have resisted the suggestion that all of these rights are available to corporations. The following case is illustrative of the type of analysis courts have gone through when determining whether a corporation is able to invoke a given right.

R. v. AGAT LABORATORIES LTD.

[1998] A.J. No. 304, 17 C.R. (5th) 147 (Prov. Ct.)

[The accused corporation was charged with several environmental offences. The trial judge, at the request of the accused, ordered the Crown to disclose certain materials by the hearing date. By the time the matter came around for hearing, disclosure had not been made. The accused submitted that this failure to disclose constituted a violation of its rights under s. 7 of the *Charter*, by adversely affecting its ability to make a full answer and defence. One of the issues, therefore, was whether s. 7 applied to a corporation.]

Fradsham Prov. J. [at p. 152]: — ... The Crown submits that a corporate accused may not receive monetary compensation for a section 7 breach. Reliance is placed on *R. v. Wholesale Travel Group Inc.* (1991), 67 C.C.C. (3d) 193

(S.C.C.) and *Irwin Toy Ltd. c. Québec (Procureur général)* (1989), 58 D.L.R. (4th) 577 (S.C.C.).

A consideration of that issue requires one to examine chronologically the development of the law relating to section 7 of the Charter and corporations generally.

In 1989, the Supreme Court of Canada decided *Irwin Toy, supra.* At pp. 632-633, the Court said:

> In order to put forward a s. 7 argument in a case of this kind where the officers of the corporation are not named as parties to the proceedings, the corporation would have to urge that its own life, liberty or security of the person was being deprived in a manner not in accordance with the principles of fundamental justice. In our opinion, a corporation cannot avail itself of the protection offered by s. 7 of the Charter. First, we would have to conceive of a manner in which a corporation could be deprived of its 'life, liberty or security of the person'. We have already noted that it is nonsensical to speak of a corporation being put in jail. To say that bankruptcy and winding-up proceedings engage s. 7 would stretch the meaning of the right to life beyond recognition. The only remaining argument is that corporations are protected against deprivations of some sort of 'economic liberty'.
>
> There are several reasons why we are of the view that this argument can not succeed. It is useful to reproduce s. 7, which reads as follows:
>
> 7. Everyone has the right to life, liberty and security of the person and the right not to be deprived thereof except in accordance with the principles of fundamental justice.
>
> What is immediately striking about this section is the inclusion of 'security of the person' as opposed to 'property'. ... [W]e find the ... effect of the inclusion of 'security of the *person*' to be that a *corporation's* economic rights find no constitutional protection in that section.
>
> That is, read as a whole, it appears to us that this section was intended to confer protection on a singularly human level. A plain common sense reading of the phrase 'Everyone has the right to life, liberty and security of the person' serves to underline the human element involved; only human beings can enjoy these rights. 'Everyone' then, must be read in light of the rest of the section and defined to exclude corporations and other artificial entities incapable of enjoying life, liberty or security of the person and include only human beings.

In 1990, The Supreme Court of Canada issued its judgement in *Dywidag Systems International Canada Ltd. v. Zutphen Brothers Construction Ltd.* (1990), 68 D.L.R. (4th) 147 (S.C.C.). The Court re-emphasised that only human beings were protected by section 7 of the *Charter*, with one exception related to attacks on the constitutionality of a statute. At p. 149, Cory, J., speaking for the Court, said:

> There can now be no doubt that a corporation cannot avail itself of the protection offered by s. 7 of the Charter. ... It is true that there is an exception to this general principle that was established in *Big M Drug Mart*, where it was held that '[a]ny accused, whether corporate or individual, may defend a criminal charge by arguing that the law under which the charge is brought is constitutionally invalid'.

Then, in 1991, the Supreme Court of Canada issued its decision in *R. v. Wholesale Travel Group Inc., supra.* The Court again reaffirmed its view that section 7 of the *Charter* applied only to human beings, with the exception previously noted. At pp. 208-210, Lamer, C.J.C., speaking for the majority on this point, said:

...

> Thus, it is my view that Wholesale Travel does have standing to challenge the constitutionality of the false/misleading advertising provisions under ss. 7 and 11(d) of the Charter and may benefit from a finding that these provisions are unconstitutional. However, this is *not* to say that if the same provisions were enacted so as to apply *exclusively* to corporations, a corporation would be entitled to raise the Charter arguments which have been raised in the case at bar... Once the provisions are held to be of no force or effect, they cannot apply to *any* accused, whether corporate or individual...

To this point, the jurisprudence seemed clear: with the exception of challenging the constitutionality of a statute itself, (and even then, *Wholesale Travel, supra,* raised the possibility of the exception not applying if the statute only pertained to corporations), section 7 of the *Charter* did not apply to corporations. However, that position softened in 1992 with the release by the Supreme Court of Canada of its decision in *R. v. C.I.P. Inc.,* [1992] 1 S.C.R. 843 (S.C.C.).

In *C.I.P., supra,* the issue was whether a corporation had a *Charter* right to trial within a reasonable time under section 11(b). The Crown submitted that a corporation could not invoke section 11 of the *Charter* unless it was contesting the constitutional validity of the charging statute. Justice Stevenson, speaking for the Court, disagreed. His Lordship said at p. 852:

> In my opinion, the respondent's argument on this first issue overlooks the generally accepted contextual and purposive approach to *Charter* analysis. In *Irwin Toy Ltd.,* it was not the absence of penal proceedings *per se* that precluded the respondent corporation from invoking s. 7. Rather, the Court focused on the language of the right in combination with the nature of the specific interests embodied therein, and concluded that in that context, s. 7 could not logically apply to corporate entities. I do not read that decision as ruling out the possibility of corporations asserting other *Charter* guarantees.

Justice Stevenson then set out the test to be applied (at p. 852):

> ... *Irwin Toy Ltd.* went only so far as to establish an appropriate analytical framework: whether or not a corporate entity can invoke a *Charter* right will depend upon whether it can establish that it has an interest falling within the scope of the guarantee, and one which accords with the purpose of the provision.

He noted that in *Slaight Communications Inc. v. Davidson,* [1989] 1 S.C.R. 1038 (S.C.C.), the Court had found that section 2(b)'s protection of freedom of expression applied to corporations. At p. 853 of *C.I.P., supra,* His Lordship said:

> What is of importance here is the fact that the corporate appellant was unanimously recognized as having the right to invoke s. 2(b) in circumstances other than those set out in *R. v. Big M Drug Mart Ltd.* No one took issue with the appellant's standing.

Justice Stevenson then directly considered the position of a corporate accused in relation to section 11(b). Applying the analytical framework he had previously set out, he held that the corporate accused had an interest in being tried within a reasonable time. At p. 856 he said:

> I am of the view that the appellant has a legitimate interest in being tried within a reasonable time. The right to a fair trial is fundamental to our adversarial system.

Parliament has seen fit to accord that right constitutional protection. I can find no principled reason for not extending that protection to *all* accused.

At pp. 856-7, he quoted with approval the following words of the Honourable Judge MacDonnell in *R. v. 741290 Ontario Inc.* (1991), 2 O.R. (3d) 336 (Ont. Prov. Div.), at pp. 351-52:

> Any accused, corporate or human, can be denied full answer and defence by reason of delay. A corporation is just as vulnerable to the deterioration of recollection which can prejudice any person on trial for an offence. Its witnesses, like those of any accused, can die, move away, or disappear. If, as seems clear, the right of an accused to make full answer and defence is a fundamental principle of the Canadian system of justice, and if that system regards corporations as being susceptible to the same criminal process as human, it would seem to follow that protection of the fairness of a corporation's trial is a concern which is well within … s. 11(b).

In concluding that portion of his analysis, Stevenson, J., said (at pp. 858-9):

> In my view, the societal interest applies to corporate offenders as it does to individual accused. To hold otherwise would be to suggest that the community is somehow less interested in seeing the former brought to trial. It would also suggest that the status of an accused can determine whether that accused is to be accorded 'fair' and 'just' treatment. I am not prepared to accept either of those propositions. I therefore conclude that the phrase 'Any person charged with an offence' in the context of s. 11(b) of the *Charter* includes corporations.

Though *R. v. C.I.P.*, *supra*, dealt with section 11(b) of the *Charter*, its analytical approach (i.e., does the corporate accused have an interest falling within the scope of the right protected by the *Charter* section?) is helpful in determining whether any of the rights protected by section 7 of the *Charter* are available to corporate accused.

When considering section 7 of the *Charter* for the purposes of answering that question, one must remember the impact on our understanding of section 7 of *R. v. Stinchcombe* (1991), 130 N.R. 277 (S.C.C.). In *Stinchcombe*, *supra*, Sopinka, J., speaking for the Court, held that the Crown's obligation to disclose its case to the accused stems from section 7's protection of the right to make full answer and defence. At p. 287, Sopinka, J., said:

> … there is the overriding concern that failure to disclose impedes the ability of the accused to make full answer and defence. This common law right has acquired new vigour by virtue of its inclusion in s. 7 of the *Canadian Charter of Rights and Freedoms* as one of the principles of fundamental justice… The right to make full answer and defence is one of the pillars of criminal justice on which we heavily depend to ensure that the innocent are not convicted.
>
> …

One can therefore fairly conclude the following:

(1) section 7 of the Charter protects, amongst other things, the right to make full answer and defence being one of the principles of fundamental justice;

(2) all accused (whether they are human beings or corporations) have an identical interest in being able to make full answer and defence when charged with an offence;

(3) it follows that a corporate accused has an interest (the right to make full answer and defence) which falls within section 7 of the *Charter* and may therefore invoke section 7 *to protect that interest.*

NOTES AND QUESTIONS

1.   As Fradsham J. indicated, the current judicial approach asks:

(a)   what constitutional value a given provision protects; then

(b)   whether this value requires that the right be available to corporations.

Are all corporations created equal for the purposes of *Charter* analysis? Consider s. 15(1) of the C.B.C.A.:

15(1) A corporation has the capacity and, subject to this Act, the rights, powers and privileges of a natural person.

Compare this with s. 30 of the British Columbia *Business Corporations Act*, S.B.C. 2002, c. 57, which says:

30. A company has the capacity and the rights, powers and privileges of an individual of full capacity.

What is the effect, if any, of the different wording in these sections?

2.   Can a legislature, which undoubtedly could define an unborn child as an individual, indirectly extend full *Charter* rights to a corporation? Has this been done already? If not, what is the meaning of the word "rights" in C.B.C.A., s. 15?

3.   As mentioned previously, the courts ask what value a given *Charter* right is protecting, then determine whether it is available to corporations. In *Irwin Toy Ltd. v. Quebec*, [1989] S.C.J. No. 36, [1989] 1 S.C.R. 927, 58 D.L.R. (4th) 577 for example, the court said that s. 7 was intended to confer protection on a "singularly human level". Similarly, in *R. v. Amway Corp.*, [1989] S.C.J. No. 3, [1989] 1 S.C.R. 21, 56 D.L.R. (4th) 309, the court held that the right in s. 11(c) did not apply to corporations on the basis that a corporation cannot be a witness. It said that the function of the section is to prevent the affront to dignity which comes from testifying against oneself, and decided that this indignity would not occur for a corporate accused. In *PPG Industries Canada Ltd. v. Canada (Attorney General)*, [1983] B.C.J. No. 2260, 42 B.C.L.R. 334, 146 D.L.R. (3d) 261 (C.A.), it was held by a majority that corporations do not enjoy the right to a jury trial under s. 11(f). The majority relied partly on the meaning of the word "person", and that part of the reasoning is doubtful, but they also relied on the fact that a corporation cannot be imprisoned.

4.   How does a judge *know* that a corporation cannot be imprisoned? Must it be proved by evidence at trial? Is it a notorious fact? How else might a judge (as opposed to an ordinary citizen) "know" something?

5.   The other important point the judges have noted is that where a corporation is charged, it can raise in its defence constitutional defects in the supposed law, even if the defects are based on constitutional rights which are only enjoyed by individuals: *R. v. Big M Drug Mart Ltd.*, [1985] S.C.J. No. 17, [1985] 1 S.C.R. 295. This point was

further discussed in *Canadian Egg Marketing Agency v. Pineview Poultry Products Ltd.*, [1998] S.C.J. No. 78, 166 D.L.R. (4th) 1 (*"Canadian Egg"*). The Supreme Court applied the same reasoning to allow corporations to invoke the *Charter* when they are defendants in civil proceedings instigated by the state pursuant to a regulatory scheme. Justices Iaccobucci and Bastarache wrote (at pp. 22-25):

> In our opinion, the logic of *Big M Drug Mart* extends to give standing as of right to the respondents. While they might seek public interest standing, we do not believe they need do so. They do not come before the court voluntarily. They have been put in jeopardy by a state organ bringing them before the court by an application for an injunction calling in aid a regulatory regime. Success of that application could result in enforcement by contempt proceedings. *If the foundation for these remedies is an unconstitutional law, it appears extraordinary that a defendant cannot be heard to raise its unconstitutionality solely because the constitutional provision which renders it invalid does not apply to a corporation.*
>
> It seems wrong to us that someone in the position of the respondents should have to seek "public interest" standing. They do not seek to attack the legislation out of public interest. They seek to defend themselves against a law that is sought to be applied to them against their will which will directly affect their "private" interest. ...
>
> If the penal proceedings requirement were allowed to stand, a corporation that was the subject of a civil injunction issued at the urging of a state agency would be barred from challenging the constitutionality of the law that authorized those proceedings. But if it violated the injunction, it could be cited for contempt. It would then face more severe penalties. Yet, at this latter stage, even though it faced possible penal sanctions, it would not be allowed to challenge the law under the Charter because the penal sanctions were authorized, not by that law, but by the contempt powers of the court.
>
> (emphasis added.)

While none of this reasoning is peculiar to state-instituted proceedings, the court stopped short of saying that a corporation would be permitted to raise the *Charter* as of right in any proceeding. See, for example, the following passage from p. 24 (D.L.R.):

> Our expanding the *Big M Drug Mart* exception to civil proceedings in these limited circumstances is not intended to provide corporations with a new weapon for litigation.

What reasons might there be for limiting the availability of the *Charter* to corporations defending state-instituted actions? Does the decision in *Canadian Egg* have this effect, or is the court merely taking a gradualist approach? For more on this issue, see A. Bernstein, "The Yoke of *Canadian Egg*: Corporate Standing under the Charter" (2000), 33 Can. Bus. L.J. 247.

6.   In *R. v. Wholesale Travel Group Inc.*, [1991] S.C.J. No. 79, 67 C.C.C. (3d) 193, the majority rejected an argument that in such a situation the offending provisions could be "read down" so as to apply only to corporations. However, the majority also noted that if the statute were re-drafted so as to apply only to corporations, then corporations would not be able to attack it on the basis of rights enjoyed only by individuals. In explaining why the corporate accused could rely on *Charter* arguments, the majority did not distinguish between the corporation's arguments based on s. 7 and those based

on s. 11(*d*); but probably they did not intend to suggest that corporations cannot directly assert a s. 11(*d*) right.

7.   A related issue was decided in *Little Sisters Book and Art Emporium v. Canada (Minister of Justice)*, [1996] B.C.J. No. 71, 131 D.L.R. (4th) 486 (S.C.) [affd [1998] B.C.J. No. 1507, 160 D.L.R. (4th) 385 (C.A.), revd in part [2000] S.C.J. No. 66, [2000] 2 S.C.R. 1120]. The corporate accused was charged under several provisions of the *Customs Tariff* and the *Customs Act*, relating to the importing of pornographic materials. These provisions were attacked on the grounds that they were a violation of freedom of expression, as guaranteed by s. 2(*b*) of the *Charter*. In addition, the corporation alleged that the application of these provisions in this case was discriminatory, and therefore contravened s. 15 of the *Charter*. The trial judge ruled that, once standing is established with respect to one ground of constitutional challenge, corporate status is irrelevant for the purposes of other grounds of challenge. Accordingly, the corporate accused was allowed to raise a defence under s. 15 of the *Charter*, by virtue of the fact that it had standing to bring a challenge under s. 2(*b*).

8.   In *Slaight Communications Inc. v. Davidson*, [1989] S.C.J. No. 45, [1989] 1 S.C.R. 1038, 93 N.R. 183, the court held that a corporation's s. 2(*b*) right was violated but that the violation was saved by s. 1. *Irwin Toy Ltd. v. Quebec* also held that the plaintiff corporation could assert the s. 2(*b*) right to freedom of expression, and that advertising is a form of expression protected under s. 2(*b*), but again the legislation was saved under s. 1 of the *Charter*. See also *Ford v. Quebec (Attorney General)*, [1988] S.C.J. No. 88, [1988] 2 S.C.R. 712, 54 D.L.R. (4th) 577, where the opposite conclusion was reached on s. 1 in relation to Quebec's French-only sign law. In *RJR-MacDonald Inc. v. Canada*, [1995] S.C.J. No. 68, [1995] 3 S.C.R. 199, 127 D.L.R. (4th) 1, the court approved of the Attorney General's concession that restrictions on tobacco advertising violated the s. 2(*b*) rights of the plaintiff corporations. The requirement of unattributed health warnings on cigarette packages was not conceded to be a violation of s. 2(*b*), but it was held to be such by a 5–4 majority. By the same majority, the court held that the infringements were not saved by s. 1. In *Hunter v. Southam Inc.*, [1984] 2 S.C.R. 145, 11 D.L.R. (4th) 641, the Supreme Court implicitly recognized that a corporation enjoys the right provided by s. 8.

9.   As noted in *R. v. Agat Laboratories Ltd.*, [1998] A.J. No. 304, 17 C.R. (5th) 147 (Prov. Ct. Crim. Div.), above, corporations are entitled to the benefit of s. 11(*b*): see *R. v. 741290 Ontario Inc.*, [1991] O.J. No. 215, 2 O.R. (3d) 336 (Prov. Div.) and *R. v. CIP Inc.*, [1992] S.C.J. No. 34, [1992] 1 S.C.R. 843. However, the latter two cases also held that the content of the s. 11(*b*) right could be different for corporations than for individuals. There are similar suggestions about other sections, at least via the s.1 analysis, in *Reference re s. 94(2) of the Motor Vehicle Act (British Columbia)*, [1985] S.C.J. No. 73, [1985] 2 S.C.R. 486 and in *R. v. Wholesale Travel Group Inc.*, [1991] S.C.J. No. 79, 67 C.C.C. (3d) 193. The latter case appears to have approved of regulatory offences, which are liable to have features of strict or absolute liability and thus reversal of onus. This has important implications for corporations, since they are more likely than individuals to be charged with this type of offence. On this point, see S. Requadt, "Regulatory Offences Since *Wholesale Travel*" (1993), 22 Can. Bus. L.J. 407.

10.   The mobility right in s. 6(2) of the *Charter* provides that "every person who has the status of a permanent resident of Canada has the right ... (*b*) to pursue the gaining of a livelihood in any province." Can corporations be permanent residents of Canada? If this section applies to corporations, what is the difference between a provincial corporation and a federal corporation, so far as doing business in another province is concerned?

11. On the whole question of corporations and the *Charter*, see W. Mackay, "The Charter of Rights and the Corporation", in F. McArdle, ed., *Cambridge Lectures 1989* (Montreal: Yvon Blais, 1990); Hon. J. Sopinka, "The Charter of Rights and Corporations", *op. cit.*; E. Foster, "Corporations and Constitutional Guarantees" (1990), 31 Cahiers de Droit 1125 and C. Tollefson, "Corporate Constitutional Rights and the Supreme Court of Canada" (1993), 19 Queen's L.J. 309.

CHAPTER 3

THE CORPORATE CONSTITUTION

A. THE FUNCTION OF A CONSTITUTION

The study of all business organizations is largely about finding out the answers to three fundamental questions: (1) who is in control? (2) who gets the profits? (3) who is liable? The corporate constitution answers the first two of those questions, and gives part of the answer to the third. Other parts of the answer to the third question come from the principle of corporate personality, and general laws governing personal and vicarious liability.

The purpose of this chapter is to develop a conceptual framework for analyzing intracorporate governance, which is primarily regulated by the corporate constitution. Understanding corporate constitutions requires a familiarity with the different models of corporate government currently found in Canada and elsewhere.

Corporations are like other organizations in that they have members (called shareholders) associated under a constitution. The primary function of any organization's constitution is to prescribe how the internal government of the organization is to operate. This involves allocating rights, duties, obligations and access to grievance procedures among the membership and their elected or appointed officials. A corporate constitution will also have some impact on interaction with the outside world. However, modern legislative and judicial developments have simplified the legal analysis of how corporations act as parties in relationships with outsiders, with the result that most details of the corporate constitution do not matter in most external problems. The impetus for these developments has been the idea that outsiders dealing with the corporation should not have to be concerned about the details of its internal government. Later chapters will explore in more detail interactions between the corporation and outsiders. The focus in this chapter will be on internal structures and relationships.

The next part of this chapter will consider the different groups that interact in the context of the corporate constitution. At this point, consider the question: what are the values a corporate constitution must balance?

WELLING, CORPORATE LAW IN CANADA: THE GOVERNING PRINCIPLES

(3rd ed., 2006), pp. 62-63

Corporate law in Canada is now built upon four major principles:

(a) corporate personality, the principle that a corporation's behaviour is to be legally analyzed by analogy to the behaviour of human beings;

(b) managerial power, the principle that the daily operation of corporate business is to be done by a relatively independent managerial group;

(c) majority rule, the principle that internal corporate decisions are to be made by a democratic process among those constitutionally enfranchised on any particular issue; and,

(d) minority protection, the principle that certain corporate, managerial or majority shareholder inclinations ought to be restrained from injuring the minority members of any group created by the corporate constitution.

Any number of authorities can be cited supporting each of these principles. The real problem for corporate analysts is which prevails when two of the principles conflict. The history of corporate law, and everyday corporate practice, are full of examples. ...

It is the function of a corporate statute to create a system of rules for determining which principle prevails when two or more come into conflict.

QUESTIONS

1. Do you agree with Welling's view of the main principles underlying corporate law? Can you think of other principles?

2. Is it possible to rank principles in order of importance in the abstract? Or is it only possible to do so in a factual matrix?

B. CORPORATE CONSTITUENCIES

1. Introduction

In this section, we will look at the different constituencies or groups that interact in different ways with, and within, the corporation. Some of these groups are external to the corporation; they interact with the corporation, but are not involved in its government. Some of these interactions are covered in later chapters, while some are outside the scope of corporate law as such, having acquired a subspecialty classification over the years.

The primary function of a corporate constitution is to prescribe how the internal corporate government is to operate, and to balance the competing interests of the internal groups. Each of the internal constituencies will therefore have an explicit role in the corporate constitution. Some groups are not recognized in general as having a role to play in the corporation's government. Although they are therefore external, nonetheless their interests receive limited recognition in some situations.

2. External Constituencies

(a) The General Public

The general public has a close economic relationship with corporate activity in every western industrial state. In Canada, virtually every citizen is affected by the inflation rate, by unemployment levels, by foreign and domestic trade figures. All of these are intimately connected with ongoing corporate success and failure; none can be dealt with in a basic survey of corporate law. On a less global scale, any particular individual or group in Canada is liable to be affected from time to time as a victim of corporate crime, such as pollution of the air or waterways. Corporate crime is dealt with in a general way in Chapter 5, but the general public interest in corporate activity is reflected in other ways. You may sometimes hear the corporations described as a "nexus of contracts". This is an understanding of the corporate constitution as representing merely a kind of multilateral contract among all the shareholders, directors, managers and other employees. On this view, corporate law provides default terms for those contracts, and these can be changed as the parties choose. This analysis omits the fact that corporate statutes do, at least in a limited way, include features that reflect the *public* interest in what corporations do. Examples include mandatory rules about publicity of the corporate constitution and the identity of directors, mandatory rules creating offences for the violation of corporate law (*e.g.*, C.B.C.A., ss. 250-51), and rules about investigations of corporations (*e.g.*, C.B.C.A., s. 119, Part XIX). These rules are not found in the private law of contracts. For a discussion of the public law side of corporate law, see W.T. Allen, "Our Schizophrenic Conception of the Business Corporation" (1992), 14 Cardozo L.R. 261.

The public interest in corporate behaviour is often discussed under the rubric of "corporate social responsibility". That is simply the idea that the management of corporations needs to be conducted with a view to the broader interests of society, and not exclusively in the financial interests of the shareholders. We will return to this debate in Chapter 4, section E, on Corporate Purpose, and also in Chapter 7, where the duties of corporate management are addressed in detail.

Members of the public may also become involved with corporations through the purchase or sale of "securities": corporate shares or debt obligations that trade on stock exchanges or elsewhere. To the extent that these transactions make people creditors or shareholders of a corporation, they cease to be simply members of the public in relation to that corporation, and they fall instead into one of the other groups discussed here. Activities in the securities markets themselves are primarily supervised by regulatory bodies such as provincial securities commissions. This regulation became recognized as a subspecialty of its own, "securities law", in the latter half of the twentieth century.

On an even more personal level, members of the public might interact with the corporation as trade suppliers or as customers. This too might make them into creditors. It is also likely to bring into play a range of legal subjects that are outside the scope of corporate law. The interaction might require reference to the basic subjects of contract, tort and property; or, to more advanced matters such as sales law, secured lending, or business practices legislation. Generally, the interests in question in these dealings will not be reflected in the corporate constitution.

(b) The Government

Governments relate to corporations in three different ways. The first is by the provision of a legislative regime which allows for the creation of corporations and which regulates general business activity. This is not particularly a matter for discussion in this chapter, but is to a large degree the subject matter of this book. A second is the creation and administration of various anti-monopoly, tax incentive, foreign investment review and other political-economic statutory controls. These are outside the generally accepted scope of corporate law. A third type of government participation in corporate affairs is by involvement as a shareholder of a particular corporation. This might be as a vocal and powerful minority shareholder, or as a 100 per cent shareholder of a Crown corporation. In both situations, the government's position as a shareholder will be generally described by the rules set out in this book, but the powerful bargaining position of a provincial or federal government will obviously greatly change the nature of the game to which these technical rules apply.

(c) Employees

Employees, and their relationships with the corporate employer, are not generally addressed in the field of corporate law. While the actions of various employees, particularly when they are dealing with suppliers and customers, create corporate law problems, the field of employees' rights and obligations *vis-à-vis* the corporation have traditionally been dealt with elsewhere. For unionized employees, these matters fall within the well-established field of labour law. For other employees, the relevant field is the somewhat looser collection of rules known as "employment law". This area includes "master-servant" and contract rules from the common law, circumscribed by employment standards and minimum wage legislation.

To this general statement, that relations with employees are not addressed as part of corporate law, there can be added one important qualification. The principle of corporate personality normally dictates that when directors of a corporation are acting as such, their acts are corporate acts and not individual acts; hence they are not liable as individuals for what they do. Consider, however, *C.B.C.A.*, s. 119:

> 119(1) Directors of a corporation are jointly and severally, or solidarily, liable to employees of the corporation for all debts not exceeding six months wages payable to each such employee for services performed for the corporation while they are such directors respectively.

What does the word "respectively" mean here?

Subsection (2) imposes significant limitations on the employee's ability to sue a director successfully. Subsection (3) provides for a two-year limitation period from the date of resignation of the director. Liability is restricted even further by A.B.C.A., s. 119(2), which excuses directors if they reasonably believe that the corporation can pay the debts as they come due, and also for debts payable for services performed while the corporation is in receivership or liquidation. You might think that this unduly restricts employee protection. On the other hand, the next time you are reading about a C.B.C.A. corporation that is on the verge of insolvency, you should make a point of noting whether the whole board of directors has resigned. (For specific examples, see R. Daniels, "Must Boards Go Overboard?" (1995), 24 C.B.L.J. 229, at 229-30.) Employees also get some protection in the bankruptcy of their corporate employer inasmuch as their claims against the corporations are given preferential treatment by the federal *Bankruptcy and Insolvency Act*, R.S.C. 1985, c. B-3, ss. 136(1)(*d*), (*h*), (*i*). For new legislation protecting wage earners, see page 325, note 4.

QUESTIONS AND NOTE

Do you agree that directors should be made personally liable for employees' wages? What do you think of *Barrette v. Crabtree Estate*, [1993] S.C.J. No. 37, [1993] 1 S.C.R. 1027, in which the Supreme Court of Canada held that this section does not make a director liable on a judgment that an employee has obtained against the corporation for wrongful dismissal?

The A.B.C.A., s. 106(9)(*b*), provides that the corporate constitution may provide for the election or appointment of a director or directors by creditors or employees of the corporation. A.B.C.A., s. 122 (which corresponds to C.B.C.A., s. 122) sets out the duties of directors and officers; subs. (4) provides:

(4) In determining whether a particular transaction or course of action is in the best interests of the corporation, a director, if he is elected or appointed by [shareholders or creditors] may give special, but not exclusive, consideration to the interests of those who elected or appointed the director.

Do you think this permission to focus on a particular constituency is a good idea? An empirical study of 553 A.B.C.A. corporations found that none of them had employee or creditor directors: R.J. Wood, M.T. Brown, and R.W. Bauman, "Modifications to Corporate Constitutions in Alberta: An Empirical Study" (1993), 31 Alta. L. Rev. 263.

(d) Creditors

A creditor of the corporation is someone to whom the corporation owes money. The debt could arise in a number of different ways. A person might buy a corporate bond, which is a right to periodic interest payments and a principal sum on maturity. A bank or other lending institution might similarly lend the corporation a large sum for a period of years, or it might make available a line of credit up to a fixed limit; probably in either event it will take security over property of the corporation. Suppliers of inventory, office supplies and equipment, and of services are likely to extend credit to the corporation, some with security and some without. Employees of the corporation are creditors some of the time, unless they are paid in advance; and even someone who has obtained a judgment in tort against the corporation is a creditor of it. Most of these relationships arise through contract; corporate contracts are dealt with in Chapter 5, as are corporate torts.

In traditional legal analysis, creditors have been considered outsiders to the corporate constitution. Thus, like all of the other groups discussed to this point, they have not generally been given any explicit recognition in corporate constitutions. Modern Canadian statutes, however, provide access to grievance procedures for "complainants"; "complainant" is defined to include a holder of a security, and "security" is defined to include debt securities. Access to some grievance procedures is wider still, in that they are available to a complainant *or* a creditor. A creditor still does not have the rights of a shareholder; nonetheless, he or she has more "say" under this type of constitution than has traditionally been the case. See also the discussion of A.B.C.A., s. 106(9), in the Note to the previous section.

Creditors can have a great deal of involvement in a corporation's affairs when it is in financial difficulties. This may occur if a secured creditor (or the court) appoints a "receiver" or a "receiver-manager" to take control of property for the benefit of that creditor. The appointment of a receiver under the terms of an agreement has historically been understood as a matter of contract law, governed by the agreement. Under new-model corporate statutes, however, the practice is recognized and subjected to some slight regulation: see C.B.C.A., Part IX. There is also some regulation under the *Bankruptcy and Insolvency Act*, R.S.C. 1985, c. B-3, Part XI. Creditors also effectively take over a corporation's property if the corporation becomes bankrupt. A bankruptcy can arise from the bankrupt's own "assignment" or from a creditor's "petition". The effect either way is (in brief) to transfer the bankrupt's assets to a "trustee in bankruptcy", who holds them for the benefit of unsecured creditors (the trustee takes the assets subject to pre-existing rights of secured creditors). The trustee's role is to turn the assets into cash and pay the creditors, in proportion to the debts they are owed. It is sometimes possible to forestall receivership or bankruptcy proceedings in an effort to get the corporation back on its financial feet, either under Division 1 of Part III of the *Bankruptcy and Insolvency Act* or under the *Companies' Creditors Arrangement Act*, R.S.C. 1985, c. C-36 (only for large corporations).

3. Internal Groups

From the outside, the corporation is treated as a person. Even in relation to the internal groups, the corporation is a separate person from any member of one of those groups. The difference between the internal and external groups is that the internal groups determine how the corporation behaves. For example, someone might make an offer to the corporation to enter into a contract. The corporation needs to decide whether it will accept this offer. Even though it is treated as a person for legal analysis, it is incapable of making a decision except through the instrumentality of other persons acting in certain capacities. A principal function of the corporate constitution is to allocate the power to decide what the corporation will do in a given situation. In the example of the contractual offer, the constitution determines who has the power to decide whether the corporation will accept the offer.

(a) Shareholders

A principal function of the corporate constitution is to answer the fundamental question, "who is in control"? Who makes the business decisions that determine the corporate destiny? The universal answer, for all corporate constitutions, is that shareholders are ultimately in control. The shareholders are the ones who have provided the funds that the corporation uses to carry on business. This means that in economic terms, they are like the owners of the business, although the principle of corporate personality means that in legal terms, it is the corporation that owns the business. But the corporation cannot control itself, and the economic status of shareholders as owners or proprietors naturally means that they should ultimately be the ones in control, just as the partners in a partnership are in control of the partnership. In a corporation, however, shareholder power is usually indirect. It is exercised through the shareholders' power to elect the directors. The shareholders do not make the day-to-day business decisions, but they elect those who do.

WELLING, CORPORATE LAW IN CANADA: THE GOVERNING PRINCIPLES

(3rd ed., 2006), pp. 478-79

Shareholders in Canadian corporations can be analogized to the general populace in the Canadian political system. They periodically elect others to manage the affairs of the enterprise and they must be reported to at regular intervals. They do not usually have direct managerial powers, but they determine the identity of those who do.

Corporations are democratic institutions. They differ from western political democracies in that they encourage the buying and selling of votes. The number of votes a shareholder has is usually determined by the number and type of shares held. As with most democratic institutions, the fundamental rule is that the majority — meaning, in corporate law, those who hold the majority of the voting shares — govern.

...

Shareholders are, from the point of view of management, a source of capital and a constituency to whom to report. Corporate law theory, however, assigns a far greater role to the shareholders. The personification of the corporation deprives them of any legal status as proprietors, but they are far more than mere creditors. While not necessarily involved directly in management, their intended role is more like that of an absentee proprietor than of the beneficiary under a trust. The corporation is primarily a vehicle for raising and using capital in the pursuit of profit. It is intended to serve the wants of capitalists, and capitalists are precisely what shareholders are, however small their investments. Corporate statutes are designed to give the collective group of shareholders a major say, however indirectly, in how the business is to be run.

The extract from Welling focuses on the principal voting power of shareholders, which is in the election of directors. As we will see in more detail in Chapter 7, this power can become somewhat illusory in the case of a large corporation whose shares are held by thousands or even millions of people. It is very real, however, in small and "closely held" corporations.

Depending on the corporate constitution, shareholders are likely to have the power to determine a range of other matters (such as amendments to the corporate constitution) by vote. If the corporate constitution creates different classes of shares, then voting powers may well be different across different classes of shares. This is examined in more detail in Chapter 10.

Another fundamental question for any business organization is, "who gets the profits"? The universal answer is, again, that the profits go to the shareholders. The reasoning is the same. They provide the capital on which the business runs, so the profits should go to them. Again, however, the full answer is more nuanced. The profits of a corporation belong to the corporation. The directors have the power (but not the obligation) to declare dividends, which are distributions of profits to the shareholders. So it is only through the decision of the directors (who themselves are elected by the shareholders) that corporate profits are distributed to shareholders. Furthermore, if the corporate constitution creates different classes of shares, the entitlement to participate in dividends may vary among those classes.

Shareholders are often described as the "owners" of a corporation. This is not true in legal analysis. Shareholders do not own the corporation, which is a legal person, nor do they own the corporate assets, which belong to the corporation. There is however an economic sense in which shareholders are owners. If the corporation were to be "wound up" or terminated, the first step would be to pay its debts. Once that is done, the remaining property is distributed to the shareholders. It will be distributed equally if there is only one class of shares, but if there are multiple classes the distribution could be more complex. In this sense, the ultimate economic benefit of the corporate assets "belongs" to the shareholders, and this is the case even if there is no prospect that the corporation will be wound up any time soon. If you hold property in a house that is rented out to tenants, the estate in land is yours even if you have no intention of ever selling it.

As the economic proprietors of the corporate enterprise, shareholders are entitled to information. This includes lists of shareholders (*e.g.*, C.B.C.A., s. 21) and disclosures of management conflicts of interest (*e.g.*, C.B.C.A., s. 120(6.1)). Shareholders are entitled to periodic financial reporting by management; this regular disclosure is part of the business of the annual meeting of the shareholders, discussed in Chapter 8. At the same meeting, the shareholders elect an auditor, whose role is to certify that the financial information produced by the directors presents a fair picture of the corporation's situation.

Shareholders have remedies available to them to enforce compliance with the corporate constitution. The nature of these rights and remedies, and the theoretical basis of shareholder power, varies depending on the type of constitution in issue. The different types are discussed in Section C, below.

The third fundamental question for any business organization is, "who is liable"? Who can be sued for liabilities arising in the course of the conduct of the business? Shareholders, generally, cannot. This is one of the fundamental attractions of the corporate form. The insulation of the investors from liability does not follow automatically from the treatment of the corporation as a separate legal person. It is quite possible for one person (whether a legal or a natural person) to be vicariously liable for the actions of another (legal or natural) person. This happens when the second person is the agent or employee of the first, or when the two persons are in partnership. It also happens for shareholders, in the case of professional corporations or "unlimited liability corporations". Conversely, with legislative intervention it is possible to exclude investor liability even without corporate personality, as in the case of the limited partnership or the limited liability partnership (See Chapter 1). General business corporations statutes personify the corporation (*e.g.*, C.B.C.A., s. 15), and also make clear that shareholders are not liable in their capacity as such (*e.g.*, C.B.C.A., s. 45).

(b) Directors and Officers

WELLING, CORPORATE LAW IN CANADA: THE GOVERNING PRINCIPLES

(3rd ed., 2006), pp. 318-26 (Footnotes deleted.)

Corporate management comprises two inter-dependent groups. Directors oversee corporate strategy. Officers function as tacticians, supervising other functionaries in the corporation's daily business life. ...

Legal analysis traditionally concentrated on directors, the less important of the two groups in the modern world. Moreover, our corporate law does not differentiate the managerial role in large corporations with widely dispersed shareholdings from that of managers in small corporations with few shareholders.

...

(a) Directors in Theory and Practice

Canadian corporate statutes typically create a board of directors to manage or supervise the management of the corporation. Individual members of the board are elected to their positions by a theoretical shareholder democracy. The directors, once elected, are collectively given the power to determine the direction of corporate business and have imposed upon them a correlative statutory obligation to exercise their powers "with a view to the best interests of the corporation".

Corporate directors do not operate as agents of their electors. Just as democratically elected Parliamentarians need not follow the day-to-day advice of the members of the electorate, or even of a majority of the electorate, so the board of directors collectively exercise independent power. They, like politicians, may be thrown out of office by the democratic process. However, their power, and indeed their duty, is to run the business as they see fit, not as dictated by someone else.

Nor are the directors simple agents of the legally personified corporate entity. They will from time to time operate as agents of the corporation, in the sense that most corporate activity is perceived by the outside world as having been accomplished through the mechanism of human intervention. However, they are not agents doing the bidding of a principal. They must exercise their powers for the benefit of the corporation, but it is they who determine what the corporation wishes to be done.

That is the theory. The practice, which has been exposed primarily by business analysts but largely ignored by lawyers, is less dramatic. Most boards of directors operate as review bodies and sounding boards for the ideas and performance of their corporation's professional managers. Their theoretically powerful voices are modulated more by the custom of the boardroom than by legal rules. Management studies tend to debunk most of the conclusions drawn from legal analysis about the role and behaviour of directors.

...

In sum, the board of directors are an elected body exercising independent decision-making powers in the business world. Traditional corporate law dwelt on the legal responsibilities of directors and largely ignored corporate officers. The officers of a typical corporation are far more important in the business world.

(b) Officers in Theory and Practice

Officers are employees. They run the day-to-day operations of the corporation within long-range policies set by the board of directors. That is the legal position.

Practically speaking, for the largest and most financially important corporations in Canada, officers determine the corporate destiny. Chief executive officers effectively appoint the board of directors, select their own successors, and regard shareholders as a necessary rubber stamp in accomplishing their long-term managerial goals. These facts of business life contrast nicely with the legal view that corporate officers are managers of day-to-day operations and are appointed, directed, and dismissed by a farsighted board of democratically elected directors, who are themselves selected for their visionary skills by a profit maximizing shareholder constituency. In small corporations the controlling shareholders also serve as directors and fill the important managerial positions. However, large commercial empires with widely dispersed shareholdings tend to be run by the officers.

This separation of responsibilities and powers between directors and officers is broadly similar in any corporate constitution. As with shareholders, the type of corporate constitution and its particular provisions will determine the position at a more detailed level, as well as determining the theoretical source of management power. The different types of constitution are discussed in Section C, below.

4. Corporate Constitutions in Action

(a) The Division of Powers

One of the most important functions of the constitution is to divide powers among the internal groups. In this way the constitution determines, for a particular question, who is able to decide what the corporation will do. In general, business decisions belong to the directors, who will delegate to a greater or lesser extent to officers and other employees. In *Hollinger Inc. v. Hollinger International Inc.*, 858 A.2d 342 (Del. Ch. 2004), Hollinger Inc. (or "Inc.") was the controlling shareholder of a corporation called Hollinger International Inc. (or "International"). In this litigation, Inc. (which in turn was controlled by Conrad Black) tried to obtain an injunction against the directors of International, to prevent them from selling one of International's most valuable assets. Chancellor Strine held that the case was outside § 271 of the Delaware General Corporation Law, which is roughly equivalent to C.B.C.A., s. 189(3). This provision requires the directors to obtain shareholder approval if they are selling "all or substantially all" of the corporation's assets. The justification for this provision is that a sale of that nature is an extraordinary step, which justifies a rule that the directors obtain shareholder approval. But normally, business decisions belong to the directors. As Chancellor Strine went on to hold (at pp. 386-87):

> In its complaint, Inc. argues that even if § 271 does not require a vote, equity demands that it be afforded one. In its early manifestation, this argument was premised largely on the idea that Inc.'s controlling stockholder, Conrad Black, and his affiliates on the International board — his wife, Barbara Amiel Black, and his managerial subordinate, Daniel Colson — have been unfairly excluded from the [decision-making process]. Because this court's injunction and the federal Consent Order have (Inc. asserts) inhibited it from removing the International board majority it had earlier installed, Inc. now finds itself in the position of being a helpless bystander while an independent board majority manages International. This, Inc. contended, constituted some sort of violation of Inc.'s natural rights as a controlling stockholder that this court, in equity, must remedy.

> Neither the law nor the factual record provides any support for Inc.'s piteous plea, however. I begin with the law.

> The reality is that controlling stockholders have no inalienable right to usurp the authority of boards of directors that they elect. That the majority of a company's voting power is concentrated in one stockholder does not mean that that stockholder must be given a veto over board decisions when such a veto would not also be afforded to dispersed stockholders who collectively own a majority of the votes. Like other stockholders, a controlling stockholder must live with the informed (i.e., sufficiently careful) and good faith (i.e., loyal) business decisions of the directors unless the [Delaware General Corporation Law] requires a vote. That is a central premise of our law, which vests most managerial power over the corporation in the board, and not in the stockholders.

The division of powers also determines who makes other decisions, such as whether to issue shares, whether to amend the corporation's constitution, and whether and how to hold meetings.

CANADIAN JOREX LTD. v. 477749 ALBERTA LTD.

[1991] A.J. No.1108, 85 Alta. L.R. (2d) 313, 117 A.R. 222 (C.A.)

Fraser J.A. (for the Court): — This appeal involves a narrow question. Do the directors of a federal corporation have the power to cancel a special meeting called by them in advance of its scheduled date? The chambers judge concluded they do not. We disagree.

The facts are not in dispute. A special meeting of Canadian Jorex Limited ("Jorex") was called for December 10, 1991. By notice dated November 27, 1991, the board of directors of Jorex purported to cancel the special meeting. 477749 Alberta Ltd., a shareholder of Jorex, and Mannville Oil and Gas Ltd., the parent of 477749 Alberta Ltd., then applied to the Court of Queen's Bench for an order confirming that the directors' notice of cancellation of the special meeting was of no force and effect. That order was granted by the chambers judge who concluded that once the Jorex directors called a special meeting, they had no right to cancel it. It is from this decision that Jorex now appeals.

Jorex contends that because nothing in its by-laws, the *Canada Business Corporations Act* ("C.B.C.A."), or any unanimous Shareholders Agreement ("U.S.A.") restricts the directors' ability to cancel special meetings called by them, the directors enjoy this power given the corporate model embraced by the C.B.C.A. In particular, Jorex relies on s. 102 of the C.B.C.A. which provides that "the directors shall manage the business and affairs of a corporation". In turn, s. 2(1) defines "affairs", in part, as meaning "the relationships among a corporation, its affiliates and the shareholders, directors and officers of such bodies corporate". Jorex points out that under s. 16(1) "it is not necessary for a by-law to be passed in order to confer any particular power on the corporation or its directors". Therefore, argues Jorex, the cumulative effect of these sections is to confer upon a corporation's directors the right to cancel any special meetings called by them. Their approach is an inclusive one: unless the C.B.C.A. or the bylaws expressly prohibit the directors' cancellation of special meetings, the directors, residual powers under s. 102 include the right to do so.

477749 Alberta Ltd. and Mannville dispute this analysis. Their approach is an exclusionary one: unless the C.B.C.A. or the bylaws contain an express power on the directors' part to cancel meetings, this power does not exist. (No U.S.A. has been executed by the Jorex shareholders.) And in this case, neither the C.B.C.A. nor Jorex's bylaws expressly confer upon the directors the right to cancel meetings. Nor can it be argued, in the respondents' view, that the directors' residual powers under s. 102 extend to the right to cancel special meetings. Their reasoning is as follows: the C.B.C.A. contains extensive provisions dealing with shareholders' meetings, most of which are designed for the protection of a corporation's shareholders. These statutory provisions were intended to be exhaustive on the question of shareholders' meetings. This being so, the directors enjoy no powers concerning the calling or holding of shareholders' meetings other than those expressly stipulated in the C.B.C.A. To find otherwise would undermine the integrity of those protective measures dealing with shareholders' meetings statutorily implemented for the shareholders' benefit.

The respondents also point out that the Jorex bylaws themselves include no reference to the directors' right to cancel meetings. Indeed, as with the C.B.C.A., the bylaws provide only for the adjournment of a meeting once convened. And, in that regard, the respondents emphasize that the Jorex bylaws specify that only the Jorex shareholders may adjourn the meeting. They argue that cancellation prior to commencement of the meeting is tantamount to adjournment of the meeting. The end result, therefore, in their view, is that the bylaws, by including provisions limiting the adjournment of meetings, also have the effect of restricting the directors' ability to cancel a meeting in advance of its scheduled date.

The primary right which the respondents claim that they would lose if the Jorex directors are permitted to cancel the December special meeting involves the shareholders' examination of the auditors under s. 168 of the C.B.C.A. The shareholders are correct on this point. They will lose this specific opportunity. But the shareholders' loss of the right to examine the auditors at a particular meeting is not, by itself, sufficient reason to conclude that the Jorex directors lack the power under either the C.B.C.A. or the bylaws to cancel a scheduled meeting.

One must distinguish between a power which the directors of a corporation enjoy and the manner in which that power is exercised. Here, we are concerned solely with the first question. Counsel did not suggest that the Jorex directors exercised the power to cancel the December special meeting for any improper purpose. Of course, if the directors had done so, then that might have been a sufficient reason to treat the purported exercise of the power as having been of no force or effect: *Teck Corporation Ltd. v. Millar*, [1973] 2 W.W.R. 385 (B.C.S.C.).

This then brings us to the central question. Do the directors of a federal corporation have the power to cancel a special meeting called by them? We have concluded that the answer is "Yes". Under the corporate model adopted by the C.B.C.A., the residual power to manage the corporation's affairs rests with the directors. This power is given by statute and is not derived from the delegation of powers by the shareholders. This must be contrasted with the British model of corporate law under which the directors enjoy only those powers delegated to them by the shareholders. The distinction is important in assessing the rationale for the court's decision in the main authority relied upon by the Respondents, *Smith v. Paringa Mines Ltd.*, [1906] 2 Ch. 193. In that case, Kekewich, J. concluded that, in the absence of express authority in the articles of association, the directors of a company have no power to postpone a general meeting. Considerable significance was placed on the fact that the articles in that case provided for the adjournment of a general meeting in certain circumstances but contained no provision for postponement. On this basis, Kekewich, J. concluded, without any real analysis of the issue, that the directors did not have the right to postpone the general meeting.

The respondents contend that the same reasoning should be applied here. Why? Because neither the C.B.C.A. nor the Jorex bylaws provide for cancellation of a meeting but only for adjournment of the meeting once convened. Therefore, on the authority of *Paringa*, cited with approval by numerous authors of corporate law texts, the directors lack the authority to cancel a meeting once called.

Several reasons exist for rejecting this unduly restrictive approach to directors' powers. First, as noted earlier, s. 102 of the C.B.C.A. statutorily confers on the directors of a corporation all residual powers to manage a corporation's affairs. To suggest that the directors enjoy no specific power unless it has been expressly granted to them by the C.B.C.A. would effectively render the s. 102 "basket clause" redundant. This result would run counter to the philosophy underlying the basket clause. The effect of this clause is that the directors' powers to manage a corporation's affairs are unlimited except to the extent these powers may have been circumscribed by the corporation's bylaws or a U.S.A. Of course, in keeping with the fundamental principles of corporate law, the directors' powers must be exercised for proper purposes.

Second, a rigid no-exceptions approach to cancellation can lead to unreasonable results. If, for example, a special meeting were convened to discuss a takeover bid and that bid were withdrawn before the date of the scheduled meeting, why should the directors be required to proceed with the holding of a pointless meeting? Other equally valid examples spring to mind. An interpretation of the directors' powers giving rise to any absurd or unintended results must be rejected.

Third, contrary to what the respondents suggest, the interpretation we propose would not necessarily affect the shareholders' right to requisition a special meeting. Under the terms of both the C.B.C.A. and the Jorex bylaws, which mirror the provisions in the C.B.C.A., a special meeting shall be called on request of those Jorex shareholders holding not less than 5 of the issued voting shares of Jorex. The respondents contend that the shareholders' ability to force a special meeting would be compromised if the directors had the right to cancel at their whim any meeting so called.

However, the decision we make does not go this far. Nor need it. The directors' residual powers under s. 102 must be interpreted in conjunction with any other statutory provisions limiting those powers. The shareholders' right to call a special meeting may well be adversely affected if the directors were entitled under s. 102 to cancel a special meeting *called on requisition of the shareholders*. This cannot have been intended by Parliament. Reading s. 102 of the C.B.C.A. in conjunction with s. 143 arguably means that the directors' residual powers under s. 102 would not extend to the unilateral cancellation of any meeting properly convened on the shareholders' request. At the very least, any exercise of the powers of the directors in these circumstances would be subject to close scrutiny by the courts.

Finally, the respondents assert that if the directors can simply cancel a scheduled meeting, the shareholders automatically lose the right to examine Jorex's auditors as they are entitled to do under s. 168. And, as a consequence, the shareholders are deprived of any meaningful protection. But this is not so. Several avenues remain open to the shareholders. First, they have the oppression remedies under the C.B.C.A. which may be relied upon where the directors breach their duties in exercising their power to cancel a meeting. Second, the shareholders can requisition the calling of a meeting. Third, the shareholders have the right to apply to court under s. 144 of the C.B.C.A. for an order directing that a meeting proceed even though cancelled by the directors. The court's powers in this regard are broad. It may order a meeting for any reason the court thinks fit. Fourth, the directors' power to cancel a *general* meeting is limited by the statutory requirement that an annual general meeting be held no later than 15 months from the preceding general meeting. Thus, the directors have no power to cancel a general meeting where the effect of doing so would be to contravene this provision. Fifth, at the annual general meeting, the shareholders may remove the directors. And sixth, and most importantly, the shareholders retain the right to eliminate the directors' power to cancel meetings called by them by including a provision to this effect in the bylaws or a U.S.A.

For these reasons, therefore, we have concluded that the Jorex directors do have the power to cancel a special meeting called by them in advance of its scheduled date. Accordingly, the appeal is allowed and the order directing that the December special meeting proceed as scheduled is vacated. The cancellation of the special meeting by Jorex's directors remains in effect.

NOTE

This decision was followed in *Oppenheimer & Co. v. United Grain Growers Ltd.*, [1997] M.J. No. 510, 120 Man. R. (2d) 281, 36 B.L.R. (2d) 54 (Q.B.), on the question whether the directors could postpone a special meeting of shareholders, called by shareholders pursuant to C.B.C.A., s. 143.

(b) Grievance Procedures

Another important function of the constitution is to provide for procedures that offer redress for potential or past violations of the other provisions of the constitution.

ROLES v. 306972 SASKATCHEWAN LTD.

[1992] S.J. No. 669, 105 Sask. R. 300, [1993] 4 W.W.R. 68 (C.A.)

The judgment of the Court was delivered by

Jackson J.A.: — Clemence Roles, in his capacity as a director of 306972 Saskatchewan Ltd. (Sask. Ltd.), applied to a judge for an order to inspect the accounting records of the company. The learned chambers judge refused to make such an order saying Roles already had or would shortly have access to all the records he needed because he was going to be given access to the financial statements. Four days after this decision, at the annual general shareholders' meeting of Sask. Ltd., the number of directors was reduced and Roles was not re-elected as a director. Roles appealed the decision denying him access to the accounting records. The broad issues on this appeal are (i) did the judge err in concluding that Roles had been given access to the accounting records; (ii) what effect does the fact that Roles is no longer a director have on his right to access.

Facts

Roles was a director of Sask. Ltd. and its predecessor company, United Chemicals Ltd., from the early 1960's until August 10, 1992. He was also chair of the board of directors from 1983 until 1989. In 1987 United Chemicals Ltd. sold its major business to Sherritt Gordon Mines Ltd. In 1988 Roles began lobbying for more corporate information from Sask. Ltd.'s chief operating officer and president, Bruno Riemer. In 1989, Arthur Shoquist succeeded Roles as chair of the board. As time passed Roles's requests for information intensified. Finally, Roles served and filed an application by way of originating notice, returnable August 6, 1992, for an order that (i) Sask. Ltd. and the individual respondents provide access to "the accounting records, bylaws and articles of incorporation"; (ii) certain minutes of directors' meetings be corrected; (iii) Sask. Ltd. be restrained from holding the annual directors' meeting on August 10, 1992 until such time as Sask. Ltd. complied with *The Saskatchewan Business Corporations Act*, S.S. 1978, c. B-10 concerning proper notice, financial disclosure, and in essence, provided access as requested above.

The application was made pursuant to s. 240 of the S.B.C.A. On August 6, 1992, the chambers judge issued the following fiat:

I have read all the material filed in this application, and I have had the benefit of hearing both counsel capably and thoroughly addressing all the issues, and I remain unconvinced of the merits of the relief prayed for.

I remain unconvinced because it does not appear to me that the applicant Roles is not already in possession of the information he seeks. If he is not, and I do not believe that to be the case, then I am satisfied that Mr. Richardson will deliver to Roles's solicitor, before August 10, 1992, copies of the articles of incorporation for the company in question, the company bylaws, current financial statements prepared by Price Waterhouse, copies of the minutes of the last corporate annual meeting, and copies of the minutes of the more recent meetings of the board of directors.

Four days later, as indicated, Mr. Roles was no longer a director of Sask. Ltd. Subsequently, he launched this appeal.

Whether Access to the Accounting Records had already been Granted

The applicable section is s. 20 of the S.B.C.A. and the relevant parts of this section are as follows:

20(1) A corporation shall prepare and maintain, at its registered office or at any other place in Saskatchewan designated by the directors, records containing:

(a) the articles and the bylaws, and all amendments thereto, and a copy of any unanimous shareholder agreement;

(b) minutes of meetings and resolutions of shareholders;

(c) copies of all notices required by section 101 or 108; and

(d) a securities register complying with section 46.

(2) In addition to the records described in subs. (1), a corporation shall prepare and maintain adequate accounting records and records containing minutes of meetings and resolutions of the directors and any committee thereof.

. . .

(4) The records described in subs. (2) shall be kept at the registered office of the corporation or at such other place in Saskatchewan as the directors think fit and shall at all reasonable times be open to inspection by the directors.

The right which Roles sought to enforce is contained in s. 20(4).

We agree with counsel for Roles that the provision of annual financial statements is not what is meant by "accounting records" in s. 20(2). In fact, the kind of annual financial statements referred to by the chambers judge are the subject of s.149 of the S.B.C.A. That section requires the directors to place before the shareholders at every annual meeting "comparative financial statements". Yet s. 20 of the S.B.C.A. gives directors, but not shareholders, the right to inspect accounting records. Accordingly, the accounting records which a director has the right to inspect must be more extensive than financial statements which are prepared from accounting records.

On this point we accept counsel's contention that what constitutes adequate accounting records is described in Palmer's Company Law, by C.M. Schmitthoff, (23rd Ed.) at vol. 1, para. 70-01 where the author refers to the British statutory definition:

The accounting records shall disclose with reasonable accuracy, at any time, the financial position of the company at that time, and shall contain a record of the assets and liabilities of the company and entries from day to day of all monies received and paid out and of the matters in respect of which these payments occurred.

It is reasonable to suppose that adequate accounting records consist at least of "entries from day to day of all monies received and paid out and of the matters in respect of which these payments occurred."

Accordingly, we find that the chambers judge erred in denying access to the accounting records on the basis that access had been or would be given by giving access to the financial statements alone.

The Effect of Roles's Changed Status

The application to obtain the accounting records was made pursuant to s. 240 of the S.B.C.A.:

> 240. If a corporation or any director, officer, employee, agent, auditor, trustee, receiver, receiver-manager or liquidator of a corporation does not comply with this Act, the regulations, articles, bylaws, or a unanimous shareholder agreement, a complainant or a creditor of the corporation may, in addition to any other right he has, apply to a court for an order directing any such person to comply with, or restraining any such person from acting in breach of, any provisions thereof, and upon such application the court may so order and make any further order it thinks fit.

Counsel for Sask. Ltd. and the other respondents submitted that the right of a director to have access to the corporate records is not an absolute right. Whether or not access will be granted under s. 240 is a discretionary matter and access can be refused if, among other things, the court is satisfied that the purpose for which access to the records is sought is an improper one. With even greater strength, counsel for Sask. Ltd. argued that there can be no purpose remaining after a person has ceased to be a director.

The issues flowing from this aspect of the case are more difficult. It should be pointed out that this case has been proceeded with on the basis of an appeal from the judge's decision refusing to allow access to the accounting records. No appeal was taken with respect to any other aspect of the judge's decision, i.e. his apparent refusal to postpone the annual directors' meeting. It was admitted that Roles was no longer a director after August 10, 1992, and it was not argued by counsel for Roles that this court could only look at the decision of the chambers judge as of the time when he rendered his decision. In any event we could not ignore the fact that he is no longer a director, and the case has been considered on that basis.

There are few judgments considering the position of someone like Roles who has requested access to corporate records. The first is *State of Delaware v. Seiberling Rubber Company* (1961), 168 A.2d 310 (S.C. Delaware). The court held that a director has a right to inspect corporate books only so long as his purpose is not in derogation of the interest of the corporation, and if his motives are improper or he is no longer performing corporate duties, the right to inspect ceases to exist. At p. 312 the court states that the right of a director to examine corporate records springs from his duty to protect and preserve the corporation. Thus, when he is no longer able to perform corporate duties, the court stated that the right to inspect the books should immediately end.

In *Re South Queensland Broadcasting Holdings Pty. Ltd.*, [1976] Qd. R. 69 (Queensland F.C.), the court was considering an appeal from an order authorizing chartered accountants to inspect, on behalf of the directors, certain accounting records. The court dismissed the appeal but it amended the order appealed from to make it subject to the condition that it was to be effective only for such time as the respondent was a director of the company. The court said at p. 72 that after ceasing to be a director, a person could not claim to carry on with an inspection of accounting records bona fide and for the purposes for which the power was conferred. The court considered in passing what happens when a director makes a bona fide request for information which is granted by the court and then the order of the court is rendered nugatory by the removal of the director from office so as to prevent access to the records. The court concluded that if the company or the other directors had the authority to remove the director in question from office and exercises that authority, the basis for the director's examination or inspection of the records would be gone. His interest in having such an inspection could not be for the purpose for which it was conferred.

In *Conway et al. v. Petronius Clothing Co. Ltd. et al.*, [1978] 1 All E.R. 185 (Ch. D.) the court considered the nature and extent of a director's right of inspection in the context of the likelihood of the director being removed from office. It was found that the applicable statute did not confer a civil right of action to enforce the director's right to inspect, but that such a right existed at common law. Application had been made by a director at a time when a general meeting of the company had been convened for the purpose of removing the director. The court held it would intervene to assist the director in such a position only if it considered such intervention necessary for the protection of the company. The court states at p. 202 that

> in particular circumstances, the court may consider it essential for the protection of the company or indeed for the personal protection of the director that he be allowed to inspect the company's books even though a resolution for his removal as a director is shortly thereafter to be considered by the company's members.

In the case before the court, the court concluded that no immediate order for inspection should be made until after the general meeting was held, as it was possible, in the circumstances of the case, that the immediate order for inspection would cause irremediable damage to the company. Although the court was considering the court's common law powers, comments of the court are still instructive. The court held that the right of a director to inspect the company's books of account must determine on removal of the director from office (see p. 201).

The right which Roles seeks to enforce is the right of a "director" to enable him to carry out his duties as a director. While a director, it would be rare that a court would require him to state the reason for wanting to peruse the records. It would be presumed that his purpose would be consistent with his responsibility as a director. But it is not sufficient to say that the chambers judge should have allowed the exercise of the right when Roles is no longer a director.

The common law right referred to in the *Conway* case was said by the court to "determine on removal of a director from office". Whether or not the statutory right exists after a director has been removed from office, it is, at the very least, incumbent on a person in Roles's position, who is no longer a director, to demonstrate that the reason for wanting access is for the benefit of the company. The reason for Roles's desire to have access to the records remains unclear.

Furthermore, we are unable to see how access would help him to fulfil any obligations that may rest upon him as a past director of the company. In the affidavit material before the chambers judge, Roles stated the reason for having lobbied for further information was to monitor the company's performance. Apparently this was to enable him to evaluate the annual payments received from Sherritt Gordon which were part of the sale price and dependant on the performance of the company. We cannot see that this purpose can assist the company at this time. To give Roles access now would require more than the assertion that he had a right to access when he was a director, if access to a person no longer a director would ever be allowed on the basis of having been a director at some time in the past.

Accordingly, the appeal must be dismissed. In the circumstances, there will be no order as to costs.

C. TYPES OF CORPORATE CONSTITUTION

1. Theoretical Differences

Imagine that someone asked you this question: "Are members of the Senate elected or appointed?" Would you respond:

(a) "Elected";

(b) "Appointed"; or

(c) "Which Senate are you talking about?"

You would probably choose (c). If your interlocutor was asking about the U.S. Senate, the answer would be "elected"; if the Canadian Senate, the answer would be "appointed"; if the Senate of your University, the answer might be "some are elected and some are appointed"; and if the U.K. Senate, the answer would be "does not compute; there is no Senate in the U.K. constitution".

Constitutions are of different types or models. They do not all have the same elements; and even where two constitutions have elements with the same name, there is no guarantee that they are parallel in any other way. To take another example from the world of politics, the powers and role of the President of the U.S. are very different from those of the President of the Republic of Ireland.

Corporate constitutions are the same way. Theoretically, there could be any number of types of corporate constitutions, just as there could be in the case of national constitutions. In practice, and again like national constitutions, there are not that many different basic models. People copy models that have worked, making amendments to take account of local conditions and to correct perceived shortcomings. In this section, the goal is to examine the different types of corporate constitution which exist and which have existed in Canada. It is obviously important, for purely practical reasons, to understand the type of corporate constitution that exists under the C.B.C.A. and under the corporations statute of your provincial jurisdiction. But it is also necessary to understand the other types, for a number of reasons. First, all of them still exist in one place or another; indeed, all of them (except perhaps charter corporations) still exist in Canada. True, they may be rather uncommon because they are no longer used for business corporations in most Canadian jurisdictions, but they remain important for Crown corporations and not-for-profit corporations. Second, you need to be aware of the different types of constitutions in order to understand the cases you read. A case from another jurisdiction, or a Canadian case from an earlier era, is liable to be concerned with a different type of corporate constitution. You need to understand the different types in order to understand the case, and to know whether it has any bearing on the type of corporation with which you are concerned. To return to the analogy of national constitutions, a case on the U.S. Bill of Rights might be relevant to the analysis of a provision of the *Canadian Charter of Rights and Freedoms*, Part I of the *Constitution Act, 1982*, being Schedule B to the *Canada Act 1982* (U.K.) 1982, c.11; on the other hand, a case on the powers of the U.S. Senate would be of no use in analyzing the powers of the Canadian Senate. Finally, an understanding of different types of corporate constitutions provides a historical context for the relatively recent adoption in most Canadian jurisdictions of a particular type of corporate constitution.

In examining each type of constitution, we will consider a number of different factors. First, what are the constitutional documents of the corporation? Second, what is the basis of the powers held by the different internal groups? Third, what is the nature and availability of the grievance mechanism for ensuring compliance with the corporate constitution?

(a) Charter Corporations

Charter corporations were the first type of corporation to be created by executive act. The executive power by which they were created was the royal prerogative, a discretionary power of the Crown. The history of the royal prerogative has been that over the centuries, its exercise has passed from the monarch to the government of the day, and more importantly that its scope has continually diminished in favour of legislative or parliamentary power. In Canadian history, perhaps the most significant example of a charter corporation is the Governor and Company of Adventurers Trading into Hudson's Bay, which was chartered in 1670 (although it became a C.B.C.A. corporation in 1978). In Canada, although there are some charter corporations (including certain universities), there are no more business corporations that are charter corporations.

The basic constitutional document of a charter corporation is its charter. This is a document, bearing the royal seal, by which the corporation is created. A charter is sometimes called "letters patent", since it is like a letter addressed to all the world; "patent" is the opposite of "latent" and means "open" or "obvious". A charter usually begins with the words, "To all to whom these presents shall come, greeting." To the extent that it defines the nature of the corporate constitution, the charter is the governing document. On the other hand, the charter might provide only a skeleton of a constitution. In this case, corporate by-laws will be required to flesh out the detail. These will be in the nature of subordinate legislation, like regulations under a statute: they must be consistent with the superior source. They are also likely to be relatively easy to change, while a change to the charter would effectively require a new charter.

The source of the powers belonging to any group within the constitution of such a corporation is the charter itself. Questions of detail as to the distribution of powers between the directors and the shareholders are likely to be resolved by construction of the particular charter. As for grievance procedures, the common law of standing will determine whether a court will listen to a particular person's argument that someone else (such as the corporation) is not complying with the charter. The common law had a proceeding (and a writ) called *scire facias*, by which a charter could be forfeited for non-compliance;

this could be used against a charter corporation to seek the forfeiture of the charter, which would mean the end of the corporation.

(b) Special Act Corporations

A special Act corporation is created by a particular act of the legislature. This type of corporation was common in the nineteenth century, but is less so now. There are still some examples in Canada, although they are not-for-profit corporations (*e.g.*, *Canadian Red Cross Society Act*, S.C. 1909, c. 68, still in force though not consolidated; *Communities Economic Development Fund Act*, C.C.S.M., c. C155). Probably the main difference from the charter corporation is that the source of power is legislative rather than executive.

The basic constitutional document is of course the relevant Act by which the corporation is created. Like a charter, it is the governing document, although it is likely to provide more details of the corporate constitution than is a charter. It is also likely to provide explicitly for the enactment of by-laws. These will be relatively easy to change, whereas a change to the special Act would require legislative intervention. Again like the charter, the source of power within the corporate constitution is the Act, and construction of the Act is required to determine distribution of powers. Grievance procedures may be provided explicitly in the special Act. If not, a dissatisfied party must rely on the general principles governing the situation where someone acts inconsistently with a statute, including the law of standing.

Charter corporations and special act corporations have this in common: they are created by a particular Act, of the executive or the legislature. The vast majority of corporations are not created in this way, and have not been since the late nineteenth century. At that time, the business corporation was in the ascendant as the preferred form of business organization for most purposes. This position was sealed by the definitive recognition of corporate personality for contractarian corporations by the House of Lords in 1897 (*Salomon v. Salomon*, [1897] A.C. 22 (H.L.)); but even before then, legislatures had responded to the increasing demand for access to the corporate form by enacting general incorporation statutes. The nature of these statutes is to allow members of the public to create corporations through the registration of particular documents (and the payment of a fee). The remaining three types of corporate constitution arise under different types of general incorporation statutes.

(c) Letters Patent Corporations

A "letters patent" corporation is one incorporated under a registration statute that adopts the charter corporation as its model. Until 1970, the federal jurisdiction and five provinces had general incorporation statutes which followed this model. Currently only P.E.I. retains this model for new business corporations (*Companies Act*, R.S.P.E.I. 1988, c. C-14). The Quebec *Companies Act*, R.S.Q. c. C-38, still provides in its Part I for the creation of letters patent corporations, while Part IA (enacted in 1980) provides for "division of powers" corporations, discussed below. New companies must be created under Part IA, although unusually in Canada, companies created earlier under Part I are not required to migrate to the new system. You should note, however, that in those jurisdictions which used to use this model for business corporations, it is generally still in place for not-for-profit corporations: see, *e.g.*, *Canada Corporations Act*, R.S.C. 1970, c. C-32 (which is still in force although it was not consolidated in the R.S.C. 1985); *Companies Act*, R.S.Q., c. C-38, Part III.

One characteristic that distinguishes this type of corporation from the other types of registration statute corporations is the retention of a discretionary element in the creation of the corporation. Letters patent statutes always provide that the relevant governmental official "may" issue the letters patent, while contractarian and division of powers statutes say "shall".

The basic constitutional documents of a letters patent corporation are its letters patent, and also the statute under which they were granted. Like all corporations created under a registration statute, the corporation is as much a creature of the statute as of the letters patent. Indeed, since the letters patent are issued under the authority of the Act, they must be seen as subordinate to it, and therefore must comply with it. The letters patent are the most basic document that is particular to the corporation, and they will set out its name, capital structure, and other basic features. The statute will also provide for the creation of by-laws, which are subordinate to the letters patent and also to the statute. By-laws will be easier to change than the letters patent. Because it is a change to the fundamental constitutional document, an amendment of the letters patent will require a "special majority" vote of the shareholders: usually, a two-thirds majority. The change will take the form of supplementary letters patent, and again is subject to a ministerial discretion. Note that while there is a minimum content for the letters patent, it is usually permissible for them to contain more than the minimum. For example, s. 7 of the P.E.I. Act provides that any provision that could be in a by-law may be put in the letters patent. Placing a feature of the constitution in the letters patent, rather than in a by-law, makes it much harder to change.

The division of constitutional powers will be set out in the statute. The usual technique is to grant managerial power to a board of directors. The shareholders are given the power to elect the directors, and also particular powers in special situations, such as the approval of changes to the letters patent. By-laws can be created, amended and repealed by the directors, but the shareholders must approve any such change. This approval requires a simple majority, which is why by-laws are easier to change than the letters patent.

In general, letters patent statutes do not provide for grievance procedures to correct or restrain violations of the corporate constitution. On principle, one would assume that the relevant principles would be those applicable to charter corporations; that is, those deriving from the general law of standing. In fact, Canadian courts tended to look to English precedent on this matter. English corporations statutes have always adopted the contractarian model discussed in the next section, and so courts in those Canadian jurisdictions that adopted this model had every reason to consult English jurisprudence. As we will see, however, the basis of shareholders' power and standing to complain under the contractarian model is totally different from the letters patent model. Following the English lead was therefore a false step for letters patent jurisdictions, but as this model is now almost obsolete the point is not overly important.

(d) Contractarian Corporations

Contractarian corporations are also called "English-model companies" or "memorandum and articles" corporations. This type of corporation is different in many ways from charter corporations and thus from letters patent corporations. This is not surprising in the light of the historical context. (For details on the history, see P.L. Davies, *Gower's Principles of Modern Company Law*, 6th ed. (London: Sweet & Maxwell, 1997), chapters 2 and 3; in the current 7th ed. (2003), most of the history has been deleted.) In the eighteenth century chartered companies were common in England, and there was actually a trade in charters in which a new business, rather than obtaining the grant of a new charter, might simply buy the charter of an existing but moribund corporation. The fact that the new business had little to do with the objects set out in the charter did not bother anyone at this time. One corporation that was active at this time was the South Sea Company. It was regularly chartered, but it was tainted by corruption and it carried on little business of its own; in a sense, it was an early pyramid scheme. In 1720, the "South Sea Bubble" burst: the South Sea Company and many others collapsed. There followed a prolonged period of public distrust in chartered corporations as business organizations.

Lawyers responded by developing the "deed of settlement" company, which was an unincorporated association implemented through a trust. The persons wishing to create a company would execute a deed setting out their agreement and the trust. Each of them would provide part of the company's capital, and the total amount (the "joint stock") would be divided into a specified number of shares. This capital, and the company's property later acquired with it, would be held by trustees for the benefit of the venturers. Shares in the stock could be transferred, making the transferee a party to the original deed. The deed could be varied by a specified majority of the venturers. In law, these companies were partnerships; it has never been possible in the common law for citizens to create a corporation without the imprimatur of the state. This type of organization underlies the use of the word "company" to describe a corporation; when these companies were first created, they were companies (groups of people with a common goal) but not corporations.

Legislation beginning in 1844 regularized these companies, primarily by requiring registration. This was seen to guard against fraudulent promotions, because anyone could consult the public register to see a company's constitution. The legislation was important because it provided for registration as of right; the registrar did not have discretion to refuse registrations. In 1855, another important development occurred, through legislation providing that stockholders in joint stock companies could not be made liable for the company's debts once they had paid for their shares. This was an important step away from the roots in partnership law. It was this legislation that required companies to add "Limited" to their names to warn the public of their nature. Finally, in 1897 it was held that these joint stock companies were corporations, and thus independent persons in law (*Salomon v. Salomon & Co. Ltd.*, [1897] A.C. 22 (H.L.)); this provided a more robust form of "limited liability", since generally one person is not liable for another's debts.

Legislation deriving from these nineteenth century statutes is still in place in the U.K., and in most of the common law world outside North America. In Canada, only two jurisdictions retain the contractarian model for business corporations: Nova Scotia (*Companies Act*, R.S.N.S. 1989, c. 81) and British Columbia (*Business Corporations Act*, S.B.C. 2002, c. 57). Note, however, that in a jurisdiction that used to use this model for business corporations, it may still apply to not-for-profit corporations (*e.g.*, *Companies Act*, R.S.A. 2000, c. C-21, Part 9).

The basic constitutional documents of this type of corporation are (in addition to the governing statute) a "memorandum of association" and "articles of association". The memorandum is the shorter document, containing the name of the company, its objects, its share capital, and perhaps some other details. In B.C. the memorandum is now called the "notice of articles". The articles are much longer, setting out all of the details of the corporate constitution, including anything that would be a by-law in another type of corporation. This two-part constitution is perhaps the only feature that this type of corporation owes to charter corporations; the memorandum can be seen to correspond to the charter, and the articles to the by-laws. For the same reason, the memorandum was originally considered to be the more basic of the two, in the sense that any inconsistency was resolved in favour of the memorandum, and in the sense that originally it could not be changed. Now, both parts of the constitution can be amended.

This similarity to charter corporations, however, is superficial, and does not go beyond the two-part nature of the constitution. The most important characteristics of the contractarian corporation derive from its origin in the "deed of settlement" company. The name "contractarian" derives from the presence in the governing statute of a provision like this one, which is s. 24(1) of the Nova Scotia *Companies Act*:

> 24(1) The memorandum and articles shall, when registered, bind the company and the members thereof to the same extent as if they respectively had been signed and sealed by each member, and contained covenants on the part of each member, his heirs, executors and administrators, to observe all the provisions of the memorandum and of the articles, subject to this Act.

Compare B.C.B.C.A., s. 19(3). True to the origins of a constitution that was a deed, the constitution of this type of corporation is treated as a binding contract among all of the shareholders (or "members") and the corporation itself.

The origin of contractarian corporations also explains the fact that the shareholders are the theoretical source of all power within the corporate constitution. The directors are not usually given any managerial powers by the statute (but see B.C.B.C.A., s. 136). If they are to have any such powers, they must come from the shareholders, as a delegation set out in the Articles of Association (see *Canadian Jorex Ltd. v. 477749 Alberta Ltd.*, *supra*). Residual power therefore rests in the shareholders. Note that while the statute is of course paramount, there is great flexibility in setting up the Articles of Association. The statute generally provides a standard set of Articles of Association (usually called "Table A"), which apply unless they are displaced by the company's original Articles. The Articles of Association can be changed only by a special majority vote of shareholders, usually a three-quarters majority. In this way, the terms of the contract that is the corporate constitution can be altered by the corporation, with the shareholders being empowered to speak for the corporation on this issue.

The B.C.B.C.A., s. 136 gives managerial authority to the directors, but the contractarian nature of the corporation is re-asserted in s. 137, which provides for the articles to allocate some or all of those managerial powers to the shareholders, or indeed to anyone else. This is the contractarian version of the "unanimous shareholder agreement" discussed below in the context of division of powers corporations. It is premised on the idea that all power flows from the shareholders, and so it is up to them whether they give it to the directors or anyone else. Managerial power can be taken from the directors by the original articles, or by a special resolution, just as in the case of any amendment to the articles; unanimity is not required, as it is in a division of powers corporation.

A great difficulty that has plagued this type of corporation is the question of grievance procedures to secure compliance with the corporate constitution. The

U.K. legislation added an "oppression" remedy, which has been adopted in B.C. and Nova Scotia (and in division of powers corporations), but this is a discretionary remedy and is not specifically concerned with enforcing the corporate constitution. Under the contractarian model, a claim to enforce the corporate constitution might have been framed simply as a claim to enforce the contract that is the constitution, but the English courts for some reason did not follow this path. Many cases got bogged down in asking whether a shareholder was suing "as a shareholder" and was thus entitled to enforce the contract. Another question was whether the corporation itself was a party to the contract; the original legislation predated *Salomon* and did not say so explicitly, referring only to the shareholders. Later versions (like the Nova Scotia provision set out above) include the corporation; and elsewhere, it has been decided that the corporation is a party even if the statute does not say so (*Hickman v. Kent or Romney Marsh Sheepbreeders' Assn.*, [1915] 1 Ch. 881 (Ch. D.)).

Although B.C. and Nova Scotia retain the contractarian model, they have followed the division of powers jurisdictions by adding a range of grievance procedures, including a procedure specifically aimed at the enforcement of the corporate constitution (B.C.B.C.A., s. 228; N.S.C.A., s. 135A and Schedule 3, s. 6).

(e) Division of Powers Corporations

The last model to be considered is now the dominant one in Canada. It applies for business corporations in all jurisdictions except British Columbia, P.E.I. and Nova Scotia. It derives from a U.S. model, and was created to try to rationalize corporate law and remove some of the difficulties that had developed in cases interpreting the contractarian corporation.

The division of powers model is so called because the statute expressly divides powers within the corporate constitution between shareholders and management. This type of corporation therefore has a lot in common with the letters patent corporation. An important difference from that type of corporation is that there is no discretion to refuse to register a division of powers corporation. Also, the division of powers model tends to be more thorough in fleshing out the division of powers, and in providing grievance procedures for the enforcement of the corporate constitution.

The basic constitutional document of a division of powers corporation (in addition to the governing statute) is called the Articles of Incorporation. In terms of its content, this document corresponds to the Memorandum of Association in the contractarian model, or the letters patent in the letters patent model. It *must* set out the name, capital structure, and a few other basic features. As in the other models, it *can* set out other things; anything which could be put in a by-law can also go into the articles of incorporation (*e.g.*, C.B.C.A., s. 6(2)). The articles of incorporation are difficult to change, requiring a special majority (two-thirds) vote of the shareholders; thus, putting a constitutional feature in the articles entrenches it. An empirical study (R.J. Wood, M.T. Brown and R.W. Bauman, "Modifications to Corporate Constitutions in Alberta: An Empirical Study" (1993), 31 Alta. L. Rev. 263) found that most of the possibilities that the statute allows for customizing the articles are not much used.

The basic division of powers is like that in the letters patent model. The directors are given the power to manage, or to supervise the management of, the business and affairs of the corporation. The shareholders are given the power to elect the directors, and also particular powers in particular situations. These will include the power to approve changes to the corporate constitution, and other fundamental changes such as a corporate emigration to another jurisdiction, or a sale of all of the business of the corporation. Shareholders can also propose such changes. As in the letters patent model, the division of powers model provides for by-laws. These can be created, amended and repealed by the directors, but the shareholders must approve any such change by an ordinary resolution. There is also a mechanism for shareholders to propose new by-laws.

Division of powers corporations may have a constitutional document that is unique to this model, called a "unanimous shareholder agreement" ("U.S.A."). Agreements among shareholders, even unanimous ones, are nothing new in corporate law. In "private" corporations, that is, corporations with only a small number of shareholders who probably know each other personally, it is common for agreements to be signed concerning various matters relating to the corporation. The parties might be all of the shareholders, and possibly the corporation as well. Under other constitutional models, though, such agreements could never attain the status of being part of the corporate constitution unless they were incorporated into it (see B.C.B.C.A., s. 137, which operates on this model). Standing on their own, they could only be contracts, possibly combined with trusts. The division of powers model contemplates that some agreements among shareholders can become constitutional documents of the corporation, although most of the Canadian statutes require that the agreement must divest some managerial power from the directors in order to qualify as a U.S.A. (see C.B.C.A., s. 146; *Duha Printers (Western) Ltd. v. Canada*, [1998] S.C.J. No. 41, [1998] 1 S.C.R. 795, 159 D.L.R. (4th) 457, paras. 57-73). It is important to notice that to the extent the U.S.A. takes powers away from the directors, it also takes away their obligations and transfers those to the shareholders (*e.g.*, C.B.C.A., s. 146(5)). The statutory provisions governing U.S.A.'s are somewhat scanty in most jurisdictions. For example, they say nothing about procedures for amendment or termination. Although a well-drafted U.S.A. would provide for these matters, a default rule is required. Moreover, since these agreements must be unanimous in the first place, should there be a *mandatory* rule that any amendment to the agreement must itself be agreed unanimously? See A.B.C.A., s. 146(8), which enacts such a rule; contrast O.B.C.A., s. 108(6)(a). A.B.C.A., s. 146 also provides that a U.S.A. can perform other functions than taking managerial power away from the directors.

Division of powers models are usually more thorough in providing grievance procedures. They provide the discretionary oppression remedy seen in some contractarian statutes. They also provide a mechanism by which a shareholder can ask a judge to allow the shareholder to enforce a right that belongs to the corporation; this provides a solution when the directors may be refusing to enforce such a right (for example, it might be a claim against one of the directors). When there are fundamental changes to the corporate constitution, the statute ensures that shareholders have a vote, and where they are outvoted it allows them to force the corporation to buy their shares at a fair value, so that a shareholder who disagrees with the way a corporation is going has a way to get out. All of these remedies are dealt with in detail later in this book. The concern here is primarily with the one that bears directly on the enforcement of the corporate constitution. It is called the "compliance and restraining order". See, for example, C.B.C.A., s. 247:

> 247. If a corporation or any director, officer, employee, agent, auditor, trustee, receiver, receiver-manager or liquidator of a corporation does not comply with this

Act, the regulations, articles, by-laws, or a unanimous shareholder agreement, a complainant or a creditor of the corporation may, in addition to any other right they have, apply to a court for an order directing any such person to comply with, or restraining any such person from acting in breach of, any provisions thereof, and on such application the court may so order and make any further order it thinks fit.

This was discussed in the context of the S.B.C.A. in *Roles v. 306972 Saskatchewan Ltd., supra*. Note how it gives standing to complain to "a complainant or a creditor". "Complainant" is defined in C.B.C.A., s. 238. By also allowing creditors to enforce the corporate constitution, the act gives standing to a group that traditionally would not have had it.

NOTES AND QUESTION

1.   In *119629 Canada Inc. v. Heath Holdings (Canada) Inc.*, [1989] Q.J. No. 110 (S.C.), a shareholder brought proceedings to require other shareholders to comply with a unanimous shareholder agreement. It was admitted that the agreement had been violated. Part of the proceeding was framed as an application under C.B.C.A., s. 247. Justice Guthrie said:

> "Shareholder" is conspicuously absent from the list of persons against whom an order of the Court can be obtained directing compliance with, or restraining a breach of, a unanimous shareholders' agreement.

Does this seem right to you? Note that A.B.C.A., s. 248 includes "shareholder" in the list of persons against whom an order can be made.

2.   In Quebec, although Part IA of the *Companies Act* is a division of powers model, it does not include the usual panoply of shareholder remedies found in other jurisdictions. It may be that similar solutions can nonetheless be found. In particular, the Civil Code of Quebec, art. 313 indicates that corporate by-laws are to be viewed as creating a contractual relationship, which provides a contractarian route to enforce the constitution. Article 316 of the Code may allow shareholder enforcement of corporate rights. As for the oppression remedy, one case has suggested that a similar outcome can be reached under Quebec law (*Combest Corp. v. Développements Urbains Candiac Inc.*, [1993] A.Q. no 841, 56 Q.A.C. 262 (C.A)); this may be especially true now that the Civil Code of Quebec imposes a general obligation of good faith (arts. 6, 7, 1375).

2. Practical Differences

Some corporate law issues can be resolved independently of the type of corporate constitution under which they arise. For example, you will see that directors owe fiduciary obligations to the corporation; this is true regardless of the type of constitution. The solutions to some problems, however, will depend largely or entirely on the type of constitution involved. You have already seen an example of this in *Canadian Jorex Ltd. v. 477749 Alberta Ltd., supra*.

(a) The Location of Particular Constitutional Provisions

The following note illustrates that the type of constitution in issue can determine the proper place for a given provision. It also illustrates some typical features of corporate constitutions, particularly of closely-held corporations.

The context for this note is that in most jurisdictions, when a new statute was enacted, corporations were required to be "continued" under the new statute. Continuation is a kind of corporate emigration: the corporation leaves the old statutory system and enters the new one. This requires the creation of a new corporate constitution, under the new statute. The author addresses continuance from the old (contractarian) Aberta *Companies Act* to the new (division of powers) *Business Corporations Act*.

R.W. EWASIUK, "THE BUSINESS CORPORATIONS ACT — THE DISTINCTION BETWEEN BYLAWS AND ARTICLES OF ASSOCIATION"

(1983), 21 Alta. L. Rev. 381 (Most footnotes deleted.)

Since the proclamation of the Business Corporations Act, a rather unfortunate practice has grown up among many of Alberta's practitioners concerning the treatment and content of a corporation's Bylaws. On continuation of client corporations, many practitioners have merely reinstated slightly modified versions of the existing Articles of Association and have termed them "the Bylaws". Similarly, with respect to new incorporations, many practitioners have simply enacted modified versions of their old Articles of Association precedents. Other practitioners, while recognizing the necessity for major modifications to the Articles of Association on continuation have, nonetheless, deemed it advisable to preserve certain provisions of the Articles of Association in the Bylaws on the theory that it is most often desirable to preserve the *status quo*. The rationale for placing such provisions in the Bylaws is that subsequent alterations would not require the unanimous consent needed if the provisions were placed in a Unanimous Shareholder Agreement, or the 2/3 majority required (and would avoid the risk of a possible triggering of dissenting shareholders' rights) if the provisions were placed in the Articles of Continuation (or Articles of Incorporation, as the case may be).

The purpose of this note is to briefly illustrate the fundamental differences between the Bylaws, as contemplated by the Business Corporations Act, and the Articles of Association as contemplated by the Alberta Companies Act. Specific examples will be used to point out the risks of incorporating into the Bylaws of a corporation continued or incorporated under the Business Corporations Act any provision not specifically authorized by the Act to be in the form of a Bylaw.

The Business Corporations Act does not contain any provisions which attempt to define exactly what the "Bylaws" of a corporation are. Similarly, no attempt has been made in the Act to outline what effect the Bylaws have upon the shareholders, the corporation, or the directors. Rather, the Act, in any given instance, makes mention of the Bylaws in one of two ways. In some cases it may be stated expressly that the Bylaws "may" provide for some matter or, alternatively, that some thing will be or that some result will follow "unless the Bylaws otherwise provide". In other case there is only the implication that the Bylaws can provide for some matter by wording to the effect that "subject to the Bylaws" some thing will be or some result will follow. Aside from these references, however, nothing more is said.

It is suggested that the result of such wording (or lack of wording) is that a provision placed in the Bylaws of a corporation that is not specifically authorized by the Act is not enforceable either as against the corporation or the shareholders. After all, in the absence of a contract or of a statutory provision imposing the enforceability of such a provision, it is difficult to imagine any principle of law which would make such provisions binding in all cases.

On first reflection, that same argument may seem equally applicable to the Articles of Association, yet no one (at least recently) has seriously disputed the enforceability of provisions in the Articles of Association not specifically authorized by the Companies Act or its predecessors. However, the differences between the Bylaws contemplated by the Business Corporations Act and the Articles of Association contemplated by the Companies Act are fundamental:

(a) *Public Record:* Unlike the Articles of Association, the Bylaws are not an incorporating document. Indeed, there is no requirement under the Business Corporations Act that there be any Bylaws at all. This has the consequence that the Bylaws are not filed with the Registrar and hence are not available for inspection by the public. Furthermore, the Business Corporations Act specifically excludes the application of the old constructive notice doctrine. It follows that a person purchasing shares in a corporation will not be artificially deemed to have knowledge of the contents of the Bylaws even if they were, for some reason, filed with the Registrar. Under the Companies Act, on the other hand, everyone, including a creditor or prospective share purchaser, is deemed to be fully appraised of the Company's Articles of Association and no one can successfully contend that he entered into a transaction in ignorance of their content.

(b) *Execution:* Under the Companies Act, the Articles of Association have to be signed by all of the incorporating shareholders and their signatures witnessed. Hence, the Articles of Association constitute an initial unanimous agreement between the existing shareholders of the company. Under the Business Corporations Act, the Bylaws need never be signed by anyone and a unanimous agreement is not required at any time whatsoever.

(c) *Enactment and Amendment*: Although unanimous consent is required to enact a company's first set of Articles of Association, the Companies Act statutorily provides that amendments can be made by a special shareholders' resolution, which, under that Act, requires a 75 per cent majority. Under the Business Corporations Act, however, the Bylaws can be enacted or amended by an *ordinary* resolution of the *Directors*. The Bylaws thus enacted or amended are fully operative and binding until the next shareholders' meeting at which time they may be confirmed or rejected by the shareholders, by mere ordinary resolution.

(d) *The Articles as a Contract*: Section 29(1) of the Companies Act provides as follows:

29(1) The memorandum and articles, when registered, bind the company and the members thereof to the same extent as if they respectively had been signed and sealed by each member, and contained covenants on the part of each member, his heirs, executors, and administrators, and in the case of a corporation, its successors, to observe all the provisions of the Memorandum and of the Articles, subject to the provisions of this Act.

This section is subject to varied interpretations, but it and its predecessors, viewed together with the points raised above, have given rise to the now well-established principle that the Articles of Association are a contract between the corporation and the shareholders, and between the shareholders inter se. The Business Corporations Act has no section comparable to section 29(1) of the Companies Act. In the absence of such a section, and given the points raised above, it is difficult to imply a similar contract in respect of the provisions of the Bylaws.

(e) *Table A*: Aside from section 29(1), the Companies Act, like the Business Corporations Act with respect to its Bylaws, does not attempt to define what the Articles of Association are. However, Table "A", by implication, provides examples of what sorts of provisions (for example, "the casting vote provision") are permissible. Once again, however, there is no provision or schedule in the Business Corporations Act comparable with Table "A".

It is in the nature of corporate law that the corporate constitution, particularly in the case of private companies, is seldom relied upon or enforced (or even looked at) unless there is a dispute between the shareholders. Hence it is really only in litigation or in contemplation of litigation that the Bylaws will be looked at in detail and, obviously, at that time there will be at least one party that will be seeking to find some grounds for attacking a Bylaw's enforceability. Many of the provisions now being placed in the Bylaws of corporations would be of fundamental importance in just such an event. Some examples of such provisions are the following:

(a) *Pre-emptive Rights*: Under the Companies Act, a provision in the Articles of Association that shares of the corporation cannot be issued to a non-shareholder without first offering those shares to the existing shareholders is not uncommon. Section 25(1) [now s. 27(1)] of the Business Corporations Act reads as follows:

25(1) Subject to the Articles, the Bylaws and any Unanimous Shareholder Agreement, and to Section 28, shares may be issued at the times and to the persons and for the consideration that the directors determine.

At first glance, the wording in section 25(1) seems to imply that the Bylaws could contain a restriction on issuance in the nature of a pre-emptive right. However, section 28(1) [now s. 30(1)] provides as follows:

28(1) If the Articles or a Unanimous Shareholder Agreement so provide, no shares shall be issued unless the shares have first been offered to the shareholders holding shares of that class, and those shareholders have a pre-emptive right to acquire the offered shares in proportion to their holdings of the shares of that class, at the same price and on the same terms as those shares are to be offered to others.

It appears, therefore, that pre-emptive rights, while permissible in the Articles or in a Unanimous Shareholder Agreement, are not to be provided for in the Bylaws. In comparison with section 28(1), the wording in section 25(1) appears to be more permissive in nature, in that it provides for what the directors can do, as opposed to what restrictions can be placed in the Bylaws. In other words, the proper interpretation of section 25(1) is probably that the directors have the power to issue shares provided such issuance is not contrary to *valid* provisions of the Bylaws, whatever they may be. It is merely an exception and does not of itself imply what provisions are valid.

(b) *Rights of First Refusal*: As in the case of the pre-emptive right, a provision in the Articles of Association that a share of the corporation cannot be transferred to a non-shareholder without first offering that share to the existing shareholders, is not uncommon. In this case, however, there are no provisions in the Business

Corporations Act comparable to section 25(1) [now s. 27(1)] to even imply that such a provision is permissible in the Bylaws. Furthermore, section 6(1)(c) provides as follows:

6(1) The Articles of Incorporation shall be in the prescribed form and shall set out, in respect of the proposed corporation …

(c) if the right to transfer shares of the corporation is to be restricted, a statement that the right to transfer shares is restricted and either

(i) a statement of the nature of the restrictions, or

(ii) a statement that the nature of the restrictions appears in a Unanimous Shareholder Agreement.

Once again it seems clear that a restriction on transfer, while permissible in the Articles of Incorporation or in a Unanimous Shareholder Agreement, ought not to be placed in the Bylaws. This, after all, only makes sense. It would be an absurd situation if the directors of a corporation were allowed to fundamentally affect the ability of the shareholders, even temporarily, to deal with their shares.

(c) *Casting Vote*: Once again, it is not uncommon under the Companies Act to provide in the Articles of Association that the Chairman of a Shareholders' or Directors' meeting has an additional vote in the event of a tie. Needless to say, the casting vote provision is an extremely important one and may ultimately determine control of the corporation. However, the Business Corporations Act is completely silent about casting votes. It may be permissible to deal with casting votes by a Unanimous Shareholder Agreement on the argument that such a provision, in respect of shareholders' meetings, is a regulation of the rights and liabilities of the shareholders as between themselves, as contemplated by section 140(1)(a) [now s. 146(1)(a)]. With respect to Directors' meetings, it could be argued that such a provision is for the management of the business and affairs of the corporation, as contemplated by section 140(1)(c) [now s. 146(1)(c)]. It is also possible that by implication of section 134(1) [now s. 139(1)], the provision can be placed in the Articles of Incorporation. However, it seems quite clear that such a provision cannot be placed in the Bylaws.

(d) *Limitation on Numbers*: Under the Business Corporations Act, the distinction between "private" and "public" companies has been abolished in favour of a distinction based upon what has actually taken place in the distribution of a corporation's shares. The Business Corporations Act now distinguishes between corporations having 15 or fewer shareholders, corporations having more than 15 shareholders and whose issued shares were a part of a distribution to the public (known as "distributing corporations"), and corporations having more than 15 shareholders which are not distributing corporations.

[Nonetheless, for reasons relating to securities legislation, a number of practitioners have tried to create corporate constitutions that preclude distributions of shares to the public.] Many have been doing this by placing the restrictions in the Articles of Incorporation. While this method is not entirely without difficulty, it is certainly preferable to placing these restrictions in the Bylaws. [Footnote from original text: Section 6 (1) (c) [A.B.C.A.] deals only with the *transfer* of shares. *Quaere*, whether s. 25 [now s. 27] of the Business Corporations Act is worded broadly enough to allow the Articles of Incorporation to contain a restriction on *issuance*.] Such a restriction constitutes both a restriction on issuance and on transfer, and as stated above, there is nothing in the Business Corporations Act, outside of section 25(1) [now s. 27(1)], which can be taken as authorizing such a placement. In any event, the Securities Act makes it clear that for the exemption to apply such a restriction must be placed in the corporation's "instrument of incorporation". The Bylaws clearly are not an instrument of incorporation.

The above are, of course, only examples, and there are other provisions commonly contained in the Articles of Association that ought not to be carried forward into the Bylaws. Such provisions may not be of such major impact as the examples given above, but they may, in any given situation, be clauses that must be relied upon by a shareholder or by the corporation. With respect, it must be recognized that at the very least, there are considerable risks in placing these provisions in the Bylaws. Such risks far outweigh any advantage to be gained by placing them in the Bylaws for the sake of easy amendment.

NOTES AND QUESTIONS

1. Ewasiuk argues that "a provision placed in the Bylaws of a corporation that is not specifically authorized by the Act is not enforceable either as against the corporation or the shareholders". Do you think this is right? C.B.C.A., s. 103(1) (which is the same as A.B.C.A., s. 102(1)) provides the general jurisdiction of directors over the by-laws, and refers to by-laws "that regulate the business or affairs of the corporation". Note that "affairs" is a defined term. What do you understand by the word "regulate"? It comes from the Latin noun "regula" meaning "rule". Is a corporate decision to buy a boat the proper subject matter of a by-law, or, as a business decision, should it be made by a resolution of the directors? See *North-West Transportation Co. v. Beatty* (1887), 12 App. Cas. 589 (J.C.P.C., Ont.).

2. Ewasiuk notes that s. 30(1) of the A.B.C.A. provides for restrictions on share transfers in a U.S.A. This is not the case in C.B.C.A., s. 28(1) or elsewhere. The explanation, as noted above, is that under the A.B.C.A. a U.S.A. can deal with a wider range of matters than under other the statutes in other jurisdictions. The same explanation is applicable to the differences between A.B.C.A., s. 6(1)(*c*) and C.B.C.A., s. 6(1)(*d*).

(b) Constitution Shopping: The Permissibility of Particular Constitutional Provisions

Some kinds of corporate constitutions may be more flexible than others, in respect of whether it is permissible to include particular provisions in the constitution. In particular, the contractarian model tends to be more flexible than other models, since it is founded conceptually on a contract, itself a flexible legal institution. Such flexibility as the law allows is often utilized in favour of making it more difficult to remove directors from office. While in theory the constitution does not "belong" to management any more than it belongs to the shareholders, the factual reality is that management has more control over the terms of the constitution than do the shareholders. The reasons for this will be considered in Chapter 7.

Bushell v. Faith, [1970] A.C. 1099, is a good example of the flexibility of contractarian constitutions. Under s. 184 of the *Companies Act 1948* (U.K.), then in force, it was provided that "A company may by ordinary resolution remove a director before the expiration of his period of office, notwithstanding anything in its articles [of association]." An ordinary resolution means a resolution passed by simple majority (more than half the votes). This provision clearly seems aimed at empowering shareholders to remove directors, and that, in a way that the articles (corporate constitution) cannot override. Nonetheless, the House of Lords held that it was permissible for a company to have a provision in its articles of association that on a resolution to remove a director from office, any shares held by that director carried three votes per share.

A parallel attempt to prevent management entrenchment exists in Canadian provisions such as C.B.C.A., s. 6(4). In *Bowater Canadian Ltd. v. R.L. Crain Inc.*, [1987] O.J. No. 1157, 62 O.R. (2d) 752 (C.A.), the Ontario Court of Appeal held that a C.B.C.A. corporation could not have a provision in its articles of incorporation to the effect that shares carried 10 votes each in the hands of the person to whom they were initially issued, but only one vote each in the hands of a transferee.

The possibility that one model of constitution may be more flexible than another opens up the possibility of shopping for corporate law. In *Jacobsen v. United Canso Oil & Gas Ltd.*, [1980] A.J. No. 572, 23 A.R. 512, [1980] 6 W.W.R. 38, 113 D.L.R. (3d) 427 (Q.B.), a C.B.C.A. corporation had a by-law that provided that no one shareholder could have more than 1,000 votes, regardless of the number of shares he or she held. This of course is contrary to the basic principle of corporate law, that each voting share carries one vote. Justice Forsyth held that the by-law was invalid when it was first enacted, at a time when the corporation was a federal letters patent corporation. He held that the by-law was also invalid when the corporation was continued under the C.B.C.A. In the light of ss. 6, 24 and 140, he held that the only way to create different voting rights among shareholders under the C.B.C.A. was by the creation of different classes of shares. His decision was rendered on 12 June 1980. But before he even rendered his decision, the corporation had been continued under the (contractarian) Nova Scotia *Companies Act.* (This continuation had been approved at a shareholder meeting held on 25 October 1979, at which each share was allowed a vote, under what is now C.B.C.A., s. 188.) An annual meeting of shareholders was called for 23 June 1980 in Halifax. One shareholder (who held 100,000 shares) commenced proceedings on 13 June 1980 in the Nova Scotia Supreme Court: *Jacobsen v. United Canso Oil & Gas Ltd.*, [1980] N.S.J. No. 482, 40 N.S.R. (2d) 692, 73 A.P.R. 692 (S.C.T.D.). He sought an injunction that in the upcoming annual meeting, the corporation could not apply the 1,000-vote limit, which was now part of the articles of association of the contractarian corporation. Justice Hallett did not purport to resolve the issue definitively, but he refused to grant the injunction. He said (at paras. 6, 28, 30, 31):

> These applications arise out of a dissatisfaction by the shareholders committee (a group of eleven who hold approximately six per cent of the outstanding shares of the company) with the management of the company by the incumbent board of directors, who hold approximately one-third of one per cent of the outstanding shares. The present board of directors has been re-elected from year to year by the shareholders for approximately the past sixteen years. ...

> ...

> On the other major issue before me, I am not prepared to grant the relief sought in the *Interlocutory* Notice of Motion of June 13, 1980, that the company be restrained from applying the 1,000 vote rule at the shareholders meeting of June 23, 1980, by reason of the decision of Forsyth, J., that the 1,000 vote by-law was invalid under the *Canada Business Corporations Act.*

> ...

> Considering (1) the accepted principle that the courts should not interfere with the management of the affairs of a company in the absence of fraud, illegality and,

now, oppressive conduct, and (2) the principle that where a party is seeking injunctive relief, he must prove irreparable harm if the order is not made, I have concluded that the order requested should not be granted. There is no suggestion of fraud, there may or may not be illegality in applying the 1,000 vote rule but, *at this point in time*, I am not satisfied that the 1,000 vote rule is illegal. This voting restriction was approved by a majority of the shareholders at the meeting of October 25, 1979, on a vote taken on a one vote one share basis. That meeting approved the continuation of the voting restriction when the company would come under the jurisdiction of the Nova Scotia *Companies Act* which, in fact, happened on June 6, 1980. For the chairman to apply that by-law at the shareholders meeting on June 23, 1980, is, in my opinion, not oppressive or unfairly prejudicial to the plaintiff. He bought his shares with notice of the restriction and he had the right to be paid out at fair value when it was decided at the October 25, 1979, meeting that the directors be authorized to apply for a continuance in Nova Scotia and the meeting approved the inclusion in the articles of continuance of the voting restriction. As to the second point, the plaintiff has not shown, as is necessary on an interlocutory motion for injunctive relief, that he will suffer irreparable harm if the order is not granted. If there was evidence of irreparable harm, the balance of convenience would dictate the application of the voting restriction at the shareholders meeting as it was approved by the shareholders. The issue as to the validity of the voting restriction now that the company is governed by the Nova Scotia *Companies Act* should be decided in proceedings commenced by Originating Notice.

...

The shareholders approved of the continuance of the voting restriction at the shareholders meeting less than one year ago; until the issue of the legality of the voting restriction is finally resolved as it applies to a Nova Scotia company, which the company now is, it would be improper for the court to impose on the company and its shareholders a method of counting votes that was other than that adopted by the shareholders.

NOTES AND QUESTIONS

1.   If you wanted to create a Canadian corporation in which no shareholder could amass a significant amount of voting power, or in which original shareholders had more voting power than transferees, or in which directors could prevent their own removal, which jurisdictions might you choose to incorporate in? Would it matter that you wanted a corporation that could carry on business anywhere in Canada?

   Is the contractarian constitution more flexible, in general terms, than the division of powers constitution? In this context, does "more flexible" inevitably mean "less regulated" and therefore "more management-oriented"?

2.   In the U.S. there are no federally-incorporated business corporations. Although the State of Delaware contains only a fraction of 1 per cent of the population of the U.S., around half of the corporations listed on the New York Stock Exchange are incorporated in Delaware. Part of the historical explanation for this appears to be a competition among states (which Delaware won) to provide a less regulated corporate law regime: see Brandeis J., dissenting in *Liggett Co. v. Lee*, 288 U.S. 517 (1933), at p. 559: "The race was not of diligence but of laxity." More recently, though, Delaware law has been restricting management latitude in favour of shareholder rights. The state retains its popularity as a jurisdiction for incorporation for a number of reasons. There is an ongoing effort to facilitate incorporation, and the legislation is amended on a continuing basis in consultation with the Bar. Perhaps most important, there is a developed body of corporate law jurisprudence. The Chancellor of the Delaware Court of Chancery claimed that that court is, in effect, "the nation's only specialized court of

corporation law": see W.T. Allen, "Our Schizophrenic Conception of the Business Corporation" (1992), 14 Cardozo L.R. 261 at 261*n*.

3. Can the continued availability of the contractarian model in some Canadian provinces be viewed as a kind of provincial competition for incorporations? See R. Daniels, "Should Provinces Compete? The Case for a Competitive Corporate Law Market" (1991), 36 McGill L.J. 130.

4. Another form of interprovincial competition in corporate constitutions relates to "unlimited liability corporations". This might seem like an odd choice for a business organization, but there are taxation reasons for it. Normally, if a U.S. corporation has a Canadian subsidiary, the two are independent for taxation purposes. If, however, the Canadian subsidiary is an unlimited liability corporation, then any losses suffered by the subsidiary can be transferred to the U.S. parent, reducing the parent's income tax bill. With its old English-model statute, Nova Scotia was for many years (and probably inadvertently) the only jurisdiction in Canada offering the possibility of an unlimited liability corporation. The tax implications of the Nova Scotia unlimited liability company were mentioned in R. Raizenne, "Hybrids and Joint Ventures," [1994-95] Meredith Lectures 79, at pp. 106-107. The number of such entities has risen steadily over the last 10 years.

    This phenomenon was not lost on the government of the province. To incorporate a "normal" company in Nova Scotia, there is a fee of $270, which is in line with the fees in other provinces and for federal corporations. In 2002 (S.N.S. 2002, c. 5, s. 5), it was enacted that in the case of unlimited liability companies, this fee should be replaced by an "incorporation tax" of $2,000. In 2004, this tax was raised to $4,000 (S.N.S. 2004, c. 3, s. 2; see now N.S.C.A., s. 5(2), (3)). In addition, under the Corporations Registration Act, R.S.N.S. 1989, c. 101, there is a tax of $2,000 that must be paid upon incorporation (s. 5(4)), and annually thereafter (s. 12(3A)).

    Not to be outdone, Alberta has created the possibility of unlimited liability corporations by amendments to the A.B.C.A. (ss. 15.1-15.9), which took effect in 2005. The incorporation fee is $100, the same as for ordinary A.B.C.A. corporations, and there is no annual renewal fee.

CHAPTER 4

THE CORPORATION AS A LEGAL PERSON

A. WHAT IS A CORPORATION?

Corporations are creatures of the law. They do not exist in the natural world. As a matter of logic, they do not need to exist in a legal system, but all developed legal systems provide for them. A corporation is an *artificial person*. It is treated as a person in legal analysis, even though it is not a person outside of legal analysis. Within the legal system, it can do many of the things that human beings can do: hold property, contract with others, commit torts, and so on. We can distinguish the corporation or artificial person from a *natural person*, that is, a human being. In distinguishing them from corporations, natural persons are also referred to as *individuals*.

Corporations existed in Roman law, which is the foundation of all civil law systems. They have also existed in the common law since the earliest times; see, generally, W.S. Holdsworth, *A History of English Law* (London: Methuen, 1926), vol. 3, pp. 469-90; vol. 9, pp. 45-71. The first corporations recognized by the common law were ecclesiastical offices, such as those of bishops and vicars. The Crown was later seen as a similar case. "The King is dead, long live the King": this expresses the idea that the individual office holder is separate from the office. The individual is mortal and eventually dies, but the office itself does not. The office is a legal person, separate from the holder.

Offices such as the Crown were called "corporations sole" by the common law, because they were occupied by a single person at a time. There were also "corporations aggregate", such as monastic orders. These were also recognized early on. This made it possible for land or other assets to be held by an order of monks, and not by any individual monk. The transfer of land to corporations had serious effects on the feudal system of land tenure, which provided for benefits to lords on the death of their tenants. Corporations did not die with the same predictable regularity as individuals, and the result was a legislative response to corporate land holding which continued to have repercussions until very recently. This legislation, dating from the Magna Carta in 1215, was called "mortmain legislation" (see A.H. Oosterhoff, "The Law of Mortmain: An Historical and Comparative Review" (1977), 27 U.T.L.J. 257).

Like Roman law, the common law has always taken the view that the creation of a corporation is a privilege deriving from the power of the state; citizens do not have the power to create corporations on their own. (The matter is less settled in modern civilian systems: J.E.C. Brierley and R.A. Macdonald, eds., *Quebec Civil Law* (Toronto: Emond Montgomery, 1993), pp. 225-26.) As the common law developed, it recognized the creation of corporations by royal charter or letters patent. Both of these are documents signed by the Crown and used to grant powers or privileges. In this way, towns, universities and guilds came to be recognized as typical corporations. Later, as power passed from the Crown to the legislature, corporations were created by special statutes: statutes which created a single corporation and governed its powers, purposes, and so on. Finally, the late nineteenth century saw the adoption of registration statutes, which granted civil servants the authority to create corporations on the application of members of the public. These registration statutes provide a general set of rules governing all corporations created under them, but allowing a greater or lesser degree of customization for the constitutions of particular corporations.

B. THE PRINCIPLE OF CORPORATE PERSONALITY

1. Theoretical Basis

One of the most dramatic consequences of incorporation is the creation of a new legal person, separate in law from its shareholders.

Business relationships could be analyzed without a theory of corporate personality. An obvious alternative would be to treat the corporation as merely the collective name by which legal analysis could be focused on an aggregate of individual humans. This is roughly how partners are seen in our legal system, as discussed in Chapter 1. The partnership name can be used to launch legal proceedings, for example. However, that's all a "partnership" is — a name that identifies the sum of the individual partners acting collectively. A corporation, in the common law system, is more.

The basic principle of corporate personality was settled in the *Salomon* case in 1897. The English House of Lords reversed the lower courts' decisions, explained the legal consequences of incorporation, and laid the cornerstone of modern corporate law.

SALOMON v. SALOMON

[1897] A.C. 22, 66 L.J. Ch. 35, 75 L.T. 426,
45 W.R. 193, 41 Sol. Jo. 63 (Eng. H.L.)

[The appellant, Aron Salomon, incorporated his leather merchant and wholesale boot manufacturing business by registering the memorandum of association required by the governing corporate statute. The statute also required that a new corporation have seven shareholders. The corporation, "Aron Salomon and Company, Limited," issued one share to each of the appellant's wife, a daughter and four sons, and 20,001 shares to the appellant. The corporation adopted an agreement whereby the appellant would be beneficial holder of some debentures. These debentures were issued to B. as security for a loan made by B. to the appellant.

The appellant defaulted on payment of interest on the loan. B. sought to enforce his security against the assets of the corporation. After paying the debt owed to B., there would remain, from the corporation's assets, a balance of £1,055, which was claimed by the appellant as beneficial holder of the debentures. A counter claim was made by the unsecured creditors of the corporation that the corporation or the liquidator was entitled to be indemnified by the appellant against the whole of the corporation's debts. The basis of this argument was that the corporation was the agent of the appellant.

At trial, the court held the appellant liable for the corporation's debts. The Court of Appeal dismissed the appellant's appeal. The appellant appealed to the House of Lords.]

Lord Halsbury L.C.: — My Lords, the important question in this case, I am not certain it is not the only question, is whether the respondent company was a company at all — whether in truth that artificial creation of the Legislature had been validly constituted in this instance; and in order to determine that question it is necessary to look at what the statute itself has determined in that respect. I have no right to add to the requirements of the statute, nor to take from the requirements thus enacted. The sole guide must be the statute itself.

Now, that there were seven actual living persons who held shares in the company has not been doubted. As to the proportionate amounts held by each I will deal presently; but it is important to observe that this first condition of the statute is satisfied, and it follows as a consequence that it would not be competent to any one — and certainly not to these persons themselves — to deny that they were shareholders.

I must pause here to point out that the statute enacts nothing as to the extent or degree of interest or influence possessed by one or the majority of the shareholders over the others. One share is enough. Still less is it possible to contend that the motive of becoming shareholders or of making them shareholders is a field of inquiry which the statue itself recognizes as legitimate.

… In saying this, I do not at all mean to suggest that if it would be established that this provision of the statute to which I am adverting had not been complied with, you could not go behind the certificate of incorporation to show that a fraud had been committed upon the officer entrusted with the duty of giving the certificate, and that by some proceeding in the nature of *scire facias* you could not prove the fact that the company had no real legal existence. But short of such proof it seems to me impossible to dispute that once the company is legally incorporated it must be treated like any other independent person with its rights and liabilities appropriate to itself, and that the motives of these who took part in the promotion of the company are absolutely irrelevant in discussing what those rights and liabilities are.

I will for the sake of argument assume the proposition that the Court of Appeal lays down — that the formation of the company was a mere scheme to enable Aron Salomon to carry on business in the name of the company. I am wholly unable to follow the proposition that this was contrary to the true intent and meaning of the Companies Act. I can only find the true intent and meaning of the Act from the Act itself; and the Act appears to me to give a company a legal existence with, as I have said, rights and liabilities of its own, whatever may have been the ideas or schemes of those who brought it into existence.

I observe that the learned judge (Vaughan Williams J.) held that the business was Mr. Salomon's business, and no one else's, and that he chose to employ as agent a limited company; and he proceeded to argue that he was employing that limited company as agent, and that he was bound to indemnify that agent (the company). I confess it seems to me that that very learned judge becomes involved by this argument in a very singular contradiction. Either the limited company was a legal entity or it was not. If it was, the business belonged to it and not to Mr. Salomon. If it was not, there was no person and no thing to be an agent at all; and it is impossible to say at the same time that there is a company and there is not.

…

My Lords, the learned judges appear to me not to have been absolutely certain in their own minds whether to treat the company as a real thing or not. If it was a real thing; if it had a legal existence, and if consequently the law attributed to it certain rights and liabilities in its constitution as a company, it appears to me to follow as a consequence that it is impossible to deny the validity of the transactions into which it has entered.

...

My Lords, the truth is that the learned judges have never allowed in their own minds the proposition that the company has a real existence. They have been struck by what they have considered the inexpediency of permitting one man to be in influence and authority of the whole company; and, assuming that such a thing could not have been intended by the legislature, they have sought various grounds upon which they might insert into the Act some prohibition of such a result. Whether such a result be right or wrong, politic or impolitic, I say, with the utmost deference to the learned judges, that we have nothing to do with that question of this company [which] has been duly constituted by law; and, whatever may be the motives of those who constitute it, I must decline to insert into that Act of Parliament limitations which are not to be found there.

I have dealt with this matter upon the narrow hypothesis propounded by the learned judges below; but it is, I think, only justice to the appellant to say that I see nothing whatever to justify the imputations which are implied in some of the observations made by more than one of the learned judges. The appellant, in my opinion, is not shown to have done or to have intended to do anything dishonest or unworthy, but to have suffered a great misfortune without any fault of his own.

The result is that I move your Lordships that the judgments appealed from be reversed, but as this is a pauper case, I regret to say it can only be with such costs in this House as are appropriate to that condition of things, and that the cross-appeal be dismissed with costs to the same extent. ...

[**Lords Herschell, MacNaghten, Watson** and **Davey** delivered similar judgments and **Lord Morris** concurred in the decisions and reasons of the court.]

NOTES

The most significant feature of incorporation is the segregation of business profits and losses from the personal accounts of the individual participants.

Throughout the nineteenth century, the merits and drawbacks of this idea were much debated in terms of granting "limited liability" to corporate investors. The description was misleading then and is obsolete now. It originally meant that one who "subscribed for a share" prepaid only part of the issue price, but contracted to contribute further sums on future "calls" up to the maximum "par value" of the share. The par value was a notional value set by the corporation and had nothing to do with the market value of the share which, of course, would fluctuate as the corporation prospered or didn't. The corporation had no power to compel further investment beyond that par value, nor did the corporation's creditors. Thus, it was popularly conceived, a shareholder had only a "limited liability" to discharge corporate debts.

The analysis is now much simpler. The practice of issuing partly paid shares has long since been abandoned. Indeed, it is illegal in most Canadian jurisdictions: see, for example, C.B.C.A., s. 25(3). One acquires a corporate share the same way as one acquires ownership of a new toothbrush: the full price is paid at the time of purchase and the vendor can't subsequently compel the holder to pay more. Moreover, since the *Salomon* case corporations have been recognized as legal persons, separate from and independent of their shareholders. Consequently, it makes no more sense to say that a shareholder's liability to pay corporate debts is "limited" to the amount paid for her shares than to say that a sister's liability to pay her brother's debts is "limited" to the amount of money she gave him for his birthday last year. Neither the shareholder nor the sister owes any obligation to someone else's creditors. This proposition, which flows directly from the *Salomon* ruling, is commonly reinforced by sections like C.B.C.A., ss. 15(1) and 45(1):

15(1) A corporation has the capacity and, subject to this Act, the rights, powers and privileges of a natural person.

...

45(1) The shareholders of a corporation are not, as shareholders, liable for any liability, act or default of the corporation except under subsection 38(4), 118(4) or (5), 146(5) or 226(4) or (5). [Certain peculiar circumstances specified in the aforementioned subsections.]

Would it be feasible to make an incorporator bear some risk for the business errors of a fledgling corporation? Would it be desirable? How would you go about imposing and limiting such risks? In the *Salomon* case, Lord Herschell noted:

It may be that a company constituted like that under consideration was not in contemplation of the Legislature at the time when the Act authorizing limited liability was passed; that if what is possible under the enactments as they stand had been foreseen a minimum sum would have been fixed as the least denomination of share permissible; and that it would have been made a condition that each of the seven persons would have had a substantial interest in the company.

Would such a plan work? For some further suggestions along these lines, see Ziegel, "Is Incorporation (with Limited Liability) Too Easily Available?" (1990), 31 Les Cahiers de Droit 1075.

You should be aware that in addition to establishing the separate personality of the corporation, *Salomon* also confirmed that corporate registration statutes mean what they say. The statute required seven shareholders, and the courts below interpreted this as meaning seven "substantial" shareholders, rather than six holders of one share and one holder of 20,001. The House of Lords pointed out that there was no warrant for this in the statute. As Lord Herschell noted, there did not even need to be one "substantial" shareholder, in the sense of a minimum share price or minimum number of shares held; thus, each of seven shareholders could buy a £1 share, so the corporation would start life with the princely sum of £7 to its name.

WELLING, CORPORATE LAW IN CANADA: THE GOVERNING PRINCIPLES

(3rd ed., 2006), pp. 131-134 (Footnotes deleted.)

A sterling example of the traditional technique can be found in the 1925 *Indian idol case*, decided by the Judicial Committee of the Privy Council. The case involved the interpretation of a will in India where succession law was religion based. The will left a sum of money, stated that each of the testator's three sons was to be the sole manager (*shebait*) of the idol for one-third of each year, and stipulated that the idol was not to be moved from the place of worship (*thakubari*) where it had been housed since its consecration a half-century earlier. A dispute among the sons arose when one of them decided during his term as *shebait* to move the idol closer to his home. He took the position that the restrictive provisions of the will could not restrict the movements of a Hindu deity. The other two brothers characterized the case as a property dispute. The Judicial Committee, sitting as a Hindu Court of Appeal, heard argument and concluded that an idol consecrated as a family divinity was a legal person in Hindu law.

> A Hindu idol is, according to long established authority, founded upon the religious customs of the Hindus and the recognition thereof by Courts of Law, a "juristic entity". It has a juridical status with the power of suing and being sued. Its interests are attended to by the person who has the deity in his charge and who is, in law, its manager with all the powers which would, in such circumstances, on analogy, be given to the manager of the estate of an infant heir.
>
> ...
>
> [Defendant's counsel] said that [the father] might, if he had so pleased, have thrown it in the river. The appellate Court rejected that proposition. And this Board can give no countenance to it. ... Their Lordships do not think that [cases cited by the defendants] form any ground for the proposition that Hindu family idols are property in the crude sense maintained, or that their destruction, degradation or injury are within the power of their custodian for the time being. ... The duties of piety ... are duties to something existing which though symbolizing the Divinity, has in the eye of the law a status as a separate persona.

The defendants thus lost the first issue, having failed to prove a proprietary claim. Whether the idol had magical powers, whether it might be sentimentally attached to its *thakubari*, what its exact religious significance was, were questions to which the Judicial Committee had no answers. They had been asked a legal question: was there property in a Hindu idol, according to Hindu law? They gave a clear and principled legal answer: the idol was a legal person and could not be the subject of a proprietary claim.

The analysis proceeded to the second issue: was the plaintiff entitled to exercise his *shebait* powers to move the idol notwithstanding the objections of his brothers, or were there some restraints on his decision-making powers imposed by Hindu law?

The Hindu religion regarded the idol as serving family interests. But it was unclear from the evidence whether the plaintiff, who wished to move the idol for his own convenience, had considered the wishes of other family members. The legal problem became how to make a *shebait* elevate family interests above self-interest in making decisions. Consistent with their conclusion that the idol was a separate legal person, the Judicial Committee determined that the solution was to find out what Sri Sri Radha Shamsunderji wanted to do!

> [T]he idol is not otherwise represented in the proceedings, though the result might conceivably vitally affect its interests. Their Lordships are accordingly of opinion that it would be in the interests of all concerned that the idol should appear by a disinterested next friend appointed by the Court.

Sceptics might smile at this seeming flight of judicial fancy. The careful analyst will see that the solution was obvious and correct. If the Hindu idol was a legal person, then it had legal rights to be protected. The idol was entitled to have its interests considered. Asking the idol what it wanted done would avail nothing: to the secular judges hearing the case, the idol was like a sane adult with a communicative disorder. The solution was to appoint a "next friend", a lawyer whose function was not so much to determine what the idol wanted, if anything, but to ensure that whatever was decided by the *shebait* was a decision *in the idol's best interest*. The idol existed for the family, not for the manager, so this ruling indirectly protected the interests of all family members. Note the methodology: the family members were not directly involved and were not legally entitled to have their preferences consulted; the idol was directly involved, and was entitled to have its interests considered and protected.

Not coincidentally, that is pretty much how we treat corporations, using the equitable concept of fiduciary duties. A corporate manager (like an idol's *shebait*) can be relied on to protect the interests of the legally personified corporation (idol) in most circumstances. However, in situations where the manager's (*shebait's*) self-interest conflicts with that of the corporation (idol), equitable rules (principles of Hindu law) are imposed to protect the corporation's legal (idol's religious) rights and liberties. There is no mysticism involved. There is only the application of law to ensure the protection of what the law has personified.

Corporations, like Hindu idols, can't be owned. People sometimes speak of shareholders owning the corporation, but that is just sloppy terminology. The form of property acquired upon becoming a shareholder is called a corporate share. A Canadian corporation has the rights and liberties of an individual. An individual can't be made a slave in the common law system. Therefore, neither can a corporation. A corporate share, like any other form of property, is a legal relationship.[1] The share defines the set of legal relations between the shareholder and the corporation, determining how each will be legally required to behave in various circumstances.

NOTES ON "FICTION", "REALISM" AND LEGAL ANALYSIS

The recognition of commercial corporations as legal entities has led to much difficulty and has spawned several theories, notably the "fiction theory" and the "realist theory". Their shortcomings, and their excesses, were long ago exposed by H.L.A. Hart in "Definition and Theory in Jurisprudence" (1954), 70 L.Q.R. at 49-70; but these theories are quite adequate provided their application is restricted to the field of law and that flights of metaphysical fancy are eschewed.

The so-called "fiction" theory assures us that, although no sane human being could seriously conceive of corporations as *really* being persons, we pretend by *legal fiction* that they are. The notion is commonly traced to a comment by Sir Edward Coke in *The Case of Sutton's Hospital* (1612), 10 Co. Rep. at 32b: "[a] corporation ... is invisible, immortal, and exists only in intendment and consideration of the law". Later commentators have

---

[1]   A corporate share belongs to the category "property other than property in things", being neither property in land nor property in a thing. Like all forms of property (eg an estate in land, possession of a dog) a corporate share conforms to the following definition of property [Welling *Property in Things in the Common Law System* (Australia Scribblers Publishing 1996) at 6].

> Property is a relationship. There are always three people in the relationship. The first person is the state.

> The second person is someone whom the state has concluded is the holder of a specified form of property. The third is any other person whom the state has not concluded is the holder of that specified form of property.

> The state will suppress the civil liberties of the third person to the extent they fall within the scope of the form of property held.

focused on how silly the theory that corporations are people becomes when used to explain non-legal matters. They ignore the word "only" in Coke J.'s statement. Corporate personality is a theory of law. It tells us that a corporation — unlike a hamster or a ham sandwich — has legal rights and legal obligations. It directs us legal analysts to deal with those rights and obligations at law as we would deal with the rights and obligations of an individual. How the corporation is thought of or dealt with in non-legal analysis is of no concern.

To classify the corporation as a legal entity is to consign it to legal treatment *by analogy*. The analogy is to the best known person in our society, the individual human being. This statement of corporate personality is axiomatic to modern corporate law. If accepted as such, it produces both rationally defensible and socially acceptable results. However, as happens with other legal theories, the logical implications of corporate personality are not always fully accepted by judges. The jurisprudence on corporate personality is still developing, and it is unclear to what extent the analogy can be taken.

2. Practical Consequences

A few obvious consequences flow from the principle that a corporation is a legal person, separate from the individuals who participate in the running of the corporation's business. Corporations make decisions, hold property, and complete legal transactions. So do individuals. Some physical acts and transactional details that we think we see performed by individuals can be legally attributed to a corporation. There must be a way of reaching that conclusion without contravening the *Salomon* analysis.

Despite his unnecessarily graphic analysis by anatomical analogy in *Bolton (Engineering) Co. v. Graham and Sons*, [1956] 3 W.L.R. 804 (Eng. C.A.), Lord Denning was correct in his conclusions concerning the locus of corporate intent. He said:

> Directors and managers … represent the directing mind and will of the company and control what it does. The state of mind of these managers is the state of mind of the company and is treated by the law as such. … Whether their intention is the company's intention depends on the nature of the matter under consideration, the relative position of the officer or agent and the other relevant facts and circumstances of the case.

The same principle was stated in *Daimler Co. v. Continental Tyre and Rubber Co.*, [1916] 2 A.C. 307 at 340 (Eng. H.L.):

> The acts of a company's … directors, managers, secretary, and so forth, functioning within the scope of their authority, are the company's acts.

It will be seen later that the acts of a company's directors and employees can be the company's acts, even when the individuals are not functioning within the scope of their authority.

QUESTIONS

1. The principal shareholder and *de facto* controller of a corporation gave evidence in a court case in which the corporation was plaintiff. Most of his testimony was rejected, the judge plainly perceiving some terminological inexactitude in his testimony. Despite this, the corporation won the case. Should the judge deny the corporation its

costs on the ground that the corporation had lied? See *Baylis Baxter Ltd. v. Sabath*, [1958] 1 W.L.R. 529 (Eng. C.A.).

2.   A corporation, party to an action, is ordered "to obtain a listing on the London Stock Exchange". A prerequisite imposed by the stock exchange was approval of "the company in general meeting" (*i.e.*, the shareholders). If the shareholders vote against applying for a stock exchange listing, is the corporation in contempt of court? See *Northern Counties Securities Ltd. v. Jackson and Steeple Ltd.*, [1974] 2 All E.R. 625 at 634-36.

3.   A corporation is involved in civil litigation in a small northern town. The other side has hired the only law firm in town. The usual lawyers' monopoly rule prevents non-lawyers from acting as agents in court proceedings. Can a corporate officer argue the case? Can the corporation present its own case? See *Northern Homes Ltd. v. Steel-Space Industries Ltd.* (1975), 57 D.L.R. (3d) 309, [1975] 5 W.W.R. 115 (N.W.T.S.C.) and *Maclab Enterprises Inc. v. Radwah* (1983), 27 Alta. L.R. (2d) 164 (Q.B.). In *92417 Canada Ltd. v. Bomac Batten Ltd.* (1984), 45 O.R. (2d) 593 (S.C.), some nice distinctions were drawn between barristers' and solicitors' work, to what end it is not clear.

4.   A assigned property in all the timber on his land to I Ltd. in consideration for all the shares of that corporation. As well as being the only shareholder, A became a creditor of the corporation. The timber was cut and lying on A's land when a fire destroyed the greater part of it. A's insurance policy covers things in which A has an "insurable interest". Can A recover from the insurer for the loss of the timber?

Lord Buckmaster addressed these facts in *Macaura v. Northern Assurance Co.*, [1925] A.C. 619, 94 L.J.P.C. 154, 133 L.T. 152, 69 Sol. Jo. 77 (Eng. H.L.).

MACAURA v. NORTHERN ASSURANCE CO.

[1925] A.C. 619, 94 L.J.P.C. 154, 133 L.T. 152, 69 Sol. Jo. 77 (Eng. H.L.)

Lord Buckmaster: — My Lords, the appellant is the owner of the Killymoon estate in the county of Tyrone. The respondents are five insurance companies with whom at various dates in January and February of 1922, the appellant effected insurance against fire on timber and wood goods in the open situate on the Killymoon domain not within a hundred yards of any saw mill or any building in which wood working by power other than wind or water was carried on. Neither the amounts nor the exact language of the policies are material for the purposes of the present appeal, nor is the fact that the policies were really effected in the name of the appellant and the Governor and the Company of the Bank of Ireland, for the real questions that arise for determination are these:

1.   Whether the appellant had any insurable interest in the goods the subject of the policies, and

2.   Whether the respondents were, in the circumstances, at liberty to raise the contention that he had no such interest in the manner in which it was raised in the course of these proceedings.

The history of the matter can be stated in a few sentences. The appellant upon whose estate the timber in question was originally standing on December 30, 1919, assigned the whole of it to a company known as the Irish Canadian Saw Mills, Ld., the amount to be paid for the timber felled and unfelled being 27,000*l.*, while a further 15,000*l.* was to be paid for the cost incurred by the appellant in felling the timber that was then down. The total price paid was therefore 42,000*l.*, satisfied by the allotment to the appellant or his nominees of 42,000*l.* fully paid 1*l.* shares in the company; no further shares than these were ever issued. ... In the course of these operations the appellant had become the creditor of the company for 19,000*l.*, and beyond this it is stated that the debts of the company were trifling in amount. The timber when cut remained lying on the appellant's land, and on February 22, 1922, the greater part of it was destroyed by fire. The appellant accordingly claimed against the companies upon the policies and, on May 30, 1922, in an answer sent on behalf of all the companies, it was stated that the companies must decline to accept liability ... The appellant and the Bank of Ireland accordingly instituted proceedings by issuing writs against each of the respondent companies ...

On production of the policies all these actions must have been dismissed, since each policy contained a clause referring all disputes to arbitration and making the award of the arbitrator a condition precedent to any liability on the part of the companies. Instead of pleading this as a defence the companies applied to stay the actions and refer the matters in dispute to arbitration, and on July 21, 1922, an order was made to that effect. Upon the hearing of the arbitration ... the arbitrator decided in the appellant's favour, but he held that in the circumstances the appellant had no insurable interest in the timber, and this view has been supported in the Court of King's Bench and in the Court of Appeal.

... It must, in my opinion, be admitted that at first sight the facts suggest that there really was no person other than the plaintiff who was interested in the preservation of the timber. It is true that the timber was owned by the company, but practically the whole interest in the company was owned by the appellant. He would receive the benefit of any profit and on him would fall the burden of any loss. But the principles on which the decision of this case rests must be independent of the extent of the interest held. The appellant could only insure either as a creditor or as a shareholder in the company. And if he was not entitled in virtue of either of these rights he can acquire no better position by reason of the fact that he held both characters. As a creditor his position appears to me quite incapable of supporting the claim. If his contention were right it would follow that any person would be at liberty to insure the furniture of his debtor, and no such claim has ever been recognized by the Courts. ...

Turning now to his position as shareholder, this must be independent of the extent of his share interest. If he were entitled to insure holding all the shares in the company, each shareholder would be equally entitled, if the shares were all in separate hands. Now, no shareholder has any right to any item of property owned by the company, for he has no legal or equitable interest therein. He is entitled to a share in the profits while the company continues to carry on business and a share in the distribution of the surplus assets when the company is wound up. If he were at liberty to effect an insurance against loss by fire of any item of the company's property, the extent of his insurable interest could only be measured by determining the extent to which his share in the ultimate distribution would be diminished by the loss of the asset — a calculation almost impossible to make. ... Neither a simple creditor nor a shareholder in a company has any insurable interest in a particular asset which a company holds.

[**Lords Atkinson, Sumner, Wrenbury** and **Phillimore** delivered concurring judgments.]

The conclusions arrived at in *Macaura* were anticipated by the Ontario Court of Appeal in *A.G. Peuchen Co. v. City Mutual Fire Insurance Co.* [1891] O.J. No. 26, 18 O.A.R. 446. Later in *General Accident Fire Life Assurance Corp. v. Midland Bank Ltd.*, [1940] 2 K.B. 388 at 401 (Eng. C.A.), it was admitted by Sir Wilfrid Greene M.R. that a parent corporation holding a controlling interest in the shares of a subsidiary corporation had a "business interest" in the subsidiary's assets, but that it held no insurable interest therein. What does "business interest" mean?

In *Bridgewater Hardware Ltd. v. Scottish Union and National Insurance Co.*, [1953] 2 D.L.R. 327 (N.S.T.D.), the plaintiff hardware corporation, whose principal shareholder was E.R. Goudey, sought to recover on a fire insurance policy in which the insured was described as "E.R. Goudey, operating as Bridgewater Hardware" and the property insured as "stock consisting of hardware (excluding automobile accessories, parts and automotive vehicles) the property of the insured". Between the date of the policy and the fire the business had been sold to the corporation as a going concern. Held, the corporation could not sue. Also, it was stated that Goudey had no insurable interest.

In contrast to these findings, see the judgment of the Ontario Court of Appeal in *Kosmopoulos v. Constitution Insurance Co. of Canada* (1983), 42 O.R. (2d) 428, 149 D.L.R. (3d) 77 (C.A.), affd [1987] S.C.J. No. 2, [1987] 1 S.C.R. 2, 34 D.L.R. (4th) 208.

KOSMOPOULOS v. CONSTITUTION INSURANCE CO. OF CANADA

(1983), 42 O.R. (2d) 428, 149 D.L.R. (3d) 77 (C.A.)

[Kosmopoulos was a Greek immigrant, not fluent in English, who operated a leather goods store. On the advice of his solicitor, he had incorporated his business and was the company's sole shareholder and director. Following the incorporation, Kosmopoulos believed he still owned the business. The lease of the business premises continued in his name and was never assigned to the corporation. Meanwhile, the insured under the insurance policy covering the business continued to be shown as "Andreas Kosmopoulos O/A Spring Leather Goods".

A fire broke out at an adjacent store and the leather goods store suffered damage from fire, smoke and water. The insurance companies now holding the policies sought to deny Kosmopoulos' claim for the damages suffered.]

Zuber J.A.: — ... Although a number of issues were raised at trial the single argument now advanced by the appellants is that the plaintiff Andreas Kosmopoulos, as a shareholder of the corporation, has no insurable interest in the assets of that corporation and his claim must fail. ...

...

The concept of "insurable interests" is described in Brown and Menezes, *Insurance Law in Canada* (1982), at p. 67 as follows:

It is the very essence of insurance that the risk of potential loss to the insured is being contractually shifted to the insurer. This feature distinguishes insurance contracts from wagers. The shifting of the risk may, however, lead to anti-social behaviour if there is a profit to be made as a result. Doctrines have developed to ensure that this "moral hazard" is minimized. One of the most important is that the validity of the contract itself is dependent on the interest the insured has in the subject matter of the contract. The concept is unique to insurance law; hence, not too surprisingly, it is termed an "insurable interest".

...

... It is obvious that the plaintiff, Andreas Kosmopoulos was "so circumstanced" with respect to the assets of his limited company that he had "benefit from its existence, prejudice from its destruction".

[**Zuber J.A.** then considered the *Macaura* case]

In *Macaura* the plaintiff was not the sole owner of the company; he owned "practically the whole interest" or "almost all the shares". In the case at hand, Mr. Kosmopoulos was the sole owner and the problems of calculating the interest of an insured shareholder envisaged by Lord Buckmaster would be greatly simplified. However, it must be conceded that the reasoning in *Macaura* is not dependent on the extent of the plaintiff's shareholding. The *rationale* of the case is summed up by Lord Wrenbury who said at p. 633:

> My Lords, this appeal may be disposed of by saying that the corporator even if he holds all the shares is not the corporation, and that neither he nor any creditor of the company has any property legal or equitable in the assets of the corporation.

...

The question then is whether this court is obliged to accept *Macaura* as the law in Ontario. *Macaura* has been twice referred to in the Supreme Court of Canada.

...

... I conclude ... that the Supreme Court of Canada has accepted the rule in *Macaura* only to the extent that it needed to decide the *Aqua-Land* case [*Guarantee Co. of North America v. Aqua-Land Exploration Ltd.*, [1966] S.C.R. 133, 54 D.L.R. (2d) 229], *i.e.*, that one shareholder of three had no insurable interest in the assets of the corporation. Therefore, the issue of whether a sole shareholder has an insurable interest in the assets of the corporation, in my view, remains open in this province.

... The question, then, is whether the *Macaura* rule should be accepted in its entirety in Ontario to compel a court to hold that the sole owner of a single-shareholder, single-director company can have no insurable interest in the assets of that company. In my view the rule should not be accepted to this extent as part of the Ontario law. ... I can see no reason for imposing the rigidity of the *Macaura* rule on this recent development in company law [allowing for corporations with a single director and shareholder].

...

In some future case where the sole owner of a corporation takes out insurance in his own name to cover the assets of his corporate *alter ego*, an insurer may be able to show that this amounted to a misstatement material to the risk and thereby avoid liability. Such a case is not easy to imagine and, in any event, is not this case. ...

Appeal dismissed.

Upon further appeal to the Supreme Court of Canada, the Court of Appeal's decision was affirmed, although on different grounds.

KOSMOPOULOS v. CONSTITUTION INSURANCE CO. OF CANADA

[1987] S.C.J. No. 2, [1987] 1 S.C.R. 2, 34 D.L.R. (4th) 208

Wilson J.: — ... As a general rule a corporation is a legal entity distinct from its shareholders: *Salomon v. Salomon & Co.*, [1897] A.C. 22 (H.L.). The law on when a court may disregard this principle by "lifting the corporate veil" and regarding the company as a mere "agent" or "puppet" of its controlling shareholder or parent corporation follows no consistent principle. ...

There is a persuasive argument that "those who have chosen the benefits of incorporation must bear the corresponding burdens, so that if the veil is to be lifted at all that should only be done in the interests of third parties who would otherwise suffer as a result of that choice": Gower, *supra*, at p. 138 [L.C.B. Gower, *Modern Company Law*, 4th ed. (London: Stevens & Sons, 1979)]. Mr. Kosmopoulos was advised by a competent solicitor to incorporate his business in order to protect his personal assets and there is nothing in the evidence to indicate that his decision to secure the benefits of incorporation was not a genuine one. Having chosen to receive the benefits of incorporation, he should not be allowed to escape its burdens. He should not be permitted to "blow hot and cold" at the same time.

...

... If the corporate veil were to be lifted in this case, then a very arbitrary and, in my view, indefensible distinction might emerge between companies with more than one shareholder and companies with only one shareholder ... In addition, it is my view that if the application of a rule leads to harsh justice, the proper course to follow is to examine the rule itself rather than affirm it and attempt to ameliorate its ill effects on a case-by-case basis.

For all these reasons, I would not lift the corporate veil in this case. The company was a legal entity distinct from Mr. Kosmopoulos. It, and not Mr. Kosmopoulos, legally owned the assets of the business.

...

Mr. Kosmopoulos, as sole shareholder of the company, was so placed with respect to the assets of the business as to have benefit from their existence and prejudice from their destruction. He had a moral certainty of advantage or benefit from those assets but for the fire. He had, therefore, an insurable interest in them capable of supporting the insurance policy and is entitled to recover under it.

...

McIntyre J.: — I have read the reasons of my colleague, Madame Justice Wilson, in this appeal. I agree with her result. I would dismiss the appeal. In doing so, however, I would not go as far as my colleague has gone in rejecting totally the limited definition of an insurable interest in *Macaura* ... I would prefer to adopt the approach of Zuber J.A. in the Court of Appeal. Modern company law now permits the creation of companies with one shareholder. The identity then between the Company and that sole shareholder and director is such that an insurable interest in the Company's assets may be found in the sole shareholder. ...

Appeal ... dismissed.

NOTE

Kosmopoulos held that the concept of "insurable interest" was broader than in the earlier cases. It stands for the proposition that a sole shareholder, though lacking any proprietary interest in the corporation's assets, had an "insurable interest" in them. The result is that the corporate personality point from *Macaura* was upheld, but the insurance law point was broadened. This conclusion on the issue of corporate personality was affirmed in *Transamerica Life Insurance Co. of Canada v. Canada Life Assurance Co.*, [1996] O.J. No. 1568, 28 O.R. (3d) 423 (Gen. Div.) [affd [1987] O.J. No. 3754 (C.A.)].

QUESTION

What (if any) property does one acquire by becoming a corporate shareholder?

Suppose 100 corporate shares are issued, all to X in exchange for a transfer of ownership of X's truck, worth $10,000. If the corporation holds no other property, how much would Y pay for:

(i)   all the assets of the corporation;

(ii)   all the shares of the corporation;

(iii) 60 of X's shares?

Suppose X sells 60 of the shares to Y and 40 of the shares to Z. Who owns the truck? Who owns the corporation? Does Y have an insurable interest in the truck? Does Z?

LEE v. LEE'S AIR FARMING LTD.

[1961] A.C. 12, [1960] 3 All E.R. 420, [1960] 3 W.L.R. 758,
104 Sol. Jo. 869 (N.Z. J.C.P.C.)

[Section 3(1) of the *Workers' Compensation Act, 1922*, of New Zealand, provided that if "personal injury by accident arising out of and in the course of the employment is caused to a worker, his employer shall be liable to pay compensation", and "worker" is defined in section 2 as "any person who has entered into or works under a contract of service ... with an employer ... whether remunerated by wages, salary, or otherwise". The appellant's husband, who had formed the respondent corporation for the purpose of carrying on the business of aerial top-dressing, was the controlling shareholder and was by the articles of association appointed governing director and employed at a salary as its chief pilot. In his capacity as governing director and controlling shareholder he exercised full and unrestricted control over all the operations of the corporation. Pursuant to its statutory obligations the corporation had insured itself against liability to pay compensation in the case of an accident to him. While he was piloting an aircraft belonging to the corporation in the course of aerial top-dressing operations, the aircraft crashed and he was killed. The Court of Appeal of New Zealand upheld the Compensation Court which had ruled that the appellant's deceased husband could not hold the office of governing director of the respondent corporation and also be its servant.]

Lord Morris of Borth-y-Gest: — ... The Court of Appeal recognized that a director of a company may properly enter into a service agreement with his company, but they considered that, in the present case, inasmuch as the deceased was the governing director in whom was vested the full government and control of the company he could not also be a servant of the company.

...

The substantial question which arises is, as their Lordships think, whether the deceased was a "worker" within the meaning of the Workers' Compensation Act, 1922, and its amendments. Was he a person who had entered into or worked under a contract of service with an employer? The Court of Appeal thought that his special position as governing director precluded him from being a servant of the company. On this view it is difficult to know what his status and position was when he was performing the arduous and skilful duties of piloting an aeroplane which belonged to the company and when he was carrying out the operation of top-dressing farm lands from the air. He was paid wages for so doing. The company kept a wages book in which these were recorded. The work that was being done was being done at the request of farmers whose contractual rights and obligations were with the company alone. It cannot be suggested that when engaged in the activities above referred to the deceased was discharging his duties as governing director. ... It was never suggested (nor in their Lordships' view could it reasonably have been suggested) that the company was a sham or a mere simulacrum. It is well established that the mere fact that someone is a director of a company is no impediment to his entering into a contract to serve the company. If, then, it be accepted that the respondent company was a legal entity their Lordships see no reason to challenge the validity of any contractual obligations which were created between the company and the deceased. ...

Nor in their Lordships' view were any contractual obligations invalidated by the circumstance that the deceased was sole governing director in whom was vested the full government and control of the company. ... The circumstance that in his capacity as a shareholder he could control the course of events would not in itself affect the validity of his contractual relationship with the company. When, therefore, it is said that "one of his first acts was to appoint himself the only pilot of the company", it must be recognised that the appointment was made by the company, and that it was none the less a valid appointment because it was the deceased himself who acted as the agent of the company in arranging it. In their Lordships' view it is a logical consequence of the decision in *Salomon's* case, [1897] A.C. 22, that one person may function in dual capacities. It is said that therein lies the difficulty, because it is said that the deceased could not both be under the duty of giving orders and also be under the duty of obeying them. But this approach does not give effect to the circumstance that it would be the company and not the deceased that would be giving the orders. Control would remain with the company whoever might be the agent of the company to exercise it. The fact that so long as the deceased continued to be governing director, with amplitude of powers, it would be for him to act as the agent of the company to give the orders does not alter the fact that the company and the deceased were two separate and distinct legal persons. If the deceased had a contract of service with the company then the company has a right of control. The manner of its exercise would not affect or diminish the right to its exercise. But the existence of a right to control cannot be denied if once the reality of legal existence of the company is recognised. ...

Ex facie there was a contract of service. Their Lordships conclude, therefore, that the real issue in the case is whether the position of the deceased as sole governing director made it impossible for him to be the servant of the company in the capacity of chief pilot of the company. In their Lordships' view, for the reasons which have been indicated, there was no such impossibility. There appears to be no greater difficulty in holding that a man acting in one capacity can give orders to himself in another capacity than there is in holding that a man acting in one capacity can make a contract with himself in another capacity. Their Lordships consider, therefore, that the deceased was a worker and that the question posed in the case stated should be answered in the affirmative.

Appeal allowed.

NOTES

The theory of corporate personality cuts two ways. On its face, it says that certain acts are acts of the corporate person. What this implies, though, is that such acts are *not* acts of any individuals who might have been involved in some way. Assume that a corporation, under the control of its directors and therefore indirectly of its shareholders, enters into a contract. The corporation is liable on the contract. If, however, the act of contracting was also treated as an act of the individuals involved, then they too would be liable on the contract, which would make nonsense of the theory of corporate personality.

It would seem to follow that if an act is a corporate act, it cannot generally also be an act of the individuals involved. *Salomon*, for instance, decided that a corporate act is not the act of an individual merely because that individual is a controlling shareholder. *Lee v. Lee's Air Farming Ltd.*, above, shows, however, that just because an individual is a controlling shareholder and a director of a corporation, he does not thereby forfeit his individual personality. He can act in different capacities, or "wear different hats" within the corporate structure. Thus if Lee, acting as the "sole governing director", had caused the corporation to commit a tort, then presumably that would be a corporate tort, and it would seem to follow that Lee would not personally have committed a tort. On the other hand, it was perfectly possible for Lee, acting in his personal capacity, to become an employee of the corporation.

Lee demonstrates that what needs to be ascertained is the capacity in which the individual in question is acting, or which "hat" the individual is wearing, at the relevant point in time in order to determine liability. How can we determine this?

QUESTIONS

1. Assume that an individual, X, creates a C.B.C.A. corporation but keeps it a secret. X carries on a business in his own name, never making any mention of the corporation in any of his business dealings. When faced with some unfortunate business outcome involving large liabilities, can X spring out the corporation and deny that any of the liabilities accrue to X? Why not? Would it make any difference to your conclusion if X had transferred all of the assets of the business to the corporation?

    Does your conclusion depend on the fact that X was in violation of C.B.C.A., s. 10(5)? See *Wolfe v. Moir* (1969), 69 W.W.R. 70 (Alta. T.D.); *CHED-CKNG FM v. Goose Loonies Inc.*, [1995] A.J. No. 596, 31 Alta. L.R. (3d) 242 (Master).

2. F was the president and sole shareholder of a corporation. One of the corporation's employees slipped on the sidewalk when leaving work after a snowstorm. The evidence established that the sidewalk had not been adequately cleared. The applicable legislation, the *Workmen's Compensation Act*, R.S.O. 1970, c. 505, gave compensation for such work-related injuries, but prevented tort actions against the employer. The injured employee sued F.

    (a) Had the statute not been in existence, could the employee have succeeded in a lawsuit against the corporation in negligence?

    (b) If the plaintiff had been a customer rather than an employee, would the action have succeeded against the corporation? Against F?

    (c) Is F liable in negligence to the employee? If so, what was F's duty of care?

    (d) Suppose a stranger passing by had noticed the icy sidewalk but done nothing. Could the plaintiff have collected damages from the stranger?

In *Berger v. Willowdale A.M.C.* (1983), 145 D.L.R. (3d) 247 (Ont. C.A.), the majority found F to be liable for the tort of negligence on the above facts. The dissent concluded that F had violated his obligations to the corporation, but owed no duty to the plaintiff. With which decision do you agree?

NOTES

The foregoing cases have involved small corporations with few shareholders. The theory of corporate entity, however, applies equally to monolithic commercial corporations. With these, it is the corporation which is the practical, as well as the legal reality. Problems may arise because of intra-corporate misunderstandings in situations where, figuratively, the left hand does not know what the right hand is doing. This is hardly surprising if one considers that the two "hands" may be different divisions, each of which is thousands of kilometres from the other and from the head office. Indeed, with multinational corporations, branch operations of the same legal entity may be carried on in different countries simultaneously. Should the legal theory be refined to classify such distant operations as legal entities in their own right?

Consider the situation in which two branch operations of a large corporation have agreed, unknown to each other, to act as agents for the vendor and the purchaser in a real estate transaction. In law, the corporation was acting for both parties in a conflict of interest situation. Can the corporation successfully sue the vendor or the purchaser for its commission? See *Harrods Ltd. v. Lemon*, [1931] 2 K.B. 157 (Eng. C.A.). Is it misleading, in a legal discussion, to describe this situation as one in which two branch operations, unknown to each other, agreed to act as agents?

C. QUESTIONING THE PRINCIPLE: THE "CORPORATE VEIL" THEORY

Judges have not always approached the question of individual liability by examining the capacities in which persons have acted. In *Lee v. Lee's Air Farming Ltd.*, [1961] A.C. 12, [1960] 3 All E.R. 420, [1960] 3 W.L.R. 758, 104 Sol. Jo. 869 (N.Z. J.P.C.), above, Lord Morris of Borth-y-Gest noted that no one had suggested that the corporation was "a mere sham or simulacrum". What he was referring to was the so-called "doctrine of lifting the corporate veil". This doctrine was referred to in the earlier excerpt from the Supreme Court of Canada's judgment in *Kosmopoulos v. Constitution Insurance Co. of Canada*, [1987] S.C.J. No. 2, [1987] 1 S.C.R. 2, 34 D.L.R. (4th) 208. This label is commonly used to describe situations in which judges have presumed to simply ignore the existence of the corporate person and fix liability on the managers or the shareholders. It is not obvious where a judge would get such power. Nevertheless, cases have articulated scenarios in which "lifting" or "piercing" the corporate veil would be appropriately done.

In *Clarkson Co. Ltd. v. Zhelka*, [1967] 2 O.R. 565, 64 D.L.R. (2d) 457 (H.C.), Thompson J. said:

> The cases in which the Courts ... have seen fit to disregard the corporate entity or personality, and instead to consider the economic realities behind the legal facade, fall within a narrow compass. The Legislature, in the fields of revenue and taxation, ... has made much greater departure in this respect. Such cases as there are illustrate no consistent principle. The only principle laid down is that in the leading case of *Salomon v. Salomon & Co. Ltd.*, [1897] A.C. 22; and in general such principle has been rigidly applied. Briefly stated, it is that the legal *persona* created by incorporation is an entity distinct from its shareholders and directors and that even in the case of a one-man company, the company is not an alias for the owner.

> The exceptions would appear to represent refusals to apply the logic of the *Salomon* case where it would be flagrantly opposed to justice.

> ... If a company is formed for the express purpose of doing a wrongful or unlawful act, or, if when formed, those in control expressly direct a wrongful thing to be done, the individuals as well as the company are responsible to those to whom liability is legally owed.

> In such cases, or where the company is the mere agent of a controlling corporator, it may be said that the company is a sham, cloak or *alter ego*, but otherwise it should not be so termed.

In *Littlewoods Mail Order Stores Ltd. v. Inland Revenue Commissioners*, [1969] 3 All E.R. 855 (Eng. C.A.), Lord Denning M.R. made the following comments about the viability of piercing the corporate veil:

> The doctrine laid down in *Salomon* ... has to be watched very carefully. It has often been supposed to cast a veil over the personality of a limited company through which the courts cannot see. But that is not true. The courts can and often do draw aside the veil. They can, and often do, pull off the mask. They look to see what really lies behind. The legislature has shown the way with group accounts and the rest. And the courts should follow suit.

More recently, in *Transamerica Life Insurance Co. of Canada v. Canada Life Assurance Co.*, [1996] O.J. No. 1568, 28 O.R. (3d) 423 at 433-34 (Gen. Div.), Sharpe J. formulated the following criteria as bases for disregarding the notion of separate corporate personality:

> There are undoubtedly situations where justice requires that the corporate veil be lifted. ... [I]t will be difficult to define precisely when the corporate veil is to be lifted, but that lack of a precise test does not mean that a court is free to act as it pleases on some loosely defined "just and equitable" standard. ...

> [T]he courts will disregard the separate legal personality of a corporate entity where it is completely dominated and controlled and being used as a shield for fraudulent or improper conduct. The first element "complete control", requires more

than ownership. It must be shown that there is complete domination and that the subsidiary company does not, in fact, function independently ...

The second element refers to the nature of the conduct: is there "conduct akin to fraud that would otherwise unjustly deprive claimants of their rights"?

(References omitted.)

The general principle behind corporate veil theory is that a corporation is to be analyzed by analogy to the individual human being. Where does the judicial power to ignore the existence of the corporation come from? It clearly is not authorized by statute. In fact, legislative statements like C.B.C.A., s. 15(1) ["A corporation has the capacity and, subject to this Act, the rights, powers and privileges of a natural person"] suggest that there is no "corporate veil" that can be drawn aside. The mystery only deepens when one examines those situations in which individual judges have attempted to explain when (though never how) a judge may violate a corporation's civil rights by "piercing the corporate veil".

ROTMAN, FIDUCIARY LAW

(2005), pp. 427, 429-32 (Footnotes deleted.)

As entities dependent upon law and whose existence is a privilege derived from the power of the state, corporations cannot ignore the limitations inherent in their statutory basis. "Incorporation," as Welling explains, "entails the severing of all legal connections between the individual shareholders and the assets, liabilities, and direct control over the business". In a legal sense, therefore, corporations are not, as some courts have described them, the alter egos of their shareholders. This is true even where only one shareholder exists. Because the process of incorporation allows for individuals' financial participation in corporate activities without the corresponding assumption of liability, some meaningful separation between corporate and investor personality must remain.

...

While the legal basis of the corporation cannot, and should not, be ignored, as Farrar indicates, "[t]his legal personification should not distort the underlying social reality". Thus, maintaining fidelity to the separate legal identity of the corporation from its shareholders does not necessitate the slavish adherence to an acontextual and absolutist vision of the corporation. Rather, it ought to allow for analysis of the effects of the corporate form on commercial realities that corporate statutes may not have adequately accounted for.

From a contemporary perspective, it is evident that the *Salomon* case resulted in a host of unforeseen problems stemming from the implications of the Judicial Committee's conclusions. The relative ease with which incorporation may be obtained potentially allows for the abuse of the corporation's independent legal existence by using the corporate vehicle as a means to shield the socially or economically inappropriate conduct of its investors. Examples of such scenarios include the intentional undercapitalizing of a corporation or the use of corporations to commit fraud. Where these scenarios exist, persons with bona fide claims against corporations may be prevented from obtaining relief since incorporation shields shareholders from financial responsibility for the corporation's actions. Judicial reaction to the perceived inequity of such scenarios led to what is commonly referred to as "piercing the corporate veil".

The attempt to foist liability upon a corporation's investors by invoking corporate veil theory is an attempt to circumvent the implications of incorporation. In order to get to the proverbial "deep pockets" needed to satisfy a judgment where a corporation is insufficiently capitalized, it is necessary to establish that a corporation's investors are directly responsible for the corporation's actions. To do this, judges have sometimes sought to "disregard the corporate entity or personality, and instead to consider the economic realities behind the legal façade...". Effecting this desire is difficult to justify in light of the legal implications of incorporation. Nonetheless, courts have seized the jurisdiction to do precisely this, using rationales similar to that expressed in *Stockton v. Central R.R. Co.*, "[i]t must not be thought that courts are powerless to strip off disguises to thwart the purposes of the law. Whenever such disguises in fact appear, they can readily be disrobed. The difficulty is in showing the disguises, not in penetrating them when they appear".

It has been suggested that the corporate form may be pushed aside where "it would be flagrantly opposed to justice," where "a company is formed for the express purpose of doing a wrongful or unlawful act, or, if when formed, those in control expressly direct a wrongful thing to be done," or "where the company is the mere agent of a controlling corporator". In these circumstances, "it may be said that the company is a sham, cloak or alter ego, but otherwise it should not be so termed". A variation on this theme is expressed by Wormser:

> When the conception of corporate entity is employed to defraud creditors, to evade an existing obligation, to circumvent a statute, to achieve or perpetuate monopoly, or to protect knavery or crime, the courts will draw aside the web of entity, will regard the corporate company as an association of live, up-and-doing, men and women shareholders, and will do justice between real persons.

Allowing the corporate form to be ignored in these scenarios suggests, by implication, that it may not be disregarded where it is used for less unseemly purposes. Thus, in *Stubart Investments Ltd. v. The Queen*, the Supreme Court of Canada determines that a corporate affiliate that was established solely for tax planning purposes and demonstrated no bona fide business purpose did not justify piercing the corporate veil.

Certainly, it is axiomatic that statutes may not be used as instruments of fraud. Corporate statutes are no exception. Absent situations of fraud, however, reliance is often placed on the perceived equities of a situation to justify "piercing" the corporate veil. Unfairness, on its own, is not a sufficient justification for dismantling the corporate structure. It is axiomatic that what is "legal" is not necessarily "fair". Instead, a reasoned and legally sustainable basis for ignoring the legal implications of incorporation must be demonstrated. For this to exist, the inequitable conduct must be shown to be inextricably linked with corporate activity and be inimical to the purposes for which the separation of corporate and shareholder liability is granted through incorporation. This is a high threshold that will not be met simply because a result is "unfair".

Eliminating the separation of corporate and shareholder liability in this way is not done because, as Wormser suggests, "equity, less abashed by forms or fictions than a court of law, is more willing to draw aside the veil and look at the real parties in interest". Equity may only peer through what is sometimes called the corporate "façade" where it is necessary to scrutinize the corporation's existence in light of the conduct complained of (where the two are demonstrated to be associated in a meaningful way) and that conduct renders the implications of incorporation on shareholder liability unsustainable. However, an equitable approach that looks to substance rather than legal form may only be properly undertaken where there is an equitable cause of action which justifies and supports it. Broad notions of fairness do not provide a sufficient basis for ignoring investor safeguards instituted by legislation. That does not entail that "piercing the corporate veil" cannot be done, but that it will be rarely done and only where a sufficiently principled basis exists.

The difficulty associated with "piercing the corporate veil," then, is that while it may result in broad notions of justice being achieved in terms of result, it may only accomplish this by subverting the legitimate scheme for separating investor and corporate identities legalized through the process of incorporation. The tension between the need to maintain the efficacy of the corporate form and the desire to alleviate the harsh effects of incorporation where fraud or similar conduct exists is captured by Sharpe J. in *Transamerica Life Insurance Co. of Canada v. Canada Life Assurance Company*:

> There are undoubtedly situations where justice requires that the corporate veil be lifted. ... [I]t will be difficult to define precisely when the corporate veil is to be lifted, but that lack of a precise test does not mean that a court is free to act as it pleases on some loosely defined "just and equitable" standard. ...

> [T]he courts will disregard the separate legal personality of a corporate entity where it is completely dominated and controlled and being used as a shield for fraudulent or improper conduct. The first element, "complete control", requires more than ownership. It must be shown that there is complete domination and that the subsidiary company does not, in fact, function independently ...

> The second element refers to the nature of the conduct: is there "conduct akin to fraud that would otherwise unjustly deprive claimants of their rights"?

NOTE

In a commentary predating the *Transamerica Life* case, Welling posits the following situations in which piercing the corporate veil has been proposed.

WELLING, CORPORATE LAW IN CANADA: THE GOVERNING PRINCIPLES

(3rd ed., 2006), pp. 127-30 (Footnotes deleted.)

Judges have claimed the power to "pierce the corporate veil" in three types of situations.

One is based on the straightforward judicial conclusion that "it's just not fair". This is essentially all there is to the American "Deep Rock doctrine". It evolved out of an attempt by Justice Douglas to explain why the claim of a controlling shareholder was subordinate to claims of corporate creditors. He said:

> At times equity has ordered disallowance or subordination by disregarding the corporate entity. That is to say, it has treated the debtor corporation simply as a part of the stockholder's own enterprise. ... [A] sufficient consideration may be simply the *violation of rules of fair play and good conscience* by [the majority shareholder],

> a breach of the fiduciary standards of conduct which he owes the corporation, its stockholders and creditors.

Little need be said about this rationale, other than that it simply won't do. There are, so far as I am aware, no broadly enforceable standards of "fair play and good conscience", at least in Canadian corporate law. Standards of sportsmanship and gentlemanly conduct have been enforced traditionally by one's peers and by the marketplace, not by referees and judges. To the extent that such standards are legally relevant, they apply only within the confines of the fiduciary obligations that corporate directors and officers owe to their corporations; the broader equitable relationships referred to above just do not exist. Pretending they do is a lame excuse for pretending that corporations don't.

Some have advanced the rather confused notion that judges can disregard corporate entity whenever a corporation was created or managed for nefarious purposes. Judicial views in this category tend to be self-contradictory. An example can be found in a 1974 Federal Court case. As we shall see later in this chapter, the result in the case can be explained by simple analogy to the character of an individual. Contrast the following extract from the reasons for judgment.

> In the present instance it is evident that [the defendant] is nothing but an instrument in the hands of the parent companies and the rule of instrumentality should be applied to lift the veil in order to assess the course of conduct of (the defendant) and of the group. ... The Court reiterates and underlines that it does not consider [the defendant] as an entity having no life of its own or as an agent.

What did he mean? The two sentences contradict one another.

The third category is more of a threat to rational decision making. It includes cases in which judges, after having reasoned their way to logical conclusions, proceed to let off steam in unprincipled invective. The proper legal term for such judicial comments is, of course, *obiter dicta*. Yet the fact that the comments are made allows future litigants to cite the *dicta* and tempts other judges to discard reasoned analysis in favour of glib, stock phrases. An oft-cited example is *Clarkson Co Ltd v Zhelka*. The case involved a complex bankruptcy situation. Justice Thompson did an admirable job of sorting out the facts and reaching a reasoned conclusion. Unfortunately, he did not stop there. His follow-up *dicta* on "piercing the corporate veil" have been trotted out with distressing regularity in subsequent cases. Again, note the inherent contradictions.

> The cases in which the Courts, both in this Province and in England, have seen fit to disregard the corporate entity or personality, and instead to consider the economic realities behind the legal facade, fall within a narrow compass. ... Such cases as there are illustrate no consistent principle. ... If a company is formed for the express purpose of doing a wrongful or unlawful act, or if when formed, those in control expressly direct a wrongful thing to be done, the individuals as well as the company are responsible to those to whom liability is legally owed.

But how? And why? Perhaps those who direct [*ie* counsel] a corporation to commit an unlawful act will themselves incur legal liability. If so, it will be by virtue of a legal rule, not as a result of calling a legal person a "façade". The judge continued.

> In such cases, *or where the company is the mere agent* of a controlling corporator, it may be said that the company is a sham, cloak or alter ego, but otherwise it should not be so termed. (*Emphasis added.*)

This slapdash approach was criticized in a 1989 British Columbia case, where it was pointed out that "If it were possible to ignore the principles of corporate entity when a judge thought it unfair not to do so, *Salomon's* case would have afforded a good example for the application of that approach". More recently in Ontario, Justice Sharpe narrowed the range of considerations that he thought judges could use in "piercing the corporate veil".

> [T]he courts will disregard the separate legal personality of a corporate entity where it is completely dominated and controlled and being used as a shield for fraudulent or improper conduct. The first element, "complete control", requires more than ownership. It must be shown that there is complete domination and that the subsidiary company does not, in fact, function independently. ... The second element refers to the nature of the conduct: is there "conduct akin to fraud that would otherwise unjustly deprive claimants of their rights"?

Judges in subsequent cases have taken to citing Justice Sharpe and applying that test to the facts.

Courts in Canada have yet to take the final step and acknowledge that they have no inherent power to pretend that a corporation does not exist. I suspect the reason is simple. Most barristers concede the judge has power to "pierce the corporate veil", then argue that this is not an appropriate case in which to use the power. They are conceding too much and they are ignoring the clear wording of Canadian corporate statutes. It is time for someone to stand up and say "*quo warranto?*".

NOTE

In *Kosmopoulos v. Constitution Insurance Co. of Canada*, [1987] S.C.J. No. 2 [1987] 1 S.C.R. 2, 34 D.L.R. (4th) 208, Wilson J. said, for the majority (at p. 10 [S.C.R.]):

> As a general rule a corporation is a legal entity distinct from its shareholders: *Salomon v. Salomon & Co.*, [1897] A.C. 22 (H.L.). The law on when a court may disregard this principle by "lifting the corporate veil" and regarding the company as a mere "agent" or "puppet" of its controlling shareholder or parent corporation follows no consistent principle. The best that can be said is that the "separate entities" principle is not enforced when it would yield a result "too flagrantly opposed to justice, convenience or the interests of the Revenue": L.C.B. Gower, *Modern Company Law* (4th ed. 1979), at p. 112. I have no doubt that theoretically the veil could be lifted in this case to do justice ... [b]ut a number of factors lead me to think it would be unwise to do so.
>
> ...
>
> ... In addition, it is my view that if the application of a rule leads to harsh justice, the proper course to follow is to examine the rule itself rather than affirm it and attempt to ameliorate its ill effects on a case-by-case basis.

D. CORPORATE PERSONALITY IN PRACTICE: SOME PROBLEM AREAS

1. Corporate Character Traits

WELLING, CORPORATE LAW IN CANADA: THE GOVERNING PRINCIPLES

(3rd ed., 2006), pp. 143-44

Corporate personality is a precise analytical tool, if used with other principles of common law and Equity. Used alone, it resembles a poorly designed club.

The principle that a corporation is a separate legal entity does not mean that one is expected to ignore the identity of the individual shareholders and managers. In fact, their character and behaviour patterns are key factors in constructing a unique personality for the corporation. One way of looking at the corporation is to consider it as a relatively unimaginative person whose behaviour can usually be predicted because it tends to mimic the character traits of certain people influential in its organization.

The fact that a corporation is likely to bear familial resemblance to its founders or dominant managerial group has influenced judicial attitudes in the past and will continue to do so. The practice is often defensible because the analogy between a newly-created corporation and a fully capable individual is strained in certain circumstances. Gathering evidence to establish a pattern of a person's past behaviour is a case in point. An individual will probably have left a trail of idiosyncratic behaviour. Any adult individual, even one who has just reached the age of majority, may have enjoyed years of diminished responsibility for his past actions, but he was not born yesterday. A fully capable corporation may well have been born yesterday. Does the law permit us to look inside the corporation's equivalent of a family to establish a pattern of behaviour? A cautious "yes" can be advanced, provided the principle of corporate personality is not sacrificed.

BIG BEND HOTEL LTD. v. SECURITY MUTUAL CASUALTY CO.

[1980] B.C.J. No. 1427, 19 B.C.L.R. 102 (S.C.)

[Kumar was the president and sole shareholder of the plaintiff corporation. The corporation contracted for an insurance policy with the defendant to insure a hotel, the sole corporate asset. The hotel burned. Kumar had previously been the president and principal shareholder of another corporation whose hotel had burned less than three years earlier.]

Callaghan J.: — The insurers ... denied coverage on the basis that the plaintiff or its agent at the time of the application for insurance fraudulently omitted to communicate the circumstances that were known to be material to the insurers in order to enable them to judge of the risk to be undertaken.

...

The defendant insurers learned for the first time following the destruction of the Big Bend Hotel of the previous fire loss sustained by the Fort Hotel and the insurance cancellations referred to, and consequently denied benefits under the policy.

Counsel for the plaintiff ... submitted that Big Bend Hotel Ltd. and K. & S. Enterprises Limited, although personally controlled by Vincent Kumar, were separate entities and Kumar could not be expected to set out in the application a prior fire loss suffered by K. & S. Enterprises Limited when the application was made on behalf of Big Bend Hotel Ltd. He then went on and said that this was not a proper case for lifting the corporate veil.

...

Section 14 [now s. 28] of the *Insurance Act* reads:

14(1) No contract is rendered void or voidable by reason of any misrepresentation, or any failure to disclose on the part of the insured in the application or proposal for the insurance or otherwise, unless the misrepresentation or failure to disclose is material to the contract.

(2) The question of materiality is one of fact.

...

There is no question on the evidence of Geoffrey Wells of Reed Shaw Stenhouse Limited and of Messrs. Boyd, Akri and Schwabb, representatives of some of the underwriters, that because Vincent Kumar personally controlled both private companies the previous fire loss to the Fort Hotel was material and the failure to complete the form in that regard led the insurers to believe that Kumar had sustained no prior loss. The test is not what is material to the plaintiff but what a reasonable insurer would have done or how a reasonable insurer would have reacted to the true facts: *Gore Mut. Ins. Co. v. Barton, Black & Robertson Ltd.* (1979), 12 B.C.L.R. 261 (S.C.).

Kumar knew information of a prior fire loss had to be disclosed. ... It is patently obvious that he failed to disclose the prior loss because he knew from previous cancellations that if he did so he would be unable to obtain insurance for the hotel. ... Clearly Vincent Kumar was cognizant of the importance or materiality of the prior fire loss and declined to make a full and frank disclosure thereof and, accordingly, I can only conclude that his failure so to do was to mislead or deceive the insurers.

Applying the test set out in *Gore Mut. Ins. Co.*, *supra*, to the evidence led in this case, I have concluded that the insurers, if they had known of the prior fire loss, would have declined to accept the risk.

...

On the whole, Canadian and English courts rigidly adhere to the concept set out in Salomon ..., that a corporation is an independent legal entity not to be identified with its shareholders.

However, there are exceptions to the general rule and courts have lifted the corporate veil to take into account the actions of the individual members, particularly in cases of improper conduct or fraud. In *Gilford Motor Co. v. Horne*, [1933] Ch. 935 (C.A.), the defendant had contracted with the plaintiff company, his former employer, not to solicit that company's customer. In order to avoid this undertaking, the defendant formed a company and the company solicited the customers. The English Court of Appeal held that the plaintiff was entitled to an injunction against both the defendant and his company, notwithstanding that the company was not a party to the covenant, as the defendant company was a "mere cloak or sham".

...

Here, Vincent Kumar clearly omitted to disclose a fact which he knew was material to the insurers and such failure to disclose is fraudulent. In these circumstances, it is appropriate to lift the corporate veil; equity will not allow an individual to use a company as a shield for improper conduct or fraud.

In the result, the plaintiff's action must be dismissed, with costs.

Action dismissed.

NOTES

Go back to the quote "I have concluded that the insurers, if they had known of the prior fire loss, would have declined to accept the risk". Now turn forward to the last line of the judgment. Are any of the intervening statements relevant to the issue?

Suppose an individual motelier knew that her night manager was a compulsive pyromaniac, but neglected to mention this fact when contracting for fire insurance. Do you think the night manager's tendencies are material to the risk? Must you "pierce the individual's veil" in order to answer that question?

In *London Computer Operators' Training Ltd. v. British Broadcasting Corp.*, [1973] 1 W.L.R 424 (Eng. C.A.), the defendant was sued in defamation for having denounced the plaintiff's computer school as a "financial racket". The defendant tried to introduce evidence that the founder of the corporation had previously been convicted on eight charges of larceny. Is this evidence relevant to the issue?

Would your answers to the foregoing questions be different if the key individual held 70 per cent of the corporation's shares? What about 10 per cent? What if he held 60 per cent of the shares of another corporation which held 60 per cent of the shares of the corporation in question?

In *Houle v. Canadian National Bank*, [1990] S.C.J. No. 120, [1990] 3 S.C.R. 122 at 177-80, the Supreme Court of Canada made the following comments on the appropriateness of piercing the corporate veil in a circumstance where the corporation in question was a family business and the respondent had had dealings with the corporation and other businesses run by family members:

> Both the trial judge and the Court of Appeal accepted the respondents' position that the "corporate veil" should be lifted, in the circumstances of this case, and the respondents' action was allowed on this basis. In the Superior Court, the judge elaborates on his reasons for so doing:

>> [TRANSLATION] In the case before the Court, whereas Hervé Houle Ltée was and has always been a family business, whereas the Houle Family had been doing business with defendant as such for over fifty years, whereas defendant required not only from the Houle brothers, the plaintiff-shareholders, but from the widow of Hervé Houle, who was not a shareholder in the "company", a letter of surety which amounted in October 1973 to $1,000,000, and whereas, further, defendant also required that Les Porcheries Houle Ltée, another family business whose shares were also held by plaintiffs, sign the said letter of surety, whereas in short all the personal assets of the Houle family, including the assets in the estate of Hervé Houle, were pledged in the business of Hervé Houle Ltée, at the express request of the defendant, THE COURT must conclude that Hervé Houle Ltée was only an intermediary between defendant and the people with whom it was really doing business, namely plaintiffs.

> After reviewing the same facts, the Court of Appeal arrives at the same conclusion (at p. 1523):

[TRANSLATION] The special nature of this case indicates that the bank was doing business not just with the company but also with respondents. The latter accordingly had a right of action for damages against the bank.

With respect, I cannot agree that the lifting of the corporate veil is a proper basis to ground the respondents' claim in the circumstances of this case.

Almost a century ago, the case of *Salomon v. A. Salomon and Co.*, *supra*, established the concept of an independent legal personality of a corporation, and it is often this very fact that attracts individuals to incorporate. The limitation of liability to the interest one possesses as a shareholder, with the resulting exclusion of certain personal liability for the debts of the corporation is a key feature of the corporate format, which carries other advantages, including fiscal ones. However, by choosing the benefits of this business structure, individuals must be prepared to accept the necessary consequences.

One of these consequences is that it is the corporation which suffers damages when there is a wrong to the corporation. As early as 1901, Lord Davey of the Privy Council expressed this principle, in *Burland v. Earle*, [1902] A.C. 83, at p. 93:

> Again, it is clear law that in order to redress a wrong done to the company or to recover moneys or damages alleged to be due to the company, the action should prima facie be brought by the company itself.

Quebec courts have been extremely reluctant to allow shareholders' actions where the damage is suffered by the corporation. In the leading case of *Silverman v. Heaps*, [1967] C.S. 536, Mayrand J. so states, at p. 539:

> The shareholder of a company has no action against the person who causes damage to the company. One cannot limit his responsibility by investing in a company and still consider as a personal damage any damage caused to such company; the shareholder's damage is indirect.

This is a clearly established principle and, I conclude, the correct position concerning shareholders' recourses.

The consequences of any other position would not be logical. There would be no value to the corporate structure if whoever does business with a corporation would, at the same time, become liable not only to the company but also to every shareholder for any damage that may be caused to the company. Wilson J. in *Kosmopoulos v. Constitution Insurance Co.*, [1987] 1 S.C.R. 2, so says, at p. 11:

> Having chosen to receive the benefits of incorporation, he [Mr. Kosmopoulos] should not be allowed to escape its burdens. He should not be permitted to "blow hot and cold" at the same time.

...

With deference for the opinion of the lower courts, on the facts of this case I cannot find any factor that would justify the lifting of the corporate veil. Notwithstanding the "family" nature of the business, the family members, here the respondents, chose the corporate structure rather than do business in their own name. The sureties provided by the respondents are common in financial relations involving small corporations, as the bank often requires more security than the corporation itself can provide. In addition, the fifty-eight years of collaboration between the respondents and the bank, as well as the personal guarantees given by the respondents as security for the loan, do not alter the fact that the loan agreement was signed only by the company, not by the respondents, and that the latter were not requested to honour such guarantees. Therefore, I find nothing in this case to distinguish it from the other cases cited above and the general principles which have served our law over the past century. Consequently, this is not a case where the corporate veil should be lifted and the respondents' action cannot, in my view, succeed on this ground.

Compare this with what the Supreme Court said some years later in *Hercules Managements Ltd. v. Ernst & Young*, [1997] S.C.J. No. 51, [1997] 2 S.C.R. 165, 146 D.L.R. (4th) 577, which is excerpted below.

HERCULES MANAGEMENTS LTD. v. ERNST & YOUNG

[1997] S.C.J. No. 51, [1997] 2 S.C.R. 165, 146 D.L.R. (4th) 577

[Two companies, Northguard Acceptance Ltd. ("NGA") and Northguard Holdings Ltd. ("NGH") were engaged in the business of lending and investing money on the security of real property mortgages. The appellants, Hercules Managements and Max Freed, were shareholders in NGA. Ernst & Young was the long-standing auditor of both companies. In 1984, both NGA and NGH went into receivership. The appellants sought a determination that the audit reports prepared on behalf of NGA and NGH for 1980-82 by Ernst & Young were negligently prepared, as well as damages for financial losses stemming from their reliance on those reports.]

La Forest J. (for the court): — This appeal arises by way of motion for summary judgment. It concerns the issue of whether and when accountants who perform an audit of a corporation's financial statements owe a duty of care in tort to shareholders of the corporation who claim to have suffered losses in reliance on the audited statements. It also raises the question of whether certain types of claims against auditors may properly be brought by shareholders as individuals or whether they must be brought by the corporation in the form of a derivative action.

[Part of the judgment concerned with who may bring the claims against the auditors is reproduced below. Other elements are excerpted in Chapter 9.]

. . .

The claims of Hercules and Mr. Freed with respect to their 1982-83 investments can be addressed quickly. The essence of these claims must be that these two appellants relied on the respondents' reports in deciding whether or not to make further investments in the audited corporations. In other words, Hercules and Mr. Freed are claiming to have relied on the audited reports for the purpose of making personal investment decisions.

. . .

With respect to the claim concerning the loss in value of their existing shareholdings, the appellants make two submissions. First, they claim that they relied on the 1980-82 reports in monitoring the value of their equity and that, owing to the (allegedly) negligent preparation of those reports, they failed to extract it before the financial demise of NGA and NGH. Secondly, and somewhat more subtly, the appellants submit that they each relied on the auditors' reports in overseeing the management of NGA and NGH and that had those reports been accurate, the collapse of the corporations and the consequential loss in the value of their shareholdings could have been avoided.

. . .

... The essence of the appellants' submission here is that the shareholders would have supervised management differently had they known of the (alleged) inaccuracies in the 1980-82 reports, and that this difference in management would have averted the demise of the audited corporations and the consequent losses in existing equity suffered by the shareholders. At first glance, it might appear that the appellants' claim implicates a use of the audit reports which is commensurate with the purpose for which the reports were prepared, i.e., overseeing or supervising management. One might argue on this basis that a duty of care should be found to inhere because, in view of this compatibility between actual use and intended purpose, no indeterminacy arises. In my view, however, this line of reasoning suffers from a subtle but fundamental flaw.

... [T]he purpose for which the audit reports were prepared in this case was the standard statutory one of allowing shareholders, *as a group*, to supervise management and to take decisions with respect to matters concerning the proper overall administration *of the corporations*. In other words, it was ... to permit the shareholders to exercise their role, *as a class*, of overseeing the *corporations'* affairs at their annual general meetings. The purpose of providing the auditors' reports to the appellants, then, may ultimately be said to have been a "collective" one; that is, it was aimed not at protecting the interests of individual shareholders but rather at enabling the shareholders, acting as a group, to safeguard the interests of the corporations themselves. On the appellants' argument, however, the purpose to which the 1980-82 reports were ostensibly put was not that of allowing the shareholders as a class to take decisions in respect of the overall running of the corporation, but rather to allow them, as *individuals*, to monitor management so as to oversee and protect their own personal investments. Indeed, the nature of the appellants' claims (i.e. personal tort claims) *requires* that they assert reliance on the auditors' reports *qua* individual shareholders if they are to recover any personal damages. In so far as it must concern the interests of each individual shareholder, then, the appellants' claim in this regard can really be no different from the other "investment purposes" discussed above, in respect of which the respondents owe no duty of care.

...

... As I have already explained, the appellants allege that they were prevented from properly overseeing the management of the audited corporations because the respondents' audit reports painted a misleading picture of their financial state. They allege further that had they known the true situation, they would have intervened to avoid the eventuality of the corporations' going into receivership and the consequent loss of their equity. The difficulty with this submission, I have suggested, is that it fails to recognize that in supervising management, the shareholders must be seen to be *acting as a body* in respect of the corporation's interests rather than as individuals in respect of their own ends. In a manner of speaking, the shareholders assume what may be seen to be a "managerial role" when, as a collectivity, they oversee the activities of the directors and officers through resolutions adopted at shareholder meetings. In this capacity, they cannot properly be understood to be acting simply as individual holders of equity. Rather, their collective decisions are made in respect of the corporation itself. Any duty owed by auditors in respect of this aspect of the shareholders' functions, then, would be owed not to shareholders *qua* individuals, but rather to all shareholders as a group, acting in the interests of the corporation. And if the decisions taken by the collectivity of shareholders are in respect of the corporation's affairs, then the shareholders' reliance on negligently prepared audit reports in taking such decisions will result in a wrong to the corporation for which the shareholders cannot, as individuals, recover.

...

Appeal dismissed with costs.

2. Corporations as Agents and Partners

Corporations, like any other legal persons, can act as agents. Agency may arise by express agreement between principal and agent or by implication from their dealings. It is only with the latter method that we are concerned here. Within the scope of an agent's authority, he can bind his principal to a contract. Also, a principal is liable for torts committed by his agent within the scope of the agency. Thus, if you can show that a corporation was acting as the agent of another person, you will have the prospect of making that person liable for what the corporation has done. Note that this does not involve ignoring the corporation's separate personality. Indeed, as the House of Lords pointed out in *Salomon*, agency is a relationship thaat requires two legal persons.

Salomon stands for the proposition that the relationship of controlling shareholder and corporation does not in general constitute a relationship of principal and agent. If the courts make use of the agency concept to circumvent *Salomon*, they must distinguish between the situation where the corporation is acting as an agent of its controlling interest, from that where the controlling interest is merely exercising the prerogative of control. Distinguishing these situations requires an examination of the capacity in which the shareholder was acting. Unless the shareholder acted in a personal capacity, then there will only be one person involved in the business — the corporation.

How do we decide that an individual is acting in a personal capacity? Obviously some factors other than control of the corporation are required, otherwise the corporation would *ipso facto* be treated as an agent of the majority shareholder. Isolating these factors isn't easy.

Only periodically have the courts used agency concepts to treat the corporation as an agent of its controlling interest. Thus, in *Apthorpe v. Peter Schoenhofen Brewing Co.* (1899), 15 T.L.R. 245, 80 L.T. 395 (Eng. C.A.), the court, for tax purposes, was willing to treat an American subsidiary as agent for its English parent. Contrast the contrary finding in *Re F.G. Films Ltd.*, [1953] 1 W.L.R. 483. Professor O. Kahn-Freund, "Some Reflections on Company Law Reform" (1943), 7 Mod. L. Rev. 54, at p. 55 has stated, however, that there has been a complete failure by "the courts to mitigate, through the mechanism of the law of agency, the rigidities of the 'folklore' of corporate entity in favour of the legitimate interests of the company's creditors".

An attempt was made in the following case to specify the criteria which, if satisfied, would indicate that a subsidiary was carrying on the business of the parent corporation.

SMITH, STONE AND KNIGHT LTD. v. BIRMINGHAM CORP.

[1939] 4 All E.R. 116, 104 J.P. 31, 161 L.T. 371, 83 Sol. Jo. 961 (Eng. K.B.)

[The plaintiff corporation held property in land, which it rented to its subsidiary corporation. The City of Birmingham expropriated the land under a statute which required compensation to be paid to estate holders who carried on business on the land, but allowed the City to evict tenants without compensation. The plaintiff claimed compensation on the ground that it, not the subsidiary, was carrying on business on the premises, through the agency of the subsidiary. The plaintiff had run the business by itself prior to turning the operation over to the subsidiary.]

Atkinson J.: — ... There was no agreement of any kind made between the two companies, and the business was never assigned to the waste company [the subsidiary]. There was no suggestion that anything was done to transfer the beneficial ownership of it to the waste company. ... If, either physically or technically, the waste company was in occupation, it was for the purpose of the service it was rendering to the claimants, such occupation was necessary for that service, and I think that these facts would make that occupation in law the occupation of the claimants. An analogous position would be where servants occupy cottages or rooms for the purposes of their business, and ... if they have to occupy those premises for the purposes of their business, their occupation is the occupation of their principal ... [**Atkinson J.** then attempted to identify criteria which would indicate such an agency between a subsidiary corporation and its controlling shareholder:]

Were the profits treated as profits of the company? — when I say "the company" I mean the parent company — Secondly, were the persons conducting the business appointed by the parent company? Thirdly, was the company the head and brain of the trading venture? Fourthly, did the company govern the venture, decide what should be done and what capital should be embarked on the venture? Fifthly, did the company make the profits by its skill and direction? Sixthly, was the company in effectual and constant control?

NOTES

1. See the note on this case by O. Kahn-Freund in (1940), 3 Mod. L. Rev. 226.

2. When a corporation is the controlling shareholder of another corporation, it is said to be the "parent" corporation and the other corporation is called its "subsidiary". Compare C.B.C.A., s. 2(3)-(5). Some courts have adopted a theory of "enterprise entity", suggesting that a parent corporation and its subsidiaries should be treated as a single entity. For example, in *De Salaberry Realties Ltd. v. M.N.R.* (1974), 46 D.L.R. (3d) 100 (F.C.T.D.), mentioned above, this was thought necessary in order to draw a conclusion about the nature of a corporation's intention in relation to certain transactions. In most cases, the idea is invoked in order to attach the liabilities of a subsidiary corporation to the parent. It is commonly used in the United States; see, for example, *Steven v. Roscoe Turner Aeronautical Corp.*, 324 F.2d 157 (7 Cir. Ind. 1963). The court there said that what was required was (a) control of the subsidiary by the parent; (b) an unlawful act by the parent through the subsidiary and (c) "unjust loss" to the plaintiff. The control requirement is assessed using factors much like those set out in *Smith, Stone and Knight Ltd. v. Birmingham Corp.*, [1939] 4 All E.R. 116, 104 J.P. 31, 161 L.T. 371, 83 Sol. Jo. 961 (Eng. K.B.), above, and it is unclear how this doctrine differs from a simple finding of agency.

   In *Sun Sudan Oil Co. v. Methanex Corp.*, [1992] A.J. No. 1003, (1992), 5 Alta. L.R. (3d) 292, 134 A.R. 1 (Q.B.), the plaintiff had contractual claims against the subsidiary, and argued that the parent should be liable. Although Hunt J. made reference to "piercing the veil," she applied the agency tests from *Smith, Stone and Knight Ltd.* and decided that the parent was not liable since the use of subsidiaries in that case was consistent with "legitimate business reasons".

   Is there any reason why corporate shareholders should be made to answer for the liabilities of the corporations in which they hold shares, to a greater degree than individual shareholders?

3. See also on the agency point *Tunstall v. Steigman*, [1962] 2 Q.B. 593; *Chenier v. Johnson* (1964), 48 D.L.R. (2d) 380 (B.C.S.C.); *Patton v. Yukon Consolidated Gold*

Corp., [1934] 3 D.L.R. 400, [1934] O.W.N. 321 (C.A.); *Ebbw Vale Urban Dist. Council v. South Wales Traffic Area Licensing Authority*, [1951] 2 K.B. 366 (Eng. C.A.) and *Rural Mun. of Assiniboia v. Suburban Rapid Transit Co.*, [1931] 2 D.L.R. 862 (Man. C.A.).

4.   This section has been addressing the possibility that an individual can be made liable as the principal of a corporate agent. Note that even in the more common case in which an individual acts as the agent of a corporation, the individual may be personally liable. If the parties so intend, then a third party dealing with an agent may have the option of enforcing a contract against either the principal or the agent. See *The Swan*, [1968] 1 Lloyd's Rep. 5 (Adm. Div.).

5.   Property in land is being expropriated under a statute which provides greater compensation to estate holders who operate their own businesses on the land. Compensation under the statute is to be paid for the value of the estate and, above that, for disturbances of the business of the estate holder. The business consists of buying, warehousing, trucking and selling produce. For some reason, the property in land is held by one subsidiary (S1), the trucks are owned by another subsidiary (S2), while the rest of the business assets are owned by the parent corporation (P). As a result of the estate's being expropriated from S1, the business must be closed down and all three corporations will be liquidated. The city council proposes to compensate S1 for the value of the estate, but maintains that, as P and S2 ran the business, no extra compensation is payable to S1.

   a.   How does the way the business assets are held affect the application of the statute?

   b.   How can you, as a lawyer, get around the corporate personality problem to reach an outcome more favourable to P, S1 and S2?

   c.   Can you do it without "piercing the corporate veil"?

The problem involving P, S1 and S2 arose in *D.H.N. Food Distributors Ltd. v. Tower Hamlets London Borough Council*, [1976] 1 W.L.R. 852 (Eng. C.A.). The English Court of Appeal held that the corporations, as a group, were entitled to compensation not only for the value of the estate in land, but also for disturbances to the business. Lord Denning M.R. analyzed the problem as follows:

> This group is virtually the same as a partnership in which all the three companies are partners. They should not be treated separately so as to be defeated on a technical point. They should not be deprived of the compensation which should justly be payable for disturbance. The three companies should, for present purposes, be treated as one, and the parent company D.H.N. should be treated as that one. So D.H.N. are entitled to claim compensation accordingly.

Why would the fact that "the group is virtually the same as a partnership" make any difference? Refer back to the discussion of partnership principles in Chapter 1.

QUESTIONS

Do you agree with the conclusion in *D.H.N. Food*? Do you approve of the analysis?

Would the judgment have been the same if P, S1 and S2 were a mother and her two sons, rather than corporations? Would the reasons for judgment have been different?

Compare the even less principled analysis in *Wallersteiner v. Moir*, [1974] 1 W.L.R. 991, [1974] 3 All E.R. 217 (Eng. C.A.). Contrast the much more clearly reasoned approach in *Woolfson v. Strathclyde Regional Council*, [1978] S.L.T. 159 (Scot. H.L.), where property was being expropriated and the majority shareholder tried, but failed, to establish that he was the holder of the corporate property.

3. Corporate Personality: Some Innovative Approaches

Judges have rarely been clear when explaining how corporate personality works. This is due in part to the facile notion that they are at liberty to disregard the separate existence of the corporate entity. There are, however, some reported cases that clearly illustrate the application of well-known remedies, mostly in tort situations, but some from the field of equity. Using them as examples one can formulate a principled approach that treats corporate personality as a solution rather than a problem.

(a) Inducing Breach of Contract

Students of contract law will be familiar with the use of, and limitations on, restrictive covenants in contracts. Those who have studied tort or the history of the labour movement may have come across this statement from *Quinn v. Leathem,* [1901] A.C. 495 (Eng. H.L.):

> A violation of legal right committed knowingly is a cause of action and it is a violation of legal right to interfere with contractual relations recognized by law if there be no sufficient justification for the interference.

A contractor who violates a term can be sued for breach of contract. Anyone who knowingly induced the breach of contract can be sued in tort. Complications arise when a corporation is alleged to have done either of the above.

GARBUTT BUSINESS COLLEGE LTD. v. HENDERSON SECRETARIAL SCHOOL LTD.

[1939] 3 W.W.R. 257, [1939] 4 D.L.R. 151 (Alta. C.A.)

[H., a well-known teacher, had a restrictive covenant in his long-standing employment contract with the plaintiff corporation. The contract restrained him from engaging in or managing a rival business college in Calgary for five years. H. resigned and incorporated a rival business college that used his surname as part of the corporate name and contracted with him to teach there. All the new corporation's shares were held by H., except for three held by his wife and daughter. Enrolment at the plaintiff's college declined as students flocked to the Henderson name.]

Harvey C.J.A.: — [The restraining covenant was upheld. The judge then turned to consideration of the case against the corporate defendant.]

As regards the damages however the identification found by the trial Judge as existing between the two defendants calls for some analysis.

The damages awarded against Henderson are for breach of contract but the company however much of a cloak it may be is a separate entity and as such has no contract with the plaintiff and therefore cannot be held liable for damages on the same ground as Henderson is. If liable it must be for tort. It is found by the trial Judge on evidence which leaves no room for doubt that the company and all its officers well knew that what it was doing in employing Henderson was in breach of his agreement with the plaintiff. It is argued that it could only be liable if it wilfully induced Henderson to break his contract. I can see no sanctity in the word "induce," nor do I think that wilfulness beyond knowledge is essential. Every day that Henderson was in the employ of the defendant company he was being aided and encouraged and paid to break his contract with the plaintiff and that deliberately and knowingly by his co-defendant, and it is alleged in the statement of claim that this was wrongful.

In my opinion the defendant company thereby committed a tort rendering itself liable for damages to the plaintiff upon the principle of *Quinn v. Leathem*, [1901] A.C. 495, 70 L.J.P.C. 76, expressed by Lord Macnaghten as follows (p. 510):

> a violation of legal right committed knowingly is a cause of action, and it is a violation of legal right to interfere with contractual relations recognized by law if there be no sufficient justification for the interference.

Ford J.A.: — ... The judgment of damages against the defendant corporation, Henderson Secretarial School Ltd., is, in my opinion, supportable only by the application of the principle enunciated in *Lumley v. Gye* (1854), 2 El. & Bl. 216, 118 E.R. 749; 3 El. & Bl. 114, 118 E.R. 1083, as explained in Bowen v. Hall (1881), 6 Q.B.D.333, 50 L.J.Q.B. 305, and *Quinn v. Leathem*, [1901] A.C. 495, 70 L.J.P.C. 76. See also *South Wales Miners' Federation v. Glamorgan Coal Co.*, [1905] A.C. 239, 74 L.J.K.B. 525. With respect I think it cannot be based upon the idea of the identity of the corporation with Henderson however much it may be said to be his creation or a cloak to cover his breach of contract. Where there is a valid and enforceable contract between A. and B., and C., without justification, knowingly induced B. to break his contract, A., subject to the rule that the same damages may not be recovered twice, may sue for and recover damages both against B. and C. in one action in which they are joined as defendants. The remedies are, however, based upon different causes of action, that against B. being for breach of contract and the other for the tort of inducing the breach. The damages for the tort may in some cases, but will not generally, exceed those recoverable for the breach and may in some cases be less, where, for instance, the wrongdoer is not responsible for a continuation of the breach during which the pecuniary loss continues to arise from the breach of contract.

While proof of special damage in the ordinary sense of that term need not be given and, "if the breach which has been procured by the defendant has been such as must in the ordinary course of business inflict damage upon the plaintiff, then the plaintiff may succeed without proof of any particular damage", to quote the language of Nevill, J. in *Goldsoll v. Goldman*, [1914] 2 Ch. 603, at 615 ... and while as McCardie, J. said in *Said v. Butt*, [1920] 3 .B. 497, at 504, 90 L.J.K.B. 239, "the damages against the wrongdoer are at large", I take it that in order to obtain an award of a substantial sum there must be proof of the actual or real damages arising from the commission of the tort. ...

In the present instance I agree that there is ample evidence to support the judgment for at least as much as has been awarded.

While it is not possible to define exactly what is meant by inducement, the employing or continuing of the employment of Henderson by the defendant corporation at a salary or share of profits is clearly an inducement and a continuing one. I think also that the pleading which alleges that the defendant corporation "wrongfully employed" its co-defendant is sufficient to put in issue the claim for damages arising from the tort committed.

... I concur in the view of the Chief Justice in support of the injunction and would like to add this, that while it cannot be said that the corporation was a mere cloak or sham to enable Henderson to break his contract it was to the knowledge of the company the channel by which, after its incorporation, he continued his breach of contract so as to bring it within the reasoning in *Gilford Motor Co. v. Horne*, [1933] 1 Ch. 935, 102 L.J. Ch. 212 (Eng. C.A.), if, indeed, it may not be said that the corporation is for this purpose in the nature of an agent of Henderson who may be enjoined. ...

QUESTIONS

1. Would the result be different if all H. had done was quit his former job and set up the same corporation, thus capitalizing on his name as a draw for students, but hired an independent manager and refrained from doing any teaching?

2. Does the public policy limitation which restricts the contractual reach of restrictive covenants also limit the tort obligation?

3. The individual defendant contracted to sell real estate to the plaintiffs for £5,250. Prior to closing, he transferred the estate to a corporation. The individual defendant and his lawyer's clerk were the sole shareholders. The transfer price was £3,000, of which the corporation borrowed £1,564 from a bank and owed the rest to the individual defendant.

    (a) Who holds property in the land now?

    (b) Can the plaintiffs sue the individual defendant in contract? In tort?

    (c) What remedy can be awarded to the plaintiffs if they win against the individual defendant in contract?

    (d) Can the plaintiffs sue the defendant corporation in contract? In tort?

    (e) If the plaintiffs were to win a lawsuit against the defendant corporation, what remedy could they seek?

    (f) Is there an alternative cause of action in equity, based on what you learned in first-year Property?

    These facts were considered in *Jones v. Lipman*, [1962] 1 All E.R. 442, [1962] 1 W.L.R. 832 (Eng. Ch.). Mr. Justice Russell decided to "lift the corporate veil" and make an order against both defendants to specifically perform the terms of the agreement between the plaintiff and the first defendant. Do you agree with this judgment? Would the result be the same if the individual had transferred the property to his grandmother?

4.   Property was listed with a real estate agent on terms that a commission was payable within three months of the expiry of the listing if the property was sold to anyone introduced by the agent. Two months after expiry of the listing the estate holder sold the property to a corporation formed by A, B and C for the purpose of buying and developing the property. A, B and C had been introduced by the agent, who now sues for his commission. What is the result? See *Circle Realty Ltd. v. Bert Long & Kingsway Refrigeration Co.* (1960), 25 D.L.R. (2d) 184 (B.C.S.C.).

5.   Compare *Associated Growers of B.C. Ltd. and Kelowna Growers Exchange v. Edmunds*, [1926] 1 D.L.R. 1093 (B.C.C.A.), in which the defendants entered into a contract with the plaintiffs to sell them all the fruit they produced. The contract contained the following clause:

> If the grower transfers any or all of his fruit and vegetable land, or any or all of the fruits or vegetables controlled by him which are not the subject of this agreement, to any member of his family by blood relationship or marriage, or any trustee for themselves or any such member of his family, any such transferee shall be deemed to be a grower and be bound by the terms of this agreement.

The defendants created a corporation to which they transferred this property in return for all the corporate shares. The court upheld the scheme. In the course of his reasons for judgment, McPhillips J.A. stated (at p. 1097):

> It cannot be said that the sale made was a breach of contract nor can it, in my opinion be said to be in any way contrary to good faith in that it was the doing of an act which was plainly unprovided against. We have not here the well-known and understood negative covenant so essential and necessary to accomplish what the appellants are contending for and they failed to make out their case in the court below, and in my opinion the trial judge arrived at the right conclusion.

Is he correct?

EINHORN v. WESTMOUNT INVESTMENTS LTD.

(1969), 6 D.L.R. (3d) 71, 69 W.W.R. 31 (Sask. Q.B.)

Disbery J.: — This is an action brought by the administratrix of the estate of Jacob Einhorn, deceased, hereafter referred to as "Einhorn" against Westmount Investments Ltd., hereafter referred to as the "corporate defendant", and three individual defendants, namely, Hyman, William and Samuel Belzberg, hereafter referred to as "the Belzbergs". The application before me is brought by the three Belzbergs to strike out the statement of claim on the ground that it discloses no reasonable cause of action against them personally.

When a defendant sallies forth to attack a statement of claim on this ground he must accept all the facts alleged in the pleading as being true; and he can only succeed if he is able to demonstrate to the Court that such facts do not disclose a reasonable cause of action against him which the plaintiff should be entitled to have adjudicated. …

The Belzbergs were "at all material times in complete control" of the corporate defendant. Einhorn was a duly licensed real estate agent carrying on his business in the City of Regina, in this Province. An agreement was entered into between

Einhorn and the corporate defendant whereby Einhorn was to assist the said defendant to acquire a property in Regina known as the "Old City Hall", and for his services Einhorn was to be paid a maximum commission of $20,000 by the corporate defendant contingent upon it obtaining the property. The said defendant "with the assistance of" Einhorn purchased the property from the City of Regina but, in breach of the agreement, the corporate defendant paid nothing to Einhorn for his services. ...

One set of facts alleged in the attacked pleading is that the Belzbergs were in complete control of two companies, namely, the corporate defendant and Regina Midtown Centre Ltd., hereafter referred to as "Midtown", and that they knowingly and *mala fides* caused the corporate defendant to transfer the said property to Midtown with the intent and purpose of denuding the corporate defendant of its assets thereby rendering it impossible for the corporate defendant to perform its contract to pay Einhorn the $20,000 under its contract with him. In short, that they siphoned off the assets of the corporate defendant into Midtown which they controlled to place them beyond the reach of Einhorn; and as they controlled both companies it was done for their own mercenary benefit and gain. It is also alleged that the Belzbergs conspired to bring this about and that they induced the corporate defendant to break its contract with Einhorn. The torts of conspiracy, of wrongful procurement of a breach of contract and of actionable interference with Einhorn's contractual relations with the corporate defendant are raised in the statement of claim against the Belzbergs as individual defendants and damages are claimed therefor.

...

The judicial development of the principle laid down in Lumley v. Gye was recently traced by Denning, M.R., in *Torquay Hotel Co. Ltd. v. Cousins*, [1969] 1 All E.R. 522 (Eng. C.A.). At pp. 529-530 he said:

> The principle of *Lumley v. Gye* is that each of the parties to a contract has a "right to the performance" of it; and it is wrong for another to procure one of the parties to break it or not to perform it. That principle was extended a step further by *Lord Macnaghten in Quinn v. Leathem*, [1901] A.C. 495, [1900-03] All E.R. Rep. 1, so that each of the parties has a right to have his "contractual relations" with the other duly observed. He said ([1901] A.C. at p. 510, [1900-03] All E.R. Rep. at p. 9): "... it is a violation of legal right to interfere with contractual relations recognized by law if there be no sufficient justification for the interference".

> That statement was adopted and applied by a strong Board of the Privy Council in *Jasperson v. Dominion Tobacco Co.*, [1923] A.C. 709. It included Viscount Haldane and Lord Sumner. The time has come when the principle should be further extended to cover "deliberate and direct interference with the execution of a contract without that causing any breach". That was a point left open by Lord Reid in *J.T.Stratford & Son, Ltd. v. Lindley*, [1964] 3 All E.R. 102 at p. 107; [1965] A.C. 269 at p. 324. But the common law would be seriously deficient if it did not condemn such interference. It is this very case. The principle can be subdivided into three elements: First, there must be *interference* in the execution of a contract. The interference is not confined to the procurement of a *breach* of contract. It extends to a case where a third person *prevents* or *hinders* one party from performing his contract, even though it be not a breach. Secondly, the interference must be deliberate. The person must know of the contract or, at any rate, turn a blind eye to it and intend to interfere with it, see *Emerald Construction Co., Ltd. v. Lowthian*, [1966] 1 All E.R. 1013; [1966] 1 W.L.R. 691 (Eng. C.A.). Thirdly, the interference must be *direct*. Indirect interference will not do. Thus, a man who "corners the

market" in a commodity may well know that it may prevent others from performing their contracts, but he is not liable to an action for so doing. A trade union official, who calls a strike on proper notice, may well know that it will prevent the employers from performing their contracts to deliver goods, but he is not liable in damages for calling it. *Indirect interference* is only unlawful if unlawful means are used.

This statement of Lord Denning, M.R., in my opinion also correctly expresses the law of this jurisdiction and, with respect, I adopt and apply it.

...

Ordinarily, an agent is subject to the control of another person, his principal. A company perforce is only able to act through its agents and servants. Consequently while company directors are referred to as "agents" the cold fact is that they control the company. As the directors pull the strings so the company must of necessity jump. Particularly is this true where, as here, the individual defendants were in "complete control" of the company. This Court in the exercise of its common law jurisdiction in the field of tort considers the realities of the situations which come before it for decision, and the Court is not restricted in so doing because individuals carry out intentional tortious acts through the medium of a puppet corporation whose every action they control. Individuals guilty of intentional tortious acts do not escape personal liability by this device of clothing themselves in a corporate veil of their own spinning.

One way in which a third party intending either to wrongfully interfere with the contractual rights of another or to procure a breach of another's contract of which he has knowledge, is to take such action as will render performance impossible. In the *Torquay* case Denning M.R., cites as an example the giving of a potion to a singer causing her to become ill and thus unable to perform a contract to sing. In *D.C. Thomson & Co. Ltd. v. Deakin*, [1952] 1 Ch. 646, Morris, L.J., gives the example of taking away tools essential for use in the performance of a contract. Where, as here, the performance by one of the contracting parties consists of making a money payment, I am unable to think of a more effective method of rendering performance impossible than that of emptying the till by transferring the contracting party's assets to other persons. At trial the Court is free to consider the predominant purpose underlying the Belzberg's conduct.

I find that the statement of claim discloses reasonable causes of action against the Belzbergs personally for actionable interference with Einhorn's contractual relations with the corporate defendant and for wrongful procurement of a breach of his contract with the said defendant. In view of this finding it becomes unnecessary for me to consider the additional cause of action raised in the pleading, namely, civil conspiracy. ...

NOTES AND QUESTIONS

1. The courts are slowly moving away from the habit of using such hackneyed metaphorical epithets as "sham," "alter ego" and "puppet" to found liability in these cases. However, the *Einhorn* case is typical in that the terminology still appears, even when liability is based upon the proper application of tort remedies with full recognition of the legitimacy of the corporate entity. The decision was affirmed by the Saskatchewan Court of Appeal [(1970), 73 W.W.R. 161, 11 D.L.R. (3d) 509].

2. In *Garbutt Business College*, the defendant corporation was liable for inducing the breach of contract by its shareholder. In *Einhorn*, the defendant shareholders were

held to be potentially liable for inducing a breach of contract by the corporation of which they were shareholders. Do you think this makes any difference?

As in the agency context, the tort of inducing breach of contract requires two persons: a breacher and an inducer. If the breacher is the corporation and a shareholder is alleged to be the inducer, must it be shown that the shareholder acted in a capacity other than as a shareholder?

McFADDEN v. 481782 ONTARIO LTD.

(1984), 47 O.R. (2d) 134, 27 B.L.R. 173 (H.C.)

[The plaintiff had a contract of employment with the corporation PMAI, under which he was entitled to work until 1 July 1982. On 30 June 1981, PMAI sold its Canadian business to another corporation, PMAC. Norman Taylor and Mary Taylor were the sole shareholders and directors of PMAC. The plaintiff began to work for PMAC, and the trial judge found that there was an implied contract of employment between him and PMAC, on the same terms as his contract with PMAI. PMAC's business was not, however, a success, and within a year PMAI was offering to buy back the business. This offer was accepted and was executed on 2 April 1982. On 5 April 1982, the plaintiff was told by Norman Taylor that he no longer had a job, which the judge found was a breach by PMAC of the plaintiff's employment contract with PMAC. In March and April of 1982, the Taylors caused PMAC to pay them $32,500, which left PMAC with no money.]

Callon J. (at p. 141 [O.R.]): — I find, for the same reasons as stated above, that all of these payments were unauthorized by either corporate by-law or by statute, and were made in breach of Mary and Norman Taylor's statutory obligations as directors and officers of the company. Furthermore, I find that they were made with the intention of defeating any claim the plaintiff might have against the corporation. It was done, in other words, to ensure that Norman and Mary Taylor would have the funds to which they felt they were entitled without any allowance for funds otherwise owing by the company to the plaintiff. In doing so, I find that they were acting with a view to their own interests, rather than those of the company.

[The judge assessed the damages for breach of contract by PMAC in the amount of $16,000.]

The next issue to be decided is whether the individual defendants Norman Taylor and Mary Taylor are personally liable to the plaintiff for the amount awarded against the defendant company. The plaintiff rested his case against the individual defendants on two grounds. First, the payments made by PMAC to the defendants Norman and Mary Taylor in March and April of 1981 [*sic*] were fraudulent preferences under the *Fraudulent Conveyances Act*, R.S.O. 1980, c. 176, and should be set aside in favour of the plaintiff pursuant to s. 2 of the Act. Second, the individual defendants were personally liable under the tort of inducing breach of contract.

It is clear that the plaintiff, as a contract creditor, does have status to sue under the *Fraudulent Conveyances Act*; but it is equally clear that, prior to obtaining judgment, he must sue on behalf of himself and all other creditors: *Longeway v. Mitchell* (1870), 17 Gr. 190; *Parker v. Tain et al.* (1907), 15 O.L.R. 187 (Div. Ct.); *Hopkinson v. Westerman* (1919), 45 O.L.R. 208, 48 D.L.R. 597 (C.A.). The plaintiff did not sue on behalf of himself and all other creditors, but such an omission is a purely technical objection to the form of the action and I would grant leave to the plaintiff to amend the style of cause to meet the omission: *Bell v. Williamson et al.*, [1945] O.R. 484 at p. 492, [1945] 4 D.L.R. 253 at p. 261; affirmed [1945] O.R. 844, [1946] 1 D.L.R. 372 (C.A.). However, the plaintiff is entitled to set aside only those transfers of funds that occurred on and after April 5, 1981, inasmuch as I have found that it was only those transfers that were made with the express intention of defeating the plaintiff's claim on the corporation. Those transfers amount to the sum of $22,250.

The tort of inducing breach of contract is committed when D, knowing of a contract between P and a third party and intending to procure a breach of that contract to the injury of P, induces the third party without justification to break that contract: *Quinn v. Leathem*, [1901] A.C. 495 at p. 510; *D. C. Thomson & Co. Ltd. v. Deaken et al.*, [1952] 1 Ch. 646 (C.A.). In the circumstances of this case, I would have had no hesitation in finding that the defendants Norman and Mary Taylor had induced the defendant PMAC to breach its contract of employment with the plaintiff. However, it has been said by McCardie J. in *Said v. Butt*, [1920] 3 K.B. 497 at p. 506, that:

> ... if a servant acting bona fide within the scope of his authority procures or causes the breach of a contract between his employer and a third person, he does not thereby become liable to an action of tort at the suit of the person whose contract has thereby been broken.

Said v. Butt, *supra*, was approved by Lord Evershed M.R. in *Thompson v. Deaken*, *supra*, wherein he adopted at p. 681 the following passage from *Winfield's Law of Torts*, 5th ed. (1950), p. 603:

> If my servant acting bona fide within the scope of his authority, procures or causes me to break a contract that I have made with you, you cannot sue the servant for interference with the contract; for he is my alter ego, and I cannot be sued for inducing myself to break a contract.

He went on to adopt a later statement from the same text to the effect that: "If the servant does not act bona fide, presumably he is liable on the ground that he has ceased to be his employer's alter ego".

I note that McCardie J. in *Said v. Butt*, *supra*, premised his statement on the condition that the servant was "acting bona fide within the scope of his authority". This requirement has been noted in a number of subsequent cases, including that of *Thompson v. Deaken*, *supra*: see for example, *De Jetley Marks v. Greenwood (Lord) et al.*, [1936] 1 All E.R. 863 at pp. 8723 (K.B.); *Official Assignee et al. v. Dowling et al.*, [1964] N.Z.L.R. 578 at p. 581; *Einhorn v. Westmount Investments Ltd.* (1970), 11 D.L.R. (3d) 509, 73 W.W.R. 161 (Sask. C.A.); *Posluns v. Toronto Stock Exchange et al.*, [1964] 2 O.R. 547 at p. 623, 46 D.L.R. (2d) 210 at p. 286; affirmed [1966] 1 O.R. 285, 53 D.L.R. (2d) 193; affirmed [1968] S.C.R. 330, 67 D.L.R. (2d) 165.

I have some difficulty with the *rationale* offered for the decision in *Said v. Butt*, *supra*, by the learned authors of *Winfield's Law of Torts*, *supra*. The fact that the agent is an *alter ego* of the corporation may afford a defence to the corporation (since it makes no sense to sue it for both breaching and inducing itself to breach a contract), but it is not clear why that should relieve the agent. For as a general rule, an agent is always liable personally for his tortious acts, notwithstanding that his acts (and hence his liability) may in law also be those of the corporation: *The "Koursk"*, [1924] P. 140 at p. 155 (C.A.); *Weir v. Bell et al.* (1878), 3 Ex. D. 238

at p. 248 (C.A.). And it is also accepted that a principal may be relieved of liability for the tortious act of his agent, where the act is outside the agent's scope of authority, real or implied — though the agent himself remains liable: *Richards v. West Middlesex Waterworks Co.* (1885), 15 Q.B.D. 660 at pp. 6634; *Weir v. Bell, supra*, at p. 244.

It appears to me that the real reason for relieving the agent of liability lies instead in the realm of justification, inasmuch as an act of inducement may be excused if there is "sufficient justification" for it: *per* Lord Macnaghten, *Quinn v. Leathem, supra*, at p. 510. And it is clear that under both statute and common law a director or officer of a company is under a duty to act with a view to the best interests of the company. Acts of inducement are justified where they are "taken as a duty": *De Jetley Marks v. Greenwood, supra*, at p. 873; *Posluns v. Toronto Stock Exchange, supra*, at p. 608 O.R., p. 271 D.L.R.; and see the discussion in Richardson, "Making an End Run Around the Corporate Veil: The Tort of Inducing Breach of Contract", 5 Adv. Q. (1984), pp. 1039.

In short, if an officer or director of a corporation is to be relieved, as an agent, of the consequences of his otherwise tortious act of inducement, it is not because he is the company's *alter ego*. Rather, it is because in so acting he acts under the compulsion of a duty to the corporation. His act is thus justified. But where he does not act under such a duty, as, for example, where he fails to act *bona fide* within the scope of his authority, his act is no longer justified, and he becomes liable. The corporation remains insulated from the legal consequences of such an act, inasmuch as the director or officer has acted outside the scope of his authority.

Thus if it could be said that in acting as they did Norman and Mary Taylor were acting in furtherance of their duties and obligations as directors and officers of PMAC, then they would have available to them the defence of justification for any breach of contract they induced. But in procuring and inducing the breach of the plaintiff's contract with PMAC, they were not acting in furtherance of any such duties and obligations.

There is nothing in the contract of sale of the assets of PMAC to PMAI that required the termination of the plaintiff's contract. There was no restrictive covenant in the contract of sale that precluded either PMAC or Norman or Mary Taylor from continuing on in the same line of business. Indeed, Norman Taylor and Mary Taylor incorporated a new company, Taylor-Wainman Associates Limited, shortly after the sale to carry on essentially the same business as that which had hitherto been conducted by PMAC. I find that in procuring the breach the individual defendants were not acting *bona fide* with a view to the best interests of the defendant PMAC, but were rather acting to secure the transfer of the greatest possible amount of PMAC's funds to themselves unhindered by any obligations that PMAC might have to the plaintiff. They sought to feather their own nest, rather than that of the company they were under a duty to serve. By effecting the sale of PMAC's assets to PMAI, the defendants sought as well to carry on its business without any of its existing liabilities. The unauthorized transfer of funds is evidence that in acting as they did, the defendants Norman and Mary Taylor acted with a view to their own best interests rather than those of PMAC. They were not, in other words, acting under a compulsion of a duty to PMAC. That being the case, they fall outside the protection that would otherwise be afforded them by the principle enunciated in *Said v. Butt, supra*, and are so liable for inducing a breach of contract.

Accordingly, the plaintiff shall have judgment against the defendants Norman and Mary Taylor in the same amount that he has against the defendant PMAC. I wish to receive the submissions of counsel and of the defendant Norman E. Taylor concerning the disposition of the costs of the action. I leave it to counsel to arrange a time and date for their attendance upon me for that purpose.

Judgment for plaintiff.

QUESTIONS

1. Remember that the tort of inducing breach of contract requires a breacher and an inducer. The judge said that if the officers or directors breach their duties to the corporation, then the latter "remains insulated from the legal consequences of such an act, inasmuch as the director or officer has acted outside the scope of his authority". Which act or acts of Norman and Mary Taylor (as individuals) do you think the judge saw as inducements to the corporation to breach its contract? Was it telling McFadden that he had no job? Does this mean that when Taylor told McFadden that he had no job, Taylor was acting as an individual? If so, did the corporation ever breach its contract with McFadden? Or was Taylor acting as the corporation? If so, who induced it to breach its contract?

   Alternatively, when Norman and Mary Taylor cashed cheques drawn by the corporation, it seems clear they were acting as individuals. But can this be an inducement to breach the employment contract? Is inducing breach of contract the same thing as inducing the inability to pay damages for a breach of contract? Note that all provincial and territorial jurisdictions have legislation on fraudulent preferences (payments to one creditor in preference to others) and fraudulent conveyances (payments to non-creditors intended to defraud creditors). Note too that if a person (including a corporation) becomes bankrupt, this invokes a federal jurisdiction under s. 91, art. 21 of the *Constitution Act, 1867*. A bankruptcy is administered by a trustee in bankruptcy, who has standing under the *Bankruptcy and Insolvency Act*, R.S.C. 1985, c. B-3 to have transactions set aside which have put assets of the bankrupt out of the reach of creditors. In some cases transactions that took place up to five years before the bankruptcy can be set aside.

   Can it be right that whenever a director or officer breaches her or his duty to act in what she or he believes to be the corporation's best interests, the director or officer thereby ceases to act on behalf of the corporation? If so, could corporations ever breach contracts? Could they commit torts or crimes? Should a legal wrong committed by a director against his or her corporation be relevant in determining the rights an ex-employee of the corporation has against the director?

   Assume that the directors breached their duties to the corporation, and as a result they owed it money. That cause of action would be a corporate asset. Is there any reason that one of the corporation's creditors should have privileged access to that corporate asset? Would it be more logical to have a procedure by which a creditor could cause the corporation to sue its directors? See Chapter 9.

2. If some kinds of conduct lead to the conclusion that individuals were acting as individuals rather than as the corporation, then not only could such individuals be liable for inducing corporate wrongdoing, they could also be directly liable for individual wrongdoing. In *Mentmore Manufacturing Co. v. National Merchandise Manufacturing Co.*, [1978] F.C.J. No. 521, 22 N.R. 161, 89 D.L.R. (3d) 195 (Fed. C.A.), a corporation breached the plaintiff's patent by making a certain type of pen. The corporation had two shareholders, one of whom was also its president. The plaintiff alleged that this individual was liable for infringement of the patent. Justice Le Dain, for the court, affirmed the dismissal of this part of the action. He said (at p. 170 [N.R.]):

What is involved here is a very difficult question of policy. On the one hand, there is the principle that an incorporated company is separate and distinct in law from its shareholders, directors and officers, and it is in the interests of the commercial purposes served by incorporated enterprise that they should as a general rule enjoy the benefit of the limited liability afforded by incorporation. On the other hand, there is the principle that everyone should answer for his tortious acts. ... There is no reason why the small, one-man or two-man corporation should not have the benefit of the same approach to personal liability merely because there is generally and necessarily a greater degree of direct and personal involvement in management on the part of its shareholders and directors.

...

What, however, is the kind of participation in the acts of the company that should give rise to personal liability? It is an elusive question. It would appear to be that degree and kind of personal involvement by which the director or officer makes the tortious act his own. It is obviously a question of fact to be decided on the circumstances of each case. I have not found much assistance in the particular cases in which courts have concluded that the facts were such as to warrant personal liability. But there would appear to be have been in these cases a knowing, deliberate, wilful quality to the participation.

...

But in my opinion there must be circumstances from which it is reasonable to conclude that the purpose of the director or officer was not the direction of the manufacturing and selling activity of the company in the ordinary course of his relationship to it but the deliberate, wilful and knowing pursuit of a course of conduct that was likely to constitute infringement or reflected an indifference to it.

In the following case, the Alberta Court of Appeal outlined seven elements to be established in order to find that a person intentionally induced a breach of contract. Do they provide the same criteria indicated in the cases above?

369413 ALBERTA LTD. v. POCKLINGTON

[2000] A.J. No. 1350, 88 Alta. L.R. (3d) 209, 194 D.L.R. (4th) 109 (C.A.)

The judgment of the Court was delivered by

Fruman J.A.: — Gainers was in deep financial trouble. Negotiations with the province of Alberta, its largest creditor, had collapsed. The day before Alberta called Gainers' loans and began to seize its assets, Peter Pocklington, the sole director and beneficial shareholder of Gainers, transferred a valuable asset from Gainers to a company he owned. The transfer, made without Alberta's knowledge or consent, placed the asset beyond Alberta's reach. Complaining that the transaction breached its loan agreement with Gainers, Alberta sued Pocklington for intentionally inducing Gainers to breach that contract. The trial judge decided that the transfer did not breach the loan agreement and dismissed the action. I would allow the appeal.

FACTS

Pocklington purchased Gainers, a meat-packing company, in 1978. His personal corporate empire consisted of several companies, including Pocklington Financial Corporation, Pocklington Holdings Inc. and Pocklington Foods Inc. In September 1985, Pocklington Foods acquired the shares of Gainers, and was Gainers' sole shareholder until October 6, 1989, when Alberta seized the shares. Pocklington also owned Gainers Properties Inc., which owned all Gainers' land, plants, machinery and equipment. After September 1987, Pocklington was the sole director of both Gainers companies.

Gainers' union began a long and bitter strike in 1986. Gainers then began to experience substantial losses: more than $10 million in 1986, $14 million in 1987 and $17 million in 1989. Pocklington and Alberta negotiated a $67 million bail-out consisting of a $55 million loan guarantee in favour of another Gainers' creditor, Lloyds Bank, and a $12 million term loan. In return, Alberta was granted a secured charge against all Gainers' and Gainers Properties' assets, both existing and after-acquired. In addition, all Gainers' shares were escrowed in favour of Alberta. The terms of this arrangement were documented in a lengthy Master Agreement and scheduled collateral security documents, effective September 25, 1987.

By the end of May 1989, Gainers had defaulted on both the Master Agreement and its loan agreement with Lloyds Bank. After another round of negotiations, the parties hammered out a 90-day standstill arrangement. Under this agreement, Lloyds Bank and Alberta agreed not to realize on their security if a complicated chain of conditions were met. Essentially, Alberta agreed to give up $5 million of security it held on Gainers Properties' assets, in favour of Lloyds Bank. Pocklington would make up this $5 million by a guarantee to Alberta for that amount, secured by a $5 million first mortgage on lands in Calgary and Edmonton, known as the Carma Lands.

It is the last step, the $5 million mortgage on the Carma Lands, that forms the backdrop for this action. At the time the deal was negotiated, the Carma Lands were owned by another Pocklington company, Hartford Properties Inc. That company would have had to guarantee Gainers' loan and grant the mortgage to Alberta. However, s. 42 of the Alberta *Business Corporations Act*, S.A. 1981, c. B-15 ("ABCA") restricted the ability of companies to provide financial assistance to related companies, and the parties were concerned that Hartford Properties would be unable to meet the statutory requirements. The transaction was therefore structured using a shell company, 350151 Alberta Ltd. Gainers acquired the shares of 350151; 350151 acquired the Carma Lands from Hartford Properties for $1.9 million; 350151 issued a promissory note to Hartford Properties for that amount; 350151 then granted a guarantee to Alberta; and finally, 350151 secured the guarantee by a $5 million mortgage in Alberta's favour registered against the Carma Lands. These arrangements were documented in a Standstill Agreement and accompanying collateral security documents, effective August 8, 1989.

Further defaults occurred; further attempts to negotiate proved fruitless. On October 4, 1989, one day before Alberta gave notice of its intention to exercise its rights under its various security agreements, Pocklington signed a Gainers director's resolution transferring the 350151 shares from Gainers to his own company, Pocklington Holdings, for $100. The $100 payment for the shares was not tendered until November 13, 1989, and was never accepted by Gainers. On October 6, 1989, Alberta exercised its rights under its various security documents, began to realize on Gainers' assets, and became the sole shareholder of Gainers. Because Pocklington Holdings had not guaranteed Gainers' debts, Pocklington Holdings' assets, including the newly acquired 350151 shares, could not be seized by Alberta.

Alberta contends that the transfer of the 350151 shares from Gainers to Pocklington Holdings breached its original loan agreement with Gainers, the

Master Agreement. Under s. 13.03(1), Gainers agreed not to sell or otherwise dispose of its assets without the prior written consent of Alberta, except in the ordinary course of business. Alberta was neither informed of the share transfer before it took place, nor was its written consent to the transfer requested. It sued Pocklington for intentionally inducing Gainers to breach the loan agreement, asking for the return of the 350151 shares to Gainers or, alternatively, for monetary damages.

...

ELEMENTS OF INDUCING BREACH OF CONTRACT

In order to find that a defendant intentionally induced a breach of contract, seven elements must be established:

i)   the existence of a contract;

ii) knowledge or awareness by the defendant of the contract;

iii) a breach of the contract by a contracting party;

iv) the defendant induced the breach;

v)   the defendant, by his conduct, intended to cause the breach;

vi) the defendant acted without justification; and

vii) the plaintiff suffered damages.

See *Ed Miller Sales & Rentals Ltd. v. Caterpillar Tractor Co.* (1996), 41 Alta. L.R. (3d) 217 (C.A.); and *Jackson v. Trimac Industries Ltd.* (1993), 6 Alta. L.R. (3d) 225 (Q.B.), varied on other grounds (1994), 20 Alta. L.R. (3d) 117.

The first two elements were admitted. In fact, Pocklington was a party to the Master Agreement and had signed it both in his personal and corporate capacities. As Pocklington was the sole director of Gainers, and signed the director's resolution which transferred the shares, the fourth element was also not contentious. The other four elements were, and are, in issue.

[The court found that the Master Agreement was breached by Pocklington, since the sale of shares in question was not a transaction in the ordinary course of Gainers' business.]

...

INTENT

The Law

In order to find liability, a plaintiff must demonstrate that the defendant had an "intent" to induce the breach of contract. The intent component of the tort is the most difficult to understand. Malicious motive, unlawful conduct, hatred or intention to harm are not required elements of intent: *Allen v. Flood*, [1898] A.C. 1 (H.L.(E.)); *Parks West Mall Ltd. v. Jennett* (1996), 36 Alta. L.R. (3d) 44 at 49 (C.A.); and *Atcheson v. College of Physicians and Surgeons (Alberta)*, [1994] 6 W.W.R. 239 at 246 (Alta. Q.B.). However, what is required is less clear. The requisite intent has been described with "loose, vague and conflicting statements" that sometime appear to be irreconcilable: *Ed Miller Sales, supra*, at 230.

Originally, the tort required the breach to be the result of wilful, deliberate and direct conduct which the defendant knew or hoped would result in a violation of the plaintiff's contractual rights. See for example, *Lumley v. Gye* (1853), 118 E.R. 749; 2 El. & Bl. 216 (Q.B.); and *Quinn v. Leathem*, [1901] A.C. 495 (H.L.(I.)).

However, courts soon recognized that intent can also be inferred when the consequences of the conduct were a necessary or reasonably foreseeable result, because "people are presumed to intend the reasonable consequences of their acts": *South Wales Miners' Federation v. Glamorgan Coal Company, Limited*, [1905] A.C. 239 at 244 (H.L.(E.)). In *Posluns v. Toronto Stock Exchange and Gardiner* (1965), 46 D.L.R. (2d) 210 at 267 (Ont. H.C.); affirmed (1966), 53 D.L.R. (2d) 193 (C.A.); affirmed [1968] S.C.R. 330, the court held that liability would attach if the defendant's conduct resulted in the breach of a contract "of which it was or ought to have been aware". The intention to bring about a breach of contract need not be the primary object; it is sufficient if the interference is necessarily incidental to attaining the defendant's primary objective: *Fraser v. Board of Trustees of Central United Church* (1983), 38 O.R. (2d) 97 at 103 (H.C.J.); and *Bank of Nova Scotia v. Gaudreau* (1985), 48 O.R. (2d) 478 (H.C.J.).

Intention can also be established when the defendant was reckless or wilfully blind to a breach. The defendant need not have actually known the precise terms of the contract or that his object only could be accomplished through breach of the contract. "If — turning a blind eye — he went about it regardless of whether it would involve a breach, he will be treated just as if he had knowingly procured it": J.G. Fleming, *The Law of Torts*, 8th ed. (Sydney: Law Book Co., 1992) at 694.

Turning a blind eye may include situations in which the defendant failed to seek advice or employ the means available to obtain the necessary knowledge. For example, in *Royal Bank of Canada v. Wilton* (1995), 165 A.R. 261 (C.A.), the defendant was uncertain about the enforceability of a contract, had the "means of knowledge" to determine if a legitimate contract existed, but made no efforts to seek advice. This court found the defendant liable because he deliberately chose not to acquire the information, but proceeded on the basis that the contract was unenforceable. Similarly, when there are competing legal interpretations and the defendant adopts an interpretation which will interfere with the plaintiff's rights, the defendant "must at least show that he was advised and honestly believed that he was legally entitled to take that course": *Swiss Bank v. Lloyds Bank*, [1979] Ch. 548 at 580 (Ch.D.); reversed on other grounds [1982] A.C. 584 (C.A.); affirmed [1982] A.C. 604 (H.L.(E.)).

If the defendant acted under a bona fide belief that contractual rights would not be infringed, liability will not be found even though the belief turned out to be mistaken. But for a mistaken belief to be bona fide, rather than the result of recklessness or wilful blindness, some basis for the belief must exist, and some reasonable effort must have been made by the defendant to learn the truth. In *British Industrial Plastics Ltd. v. Ferguson*, [1940] 1 All E.R. 479 (H.L.(E.)), defendants who had made the effort to seek advice were not found liable even though their belief was described as "illogical". In *Z-Mark International Inc. v. Leng Novak Blais Inc.* (1996), 12 O.T.C. 33 (Gen. Div.), appeal dismissed (1999), 122 O.A.C. 341, a defendant made enquiries and obtained assurances and a warranty. The court found that the defendant had no reason to doubt the assurance or the warranty and therefore the defendant was not knowingly or recklessly indifferent to a breach of contract.

In some cases a distinction is drawn between direct interference, for which the breach must be a foreseeable or reasonable consequence of the conduct, and indirect interference, for which the breach must be a necessary or substantially certain consequence. See, for example, L.N. Klar, *Tort Law*, 2nd ed.

(Scarborough: Carswell, 1996) at 498 and 507; *Fleming, supra*, at 694; *D.C. Thomson & Co. Ltd. v. Deakin*, [1952] Ch. 646 (C.A.); *Bank of Nova Scotia, supra; Garry v. Sherritt Gordon Mines Ltd.*, [1988] 1 W.W.R. 289 (Sask. C.A.); and *Atcheson, supra*.

As this case involves direct interference, this distinction does not arise. Pocklington, as the director of Gainers, executed the documents to complete the transfer of the 350151 shares to his own company. The transfer caused Gainers to breach s. 13.03(l) of the Master Agreement, which prohibited dispositions of assets without Alberta's consent. Therefore, if the breach was a reasonable or foreseeable consequence of that transfer, or alternatively, if Pocklington completed the transfer recklessly, was wilfully blind to its consequences, or was indifferent as to whether or not it caused a breach, the necessary intent element for the tort will be met.

The Evidence

...

Pocklington's evidence demonstrates he did not care whether his actions constituted a breach. He admitted that he was acting in his own interests and that he had no loyalty to Gainers (AB 742:17-37). His acknowledged that he was trying to defeat the entirety of the mortgage (AB 1094:5-11; 1095:4-6; 1052:46-1053:10; 1096:29-30). It is not much of a defence to a charge of intentionally breaching the Master Agreement to show that Pocklington intended to breach the Standstill Agreement instead.

...

... Prudent business people, concerned about honouring contractual commitments, make appropriate inquiries before embarking on transactions that involve complex legal documents. Consulting legal counsel may not be necessary in every case, but the circumstances here cry out for legal advice: negotiations with Alberta had collapsed and Pocklington knew that realization of the loan was imminent; Gainers was insolvent with no equity left in the company; Gainers' assets and shares were secured and its business activities were restricted by binders full of loan and security agreements; and Gainers' sole beneficial shareholder proposed to transfer a valuable asset to himself for nominal consideration, signing the resolutions as sole director. Pocklington, both personally and in his capacity as a director of Gainers, had an obligation to obtain legal advice about the propriety of the transaction. If he failed to do so, or ignored the legal advice he received, he proceeded at his peril.

...

The share transfer documents were prepared by Ogilvie and Company, "on instructions received from Gainers Inc. on the 3rd day of October, 1989" (AB XVIII at 3606), just as negotiations with Alberta collapsed. They were signed the next day. Lloyd was uncertain whether Ogilvie and Company brought s. 13.03(l) to Pocklington's attention. At first he acknowledged this had occurred:

Q   [...] And, sir, I take it that you're also aware that your firm drew Article 13.03(l) to Mr. Pocklington's attention at the time the shares were transferred from Gainers to Pocklington Holdings Inc.?

A   I think that's correct. I think that there was — these — these sections were — now, I think that's correct.

(AB 862:24-31)

Later, he changed his mind:

> A   I think that there were discussions with respect to the people at Ogilvie
> about them and I'd — I'm not certain — I'm not that certain in fact — I
> can't recall whether or not Mr. Pocklington was specifically directed to
> the sections or not.

(AB 874:23-28)

Correspondence from Ogilvie and Company provides some clarification. On
November 15, 1989, after Alberta got wind that the shares had been transferred, its
counsel wrote Ogilvie and Company asking for details. Alberta's counsel referred
to a possible breach of s. 13.03(l) of the Master Agreement, noting that Alberta's
consent had not been obtained, and that the transfer was not in the ordinary course
of Gainers' business (AB XVIII at 3586-87).

Ogilvie and Company responded by letter dated November 16, 1989, which stated:

> We are also able to advise you that our firm raised with our client the exact
> provision of the Master Agreement which your letter raises [s. 13.03(l)], however
> our client takes the view that the transaction is not off side the terms of the Master
> Agreement.

(AB XVIII at 3606, para. 3) [Emphasis added.]

The clear implication of Ogilvie and Company's carefully worded letter is that
either the lawyers did not share their clients' views, or they were invited to keep
their legal advice to themselves. Pocklington nevertheless signed the documents to
give effect to the share transfer, and retained the shares despite Alberta's early
protests and Ogilvie and Company's apparent reservations. He had the means of
knowledge, but chose to act without legal advice. Pocklingon was wilfully blind to
the consequences of his actions and showed clear indifference to the breach. The
intent component of the tort is satisfied.

JUSTIFICATION

In some situations, a defendant's plea of justification may avoid liability: *South
Wales Miners' Federation, supra,* and *Quinn, supra.* The defence of justification
is available when the defendant caused the breach while acting under a duty
imposed by law. The issue in each case is whether, upon consideration of the
relative significance of all the factors, the defendant's conduct should be tolerated
despite its detrimental effect on the interests of others: *Fleming, supra,* at 657.

Directors of companies owe duties to the corporation; they are obliged both at
common law and under statute to act in the best interests of the company: *Re
Cawley & Co.* (1889), 42 Ch. 209 at 233 (C.A.). For example, s. 117(1)(a) of the
ABCA provides: "Every director and officer of a corporation in exercising his
powers and discharging his duties shall act honestly and in good faith with a view
to the best interests of the corporation [...] ".

Therefore, when the interests of the company are best served by breaking its
contractual commitments, the director's act of inducement is justified because it is
"taken as a duty": *De Jetley Marks v. Greenwood (Lord),* [1936] 1 All E.R. 863
(K.B.) at 873; and *Imperial Oil Ltd. v. C & G Holdings Ltd.* (1990), 62 D.L.R.
(4th) 261 (Nfld. C.A.). The rationale for this defence is that a director acting in

compliance with a duty imposed by law should not be personally liable because the director's act induced a breach of the company's contract.

But if the director is not complying with that duty, the rationale for relieving personal liability disappears. Although the director may have acted in the name of the company, justification is not available as a defence. See W.A. Richardson, "Making an End Run Around the Corporate Veil: The Tort of Inducing Breach of Contract" (1984) 5 Advocates' Q. 103.

For example, in *McFadden v. 481782 Ontario Ltd. et al.* (1984), 47 O.R. (2d) 134 at 146-47 (H.C.J.), the court found that the defendant directors were liable when "[t]hey sought to feather their own nest, rather than that of the company they were under a duty to serve". In transferring corporate funds to themselves, they were acting with a view to their own best interests rather than the corporation's. Therefore, they were not acting "under a compulsion of a duty", justification was not available as a defence, and the directors were personally liable for inducing a breach of contract. Similarly, immunity did not extend to directors who took advantage of their office to commit a tort for their own ends: *Jackson, supra.*

...

Although justification is a defence to the tort, the burden is fairly placed on the plaintiff to prove the director was not acting in the best interest of the corporation, and therefore stepped out from under the protective umbrella of the director's corporate duties. If a director wishes the plaintiff to prove more, in my view the director must at least demonstrate that some legitimate interest of the corporation could have been served by the conduct. This information is well within the director's knowledge and a requirement to demonstrate it on a prima facie basis, rather than to prove it on a balance of probabilities, does not unduly open the company's business to third party scrutiny.

If the court concludes the director's conduct is capable both of serving the interests of the corporation and of achieving some less worthy purpose, the court should go on to consider whether the plaintiff has proven that the director's act was aimed at depriving the aggrieved party of the benefits of the contract. But where, as in *McFadden, supra*, it is readily apparent that the conduct could only be intended for the director's own benefit and not the company's, the court need not address the director's dominating concern. In such direct interference cases, proof of intent as it has developed through the case law, and proof that the director was not acting in the best interests of the corporation, will be sufficient to ground liability.

In this case Pocklington acquired a valuable asset for nominal consideration at the expense of Gainers' creditors. Since Gainers was insolvent at that time, its creditors' interests were the interests of the company: L.C.B. Gower, *Gower's Principles of Modern Company Law*, 6th ed. (London: Sweet & Maxwell, 1997) at 603; and *Levy-Russell Ltd. v. Tecmotiv Inc.* (1994), 13 B.L.R. (2d) 1 (Ont. Gen. Div.) at 189-90. Promoting the interests of one shareholder at the expense of the creditors is not in the best interests of the company: *Levy-Russell* at 169. A director who pursues these objectives is not acting in furtherance of his corporate duty, and there is no justification for his deeds.

Pocklington has not demonstrated any legitimate business interest of Gainers that could have been served by the 350151 share transfer. In fact, he candidly admitted he was acting only in his own interests, with no benefit to Gainers (AB 742:16-37):

Q I am talking about on October the 4th when Gainers sold the shares —

A To me?

Q — in the numbered company to Pocklington Holdings Inc.?

A Right.

Q Was there any benefit to Gainers in that transaction?

A I guess I was more interested in my own personal well-being than Gainers' well-being at that particular date. I felt, as I said, by that time a lot of my trust had left my partners called the government.

Q All right, so you were acting —

A In short, I realized that I was getting screwed by them.

Q You were acting to further the interests of PHI and yourself and you weren't too concerned with Gainers at that time?

A My loyalty to Gainers had been squeezed at that time.

By transferring the 350151 shares to his own company, Pocklington was not discharging his legal duty to act honestly and in good faith with a view to the best interests of Gainers; he was acting solely in his own interests. As no legitimate interest of Gainers could possibly be served by the transaction, the court need not go on to consider whether Pocklington's act was aimed at depriving Alberta of the benefits of its contract. Pocklington's position as director cannot provide justification for his actions.

DAMAGES

...

The damage element of the tort is met.

...

Damages ... are assessed at the $6.6 million value of the Carma Lands, less the $1.9 million balance owing, for a total of $4.7 million. Because the 350151 shares were valued at the date of the trial, it is not appropriate to order prejudgment interest on this amount.

Appeal allowed.

NOTES AND QUESTIONS

Is it always the case that directors or officers who induce a breach of contract by a corporation will be held personally liable for the inducement? What if the directors or officers, by inducing a breach of contract, were fulfilling their fiduciary duties to the corporation mandated by statute? Consider what is said in the following case:

ADGA SYSTEMS INTERNATIONAL INC. v. VALCOM LTD.

[1999] O.J. No. 27, 43 O.R. (3d) 101 (C.A.)

The judgment of the court was delivered by

Carthy J.A.: — This appeal presents for consideration once again the troublesome issue of the liability of officers and directors of a corporation for acts done in pursuance of a corporate purpose.

The plaintiff, ADGA Systems International Ltd., has claimed that a competitor, the defendant Valcom Ltd., raided its employees and caused the plaintiff economic damage. The plaintiff also claims against three of its own employees for breach of fiduciary duty in acceding to the importunes of Valcom Ltd. The issue in controversy on this particular appeal is the claim by the plaintiff against the director and two employees of Valcom Ltd. for their personal involvement in this recruitment program. Those three defendants brought a motion for summary judgment seeking to dismiss the claim against them. The motion was dismissed by Mercier J. The Divisional Court then heard an appeal from that order, allowed the appeal, and dismissed the claim against those three defendants. The plaintiff now appeals to this court and seeks to justify proceeding to trial against MacPherson, the Director of Valcom Ltd. and Ewing and McKenzie, senior employees of Valcom Ltd. The question is whether the respondents can be sued for their actions as individuals, assuming those actions were genuinely directed to the best interests of their corporate employer. In my view a cause of action does exist against the respondents and a trial is required to determine the merits of that action.

Facts

For purposes of this appeal, a simple sketch of the background facts is sufficient. The plaintiff ADGA and the defendant Valcom were competitors, and for some years the plaintiff had a substantial contract with Correctional Services Canada for technical support and maintenance of security systems in the federal prisons. In 1991 the contract was coming up for renewal and the Department of Supply and Services called for tenders. One of the conditions of the tender was that the tendering party provide the names of 25 senior technicians together with their qualifications, thus assuring that the tendering company would be competent to perform the work required under the contract. Through its long association with this contract, the plaintiff had 45 such employees. Valcom is alleged to have had none. The pleadings and the evidence indicate that Valcom, through its sole director MacPherson and the two senior employees Ewing and McKenzie, set out to interview the senior representatives of the plaintiff's technical staff to convince them of the following: to permit their names to be used on the tendering document; to come to work for Valcom if the tender was successful; and to use their efforts to convince the other employees on the technical staff of the plaintiff to do likewise. In the result, all but one of the 45 members of the plaintiff's technical staff apparently "signed on" with Valcom. Both companies presented the same staff in their tender offerings, and Valcom was the successful bidder.

...

Analysis

... The issue that I must deal with is whether, on the assumption that the defendant Valcom committed a tort against the appellant, the sole director and employees of Valcom can be accountable for the same tort as a consequence of their personal involvement directed to the perceived best interests of the corporation.

My first observation is that I recognize the policy concern expressed by the Divisional Court, and other General Division judges, over the proliferation of claims against officers and directors of corporations in circumstances which give the appearance of the desire for discovery or leverage in the litigation process. This is a proper concern because business cannot function efficiently if corporate officers and directors are inhibited in carrying on a corporate business because of a fear of being inappropriately swept into lawsuits, or, worse, are driven away from involvement in any respect in corporate business by the potential exposure to ill-founded litigation. That being said, it is not appropriate to extend the reasoning of *ScotiaMcLeod* [*Montreal Trust Co. of Canada v. ScotiaMcLeod Inc.* (1995), 26 O.R. (3d) 481, 129 D.L.R. (4th) 711 (C.A.)] beyond its intended application by reading it as protecting all conduct by officers and employees in pursuit of corporate purposes. The common law should not develop on an *ad hoc* basis to put out fires. When a policy issue arises, here from modern business realities, the courts must proceed on a principled basis to establish a framework for further development which recognizes the new realities but preserves the fundamental purpose served by that area of law. For this reason I intend to analyze the development of law in this field from its beginnings.

That beginning is found in the House of Lords' decision in *Salomon v. Salomon & Co. Ltd.*, [1895-9] All E.R. 33 (H.L.), which established that a company, once legally incorporated, must be treated like any other independent person, with rights and liabilities appropriate to itself. From time to time, litigants have sought to lift this "corporate veil", by seeking to make principals of the corporation liable for the obligations of the corporation. However, where, as here, the plaintiff relies upon establishing an independent cause of action against the principals of the company, the corporate veil is not threatened and the *Salomon* principle remains intact.

The distinction between an independent cause of action and looking through the corporation was confirmed by the subsequent case of *Said v. Butt*, [1920] 3 K.B. 497. This is a King's Bench decision but has been adopted in Canada and throughout the United States. ...

In *Said v. Butt*, the plaintiff was engaged in a dispute with an opera company which refused to sell him tickets to a performance. The plaintiff purchased a ticket through an agent and when he appeared at the opera the defendant, an employee of the opera company recognized him and ejected him. The plaintiff sued the employee for wrongfully procuring the company to break a contract made by the company to sell the plaintiff a ticket.

The court held that there was no contract because the company would not knowingly have sold a ticket to the plaintiff. Nevertheless, on the assumption that there was a contract, the court considered the implications to the defendant employee. McCardie J. stated at p. 504:

> It is well to point out that Sir Alfred Butt possessed the widest powers as the chairman and sole managing director of the Palace Theatre, Ld. He clearly acted within those powers when he directed that the plaintiff should be refused admission on December 23. I am satisfied, also, that he meant to act and did act *bona fide* for the protection of the interests of his company. If, therefore, the plaintiff, assuming that a contract existed between the company and himself, can sue the defendant for wrongfully procuring a breach of that contract, the gravest and widest consequences must ensue.

After detailing the mischief that would flow from permitting such claims to be made McCardie J. concluded at p. 506:

> I hold that if a servant acting *bona fide* within the scope of his authority procures or causes the breach of a contract between his employer and a third person, he does

not thereby become liable to an action of tort at the suit of the person whose contract has thereby been broken. ... Nothing that I have said to-day is, I hope, inconsistent with the rule that a director or a servant who actually takes part in or actually authorizes such torts as assault, trespass to property, nuisance, or the like may be liable in damages as a joint participant in one of such recognized heads of tortious wrong.

For present purposes, I extract the following from McCardie J.'s reasons. First, this is not an application of *Salomon*. That case is not mentioned anywhere in the reasons. Second, it provides an exception to the general rule that persons are responsible for their own conduct. That exception has since gained acceptance because it assures that persons who deal with a limited company and accept the imposition of limited liability will not have available to them both a claim for breach of contract against a company and a claim for tortious conduct against the director with damages assessed on a different basis. The exception also assures that officers and directors, in the process of carrying on business, are capable of directing that a contract of employment be terminated or that a business contract not be performed on the assumed basis that the company's best interest is to pay the damages for failure to perform. By carving out the exception for these policy reasons, the court has emphasized and left intact the general liability of any individual for personal conduct.

The third point of interest arises from this excerpt from the reasons at p. 505:

The explanation of the breadth of the language used in the decisions probably lies in the fact that in every one of the sets of circumstances before the Court the person who procured the breach of contract was in fact a stranger, that is a third person, who stood wholly outside the area of the bargain made between the two contracting parties. If he is in the position of a stranger, he will be *prima facie* liable, even though he may act honestly, or without malice, or in the best interests of himself; or even if he acts as an altruist, seeking only the good of another . . .

The court was there referring to the stranger as the wrongdoer but the same principle might be applied in the converse situation where the stranger is the victim. This suggestion, was picked up later in the dissenting reasons of La Forest J. in *London Drugs Ltd. v. Kuehne & Nagel International Ltd.*, *infra*, to the effect that a jurisprudential division line might be drawn between those who contract with the company, or voluntarily deal with it, and can be taken to have accepted limited liability, and strangers to the company whose only concern is not to be harmed by the conduct of others. On that theory, those harmed as strangers to the corporate body naturally look for liability to the persons who caused the harm and those who have in some manner accepted limited liability in their dealings with the company would be limited in recourse to the company. As evidenced by the decision in *London Drugs v. Kuehne* that theory of demarcation of liability has not been adopted in Canada.

The consistent line of authority in Canada holds simply that, in all events, officers, directors and employees of corporations are responsible for their tortious conduct even though that conduct was directed in a bona fide manner to the best interests of the company, always subject to the *Said v. Butt* exception.

...

The Supreme Court of Canada ... considered the issue of an employee's liability for acts done in the course of his duties on behalf of the employer in *London Drugs Ltd. v. Kuehne & Nagel International Ltd.*, [1992] 3 S.C.R. 299, 97 D.L.R. (4th) 261. The plaintiff delivered a transformer to a warehouse company for storage. An employee of the warehouse company negligently permitted the transformer to topple over, causing extensive damage. Even though there was a contractual relationship between the company and the customer, the majority held in favour of the claim against the employee.

Iacobucci J. stated at pp. 407-08:

> There is no general rule in Canada to the effect that an employee acting in the course of his or her employment and performing the "very essence" of his or her employer's contractual obligations with a customer does not owe a duty of care, whether one labels it "independent" or otherwise, to the employer's customer. ...
>
> ... The mere fact that the employee is performing the "very essence" of a contract between the plaintiff and his or her employer does not, in itself, necessarily preclude a conclusion that a duty of care was present.

La Forest J. dissented on this issue and was prepared to relieve the employee from personal liability in tort where the tort occurred in the context of a breach of contract between the employer and the customer, and so long as the employee's tort was in the course of duties. His analysis of the distinction between the voluntary and involuntary creditor is, and will continue to be, of interest as policy questions impact upon the evolving jurisprudence in this area. At p. 349 he stated:

> The distinction between voluntary and involuntary creditors is also useful in this area. As commentators have pointed out (Halpern, Trebilcock and Turnbull, "An Economic Analysis of Limited Liability in Corporation Law" (1980), 30 U.T.L.J. 117), different types of claimants against the corporation have differing abilities to benefit from being put on notice with respect to the impact of the limited liability regime. At one end, creditors like bond holders and banks are generally well situated to evaluate the risks of default and to contract accordingly. These "voluntary" creditors can be considered to be capable of protecting themselves from the consequences of a limited liability regime and the practically systematic recourse by banks to personal guarantees by the principals of small companies attests to that fact.
>
> At the other end of the spectrum are classic involuntary tort creditors exemplified by a plaintiff who is injured when run down by an employee driving a motorcar. These involuntary creditors are those who never chose to enter into a course of dealing with the company and correspond to what I have termed as the classic vicarious liability claimant.

These Canadian authorities at the appellate level confirm clearly that employees, officers and directors will be held personally liable for tortious conduct causing physical injury, property damage, or a nuisance even when their actions are pursuant to their duties to the corporation.

...

An excerpt from the reasoning of Finlayson J.A. in *ScotiaMcLeod Inc.*, at pp. 490-91 O.R., pp. 720-21 D.L.R., has been quoted from time to time by General Division judges and, here, by the Divisional Court, as suggesting some limitation on the liability of directors and officers who are acting in the course of their duties:

> The decided cases in which employees and officers of companies have been found personally liable for actions ostensibly carried out under a corporate name are fact-specific. In the absence of findings of fraud, deceit, dishonesty or want of authority on the part of employees or officers, they are also rare. Those cases in which the corporate veil has been pierced usually involve transactions where the use of the corporate structure was a sham from the outset or was an afterthought to a

deal which had gone sour. There is also a considerable body of case-law wherein injured parties to actions for breach of contract have attempted to extend liability to the principals of the company by pleading that the principals were privy to the tort of inducing breach of contract between the company and the plaintiff: see *Ontario Store Fixtures Inc. v. Mmmuffins Inc.* (1989), 70 O.R. (2d) 42 (H.J.C.), and the cases referred to therein. Additionally there have been attempts by injured parties to attach liability to the principals of failed businesses through insolvency litigation. In every case, however, the facts giving rise to personal liability were specifically pleaded. Absent allegations which fit within the categories described above, officers or employees of limited companies are protected from personal liability unless it can be shown that their actions are themselves tortious or exhibit a separate identity or interest from that of the company so as to make the act or conduct complained of their own.

The operative portion of this paragraph is the final sentence which confirms that, where properly pleaded, officers or employees can be liable for tortious conduct even when acting in the course of duty. That this is clearly the intent of what was being stated is evidenced by the conclusion that the action should proceed against two defendants; against whom negligent conduct had been properly pleaded. The reasoning of *ScotiaMcLeod* has been recently applied by this court in decisions which confirm my interpretation.

...

Conclusion

It is my conclusion that there is no principled basis for protecting the director and employees of Valcom from liability for their alleged conduct on the basis that such conduct was in pursuance of the interests of the corporation. It may be that for policy reasons the law as to the allocation of responsibility for tortious conduct should be adjusted to provide some protection to employees, officers or directors, or all of them, in limited circumstances where, for instance, they are acting in the best interests of the corporation with parties who have voluntarily chosen to accept the ambit of risk of a limited liability company. However, the creation of such a policy should not evolve from the facts of this case where the alleged conduct was intentional and the only relationship between the corporate parties was as competitors. Any such evolution should await facts which are apposite to the policy concerns and should probably be articulated as a definitive extension of the defence in *Said v. Butt*. Such a development would be in the direction indicated by La Forest J. in his dissenting reasons in *London Drugs* and thus may have to await further consideration by the Supreme Court. In the meantime the courts can only be scrupulous in weeding out claims that are improperly pleaded or where the evidence does not justify an allegation of a personal tort. A principled development of jurisprudence is the tradition and the strength of the common law and must take precedence over incidental attempts to abuse the law as it develops.

...

Appeal allowed.

NOTES AND QUESTIONS

In *ADGA Systems*, Carthy J.A. said that the precedent in *Said v. Butt*, [1920] 3 K.B. 497 provides an exception to the general rule that "in all events, officers, directors and employees of corporations are responsible for their tortious conduct even though that conduct was directed in a *bona fide* manner to the best interests of the company".

Is this what the precedent in *Said v. Butt* truly stands for? Does it entail that the director commits a tort, but is exempted from liability for its commission, or does it entail that the director commits no tort at all? Does the restatement of the precedent in *Said v. Butt* by Carthy J.A. in *ADGA Systems* change how it is now understood in Canadian law?

As a result of the judgment in *ADGA Systems*, what is the legal result where directors must choose between (i) inducing a breach of contract because doing so is in the best interests of the corporation and (ii) acting contrary to the interests of the corporation in order to avoid inducing a breach of the corporation's contract? Are the directors liable in tort for inducing the breach of contract in order to fulfil their fiduciary duties owed to the corporation? Alternatively, if the directors do not induce the breach of contract, will they then be liable for breaching the fiduciary duties they owe to the corporation? Would you want to be a director placed in this situation?

If one of the above duties is equitable (*e.g.*, the fiduciary duty owed to the corporation) and the other is merely a common law duty (a duty not to induce a breach of contract), will the equitable duty prevail, thereby providing a defence to what would otherwise constitute a breach of the common law duty? Would your answer change if the duty owed to the corporation is statutory (which would include both fiduciary duties and the duty to manage the business and affairs of the corporation)?

Is there a policy basis for holding directors and officers personally liable for inducing corporations to engage in unlawful behaviour where those directors and officers are merely fulfilling the best interests of the corporation? Compare the issue of "Thin Capitalization", discussed below.

Does *ADGA Systems* create a distinction between directors who induce their corporations to breach contracts and directors who induce third parties to breach contracts?

Are there different standards for the liability of employees versus that of corporate directors and officers where each acts within the scope of his or her duties? Should there be? Compare the result in *ADGA Systems* with that in *London Drugs Ltd. v. Kuehne & Nagel International Ltd.*, [1992] S.C.J. No. 84, [1992] 3 S.C.R. 299, 97 D.L.R. (4th) 261, which is discussed in *ADGA Systems*.

(b) Knowing Assistance in a Breach of Trust

Trusts arise in many contexts, and corporations can be trustees. It is an equitable wrong to breach a trust, and this wrong can be committed innocently, in the sense that the trustee is liable to the beneficiary for breach of trust even if it thought it was acting lawfully. When a trust is breached, two kinds of accessory liability can arise — that is, liability of so-called strangers to the trust. One is sometimes called "knowing receipt of trust property". If a third party acquires trust property from the trustee in connection with a breach of trust, then the property must be returned unless the third party was a *bona fide* purchaser for value and had no knowledge of the plaintiff's equitable rights. If the third party no longer holds the trust property, it will still be personally liable to the beneficiary if it knew that the property was transferred in breach of trust. For the standard of knowledge required for "knowing receipt" in Canada, see *Citadel General Assurance Co. v. Lloyds Bank Canada*, [1997] S.C.J. No. 92, [1997] 3 S.C.R. 805, 152 D.L.R. (4th) 411 and

Gold v. Rosenberg, [1997] S.C.J. No. 93, [1997] 3 S.C.R. 767, 152 D.L.R. (4th) 385.

The other kind of accessory liability does not depend on acquisition of any property by the third party. It is sometimes called "knowing assistance in a fraudulent or dishonest breach of trust". That lengthy name indicates the traditional view, which is that this third party liability cannot arise unless (a) the *trustee's* breach was fraudulent or dishonest; and (b) the *third party* whose liability is in issue must have had knowledge of the trustee's dishonest scheme. Thus, the states of mind of two different people are in issue.

The concept of "knowing assistance" was discussed in *Air Canada v. M & L Travel Ltd.*, [1993] S.C.J. No. 118, [1993] 3 S.C.R. 787, 108 D.L.R. (4th) 592.

AIR CANADA v. M & L TRAVEL LTD.

[1993] 3 S.C.R. 787, 108 D.L.R. (4th) 592

[The defendant corporation ran a travel agency. Its directors and shareholders were Mssrs. Martin and Valliant. Under M & L's working agreement with the plaintiff airline, the corporation was to hold the proceeds of ticket sales in trust for the plaintiff. Instead, M & L placed these proceeds into its general operating account, from which its general operating expenses were paid. As a result of financial difficulties experienced by the corporation and disputes between Martin and Valliant, the plaintiff airline was owed some $25,079.67 for ticket sales. It commenced an action against the directors personally for the amount it was owed.]

The judgment of La Forest, Sopinka, Gonthier, Cory, Iacobucci and Major JJ. was delivered by

Iacobucci J.: — ... Two main questions are raised on this appeal. First, was the relationship between the corporation and the respondent airline one of trust? Second, if so, is the appellant director personally liable for the breach of trust by the corporation?

...

IV. Analysis

1. The Nature of the Relationship between M & L and Air Canada

In this Court, the appellant initially argued that the relationship between M & L and the respondent airline was one of debtor and creditor, rather than one of trust. However, at the hearing, the appellant properly conceded that the relationship was one of trust. Given this concession, I will consider this question only briefly.

The appellant relied on the fact that the agreement between the airline and M & L did not require it to keep the proceeds of Air Canada tickets in a separate account or trust fund, or to remit the funds forthwith. Rather, M & L was permitted to keep such funds for a period of up to 15 days, and then for a further 7-day grace period. Furthermore, M & L was liable for the total sale price of all tickets sold, less its commission, regardless of whether it had actually collected the full amount from its customers. That is, M & L was free to sell Air Canada tickets on credit to its customers. Prior to his concession on this point, the appellant submitted that, in these circumstances, M & L was not a trustee of the sale proceeds of the Air Canada tickets.

In concluding that the relationship between M & L and the airline was one of trust, the Court of Appeal relied on *Canadian Pacific Air Lines, Ltd. v. Canadian*

Imperial Bank of Commerce (1987), 61 O.R. (2d) 233. Although the Court of Appeal's decision in that case (1990), 71 O.R. (2d) 63 (note), was brief, the reasons of the trial judge, at p. 237, went into greater depth:

> In order to constitute a trust, an arrangement must have three characteristics, known as the three certainties: certainty of intent, of subject-matter and of object. The agreement ... is certain in its intent to create a trust. The subject-matter is to be the funds collected for ticket sales. The object, or beneficiary, of the trust is also clear; it is to be the airline. The necessary elements for the creation of a trust relationship are all present. I find that such a relationship did exist between CP and the two travel agencies.

This analysis is clearly applicable to the facts of the present case. That the intent of the agreement is to create a trust is evident from the following wording: "All monies, less applicable commissions to which the Agent is entitled hereunder, collected by the Agent for air passenger transportation (and for which the Agent has issued tickets or exchange orders) shall be the property of the Airline, and shall be held in trust by the Agent until satisfactorily accounted for to the airline". The object of the trust is the respondent airline, and its subject-matter is the funds collected for ticket sales.

...

In conclusion, it is well established that the nature of the relationship between the parties is a matter of intention. In the present case, the relationship of trust is further evidenced by the express prohibition restricting the use of the funds, and the supervision and control of the carrier over the financial dealings of M & L. ... [T]he absence of a prohibition on the commingling of funds is not determinative, although it may be a factor to be taken into account by the trial judge, as it was here. Moreover, in the present case M & L acted in accordance with that intention and set up trust accounts, which, although never used, confirm that the relationship was viewed by the directors as a trust relationship. Finally, it must be noted that the nature of the relationship is consistent with trust as the IATA agreement allowed M & L to affect Air Canada's legal responsibilities.

2. Personal Liability of the Directors as Constructive Trustees

(a) General Principles

Having found that the relationship between M & L and the respondent airline was a trust relationship, there is no question that M & L's actions were in breach of trust. M & L failed to account to the respondent for the monies collected through sales of Air Canada tickets. What remains to be decided is whether the directors of M & L should be held personally liable for the breach of trust on the basis that they were constructive trustees. Whether personal liability is imposed on a stranger to a trust depends on the basic question of whether the stranger's conscience is sufficiently affected to justify the imposition of personal liability. See *In re Montagu's Settlement Trusts*, [1987] Ch. 264, at p. 285. The authorities reflect distinct approaches to answer this question depending on the circumstances of the case, and it is to these that I shall now turn.

There are two general bases upon which a stranger to the trust can be held liable as a constructive trustee for breach of trust. First, although not directly relevant to this appeal, strangers to the trust can be liable as trustees *de son tort*. Such persons, although not appointed trustees, "take on themselves to act as such and to possess and administer trust property". ...

This type of liability is inapplicable to the present case because the directors of M & L did not personally take possession of trust property or assume the office or function of trustees. ...

Second, strangers to the trust can also be personally liable for breach of trust if they knowingly participate in a breach of trust. ...

...

[T]here were traditionally therefore two ways in which a stranger to the trust could be held personally liable to the beneficiaries as a participant in a breach of trust: as one in receipt and chargeable with trust property and as one who knowingly assisted in a dishonest and fraudulent design on the part of the trustees. The former category of constructive trusteeship has been termed "knowing receipt" or "knowing receipt and dealing", while the latter category has been termed "knowing assistance".

The former category of "knowing receipt" of trust property is inapplicable to the present case because it requires the stranger to the trust to have received trust property in his or her personal capacity, rather than as an agent of the trustees. ... As I have already noted, the courts below found that the directors of M & L did not personally control the trust funds in the present case, and this finding was not challenged before us.

Thus the only basis upon which the directors could be held personally liable as constructive trustees is under the "knowing assistance" head of liability. To repeat, in *Barnes v. Addy*, [(1874), L.R. 9 Ch. App. 244] ... at p. 252, Lord Selborne L.C. stated that persons who "assist with knowledge in a dishonest and fraudulent design on the part of the trustees" will be liable for the breach of trust as constructive trustees. See also, *Soar v. Ashwell*, [1893] 2 Q.B. 390 (C.A.). This basis of liability raises two main issues: the nature of the breach of trust and the degree of knowledge required of the stranger.

(b) Degree of Knowledge of the Stranger

The latter point may be quickly addressed. The knowledge requirement for this type of liability is actual knowledge; recklessness or wilful blindness will also suffice. See *Belmont Finance, supra*, at pp. 130, 136; *In re Montagu's Settlement Trusts, supra*, at pp. 271-72, 285; *Carl-Zeiss-Stiftung v. Herbert Smith & Co. (No. 2)*, [1969] 2 All E.R. 367 (C.A.), at p. 379. In the latter case, Sachs L.J. stated that to be held liable the stranger must have had "both actual knowledge of the trust's existence and actual knowledge that what is being done is improperly in breach of that trust — though, of course, in both cases a person wilfully shutting his eyes to the obvious is in no different position than if he had kept them open". Whether the trust is created by statute or by contract may have an impact on the question of the stranger's knowledge of the trust. If the trust was imposed by statute, then he or she will be deemed to have known of it. If the trust was contractually created, then whether the stranger knew of the trust will depend on his or her familiarity or involvement with the contract.

If the stranger received a benefit as a result of the breach of trust, this may ground an inference that the stranger knew of the breach. See *Shields v. Bank of Ireland*, [1901] 1 I.R. 222, at p. 228; *Gray v. Johnston* (1868), L.R. 3 H.L. 1, at p. 11, *per* Lord Cairns, L.C.; *Selangor, supra*, at p. 1101; *Coleman v. Bucks and Oxon Union Bank*, [1897] 2 Ch. 243, at p. 254; *Waters, supra*, at p. 401; *Fonthill Lbr. Ltd. v. Bk. of Montreal*, [1959] O.R. 451 (C.A.), at p. 468; *Groves-Raffin Construction Ltd. v. Bank of Nova Scotia* (1975), 64 D.L.R. (3d) 78 (B.C.C.A.), at pp. 116-17. The receipt of a benefit will be neither a sufficient nor a necessary condition for the drawing of such an inference.

The reason for excluding constructive knowledge (that is, knowledge of circumstances which would indicate the facts to an honest person, or knowledge of facts which would put an honest person on inquiry) was discussed in *In re Montagu's Settlement Trusts*, *supra*, at pp. 271-73, 275-85. Megarry V.-C. held, at p. 285, that constructive notice was insufficient to bind the stranger's conscience so as to give rise to personal liability. While cases involving recklessness or wilful blindness indicate a "want of probity which justifies imposing a constructive trust", Megarry V.C., at p. 285, held that the carelessness involved in constructive knowledge cases will not normally amount to a want of probity, and will therefore be insufficient to bind the stranger's conscience. ...

(c) Nature of the Breach of Trust

With regard to the first issue, the nature of the breach of trust, the authorities can be divided into two lines. Most of the English authorities have followed the *Barnes v. Addy* standard which requires participation by the stranger in a dishonest and fraudulent design. ...

...

The English "fraudulent and dishonest design" analysis was adopted by the Saskatchewan Court of Appeal in *MacDonald v. Hauer* (1976), 72 D.L.R. (3d) 110. In that case, one of the trustees opened a margin account in his own name for the purpose of securities trading. He pledged securities belonging to the estate for which he was trustee with a broker as security for the margin, and gave his business associate Hauer his power of attorney on the account. The profits on the account were to be shared equally between the trustee and Hauer. The estate's securities were eventually sold by Hauer. Bayda J.A. (as he then was) found Hauer liable in equity for breach of trust as a constructive trustee. Relying on *Barnes v. Addy*, *supra*, Bayda J.A. held at p. 121 that the three essential elements for finding a stranger to a trust to be a constructive trustee were: "(1) assistance by the stranger of a nominated trustee (2) with knowledge (3) in a dishonest and fraudulent design on the part of the nominated trustee (or fraudulent or dishonest disposition of the trust property)", although it should be noted that Bayda J.A. appears later in his analysis also to rely on a passage from *Selangor*, *supra*, which is characteristic of the second approach, discussed below.

Barnes v. Addy was also followed in *Scott v. Riehl* (1958), 15 D.L.R. (2d) 67 (B.C.S.C.). In that case, the two defendants were the directors of a construction company. The directors had failed to comply with the provisions of the *Mechanics' Lien Act, 1956*, S.B.C. 1956, c. 27, requiring certain monies to be held in trust. All monies received were deposited into one bank account, which was always overdrawn. The director and president of the corporation, Riehl, "knew that monies deposited, such as those received from the plaintiffs, must [not] be used for the general purposes of the company in abuse of the trust created by s. 3 of the Act. He knowingly created, maintained and operated this unlawful system. The company was the instrument of its operation, but he was the director" (p. 70). Wilson J. (as he then was) concluded at pp. 73-74 as follows:

> ... on the facts here Riehl, as agent received and misdirected trust funds. The acts of reception and application of these particular monies may not physically have been his, but they were entirely directed by him, with the possible, although not proven, collusion of the defendant Schumak. Riehl received a benefit, through the payment

of his salary out of the account into which these trust funds were paid. His complicity in the misappropriation of these funds is proven; it was not an act of negligence or a mistake of judgment but a wrongful act knowingly done. In these circumstances not only the principal but the agent is liable.

I have not ignored the numerous cases cited to me by defence counsel in which it has been held that directors are not personally responsible to strangers for acts done by them on behalf of the company but are at most responsible to the company. I only say that none of these cases goes so far as to say that where a fraudulent breach of trust known by the director to be fraudulent, is done by the company at his direction, so that he is not only a party to but the instigator of the fraudulent breach of trust and benefits from the breach of trust he is not to be held liable.

...

There is, however, a second line of Canadian authority, holding that a person who is the controlling or directing mind of a corporate trustee can be liable for an innocent or negligent breach of trust if the person knowingly assisted in the breach of trust. That is, in these cases, proof of fraud and dishonesty has not been required. ...

...

The modified standard found in many of the Canadian cases involving directors of a closely held corporation reflects a difficulty with the application of the strict *Barnes v. Addy* standard to cases in which the corporate trustee is actually controlled by the stranger to the trust. In *Barnes v. Addy*, Lord Selborne L.C., at p. 252, expressed concerns regarding the imposition of liability on strangers to the trust in the absence of participation in a fraudulent and dishonest design: "those who create trusts do expressly intend, in the absence of fraud and dishonesty, to exonerate such agents of all classes from the responsibilities which are expressly incumbent, by reason of the fiduciary relation, upon the trustees". Later in his reasons, Lord Selborne L.C. reiterated this position at p. 253: "if we were to hold that [a solicitor] became a constructive trustee by the preparation of such a deed, ... not having enabled any one, who otherwise might not have had the power, to commit a breach of trust, we should be acting ... without authority. ... ".

Generally, there are good reasons for requiring participation in a <u>fraudulent and dishonest</u> breach of trust before imposing liability on agents of the trustees:

Unlike the stranger who takes title, an agent who disposes of trust property has no choice in the matter. He is contractually bound to act as directed by his principal the trustee. It is one thing to tell an agent that he must breach his contract rather than participate in a fraud on the part of his principal. It is quite another to tell him that he must breach his contract any time he believes his principal's instructions are contrary to the terms of the trust. This is to tell the agent that he must first of all master the terms of his principal's undertaking and, secondly, enforce his own understanding of what that undertaking entails. In effect, it burdens him with the duties of trusteeship upon the mere receipt of trust property as agent. As we have seen, however, properly understood, the role of agent is distinct from that of trustee. An agent is not to be made a trustee *de son tort* unless he voluntarily repudiates the role of agent and takes on the job of a trustee. So long as he chooses to remain an agent, his loyalties are to his principal, the trustee, and he should be free to follow the latter's instructions short of participating in a fraud.

Ruth Sullivan, "Strangers to the Trust", [1986] *Est. & Tr. Q.* 217, p. 246.

It must be remembered that it is the nature of the breach of trust that is under consideration at this point in the analysis, rather than the intent or knowledge of the stranger to the trust. That is, the issue here is whether the breach of trust was fraudulent and dishonest, not whether the appellant's actions should be so characterized. *Barnes v. Addy* clearly states that the stranger will be liable if he or she knowingly assisted the <u>trustee</u> in a fraudulent and dishonest breach of trust. Therefore, it is the corporation's actions which must be examined. The appellant's actions will also be relevant to this examination, given the extent to which M & L was controlled by the defendant directors. The appellant's conduct will be more directly scrutinized when the issue of knowledge is under consideration. It is unnecessary, therefore, to find that the appellant himself acted in bad faith or dishonestly.

Where the trustee is a corporation, rather than an individual, the inquiry as to whether the breach of trust was dishonest and fraudulent may be more difficult to conceptualize, because the corporation can only act through human agents who are often the strangers to the trust whose liability is in issue. ... I would therefore "take as a relevant description of fraud 'the taking of a risk to the prejudice of another's rights, which risk is known to be one which there is no right to take'". In my opinion, this standard best accords with the basic rationale for the imposition of personal liability on a stranger to a trust which was enunciated in *In re Montagu's Settlement Trusts, supra,* namely, whether the stranger's conscience is sufficiently affected to justify the imposition of personal liability. In that respect, the taking of a knowingly wrongful risk resulting in prejudice to the beneficiary is sufficient to ground personal liability. This approach is consistent with both lines of authority previously discussed.

In the instant case, as a party to the contract between itself and the respondent, M & L knew that the Air Canada monies were held in trust for the respondent, and were not for the general use of M & L. Trust accounts were set up by M & L in 1978, but never used. M & L also knew that any positive balance in its general account was subject to the Bank's demand. By placing the trust monies in the general account which were then subject to seizure by the Bank, M & L took a risk to the prejudice of the rights of the respondent beneficiary, Air Canada, which risk was known to be one which there was no right to take. ... Therefore, the breach of trust by M & L was dishonest and fraudulent from an equitable standpoint.

It is clear that the appellant participated or assisted in the breach of trust. ... [T]he appellant dealt with the funds in question: in particular, he stopped payment on all cheques, and then opened a trust account and attempted to withdraw the stop payment orders and to transfer the funds into the new trust account in order to pay the respondent. The breach of trust was directly caused by the conduct of the defendant directors. As Griffiths J.A. observed, at p. 204, "[t]he movement of these directors, acting solely in their own interest to stop payment on cheques, not only prevented payment on cheques issued to Air Canada, but precipitated the seizure by the bank of the only funds available in the unprotected general account". In such circumstances, the directors are personally liable for the breach of trust as constructive trustees provided that the requisite knowledge on the part of the directors is proved.

With respect to the knowledge requirement, this will not generally be a difficult hurdle to overcome in cases involving directors of closely held corporations. Such directors, if active, usually have knowledge of all of the actions of the corporate trustee. In the instant case, the analysis is somewhat more difficult to resolve, as the appellant was not as closely involved with the day-to-day operations as was the other director, Martin. However, the appellant knew of the terms of the agreement between M & L and the respondent airline, as he signed that agreement. The appellant also knew that the trust funds were being deposited in the general bank account, which was subject to the demand loan from the Bank. This constitutes actual knowledge of the breach of trust. That is, even if the appellant could argue that he had no subjective knowledge of the breach of trust, given the facts of which he did have subjective knowledge, he was wilfully blind to the breach, or reckless in his failure to realize that there was a breach. Furthermore, the appellant received a benefit from the breach of trust, in that his personal liability to the Bank on the operating line of credit was extinguished. Therefore, he knowingly and directly participated in the breach of trust, and is personally liable to the respondent airline for that breach.

V. Disposition

For the foregoing reasons, I would therefore dismiss the appeal with costs.

The following are the reasons delivered by

McLachlin J.: — I agree with Justice Iacobucci that the relationship between the corporation and Air Canada was one of trust, not debtor and creditor. I also agree with his proposed disposition of the appeal. In my view, whatever view one adopts on the difficult issues discussed by my colleague, the appellant is clearly liable as a constructive trustee for the breach of trust which the corporation committed respecting Air Canada's account.

There is no debate on the first requirement for imposition of personal liability on a stranger to a trust: knowing participation in the breach. The next question is whether the required knowledge is subjective knowledge (i.e., actual knowledge of the breach or wilful blindness and recklessness) or objectively determined knowledge (what a reasonably diligent person would have known). Courts have divided on this issue. The courts in England require subjective knowledge. However, certain appellate courts in Canada have suggested that a subjectively determined standard of knowledge is not appropriate in the trust context, even for a stranger to the trust, and that where a stranger should reasonably have known that the trust was being breached by his or her actions, there may be circumstances where liability is appropriate. ... In this case, as my colleague points out, the evidence meets the higher English standard of subjective knowledge, given that the appellant was wilfully blind. Accordingly, it is not necessary to decide whether in some cases, an objective test might suffice. That is a difficult and important question which I would prefer to leave to a case in which it squarely arises.

The second issue is the nature of the breach which can give rise to liability. Must it be fraudulent and dishonest, or does any breach suffice? Again, the authorities are divided; as Iacobucci J. discusses, a number of Canadian courts do not adopt the dominant English view that the breach must be fraudulent and dishonest: *Horsman Bros. Holdings Ltd. v. Panton & Panton*, [1976] 3 W.W.R. 745; *Trilec Installations Ltd. v. Bastion Construction Ltd.* (1982), 135 D.L.R. (3d) 766; *Andrea Schmidt Construction Ltd. v. Glatt* (1979), 25 O.R. (2d) 567 (H.C.). Again, it is not necessary to resolve the issue in this case, since here the breach was fraudulent and dishonest in the sense discussed by my colleague of involving a risk to the property to the prejudice of the beneficiary. Given the importance and difficulty of the question, I would prefer to leave it to a case where it squarely arises.

A final matter is the effect, if any, of the fact that the appellant benefitted personally from the breach. In some Canadian cases, this has been cited as a circumstance in favour of imposing liability on the stranger to the trust: see *Scott v. Riehl* (1958), 15 D.L.R. (2d) 67; *Henry Electric Ltd.*, *supra*, and *Andrea*

Schmidt Construction Ltd., *supra*. My colleague cites it as relevant to establishing actual knowledge of the breach, and refers to it as a factor in his conclusion that the appellant is liable. Given that this factor is present in this case, it is not necessary to decide whether liability could be imposed in the absence of personal benefit. My colleague, I hasten to add, does not himself venture on this question.

While I agree with Iacobucci J. that on the facts here, liability is clearly made out, I would prefer to leave consideration of the questions to which I have referred to future cases in which they directly arise.

I would dismiss the appeal.

Appeal dismissed with costs.

NOTES

In *Royal Brunei Airlines Sdn. Bhd. v. Tan Kok Ming*, [1995] A.C. 378, 3 W.L.R. 64 (P.C.), the Judicial Committee of the Privy Council was faced with an almost identical set of facts as in *M & L Travel*. It held that there could be third-party liability for assisting in a breach, even if the trustee was innocent in breaching the trust. What mattered was the conduct of the third party. On that point, the Judicial Committee rejected the traditional options of "actual knowledge" or "negligence", and said that what was required was "objective dishonesty".

In these cases, as in inducing breach of contract, the individuals are alleged to have been involved in some wrongdoing by the corporation. As in those cases, the liability is premised on the involvement of two persons: a primary wrongdoer and an inducer or assister. How is it decided that the directors, sued for assisting in a corporate breach of trust, were acting as individuals? In *Air Canada*, Iacobucci J. said:

Although involving a corporation, the case falls to be resolved trust principles, and does not raise general questions of the personal liability of directors for the acts of the corporation.

Contrast this with the findings in *Royal Brunei*, where Mr. Tan was the controlling shareholder and director of the corporate trustee, BLT. In that case, Lord Mustill said for the Board:

Set out in these bald terms, Mr. Tan's conduct was dishonest. By the same token, and for good measure, BLT also acted dishonestly. Mr. Tan was the company, and his state of mind is to be imputed to the company.

In some situations, plaintiffs who have sought to circumvent the concept of corporate personality have attempted not just one of the possibilities canvassed thus far, but a combination of them. One such case is reproduced below.

TRANSAMERICA LIFE INSURANCE CO. OF CANADA v. CANADA LIFE ASSURANCE CO.

(1996), 28 O.R. (3d) 423 (Gen. Div.)

Sharpe J.: — ... In the period 1983 to 1989, the plaintiff, Transamerica Life Insurance Company of Canada, made 54 mortgage loans which were arranged by the defendant Canada Life Mortgage Services Ltd. ("C.L.M.S".). A number of the mortgages have fallen into default, resulting in an alleged loss of some $60 million. Transamerica assets that C.L.M.S. owed it a duty to do the underwriting (due diligence, risk assessment and analysis) for these loans, that C.L.M.S. failed in that regard, and that Transamerica has suffered loss as a consequence. In its claim against C.L.M.S., Transamerica pleads breach of contract, breach of fiduciary duty, fraud, misrepresentation, and negligence. C.L.M.S. denies that it owed Transamerica any duty to underwrite the loans, asserts that it acted throughout simply as a mortgage broker, and contends that it was for Transamerica to do its own underwriting and due diligence with respect to the loans in question.

C.L.M.S. is the wholly owned subsidiary of the Canada Life Assurance Company. Transamerica asserts that Canada Life is liable for the wrongs of C.L.M.S. on a variety of grounds and has joined Canada Life as a defendant to this lawsuit. Canada Life asserts that it had nothing to do with the mortgages in question and that there is no basis for the claim that it is legally responsible for the alleged wrongs of its wholly owned subsidiary, C.L.M.S. Canada Life brings this motion for summary judgment on the grounds that Transamerica had failed to show that there is a triable issue as to Canada Life's liability and asks that the action against it be dismissed.

ISSUES

Transamerica bases its claim against Canada Life on three grounds which, it asserts, permit the court to look behind the separate corporate existence of C.L.M.S. and attach liability to its sole shareholder, Canada Life. These assertions give rise to the following issues on this motion for summary judgment.

1. Is there a basis for "piercing the corporate veil" and holding Canada Life liable for the acts of its wholly owned subsidiary, C.L.M.S.?

2. Is there a basis for holding Canada Life liable as an accessory to a breach of fiduciary duty by C.L.M.S.?

3. Is there a basis for holding Canada Life liable for the alleged misrepresentations of C.L.M.S. either at common law or under the *Competition Act*, R.S.C. 1985, c. C-34?

[Note: Only the discussion relating to the first two issues is reproduced.]

...

C.L.M.S. was incorporated in 1974 to carry on business as a mortgage correspondent and general financial agent. Before the creation of C.L.M.S., Canada Life had regularly invested in mortgages originated by its branch offices. The branches produced more mortgage investment opportunities than Canada Life could handle and Canada Life decided to incorporate C.L.M.S. to carry on the business of mortgage correspondent and to deal with both Canada Life and other institutional investors. As C.L.M.S. was to be a wholly owned subsidiary, governing legislation required Canada Life to obtain the consent of the Department of Insurance, now Office of the Superintendent of Financial Institutions ("O.F.S.I".), to its incorporation. The Department of Insurance was satisfied that the proposed business of C.L.M.S. was ancillary to the business of insurance as required by s. 65 of the *Canadian and British Insurance Companies Act*, R.S.C. 1985, c. I-12. ...

...

In March 1981, Transamerica and C.L.M.S. established a "Master Agreement" to govern their relationship, and in the period prior to 1989, Transamerica invested in 54 mortgages originated by C.L.M.S. pursuant to this agreement. The terms of this agreement do not specifically provide that C.L.M.S. is to perform any underwriting function on Transamerica's behalf. C.L.M.S. takes the position that the agreement excludes this duty and asserts that it does not engage in the business of underwriting mortgage loan proposals for any lender. C.L.M.S. has an agreement with Canada Life in terms virtually identical to the Transamerica agreement and Canada Life does its own due diligence, review and risk assessment. ...

The relationship between C.L.M.S. and Canada Life is as follows. C.L.M.S. has its own head office and branch offices distinct from those of Canada Life. C.L.M.S. has its own bank accounts. It is and was managed and operated independently of Canada Life. C.L.M.S. management exercises independent discretion in conducting the business of C.L.M.S. Apart from the president, the senior management of C.L.M.S. is independent of Canada Life. Two vice-presidents have overall responsibility for the affairs of C.L.M.S. The president of C.L.M.S. is a Canada Life employee. He spends a very small percentage of his time on C.L.M.S. business and he plays no role in the day-to-day management of C.L.M.S. While his salary is paid by Canada Life, the portion of it attributable to the time he spends on C.L.M.S. business is charged back to C.L.M.S. Canada Life does provide C.L.M.S. with certain administrative services, including payroll, salary records and legal services. The cost of these services is billed to C.L.M.S. by Canada Life, and responsibility for hiring, promotion and remuneration of C.L.M.S. employees remains that of C.L.M.S. management. All members of the C.L.M.S. board of directors and the president of C.L.M.S. are senior executives of Canada Life.

Canada Life and C.L.M.S. take the position that the exigencies of the market required there to be an arm's-length relationship between the two companies. They contend that prospective lenders, including Transamerica, were concerned that Canada Life would be in a favoured position and "cherry-pick" the best investments, and for that reason C.L.M.S. was operated as a business entirely separate and independent of Canada Life.

...

There is no evidence, subject to what follows relating to certain meetings in 1989, that Mr. Fleming [the President and Chairman of the Board of C.L.M.S. from 1984 to 1994] or any other Canada Life officer or employee were involved in any way in the dealings between C.L.M.S. and Transamerica. The relationship between C.L.M.S. and Transamerica was not discussed by the Board of Directors of C.L.M.S. Apart from six letters from the legal department of Canada Life, acting in the capacity of solicitors for C.L.M.S., there is no evidence of any communication whatsoever between Canada Life and Transamerica in relation to the transactions at issue in this suit prior to the initiation of proceedings.

... Fleming's involvement prior to the initiation of proceedings was as follows. In 1989, senior officers from Transamerica's parent came to Toronto to conduct a review of the mortgage investment practices and procedures of Transamerica. ... For the purposes of this motion, Transamerica argues that there is evidence that Fleming became aware of the review and that his failure to set the record straight as to the nature of the service being provided by C.L.M.S. to Transamerica is sufficient to fix liability on Canada Life. The only evidence of Fleming's awareness is as follows. The defendants have produced an extract from a minute of a C.L.M.S. management meeting of June 28, 1989, of Fleming, and the two vice-presidents, Curtin and Deegan:

> Mr. Fleming was advised of a visit from the Senior Vice-President of Transamerica who was conducting an "underwriting audit" of their mortgage dealings in Canada. Attending the meetings were Joseph Barbieri, Bob Clarke and myself.
>
> Transamerica was interested in mortgage financing in Canada and their questions were mainly directed to types of financings, building construction, appraisals, etc. There was no criticism of our services either from the branch or head office.

Transamerica takes the position that this is sufficient to fix Fleming, and through Fleming, Canada Life, with knowledge of the breach of contract, breach of fiduciary duty, and misrepresentations alleged against C.L.M.S. In my view, this assertion reads far more into the minute than is warranted by the minute itself and by the balance of the evidence surrounding the meetings of the visiting Transamerica executives. Fleming denies that he was told that Transamerica thought that C.L.M.S. was doing the underwriting. ... He agreed that if he had been made aware that Transamerica was operating under the mistaken impression that C.L.M.S. was doing the underwriting for the loans, he would have instructed the C.L.M.S. staff to set the matter straight, but the information he was given did not convey that information.

ANALYSIS

1. *Is there a basis for "piercing the corporate veil" and holding Canada Life liable for the acts of its wholly owned subsidiary, C.L.M.S.?*

On behalf of Transamerica, Mr. Bates submits that the applicable legal test for piercing the corporate veil can be stated no more precisely than this: the corporate veil will be pierced when it is "just and equitable" to do so. As authority for that proposition, reliance is placed on the following passage from the judgment of Wilson J. in *Constitution Insurance Co. of Canada v. Kosmopoulos*, [1987] 1 S.C.R. 2 at pp. 10-11, 34 D.L.R. (4th) 208:

> As a general rule a corporation is a legal entity distinct from its shareholders: *Salomon v. Salomon & Co.* [1897] A.C. 22 (H.L.). The law on when a court may disregard this principle by "lifting the corporate veil" and regarding the company as a mere "agent" or "puppet" of its controlling shareholder of parent corporation follows no consistent principle. The best that can be said is that the "separate entities" principle is not enforced when it would yield a result "too flagrantly opposed to justice, convenience or the interests of the Revenue": L.C.B. Gower, *Modern Company Law* (4th ed. 1979) at p. 112. I have no doubt that theoretically the veil could be lifted in this case to do justice ... But a number of factors lead me to think it would be unwise to do so.

If accepted, the argument advanced by Transamerica would represent a significant departure from the principle established in *Salomon v. Salomon & Co.*, [1897] A.C. 22 at p. 51, [1895-9] All E.R. Rep 33 (H.L.), *per* Lord Macnaghten:

> The company is at law a different person altogether from the subscribers to the memorandum; and, though it may be that after incorporation the business is precisely the same as it was before, and the same persons are managers, and the same hands receive the profits, the company is not in law the agent of the

subscribers or trustee for them. Nor are the subscribers as members liable, in any shape or form, except to the extent and in the manner provided by the Act.

In my view, the argument advance by Transamerica reads far too much into a dictum plainly not intended to constitute an in-depth analysis of an important area of the law or to reverse a legal principle which, for almost 100 years, has served as a cornerstone of corporate law.

It was conceded in argument that no case since *Kosmopoulos* has applied the preferred "just and equitable" test. In *Kosmopoulos* itself, the Supreme Court, including Wilson J., rejected the submission that the corporate veil be lifted. Moreover, it will be noted that Wilson J. does not use the phrase "just and equitable" but rather quotes a passage from an English text which describes the test in much more stringent terms.

Two recent judgments of this court have refused to read the *Kosmopoulos* decision as granting *carte blanche* to life the corporate veil absent fraudulent or improper conduct: *W.D. Latimer Co. v. Dijon Investments Ltd.* (1992), 12 O.R. (3d) 415; *801962 Ontario Inc. v. MacKenzie Trust Co.*, [1994] O.J. No. 2015. In the *MacKenzie* case, Spence J. reviewed the case-law in detail and concluded:

> These decisions do not support a claim that the test in *Salomon v. Salomon* has been superseded by a new "business entity" or "single business entity" test. They merely illustrate the principle that, in particular fact situations, where the nature of the legal issue in dispute makes it appropriate to have regard to the larger business entity, the court is not precluded by *Salomon v. Salomon* from doing so. In a few cases, there are statements that the court will lift the corporate veil "where injustice would otherwise result". I am not able to conclude that such statements are intended to remove the authority of the *Salomon* principle. I think they may be more in the nature of a shorthand formulation reflecting the approach of the courts in the cases discussed above.

The proposition that the dictum of Wilson J. in *Kosmopoulos* suggests a fundamental shift in the law was also rejected by the British Columbia Court of Appeal in *B.G. Preeco I (Pacific Coast) Ltd. v. Bon Street Developments Ltd.* (1989), 37 B.C.L.R. (2d) 258, 60 D.L.R. (4th) 30. Seaton J.A. observed (at p. 267) that the passage quoted in *Kosmopoulos* (at p. 138) from Gower, *Modern Company Law*, 4th ed. (1979), concluded with a passage which disapproved of the free-wheeling "just and equitable" approach:

> The most that can be said is that the courts' policy is to lift the veil if they think that justice demands it and they are not constrained by contrary binding authority. The results in individual cases may be commendable, but it smacks of palm-tree justice rather than the application of legal rules.

...

It should also be noted that the most recent edition of Gower, *Modern Company Law*, 5th ed. (1992) puts the test for lifting the corporate veil in much more stringent terms. The authors review the decision of the English Court of Appeal in *Adams v. Cape Industries plc*, [1991] 1 All E.R. 433, which, they state (at p. 125) "subjected lifting the corporate veil to the most exhaustive treatment that it has yet received in the English (or Scottish) courts". The authors conclude that the *Adams* decision significantly attenuates the grounds for lifting the veil, and they make no suggestion, as they did in the earlier edition cited in *Kosmopoulos*, that the test is anything like a "just and equitable standard" (at pp. 132-33):

There seem to be three circumstances only in which the courts can do so. These are:

(1) When the court is construing a statute, contract or other document.

(2) When the court is satisfied that a company is a "mere façade" concealing the true facts.

(3) When it can be established that the company is an authorized agent of its controllers or its members, corporate or human.

In a recent judgment of the Ontario Court of Appeal, *Gregorio v. Intrans-Corp.* (1994), 18 O.R. (3d) 527 at p. 536, 115 D.L.R. (4th) 200, Laskin J.A. restated the legal principles relating to the liability of a parent company for the acts of its subsidiary as follows:

> Generally, a subsidiary, even a wholly owned subsidiary, will not be found to be the alter ego of its parent unless the subsidiary is under the complete control of the parent and is nothing more than a conduit used by the parent to avoid liability. The alter ego principle is applied to prevent conduct akin to fraud that would otherwise unjustly deprive claimants of their rights.

There are undoubtedly situations where justice requires that the corporate veil be lifted. The cases and authorities already cited indicated that it will be difficult to define precisely when the corporate veil is to be lifted, but that lack of a precise test does not mean that a court is free to act as it pleases on some loosely defined "just and equitable" standard. There may be a principal-agent relationship between two related corporations which leads to liability despite separate legal personalities: see Gower, *supra*; *Clarkson Co. v. Zhelka*, [1967] 2 O.R. 565 at p. 578, 64 D.L.R. (2d) 457 (H.C.J.). It is also the case that the courts will look behind corporate structures where necessary to give effect to legislation, especially taxation statutes: see Gower, *supra*; *Jodrey's Estate v. Nova Scotia*, [1980] 2 S.C.R. 774, 41 N.S.R. (2d) 181. Neither of these two exceptions applies to the situation of the case at bar

As just indicated, the courts will disregard the separate legal personality of a corporate entity where it is completely dominated and controlled and being used as a shield for fraudulent or improper conduct. The first element "complete control", requires more than ownership. It must be shown that there is complete domination and that the subsidiary company does not, in fact, function independently ... The evidence before me indicates that the relationship between Canada Life and C.L.M.S. was that of a typical parent and subsidiary. While C.L.M.S. is wholly owned by Canada Life and its board of directors is comprised of Canada Life executives, I have found that it does have an independent management and conducts a business separate and distinct from that of its parent. There is, in my opinion, no evidence sufficient to give rise to a triable issue that C.L.M.S. is the mere puppet of Canada Life.

The second element refers to the nature of the conduct: is there "conduct akin to fraud that would otherwise unjustly deprive claimants of their rights"? In my view, while Transamerica has alleged fraud against C.L.M.S., there is no evidence to suggest that Canada Life has any involvement in that alleged fraud, apart from the fact that C.L.M.S. is its wholly owned subsidiary. ...

2. Is there a basis for holding Canada Life liable as an accessory to a breach of fiduciary duty by C.L.M.S.?

In my view, Transamerica has failed to demonstrate that there is a triable issue on the claim that Canada Life is liable as an accessory to a breach of fiduciary duty.

This area of the law was canvassed at length in the recent decision of the Supreme Court of Canada, *Air Canada v. M & L Travel Ltd.*, [1993] 3 S.C.R. 787, 108 D.L.R. (4th) 592. That case affirms the principle that a stranger to a trust may become personally liable for a breach of trust committed by the trustee. ... On the surface, this is analogous to the case at bar where Transamerica alleges that Canada Life should be held to account for a breach of fiduciary duty committed by its wholly owned subsidiary, C.L.M.S. However, it should be noted that in the *Air Canada* case, the directors were directly and personally involved in the misappropriation of trust funds. The Supreme Court of Canada found that to support a claim against an accessory, the plaintiff must show a breach of trust of a fraudulent or dishonest nature. An innocent breach of trust will not suffice. The opinion of Iacobucci J. also makes it clear that the stranger to the trust must be involved in the breach with actual knowledge, recklessness or wilful blindness. Iacobucci J. expressly excludes the possibility of liability on the basis of constructive knowledge. ...

The information conveyed to Fleming in relation to the visit from the senior executives of Transamerica's parent in 1989 falls well short of evidence capable of grounding a triable issue on this point. ... It is apparent that this argument amounts to an attempt to overcome the limitation of liability created by the separate corporate existence of Canada Life and C.L.M.S. It is also apparent from the *Air Canada* case ... that without proof of knowing involvement in the breach of trust, the law does not impose equitable liability simply on the basis that the targeted defendant is the owner of the corporate entity which committed the equitable wrong.

...

CONCLUSION

For the foregoing reasons, I conclude that the moving party, Canada Life, has met the onus of demonstrating that there is no genuine issue for trial. ...

Motion granted.

(c) The Particular Problem of Thin Capitalization

Some countries have substantial minimum capitalization requirements for setting up new corporations. Essentially, such rules require that a specified amount of cash or property valued at that amount be given to the corporation in exchange for shares as a condition of the state's creating the new corporate entity. Minimum capitalization requirements have not been a part of the Canadian (or American, or English) corporate tradition: it is quite possible, and not at all uncommon, for new corporations to go into business having issued, for example, one share for one dollar. This can cause problems.

"Thin capitalization" is the term used to describe any situation in which a corporation is *initially set up* with an abnormally high "debt to equity ratio". In simple terms this means that most of the capital the corporation has to deal with is borrowed, rather than being invested by shareholders. What is an acceptable debt to equity ratio will vary widely with the type of business. However, the important fact to remember is that capital advanced to the corporation by way of loan will normally be secured and the lender will rank ahead of trade creditors in an insolvency situation. Shareholders will rank behind unsecured creditors. Thus, as in *Salomon* itself, one cannot determine a company's credit reliability without researching its capitalization structure, or perhaps obtaining a credit rating from an agency or financial institution. For those who deal with the corporation in terms of long-term financing contracts involving large sums of money, such a preliminary check will be a normal business practice. A casual trader extending minor trade credit or an employee contributing his labour in exchange for the promise of twice-monthly paycheques cannot be expected to take such elaborate precautions with every new corporation he encounters.

Separate corporate entities often are set up, perhaps for tax reasons, to handle each different business in which an individual dabbles. Often these corporations will be set up with virtually no working capital. Larger firms, when dealing with such corporations, commonly demand collateral contracts of guarantee with the majority shareholder. But what of the smaller firms which may not have enough bargaining power to demand such guarantees? This leads to the question as to whether thin capitalization, in and of itself, will suffice to entitle a court to ignore the corporate entity and strike at the incorporators.

What would be the rationale for such a finding? Robert Zimet has suggested that "the failure of the owners of the corporation to adequately capitalize the venture is indicative of their desire to enjoy the benefits of limited liability without paying for it with adequate capitalization. Equitably then, the court will not permit the owners to enjoy their ill-gotten immunity". See (1973), 23 Am. U. L. Rev. 208, at p. 216. Nevertheless, Zimet acknowledges that "the extent to which 'under capitalization' in and of itself might function as the sole ground for disregarding the corporate entity has been questioned".

WALKOVSZKY v. CARLTON

18 N.Y.2d 414, 223 N.E.2d 6 (Ct. App. 1966)

Fuld J.: — This case involves what appears to be a rather common practice in the taxicab industry of vesting the ownership of a taxi fleet in many corporations, each owning only one or two cabs.

The complaint alleges that the plaintiff was severely injured four years ago in New York City when he was run down by a taxicab owned by the defendant Seon Cab Corporation and negligently operated at the time by the defendant Marchese. The individual defendant, Carlton, is claimed to be a stockholder of 10 corporations, including Seon, each of which has but two cabs registered in its name, and it is implied that only the minimum automobile liability insurance required by law (in the amount of $10,000) is carried on any one cab. Although seemingly independent of one another, these corporations are alleged to be "operated … as a single entity, unit and enterprise" with regard to financing, supplies, repairs, employees and garaging, and all are named as defendants. The plaintiff asserts that he is also entitled to hold their stockholders personally liable for the damages sought because the multiple corporate structure constitutes an unlawful attempt "to defraud members of the general public" who might be injured by the cabs.

The defendant Carlton his moved … to dismiss the complaint on the ground that as to him it "fails to state a cause of action". The court at Special Term granted the motion but the Appellate Division, by a divided vote, reversed, holding that a valid cause of action was sufficiently stated. The defendant Carlton appeals to us, from the non-final order, by leave of the Appellate Division on a certified question.

The law permits the incorporation of a business for the very purpose of enabling its proprietors to escape personal liability but, manifestly, the privilege is not without its limits. Broadly speaking, the courts will disregard the corporate form, or, to use accepted terminology, "pierce the corporate veil", whenever necessary "to prevent fraud or to achieve equity". In determining whether liability should be extended to reach assets beyond those belonging to the corporation, we are guided, as Judge Cardozo noted, by "general rules of agency". (*Berkey v. Third Ave. Ry. Co.* 84, 95, 155 N.E. 58, 61, 50 A.L.R. 599). In other words, whenever anyone uses control of the corporation to further his own rather than the corporation's business, he will be liable for the corporation's acts "upon the principle of *respondent superior* applicable even where the agent is a natural person". Such liability, moreover, extends not only to the corporation's commercial dealings but to its negligent acts as well.

In the *Mangan* case (247 App. Div. 853, 286 N.Y.S. 666, mot. for lv. to app. den. 272 N.Y. 676, 286 N.Y.S. 666 supra) the plaintiff was injured as a result of the negligent operation of a cab owned and operated by one of four corporations affiliated with the defendant Terminal. Although the defendant was not a stockholder of any of the operating companies, both the defendant and the operating companies were owned, for the most part, by the same parties. The defendant's name (Terminal) was conspicuously displayed on the sides of all of the taxis used in the enterprise and, in point of fact, the defendant actually serviced, inspected, repaired and dispatched them. These facts were deemed to provide sufficient cause for piercing the corporate veil of the operating company — the nominal owner of the cab which injured the plaintiff — and holding the defendant liable. The operating companies were simply instrumentalities for carrying on the business of the defendant without imposing upon it financial and other liabilities incident to the actual ownership and operation of the cabs.

In the case before us, the plaintiff has explicitly alleged that none of the corporations "had a separate existence of their own" and, as indicated above, all are named as defendants. However, it is one thing to assert that a corporation is a fragment of a larger corporate combine which actually conducts the business. (See Berle, The Theory of Enterprise Entity, 47 Col. L. Rev. 343, 348-350.) It is quite another to claim that the corporation is a "dummy" for its individual stockholders who are in reality carrying on the business in their personal capacities for purely personal rather than corporate ends. Either circumstance would justify treating the corporation as an agent and piercing the corporate veil to reach the principal but a different result would follow in each case. In the first, only a larger corporate entity would be held financially responsible ... while, in the other the stockholder would be personally liable. ... Either the stockholder is conducting the business in his individual capacity or he is not. If he is, he will be liable; if he is not, then, it does not matter — insofar as his personal liability is concerned — that the enterprise is actually being carried on by a larger "enterprise entity".

At this stage in the present litigation we are concerned only with the pleadings and, since CPLR 3014 permits causes stated "alternatively or hypothetically" it is possible for the plaintiff to allege both theories as the basis for his demand for judgment. ... Reading the complaint in this case most favorably and liberally, we do not believe that there can be gathered from its averments the allegations required to spell out a valid cause of action against the defendant Carlton.

The individual defendant is charged with having "organized, managed, dominated and and controlled" a fragmented corporate entity but there are no allegations that he was conducting business in his individual capacity. Had the taxicab fleet been owned by a single corporation, it would be readily apparent that the plaintiff would face formidable barriers in attempting to establish personal liability on the part of the corporation's stockholders. The fact that the fleet ownership has been deliberately split up among many corporations does not ease the plaintiff's burden in that respect. The corporate form may not be disregarded merely because the assets of the corporation, together with the mandatory insurance coverage of the vehicle which struck the plaintiff, are insufficient to assure him the recovery sought. If Carlton were to be held individually liable on those facts alone, the decision would apply equally to the thousands of cabs which are owned by their individual drivers who conduct their businesses through corporations organized pursuant to section 401 of the Business Corporation Law, Consol. Laws, c. 4 and carry the minimum insurance required by subdivision 1 (par. [a]) of section 370 of the Vehicle and Traffic Law, Consol. Laws. c. 71. These taxi owner-operators are entitled to form such corporations, and we agree with the court at Special Term that, if the insurance coverage required by statute, is inadequate for the protection of the public, the remedy lies not with the courts but with the Legislature". It may very well be sound policy to require that certain corporations must take out liability insurance which will afford adequate compensation to their potential tort victims. However, the responsibility for imposing conditions on the privilege of incorporation has been committed by the Constitution to the Legislature (N. Y. Const. art. X. § 1) and it may not be fairly implied, from any statute, that the Legislature intended, without the slightest discussion or debate, to require of taxi corporations that they carry automobile liability insurance over and above that mandated dated by the Vehicle and Traffic Law.

This is not to say that it is impossible for the plaintiff to state a valid cause of action against the defendant Carlton. However, the simple fact is that the plaintiff has just not done so here. While the complaint alleges that the separate corporations were undercapitalized and that their assets have been intermingled, it is barren of any "sufficiently particular[ized] statements" that the defendant Carlton and his associates are actually doing business in their individual capacities, shuttling their personal funds in and out of the corporations "without regard to formality, and to suit their immediate convenience". Such a "perversion of the privilege to do business in a corporate form" (*Berkey v. Third Ave. Ry. Co.*, 244 58, 61, 50 A.L.R. 599, *supra*) would justify imposing personal liability on the individual stockholders. (See *African Metals Corp. v. Bullowa*, 288 N.Y. 78, 41 N. E. 2d 466, supra.) Nothing of the sort has in fact been charged, and it cannot reasonably or logically be inferred from the happenstance that the business of Seon Cab Corporation may actually be carried out by a larger corporate entity composed of many corporations which, under general principles of agency, would be liable to each other's creditors in contract and in tort.

In point of fact, the principle relied upon in the complaint to sustain the imposition of personal liability is not agency but fraud. Such a cause of action cannot withstand analysis. If it is not fraudulent for the owner-operator of a single cab corporation to take out only the minimum required liability insurance, the enterprise does not become either illicit or fraudulent merely because it consists of many such corporations. The plaintiff's injuries are the same regardless of whether the cab which strikes him is owned by a single corporation or part of a fleet with ownership fragmented among many corporations. Whatever rights he may be able to assert against parties other than the registered owner of the vehicle come into being not because he has been defrauded but because, under the principle of respondent superior, he is entitled to hold the whole enterprise responsible for the acts of its agents.

In sum, then, the complaint falls short of adequately stating a cause of action against the defendant Carlton in his individual capacity.

...

Keating J. (dissenting): —

... From their inception these corporations were intentionally undercapitalized for the purpose of avoiding responsibility for acts which were bound to arise as a result of the operation of a large taxi fleet having cars out on the street 24 hours a day and engaged in public transportation. And during the course of the corporations' existence all income was continually drained out of the corporations for the same purpose.

The issue presented by this action is whether the policy of this State, which affords those desiring to engage in a business enterprise the privilege of limited liability through the use of the corporate device, is so strong that it will permit that privilege to continue no matter how much it is abused, no matter how irresponsibly the corporation is operated, no matter what the cost to the public. I do not believe that it is.

Under the circumstances of this case the shareholders should all be held individually liable to this plaintiff for the injuries he suffered. At least the matter should not be disposed of on the pleadings by a dismissal of the complaint. "If a corporation is organized and carries on business without substantial capital in such a way that the corporation is likely to have no sufficient assets available to meet its debts, it is inequitable that the shareholders should set up such a flimsy organization to escape personal liability. The attempt to do corporate business without providing any sufficient basis of financial responsibility to creditors is an abuse of the separate entity and will be ineffectual to exempt the shareholders from corporate debts. It is coming to be recognized as the policy of law that shareholders should in good faith put at the risk of the business unencumbered capital reasonably adequate for its prospective liabilities. If capital is illusory or trifling compared with the business to be done and the risks of loss, this is a ground for denying the separate entity privilege". (Ballantine, Corporations [rev. ed., 1946], § 129, pp. 302-303).

In *Minton v. Cavaney*, 56 Cal. 2d 576, 15 Cal. Rptr. 641, 364 P.2d 473, the Supreme Court of California had occasion to discuss this problem in a negligence case. The corporation of which the defendant was an organizer, director and officer operated a public swimming pool. One afternoon the plaintiffs' daughter drowned in the pool as a result of the alleged negligence of the corporation.

Justice Roger Traynor, speaking for the court, outlined the applicable law in this area. "The figurative terminology 'alter ego' and 'disregard of the corporate entity' ", he wrote, "is generally used to refer to the various situations that are an abuse of the corporate privilege. ... The equitable owners of a corporation, for example, are personally liable when they treat the assets of the corporation as their own and add or withdraw capital from the corporation at will ...; when they hold themselves out as being personally liable for the debts of the corporation ...; *or when they provide inadequate capitalization and actively participate in the conduct of corporate affairs*". (56 Cal. 2d p. 579, 15 Cal. Rptr., p. 643, 364 P.2d p. 475; italics supplied.)

Examining the facts of the case in light of the legal principles just enumerated, he found that "[it was] undisputed that there was no attempt to provide adequate capitalization. [The corporation] never had any substantial assets. It leased the pool that it operated, and the lease was forfeited for failure to pay the rent. Its capital was 'trifling compared with the business to be done and the risks of loss'". (56 Cal. 2d, p. 580, 15 Cal. Rptr., p. 643, 364 P.2d p. 475.)

It seems obvious that one of "the risks of loss" referred to was the possibility of drownings due to the negligence of the corporation. And the defendant's failure to provide such assets or any fund for recovery resulted in his being held personally liable.

In *Anderson v. Abbott*, 321 U.S. 349, 64 S. Ct. 531, 88 L. Ed. 793, the defendant shareholders had organized a holding company and transferred to that company shares which they held in various national banks in return for shares in the holding company. The holding company did not have sufficient assets to meet the double liability requirements of the governing Federal statutes which provided that the owners of shares in national banks were personally liable for corporate obligations "to the extent of the amount of their stock therein, at the par value thereof, in addition to the amount invested in such shares" (U.S. Code, tit. 12, former § 63).

The court had found that these transfers were made in good faith, that other defendant shareholders who had purchased shares in the holding company had done so in good faith and that the organization of such a holding company was entirely legal. Despite this finding, the Supreme Court, speaking through Mr. Justice Douglas, pierced the corporate veil of the holding company and held all the shareholders, even those who had no part in the organization of the corporation, individually responsible for the corporate obligations as mandated by the statute.

"Limited liability", he wrote, "is the rule, not the exception; and on that assumption large undertakings are rested, vast enterprises are launched and huge sums of capital attracted. But there are occasions when the limited liability sought to be obtained through the corporation will be qualified or denied. Mr. Chief Judge Cardozo stated that a surrender of that principle of limited liability would be made when the sacrifice is so essential to the end that some accepted public policy may be defended or upheld". ... But they do not exhaust it. *An obvious inadequacy of capital, measured by the nature and magnitude of the corporate undertaking, has frequently been an important factor in cases denying stockholders their defense of limited liability. ... That rule has been invoked even in absence of a legislative policy which undercapitalization would defeat.* It become more important in a situation such as the present one where the statutory policy of double liability will be defeated if impecunious bank-stock holding companies are allowed to be interposed as non-conductors of liability. *It has often been held that the interposition of a corporation will not be allowed to defeat a legislative policy, whether that was the aim or only the result of the arrangement,* ... 'the courts will not permit themselves to be blinded or deceived by mere forms of law' but will deal 'with the substance of the transaction involved as if the corporate agency did not exist and as the justice of the case may require'". (321 U.S., pp. 362-363, 64 S. Ct. p. 537; emphasis added).

...

The defendant Carlton claims that, because the minimum amount of insurance required by the statute was obtained, the corporate veil cannot and should not be pierced despite the fact that the assets of the corporation which owned the cab were "trifling compared with the business to be done and the risks of loss" which were certain to be encountered. I do not agree.

The Legislature in requiring minimum liability insurance of $10,000, no doubt, intended to provide at least some small fund for recovery against those individuals and corporations who just did not have and were not able to raise or accumulate assets sufficient to satisfy the claims of those who were injured as a result of their negligence. It certainly could no have intended to shield those individuals who organized corporations, with the specific intent of avoiding responsibility to the public, where the operation of the corporate enterprise yielded profits sufficient to purchase additional insurance. ...

The defendant contends that a decision holding him personally liable would discourage people from engaging in corporate enterprise.

What I would merely hold is that a participating shareholder of a corporation vested with a public interest, organized with capital insufficient to meet liabilities which are certain to arise in the ordinary course of the corporation's business, may be held personally responsible for such liabilities. Where corporate income is not sufficient to cover the cost of insurance premiums above the statutory minimum or where initially adequate finances dwindle under the pressure of competition, bad times or extraordinary and unexpected liability, obviously the shareholder will not be held liable (Henn, Corporations, p. 208, n.7).

The only types of corporate enterprises that will be discouraged as a result of a decision allowing the individual shareholder to be sued will be those such as the one in question, designed solely to abuse the corporate privilege at the expense of the public interest.

For these reasons, I would vote to affirm the order of the Appellate Division.

QUESTIONS

Is the court's disposition of the *Walkovszky* case fair? Is fairness a material consideration here? Which of the judgments in this case do you think is more consistent with the reasoning likely to be adopted by Canadian courts?

NOTE

Part of the difficulty in sanctioning thin capitalization as a basis for piercing the corporate veil is that there is no consensus as to defining what constitutes adequate capitalization.

The question of whether there should be minimum capitalization requirements for the creation of a corporation can be seen as part of a larger question about the nature of corporations. Are they primarily creatures of private agreement, so that their characteristics should serve the needs of those who bring them into the world? Or, given their ability to affect other people, does everyone in society have an interest in the characteristics of corporations? See W.T. Allen, "Our Schizophrenic Conception of the Business Corporation" (1992), 14 Cardozo L.R. 261, and the symposium papers at (1989), 89 Columbia L.R. 1395-1774; see also L.E. Mitchell, "Groundwork of the Metaphysics of Corporate Law" (1993), 50 Wash. & Lee L. Rev. 1477-88 and the symposium papers at (1993), 50 Wash. & Lee L. Rev. 1373-1723. When you are reading the provisions of the C.B.C.A. or a provincial corporations statute, ask yourself whether the legislature has struck a good balance between the competing interests of those who create corporations and those who may later interact with them.

HENRY BROWNE & SONS LTD. v. SMITH

[1964] 2 Lloyd's Rep. 476 (Eng. Q.B.)

McNair J.: — ... The plaintiffs in this action are manufacturers and suppliers of a navigational device known as the "Sestrel-Owen" automatic helmsman, which, as the name indicates, is a device to enable a vessel to be steered without a man at the wheel by some magnetic automatic steering mechanism. In May, 1962, they supplied and fitted such an apparatus to the motor yacht Diahla, an ocean cruiser ... at a cost, with certain extras, of £381 19s 6d. In this action, they seek to recover this sum — the amount of which is not in dispute — from the defendant, Mr. Robin Smith, by whom the order was in fact placed. The defence in summary is that the order so placed was placed for and on behalf of a limited company known by the name of Ocean Charters Ltd., a private company with an authorized capital of 3,000 £1 shares of which two only have been issued. It was incorporated on Sept. 7, 1961, by the defendant Mr. Robin Smith, who is the sole director and with his wife holds the only two issues of shares.

It was submitted to me on behalf of the plaintiffs that, if the order was placed and accepted by the plaintiffs as an order on behalf of Ocean Charters Ltd., this company was a mere sham or a name under which Mr. Robin Smith traded, or alternatively, the order was placed by Ocean Charters Ltd., as agent for him, Mr. Robin Smith. Admittedly, there is a certain degree of artificiality in the whole position, since the only person who took part in the purchase on the customer's side was Mr. Robin Smith himself, who was, as already stated, responsible for the formation of the limited company and with his wife held the only two shares. It is well established that a limited company and its incorporators are distinct legal entities and it is only in very special circumstances that the difference between them can be disregarded. (See *Tunstall v. Steigmann,* [1962] 2 Q.B. 593.)

Oral evidence was called on behalf of the plaintiffs and a number of documents were referred to. No evidence was called on behalf of the defendant. The transaction started with a letter of Apr. 17, 1961, written by Mr. Dean, the commercial manager of the plaintiff company, by which certain information as to the automatic device together with an explanatory leaflet was sent to Mr. Smith personally. There was no reply to this letter and nothing further was heard of the matter by Mr. Dean until sometime in May, 1962, when he received a telephone message from Mr. Smith.

... Mr. Dean said: "There was no mention of the company, but he did say that he had an associate company and details would be sent to me of its name and address. He did not tell me in which connection the associate company was to be concerned". In cross-examination he agreed that he could not remember whether Mr. Smith said: "We are hoping" or "I am hoping" or "My yacht" or "Our yacht", and further in answer to me I think, he agreed that there was no purpose in Mr. Smith giving him the name and address of the company except as potential customers.

In due course, Mr. Diggens, the compass adjuster and engineer employed by the plaintiffs at their Barking depot, on instructions from his London office, was sent to Liverpool, where the yacht was lying, to meet Mr. Smith. His instructions were to meet Mr. Smith of Ocean Charters Ltd., this name having been apparently supplied by Mr. Smith after the telephone conversation with Mr. Dean. Mr. Diggens and Mr. Smith met at Liverpool and went down to the yacht, and between them an examination of the yacht was carried out; and the necessary particulars as to dimensions and type of steering gear were taken. In the course of this examination, Mr. Diggens handed to Mr. Smith a document in the form of a questionnaire, on which is stated: "To be completed and returned to: Henry Browne & Sons Ltd. [the plaintiffs]".

... The first question on this questionnaire is: "Customer's Name and Address" to which the answer is "Ocean Charters Limited 61, Bold St. Liverpool.1", telephone number "Royal 1042".

... According to the practice of the plaintiff company, this questionnaire, completed by the person placing the order, was accepted by the plaintiffs as the formal order.

... On July 31, 1962, the equipment was invoiced to Ocean Charters Ltd., at £381 19s 6d and no payment was made. A request for payment addressed to Ocean Charters Ltd. was repeated on Sept. 11, Oct. 3 and Oct. 16. On Nov. 5 the matter was placed in the hands of a debt collecting agency who again wrote to Ocean Charters Ltd., asking for payment, but no payment was made, and indeed, no reply was sent. On March 26, 1963, this action was commenced against Mr. Robin Smith personally, no reference being made in the statement of claim indorsed on the writ to Ocean Charters Ltd.

... On the facts so far stated, in my judgment it is clear beyond controversy that the principals to the contract were the plaintiffs, on the one hand, and Ocean Charters, Ltd. on the other, to who alone the plaintiffs were looking for payment. ...

As to the alternative contention that Ocean Charters, Ltd., were acting as agent for the defendant in placing the order, it is sufficient to say that there is no evidence at all to support this contention. ...

Judgment for defendant.

QUESTIONS

1. Is this case correctly decided?

2. Should it make any difference whether the corporation lacks funds because it was inadequately capitalized at the outset or because it has lost most of its capital in a bad business venture? What does "inadequately capitalized" mean? Was the corporation in the *Salomon* case adequately capitalized?

3. Should we be concerned about the effects of adequate corporate capitalization from a legal perspective? Should we be concerned about it from a broader, communitarian perspective? For the distinctions between these perspectives, contrast M. Friedman, "The Social Responsibility of Business is to Increase its Profits", N.Y. Times Magazine, 13 Sept. 1970 and L.E. Mitchell, "Groundwork of the Metaphysics of Corporate Law" (1993), 50 Wash. & Lee L. Rev. 1477-88.

4. Consider an alternative, *Henry Browne*-type setting. The yacht, newly fitted with its automatic steering device, is chartered from the corporation for a Sunday afternoon cruise. The steering device works perfectly. Unfortunately, the same cannot be said for the yachtsmen, who become abysmally drunk. One of them adjusts the steering device improperly, causing the yacht to run over two lovers out for a row. The lovers, in the

nature of well-advised tort victims, look around for deep pockets to sue. The manufacturer of the steering device is clearly free of liability, the chartering corporation has no money, and to make the story typical, the partygoers are all impecunious law students.

The only potential defendant with any money is Mr. Robin Smith, fresh from his successful defence in the contractual action. The victims from the rowboat sue him. Do they win? Clue: check the corporation's birthdate; to what type of person is the corporation most closely analogous; what type of person does that make Mr. Robin Smith? Describe the breach of duty alleged. Are parents liable in tort when their six-year-old children hit other children with bricks, because of their six-year-olds' (a) age; or (b) impecuniosity? Describe the extent of the injury suffered by the lovers as a result of the alleged breach of duty by Mr. Robin Smith. Is the cause of action the tort of thin capitalization, or is it something more traditional?

E. CORPORATE PURPOSE

What is the purpose or function of corporations? As we have seen, corporations provide a vehicle for investment that insulates investors from the form of liability incurred by sole proprietors and partners in partnerships (other than limited partners in limited partnerships). Thus, it would seem that the corporation is a vehicle to facilitate business. Certainly, the aim of for-profit corporations — as distinguished from charitable and other not-for-profit corporations — is to earn profits. What remain the subjects of contention, though, are the processes by which corporations seek out profits, for whose benefit those profits are sought, and to whom corporations may be found liable.

The debate over who the beneficiaries of corporate endeavours ought to be is briefly encapsulated in the following excerpt. Although its focus is on the fiduciary duties of corporate directors and officers — insofar as those persons' duties are owed to "the corporation", as dictated by both common law and Canadian corporate law statutes — the beneficiaries of those duties are also the beneficiaries of the fruits of corporate endeavours.

ROTMAN, FIDUCIARY LAW

(2005), pp. 420-25 (Footnotes deleted.)

In the 1930s, a significant debate on the use of corporate powers by management took place between Adolf A. Berle Jr. of Columbia Law School and E. Merrick Dodd Jr. of Harvard Law School that continues to have contemporary ramifications. They, like others, framed this debate in fiduciary terms. However, it is readily observed that their characterizations of the goals of directors' and officers' fiduciary duties differ. In Berle's view, the exclusive beneficiaries of these fiduciary duties are the shareholders. Thus "all powers granted to a corporation or to the management of a corporation, or to any group within the corporation … are necessarily and at all times exercisable only for the ratable benefit of all the shareholders as their interest appears". Dodd disagrees with this assessment. He contends that corporations have a much larger constituency to whom fiduciary duties are owed, including, *inter alia*, shareholder interests, the interests of corporate employees, and broader social goals. The rationale for this broader constituency is premised upon his assertion that corporate managers "are guardians of all the interests which the corporation affects and not merely servants of its absentee owners".

Although in later years Berle conceded that Dodd's broader vision of the scope of the responsibilities of commercial enterprise — as well as that of directors' and officers' fiduciary duties — had prevailed over his own, that did not quell the debate between their formerly entrenched positions. The debate between Berle and Dodd foreshadowed the contemporary controversy over the beneficiaries of directors' and officers' fiduciary duties that is now characterized as being between "shareholder primacy" or "shareholder wealth maximization" on the one hand and those championing a broader constituency to whom directors' and officers' fiduciary duties are owed. This "broader constituency," although it differs in its precise content among theorists, may include any or all of shareholders, bondholders, general creditors, employees, and social interests at large, as encapsulated by the notion of corporate social responsibility.

For the most part, this division in emphasis mirrors the division between Contractarians and anti-Contractarians. ... Contractarians regard the corporate form as a nexus of contracts between interested actors — directors, officers, managers, shareholders, creditors, and employees, to name the more obvious. Their vision is predicated upon the primacy of private ordering among these constituent groups. For present purposes, however, the most important implication of the Contractarian vision of the corporation is that shareholders are regarded as having primacy among the various corporate stakeholders. In some instances, shareholders are characterized as the principals, or "owners," of the firm.

Anti-Contractarians and others opposed to the Contractarian perspective reject the shareholder primacy norm, particularly the characterization of shareholders as the "owners" of the firm. They regard the fiduciary concept as a means to ensure directors' and officers' fidelity to corporations' interests. This, in turn, entails that the interests of various stakeholders and not merely shareholders must be accounted for.

1. Contractarian vs. Anti-Contractarian Theories of the Corporation

While the excerpt above largely portrays Contractarian and anti-Contractarian theories of the corporation as contradictory, the reality of the situation is far more complex. A greater appreciation of the distinctions between the Contractarian and anti-Contractarian approaches to corporate purposes may be obtained by considering the following cases.

DODGE v. FORD MOTOR CO.

204 Mich. 459, 170 N.W. 668 (1919)

[The Ford Motor Co. ("FMC") had been earning significant profits and had paid special dividends to its shareholders between December 1911 and October 1915 amounting to some $41 million. In 1915 alone, the company paid out $15 million in special dividends, which was in addition to the $1.2 million that it paid in regular dividends. For the year ending July 31, 1916, FMC profits were just shy of $60 million and its accumulated profits were approximately $174 million.

In November 1916, FMC declared a special dividend of $2 million. FMC's board of directors — whose chairman was Henry Ford, founder of FMC and holder of 58% of FMC shares — then decided to cease paying such large special dividends and invest the bulk of FMC's profits in order to expand the company's operation and continue its policy of manufacturing cars at a lower per-unit cost. As Henry Ford is reported to have stated in Detroit newspapers, "[m]y ambition is to employ still more men; to spread the benefits of this industrial system to the greatest possible number, to help them build up their lives and their homes. To do this, we are putting the greatest share of our profits back into the business".

The Dodge brothers, who owned 10 per cent of FMC's shares, regarded this plan as one designed "to continue the corporation henceforth as a semi-eleemosynary [charitable] institution and not as a business institution". They subsequently commenced an action against FMC, claiming that it had a duty to distribute accumulated profits to FMC's shareholders. They sought a special dividend of not less than 75 per cent of FMC's accumulated cash surplus. At trial, the court ordered the declaration of a dividend in excess of $19 million. FMC appealed the judgment.]

Ostrander, J.: — When plaintiffs made their complaint and demand for further dividends the Ford Motor Company had concluded its most prosperous year of business. The demand for its cars at the price of the preceding year continued. It could make and could market in the year beginning August 1, 1916, more than 500,000 cars. Sales of parts and repairs would necessarily increase. The cost of materials was likely to advance, and perhaps the price of labor, but it reasonably might have expected a profit for the year of upwards of $60,000,000. It had assets of more than $132,000,000, a surplus of almost $112,000,000, and its cash on hand and municipal bonds were nearly $54,000,000. Its total liabilities, including capital stock, was a little over $20,000,000. It had declared no special dividend during the business year except the October, 1915, dividend. It had been the practice, under similar circumstances, to declare larger dividends. Considering only these facts, a refusal to declare and pay further dividends appears to be not an exercise of discretion on the part of the directors, but an arbitrary refusal to do what the circumstances required to be done. These facts and others call upon the directors to justify their action, or failure or refusal to act. In justification, the defendants have offered testimony tending to prove, and which does prove, the following facts. It had been the policy of the corporation for a considerable time to annually reduce the selling price of cars, while keeping up, or improving, their quality. As early as in June, 1915, a general plan for the expansion of the productive capacity of the concern by a practical duplication of its plant had been talked over by the executive officers and directors and agreed upon, not all of the details having been settled and no formal action of directors having been taken. The erection of a smelter was considered, and engineering and other data in connection therewith secured. In consequence, it was determined not to reduce the selling price of cars for the year beginning August 1, 1915, but to maintain the price and to accumulate a large surplus to pay for the proposed expansion of plant and equipment, and perhaps to build a plant for smelting ore. It is hoped, by Mr. Ford, that eventually 1,000,000 cars will be annually produced. The contemplated changes will permit the increased output.

The plan, as affecting the profits of the business for the year beginning August 1, 1916, and thereafter, calls for a reduction in the selling price of the cars. It is true that this price might be at any time increased, but the plan called for the reduction in price of $80 a car. The capacity of the plant, without the additions thereto voted to be made (without a part of them at least), would produce more than 600,000 cars annually. This number, and more, could have been sold for $440 instead of $360, a difference in the return for capital, labor and materials employed of at least $48,000,000. In short, the plan does not call for and is not intended to produce immediately a more profitable business but a less profitable one; not only less profitable than formerly but less profitable than it is admitted it might be made. The apparent immediate effect will be to diminish the value of shares and the returns to shareholders.

It is the contention of plaintiffs that the apparent effect of the plan is intended to be the continued and continuing effect of it and that it is deliberately proposed, not of record and not by official corporate declaration, but nevertheless proposed, to continue the corporation henceforth as a semi-eleemosynary institution and not as a business institution. In support of this contention they point to the attitude and to the expressions of Mr. Henry Ford.

Mr. Henry Ford is the dominant force in the business of the Ford Motor Company. No plan of operations could be adopted unless he consented, and no board of directors can be elected whom he does not favor. One of the directors of the company has no stock. One share was assigned to him to qualify him for the position, but it is not claimed that he owns it. A business, one of the largest in the world, and one of the most profitable, has been built up. It employs many men, at good pay.

"My ambition," said Mr. Ford, "is to employ still more men, to spread the benefits of this industrial system to the greatest possible number, to help them build up their lives and their homes. To do this we are putting the greatest share of our profits back in the business".

"With regard to dividends, the company paid sixty per cent. on its capitalization of two million dollars, or $1,200,000, leaving $58,000,000 to reinvest for the growth of the company. This is Mr. Ford's policy at present, and it is understood that the other stockholders cheerfully accede to this plan".

He had made up his mind in the summer of 1916 that no dividends other than the regular dividends should be paid, "for the present".

"*Q.* For how long? Had you fixed in your mind any time in the future, when you were going to pay —

"*A.* No.

"*Q.* That was indefinite in the future?

"*A.* That was indefinite, yes, sir".

The record, and especially the testimony of Mr. Ford, convinces that he has to some extent the attitude towards shareholders of one who has dispensed and distributed to them large gains and that they should be content to take what he chooses to give. His testimony creates the impression, also, that he thinks the Ford Motor Company has made too much money, has had too large profits, and that although large profits might be still earned, a sharing of them with the public, by reducing the price of the output of the company, ought to be undertaken. We have no doubt that certain sentiments, philanthropic and altruistic, creditable to Mr. Ford, had large influence in determining the policy to be pursued by the Ford Motor Company — the policy which has been herein referred to.

It is said by his counsel that —

"Although a manufacturing corporation cannot engage in humanitarian works as its principal business, the fact that it is organized for profit does not prevent the existence of implied powers to carry on with humanitarian motives such charitable works as are incidental to the main business of the corporation".

And again:

"As the expenditures complained of are being made in an expansion of the business which the company is organized to carry on, and for purposes within the powers of the corporation as hereinbefore shown, the question is as to whether such expenditures are rendered illegal because influenced to some extent by humanitarian motives and purposes on the part of the members of the board of directors".

In discussing this proposition, counsel have referred to decisions such as *Hawes* v. *Oakland*, 104 U.S. 450; *Taunton* v. *Royal Ins. Co.*, 2 Hem. & Miller, 135; *Henderson* v. *Bank of Australasia*, L.R. 40 Ch. Div. 170; *Steinway* v. *Steinway & Sons*, 40 N.Y. Supp. 718; *People, ex rel. Metropolitan Life Ins. Co.*, v. *Hotchkiss*, 136 App. Div. 150 (120 N.Y. Supp. 649). These cases, after all, like all others in which the subject is treated, turn finally upon the point, the question, whether it appears that the directors were not acting for the best interests of the corporation. We do not draw in question, nor do counsel for the plaintiffs do so, the validity of the general propositions stated by counsel nor the soundness of the opinions delivered in the cases cited. The case presented here is not like any of them. The difference between an incidental humanitarian expenditure of corporate funds for the benefit of the employees, like the building of a hospital for their use and the employment of agencies for the betterment of their condition, and a general purpose and plan to benefit mankind at the expense of others, is obvious. There should be no confusion (of which there is evidence) of the duties which Mr. Ford conceives that he and the stockholders owe to the general public and the duties which in law he and his codirectors owe to protesting, minority stockholders. A business corporation is organized and carried on primarily for the profit of the stockholders. The powers of the directors are to be employed for that end. The discretion of directors is to be exercised in the choice of means to attain that end and does not extend to a change in the end itself, to the reduction of profits or to the nondistribution of profits among stockholders in order to devote them to other purposes.

There is committed to the discretion of directors, a discretion to be exercised in good faith, the infinite details of business, including the wages which shall be paid to employees, the number of hours they shall work, the conditions under which labor shall be carried on, and the prices for which products shall be offered to the public. It is said by appellants that the motives of the board members are not material and will not be inquired into by the court so long as their acts are within their lawful powers. As we have pointed out, and the proposition does not require argument to sustain it, it is not within the lawful powers of a board of directors to shape and conduct the affairs of a corporation for the merely incidental benefit of shareholders and for the primary purpose of benefiting others, and no one will contend that if the avowed purpose of the defendant directors was to sacrifice the interests of shareholders it would not be the duty of the courts to interfere.

We are not, however, persuaded that we should interfere with the proposed expansion of the business of the Ford Motor Company. In view of the fact that the selling price of products may be increased at any time, the ultimate results of the larger business cannot be certainly estimated. The judges are not business experts. It is recognized that plans must often be made for a long future, for expected competition, for a continuing as well as an immediately profitable venture. The experience of the Ford Motor Company is evidence of capable management of its affairs. It may be noticed, incidentally, that it took from the public the money required for the execution of its plan and that the very considerable salaries paid to

Mr. Ford and to certain executive officers and employees were not diminished. We are not satisfied that the alleged motives of the directors, in so far as they are reflected in the conduct of the business, menace the interests of shareholders. It is enough to say, perhaps, that the court of equity is at all times open to complaining shareholders having a just grievance.

Assuming the general plan and policy of expansion and the details of it to have been sufficiently, formally, approved at the October and November, 1917, meetings of directors, and assuming further that the plan and policy and the details agreed upon were for the best ultimate interest of the company and therefore of its shareholders, what does it amount to in justification of a refusal to declare and pay a special dividend, or dividends? The Ford Motor Company was able to estimate with nicety its income and profit. It could sell more cars than it could make. Having ascertained what it would cost to produce a car and to sell it, the profit upon each car depended upon the selling price. That being fixed, the yearly income and profit was determinable, and, within slight variations, was certain.

There was appropriated — voted — for the smelter $11,325,000. As to the remainder voted there is no available way for determining how much had been paid before the action of directors was taken and how much was paid thereafter, but assuming that the plans required an expenditure sooner or later of $9,895,000 for duplication of the plant, and for land and other expenditures $3,000,000, the total is $24,220,000. The company was continuing business, at a profit — a cash business. If the total cost of proposed expenditures had been immediately withdrawn in cash from the cash surplus (money and bonds) on hand August 1, 1916, there would have remained nearly $30,000,000.

Defendants say, and it is true, that a considerable cash balance must be at all times carried by such a concern. But, as has been stated, there was a large daily, weekly, monthly, receipt of cash. The output was practically continuous and was continuously, and within a few days, turned into cash. Moreover, the contemplated expenditures were not to be immediately made. The large sum appropriated for the smelter plant was payable over a considerable period of time. So that, without going further, it would appear that, accepting and approving the plan of the directors, it was their duty to distribute on or near the first of August, 1916, a very large sum of money to stockholders.

In reaching this conclusion, we do not ignore, but recognize, the validity of the proposition that plaintiffs have from the beginning profited by, if they have not lately, officially, participated in, the general policy of expansion pursued by this corporation. We do not lose sight of the fact that it had been, upon an occasion, agreeable to the plaintiffs to increase the capital stock to $100,000,000 by a stock dividend of $98,000,000. These things go only to answer other contentions now made by plaintiffs and do not and cannot operate to estop them to demand proper dividends upon the stock they own. It is obvious that an annual dividend of sixty per cent. upon $2,000,000, or $1,-$200,000, is the equivalent of a very small dividend upon $100,000,000, or more.

The decree of the court below fixing and determining the specific amount to be distributed to stockholders is affirmed. In other respects, except as to the allowance of costs, the said decree is reversed. Plaintiffs will recover interest at five per cent. per annum upon their proportional share of said dividend from the date of the decree of the lower court. Appellants will tax the costs of their appeal, and two-thirds of the amount thereof will be paid by plaintiffs. No other costs are allowed.

NOTE

Although the *Dodge* case is generally pointed to as a profound illustration of Contractarian analysis and shareholder primacy, a closer examination of the judgment shows flaws in this portrayal, as indicated in the following excerpt.

ROTMAN, FIDUCIARY LAW

(2005), pp. 469-72 (Footnotes deleted.)

Insofar as the court's judgment [in *Dodge v. Ford Motor Co.*] explicitly states that the purpose of for-profit corporations is to maximize profit for shareholders, it determines that courts may interfere with business decisions where profit maximization is not the primary motivation of directors. Nonetheless, the court does not interfere with FMC's infrastructure improvement plan. As it explains, "[i]t is recognized that plans must often be made for a long future, for expected competition, for a continuing as well as immediately profitable venture". Thus, while the court affirms the $19 million plus dividend declared by the trial court, it fails to enjoin FMC's plan to lower the price of automobiles from $440 to $360, even though that action would reduce short-term profits.

Certainly, FMC's directors did not have shareholders' immediate interests foremost in their minds when devising their plan to reinvest in improvements to FMC's infrastructure. Nevertheless, it is difficult to accept that shareholders' interests were being ignored when they had received some $41 million dollars in special dividends between December, 1911 and October, 1915 and their long-term interests, which were intricately tied with those of FMC, were being attended to via the infrastructure improvement plan. Further, with increased consolidation of the automotive sector during the period in question it was both logical and rational for the directors of FMC to seek to entrench or extend FMC's position in the automotive market and attempt to impede competitors' inroads into their market share, which would reduce FMC's profits. Thus, in order to sustain the types of profit being made prior to 1916, FMC's board of directors looked beyond the immediate satisfaction of its shareholders in an attempt to sustain those interests, as well as those of the company, in future years.

On its face, it would be difficult to characterize this plan as something other than an exercise of business judgment. However, there is reason to suggest that Ford's actions were not entirely altruistic, insofar as the Dodge brothers had formed a rival car manufacturing concern in 1914 and were depending on the continued flow of special dividends from their Ford shares to help finance it. Absent, however, proof that FMC's board did not act reasonably, soundly, or prudently, acted in bad faith, without due care, or in breach of its fiduciary duties, the court in *Dodge* ought to have deferred to the board's judgment in light of accepted practice at the time.

The benefits that FMC conferred on non-shareholders, such as employees and the public at large, were not entirely selfless, but ultimately enured to the benefit of FMC. This is consistent with the fulfillment of directors' fiduciary duties, which are owed directly to their corporations and not to corporate stakeholders except in unusual circumstances. Increased wages for employees brought more potential customers for Ford vehicles, especially when the loyalty and pride of employees — which is particularly extant in the automotive sector — is accounted for. Similarly, reducing the cost of purchasing one of its vehicles entailed that more people could afford to purchase Ford cars. While this may have resulted in less profit per vehicle, it was designed to create greater long-term profitability because of the larger volume of vehicles sold and the reduction in the costs of production envisaged by FMC's infrastructure plan. The fact that the *Dodge* court admitted that "[t]he judges are not business experts" leads, logically, to the conclusion that the judges ought to have deferred to the business judgment exercised by FMC's board of directors absent a finding that the directors were in breach of their fiduciary duties or did not properly discharge their duties of care, given the greater willingness to defer to business judgment at that time than in the present day.

By effectively holding that the directors' owed fiduciary duties directly to shareholders rather than to the corporation, the *Dodge* court found that FMC's board of directors breached its duties because it did not act foremostly to maximize shareholders' benefits. For this reason, the board's actions did not fit within the business judgment rule and no deference was required. As Ashford suggests:

> ... under the business judgment rule a modest amount of corporate philanthropy may be pursued by the corporation in the name of corporate social responsibility, but a decision to change the primary purpose of the business corporation (i.e., to maximize shareholder wealth) is a violation of fiduciary duties. The business judgment rule extends to a broad range of means, but not to a change in the end of the corporate enterprise. A change in the end is simply not a business judgment.

This characterization is not entirely correct. By not requiring FMC to completely abandon its plan, even though it did not serve the goal of maximizing shareholder profits, the court did defer, at least in part, to the business judgment exercised by FMC's board.

While the *Dodge* case is pointed to as an example of the shareholder primacy norm, it does not entirely discount the need for long-term planning in order for the corporation to prosper. In engaging in such planning, benefits may be conferred upon non-shareholders, such as employees and the public at large. This seemingly schizophrenic nature of the *Dodge* judgment is reconciled by the fact that where short term profit maximization is subordinated to longer range ideas that diminish immediate shareholder benefits while providing benefits to others, such behaviour is acceptable so long as the latter may be shown to ultimately benefit shareholders (such as by ensuring the long term profitability of the company). Thus, even though the interests of others are sometimes accounted for, they must still be subordinated to the interests of shareholders on some level under the shareholder primacy norm.

NOTE

The dictum of the *Dodge* case in favour of shareholder primacy, while the mantra of most Contractarians, has not been universally accepted. A clear example of anti-*Dodge* sentiment may be observed in another prominent case, *Shlensky v. Wrigley*, which emphasizes communitarian interests.

SHLENSKY v. WRIGLEY

237 N.E.2d 776 (Ill. App. 1968)

Sullivan J.: — This is an appeal from a dismissal of plaintiff's amended complaint on motion of the defendants. The action was a stockholders' derivative suit against the directors for negligence and mismanagement. The corporation was also made a defendant. Plaintiff sought damages and an order that defendants cause the installation of lights in Wrigley Field and the scheduling of night baseball games.

Plaintiff is a minority stockholder of defendant corporation, Chicago National League Ball Club (Inc.), a Delaware corporation with its principal place of business in Chicago, Illinois. Defendant corporation owns and operates the major league professional baseball team known as the Chicago Cubs. The corporation also engages in the operation of Wrigley Field, the Cubs' home park, the concessionaire sales during Cubs' home games, television and radio broadcasts of Cubs' home games, the leasing of the field for football games and other events and receives its share, as visiting team, of admission moneys from games played in other National League stadia. The individual defendants are directors of the Cubs and have served for varying periods of years. Defendant Philip K. Wrigley is also president of the corporation and owner of approximately 80% of the stock therein.

Plaintiff alleges that since night baseball was first played in 1935 nineteen of the twenty major league teams have scheduled night games. In 1966, out of a total of 1,620 games in the major leagues, 932 were played at night. Plaintiff alleges that every member of the major leagues, other than the Cubs, scheduled substantially all of its home games in 1966 at night, exclusive of opening days, Saturdays, Sundays, holidays and days prohibited by league rules. Allegedly this has been done for the specific purpose of maximizing attendance and thereby maximizing revenue and income.

The Cubs, in the years 1961-65, sustained operating losses from its direct baseball operations. Plaintiff attributes those losses to inadequate attendance at Cubs' home games. He concludes that if the directors continue to refuse to install lights at Wrigley Field and schedule night baseball games, the Cubs will continue to sustain comparable losses and its financial condition will continue to deteriorate.

Plaintiff alleges that, except for the year 1963, attendance at Cubs' home games has been substantially below that at their road games, many of which were played at night.

Plaintiff compares attendance at Cubs' games with that of the Chicago White Sox, an American League club, whose weekday games were generally played at night. The weekend attendance figures for the two teams were similar; however, the White Sox week-night games drew many more patrons than did the Cubs' weekday games.

Plaintiff alleges that the funds for the installation of lights can be readily obtained through financing and the cost of installation would be far more than offset and recaptured by increased revenues and incomes resulting from the increased attendance.

Plaintiff further alleges that defendant Wrigley has refused to install lights, not because of interest in the welfare of the corporation but because of his personal opinions "that baseball is a 'daytime sport' and that the installation of lights and night baseball games will have a deteriorating effect upon the surrounding neighborhood". It is alleged that he has admitted that he is not interested in whether the Cubs would benefit financially from such action because of his concern for the neighborhood, and that he would be willing for the team to play night games if a new stadium were built in Chicago.

Plaintiff alleges that the other defendant directors, with full knowledge of the foregoing matters, have acquiesced in the policy laid down by Wrigley and have permitted him to dominate the board of directors in matters involving the installation of lights and scheduling of night games, even though they knew he was not motivated by a good faith concern as to the best interests of defendant corporation, but solely by his personal views set forth above. It is charged that the directors are acting for a reason or reasons contrary and wholly unrelated to the business interests of the corporation; that such arbitrary and capricious acts constitute mismanagement and waste of corporate assets, and that the directors have been negligent in failing to exercise reasonable care and prudence in the management of the corporate affairs.

The question on appeal is whether plaintiff's amended complaint states a cause of action. It is plaintiff's position that fraud, illegality and conflict of interest are not the only bases for a stockholder's derivative action against the directors. Contrariwise, defendants argue that the courts will not step in and interfere with honest business judgment of the directors unless there is a showing of fraud, illegality or conflict of interest.

The cases in this area are numerous and each differs from the others on a factual basis. However, the courts have pronounced certain ground rules which appear in all cases and which are then applied to the given factual situation. The court in *Wheeler v. The Pullman Iron & Steel Co.*, 143 Ill 197, 207, 32 NE 420 said:

> "It is, however, fundamental in the law of corporations, that the majority of its stockholders shall control the policy of the corporation, and regulate and govern the lawful exercise of its franchise and business. ... Every one purchasing or subscribing for stock in a corporation impliedly agrees that he will be bound by the acts and proceedings done or sanctioned by a majority of the shareholders, or by the agents of the corporation duly chosen by such majority, within the scope of the powers conferred by the charter, and courts of equity will not undertake to control the policy or business methods of a corporation, although it may be seen that a wiser policy might be adopted and the business more successful if other methods were pursued. The majority of shares of its stock, or the agents by the holders thereof lawfully chosen, must be permitted to control the business of the corporation in their discretion, when not in violation of its charter or some public law, or corruptly and fraudulently subversive of the rights and interests of the corporation or of a shareholder".

The standards set in Delaware are also clearly stated in the cases. In *Davis v. Louisville Gas & Electric Co.*, 6 NJ Misc 706, 142 A 654, a minority shareholder sought to have the directors enjoined from amending the certificate of incorporation. The court said on page 659:

> "We have then a conflict in view between the responsible managers of a corporation and an overwhelming majority of its stockholders on the one hand and a dissenting minority on the other — a conflict touching matters of business policy, such as has occasioned innumerable applications to courts to intervene and determine which of the two conflicting views should prevail. The response which courts make to such applications is that it is not their function to resolve for corporations questions of policy and business management. The directors are chosen to pass upon such questions and their judgment *unless shown to be tainted with fraud* is accepted as final. The judgment of the directors of corporations enjoys the benefit of a

presumption that it was formed in good faith and was designed to promote the best interests of the corporation they serve". (Emphasis supplied.)

Similarly, the court in *Toebelman v. Missouri-Kansas Pipe Line Co.*, 41 F Supp 334, said at page 339:

> "The general legal principle involved is familiar. Citation of authorities is of limited value because the facts of each case differ so widely. Reference may be made to the statement of the rule in *Helfman v. American Light & Traction Company*, 121 NJ Eq 1, 187 A 540, 550, in which the Court stated the law as follows: 'In a purely business corporation . . . the authority of the directors in the conduct of the business of the corporation must be regarded as absolute when they act within the law, and the court is without authority to substitute its judgment for that of the directors.'"

Plaintiff argues that the allegations of his amended complaint are sufficient to set forth a cause of action under the principles set out in *Dodge v. Ford Motor Co.*, 204 Mich 459, 170 NW 668. In that case plaintiff, owner of about 10% of the outstanding stock, brought suit against the directors seeking payment of additional dividends and the enjoining of further business expansion. In ruling on the request for dividends the court indicated that the motives of Ford in keeping so much money in the corporation for expansion and security were to benefit the public generally and spread the profits out by means of more jobs, etc. The court felt that these were not only far from related to the good of the stockholders, but amounted to a change in the ends of the corporation and that this was not a purpose contemplated or allowed by the corporate charter. The court relied on language found in *Hunter v. Roberts, Throp & Co.*, 83 Mich 63, 47 NW 131, 134, wherein it was said:

> "Courts of equity will not interfere in the management of the directors unless it is clearly made to appear that they are guilty of fraud or misappropriation of the corporate funds, or refuse to declare a dividend when the corporation has a surplus of net profits which it can, without detriment to its business, divide among its stockholders, and when a refusal to do so would amount to such an abuse of discretion as would constitute a fraud or breach of that good faith which they are bound to exercise toward the stockholders".

From the authority relied upon in that case it is clear that the court felt that there must be fraud or a breach of that good faith which directors are bound to exercise toward the stockholders in order to justify the courts entering into the internal affairs of corporations. This is made clear when the court refused to interfere with the directors' decision to expand the business. The following appears on page 684:

> "We are not, however, persuaded that we should interfere with the proposed expansion of the business of the Ford Motor Company. In view of the fact that the selling price of products may be increased at any time, the ultimate results of the larger business cannot be certainly estimated. *The judges are not business experts.* It is recognized that plans must often be made for a long future, for expected competition, for a continuing as well as an immediately profitable venture. . . . We are not satisfied that the alleged motives of the directors, in so far as they are reflected in the conduct of the business, menace the interests of the shareholders". (Emphasis supplied.)

Plaintiff in the instant case argues that the directors are acting for reasons unrelated to the financial interest and welfare of the Cubs. However, we are not satisfied that the motives assigned to Philip K. Wrigley, and through him to the other directors, are contrary to the best interests of the corporation and the stockholders. For example, it appears to us that the effect on the surrounding neighborhood might well be considered by a director who was considering the patrons who would or would not attend the games if the park were in a poor neighborhood. Furthermore, the long run interest of the corporation in its property value at Wrigley Field might demand all efforts to keep the neighborhood from deteriorating. By these thoughts we do not mean to say that we have decided that the decision of the directors was a correct one. That is beyond our jurisdiction and ability. We are merely saying that the decision is one properly before directors and the motives alleged in the amended complaint showed no fraud, illegality or conflict of interest in their making of that decision.

While all the courts do not insist that one or more of the three elements must be present for a stockholder's derivative action to lie, nevertheless we feel that unless the conduct of the defendants at least borders on one of the elements, the courts should not interfere. The trial court in the instant case acted properly in dismissing plaintiff's amended complaint.

We feel that plaintiff's amended complaint was also defective in failing to allege damage to the corporation. ...

There is no allegation that the night games played by the other nineteen teams enhanced their financial position or that the profits, if any, of those teams were directly related to the number of night games scheduled. There is an allegation that the installation of lights and scheduling of night games in Wrigley Field would have resulted in large amounts of additional revenues and incomes from increased attendance and related sources of income. Further, the cost of installation of lights, funds for which are allegedly readily available by financing, would be more than offset and recaptured by increased revenues. However, no allegation is made that there will be a net benefit to the corporation from such action, considering all increased costs.

Plaintiff claims that the losses of defendant corporation are due to poor attendance at home games. However, it appears from the amended complaint, taken as a whole, that factors other than attendance affect the net earnings or losses. For example, in 1962, attendance at home and road games decreased appreciably as compared with 1961, and yet the loss from direct baseball operation and of the whole corporation was considerably less.

The record shows that plaintiff did not feel he could allege that the increased revenues would be sufficient to cure the corporate deficit. The only cost plaintiff was at all concerned with was that of installation of lights. No mention was made of operation and maintenance of the lights or other possible increases in operating costs of night games and we cannot speculate as to what other factors might influence the increase or decrease of profits if the Cubs were to play night home games.

... [I]n the instant case, plaintiff's allegation that the minority stockholders and the corporation have been seriously and irreparably damaged by the wrongful conduct of the defendant directors is a mere conclusion and not based on well pleaded facts in the amended complaint.

Finally, we do not agree with plaintiff's contention that failure to follow the example of the other major league clubs in scheduling night games constituted negligence. Plaintiff made no allegation that these teams' night schedules were profitable or that the purpose for which night baseball had been undertaken was fulfilled. Furthermore, it cannot be said that directors, even those of corporations that are losing money, must follow the lead of the other corporations in the field. Directors are elected for their business capabilities and judgment and the courts cannot require them to forego their judgment because of the decisions of directors of other companies. Courts may not decide these questions in the absence of a clear showing of dereliction of duty on the part of the specific directors and mere failure to "follow the crowd" is not such a dereliction.

For the foregoing reasons the order of dismissal entered by the trial court is affirmed.

Affirmed.

NOTES AND QUESTIONS

Interestingly, in 1988, lights were installed at Wrigley Field and night baseball is now a regular event at the stadium. Not only has the surrounding neighbourhood not deteriorated as a result, but it has experienced a resurgence with the addition of new businesses tapping into the increased attendance generated by the ballpark following the addition of night games. Peak attendance at Wrigley Field before the introduction of night baseball came in 1985, when 2,161,534 fans attended baseball games. In the first full year of night baseball in 1989, 2,491,942 fans were in attendance, while attendance since 1998 has consistently been in excess of 2.6 million, reaching a peak of just under 3 million in 2003: online: Baseball Almanac <http://www.baseball-almanac.com/teams/cubsatte.shtml> (last accessed 13 April 2006).

Do the attendance numbers associated with the introduction of night baseball at Wrigley Field, cited above, indicate that the *Shlensky* judgment was incorrectly decided? Can *Shlensky* be reconciled as an instance of a court properly deferring to the business judgment of the directors of the Chicago National League Ball Club (Inc.)?

The Supreme Court of Canada made some pertinent comments on the business judgment and concomitant duties of directors in the following case. Consider whether its comments are consistent with what was said in either *Dodge* or *Shlensky*.

PEOPLES DEPARTMENT STORES INC. (TRUSTEE OF) v. WISE

[2004] S.C.J. No. 64, [2004] 3 S.C.R. 461

[The Wise brothers were directors of a chain of department stores (Wise Stores) which purchased all of the shares in Peoples Department Stores Inc. ("Peoples") from Marks and Spencer Canada Inc. (M&S). Under the terms of a highly leveraged purchase, the Toronto-Dominion Bank ("TD Bank") loaned $5 million in cash that was paid to M&S and the balance of the $27 million purchase price was to be paid off over time to M&S. In exchange, M&S was granted a floating charge over Peoples' assets, subject only to the priority of the bank. The vendor also instituted other requirements, including a prohibition against Peoples providing financial assistance to Wise Stores.

Some time later, Wise Stores implemented a new inventory procurement policy which saw Peoples order all inventory from North American suppliers for both it and Wise Stores (which comprised 82 per cent of all combined inventory purchases). As a result of this policy, Peoples became indebted for inventory delivered to and sold by Wise Stores, which also retained the profits from those sales. The Wise brothers then completed a second public offering for Peoples that netted them $15 million in proceeds, none of which went to pay off the purchase price of Peoples. Less than a year after implementing this inventory procurement policy, Peoples and Wise Stores were both bankrupt. The TD Bank was paid in full and M&S suffered only a 1 per cent loss on the purchase price. Trade creditors remained owed approximately $21.5 million as a result of the bankruptcy. Peoples' trustee in bankruptcy subsequently brought an action against the Wise brothers, in their capacities as directors of Peoples, on behalf of Peoples' unsecured creditors. The action claimed that the Wise brothers had breached their duties under s. 122 of the *Canada Business Corporations Act*.]

The judgment of the Court was delivered by

Major and Deschamps JJ.: — ... This appeal ... is concerned only with the statutory duties owed under the CBCA. Insofar as the statutory fiduciary duty is concerned, it is clear that the phrase the "best interests of the corporation" should be read not simply as the "best interests of the shareholders". From an economic perspective, the "best interests of the corporation" means the maximization of the value of the corporation: see E. M. Iacobucci, "Directors' Duties in Insolvency: Clarifying What Is at Stake" (2003), 39 *Can. Bus. L.J.* 398, at pp. 400-1. However, the courts have long recognized that various other factors may be relevant in determining what directors should consider in soundly managing with a view to the best interests of the corporation. For example, in *Teck Corp. v. Millar* (1972), 33 D.L.R. (3d) 288 (B.C.S.C.), Berger J. stated, at p. 314:

> A classical theory that once was unchallengeable must yield to the facts of modern life. In fact, of course, it has. If today the directors of a company were to consider the interests of its employees no one would argue that in doing so they were not acting *bona fide* in the interests of the company itself. Similarly, if the directors were to consider the consequences to the community of any policy that the company intended to pursue, and were deflected in their commitment to that policy as a result, it could not be said that they had not considered *bona fide* the interests of the shareholders.

> I appreciate that it would be a breach of their duty for directors to disregard entirely the interests of a company's shareholders in order to confer a benefit on its employees: *Parke v. Daily News Ltd.*, [1962] Ch. 927. But if they observe a decent respect for other interests lying beyond those of the company's shareholders in the strict sense, that will not, in my view, leave directors open to the charge that they have failed in their fiduciary duty to the company.

The case of *Re Olympia & York Enterprises Ltd. and Hiram Walker Resources Ltd.* (1986), 59 O.R. (2d) 254 (Div. Ct.), approved, at p. 271, the decision in *Teck*, *supra*. We accept as an accurate statement of law that in determining whether they are acting with a view to the best interests of the corporation it may be legitimate, given all the circumstances of a given case, for the board of directors to consider, *inter alia*, the interests of shareholders, employees, suppliers, creditors, consumers, governments and the environment.

The various shifts in interests that naturally occur as a corporation's fortunes rise and fall do not, however, affect the content of the fiduciary duty under s. 122(1)(*a*) of the CBCA. At all times, directors and officers owe their fiduciary obligation to the corporation. The interests of the corporation are not to be confused with the interests of the creditors or those of any other stakeholders.

The interests of shareholders, those of the creditors and those of the corporation may and will be consistent with each other if the corporation is profitable and well capitalized and has strong prospects. However, this can change if the corporation starts to struggle financially. The residual rights of the shareholders will generally become worthless if a corporation is declared bankrupt. Upon bankruptcy, the directors of the corporation transfer control to a trustee, who administers the corporation's assets for the benefit of creditors.

Short of bankruptcy, as the corporation approaches what has been described as the "vicinity of insolvency", the residual claims of shareholders will be nearly exhausted. While shareholders might well prefer that the directors pursue high-risk alternatives with a high potential payoff to maximize the shareholders' expected residual claim, creditors in the same circumstances might prefer that the directors steer a safer course so as to maximize the value of their claims against the assets of the corporation.

The directors' fiduciary duty does not change when a corporation is in the nebulous "vicinity of insolvency". That phrase has not been defined; moreover, it is incapable of definition and has no legal meaning. What it is obviously intended to convey is a deterioration in the corporation's financial stability. In assessing the actions of directors it is evident that any honest and good faith attempt to redress the corporation's financial problems will, if successful, both retain value for shareholders and improve the position of creditors. If unsuccessful, it will not qualify as a breach of the statutory fiduciary duty.

For a discussion of the shifting interests and incentives of shareholders and creditors, see W. D. Gray, "*Peoples v. Wise* and *Dylex*: Identifying Stakeholder Interests upon or near Corporate Insolvency — Stasis or Pragmatism?" (2003), 39 *Can. Bus. L.J.* 242, at p. 257; E. M. Iacobucci and K. E. Davis, "Reconciling Derivative Claims and the Oppression Remedy" (2000), 12 *S.C.L.R.* (2d) 87, at p. 114. In resolving these competing interests, it is incumbent upon the directors to act honestly and in good faith with a view to the best interests of the corporation. In using their skills for the benefit of the corporation when it is in troubled waters financially, the directors must be careful to attempt to act in its best interests by creating a "better" corporation, and not to favour the interests of any one group of stakeholders. If the stakeholders cannot avail themselves of the statutory fiduciary duty (the duty of loyalty, *supra*) to sue the directors for failing to take care of their interests, they have other means at their disposal.

[The court then considered the oppression remedy available under the C.B.C.A. Discussion of the applicability of the oppression remedy to the situation in *Peoples* is excerpted in Chapter 9, Minority Protection, section D.2.(c) Oppression vs. Fiduciary Duty.]

NOTE

The *Dodge, Shlensky* and *Peoples* cases demonstrate that there is merit in analyzing corporate ends under Contractarian and anti-Contractarian schools of thought. The excerpt below suggests that Contractarian analyses are far too limited to reflect the full extent of corporate purposes. Consider what is proposed and draw your own conclusions.

ROTMAN, FIDUCIARY LAW

(2005), pp. 484-86 (Footnotes deleted.)

While shareholders certainly have interests in corporate activities, adhering to the shareholder primacy norm is problematic ... By emphasizing shareholder interests at the expense of those of other stakeholders, shareholder primacy inappropriately skews the focus of corporate directors and officers in the discharging of their duties, as well as their allocation of benefits. Blair and Stout contend that arguments in favour of shareholder primacy ignore a variety of economic arguments that suggest that it could be inefficient. These include options theory, firm-specific investment, team production analysis, and the efficient capital markets hypothesis ("ECMH").

Shareholders' interests, generally speaking, are indirectly served by corporate directors and officers. Even under the various shareholder primacy arguments ... the duties that are said to be owed to shareholders are channeled through the corporate vehicle. Similarly, under Communitarian approaches, the stakeholders whose interests are to be accounted for by directors and officers are considered by the latter in the course of discharging their fiduciary duties to their corporations. That shareholders and other stakeholders are indirect recipients of directors and officers' fiduciary duties is reflected in the fact that, as a general rule, neither shareholders nor other corporate stakeholders can directly enforce directors' and officers' fiduciary duties. If duties were owed directly to them rather than to the corporation, they would not be under this disability. Shareholders may, however, be able to enforce directors' and officers' fiduciary duties indirectly via the derivative action, although that would benefit the corporation's interests and not their own.

While the interests of shareholders are accounted for in the grand scheme of directors' and officers' considerations on behalf of their corporations, those interests are not determinants for actions taken, but merely considerations that exist alongside others, such as the interests of other stakeholders as well as the broader community affected by the corporation, whether economically or physically. Shareholders can, however, directly enforce any fiduciary duties that are owed specifically to them, which arise only in unique circumstances in which the directors or officers engage in activity outside of their usual duties.

A meaningful separation between the corporation and its shareholders (and, for that matter, its other stakeholders) is necessary since the recognition of the corporation as a legal entity distinct from its shareholders is, as Farrar states, "not simply a matter of form and fiction," but, rather, "the way in which law defines and regulates economic reality". The corporation, by definition, is not the same as its shareholders and may legitimately have different interests than some, or perhaps all, of them. When the even more varying, and legitimate, interests of other corporate stakeholders are factored in, reconciling the range of divergent interests becomes even more difficult, if not impossible, to accomplish.

CHAPTER 5

CORPORATE OBLIGATIONS

A. INTRODUCTION TO TWO THEORIES

The corporation has now been established as a legal entity whose behaviour is to be analyzed by analogy to that of a human individual in a similar situation. As in most areas of law, the analysis is often done in retrospect. Little thought is given to most problematical situations until a corporation is about to be prosecuted for a criminal offence, to sue or be sued over some alleged civil obligation. Then, the question becomes whether the corporation did one of the acts, thought one of the thoughts, or communicated one of the messages necessary to create a criminal or civil obligation. The answer usually involves a balancing act: are we to waive some of the internal formalities required by the corporate constitution or thwart some outsiders' civil liberties and transactional expectations?

Broadly speaking, a person can incur obligations in three ways. The first is personally: for example, a person may incur obligations to other people based on duties recognized in tort law or contracts. The other two ways are through agency. If your agent contracts according to your instructions, then you are bound to a contract. The liability is consensual in the sense that you authorized your agent to bind you. Note that the agent is not generally a party to the contract. Non-consensual liabilities can also be incurred through agency. If your agent commits a tort *within the scope of the agency*, then you are liable to the victim on the basis of vicarious liability or *respondeat superior*. The liability is non-consensual in that you did not want it. The difference here from the previous case is that your agent is liable in tort as well.

It often happened in the common law that two distinctly different theories arose, developed along roughly parallel lines, and were never thought to be related until their paths accidentally crossed in litigation. This happened in corporate obligations. One theory was concerned with identifying a particular human brain that could be said to have been operating as the corporate mind in particular circumstances. It led to the conclusion that the brain *was* the corporate brain, so the corporation incurred liability personally. This theory was used in most criminal and a few tort cases. The other theory saw individuals acting as corporate agents. In practice, it was concerned with the scope of the corporation's ability to avoid external liabilities by pleading limitations on its agents' powers. Agency theory was used in contract and in most tort situations.

Both theories are alive and well in Canadian corporate law. Both were simplified — the former by judicial analysis, the latter by legislative reform — in the last quarter of the twentieth century. As usual, a clear understanding of the common law and Equitable rules provides the best basis for understanding the latest developments.

B. CRIME AND TORT: ESTABLISHING CORPORATE MENS REA

In most tort situations little behavioural analysis of corporate activity is required because of the concept of vicarious liability. A corporation has a separate existence and can be summoned before the courts. A corporation is vicariously liable like any other employer for the torts of its agents.

> If it is once granted that corporations are for civil purposes to be regarded as persons, i.e., as principals acting by agents and servants, it is difficult to see why the ordinary doctrines of agency and master and servant are not to be applied to corporations as well as to ordinary individuals [Lord Lindley in *Citizens' Life Assurance Co. v. Brown*, [1904] A.C. 423, at 426 (Ont. J.C.P.C.)].

There are other situations, however, where the principle *respondeat superior* does not apply to individuals or to corporations. Many prohibited acts are criminal only if *mens rea*, the elusive guilty mind, can be proved: some torts are proved only if knowledge and default can be proved. Vicarious liability does not apply; personal liability must be shown.

In the early days it was said that a corporation could not be guilty of a crime because of the impossibility of inflicting punishment upon the incorporeal body of the defendant. See, in this regard, Lord Blackburn's comments in *Pharmaceutical Society v. London and Provincial Supply Assn.* (1880), 5 App. Cas. 857, at 869 (Eng. H.L.). This early failure to see the logical distinction between crime and punishment was soon swept aside and corporate convictions became commonplace. See *R. v. Fane Robinson Ltd.*, [1941] 2 W.W.R. 235, [1941] 3 D.L.R. 409, 76 C.C.C. 196 (Alta. C.A.) and cases cited therein.

1. The Test

Proving a particular individual's *mens rea* is a traditional criminal law problem. The corporate law problem is whether the guilty mind can be proved to have been the corporate mind in the circumstances. Put another way, if a corporation is the named defendant and the mental culpability of the defendant must be proved, then somewhere in the corporate organization must be found a guilty mind which can be identified with the mental element of corporate activity.

THE "RHONE" v. THE "PETER A.B. WIDENER"

[1993] S.C.J. No. 19, [1993] 1 S.C.R. 497, 101 D.L.R. (4th) 188

[The vessel "Peter A.B. Widener" caused a shipping accident. It was under the command of Captain Kelch, who worked for the corporation that owned the vessel. The corporation, Great Lakes Towing Co., sought to limit its liability under s. 647(2) of the *Canada Shipping Act*, R.S.C. 1970, c. S-9, which limited liability if the damage was caused without the "actual fault or privity" of the owner of the ship.]

Iacobucci J.: —

1. Is the Master of the Appellant's Tug a Directing Mind of the Corporation?
The appellant, Great Lakes, contends that Hugessen J.A. erred in concluding that there was actual fault or privity on its part on the basis that Captain Kelch was a

directing mind of the corporation and that therefore Great Lakes could not limit its liability under the *Canada Shipping Act*. Assessing the merits of this contention requires that I examine briefly both the general principles pertaining to the limitation of liability under the *Canada Shipping Act* and the development of the doctrine of corporate identification before applying the relevant principles to the facts of this case. As a preliminary matter, I believe it important to point out that the identification of particular individuals within a corporate structure as directing minds of that company is a question of mixed fact and law. As Lord Reid observed in *Tesco Supermarkets Ltd. v. Nattrass*, [1972] A.C. 153 (H.L.), at p. 170, "It must be a question of law whether, once the facts have been ascertained, a person in doing particular things is to be regarded as the company or merely as the company's servant or agent." The legal issue is concerned with identifying which functions or offices ground corporate identification; the factual issue determines who carries out these functions or fills these offices.

(a) The General Principles of Limitation of Liability and Corporate Identification

It is well settled that in an action to limit liability under s. 647(2) of the *Canada Shipping Act*, the onus is on the shipowner claiming the limitation to establish a complete absence of "actual fault or privity" on its part. The onus is a heavy one which is not discharged by showing merely that the owner was not the sole or principal cause of the mishap: *Stein v. The Ship "Kathy K"*, [1976] 2 S.C.R. 802, at p. 819.

The leading Anglo-Canadian case setting out the meaning of the words "actual fault or privity" and its application to a corporate shipowner is *Lennard's Carrying Co. v. Asiatic Petroleum Co.*, [1915] A.C. 705 (H.L.), aff'g [1914] 1 K.B. 419 (C.A.). The words "actual fault or privity" were found to denote something personal and blameworthy to a shipowner as opposed to a constructive fault arising under the doctrine of respondeat superior. In the oft quoted words of Viscount Haldane L.C. at pp. 713-14:

> It must be upon the true construction of that section in such a case as the present one that the fault or privity is the fault or privity of somebody who is not merely a servant or agent for whom the company is liable upon the footing *respondeat superior*, but somebody for whom the company is liable because his action is the very action of the company itself. It is not enough that the fault should be the fault of a servant in order to exonerate the owner, the fault must also be one which is not the fault of the owner, or a fault to which the owner is privy; and I take the view that when anybody sets up that section to excuse himself from the normal consequences of the maxim *respondeat superior* the burden lies upon him to do so.

In *Paterson Steamships, Ltd. v. Robin Hood Mills, Ltd. (The Thordoc)* (1937), 58 Ll. L. Rep. 33 (P.C.), Lord Roche adopted the meaning attributed to the words "fault and privity" by both the Court of Appeal and the House of Lords in *Lennard's, supra*, and further highlighted that the fault or privity of a shipowner must be fault or privity in respect of that which causes the loss or damage in question. See also *British Columbia Telephone Co. v. Marpole Towing Ltd.*, [1971] S.C.R. 321, at pp. 326-27, per Ritchie J.

Therefore, in the case of a corporate shipowner, it is necessary to consider whether the acts of a particular individual giving rise to liability should be attributed to that of the company itself. Said differently, the question that arises is at what point in the hierarchy of a company is the fault of a person employed in the organization to be treated as the fault of the company itself. In this connection, the nature of a corporation was aptly described by Viscount Haldane L.C. in *Lennard's, supra*, in the following manner at p. 713:

> My Lords, a corporation is an abstraction. It has no mind of its own any more than it has a body of its own; its active and directing will must consequently be sought in the person of somebody who for some purposes may be called an agent, but who is really the directing mind and will of the corporation, the very ego and centre of the personality of the corporation. That person may be under the direction of the shareholders in general meeting; that person may be the board of directors itself, or it may be, and in some companies it is so, that that person has an authority co-ordinate with the board of directors given to him under the articles of association, and is appointed by the general meeting of the company, and can only be removed by the general meeting of the company.

In *H. L. Bolton (Engineering) Co. v. T. J. Graham & Sons Ltd.*, [1957] 1 Q.B. 159, the Court of Appeal compared a corporation to a human body, describing those who control what a company does (and who therefore are the directing mind and will of a company) as the brain of an individual. Denning L.J. rejected the argument that only actions arising from a meeting of a company's board of directors can form the intention of a company. Rather, he accepted that the intention of a company can be derived from its officers and agents in some instances depending on the nature of the matter in consideration and their relative position within the company. Denning L.J. observed at p. 172:

> A company may in many ways be likened to a human body. It has a brain and nerve centre which controls what it does. It also has hands which hold the tools and act in accordance with directions from the centre. Some of the people in the company are mere servants and agents who are nothing more than hands to do the work and cannot be said to represent the mind or will. Others are directors and managers who represent the directing mind and will of the company, and control what it does. The state of mind of these managers is the state of mind of the company and is treated by the law as such.

In *Tesco Supermarkets, supra*, the House of Lords dealt with a situation in which a manager of one store in a chain of supermarkets was found to have been negligent in supervising an employee who placed improperly priced goods for sale, thereby committing a pricing offence under the *Trade Descriptions Act 1968* (U.K.), 1968, c. 29. Their lordships held that the mere fact that the manager exercised limited discretion in the performance of his assigned role did not render him part of the directing mind of the company. Lord Morris of Borth-y-Gest stated at pp. 180-81:

> A system had to be created which could rationally be said to be so designed that the commission of offences would be avoided. There was no delegation of the duty of taking precautions and exercising diligence. There was no such delegation to the manager of a particular store. He did not function as the directing mind or will of the company. His duties as the manager of one store did not involve managing the company. He was one who was being directed. He was one who was employed but he was not a delegate to whom the company passed on its responsibility. He had certain duties which were the result of the taking by the company of all reasonable precautions and of the exercising by the company of all due diligence. He was a person under the control of the company. ... He was, so to speak, a cog in the machine which was devised: it was not left to him to devise it.

Some commentators have suggested that their lordships placed too great a reliance upon form at the expense of function in their analysis: I. A. Muir, "Tesco Supermarkets, Corporate Liability and Fault" (1973), 5 N.Z.U. L. Rev. 357, at p. 365. Glanville Williams states in his *Textbook of Criminal Law* (2nd ed. 1983), at p. 973:

> In crimes requiring *mens rea* it does not greatly matter if the range of persons inculpating the company is restricted, since the purposes of deterrence are generally best served by prosecuting those who are responsible. It is in offences of negligence that the limitation of liability imposed in Tesco is most injurious. That a company should not be liable for an offence of negligence committed by its branch manager, who after all represents the company in the particular locality, is a considerable defect in the law.

Another commentator characterizes *Tesco Supermarkets* and the cases which followed it as evincing a "socially unjustifiable regression" which was incapable of providing effective deterrence against criminal conduct perpetrated by multinational corporations with complex managerial structures: E. G. Ewaschuk, "Corporate Criminal Liability and Related Matters" in (1975), 29 C.R.N.S. 44, at pp. 52-53.

This Court considered the issue of corporate identification in *Canadian Dredge & Dock Co. v. The Queen*, [1985] 1 S.C.R. 662. Estey J. found that in order for a corporation to be criminally liable under the "identification" theory, the employee who physically committed the offence must be "the 'ego', the 'centre' of the corporate personality, the 'vital organ' of the body corporate, the *'alter ego'* of the employer corporation or its 'directing mind'" (p. 682). However, he also acknowledged that there may be more than one directing mind and highlighted that there may exist the "delegation and sub-delegation of authority from the corporate centre" and the "division and subdivision of the corporate brain." In this regard, Estey J. provided the following guidance as to who may qualify as the directing mind of a corporation at p. 693, casting doubt in the process of whether the specific conclusion reached in *Tesco Supermarkets, supra,* is appropriate in the Canadian context:

> The identity doctrine merges the board of directors, the managing director, the superintendent, the manager or anyone else delegated by the board of directors to whom is delegated the governing executive authority of the corporation, and the conduct of any of the merged entities is thereby attributed to the corporation. ... [A] corporation may, by this means, have more than one directing mind. This must be particularly so in a country such as Canada where corporate operations are frequently geographically widespread. The transportation companies, for example, must of necessity operate by the delegation and sub-delegation of authority from the corporate centre; by the division and subdivision of the corporate brain; and by decentralizing by delegation the guiding forces in the corporate undertaking. The application of the identification rule in *Tesco, supra,* may not accord with the realities of life in our country, however appropriate we may find to be the enunciation of the abstract principles of law there made.

As Estey J.'s reasons demonstrate, the focus of inquiry must be whether the impugned individual has been delegated the "governing executive authority" of the company within the scope of his or her authority. I interpret this to mean that one must determine whether the discretion conferred on an employee amounts to an express or implied delegation of executive authority to design and supervise the implementation of corporate policy rather than simply to carry out such policy. In other words, the courts must consider who has been left with the decision-making power in a relevant sphere of corporate activity.

Negligence on the part of a master of a ship in the performance of his or her navigational duties does not amount to actual fault or privity on the part of a corporate shipowner. Courts have viewed masters as the "hands" of a shipping company. Obviously, if it were otherwise a corporate shipowner's right to limit its liability would be virtually nonexistent. However, having said that, the courts have moved away from allowing shipowners to wash their hands completely of all responsibility for matters of navigation by leaving everything to the discretion of their masters. Whereas in the past it may have been sufficient for a shipowner to discharge its responsibility by merely showing that it appointed a competent master, a number of decisions now make it clear that there exists an overall duty on a shipowner to supervise properly the navigation of its vessels: see, for example, *Grand Champion Tankers, supra,* and *Continental Bank of Canada v. Riedel International Inc.* (1991), 78 D.L.R. (4th) 232 (F.C.A.).

In such instances, the focus of inquiry is on whether a shipowner acted as an ordinary reasonable shipowner in the management and control of its shipping operation (e.g., in the selection of its crew and supervision of the navigation of its vessels): *The Lady Gwendolen, supra,* and *The Garden City,* [1982] 2 Lloyd's Rep. 382 (Q.B. (Adm.Ct.)). Courts have further applied a "reasonable likelihood" test in determining whether the exercise of particular duty by a shipowner would have prevented the impugned damage. For example, in *Marpole Towing, supra,* Ritchie J. accepted that damage caused by the negligent navigation of a ship does not give rise to actual fault or privity on the part of the shipowner where the navigational error committed by the tug master could not have been foreseen by the shipowner.

The issue, however, this Court is asked to consider is not whether Great Lakes breached its duty to supervise and manage its vessels properly but instead whether Captain Kelch's faults are essentially the actual faults of Great Lakes by reason of his position within the corporate hierarchy of the appellant. In this regard, it is relevant to note Hugessen J.A.'s observation at p. 213 that "if Kelch was truly a directing mind and will of the company, the fact that he was also acting as master and that his negligence was committed in that capacity is nothing to the point": see also *Wishing Star Fishing, supra,* and *Société anonyme des minerais v. Grant Trading Inc. (The Ert Stefanie),* [1989] 1 Lloyd's Rep. 349 (C.A.). The appellant did not challenge this proposition before this Court and, in light of the conclusion I have arrived at, I need not discuss this matter any further.

(b) Application of These Principles to This Case

...

With respect, I cannot agree with the conclusion reached by the courts below as to the status of Captain Kelch as a directing mind of Great Lakes. In my opinion, the facts of this case do not merely put it at "the outer margins of the application of the doctrine of corporate identification" but outside those margins.

While Captain Kelch was described as part of the "management" and a "trouble shooter" for Great Lakes ... one must look behind these labels and consider the responsibilities and functions performed by Captain Kelch within the Great Lakes' hierarchy in the context of captains of seafaring vessels. In this respect, it is clear from the totality of the evidence that Captain Kelch was essentially a port captain subject to the supervision and direction of Captain Lloyd. It is not surprising that given his twenty-five years of expertise that Kelch was given additional responsibilities in such matters as breaking in new tug captains, assisting with occasional problems, and taking care of documents for Great Lakes' fleet. However, these additional tasks, in my mind, do not denote delegation to Captain Kelch of the governing executive authority over the management and supervision of Great Lakes' fleet. This authority remained with Captain Lloyd, as is borne out by the evidence.

For example, Captain Kelch described both his and Captain Lloyd's role at Great Lakes in the following manner:

Q.   At the end of your employment with Great Lakes, you were a fleet captain?

A.   Port captain, or whatever.

Q.   What were your duties?

...

A.   Flunkie ... I was a flunkie, believe me, more or less a trouble shooter. I would make tows. I could communicate pretty good with the unions, you know, really.

...

Q.   Chick Lloyd was mentioned. Who exactly is he?

...

A.   He is the flunkie now. He was the operations manager. He was a vice-president.

Q.   He was a vice-president and operations manager. What were the nature of his duties then?

A.   Well, he could make prices on the tows. They would come to him if somebody wanted a specific tow or tug or anything like that.

Q.   Was he responsible for crewing the tugs?

A.   Well, in a way. I mean he had a lot of people that if he didn't want them on there, they didn't go. He was in charge of the whole operation, really, as far as the marine end of it, you know.

Q.   And I take it then he was your supervisor?

A.   My supervisor, my immediate supervisor, yes.

Q.   Did you report only to him?

A.   Just about. I never had any cause to report to anyone one else unless, of course, you call into the dispatcher. I mean, I was under Chick Lloyd. I did — whatever rotten job he had for me, I done.

(Captain Kelch, Commission Evidence, Appeal Book, app. I, vol. 3, at pp. 404-6; see also pp. 299 and 411.)

...

With respect, I think that the courts below overemphasized the significance of sub-delegation in this case. The key factor which distinguishes directing minds from normal employees is the capacity to exercise decision-making authority on matters of corporate policy, rather than merely to give effect to such policy on an operational basis, whether at head office or across the sea. While Captain Kelch no doubt had certain decision-making authority on navigational matters as an incident of his role as master of the tug Ohio and was given important operational duties, governing authority over the management and operation of Great Lakes' tugs lay elsewhere. Therefore, I am of the view that the courts below erred in holding that Captain Kelch was part of the directing mind and will of Great Lakes. As a result, the collision between the Rhone and the Widener did not occur with the actual fault or privity of Great Lakes.

[La Forest, L'Heureux-Dubé, Sopinka, Gonthier, Cory, and McLachlin JJ. concurred with this part of the judgment.]

QUESTIONS

1. Do you agree that the question whether someone is the "directing mind" of a corporation is a question of mixed law and fact? Why did Iacobucci J. make this point?

2. Review the test given by Iacobucci J. in *The "Rhone"* for establishing corporate *mens rea*. Apply the test to the following fact situation. Of what criminal offence, if any, is the corporation guilty?

    > The secretary and general manager of a corporation and the sales manager of its Nottingham branch sold certain of the corporation's goods. Their object was to defraud the corporation by keeping the proceeds for themselves. In furtherance of this objective the secretary, who kept the accounts, and the general manager made false returns in respect of purchase tax on the amount of sales. The two individuals and the corporate defendant were charged with making false returns with intent to deceive contrary to the *Finance (No. 2) Act 1940*, s. 35.

    Compare your answer with the analysis of Viscount Caldecote L.C.J. in *Moore v. I. Bresler, Ltd.*, [1944] 2 All E.R. 515 (Eng. Div. Ct.). The corporation was convicted, but on appeal to Quarter Sessions the conviction was discharged on the ground that the sales were not made by the officers of the Company as the agents of or with the authority of the corporation but in defrauding it. This decision was appealed to the English Divisional Court. Viscount Caldecote had this to say.

    > These two men were important officials of the company, and when they made statements and rendered returns which were proved in this case, they were clearly making those statements and giving those returns as the officers of the company, the proper officers to make the returns. Their acts, therefore ... were the acts of the company. It is only because, for some reason which I am not able to fathom, he thinks that they have converted the goods of the company and made them their own and so acted without authority, that the recorder came to the conclusion that the appeal ought to be allowed. How he came to base his decision upon the fallacious reasoning contained in his opinion, if I may say so with great respect to him, I do not know. It is sufficient for us, I think, to say that he went wrong on a point of law and on the facts stated in this case these two people acting as officers of the company made the company liable for the offence which was committed.

    > The case, therefore, ought to go back to the recorder with a direction to find the offence proved.

    Two critical questions arise from this decision.

(a) Viscount Caldecote said that the two men involved in the defrauding of the corporation were "important officials". But does this alone satisfy the test set out in *The "Rhone"*? What is required is an offence conceived by the "directing minds" of the company before the company can be held criminally liable. Does holding it liable for the actions of "important officials" suggest an element of vicarious liability?

(b) The charge alleged an attempt to defraud. Each manager tried to defraud the corporation. If the mind of the corporation was inside his head, was the corporation intending to defraud itself? Is that possible? Alternatively, could it be argued that the manager falsified the returns while thinking both as the corporation and in his individual capacity — that is, as two separate minds? How is this issue resolved outside the criminal context? Recall the cases in the last chapter on corporate agency, inducing breach of contract, and assisting in a breach of trust.

3.   Would a criminal indictment for conspiracy to defraud lie against a director where the only other party to the conspiracy is a corporation that she controls? Think out the basic principles for yourself, then see *R. v. Electrical Contractors Assn. (of Canada)*, [1961] O.R. 265, 27 D.L.R. (2d) 193 and *R. v. McDonnell*, [1966] 1 All E.R. 193.

2. A Corporate Defence

CANADIAN DREDGE & DOCK CO. v. THE QUEEN

[1985] S.C.J. No. 28, [1985] 1 S.C.R. 662, 19 D.L.R. (4th) 314

[Four corporate appellants appealed their convictions for rigging bids under ss. 338(1) and 423(1)(*d*) of the *Criminal Code*. Each corporation had a manager who conducted the business of the corporation relating to the submission of bids for contracts. Corporate criminal liability was denied by the appellants, notwithstanding the managers' positions, because these managers allegedly (i) were acting in fraud of their corporations; (ii) were acting for their own benefit; and (iii) were acting outside the scope of their employment.]

Estey J. (at 683): — It is the wrongful action of the "primary" representative which by attribution to the corporation creates "primary" rather than "vicarious" liability, according to the identification theory.... Lord Reid in *Tesco Supermarkets Ltd. v. Nattrass*, [1972] A.C. 153 (H.L.), challenged the accuracy of the expression "*alter ego*" and so joins Viscount Haldane in the use of the expression "ego" of the corporation. It follows that the management officer is not guilty additionally of the offence of conspiring with the employer to commit the wrongful act in question because in the identification theory there is only one entity, the natural, and legal person having merged into one identity, and hence the basic requirement of two persons in a conspiracy is not met. See *R. v. Martin*, [1932] 3 W.W.R. 1 (Man. C.A.), *per* Dennistoun J.A., at p. 8; *R. v. McDonnell*, [1966] 1 All E.R. 193, at p. 201; Leigh, "The Criminal Liability of Corporations and Other Groups" *supra*, at p. 257; and Ewaschuk, "Corporate Criminal Liability and Related Matters" (1975), 29 C.R.N.S. 44, at pp. 62-64; but see also *R. v. Electrical Contractors Association of Ontario and Dent, supra*, at p. 272.

The principle of attribution of criminal actions of agents to the employing corporate principal in order to find criminal liability in the corporation only operates where the directing mind is acting within the scope of his *authority*

(*Beamish, supra*, at pp. 890 and 892, and *St. Lawrence, supra*, at p. 320), in the sense of acting in the course of the corporation's business (Halsbury's 4th ed., vol. 14, p. 30, paragraph 34, *supra*). Scattered throughout the submissions on behalf of the four appellants, was a translation of the directing mind rule to a requirement that for its application the directing mind must, at all times, be acting in the scope of his employment. Conversely, the argument went, if the directing mind was acting totally outside the "scope of that employment", the attribution of the acts of the directing mind to the corporate employer would not occur. The terminological problems arise from the fact that the concept of vicarious liability in the law of torts has been traditionally fenced in by the concept of the employee acting within "the scope of his employment" and not, in the classic words, "on a frolic of his own". The identification theory, however, is not concerned with the scope of employment in the tortious sense. "Scope of employment" in the *St. Lawrence* judgment, *supra*, and the other discussions of that term in Canadian law have reference to the field of operations delegated to the directing mind. The charge by His Lordship to the jury makes this abundantly clear, as does the Court of Appeal in its analysis of this defence. The Court in *St. Lawrence, supra*, in describing the elements of the delegation theory, concluded by adding that attribution to the corporation occurred only so long as the directing will "was acting in the scope of his *employment*". The expression comes from the law of tort and agency and from master and servant law. It is not apt in relation to the identification theory. It smacks of vicarious liability and it invites the defence that criminal actions must *prima facie* be beyond the scope of an employee's duty and authority. The learned trial judge, in directing the jury, expressed it more accurately: "... so long as he was acting within the scope of the area of the work assigned to him". In *Tesco, supra*, at p. 171, Lord Reid employed the phrase acting "within the scope of delegation" of the corporation's business. The essence of the test is that the identity of the directing mind and the company coincide so long as the actions of the former are performed by the manager within the sector of [corporate] operation assigned to him by the corporation. The sector may be functional, or geographic, or may embrace the entire undertaking of the corporation. The requirement is better stated when it is said that the act in question must be done by the directing force of the company when carrying out his assigned function in the corporation. It is no defence to the application of this doctrine that a criminal act by a corporate employee cannot be within the scope of his authority unless expressly ordered to do the act in question. Such a condition would reduce the rule to virtually nothing. Acts of the ego of a corporation taken within the assigned managerial area may give rise to corporate criminal responsibility, whether or not there be formal delegation; whether or not there be awareness of the activity in the board of directors or the officers of the company; and, as discussed below, whether or not there be express prohibition. [**Estey J.** considered the evidence and found the managers to be the directing minds of their respective corporations.]

. . .

I turn to the submission by the appellants that the identification theory cannot import into the criminal law a brand of vicarious liability under any of the authorities where the wrongful acts of the directing mind were done in fraud on the employer, for the benefit of the employee, or contrary to the instructions issued by the employer. Whether there be evidence to support a finding that the employee of each of these appellants acted in fraud on the employer, for his own benefit, or contrary to instructions, I set aside until after the applicability of these defences in Canadian criminal law is examined.

The third defence, acts carried out in the face of express instructions to the contrary, is susceptible to easy disposition. ... If the law recognized such a defence, a corporation might absolve itself from criminal consequence by the simple device of adopting and communicating to its staff a general instruction prohibiting illegal conduct and directing conformity at all times with the law. That is not to say that such an element is without relevance when considering corporate liability with reference to offences of strict liability, *supra*. Where, however, the court is concerned with those mens rea offences which can in law be committed by a corporation, the presence of general or specific instructions prohibiting the conduct in question is irrelevant. The corporation and its directing mind became one and the prohibition directed by the corporation to others is of no effect in law on the determination of criminal liability of either the directing mind or the corporation itself by reason of the actions of the directing mind. This accords with the result reached in other courts.

. . .

The two remaining issues as to the effect, if any, of the directing mind of the corporation "acting in whole or in part in fraud on the corporation" or "wholly or partly for his own benefit" raise problems both of terminology and substance. The two questions in substance raise the same legal issues. The immediate question which arises is whether or not there is, in fact and in law, any controlling difference between a directing mind acting in fraud of the corporation and a directing mind acting on behalf of the corporation as its managerial arm but doing so for his own benefit. As will be mentioned below, there are fine factual distinctions which one can make between the two concepts. In substance, however, these appeals can be more usefully analyzed if the practical view is taken that the situation as between the corporation and its directing mind is the same whether the directing mind is acting in fraud of the corporation or whether he is acting against the interests of the corporation for his own benefit.

. . .

The question arises as to whether on the facts and charge of *Moore v. Bresler* there is a defence in respect of either a fraud charge or the *Tax Act* charge in the corporation by reason of the fact that the dishonest act was committed by the directing mind but in fraud on the company or wholly or partly for the benefit of the dishonest employee. Were the charge in question a charge of fraud, there would clearly be no benefit to the corporation, and indeed the design of the dishonest employee was aimed squarely at reducing the financial stature of the employer. It can hardly be said with any reality that a person designing and executing such a scheme could be, while doing so, the directing mind and the ego of the company itself. That being so, no longer would we be faced with the logical conundrum that a person however dishonest cannot defraud himself. Once the *ego* is split into its original two parts that problem disappears. The employee would be guilty of fraud and the victim of that fraud would be the company. The victim would, in all logic, have a defence against a charge that it too had committed fraud in its own right. Were the criminal law otherwise, it would not provide protection of any interest in the community. Punishment of the corporation for such acts of its employee would not advantage society by advancing law and order. It is otherwise, however, where there is benefit to the corporation, in whole or in part, from the unlawful acts of its directing mind. The charge with reference to the tax returns raises different considerations.

...

In my view, the outer limit of the delegation doctrine is reached and exceeded when the directing mind ceases completely to act, in fact or in substance, in the interests of the corporation. Where this entails fraudulent action, nothing is gained from speaking of fraud in whole or in part because fraud is fraud. What I take to be the distinction raised by the question is where all of the activities of the directing mind are directed against the interests of the corporation with a view to damaging that corporation, whether or not the result is beneficial economically to the directing mind, that may be said to be fraud on the corporation. Similarly, but not so importantly, a benefit to the directing mind in single transactions or in a minor part of the activities of the directing mind is in reality quite different from benefit in the sense that the directing mind intended that the corporation should not benefit from any of its activities in its undertaking. A benefit of course can, unlike fraud, be in whole or in part, but the better standard in my view is established when benefit is associated with fraud. The same test then applies. Where the directing mind conceives and designs a plan and then executes it whereby the corporation is intentionally defrauded, and when this is the substantial part of the regular activities of the directing mind in his office, then it is unrealistic in the extreme to consider that the manager is the directing mind of the corporation. His entire energies are, in such a case, directed to the destruction of the undertaking of the corporation. When he crosses that line he ceases to be the directing mind and the doctrine of identification ceases to operate. The same reasoning and terminology can be applied to the concept of benefits.

Where the criminal act is totally in fraud of the corporate employer and where the act is intended to and does result in benefit exclusively to the employee-manager, the employee-directing mind, from the outset of the design and execution of the criminal plan, ceases to be a directing mind of the corporation and consequently his acts could not be attributed to the corporation under the identification doctrine. This might be true as well on the American approach through respondeat superior. Whether this is so or not, in my view the identification doctrine only operates where the Crown demonstrates that the action taken by the directing mind (a) was within the field of operation assigned to him; (b) was not totally in fraud of the corporation; and (c) was by design or result partly for the benefit of the company.

[**Estey J.** found that the directing minds of the corporations (the managers) were acting partly for the benefit of the corporations and partly for their own benefit. Since the managers were not acting wholly in fraud of their employees, the corporations could not raise a defence and were held liable. The appeal was dismissed.]

NOTES AND QUESTIONS

1. Is the "identification theory" consistent with the commonly expressed idea that a corporation can only act through agents? If corporations could only act through agents, then whenever a corporation was liable for (say) the tort of negligence, that could only be through vicarious liability for the negligence of an agent. In that case, the agent would also be liable for negligence, because the vicarious liability of a principal does not excuse an agent.

2. The conspiracy cases, approved by Estey J., suggest that where an individual's mind counts as the corporate mind, it *ipso facto* ceases to be the individual's mind. There can be no conspiracy because a conspiracy requires two minds conspiring, and the individual's mind is either his own *or* the corporation's, but not both. That is consistent with the principles discussed in the last chapter. If individuals acting as the corporation are also acting as themselves, then does corporate personality have any practical effects?

    On the other hand, if this is right, then when an offence is committed it is committed by either the corporation or an individual, but not both (at least in the absence of a statute expressly imposing personal liability on directors or officers: see *R. v. Bata Industries Ltd. (No. 2)*, [1992] O.J. No. 236, 9 O.R. (3d) 329, 70 C.C.C. (3d) 394 (Prov. Div.); varied [1993] O.J. No. 1679, 14 O.R. (3d) 354 (Gen. Div.)). In *R. v. Fell* (1981), 131 D.L.R. (3d) 105 (Ont. C.A.), Martin J.A., speaking for the Ontario Court of Appeal and quoting Glanville Williams, said:

    > ... the fact that the acts of the respondent were at law those of the corporation for the purpose of imposing liability on it did not prevent the conviction of the respondent as a principal or as an aider and abettor as the facts might warrant.

    Similarly, in *Canadian Dredge & Dock Co.*, Estey J. said (emphasis added):

    > In order to trigger [the identification theory's] operation and through it corporate criminal liability for the actions of the employee (*who must generally be liable himself*), the actor/employee who physically committed the offence must be the "ego", the "centre" of the corporate personality, the "vital organ" of the body corporate, the "alter ego" of the employer corporation or its "directing mind".

    Is it any more possible to aid or abet yourself than it is to conspire with yourself or defraud yourself? Is there any reason that conspiracy should be a special case? Do you think that all of the implications of the identification theory have been worked out? Is it possible that it only works in one direction, to attach liability to the corporation, but not in the other direction, to remove liability from the individual? If so, how would this apply in the case of corporate torts? Corporate contracts?

3. The defendant corporation, a used car dealer, was charged under s. 338(1) of the *Criminal Code* for altering an odometer. The alteration was made by a mechanic who had been told to do so by G, a used car sales manager. G was neither a director nor an officer. His responsibilities were to buy used cars, clean them, do minor reconditioning work, fix the selling price, arrange advertising, and demonstrate and sell them to the public. He was supported by a staff of 12, some of whom sold and some of whom did mechanical work, but all final sales decisions were his. The president of the corporation had previously circulated written instructions to all personnel, ordering that odometers not be altered.

    (a) Who was the directing mind of the corporation?

    (b) Could the corporation be held criminally liable for G's actions? Why or why not?

    (c) What is the effect of the president's instructions?

    (d) What defences does the corporation have to a charge under the *Criminal Code*?

    (e) What would be the effect of a clause in the corporate constitution stating either

        (i) "the corporation doesn't have the capacity to change odometers";

        (ii) "the corporation doesn't have the power to change odometers";

(iii) "the corporation won't change odometers"; or

(iv) "the corporation does not have the capacity or power to commit criminal offences".

Legg D.C.J., in *R. v. Waterloo Mercury Sales Ltd.*, [1974] 4 W.W.R. 516, 49 D.L.R. (3d) 131 (Alta. Dist. Ct.) found the corporation criminally liable on the above facts.

It is not obvious what societal goals were advanced by convicting the corporation in the *Waterloo Mercury* case. G seems clearly guilty. Had he turned back the odometer following superior orders, the individual who gave the order could have been convicted of counselling the offence. Whenever a corporation is convicted of a *mens rea* offence, one element of proving the corporate guilt will be to identify some individual in the corporation as a criminal. What, if anything, is gained by complicating the case and trying to convict the corporation? Does this suggest that earlier views that the criminal law had no application to corporations were correct?

It is now clear that a corporation cannot construct a successful defence merely by showing that, as a matter of official delegation of authority on the corporation's organization chart, the individual in question was not the proper corporate official to make the decision. The courts have found corporations guilty where corporate practice has created delegated authority beyond that authorized by the corporate constitution. As yet it is unclear whether a corporation will be found guilty where *de facto* authority has inadvertently been created in low-level personnel by careless managerial practice rather than by conscious decisions to short-circuit the formal managerial hierarchy.

4.   What if the president of Waterloo Mercury Sales Ltd. had circulated a second memo to all employees after the conviction, ordering that odometers were not to be turned back? Would that serve as a corporate defence if G or his replacement did it again?

5.   Does it matter what the individual employee's motivation was? Would the corporation be convicted if someone in G's position turned back odometers to enhance his prospects of winning a vacation trip to be awarded to the highest volume sales manager? What if a corporate employee had recently been disciplined for some unrelated industrial offence and decided to turn back the odometer on some used cars in order to cause trouble for corporate management?

6.   The criminal law has recognized that those who know that they are subject to loss of control over their bodies must take greater precautions than others. But they are not convicted on a strict liability basis, or on the grounds that at the time of the incident, their hands had a mind of their own. Should our treatment of corporations be any different? On the other hand, could this principle help corporations in the case of *mens rea* offences? If we have concluded that an individual with a guilty mind was *the* directing mind of the corporation, then doesn't that imply that the corporation knew exactly what it was doing?

What types of precautions would a corporation be required to take in order to avoid the possibility of being convicted due to unauthorized acts of its personnel? In support of the principle that corporations should be allowed to show a plan of prevention as a defence, at least to certain types of offences, see the Law Reform Commission of Canada, Working Paper No. 16 (1976).

3. Non *Mens Rea* Offences

R. v. FITZPATRICK'S FUEL LTD.

[2000] N.J. No. 149 (Prov. Ct.)

[The corporation was licensed to sell beer. It was charged with selling liquor to a minor. Peter Fitzpatrick was the sole shareholder, sole director, and sole officer. There were two employees, who worked alternating shifts, alone and unsupervised. A 17-year-old minor bought six beer.]

Handrigan Prov. Ct. J.: — The business is called "Fitzpatrick's Gas Bar" and its main interest is selling fuel for motor vehicles. Beer sales are not an important part of the revenue generated by the business. They are largely a "lost leader" [*sic*] designed to entice customers to the gas bar for fuel sales, or as Peter Fitzpatrick said, a "convenience" to his customers.

The licence ... authorized the Company to sell beer to "any person not disqualified to purchase it by or under this Act or Regulations". ... In the province of Newfoundland and Labrador, the minimum age at which a person may purchase and/or consume alcoholic beverages, including "Local Brewery Products", is 19 years.

On New Year's Eve, December 31, 1999, at some time in the early evening hours, Evan Michael Brennan entered the Fitzpatrick's Gas Bar. He asked to buy beer and a half dozen Black Horse beer was presented. The lone attendant, Parviz Zamzam, an employee of Fitzpatrick's, served him. He left the store with his purchase and returned to a "party" that he had been at earlier.

Over the course of the evening, Evan Brennan drank the beer, and a large amount of other liquor products. In fact, he was taken to hospital by ambulance, in a comatose state, in the early morning hours of the New Year. He says that he remembers little of what happened to him after he drank the beer, until he awoke in hospital the next day and wondered how he had gotten there.

Zamzam testified that he was working during the evening hours of New Years' Eve. He ... did not know Evan Brennan ... He said that he is aware of the age restriction that applies for beer sales and that he follows the required practice of asking for identification and proof of age where there were any doubts as to a customer's age. He also confirmed that there were signs posted in the store that stated the policy with respect to sales to minors and other advisory notices with respect to beer sales.

...

Peter Fitzpatrick testified on behalf of the Company. He said that his is a sole corporation, of which he is the only shareholder and officer and director. He said that the company was incorporated to operate the gas bar and that the gas bar is its only undertaking. He said that he is aware of the interdiction as to beer sales to minors and that he instructs his staff accordingly. Signs are posted about the premises to this effect and the staff is directed to ask for proof of age if they are in doubt as to a customer's age. Under no circumstances are they permitted to sell beer to minors.

...

The *Liquor Control Act* is public welfare legislation. The section under which the accused is charged creates a strict liability offence. The Company will be found guilty if the Crown proves the *actus reus* of the offence, unless the Company can show that it took reasonable care, or exercised due diligence, to avoid the commission of the offence. There is no requirement to prove the *mens rea*. A guilty mind need not be shown.

[**Handrigan J.** listed his findings of fact, and concluded beyond a reasonable doubt that the *actus reus* of the offence had been proved.]

...

The question unresolved is this: despite the care exercised by its sole officer, director, and shareholder, Peter Fitzpatrick, should the Company still be held liable for the wrongful actions of Parviz Zamzam? The Crown says "Yes!" and submits that a correct application of the "identification theory" of corporations will prove as much. I turn now to a consideration of this theory.

The seminal case on the identification theory (sometimes called the "identification doctrine"), in Canadian jurisprudence, is *Canadian Dredge & Dock Co. Ltd. et al. v. The Queen* (1985), 19 C.C.C. (3d) 1. Mr. Justice Estey explored the law with respect to corporate identity, in the context of criminal prosecutions, by canvassing all of the major common law jurisdictions throughout the world. He was concerned primarily of the criminal liability of corporations charged with offences that require the Crown to prove mens rea. However, his remarks with respect to identity apply with equal relevance to strict liability offences.

It is important to understand that the criminal liability of a corporation for the conduct of the natural persons who act on behalf of the corporation is a primary responsibility. It is not a vicarious one. A full discussion of how criminal liability attaches to corporations in each of the three categories of offences is set out in this lengthy passage from *Canadian Dredge, supra*:

> The position of the corporation in criminal law must first be examined. Inasmuch as all criminal and quasi-criminal offences are creatures of statute the amenability of the corporation to prosecution necessarily depends in part upon the terminology employed in the statute. In recent years there has developed a system of classification which segregates the offences according to the degree of intent, if any, required to create culpability.

> (a)   Absolute Liability Offences

> Where the legislature by the clearest intendment establishes an offence where liability arises instantly upon the breach of the statutory prohibition, no particular state of mind is a prerequisite to guilt. Corporations and individual persons stand on the same footing in the face of such a statutory offence. It is a case of automatic primary responsibility. Accordingly, there is no need to establish a rule for corporate liability nor a rationale therefor. The corporation is treated as a natural person.

> (b)   Offences of Strict Liability

> Where the terminology employed by the legislature is such as to reveal an intent that guilt shall not be predicated upon the automatic breach of the statute but rather upon the establishment of the *actus reus*, subject to the defence of due diligence, an offence of strict liability arises. See *R. v. City of Sault St. Marie*, [1978] 2 S.C.R. 1299. As in the case of an absolute liability offence, it matters not whether the accused is corporate or unincorporate, because the liability is primary and arises in the accused according to the terms of the statute in the same way as in the case of absolute offences. It is not dependent upon the attribution to the accused of the misconduct of others. This is so when the statute, properly construed, shows a clear contemplation by the Legislature that a breach of the statute itself leads to guilt, subject to the limited defence

above noted. In this category, the corporation and the natural defendant are in the same position. In both cases liability is not vicarious but primary.

[He contrasted traditional *mens rea* offences, then summarized the position of a corporation in Canadian criminal law.]

Criminal responsibility in our courts thus far has been achieved in the *mens rea* offences by the attribution to the corporation of the acts of its employees and agents on the more limited basis of the doctrine of the directing mind or identification. Corporate responsibility in both strict and absolute liability offences has been found to arise on the direct imposition of a primary duty in the corporation in the statute in question, as construed by the court.

...

It is clear then that the liability which attaches to corporations in whichever context is appropriate does so because of the identification of the corporation with the natural persons who act on behalf of it. But just how does this occur? Once again, Mr. Justice Estey is to the rescue:

The corporation is but a creature of statute, general or special, and none of the provincial corporation statutes and business corporations statutes, or the federal equivalents, contain any discussion of criminal liability or liability in the common law generally by reason of the doctrine of identification. It is a court-adopted principle put in place for the purpose of including the corporation in the pattern of criminal law in a rational relationship to that of the natural person. The identity doctrine merges the board of directors, the managing director, the superintendent, the manager or anyone else delegated by the board of directors to whom is delegated the governing executive authority of the corporation, and the conduct of any of the merged entities is thereby attributed to the corporation.

There may be a concern as to the scope at which this doctrine operates. In that behalf ... there are conditions that attach to its application. As might be expected, it is not every wrongful act of the "directing mind(s)" of the corporation for which it will be criminally responsible:

...

The Crown submits that the Company should be held accountable for the actions of Parviz Zamzam. Even though he was no more than an employee of the Company filling the position of gas attendant/cashier, the Crown views him as the "directing mind" of Fitzpatrick's and contends that the identity of the Company "merges" with his when he is performing the duties delegated to him by his employer. As a result, it further submits, his conduct is "attributed to the company" and it is "primarily liable" for it.

At first blush, this position suffers from the doubt that it is pushing the concept of "directing mind" too far to argue that the identity of the Company can merge in that of an employee of the status of Parviz Zamzam. After all, he simply sold gas, confectionaries, cigarettes and beer for it. However ... the natural person who represents that company and who "acts" as it in providing any of the services delivered by the Company is the employee specifically authorized and instructed for that purpose. On New Year's Eve, December 31, 1999, that person was Parviz Zamzam. Peter Fitzpatrick can be identified easily as the "directing mind" of the Company but it was Parviz Zamzam, not he that Evan Brennan and all other member of the public dealt with when they transacted business at the gas bar and convenience store on that evening.

As well, when Zamzam sold the half dozen bottle of beer to Brennan the transaction fell squarely with the parameters delineated by Mr. Justice Estey in *Canadian Dredge, supra*. It was:

(a) within the field of operation assigned to him;

(b) not totally in fraud of the corporation; and,

(c) by design or result partly for the benefit of the company.

Occasionally, concern is expressed that the application of the "identification doctrine" may result in injustices being inflicted on corporation. In this case, for example, the accused might be heard to say that it could do no more than it did — post warning signs in conspicuous places about the place of business warning of the restrictions on the sale of beer to minors, and instruct its employees to be ever vigilant for minors and when in doubt as to age, ask for identification and proof of age. If customers who are under the age of majority persist in trying to buy beer despite the signs, or employees are less than circumspect in the dealings with underage customers the Company should not be visited with their omissions.

The answer to that criticism is twofold: in the first instance, there is the simple admonition that it is the price of doing business. Corporations are staples in the delivery of modern commerce and their owners enjoy all of the benefits that accompany the use of them, not the least of which is the limitation of their liabilities to their creditors. Secondly, corporations hire their employees and are obliged to exercise care that the people they hold out to do their business for them are reliable and dependable. Mr. Justice Estey made no apologies for the application of the identification doctrine in *Canadian Dredge, supra*, calling it "the product of judicial necessity brought on by the realities of the modern community". He declined to define the "outer limits" of the doctrine, except to say that it would not apply in the situation where the "directing mind" acted entirely for his own benefit and directed his principal efforts to defrauding the company. There was no fraud on Fitzpatrick's when Parviz Zamzam sold the Black Horse beer to Evan Brennan.

For these reasons, I find the charge against the accused is proved beyond a reasonable doubt.

4. Statutory Reform

Amendments to the *Criminal Code*, R.S.C. 1985, c. C-46 in 2004 altered the treatment of the criminal mind. Bill C-45 was passed with the purpose of making it easier to prosecute large corporations. A number of changes were made. First, the statute defines which individuals involved within the corporation will provide the *mens rea* element. A "senior officer" must be found. The term is defined in s. 2 to be "a representative who plays an important role in the establishment of an organization's policies or is responsible for managing an important aspect of the organization's activities". This specifically includes the directors, chief executive officer and chief financial officer.

Once a senior officer is found, s. 22.2 of the Code says that the corporation is a party to the offence if any senior officer has the intention to benefit the corporation in part and

(a) acting within the scope of their authority, is a party to the offence;

(b) having the mental state required for the offence, directs representatives to commit the prohibited act or make the omission; or

(c) knowing that a representative of the organization is or is about to be a party to the offence, does not take all reasonable measures to stop them from being a party to the offence.

For an offence requiring criminal negligence instead of intention, the standard is codified by s. 22.1 of the *Criminal Code*. This says that the corporation is a party to the offence if:

(a) a representative of the corporation is acting within the scope of his authority; and

(b) "the senior officer who is responsible for the aspect of the organization's activities that is relevant to the offence departs ... markedly from the standard of care that, in the circumstances, could reasonably be expected to prevent a representative of the organization from being a party to the offence."

For all crimes, whether they require negligence or intention, the *actus reus* element can be satisfied by any individual involved in the corporation committing the act. However, the *mens rea* element must be satisfied by a senior officer.

QUESTIONS

1. *The "Rhone"* said that the test for the appropriate individual to provide the *mens rea* for a corporation was someone who had "governing authority over the management and operations". Now the "senior officer" must be "responsible for managing an important aspect of the organization's activities". Would Captain Kelch of The "Rhone" have met this test? What about the used car sales manager in *Waterloo Mercury Sales*?

2. The statute still requires that the senior officers have the intention of at least partially benefiting the corporation. Does this do anything more then codify the existing defence used in *Canadian Dredge & Dock Co.*?

3. The identification test was confusing as judges had trouble determining if the relevant individual's mind was the corporate mind. Do the *Criminal Code* amendments change the law in this area at all?

4. Section 7 of the *Canadian Charter of Rights and Freedoms*, Part I of the *Constitution Act, 1982*, being Schedule B to the *Canada Act 1982* (U.K.), 1982, c. 11 has been held to require that a mental element be present in the accused for guilt in cases of indictable offences. Does the new approach violate the *Charter*? Does it matter whether a corporation can be imprisoned?

5. As discussed at the start of this section, punishing corporations has always been a difficult task for judges. This has also been made easier with the amendments to the *Criminal Code*. Compare the specific treatment of corporations for sentencing and probation in s. 718.21 to s. 732.1(3.2) of the Code to the general guidelines in s. 718 and s. 732.1(2). What are the goals of the provisions for corporations?

C. CONTRACTS: AGENTS, OUTSIDERS AND CORPORATE LIABILITY

1. Constitutional Restrictions on a Corporation's Abilities

The extent to which a corporation approaches the status of a fully capable human being depends on the authority that created it. The constitutional documents, whether crown patent, special statute, or articles filed under a general enabling statute, may expressly or impliedly prohibit certain corporate endeavours.

There are two possible interpretations of a statutory prohibition. One is that the intended result can't possibly occur. For example, it is impossible in Canada to contract (as opposed to agree) to murder someone. The other is that the activity is sanctioned by criminal punishment: no one seriously thinks that a "thou shalt not kill" law makes murder impossible. Be wary of leaping to one conclusion or the other when interpreting a corporate statute.

During the nineteenth century, any activity beyond the corporate capacity was usually described as being *ultra vires* the corporation. The term had the same implications as in constitutional law: someone who lacked the capacity to do something clearly didn't do it, despite appearances to the contrary. In the modern corporate setting, the label *ultra vires* has much narrower implications

It was noted in earlier chapters that corporations these days are given "capacity", "rights", "powers" and "privileges" by statute. The same statutes then enact restrictions on the activities of corporations and permit further restrictions to be set out in the corporate constitution. What is a corporate lawyer to make of such restrictions? As usual, the answer evolves from a basic understanding of earlier common law, Equitable and statutory rules.

(a) Restrictions in the Corporate Constitution

COMMUNITIES ECONOMIC DEVELOPMENT FUND v. CANADIAN PICKLES CORP.

[1991] S.C.J. No. 89, [1991] 3 S.C.R. 388, 85 D.L.R. (4th) 88

[The plaintiff was a corporation set up by a special act, *The Communities Economic Development Fund Act*, R.S.M. 1987, c. C155. Its objects, as set out in s. 3 of the Act, were "to encourage the optimum economic development of remote and isolated communities within the province ...".

It purported to make a loan of $150,000 to the defendant corporation, and to take a guarantee of this debt from Robert and June O'Donnell, the defendant's majority shareholders. The money was advanced to the defendant corporation. When it defaulted on the loan, the plaintiff sued it on the loan, and sued the O'Donnells on the guarantees.]

Iacobucci J.: — ...

V. Is the Loan *Ultra Vires*?

There can be no doubt that the appellant's loan to Canadian Pickles was contrary to the objects of the appellant as stated in s. 3 of the Act. Stony Mountain, where Canadian Pickles' operation was located, is not a remote and isolated community. In this regard, I accept the finding of Monnin C.J.M. (dissenting on other grounds): "The town of Stony Mountain is a prosperous and viable non-urban area. It is not remote nor is it an isolated community" (p. 550). Indeed, neither the trial judge nor any judge of the Court of Appeal differed on this point.

...

The making of a loan contrary to the statutory objects of the appellant is a violation of the prohibition in s. 9(7) of the Act against loans which contravene any provision of the Act. The question is, what are the consequences of this violation of s. 9(7) of the Act? Must the loan be *ultra vires* the appellant, or is some less drastic result possible? To answer these questions, a brief review of the law of *ultra vires* is warranted, following which I shall discuss the relevant legal principles as they apply to the facts of the instant case.

A. *The Law of Ultra Vires*

A review the law of *ultra vires* is important to establish the context in which the provisions of the Act should be interpreted. Of particular relevance is the distinction that has been made in the application of the *ultra vires* doctrine between common law and statutory corporations.

(1) Common Law Corporations

Shortly put, the doctrine of *ultra vires* has been applied to corporations created by statute or pursuant to statutory authority, but has not been applied to corporations created by the exercise of the royal prerogative. Corporations created by the exercise of the royal prerogative, known as "chartered", "letters patent" or "common law" corporations, are taken to have all the powers of a natural person. The actions of a common law corporation are not invalid because they are outside the stated objects of a corporation: *Sutton's Hospital Case* (1613), 10 Co. Rep. 1a, 23a, 77 E.R. 937, 960. Legal action may be taken against a common law corporation if it acts outside its objects, but the acts are not invalid.

The Judicial Committee of the Privy Council considered the powers of a letters patent corporation in *Bonanza Creek Gold Mining Co. v. The King*, [1916] 1 A.C. 566. The appellants were incorporated by letters patent issued by the Lieutenant-Governor of Ontario, under the authority both of *The Ontario Companies Act*, R.S.O. 1897, c. 191, and of all other powers and authority vested in the Lieutenant-Governor. The objects of the appellants, as stated in the letters patent, were to carry on the business of mining and exploration. The letters patent did not limit the appellants' area of operation. The appellants were carrying on mining operations in the Yukon. As a result of disagreements over certain mining leases, the appellants brought an action for damages against the respondent. The appeal came to the Judicial Committee of the Privy Council on the bare question of whether the appellants had the power to carry on operations in the Yukon.

The Judicial Committee held that the appellants did have the power to carry on operations in the Yukon, and allowed the appeal. Writing for the Committee, Viscount Haldane distinguished companies created by charter from those created by statute (at pp. 583-84):

> In the case of a company created by charter the doctrine of *ultra vires* has no real application in the absence of statutory restriction added to what is written in the charter. Such a company has the capacity of a natural person to acquire powers and rights. If by the terms of the charter it is prohibited from doing so, a violation of this prohibition is an act not beyond its capacity, and is therefore not *ultra vires*,

although such a violation may well give ground for proceedings by way of *scire facias* for the forfeiture of the charter.

Prior to the decision in *Bonanza Creek*, some Canadian courts had assumed that the doctrine of *ultra vires* did apply to chartered companies: see *Union Bank of Canada v. A. McKillop & Sons, Ltd.* (1915), 51 S.C.R. 518. After the decision, it was clear that restrictions in the charter of the company were not sufficient to make any act *ultra vires*, although other remedies might be available for breach of the charter: see F. W. Wegenast, *The Law of Canadian Companies* (1979), at pp. 141-44. However, the doctrine of *ultra vires* remained applicable to chartered companies after *Bonanza Creek* in the limited sense that an action could still be *ultra vires* the company if the act were prohibited by statute. This conclusion follows from the passage just quoted from *Bonanza Creek*, *supra*, at p. 583: "In the case of a company created by charter the doctrine of *ultra vires* has no real application *in the absence of statutory restriction added to what is written in the charter*" (emphasis added). For analysis, see *Wegenast*, *supra*, at pp. 141-50, and E. J. Mockler's helpful article, "The Doctrine of *Ultra Vires* in Letters Patent Companies", in J.S. Ziegel, ed., *Studies in Canadian Company Law* (1967).

(2) Corporations Created by or under a Statute

The presumption at common law is that corporations created by or under a statute have only those powers which are expressly or impliedly granted to them. To the extent that a corporation acts beyond its powers, its actions are *ultra vires* and invalid. Assessing the limits of the powers of a corporation created by or under a statute is a question of the interpretation of the statute and corporation's constating documents which give the corporation its powers.

If the appropriate language is used, the powers of a corporation created by or under a statute may be as wide as those of a common law corporation. The question will turn on the language used in the statute and constating documents. The point is well illustrated by the following passage from *Bonanza Creek*, *supra*, at p. 578:

> Such a creature, where its entire existence is derived from the statute, will have the incidents which the common law would attach if, but only if, the statute has by its language gone on to attach them. In the absence of such language they are excluded, and if the corporation attempts to act as though they were not, it is doing what is *ultra vires* and so prohibited as lying outside its existence in contemplation of law. The question is simply one of interpretation of the words used. For the statute may be so framed that executive power to incorporate by charter, independently of the statute itself, which some authority, such as a Lieutenant-Governor, possessed before it came into operation, has been left intact. Or the statute may be in such a form that a new power to incorporate by charter has been created, directed to be exercised with a view to the attainment of, for example, merely territorial objects, but not directed in terms which confine the legal personality which the charter creates to existence for the purpose of these objects and within territorial limits. The language may be such as to show an intention to confer on the corporation the general capacity which the common law ordinarily attaches to corporations created by charter.

(a) Memorandum Corporations

The doctrine of *ultra vires* was first applied to memorandum companies incorporated under business corporation statutes in *Ashbury Railway Carriage & Iron Co. v. Riche* (1875), L.R. 7 H.L. 653. The appellant was incorporated under the *Companies Act, 1862.* The purpose of the company, set out in its memorandum, was to carry on business as mechanical engineers and general contractors. The directors of the appellant entered into a contract with the respondent Riche. As part of the contract, the appellant was to purchase a railway concession in Belgium, and to raise money for the construction of the railway. The House of Lords held that the transaction was *ultra vires* the appellant because it was beyond the scope of its memorandum. As a consequence, the contract was null and void, and not capable of ratification by the shareholders of the appellant. Prior to the statutory abolition in most Canadian jurisdictions of the *ultra vires* doctrine for companies incorporated under the business corporation statutes, *Ashbury Railway* and *Bonanza Creek, supra,* were the law in Canada.

(b) Corporations Created by Special Act

The applicability of the doctrine of *ultra vires* to corporations created by special act was at issue in *Attorney-General v. Great Eastern Railway Co.* (1880), 5 App. Cas. 473 (H.L.). The respondent company was incorporated by an Act of Parliament. The respondent was given a variety of powers by several statutes. The respondent purported to lease locomotives to another railway company. The appellant sought an injunction to prevent the respondent from leasing its locomotives or other rolling stock, on the grounds that the directors of the respondent had exceeded their powers. The House of Lords held that the acts in question were *intra vires* the company because expressly authorized by the statutory scheme. In so finding, their Lordships stated emphatically that the principle earlier enunciated in *Ashbury Railway, supra,* applied also to statutory corporations. In the words of Lord Watson, at p. 486:

> I cannot doubt that the principle by which this House, in the case of the *Ashbury Railway Company v. Riche*, tested the power of a joint stock company registered (with limited liability) under the *Companies Act* of 1862, applies with equal force to the case of a railway company incorporated by Act of Parliament. That principle, in its application to the present case, appears to me to be this, that when a railway company has been created for public purposes, the Legislature must be held to have prohibited every act of the company which its incorporating statutes do not warrant either expressly or by fair implication.

The House of Lords affirmed the applicability of *Ashbury Railway* to corporations created by special act in *Baroness Wenlock v. River Dee Co.* (1885), 10 App. Cas. 355 (H.L.). Lord Watson held that the powers of a statutory corporation are limited by the purposes of the corporation as set out in the special act (at pp. 362-63):

> Whenever a corporation is created by Act of Parliament, with reference to the purposes of the Act, and solely with a view to carrying these purposes into execution, I am of opinion not only that the objects which the corporation may legitimately pursue must be ascertained from the Act itself, but that the powers which the corporation may lawfully use in furtherance of these objects must either be expressly conferred or derived by reasonable implication from its provisions.

The principle that a statutory corporation can do only what it is expressly or impliedly authorized to do by the statute creating it has been repeatedly applied by Canadian courts. The principle was approved by Locke J. in this Court, in *Canadian Pacific Railway Co. v. City of Winnipeg*, [1952] 1 S.C.R. 424, at p. 485. The principle was referred to as "trite law" in *Canadian Pacific Ltd. v. Telesat Canada* (1982), 133 D.L.R. (3d) 321 (Ont. C.A.), at p. 326. In *Redlin v. Governors of the University of Alberta* (1979), 8 Alta. L.R. (2d) 313, 23 A.R. 42, 98 D.L.R. (3d) 643 (Dist. Ct.), affirmed unanimously on appeal (1980), 23 A.R. 31, [1980] 4 W.W.R. 133, 110 D.L.R. (3d) 146 (C.A.), Stevenson Dist. Ct. J. (as he then was), said in reference to the same principle that, "One cannot quarrel with that general proposition" (p. 48). I would also refer to *Alberta Mortgage and Housing Corp. v. Ciereszko*, [1986] 2 W.W.R. 57, 41 Alta. L.R. (2d) 242, 67 A.R. 131 (Q.B.). The principle has been recently affirmed by the House of Lords in *Hazell v. Hammersmith and Fulham London Borough Council*, [1991] 2 W.L.R. 372 (H.L.).

(c) Abolition of the Doctrine of Ultra Vires

The doctrine of *ultra vires* has been abolished by statute for corporations incorporated under the business corporations legislation in most Canadian jurisdictions. The following statute sections reverse the presumption that corporations have limited capacity: [C.B.C.A., M.C.A., O.B.C.A., and S.B.C.A., s. 15(1), A.B.C.A., s. 16(1), B.C.B.C.A., s. 30, N.B.B.C.A., s. 13(1), N.C.A., s. 27(1), and Y.B.C.A., s. 18(1)]. The doctrine of *ultra vires* may still apply in the Northwest Territories, and in Nova Scotia. Prince Edward Island is a letters patent jurisdiction.

In my view, the general abolition of the doctrine of *ultra vires* is in accordance with sound policy and common sense. The original purposes of the doctrine, which were, in the words of the *1967 Interim Report of the Select Committee on Company Law* (tabled before the Ontario Legislative Assembly, at p. 25) "to protect creditors by ensuring that the company's funds to which creditors must look for payment were not dissipated in unauthorized activities and to protect investors by allowing them to know the objects for which their money was to be used", have been largely frustrated. Subsequent statutory and case law developments have made the doctrine a protection to no one and a trap for the unwary. No less an authority than L.C.B. Gower has recommended, in *Gower's Principles of Modern Company Law* (4th ed. 1979), at p. 179, "total abolition of the *ultra vires* rule in so far as it affects the capacity of companies" and indeed referred favourably to the approach taken by the C.B.C.A. in this respect.

However, in spite of the general trend towards abolition of the doctrine of *ultra vires*, the limited aspects of the doctrine, as seen from the above review, may be present with respect to corporations created by special act for public purposes. Not only is there a long line of cases supporting the principle, but one may argue that this protects the public interest because a company created for a specific purpose by an act of a legislature ought not to have the power to do things not in furtherance of that purpose. Of course, it is open to the legislature to rebut this presumption because, for example, the legislature may provide for other remedies short of invalidity for acts contrary to the statute. But this takes us to discussing the application of the general principles of law on *ultra vires* to the facts of this case.

[**Iacobucci J.** held that the loan was *ultra vires*. This was so even though s. 26(2) of the Act said that the Fund had "the general capacity and powers of a common law corporation". Moreover, ss. 15(1) and 16(3) of the *Corporations Act*, R.S.M. 1987, c. C225, which are the same as s. 15(1) of the C.B.C.A., applied to the Fund. His conclusion was based primarily on s. 9(7) of the Act, which said that "No loan shall be made under this Act ... if the making or giving thereof contravenes any provision of this Act." Also, s. 26(5) of the Act provided that its terms prevailed over those of the *Corporations Act* in the case of conflict. The individuals' guarantees were therefore inapplicable. Although the defendant corporation would have been liable to the plaintiff in unjust enrichment, the individuals' guarantees did not extend to this type of obligation.]

NOTES AND QUESTIONS

1. Who paid for the irrecoverable loan? Do you think the Supreme Court's finding of *ultra vires* in this case served a useful purpose?

2. Justice Iacobucci said that the doctrine of *ultra vires* may still apply in Nova Scotia. In that memorandum and articles jurisdiction, s. 26(8) of the *Companies Act*, R.S.N.S. 1989, c. 81, says: "Subject to this Act, a company has the capacity, rights, powers and privileges of a natural person". How does this differ from C.B.C.A., s. 15(1)? Do you think it abolishes *ultra vires*? Do you think it was intended to?

3. The decision of the House of Lords in *Ashbury Railway Carriage Co. v. Riche* (1875), L.R. 7 H.L. 653, 24 W.R. 794 (Eng. H.L.) is commonly understood to have established the doctrine of *ultra vires* for companies registered under the English-model statute. They lacked capacity to pursue activities outside their stated objects. As *Communities Economic Development Fund, supra*, notes, this marked a change from the principles developed in relation to "common law" corporations. The wisdom of this change, and what political and economic views may have influenced it, was questioned by L. Getz, "*Ultra Vires* and Some Related Problems" (1969), 3 U.B.C. L. Rev. 30. Note that the Lords were unclear about whether they were interpreting the incorporating statute or elaborating a common law rule. What is your view on this issue, in the light of *Communities Economic Development Fund*?

4. In *Ashbury Railway Carriage*, the Lords supported their conclusions by noting that the objects were disclosed in the memorandum of association, which was a publicly registered document. Even before *ultra vires* was firmly established, the doctrine of "constructive notice" had taken root. This rule was essentially an estoppel by registration. Because it was possible to look at the publicly registered documents, nobody was to be heard to say, "I didn't bother to look." This is sometimes expressed by saying that everyone was "deemed" to know what was in the documents; or, worse, that everyone had a duty to read them. In fact, there was a rule of evidence, by which everyone was estopped from denying knowledge of every detail of the publicly registered documents. Thus, since no one was allowed to deny that he knew all about the company's objects, it did not seem so harsh to inflict the doctrine of *ultra vires*. Note, however, that even though constructive notice supported the development of *ultra vires*, the idea that capacity is limited by objects is logically distinct from the idea of constructive notice by public registration.

5. Despite the uncompromising tenor of *Ashbury Railway Carriage Co. v. Riche*, the courts adopted certain rules of interpretation, and permitted certain drafting techniques, which greatly circumscribed the operation of the *ultra vires* rule. The courts interpreted objects clauses in such a manner as to render everything incidental

to the carrying out of the enumerated objects to be *intra vires* the company: see *A.G. v. Great Eastern Railway Co.* (1880), 5 App. Cas. 473 (Eng. H.L.). In *Cotman v. Brougham*, [1918] A.C. 514 (Eng. H.L.), a statement to the effect that each enumerated object was independent and not ancillary to any other enumerated object was upheld. Thus did the courts permit corporate designers to eliminate the application of the *ejusdem generis* rule in the interpretation of corporate constitutions.

The predictable result was the inclusion of prolix object clauses in virtually all English-model registration companies. The intended investor protection of the *ultra vires* concept was further undermined by the standard inclusion of a subjectively worded clause empowering the company "to carry on any other business which the company may consider can be conveniently carried on in connection with the business of the company". This clause was upheld by the British Columbia Court of Appeal in *H & H Logging Co. Ltd. v. Random Services Corp.* (1976), 63 D.L.R. (2d) 6, 60 W.W.R. 619, applying the similar reasoning of *Bell Houses Ltd. v. City Wall Properties Ltd.*, [1966] 2 Q.B. 656 (Eng. C.A.): compare *Christchurch Corp. v. Flamingo Coffee Lounge Ltd.*, [1959] N.Z.L.R. 986, noted (1960), 23 Mod. L.R. 561.

In 1989, a new *Companies Act* was passed in the U.K. (c. 40). Its s. 110 added a s. 3A to the *Companies Act, 1985* (c. 6), which says that if a company states that its object is to carry on business as a "general commercial company", then its object is to carry on any business or trade, and moreover it has the power to do everything incidental thereto. Companies are still free to list any objects they like, however, and so a more significant provision of the act (s. 108) amended s. 35 of the *Companies Act, 1985* to provide that a company's capacity is not restricted by its memorandum of association.

6. As the *Communities Economic Development Fund* case points out, the rule was different in those Canadian jurisdictions where incorporation was by letters patent issued under a general statute. This was recognized in *Bonanza Creek Gold Mining Co. v. The King*, [1916] 1 A.C. 566, 26 D.L.R. 373 (Ont. J.C.P.C.), set out in Chapter 2. This result met with some initial resistance in the law journals, but by 1931 Wegenast, in *Canadian Companies*, p. 139, was able to confidently pronounce the point to be "abundantly clear". The doctrine of constructive notice applied in respect of the letters patent themselves, but since that document could not limit corporate capacity, this was unlikely to cause a problem.

7. Thus, Canadian corporate law was divided into two camps prior to the reforms that began in 1970, so far as the capacity of corporations to contract with outsiders was concerned. The letters patent jurisdictions had a simple corporate personality rule while the English-model provinces had, in theory, a limited capacity rule that, in practice, was a minor nuisance that any sensible practitioner could avoid by simple planning at the incorporation stage. However, carelessness in setting up the corporate constitution could cause unforeseeable problems later in the corporation's life.

RE JON BEAUFORTE (LONDON) LTD.

[1953] Ch. 131, [1953] 1 All E.R. 634 (Eng. Ch.)

[A company had been set up to manufacture women's gowns, but eventually switched careers and began making veneered panels. This was clearly not within the objects clause, though it was reflected on the new letterhead which described the business as "Veneer Panel Manufacturers". The letterhead was used to place an order for a supply of fuel. The company went into liquidation and the liquidators refused to pay the fuel bill.]

Roxburgh J.: — [T]he argument is that the company needed fuel for its legitimate business, and that the fuel merchants cannot be prejudiced by its misapplication. I need not consider what the position might have been if the fuel merchants had not had clear notice that the business which the company was carrying on and for which the fuel was required was that of veneered panel manufacturers. The correspondence shows that they had notice of that and, as they had constructive notice of the contents of the memorandum of association, they had notice that the transaction was *ultra vires* the company.

NOTES AND QUESTIONS

1.   What do you think would have been the result if the letterhead had mentioned nothing about veneered panels? What would be the result in a letters patent system?

2.   It was noted above that constructive notice supports *ultra vires*, but they are not quite the same thing. Assume that the articles of association of an English-model corporation contained a rule that no contract could be entered into by the company unless the directors approved it by a majority. Assume further that without such authority, a director purported to contract with a supplier to buy fuel on behalf of the company, for some purpose within the corporate objects. There would be no contract, but *not* because of any lack of capacity. Rather, the director would lack the authority to contract on behalf of the company, and the supplier would be estopped (by constructive notice) from even alleging that the director had such authority. The problem arises from constructive notice, but has nothing to do with *ultra vires*. Theoretically, therefore, the same type of problem could arise with a letters patent corporation, if some limit on authority were in the letters patent. The distinctness of the two principles explains why the modern statutory reforms abolish both constructive notice and *ultra vires*.

(b) Statutory Reform of Corporate Incapacity

Since 1970, the rules restricting a corporation's capacity and powers have changed in most Canadian jurisdictions. The question is how far do the new rules go? The following sections of the C.B.C.A. are typical of the statutory changes.

6(1) Articles of incorporation shall follow the form that the Director fixes and shall set out, in respect of the proposed corporation, ...

(f)   any restrictions on the businesses that the corporation may carry on.

15(1) A corporation has the capacity and, subject to this Act, the rights, powers and privileges of a natural person.

16(2) A corporation shall not carry on any business or exercise any power that it is restricted by its articles from carrying on or exercising, nor shall the corporation exercise any of its powers in a manner contrary to its articles.

(3) No act of a corporation, including any transfer of property to or by a corporation, is invalid by reason only that the act or transfer is contrary to its articles or this Act.

17. No person is affected by or is deemed to have notice or knowledge of the contents of a document concerning a corporation by reason only that the document

has been filed by the Director or is available for inspection at an office of the corporation.

18(1) No corporation … may assert against a person dealing with the corporation … that

(a) the articles, by-laws and any unanimous shareholder agreement have not been complied with; …

(2) Subsection (1) does not apply in respect of a person who has, or ought to have, knowledge of a situation described in that subsection by virtue of their relationship to the corporation.

[The various provincial statutes contain similar sections. However they also contain some minor variations in the wording that may prove interesting in future litigation.]

QUESTIONS

1. What is the purpose of making rights, powers and privileges (but not capacity) "subject to this Act"? What is the effect?

2. Note the prohibition in s. 16(2). What are the consequences of an attempted violation of the section?

3. What does s. 16(3) mean? Did you note that it is circular?

4. What would have been the effect of omitting s. 17 from the C.B.C.A.? Be careful. Was anyone "deemed to have notice" of anything at common law? Was estoppel by constructive notice a common law rule or a statutory rule? These points are dealt with in more detail later under Section 3, "Proving Corporate Contracts in Canada".

5. On the basis of the above sections, what would be the result in each of the following variations on the facts of *Re Jon Beauforte (London) Ltd.*, [1953] 1 All E.R. 634 (Eng. Ch.)? Assume in each scenario except (1) that the corporation was incorporated under the C.B.C.A.

    (a) The articles state quite simply "the sole corporate business authorized is the manufacture of women's gowns in London".

    (b) The articles preclude the manufacture of veneered panels "unless authorized by by-law". By-law No. 3 says that veneered panels can be manufactured only as ordered by the managing director. X was appointed managing director three years ago, but died before making any orders. Y, who was hired to assist X, then began to do X's work and has continued to do so even though no board resolution to replace X has been passed. Veneered panels have been made under Y's supervision for two years.

    (c) The articles preclude the manufacture of veneered panels. The supplier had agreed to supply the fuel, but refused to deliver.

    (d) The articles authorize the manufacture of women's gowns and other unrelated products, but specifically forbid any involvement with veneered panels unless specifically authorized in advance by the board of directors. The corporate agent with whom the fuel dealer negotiated had made five different agreements with various suppliers of things used to make veneered panels in the last year, all of which had been approved after the deal was made by the board of directors and subsequently ratified by the shareholders.

(e) Would your answer in any of the above situations vary if the fuel supplier just happened to have read and remembered the contents of the corporation's articles of incorporation at the time of the transaction?

(f) The articles authorize the manufacture of women's gowns "and such other business pursuits as the directors may authorize from time to time". The fuel supplier had read the articles. The day before the fuel supply agreement was negotiated all the shareholders had signed a document saying "all the directors' power to manage corporate affairs is suspended". The shareholders had then voted (75 per cent in favour) to authorize the corporation to engage in the veneered panel business.

(g) The articles precluded the manufacture of veneered panels and the fuel supplier was a member of the board of directors of Jon Beauforte (London) Ltd., but had not read the articles.

(h) The articles specified no corporate objects at all and the fuel supplier was listed in the share register as a shareholder of Jon Beauforte (London) Ltd. at the time of the transaction.

(i) The articles precluded the manufacture of veneered panels and the supplier knew about the limitation, but the shareholders of Jon Beauforte (London) Ltd. had met after the agreement was made and voted to approve the fuel purchase?

(j) If J.B. (Ipswich) Ltd. had been incorporated in England and the facts were the same as in the 1953 *Re Jon Beauforte (London) Ltd.* case except that the plaintiff commenced the action against J.B. (Ipswich) Ltd. in Ontario, would the O.B.C.A. or the C.B.C.A. apply? What would be the result? Assume for the purposes of this scenario that the O.B.C.A. and the C.B.C.A. are identically worded except where the word "Ontario" appears instead of the word "Canada". Note the definition of "corporation" in the Act.

(c) The Canadian Constitution: Some Residual Problems

A corporation might be deprived of contractual capacity by a deficiency of legislative power in the incorporating jurisdiction. This residual application of the *ultra vires* rule evolves from the federal nature of the Canadian constitution. Some subject matters are beyond the legislative capacity of the provincial legislature; some are exclusive to the provinces and beyond the legislative capacity of the federal Parliament. It arguably follows that any matter beyond the legislative capacity of a parliamentary body cannot be pursued by a business corporation owing its existence and scope of activities to laws, whether general or particular, passed by that legislative body. Is that the way it works?

The analysis is complicated by both constitutional and corporate law considerations. It would seem that if a provincial legislature cannot pass a statute establishing an inter-provincial railway, it cannot create a corporation to do so by passing an Act to incorporate the inter-provincial railway corporation. In *Alberta Government Telephones v. Canadian Radio-television and Telecommunications Commission*, [1989] 2 S.C.R. 225, 61 D.L.R. (4th) 193, a corporation was created by the province of Alberta with the power to carry on a telephone business providing local, long-distance, inter-provincial and international services. The court held that this was a federal undertaking within ss. 91(29) and 92(10)(*a*) of the *Constitution Act, 1867*, (U.K.), 30 & 31 Vict., c. 3. On the issue of the province's powers to create this corporation, Dickson C.J.C. said, for the majority: "It is unnecessary, for the purposes of this appeal, to consider whether there are limits on provincial authority to create Crown corporations operating from the outset within the federal regulatory sphere."

Thus, the point was left open. Assuming, however, that the provincial legislature cannot set up such a corporation by a special Act, the same result would probably follow if articles of incorporation were filed under an ordinary provincial statute "in relation to ... the incorporation of companies with provincial objects" (the A.B.C.A., for example) to set up a new corporate entity with the sole stated "object" of operating an inter-provincial railway. But, as observed earlier, that is not the way business corporations are typically set up in Canada today.

Suppose a provincial incorporating statute, following the English example, required that corporate "objects" be exhaustively stated upon incorporation. The incorporators have listed the traditional objects such as tallow-chandling and receiving government grants, have stipulated that each stated object is independent of all the others and have included the phrase whereby the corporation is stated to be capable of engaging in "any business venture determined by the directors from time to time". As you might have suspected, the corporation begins operating an inter-provincial railway. An advertising agency is engaged and creates a series of television commercials clearly describing the routes available. Can the corporation escape payment on the ground that the agreement is *ultra vires* the corporate contractual power? What about a similar situation in which the incorporating statute is similar to the C.B.C.A.? Is the real problem, as noted in Chapter 2, the failure of the provinces to require the articulation of "provincial objects" in the corporate constitution or to set them out in the statute?

2. Contracting Through Corporate Agents: An Analytical Framework

WELLING, CORPORATE LAW IN CANADA: THE GOVERNING PRINCIPLES

(3rd ed., 2006), pp. 193-95 (Footnotes deleted.)

Proving a civil transaction with a corporation is easier than proving a corporate crime. One need not prove that the corporate mind was directly involved in the particular transaction. Lawyers analyze corporate contracts, and other transactions creating civil obligations, on the basis of agency principles.

...

They see [an] individual as an agent of the corporation and ask what the agent's authority was. The reasons are largely historical. The law of corporate agency relies on basic rules of evidence and civil procedure. At common law the plaintiff's evidentiary burden was eased by an estoppel rule called "ostensible authority". In Canada, the focus has been eased further by statute. The common law and statutory rules are covered under separate headings in the following pages.

Corporate agents facilitate a wide range of transactions. The easiest to understand involve outsiders negotiating with agents to contract with corporations.

There are always three people involved in a corporate agency analysis. They can be visualized in a triangular game of relationships. *The corporation* has an ongoing relationship with *the agent*; *the outsider* negotiates with *the agent*; *the outsider* claims that the negotiations created a contract with *the corporation.* Maybe they did, or maybe they didn't. The object of the game is to ascertain whether the agent can be proved to have been the appropriate type of agent through whom to arrange contracts of the sort negotiated. The outsider will no doubt allege that the agent had authority to negotiate the contract, but proof is about admissible evidence, not about facts. If the allegation of authority can't be proved in the circumstances, there is no contract between the outsider and the corporation. If the alleged scope of authority is proved (or, for whatever reason, not denied by the corporation), then the corporation is bound as a principal on whose behalf the agent contracted with the outsider.

Throughout the rest of this chapter I propose to use the above terms — *the corporation, the agent,* and *the outsider* — as convenient labels to describe the players in the corporate agency game. This will provide some consistent terminology as we move through a rather confusing series of three different theoretical approaches. As we shall see, at the beginning of the 20th century corporations were a protected species and a plaintiff needed to produce clear evidence of a corporate agent's scope of authority. By mid-century the "ostensible authority" theory had gained ascendance and corporations were treated almost exactly like human principals. In the 21st century, Canadian corporate statutes discriminate against corporate principals and in favour of outsiders in agency matters.

NOTES

Before a person can be bound to a contract, he, she or it must have capacity to enter into the contract. A principal, whether corporate or otherwise, is bound where it appoints a particular agent to conclude a particular contract and the agent does so. At the other end of the spectrum, a person cannot create a contract between two parties merely by claiming in his dealings with one of them that he is the agent of the other. What is required is the creation, between principal and agent, of an agency relationship, on which the other contracting party can rely, and by which the principal will be bound.

It is this middle ground, where the agent has some degree of authority from his principal, yet not the extended authority which he claims, with which we are concerned.

3. Proving Corporate Contracts in Canada

(a) Actual Authority at Common Law

Even where the corporation is fully capable of concluding a legal transaction, there may be further legal complications when an outsider attempts to prove a contract (or other transaction) with the corporate person. In one way or another these problems usually come down to a simple question: can it be proved that the proper steps have been taken to make the corporation a party?

Once upon a time every corporation had a corporate seal that was ritualistically affixed to documents to formally evidence corporate assent. Such formalities are now largely passé — note, *e.g.*, C.B.C.A., s. 23: "A document executed on behalf of a corporation is not invalid merely because a corporate seal is not affixed to it." Moreover, in the olde days, the fact that a corporate seal appeared on a document was not conclusive, as the question then became whether it had been affixed by the appropriate corporate official: see *Ruben v. Great Fingall Consolidated*, [1906] A.C. 439; [1904-7] All E.R. 460 (Eng. H.L.).

The real issue, stripped of legalistic verbiage, is: to what extent is a corporation permitted to prejudice outsiders by citing a failure to comply with internal corporate procedures?

PANORAMA DEVELOPMENTS (GUILDFORD) LTD. v. FIDELIS FURNISHING FABRICS LTD.

[1971] 2 Q.B. 711, [1971] 3 All E.R. 16 (Eng. C.A.)

[The plaintiff operated a car rental agency. The defendant's corporate secretary, by phone and written correspondence, secured the plaintiff's agreement to make cars available from time to time to the corporate secretary or persons sent by him. Corporate business was cited as the purpose and it was agreed that bills would be sent directly to the defendant company for payment. Eventually it was discovered that the secretary had been converting these cars to his own use. He went to jail and the defendant company denied contractual liability.]

Denning M.R.: — It is clear that these cars were hired as a result of letters which described Fidelis as the contracting party. The cars were booked by letters written on the paper of Fidelis and signed by Mr. R.L. Bayne, with the words underneath "Company Secretary". References were given as to the credit and standing of Fidelis. ... The contract for each of them was with the company and not with Mr. Bayne.

The second point of counsel for Fidelis is this. He says that the company is not bound by the letters which were signed by Mr. Bayne as "Company Secretary". He says that, on the authorities, a company secretary fulfills a very humble role and that he has no authority to make any contracts or representations on behalf of the company. He refers to *Barnett, Hoares & Co. v. South London Tramways Co.* (1887), 18 Q.B.D. 815 at 817, where Lord Esher M.R. said: "A secretary is a mere servant; his position is that he is to do what he is told, and no person can assume that he has any authority to represent anything at all... ." Those words were approved by Lord MacNaughten in *George Whitechurch Ltd. v. Cavanagh*, [1902] A.C. 117 at 124. They are supported by the decision in *Ruben v. Great Fingall Consolidated*, [1906] A.C. 439, they are referred to in some of the textbooks as authoritative. But times have changed. A company secretary is a much more important person nowadays than he was in 1887. He is an officer of the company with extensive duties and responsibilities. This appears not only in the modern Companies Acts, but also by the role which he plays in the day-to-day business of companies. He is no longer a mere clerk. He regularly makes representations on behalf of the company and enters into contracts on its behalf which come within the day-to-day running of the company's business. So much so that he may be regarded as held out as having authority to do such things on behalf of the company. He is certainly entitled to sign contracts connected with the administrative side of a company's affairs, such as employing staff, and ordering cars, and so forth. All such matters now come within the ostensible authority of a company's secretary. Accordingly, I agree with the judge that Mr. R.L. Bayne, as company secretary, had ostensible authority to enter into contracts for the hire of these cars and, therefore, the company must pay for them. Mr. Bayne was a fraud. But it was the company which put him in the position in which he, as company secretary, was able to commit the frauds. So the defendants are liable. I would dismiss the appeal, accordingly.

NOTES

The meaning of "ostensible authority" is covered in detail under the next heading.

The *Panorama* reasoning can be looked at in at least two ways. One is similar to the approach in corporate crime and tort. Lord Denning's reasoning can easily be interpreted as the familiar two-part analysis consisting of (i) finding the mind that performed the elements of the contract (clearly the rogue, Mr. Bayne); and (ii) ascertaining whether, in the circumstances, that mind can be identified as the corporate mind. The other way, though quite different, brings about the same result. Mr. Bayne was clearly an agent of the company. His agency agreement with the company gave him the authority to do a range of administrative tasks, one of which was to rent cars on behalf of the company. So long as his dealings with an outsider appeared to be within his scope of authority, the fact that he had nasty plans to defraud someone cannot affect the outsider's position. The cars had been rented from the outsider by the company, through its agent, and the subsequent defrauding of the company was a matter between the company and its agent.

One of the oddities of modern corporate law is that the former theory is never used in analyzing corporate contractual issues. The latter theory was well established in the common law of "agency" long before the analogy of corporations to human beings became settled and the concept of an agent's contracting on behalf of a "principal" — whether a single human principal or a group, such as the board of directors of a corporation — was easy to transpose to the newly recognized personality of the corporation. Some basic assumptions concerning the nature of an agency relationship are therefore useful in analyzing corporate contracts.

If an agent has "actual authority" to perform function X, an outsider may deal with her as if the agent were an extension or manifestation of the principal's own personality. Thus, when an outsider deals through an agent with a corporation, it will be a great advantage either to know in advance or to subsequently be able to prove that the agent had actual authority to conclude the agreement negotiated. An English judge described actual authority as follows:

> An actual authority is a legal relationship between principal and agent to which they alone are parties. Its scope is to be ascertained by applying ordinary principles of construction of contracts, including any proper implications from the express words used, the usages of trade, or the course of business between the parties. [*Freeman and Lockyer (a Firm) v. Buckhurst Park Properties (Mangal) Ltd.*, [1964] 2 Q.B. 480 (Eng. C.A.), per Diplock L.J.]

It is important to note that we are dealing with a tri-partite relationship here and the outsider's best case involves two points. If the outsider can prove the agent had actual authority (a question which depends on the arrangements between principal and agent), the outsider may rely on what the agent said as binding on the corporation. An agent may get actual authority from his principal in one of three ways. The agent may have express actual authority: the principal may have said in no uncertain terms to the agent "you may perform function X". The agent may have implied actual authority: the verbal or non-verbal exchanges between principal and agent might have been interpreted by the agent as authorization to "do X". Finally, the agent may have been given actual authority retroactively by the principal's "ratification" or adoption of what the agent did in excess of his actual authority: if the principal chooses to forgive the agent and to accept the agreement as negotiated, the breach of authority will be regarded as retroactively healed and cannot subsequently be legally complained of by the principal against the agent. Attempts to retroactively confer actual authority don't always work. Ratification is impossible if the unauthorized agent purported to act as a principal: *Keighley Maxsted & Co. v. Durant*, [1901] A.C. 240 (H.L.). In other words, ratification is not available to an "undisclosed principal".

Actual authority is relatively simple as a legal concept. However, it has not often been invoked in cases involving outsiders' contracts. Cases in which actual authority has been proved often involved corporate disputes with individuals who had some position with the corporation, thus differentiating them from most outsiders: see, for example, *Hely-Hutchinson v. Brayhead Ltd.*, [1968] 1 Q.B. 549, [1967] 3 All E.R. 98 (Eng. C.A.), where the "outsider" was one of the corporation's directors. One reason actual authority does not appear more often in the cases may be that it is difficult for the outsider to get access to evidence concerning the relationship between principal and agent. A second reason is the judicially created concept of "ostensible authority".

(b) Ostensible Authority at Common Law

FREEMAN & LOCKYER (A FIRM) v. BUCKHURST PARK PROPERTIES (MANGAL) LTD.

[1964] 2 Q.B. 480, [1964] 1 All E.R. 630, [1964] 2 W.L.R. 618 (Eng. C.A.)

[The plaintiffs, who carried on business as architects and surveyors, claimed £291 6s. for fees due in respect of work done during 1959 in relation to property in land held by the defendant company, Buckhurst Park Properties (Mangal) Ltd. The plaintiffs had received their instructions from Shiv Kumar Kapoor, the second defendant, a director of the defendant company. The only question was whether the liability was that of the defendant company or of the second defendant, who was never served with the proceedings since his whereabouts were unknown. The defendant company appealed a judgment against it, contending that the liability was that of the second defendant.

A few background facts will clarify the issues. In September, 1958, Kapoor contracted to purchase Buckhurst Park Estate for £75,000. Having insufficient funds, he approached Nimarjit Singh Hoon, who was willing to advance approximately £40,000. The two men agreed in writing to form a company with a nominal capital of £70,000 to be subscribed in equal shares. Kapoor and Hoon and a nominee of each were to be directors. The objective was to complete the purchase of the property and then resell it. It was agreed that Kapoor personally should defray the running expenses and be reimbursed out of the proceeds of the resale. The articles of association contained power to appoint a managing director but none was appointed. The property was conveyed to the company but the prompt resale which Kapoor had contemplated did not materialize. Kapoor engaged the plaintiffs to apply for planning permission to develop the land and to do certain other work which the plaintiffs did, and for which they claimed the fees in question.]

Diplock L.J.: — The county court judge made the following findings of fact: (1) that the plaintiffs intended to contract with Kapoor as agent for the company, and not on his own account; (2) that the board of the company intended that Kapoor should do what he could to obtain the best possible price for the estate; (3) that

Kapoor, although never appointed as managing director, had throughout been acting as such in employing agents and taking other steps to find a purchaser; (4) that Kapoor was so acting was well known to the board. The only findings which have been challenged on appeal are (3) and (4), but for the reasons given by Willmer L.J. I think that the challenge failed.

The county court judge did not hold (although he might have done) that actual authority had been conferred upon Kapoor by the board to employ agents. He proceeded on the basis of apparent authority, that is, that the defendant company had so acted as to be estopped from denying Kapoor's authority. This rendered it unnecessary for the judge to inquire whether actual authority to employ agents had been conferred upon Kapoor by the board to whom the management of the company's business was confided by the articles of association. ...

This makes it necessary to inquire into the state of the law as to the ostensible authority of officers and servants to enter into contracts on behalf of corporations.

...

An "actual" authority is a legal relationship between principal and agent created by a consensual agreement to which they alone are parties. Its scope is to be ascertained by applying ordinary principles of construction of contracts, including any proper implications from the express words used, the usages of the trade, or the course of business between the parties. To this agreement the contractor is a stranger; he may be totally ignorant of the existence of any authority on the part of the agent. Nevertheless, if the agent does enter into a contract pursuant to the "actual" authority, it does create contractual rights and liabilities between the principal and the contractor. It may be that this rule relating to "undisclosed principals", which is peculiar to English law, can be rationalised as avoiding circuity of action, for the principal could in equity compel the agent to lend his name in an action to enforce the contract against the contractor, and would at common law be liable to indemnify the agent in respect of the performance of obligations assumed by the agent under the contract.

An "apparent" or "ostensible" authority, on the other hand, is a legal relationship between the principal and the contractor created by a representation, made by the principal to the contractor, intended to be and in fact acted upon by the contractor, that the agent has authority to enter on behalf of the principal into a contract of a kind within the scope of the "apparent" authority, so as to render the principal liable to perform any obligations imposed upon him by such contract. To the relationship so created the agent is a stranger. He need not be (although he generally is) aware of the existence of the representation but he must not purport to make the agreement as principal himself. The representation, when acted upon by the contractor by entering into a contract with the agent, operates as an estoppel, preventing the principal from asserting that he is not bound by the contract. It is irrelevant whether the agent had actual authority to enter into the contract.

In ordinary business dealings the contractor at the time of entering into the contract can in the nature of things hardly ever rely on the "actual" authority of the agent. His information as to the authority must be derived either from the principal or from the agent or from both, for they alone know what the agent's actual authority is. All that the contractor can know is what they tell him, which may or may not be true. In the ultimate analysis he relies either upon the representation of the principal, that is, apparent authority, or upon the representation of the agent, that is, warranty of authority.

The representation which creates "apparent" authority may take a variety of forms of which the commonest is representation by conduct, that is by permitting the agent to act in some way in the conduct of the principal's business with other persons. By so doing the principal represents to anyone who becomes aware that the agent is so acting that the agent has authority to enter on behalf of the principal into contracts with other persons of the kind which an agent so acting in the conduct of his principal's business has usually "actual" authority to enter into.

In applying the law as I have endeavoured to summarise it to the case where the principal is not a natural person, but a fictitious person, namely, a corporation, two further factors arising from the legal characteristics of a corporation have to be borne in mind. The first is that the capacity of a corporation is limited by its constitution, that is, in the case of a company incorporated under the Companies Act, by its memorandum and articles of association; the second is that a corporation cannot do any act, and that includes making a representation, except through its agent.

Under the doctrine of *ultra vires* the limitation of the capacity of a corporation by its constitution to do any acts is absolute. This affects the rules as to the "apparent" authority of an agent of a corporation in two ways. First, no representation can operate to estop the corporation from denying the authority of the agent to do on behalf of the corporation an act which the corporation is not permitted by its constitution to do itself. Since the conferring of actual authority upon an agent is itself an act of the corporation, the capacity to do which is regulated by its constitution, the corporation cannot be estopped from denying that it has conferred upon a particular agent authority to do acts which by its constitution, it is incapable of delegating to that particular agent.

To recognize that these are direct consequences of the doctrine of *ultra vires* is, I think, preferable to saying that a contractor who enters into a contract with a corporation has constructive notice of its constitution, for the expression "constructive notice" tends to disguise that constructive notice is not a positive, but a negative doctrine, like that of estoppel of which it forms a part. It operates to prevent the contractor from saying that he did not know that the constitution of the corporation rendered a particular act or a particular delegation of authority *ultra vires* the corporation. It does not entitle him to say that he relied upon some unusual provision in the constitution of the corporation if he did not in fact so rely.

The second characteristic of a corporation, namely, that unlike a natural person it can only make a representation through an agent, has the consequence that in order to create an estoppel between the corporation and the contractor, the representation as to the authority of the agent which creates his "apparent" authority must be made by some person or persons who have "actual" authority from the corporation to make the representation. Such "actual" authority may be conferred by the constitution of the corporation itself, as, for example, in the case of a company, upon the board of directors, or it may be conferred by those who under its constitution have the powers of management upon some other person to whom the constitution permits them to delegate authority to make representations of this kind. It follows that where the agent upon whose "apparent" authority the contractor relies has no "actual" authority from the corporation to enter into a particular kind of contract with the contractor on behalf of the corporation, the contractor cannot rely upon the agent's own representation as to his actual authority. He can rely only upon a representation by a person or persons who have actual authority to manage or conduct that part of the business of the corporation to which the contract relates.

The commonest form of representation by a principal creating an "apparent" authority of an agent is by conduct, namely, by permitting the agent to act in the management or conduct of the principal's business. Thus, if in the case of a company the board of directors who have "actual" authority under the memorandum and articles of association to manage the company's business permit the agent to act in the management or conduct of the company's business, they thereby represent to all persons dealing with such agent that he has authority to enter on behalf of the corporation into contracts of a kind which an agent authorised to do acts of the kind which he is in fact permitted to do usually enters into in the ordinary course of such business. The making of such a representation is itself an act of management of the company's business. Prima facie it falls within the "actual" authority of the board of directors, and unless the memorandum or articles of the company either make such a contract *ultra vires* the company or prohibit the delegation of such authority to the agent, the company is estopped from denying to anyone who has entered into a contract with the agent in reliance upon such "apparent" authority that the agent had authority to contract on behalf of the company.

If the foregoing analysis of the relevant law is correct, it can be summarised by stating four conditions which must be fulfilled to entitle a contractor to enforce against a company a contract entered into on behalf of the company by an agent who had no actual authority to do so. It must be shown:

(1) that a representation that the agent had authority to enter on behalf of the company into a contract of the kind sought to be enforced was made to the contractor;

(2) that such representation was made by a person or persons who had "actual" authority to manage the business of the company either generally or in respect of those matters to which the contract relates;

(3) that he (the contractor) was induced by such representation to enter into the contract, that is, that he in fact relied upon it;

(4) that under its memorandum or articles of association the company was not deprived of the capacity either to enter into a contract of the kind sought to be enforced or to delegate authority to enter into a contract of that kind to the agent.

The confusion which, I venture to think, has sometimes crept into the cases is in my view due to a failure to distinguish between these four separate conditions, and in particular to keep steadfastly in mind (a) that the only "actual" authority which is relevant is that of the persons making the representation relied upon, and (b) that the memorandum and articles of association of the company are always relevant (whether they are in fact known to the contractor or not) to the questions (i) whether condition (2) is fulfilled, and (ii) whether condition (4) is fulfilled, and (but only if they are in fact known to the contractor) may be relevant (iii) as apart of the representation on which the contractor relied. [**Diplock L.J.** reviewed the conflicting precedents and continued.]

In the present case the findings of fact by the county court judge are sufficient to satisfy the four conditions, and thus to establish that Kapoor had "apparent" authority to enter into contracts on behalf of the company for their services in connection with the sale of the company's property, including the obtaining of development permission with respect to its use. The judge found that the board knew that Kapoor had throughout been acting as managing director in employing agents and taking other steps to find a purchaser. They permitted him to do so, and by such conduct represented that he had authority to enter into contracts of a kind which a managing director or an executive director responsible for finding a purchaser would in the normal course be authorised to enter into on behalf of the company. Condition (1) was thus fulfilled. The articles of association conferred full powers of management on the board. Condition (2) was thus fulfilled. The plaintiffs, finding Kapoor acting in relation to the company's property as he was authorised by the board to act, were induced to believe that he was authorised by the company to enter into contracts on behalf of the company for their services in connection with the sale of the company's property, including the obtaining of development permission with respect to its use. Condition (3) was thus fulfilled. The articles of association, which contained powers for the board to delegate any of the functions of management to a managing director or to a single director, did not deprive the company of capacity to delegate authority to Kapoor, a director, to enter into contracts of that kind on behalf of the company. Condition (4) was thus fulfilled.

I think the judgment was right, and would dismiss the appeal. [**Wilmer** and **Pearson L.JJ.** delivered concurring judgments.]

NOTES AND QUESTIONS

"Ostensible authority" and "apparent authority" appear to be synonymous labels. Another term one finds in academic and judicial analysis is "usual authority". This is used to focus attention on the position occupied within the corporate hierarchy by "the agent". The question traditionally asked was whether agents in similar positions in similar corporations usually have the scope of authority that the particular plaintiff alleges the particular agent had. This can be used to show (a) that the particular agent in question had implied actual authority, or (b) the required representation for ostensible authority, through "holding out" the particular agent as having some authority.

There are two problems with this. One is that not all corporate agents will be the incumbents of such familiar offices as "managing director" or "corporate secretary": thus, it will often be difficult to assess what is the authority wielded by someone occupying "position X". Second, to focus on the name of a position is likely to unduly narrow the search for precedent, which can give unsatisfactory answers in an evolving business world: as was shown in the *Panorama Developments* case, *supra*, someone labelled, for example, a corporate secretary may have somewhat broader powers today than when some precedent case was decided.

Even if the concept of usual authority is adopted the problem still remains of what is the usual authority in each particular case. This will vary with the nature of the transaction in question, the office held by the corporate agent, and the complexity of the structure of the corporation involved. On this see *Kreditbank Cassell G.M.B.H. v. Schenkers Ltd.*, [1927] 1 K.B. 826 (Eng. C.A.); *J.H. McKnight Construction Co. v. Vansickler* (1915), 51 S.C.R. 374, 24 D.L.R. 298; *Ontario Marble Co. v. Creative Memorials Ltd.* (1964), 45 D.L.R. (2d) 244, 48 W.W.R. 239 (Sask. C.A.); *Treasure Book Ltd. v. Laundrall Ltd.* (1963), 43 W.W.R. 193, 39 D.L.R. (2d) 94 (Sask. C.A.); *Hazlewood v. West Coast Securities Ltd.* (1974), 49 D.L.R. (3d) 46; varied (1976) 68 D.L.R. (3d) 172 (B.C.C.A.); *Wolpert v. Vizgit Properties (pty) Ltd.*, [1961] 2 S.A.L.R. 257. See also Hornby, "The Usual Authority of An Agent", [1961] Camb. L.J. 239.

What was the representation made by the corporation in the *Freeman & Lockyer* case? To whom was it made? The reasons for judgment suggest that Diplock L.J. was of the view that a representation was made to the plaintiffs. Was there any evidence of any communication between the corporation and the plaintiffs?

Is the *Freeman & Lockyer* case one of those rare (but not unheard of) judicial gems whose legal principle endures, but whose *ratio* is that the case itself is wrongly decided?

Would the decision have been the same if the architects were Americans and had been engaged to do the work by Mr. Kapoor while he was on a surfing holiday in San Diego, or while he and the architects were in Alice for the boat race? If not, why not?

CANADIAN LABORATORY SUPPLIES LTD. v. ENGELHARD INDUSTRIES OF CANADA LTD.

[1979] 2 S.C.R. 787, 97 D.L.R. (3d) 1, 6 B.L.R. 235

[The plaintiff and the defendant had an ongoing business relationship over several years. Canlab regularly bought platinum from Engelhard, used the platinum in its lab operations, and returned the scrap metal to Engelhard, who refined and recycled it. Cook ("the rogue"), one of Canlab's employees, began to take advantage of the relationship in 1962. Cook had actual authority to sell but not to buy. He contacted Engelhard and said that some secret experiment would be carried out by a scientist named Giles, that platinum would be needed for these experiments, but that their nature was sufficiently sensitive that the particulars were to be kept from Canlab's other employees. Engelhard agreed to the following arrangement: platinum shipments were ordered on regular Canlab purchase orders, but Engelhard agreed to accept scrap returns directly from Giles; payments for these scrap returns were to be made directly to Giles.

Of course, the elusive Giles was Cook in disguise. The net effect was that Canlab was paying Engelhard for platinum which Canlab never used and Engelhard was paying Cook ("Giles") for scrap platinum returns. By the time Cook's deception was uncovered, some seven years later, Cook had absconded with approximately $0.8 million.

All the Engelhard decisions had been made by the appropriate corporate officials. It therefore became a question of whether Canlab had represented to Engelhard that Cook, Canlab's employee, had authority to set up the arrangement. Three different representations were alleged:

(i) In 1962, Cook had by his own representations persuaded Engelhard to agree to the arrangement.

(ii) In 1966, Engelhard had some concerns about late payments by Canlab on platinum shipments to "Giles" and contacted the Canlab purchasing agent (incredibly, named Snook), who told Engelhard to contact Cook who would deal with their problem.

(iii) In 1968, Engelhard became curious about what "Giles" was doing with the platinum and phoned Canlab's vice-president of operations, who, upon being told that Cook was the contact in the matter, said that things should continue as they were and he would investigate the matter and get back to Engelhard.

The sole issue between Canlab and Engelhard was how the loss was to be split between them.]

Laskin C.J.C. (**Spence** and **Dickson JJ.** concurring): — The issues in this appeal arise out of an action of conversion … . The action … was founded, of course, on Canlab's claim of title to the platinum ordered through Cook for Giles and in the unlawfulness of any claim of title by Engelhard to the platinum scrap which it received directly from Giles and for which it paid by cheques issued to Giles. [**Chief Justice Laskin** first examined the question of who had property in the platinum, obviously an important point given the nature of the action. He concluded that property had been transferred to Canlab, from whom the platinum was then stolen by Cook.]

Blair J.A., in proceeding from the base of an ostensible authority exercised by Cook to purchase platinum from Engelhard, founded it on what he said was "[Canlab's] conduct in permitting [Cook] to act as he did in the conduct of [its] business with Engelhard". This was his assessment based upon the application of principles taken from *Freeman & Lockyer (a firm) v. Buckhurst Park Properties (Mangal) Ltd.*, [1964] 2 Q.B. 480, [1964] 1 All E.R. 630, quoting Diplock L.J., as he then was, at p. 502, and from *Hely-Hutchinson v. Brayhead Ltd. et al.*, [1968] 1 Q.B. 549, per Lord Pearson, at p. 593. There is, of course, no doubt in my mind that if an agent, in the exercise of an admitted authority in him in respect of his ordinary duties acts for his own benefit, his principal cannot deny liability for contracts he purports to make on behalf of the principal. It is only in such circumstances or where there is a representation from the principal that puts the agent in a position to act beyond the authority reposed in him that the principal can be bound. There is no "permitting" in the sense of binding the principal where the agent is not in the course of his ordinary duties or where there is no representation at all from the principal or from someone in a directory capacity to act for a corporate principal.

...

I agree with Lacourcière J.A., that there is nothing in the record to show that Canlab as principal had placed Cook in a position to hold himself out as having authority to arrange any of the tripartite transactions (so characterized by the majority of the Ontario Court of Appeal), at least until October, 1966. I shall deal with this phase of Lacourcière, J.A.'s reasons later on and confine myself at this stage simply to the original purchases by Canlab from Engelhard. Cook was a sales agent not a purchasing agent, and the "permitting" relied on by Blair, J.A., appears to me to be a rationalization of Cook's success not in the purchase of the platinum (backed up as that was by proper purchase orders) but in the subsequent theft and resale to Engelhard.

In saying this I do not subscribe to the proposition, in so far as it purports to be a general statement of the law, that a representation by an agent himself as to the extent of his authority cannot amount to a holding out by the principal. It will depend on what it is an agent has been assigned to do by his principal, and an overreaching may very well inculpate the principal. This, however, does not help Engelhard in the present case.

...

I come hence to the crucial question whether Engelhard must answer for the whole of the loss suffered by Canlab. Lacourcière, J.A., would have cut the loss at October, 1966, by reason of the telephone conversation between McCullough of Engelhard and one Snook, an employee of Canlab, who directed his inquirer to get in touch with Cook. What militates against this, however appealing it may be as an equitable solution in a situation where Cook duped both his employer and a third party which did business with the employer, is that Snook like Cook had no managerial authority. He was merely a purchasing agent in the purchasing department and there was no evidence of any back-up authority by which he could hold Cook out as having power to compose the difficulty, as raised by Engelhard, in settling accounts.

...

I wish to refer to a contact in 1968 between Canlab and Engelhard to see if it could have a bearing by way of limiting Engelhard's liability. Engelhard's president, one Scott, curious about the use made of the platinum by the unknown Giles, telephoned Canlab's vice-president of operations, one Fabian. The trial Judge found that Fabian, who said he did not remember receiving a call from Scott, had indeed received the call during which there was a discussion of the large number of transactions in platinum involving Canlab and Giles. Fabian, according to Scott, said he was unaware of the transactions and asked which employee of Canlab dealt with Engelhard. Informed it was Cook, Fabian undertook to investigate and call back. It was Cook who called back later that day, telling Scott he was asked to speak on Fabian's behalf. Cook undertook to make inquiries to answer Scott's question and to call back but never did.

I am of opinion that Fabian was put on inquiry as a result of the call from Scott, and that any losses suffered by Canlab by the continued deception of Cook, that is from late September or early October, 1968, must be borne by it. The trial Judge, O'Driscoll, J., took, in my opinion, too narrow a view of the matter in saying that "Mr. Scott's concern had nothing to do with the repurchase by Engelhard from Giles".

In the result, I would allow the appeal, set aside the judgment of the Ontario Court of Appeal and restore the judgment of O'Driscoll. J., but would vary it to limit the recovery of Canlab up to the time that Scott and Fabian had their conversation. If the parties cannot agree on the transactions with Giles that took place after that time, I would direct a reference before O'Driscoll J., or, failing him, another Judge of the High Court of Justice of Ontario, to settle the issue. I should add that the fact that Engelhard thought it was buying from Giles and not from Cook should not affect the limitation of Engelhard's liability as above indicated.

Estey J. (**Martland, Ritchie, Pigeon, Beetz,** and **Pratte JJ.** concurring): — I have had the benefit of reading the reasons of the Chief Justice and with respect agree with his disposition of this appeal save in one respect. The computation of damages in the Chief Justice's approach to the claims by the appellant commences in 1964 and continues until late 1968 when it was found that the respondent had alerted the appellant to the nature of the transaction so as to prevent any recovery beyond that date by the appellant. Lacourcière, J.A., in the Court of Appeal would have terminated the time of recovery in October, 1966. The learned Justice stated [78 D.L.R. (3d) 232 at p. 235, 16 O.R. (2d) 202]:

> The situation is different after McCullogh's telephone conversation with Snook in Canlab's purchase department. McCullogh was then referred to Cook with respect to direct payments to Giles for such platinum, and the request for net cash payments by Canlab for all future platinum purchases. I agree that from that date forward, October 11, 1966, Canlab can be said to have held out Cook as an authorized agent to deal with the resale of scrap platinum directly from Giles, and is thereby estopped from denying the validity of Cook's scheme which on that date became one transaction. I would dismiss Canlab's claim arising after that date.

The evidence upon which the foregoing is founded is presumably the testimony of McCullough, manager of inside sales of the respondent Engelhard ... Furthermore, it can reasonably be concluded from the evidence ... that McCullough and Snook discussed Canlab's customer, Giles, and that after such discussion McCullough was directed to call Cook. It is of considerable importance in my view that Snook was described by a witness (a former Canlab employee) called by the respondent, as being "the purchasing agent" of Canlab. As Snook was the purchasing agent and Engelhard was a supplier to Canlab, it was natural to expect that Engelhard's inquiries regarding payment by Canlab for purchases from Engelhard would be directed in the first instance to Snook, the purchasing agent, with whom, furthermore, McCullough had had many telephone contacts over the years.

It therefore seems to me that in the month of October, 1966:

(a) Canlab was apprised in sufficient detail of the Giles transaction through the discussion by an Engelhard representative with an appropriate employee of Canlab engaged in the general area of the operation in question, to put Canlab on notice of the general nature of the platinum transactions and, of Giles, and of some of Cook's involvement therein. Canlab was thereby alerted and put on its own inquiry; and,

(b) Cook was held out by a responsible authority in Canlab as an authorized agent of Canlab with whom Engelhard could deal regarding the request by Engelhard concerning the Giles matter.

It is not without significance that immediately after this discussion with Cook the payments by Canlab to Engelhard for the platinum ordered by Cook were made "on a net cash basis" ... .

Thus, as a result of McCullough's call to Snook, and McCullough's consequential call to Cook, which was in turn followed by a letter written by McCullough on the direction of Cook to Ferguson and Birk of the Canlab staff, the complaint by Engelhard of late payment by Canlab was answered by the immediate payment by Canlab to Engelhard for platinum picked up by Cook. The situation whereby Engelhard was financing Canlab on the purchase of the platinum for a 30- to 60-day period was, from Engelhard's point of view, corrected.

...

As was said by Pearson, L.J., in *Freeman & Lockyer v. Buckhurst Park Properties (Mangal) Ltd. et al.*, [1964] 2 Q.B. 480, [1964] 1 All E.R. 630 at p. 641:

> The identification of the persons whose knowledge and acquiescence constitute knowledge and acquiescence by the company depends on the facts of the particular case.

Here we have a supplier of raw material, Engelhard, seeking to rectify a lag in payment by its customer Canlab. The supplier sought out the purchasing agent of its customer. The purchasing agent, on hearing the situation described, heard at least enough to know that purchases by Canlab were being made by Cook, a Canlab employee in the internal sales department. The purchasing agent told its supplier, Engelhard, to discuss the payment problem with Cook. Engelhard did so. The situation about which Engelhard had complained was rectified immediately. This is in 1966, three years before Canlab detected the fraud of Cook. [**Justice Estey** went on to quote **Diplock L.J.**, in the *Freeman & Lockyer* case on the law of ostensible authority, then continued.]

Modern commerce at practically all levels and sectors operates through the corporate vehicle. That vehicle itself, by conglomerate grouping and divisionali-zation, has become increasingly complex. Persons, including corporate persons, dealing with a corporation must for practical reasons be able to deal in the ordinary course of trade with the personnel of that corporation secure in the knowledge that the law will match these practicalities with binding consequences. The law has long so provided. Both corporate sides to a contractual transaction must be able to make secure arrangements at the lowest level at which adequate business controls can operate. It is in the interest of both corporate and natural persons engaged in business that this be so. One alternative would be to retain corporate trading authority in the inner core of management; another would be to conduct the daily business of the undertaking on a committee basis. Neither law nor commerce has apparently found a practical alternative to the delegation of the corporate authority to agents, its employees. In undertakings of all but the smallest proportions, division of authority according to function is as necessary as it is commonplace. The day of the proprietor and the one-man operation has, for better or for worse, long departed from the main stage of business, and the corporate vehicle with attendant business structures has taken over much of the commerce of the country. The law has altered old rules and developed new ones to facilitate the conduct of trade on this larger scale. Obviously some employee must be placed in charge of buying, another of selling, another of financing, and another in charge of accounting, and so on, and each must have the authority necessary to deal responsibly with his counterpart in other trading and governmental organizations.

In this transaction, a senior employee in the sales sector of Engelhard seeks out the purchasing agent of his customer Canlab. The purchasing agent says he is not familiar with the particular purchases made by Canlab from Engelhard and so he refers him to an employee who is dealing with these matters, namely, Cook. The president of Cook's employer, Canlab, is not sure of Cook's actual and real authority to revise the timetable for payment for these purchases but another employee in the accounting division of Canlab testified that Cook had such authority. So far as Engelhard, the customer, is concerned Cook was in the position or had the authority necessary to bring about the desired results by apparently making the necessary arrangements through appropriate Canlab officials, and then reporting his success by letter to Engelhard. Thereafter, as I have said, payments were on the expedited basis as requested. In these intercorporate dealings in 1966 Engelhard apprised the purchasing agent of at least part of the Giles affair. Engelhard responded to the request of Cook, the employee to whom Canlab's purchasing agent referred Engelhard, by setting out the entire story in a letter to the comptroller of Canlab. That this letter was somehow intercepted and stolen by Cook cannot be held against the position of Engelhard. The law does not put such a high standard of duty on a customer dealing with a corporation and the practices of modern commerce make it most unwise to do so now. It is convenient to note the summary of this principle in *Palmer's Company Law*, 22nd ed. (1976), vol. I, at p. 291:

> According to this rule, while persons dealing with a company are assumed to have read the public documents of the company and to have ascertained that the proposed transaction is not inconsistent therewith, they are not required to do more; they need not inquire into the regularity of the internal proceedings — what Lord Hatherley called "the indoor management" — and may assume that all is being done regularly (*onmia praesumuntur rite ac solemniter esse acta*).

> This rule, which is based on a general presumption of law, is eminently practical, for business could not be carried on if a person dealing with the apparent agents of a

company was compelled to call for evidence that all internal regulations had been duly observed.

Thus, despite the fact that Cook, in the course of dealing with McCullough following Snook's suggestion, disavowed personal authority to actually revise the payment timetable, but rather gave directions to McCullough as to how to present their request for such revision, nothing in the ensuing evidence, including Cook's written report to Engelhard which completed the negotiations commenced with Snook, can be interpreted as undoing any representation as to Cook's status in these matters resulting from the conversation between McCullough and Snook. Cook was said to be the person to see regarding the Engelhard complaint, Cook was approached, and by McCullough's doing as directed by Cook, the complaint was remedied. How Cook actually brought about the desired result was not to be investigated by Engelhard. This, in my view, operates as an affirmative holding out by Canlab through a responsible and appropriate representative, of Cook's status in connection with the platinum dealings, both the direct purchase by Canlab from Engelhard as well as the system for repurchase by Engelhard from Giles; and this holding out took effect in law from the aforementioned conversation which occurred on October 11, 1966.

As I stated at the outset, I only diverge in my disposition of this appeal from that proposed by the Chief Justice with respect to the period during which the responsibility for Engelhard sounds in damages. I therefore would limit the recovery of damages in respect of the years 1964 and 1965 and until October 11, 1966, with a reference to the Master, Supreme Court of Ontario, should the parties be unable to agree upon the amount of such damages. I would award interest in the circumstances of this case, only from the date of judgment at trial, in the amount calculated in the above manner.

In the result, judgment at trial and in the Court of Appeal should be set aside and judgment entered in lieu thereof on the above terms with costs to the appellant in this Court and the Courts below.

Appeal allowed in part.

NOTES AND QUESTIONS

1. What exactly was the representation made to the outsider in Canlab?

2. What was the actual authority of the individual who made the representation?

3. Can one use the majority reasoning to articulate a workable rule as to when outsiders may prove "the agent's" ostensible authority?

4. Consider the assertion of Laskin C.J.C., that the required representation can sometimes come from "the agent" himself. Can you think of an example where that would be true, yet "the agent" lacked actual authority? See *First Energy (U.K.) Ltd. v. Hungarian International Bank Ltd.*, [1993] 2 Lloyds Rep. 194 (C.A.).

5. Justice Estey, near the end of his reasons for judgment, unfortunately perpetuated one of the classic dinosaurs of corporate law — the "indoor management" rule. Like many of the stock phrases of twentieth century corporate lawyers, this one had little real significance in its day, and what significance it once had is now gone through statutory reform.

The phrase appears to have been coined by analysts reviewing a mid-19th-century case, *Royal British Bank v. Turquand* (1856), 6 E. & B. 327, 119 E.R. 886 (Eng.). The case held that an outsider did not have constructive notice of (and therefore could claim ignorance of) non-public documents of the corporation. The result was undoubtedly correct, but the reasoning was confused. As Jervis C.J. put it: "Parties dealing with [registered corporations] are bound to read the statute and the deed of settlement. But they are not bound to do more."

Now that is palpable nonsense. Outsiders are not bound to read the public documents at all. They are at liberty to ignore them, although they do so at their peril where there is a doctrine of constructive notice. As was discussed above, that doctrine imposes an estoppel that prevents anyone from denying knowledge of the contents of registered documents to which it applies. However, having begun with this *faux pas*, Jervis, C.J., tumbled down the slippery slope.

> And the party here ... would find not a prohibition from borrowing, but a permission to do so on certain conditions. Finding that the authority might be made complete by a resolution, he would have a right to infer the fact of a resolution authorizing that which on the face of the document appeared to be legitimately done.

Thus was born the "indoor management" rule, a limitation on the supposed reach of constructive notice. Presumably, once constructive notice became essentially a non-factor, so did its *Turquand*-inspired limitations: as falls Wichita, so falls Wichita Falls. But before the enactment of sections like C.B.C.A., s. 17, the *Turquand* view of constructive notice as a positive doctrine (rather than the negative, estoppel generator described by Diplock L.J. in the *Freeman & Lockyer* case) inspired some rather wasteful litigation and some rather odd judicial reasoning. See, in particular, *Irvine v. Union Bank of Australia* (1877), 2 App. Cas. 366 (Rangoon, J.C.P.C.), and *Re Almur Fur Trading Co.*, [1932] S.C.R. 150, [1932] 2 D.L.R. 128.

(c) Statutory Reform

Whether a corporate agent had actual authority will depend on the facts in each particular case. Whether an outsider can establish the prerequisites to ostensible authority, and thereby preclude the corporate principal from denying the truth of some representation, will also depend on the facts. However, what the facts are in any particular case has more to do with what evidence can be mustered and presented in court than with what really happened. The reformed Canadian statutes are based on this evidentiary principle. They work by setting up a statutory rule that lists with admirable clarity certain types of facts corporations will not be permitted to "assert" against an outsider. The result is that whether a corporate agent lacked actual authority in a particular case usually will end up not being a disputed point: if the outsider alleges actual authority and the corporation presents no *admissible* evidence to disprove it and makes no statements that can be heard by the court in denial of it, then the case can only proceed to judgment on the basis that the outsider's allegations were, in effect, admitted to be true by the corporate principal. That is how the reformed Canadian statutes work.

Questions involving the corporate principal's own incapacity have already been dealt with, under the heading "Constitutional Restrictions on a Corporation's Abilities". Here, we focus primarily on limitations on the agent's authority. C.B.C.A., M.C.A. and S.B.C.A. s. 18, A.B.C.A. and O.B.C.A. s. 19, B.C.B.C.A. s. 146, N.B.B.C.A., s. 16, N.C.A., s. 31, and N.S.C.A., s. 30 have quite similar provisions. The following C.B.C.A. sections may be compared for differences in detail.

> 16(1) It is not necessary for a by-law to be passed in order to confer any particular power on the ... directors.

> ...

> 17. No person is affected by or is deemed to have notice or knowledge of the contents of a document concerning a corporation by reason only that the document has been filed by the Director or is available for inspection at an office of the corporation.

> 18(1) No corporation and no guarantor of an obligation of a corporation may assert against a person dealing with the corporation or against a person who acquired rights from the corporation that

>> (*a*) the articles, by-laws and any unanimous shareholder agreement have not been complied with;

>> (*b*) the persons named in the most recent notice sent to the Director under section 106 or 113 are not the directors of the corporation;

>> (*c*) the place named in the most recent notice sent to the Director under section 19 is not the registered office of the corporation;

>> ...

>> (*f*) a sale, lease or exchange or property referred to in subsection 189(3) was not authorized.

> 18(2) Subsection (1) does not apply in respect of a person who has, or ought to have, knowledge of a situation described in that subsection by virtue of their relationship to the corporation.

Note who is bound by the statutory preclusion in s. 18(1): a "corporation" or a "guarantor of an obligation of a corporation". See *Agricultural Credit Corp. of Saskatchewan v. Path Head Farms Ltd.*, [1994] S.J. No. 229, 121 Sask. R. 81 (Q.B.). Note also who benefits from it: "a person dealing with the corporation or ... a person who acquired rights from the corporation". The exception in s. 18(2) narrows the application of the section by providing that some "outsiders" are not pure outsiders and that, in dealing with them, the corporation is not prevented from asserting any of the details covered in paras. (*a*), (*b*), (*c*) and (*f*). The varying gradations of "outsiders" under this section will be covered after the details of the particular paragraphs are illustrated.

NOTES AND QUESTIONS

1.   What type of rules are created by s. 18? Are they evidence rules? If so, is it within the jurisdiction of Parliament to enact this section? Is it within the jurisdiction of the provincial legislature to enact the provincial equivalents?

    Subsection 15(1) of the C.B.C.A. says that "rights, power and privileges" of a corporation are limited by the Act. Perhaps the rules are not evidence rules but are corporate personality rules? If this is the case what is the effect of s. 2(*b*) of the

Canadian Charter of Rights and Freedoms, which says that "everyone has ... freedom of ... expression"?

2. Compare ss. 35A-B of the U.K. *Companies Act, 1985* (c. 6), which was added by s. 108 of the *Companies Act, 1989* (c. 40). Section 35A protects outsiders by deeming (in their favour) that the authority of the board of directors is free from limitations in the corporate constitution. Section 35B provides: "A party to a transaction with a company is not bound to enquire as to whether it is permitted by the company's memorandum... ." The newer Act, by its s. 142, also adds a s. 711A to the older Act, which abolishes constructive notice.

3. How would one characterize "the agent's" authority based on the admissible evidence that would be presented if the C.B.C.A. were applicable to each of the following scenarios?

(a) Section 114(2) of the C.B.C.A. states that a majority of the directors constitutes a quorum for a directors' meeting, but indicates that a lesser number could constitute a quorum if so stated in the by-laws. The basic, underlying principle involved is that directors can only act at a meeting and that a meeting requires a quorum. Fewer than a majority of the directors of A Furs Ltd. congregate and purport to arrange a huge, long-range supply contract with an outsider. No by-law to lower the quorum requirement has been passed. Does the outsider have a contract with the corporation? (Compare the judicial analysis pre-C.B.C.A. in *Re Almur Fur Trading Co.*, [1932] S.C.R. 150, [1932] 2 D.L.R. 128.)

(b) The articles of B Corp., which are registered with the Director, authorize the directors to borrow amounts, not exceeding a certain sum, which sum could be varied upwards from time to time by a resolution of the shareholders. No such shareholders' resolution had been passed, but the directors purported to borrow from an outsider a sum in excess of the set amount. Is the corporation liable to the outsider for the amount of the loan? (Compare the judicial analysis, pre-C.B.C.A., in *Royal British Bank v. Turquand* (1856), 6 E. & B. 327, 119 E.R. 886 (Eng. Exch. Ct.).)

(c) C Corp. had been set up only to manufacture ladies' gowns. It became engaged in the manufacture of veneered panels. The corporate letterhead, which described the business as "Veneer Panel Manufacturers", was used to order fuel. In an action for payment by the fuel supplier, can the corporation use the *ultra vires* defence? (Compare the judicial analysis in *Re Jon Beauforte (London) Ltd.*, [1953] 1 All E.R. 634 (Eng. Ch.).)

(d) The Director receives and files a notice that D has been elected to the board of directors of D Corp. It is subsequently established that D, a shareholder, purported to hold a meeting without notifying the other shareholders and thus falsely elevated himself to the board of directors. Does D now have power to act as a director? To what extent will D Corp. be bound by what D does? Can D bind the corporation in contract with an outsider? Can D issue corporate shares? (What is the relationship between C.B.C.A., s. 116 and s. 18(*d*)? (Compare *Morris v. Kanssen*, [1946] A.C. 459, [1946] 1 All E.R. 586 (Eng. H.L.), and *Oliver v. Elliott* (1960), 30 W.W.R. 641, 23 D.L.R. (2d) 486 (Alta. S.C.).)

(e) The latest notice sent to the Director under C.B.C.A., s. 19 states that the "registered office" of E Corp. is at 21 Oak Street. This is a typographical error; the real corporate address is 21 Oakley Street and 21 Oak Street is an abandoned warehouse. A plaintiff seeks to commence a civil action against E Corp. by sending a writ by registered mail to 21 Oak Street. Is the action commenced? (Is the issue more complex than C.B.C.A., s. 254 makes it seem?)

(f) What is the inter-relationship between s. 18(*f*) and s. 189(3) of the C.B.C.A.? Who may take advantage of s. 18(*f*)? Ought a purchaser to have knowledge that a sale of substantially all the assets of a corporation requires unusual internal approvals? Must a shareholder ensure these are followed? What remedies can the shareholders have if s. 189(3) is not followed?

4. The foregoing sections are relatively uncomplicated in their operation. They may be viewed as rather simple examples of the statutory technique of precluding certain evidence from being presented in litigation between corporations and outsiders. Two complications may now be introduced. The first involves representations ("holding out") by the corporation and is found in two different subsections. The second is a general, overriding rule that, in effect, removes the corporate gag in disputes with certain types of "outsiders". Both are illustrated in the following extract from C.B.C.A., s. 18.

> 18(1) No corporation ... may assert against a person dealing with the corporation ... that
>
> ...
>
> (*d*) a person held out by a corporation as a director, an officer or an agent of the corporation has not been duly appointed or has no authority to exercise the powers and perform the duties that are customary in the business of the corporation or usual for such director, officer or agent;
>
> (*e*) a document issued by any director, officer or agent of a corporation with actual or usual authority to issue the document is not valid or not genuine; ...
>
> 18(2) Subsection (1) does not apply in respect of a person who has, or ought to have, knowledge of a situation described in that subsection by virtue of their relationship to the corporation.

The world of persons dealing with the corporation may be divided into two types. Let's call a person described in s. 18(2) a "Mark II" outsider: most people dealing with a corporation won't fit that description. Let's call everyone else dealing with the corporation — which would cover the vast majority of the populace — "Mark I" outsiders. Pick any of the subsections and identify what types of details an outsider would have to know in order to lose the advantages of being in the Mark I category.

5. Analyze the following situations on the assumption that a Mark I outsider is suing the corporation and argues that the "agent" in question had actual authority and, in the alternative, ostensible authority.

(a) Assume the facts of *Freeman & Lockyer v. Buckhurst Park Property (Mangal) Ltd.*, set out *supra*.

(i) Was K. "held out" as managing director?

(ii) Does it matter if no representation was made by the corporation to the outsider?

(iii) Would the fact that a representation had previously been made to U., a person unknown to the Mark I outsider, be a sufficient "holding out" to bar the corporation from asserting "the agent's" lack of authority?

(iv) What if the representation had been made to U. prior to the Mark I outsider's dealings with "the agent", but the fact that the representation had been made to U. was not discovered by the Mark I outsider until the day of the trial?

(v) What if the representation to U. took place after the Mark I outsider's dealings with "the agent"?

(vi) Is K's own misrepresentation of the extent of his authority a sufficient "holding out" to bar the corporation's assertions?

(b) Assume the facts of *Canadian Laboratory Supplies Ltd. v. Engelhard Industries of Canada Ltd. (Canlab)*, set out *supra*.

(i) Can Snook be construed as "the corporation" in determining whether Cook was "held out"?

(ii) Will a representation from any employee of the corporation suffice?

(iii) What if the authority claimed is highly unusual for that particular officer, but is quite usual for similarly titled officers in similar corporations?

(iv) What if the authority claimed is highly unusual for that type of agent, but it is customary in the business of the corporation for such functions to be performed, albeit by much higher ranking corporate officials?

(v) Is every corporate employee "an agent" of the corporation? If it is customary in the business of the corporation to sell jet aircraft (or real estate), can a Mark I outsider confidently deal with any corporate employee, no matter how low ranking, so long as he is buying jet aircraft (or real estate)?

(vi) In seeking the protection of s. 18(d), must the Mark I outsider prove reliance on the "holding out"?

Compare *Kuklica v. Morguard Trust Co.*, [1987] M.J. No. 594, 50 Man. R. (2d) 136 (Q.B.).

(c) The corporate secretary forges share certificates in the name of M, a Mark I outsider, transfers possession of them to M in exchange for a large sum of money, and flees to South Exotica.

(i) Is the forgery of any relevance to the subsequent dispute between M and the corporation?

(ii) What do the words "valid" and "genuine" mean in C.B.C.A., s. 18(e)?

Compare *Ruben v. Great Fingall Consolidated*, [1906] A.C. 439 (H.L.).

(d) R, a rogue, sets up R Corp. to exploit a statutory loophole. In exchange for specified sums of money, R Corp. issues statements "holding out" any person whose name has been submitted by the payer as being (as requested) a director, officer or agent of any prominent North American corporation. In one such statement, R Corp. falsely names Rodney Leitch as the executive vice-president of The John W. Astor School of Dance (International) Inc. Mark, who has no affiliation whatever with either corporation, but has seen the statement, negotiates through Rodney a long-term supply agreement for dance floor wax.

(i)   Has Rodney been sufficiently "held out" to prevent his lack of authority's being asserted against Mark?

(ii)   Would your answer be different if R Corp. was incorporated in South Exotica, a well-known tax haven?

(iii) Was the sixth word in C.B.C.A., s. 18(d) meant to be "the"?

6.   Some outsiders know a lot more about the internal organizations of corporations they deal with than most people do. Canadian corporate statutes permit corporations to defend themselves differently against such outsiders. Continuing with our labels of convenience, a Mark II outsider is described by C.B.C.A., s. 18 as someone who "has, or ought to have, knowledge of a situation ... by virtue of their relationship to the corporation". The statute appears to permit the corporation to present evidence against the Mark II outsider that it could not have presented against most people.

For analytical purposes, the category of Mark II outsiders can be subdivided in two: a Mark IIA outsider is one who "has ... knowledge"; a Mark IIB outsider is one who "ought to have knowledge" but, presumably, does not. It is arguable that the two end up being treated quite differently due to the combined effect of the statute and the common law principles.

A preliminary point involves the modifying phrase "by virtue of their relationship to the corporation". The opening of s. 18(2) refers to a single person but this phrase is referring to a group of people. Can the exception apply if only one person has knowledge of a situation?

Subsection 18(2) applies to both types of Mark II outsiders. Other statutes are worded differently. For example, O.B.C.A., s. 19 has a single subsection and these words follow the last paragraph: "except where the person has or ought to have, by virtue of the person's position with or relationship to the corporation, knowledge to that effect". Will the results differ on this grammatical point? Is this phrase even necessary? Are there any situations where a person can have knowledge related to the corporation that does not come by virtue of a relationship to the corporation?

Whether one is a Mark IIA outsider — someone who knew about the limitation of authority, yet dealt with the agent — is a question of fact. It is less clear how a corporation would go about proving that someone is a Mark IIB outsider. What types of positions with the corporation, what sorts of relationships, will incline the judiciary to conclude that an outsider "ought" to know certain internal corporate details? Once the "ought" is established, however, the initial effect is the same: facts that could not otherwise have been "asserted" by the corporation may now become part of the evidence in the case.

7.   What is the effect if the outsider ("O") has *some* knowledge of "the situation" but the knowledge is insufficient in quantity or quality to have prevented O from making the impugned transaction? Can the common law rules examined earlier play a role in this instance? In *McAteer v. Devoncroft Developments Ltd.*, [2001] A.J. No. 1481, 24 B.L.R. (3d) 1 (Q.B.) *circa* para. 212, this issue was briefly examined. The court found that O had information regarding unmet restrictions on the transaction that resulted from unanimous shareholders agreements and internal procedures. However, O believed they had been followed and s. 18(2) did not apply because she "did not have, nor should she ought to have had, knowledge of the internal irregularities". The

standard here appears to be that the outsider must have sufficient knowledge to have changed her behaviour.

Contrast this to the approach taken in *Royal Bank v. Ag-Com Trading Inc.*, [2001] O.J. No. 474 (S.C.J. [Commercial List]) at *circa* para. 63, where Cameron J. said that the amount of knowledge required is "sufficient knowledge to put [the outsider] on its inquiry". Which approach is more appropriate?

8. In *Canada Mortgage and Housing Corp. v. Edinburgh House Apartments Ltd.*, [1991] A.J. No. 90, 112 A.R. 104 (Q.B.) (aff'd [1993] A.J. No. 17, 135 A.R. 244 (C.A.), the corporation (Lincoln Properties Ltd.) retained a lawyer (Rondeau) and obtained his opinion that a document which had been signed by Richard Connor on behalf of Lincoln was duly executed and was binding on Lincoln. This opinion was presented to the outsider, Maritime, who accepted it. It transpired that the directors had not passed a resolution authorizing the document, as required by a corporate by-law. Maritime, seeking to enforce the document, relied on s. 18(*a*) and (*d*) of the A.B.C.A. Lincoln argued that since it had obtained a lawyer's opinion on the document, Maritime was not relying on any apparent authority, or alternatively, it knew or ought to have known that the document was unauthorized. Justice McFayden said:

> In my view, rather than preventing the plaintiff from relying on s. 18, the presentation of Rondeau's opinion to Maritime by agents acting for Lincoln Properties Limited is the best evidence that Lincoln Properties Limited held Connor out as the officer or agent who had authority to execute the acknowledgement on its behalf.
>
> By requesting the opinion, the plaintiff did not cease to rely on the apparent authority of Connor to negotiate for Lincoln Properties Limited. The plaintiff was seeking and obtained confirmation of such authority from the solicitor for Lincoln Properties Limited. While the plaintiff may have an additional remedy in tort against the defendant's solicitor, I see no reason why this should alter the obligations of the corporate guarantor. Possible liability in tort of the guarantor's solicitor does not alter the liability of the corporation although that corporation may also have a cause of action against its own solicitor.
>
> ... Nothing in the evidence convinces me that Maritime or [its assignee] C.M.H.C. had reason to believe that Connor had no authority to act for Lincoln Properties Limited.
>
> Lincoln Properties Limited may not assert that Connor and Wright were not authorized to execute the acknowledgement on its behalf or that the bylaws were not complied with in designating these agents or officers. Lincoln Properties Limited is bound by the terms of the acknowledgement. ...

9. See also *Re Agravoice Productions Ltd.* (*sub nom. Flewitt v. Agravoice Productions Ltd. (Trustee of)*), [1986] M.J. No. 666, 61 C.B.R. (N.S.) 280 (Q.B.), in which the corporation's trustee in bankruptcy argued that a loan to the outsider was not properly authorized and therefore could not be proved in the bankruptcy. The outsider was the brother of the corporation's president. Justice Oliphant concluded that the outsider was not in a position where he knew or ought to have known of his brother's lack of authority.

10. Compare *1394918 Ontario Ltd. v. 1310210 Ontario Inc.*, [2004] O.J. No. 2967, 24 R.P.R. (4th) 203 (S.C.J.), concerning a corporation with two shareholders with equal numbers of shares. The outsider had previously signed an agreement that both shareholders had signed. In all dealings Shareholder A seemed to be the shareholder in control. Only Shareholder A signed an amendment to the agreement. Despite the

outsider's perception that Shareholder A was the decision-maker and principal shareholder, the past practice of the corporation was knowledge that should have informed the outsider that both shareholders should sign. Justice Rutherford also relied on documents the outsider had in his possession (but had not examined) that demonstrated both shareholders were equal.

11. Finally, see *Springdale Ultramar Limited v. Dorman Roberts Ltd.*, [1996] N.J. No. 338, 149 Nfld. & P.E.I.R. 219 (T.D.), in which the defendant corporation argued that the purchases for which the plaintiff (the outsider) was seeking payment were made on behalf of a third corporation, DRCL. Jason Roberts, the sole shareholder and director of the third corporation had, prior to the incorporation of DRCL, actual authority to contract on behalf of the defendant. However, at the time of the transactions in question, he no longer had actual authority. The plaintiff attempted to rely on s. 31(*d*) of the Newfoundland *Corporations Act*, R.S.N.L. 1990, c. C-36, to prevent the defendant from asserting that Jason did not have authority. Justice Barry ruled that, due to the nature and length of the relationship between the three corporations, the plaintiff *ought* to have known that Jason only had authority to contract on behalf of DRCL, and not for the defendant. At page 225, he wrote:

> I do not accept that, in the circumstances, these facts entitled Dicks to assume all work was for the account of the defendant. The plaintiff has not satisfied me that the defendant must be considered to have given Jason Roberts ... the apparent or ostensible authority to contract on behalf of the defendant, where the evidence establishes that any reasonable person in the place of the plaintiff would have been put on notice or inquiry, by the facts of the transaction, that the prior authority of Jason had been terminated and that the contract might be that of DRCL.

12. Contrast *Morris v. Kanssen*, [1946] A.C. 459, [1946] 1 All E.R. 586 (Eng. H.L.), where Morris was acting as a director in the transaction in issue, which was a share issue to him. He argued that the transaction was effective, even though he had not been properly appointed as a director. It was held that Morris could not take the benefit of the "indoor management rule" and so the transaction was ineffective. Would Morris have been able to take the benefit of a section like C.B.C.A., s. 18?

13. Work through the foregoing examples again, first assuming a Mark IIA outsider, second assuming a Mark IIB outsider. Summarize your conclusions by answering the following general questions.

    (a) If the outsider is a Mark I outsider, will the case always be decided on the basis of actual authority? Be careful to distinguish between evidence and fact in answering this question.

    (b) If the outsider is a Mark IIA outsider, will the corporation always be able to rely on the limitation and win?

    (c) Is the Mark IIB outsider best advised to plead his case in ostensible authority and frankly confess "maybe I *ought* to have known, but I didn't know and I relied on the corporation's representation"?

    (d) Apart from Question 3, is ostensible authority of any use to outsiders under the reformed Canadian statutes, or do sections like C.B.C.A., s. 18 provide simpler routes to the same conclusion?

CHAPTER 6

INCORPORATION AND PRE-INCORPORATION TRANSACTIONS

A. THE DETAILS OF INCORPORATION

1. Registration

The procedure for incorporation in most Canadian jurisdictions is quite simple. The incorporators submit an application to the appropriate official. If the application is in order the official must issue a certificate of incorporation and the corporation is born. The C.B.C.A. official is "the Director" and her duties in this regard are set out in C.B.C.A., ss. 8 and 262. In other jurisdictions the equivalent public official is sometimes called "the Registrar", but the duties are the same so far as the creation of new corporations is concerned. See, for example, B.C.B.C.A. ss. 13 and 14. Only in P.E.I., the last letters patent jurisdiction, does the official have discretion: see *Companies Act*, R.S.P.E.I. 1988, c. C-14, s. 4.

The corporate birth date is set by C.B.C.A., s. 9: "A corporation comes into existence on the date shown in the certificate of incorporation." The certificate of incorporation is the document signed and returned to the incorporators by the Director and may conveniently be analogized to your own birth certificate. When the date on the certificate is the date it was issued, C.B.C.A. s. 9 causes no problems. However, when a document alleged to be a certificate bears a date other than the date it was issued, complications arise.

PROBLEM

Consider s. 256(2) of the C.B.C.A. and the following fact situation.

> (2) Except in a proceeding under section 213 to dissolve a corporation, a certificate referred to in subsection (1) or a certified copy thereof, when introduced as evidence in any civil, criminal or administrative action or proceeding, is conclusive proof of the facts so certified without proof of the signature or official character of the person appearing to have signed the certificate.

The defendant, a distributor, signed a contract binding himself personally for the purchase of at least 5,000 units of the plaintiff wholesaler's product. The minimum number of units had to be ordered either by the defendant or a corporation by 15 June. The plaintiff became apprehensive that the defendant's financial and administrative situation boded ill for the distributorship, and was not enthusiastic about continuing with the contract. On 15 June, the plaintiff received an order for delivery of the remainder of the 5,000 units. The order form was made out in a corporate name and signed by the defendant as president of the corporation. Assume that the certificate of incorporation had not been issued until 16 June, although it bore the date of 15 June. The plaintiff took the position that the defendant had not met the order deadline, refused to deliver the units, and sought damages for breach of contract.

When was the corporation in this hypothetical situation born? What is the effect of s. 9 and s. 256 of the C.B.C.A. on this question? What is a certificate?

Similar facts, under a different statute, came before the Alberta courts. The trial judge held that the corporate order was placed before the deadline, having declined to hear evidence about backdating a certificate of incorporation.

C.P.W. VALVE AND INSTRUMENT LTD. v. SCOTT

[1978] A.J. No. 603, 84 D.L.R. (3d) 673, 3 B.L.R. 204 (C.A.)

McDermid J.A. (dissenting): — I ... would ... dismiss the appeal ...

... I wish to express my reasons ... as to the admissibility of evidence that the company, S. & V. Fluid Gauge Ltd., was not incorporated on June 15, 1971, the date stated in the certificate of incorporation issued by the Registrar of Companies, but was incorporated on June 16th and the certificate was back-dated. The learned trial Judge ruled that such evidence was not admissible and that the witness from the Companies Branch could not be asked "the date upon which the Registrar actually put his stamp upon the memorandum (of association) and actually issued the certificate of incorporation".

...

The applicable provisions of the *Companies Act* as amended are:

25. The applicants for incorporation shall deliver the memorandum and the articles, if any, to the Registrar, and if all other requirements of this Act precedent to incorporation have been complied with, the Registrar shall retain and register them.

...

27. A certificate of incorporation given by the Registrar in respect of a company is conclusive proof that all the requirements of this Act in respect of registration and of matters precedent and incidental to incorporation have been complied with, and that the company is a company authorized to be registered and duly registered under this Act.

28. From the date of incorporation mentioned in the certificate of incorporation the subscribers, together with such other persons as may from time to time become members of the company, are a body corporate by the name contained in the memorandum, capable of exercising all the functions of an incorporated company, and having perpetual succession and a common seal, with power to hold lands, but with such liability on the part of the members to contribute to the assets of the company in the event of its being wound up as is mentioned in this Act.

In deciding the point in issue the main case that I need examine is *Letain v. Conwest Exploration Co. Ltd.* (1960), 26 D.L.R. (2d) 266, [1961] S.C.R. 98, 33 W.W.R. 635. The facts were set out in the judgment of Chief Justice Kerwin, in whose judgment Taschereau, Fauteux, and Judson, JJ., concurred. Ritchie, J., gave the majority judgment and his judgment was concurred in by Locke, Cartwright, Abbott and Martland JJ.

The Chief Justice said at pp. 267-8 D.L.R., pp. 99-100 S.C.R.:

The action arises out of an option agreement, dated July 26, 1955, between the appellant and the respondent therein called Conwest, whereby the appellant for valuable consideration granted an option to the respondent to purchase certain mineral claims. Clause 7 of the agreement reads as follows:

> In the event of Conwest electing to exercise fully the option hereby granted, it may do so by causing to be incorporated on or before the 1st day of October, 1958, under the Companies Act of Canada, or under the laws of such other jurisdiction in Canada as Conwest shall choose, a mining company to which reference is herein made as the proposed company, with an authorized capital comprising three million shares, either without nominal or par value, or of the par value of $1.00 each, as Conwest shall decide. The proposed company, if incorporated, shall, in due course, be organized by Conwest, whereupon the said claims and such other mineral claims, if any, as Conwest shall elect, shall be transferred to the proposed company free of encumbrance.

> The agreement provided for the transfer of the mineral claims to the company to be incorporated as provided in cl. 7 in return for 50,000 shares of the proposed company. It also provided for the transfer forthwith of the claims to the respondent and that in the event that Conwest should not duly exercise the option thereby granted, Conwest would, at the request of the appellant, re-transfer the said claims to the appellant. Other agreements were made later between the parties but their provisions do not materially affect cl. 7 of the original.

The Chief Justice goes on to further state that the respondent in that case caused an application to be made under the *Companies Act* of Canada [then R.S.C. 1952, c. 53] on September 15, 1958, and letters patent of incorporation were issued bearing date September 25, 1958. It was clear, however, that the letters patent were actually signed, sealed and issued after October 1, 1958, the relevant date for the exercise of the option. At p. 270 D.L.R., p. 103 S.C.R., the Chief Justice says:

> Kutcho Creek Asbestos Co. Ltd. [the company incorporated] is not a party to this action; it continues to exist and not one of its powers is affected. The rights of the appellant and respondent are to be determined by the meaning to be ascribed to c.7 of the original agreement between them and the appellant is not precluded by the mere production of the letters patent from showing at the trial that Conwest did not exercise the option in accordance with its terms.

...

This case turns upon the interpretation that is to be placed upon the distributorship agreement. In the *Letain* case, in order to exercise the option, a company had to be in existence on a certain date so a third party could exercise the option. It was a point of time that was of importance, and, as decided by the Supreme Court, if the company had in fact not been incorporated at that point of time, then the condition upon which the exercise of the option depended had not been fulfilled and it could not be exercised.

In the case at bar the question is whether the terms of the distributorship contract were fulfilled in respect of the order for gauges. On June 15th there were orders handed to the appellant signed by the proposed company; undoubtedly the company was bound by those orders even if it were not placed on the register until June 16th. Its certificate of incorporation stated it was on the date of the certificate "incorporated under The *Companies Act* of the Province of Alberta as a limited company" and the certificate was dated June 15th, 1971. Accordingly, as provided for in s. 28, from the date of incorporation mentioned in the certificate of incorporation, which was June 15, 1971, the subscribers were a body corporate, capable of exercising all the functions of an incorporated company. On that date the company gave an order which was signed by the president of the newly formed company, and it would appear to me that the company was bound by the terms of that order to take the gauges so ordered. If such be the case, then the terms of the distributorship agreement had been satisfied. Even if the company had not been placed on the register until June 16th it was bound by the terms of the order to take the gauges. Accordingly, the evidence would not have changed the decision of the trial Judge. I therefore agree with the trial Judge and would dismiss the appeal and cross-appeal with costs.

Clement J.A. (Lieberman J.A. concurring): — This appeal raises, as the first point for consideration, the scope and operation of s. 27 of the *Companies Act*, R.S.A. 1970, c. 60, which declares the conclusiveness of a certificate of incorporation of a company issued pursuant to s. 26. The facts relevant to the issue are not in dispute and are detailed in the reasons for judgment of Moshansky J. at trial.

...

In the result, C.P.W. has sued Scott for damages for breach of the covenant to purchase units. Scott and S. & V. Fluid Gauge Ltd. have counterclaimed, alleging that C.P.W. had repudiated the agreement by its letter of June 24th, and asserting damages sustained thereby. Neither party contends that the purchase order should be treated as a purchase by Scott personally pursuant to the distributorship agreement.

C.P.W. tendered evidence that, if admitted, would presumably have established that the certificate of incorporation had not in fact been actually signed and sealed by the Registrar, nor given by him, until June 16th. Such evidence would enable C.P.W. to argue that S. & V. Fluid Gauge Ltd. was not legally in existence at the time its purported purchase order was delivered, and that the subsequent issue of a certificate of incorporation dated June 15th had no effect in law on that state of affairs. The matter has stood there. Neither Scott nor S. & V. Fluid Gauge Ltd. has purchased any units since, nor has the latter purported to adopt the purchase order.

Scott and S. & V. Fluid Gauge Ltd. contend that the latter had a legal existence on June 15th, the date stated on the certificate of incorporation, because of s. 27 of the Act, with which, I think, must also be read s. 28: [**Clement J.A.** set out ss. 27 and 28.]

The learned trial Judge ruled against the admissibility of such evidence, relying not only on s. 27, but on *Letain v. Conwest Exploration Co. Ltd.* (1960), 26 D.L.R. (2d) 266, [1961] S.C.R. 98, 33 W.W.R. 635; *Re Barned's Banking Co., Peel's Case* (1867), L.R. 2 Ch. App. 674; *Re Laxon & Co.*, [1892] 3 Ch. 555; and *Kerr v. John Mottram, Ltd.*, [1940] Ch. 657. This ruling is in appeal.

I am of opinion that the ruling extends s. 27 beyond the plainly worded limits of its operation and projects it with decisive force into an area in which other considerations apply.

...

The point of law taken [in *Letain v. Conwest, supra*] was that although the letters patent had in fact been signed, sealed and delivered after October 1, 1958, which is to say after the right to exercise the option had expired, s. 133 of the *Companies Act* of Canada established conclusively its legal existence on September 25th and prevented the admission of any evidence as to when the letters patent had in fact been issued:

133. Except in any proceeding by *scire facias* or otherwise for the purpose of rescinding or annulling letters patent or supplementary letters patent issued under this Part, such letters patent or supplementary letters patent, or any exemplification or copy thereof certified by the Registrar General of Canada, shall be conclusive proof of every matter and thing therein set forth.

Ritchie, J., speaking for the majority, held that this section conclusively vested the company with corporate status on September 25th, since that date was a matter set forth in the letters patent.

This brought the incorporation to the same point reached above in consideration of the *Companies Act* of Alberta. But that point was held to be only background to the real matter in issue, namely, whether in law and on the facts the option had been duly exercised. The case was remitted for trial of the facts on that issue, to which s. 133 had of itself no decisive application. This passage in the judgment of Ritchie, J., at pp. 273-4 D.L.R., pp. 106-7 S.C.R., is instructive:

Kutcho Creek Asbestos Co. Ltd. is a company incorporated under the authority of the Dominion *Companies Act*, endowed with the characteristics enumerated in that statute and in its letters patent granted pursuant thereto, one of which is that its date of incorporation is to be conclusively taken for all purposes of its corporate dealings and activities as being September 25, 1958. The date of incorporation is one of the badges of a company's status and identity, it is an integral part of its corporate personality which flows from its charter as do the other ingredients of its status, the determination of which is, as has been said, a matter within the exclusive jurisdiction of Parliament. With the greatest respect, however, it seems to me that it is not the status of Kutcho Creek Asbestos Co. Ltd. but the actions of the respondent Conwest Explorations Co. Ltd. which are at issue in this case, and I am unable to see how conclusive proof of the fact that the former company has acquired status with effect from September 25th for the purposes of the Dominion *Companies Act* can preclude the appellant from proving whether or not the latter company exercised its option on or before October 1st.

The only method of creating a body corporate under Part I of the Dominion *Companies Act* is for the Secretary of State to grant a charter by letters patent under his seal of Office [see s. 5(1)]. If the charter so granted bears a date earlier than that upon which the seal was affixed, then, by virtue of s. 133, the company acquires status with effect from the earlier date. The question here, however, is not whether or not Kutcho Creek Asbestos Co. Ltd. is to be conclusively taken as having the status of a company incorporated on September 25th, but rather whether or not the respondent caused it to be "incorporated on or before the 1st day of October, 1958" within the meaning of those words as they are used in para. 7 of the agreement pursuant to which this action is brought.

I am of opinion that the fact that the letters patent of Kutcho Creek Asbestos Co. Ltd. bear date September 25th and that company has status as from that date for the purposes of the Dominion *Companies Act* in no way precludes the appellant from adducing evidence to prove whether or not this option was exercised by the respondent in accordance with the terms of the contract now sued upon, and I would accordingly dispose of this appeal as proposed by the Chief Justice.

These words are applicable here, and we must now determine what effect s. 28 would have if evidence had been given that the Registrar had not in fact completed his duties and registered the documents pursuant to s. 25 until June 16th, since that determination must be made before it can be concluded whether or not such evidence is relevant.

On this hypothesis, during the whole of the time period of June 15th S. & V. Fluid Gauge Ltd. had in fact no legal existence. It is not possible in law for a non-existent person to perform a legal act such as purchasing a quantity of goods. It follows that the purchase order purportedly given by S. & V. Fluid Gauge Ltd. on that day had no legal validity at any moment of the critical period prior to June 16th and cannot be relied on by Scott as performance of his obligation under the distributorship agreement. It existed only as a concept for which legal validity could only be secured by a statutory fiction reaching backwards to give legal substance and life to the concept. Section 28 may well have such effect for the purposes of the Act, particularly those mentioned in the section, but I would think it would take very clear words to enable a Court to say that the creation of status for a corporation can operate to negate a breach of contract that had already existed, the contract being between parties other than the ex post facto company. Section 28 is not directed by its wording or intent to that end. I would remit the action to the learned trial Judge to hear the evidence that had been tendered by C.P.W.

NOTES

To what extent is a civil servant's dating of a document conclusive evidence of the date of incorporation? The cases seem inconsistent.

In *Letain v. Conwest Exploration Co.*, [1961] S.C.R. 98, 26 D.L.R. (2d) 266 (*Conwest No. 1*), the Supreme Court of Canada considered s. 133 of the *Canada Corporations Act*, R.S.C. 1952, c. 53.

> 133. ... letters patent or supplementary letters patent, or any exemplification or copy thereof certified by the Registrar General of Canada, shall be conclusive proof of every matter and thing therein set forth.

The issue was whether the plaintiff had complied with the terms of a contract between the plaintiff and the defendant. The contract required the plaintiff's "causing a company to be incorporated" prior to 1 October 1958. The plaintiff's application for letters patent had been submitted on 18 September; the letters patent were not issued until 20 October, but were backdated to 25 September. The Supreme Court of Canada ruled in *Conwest No. 1* that s. 133 of the Canada *Corporations Act* did not render inadmissible the plaintiff's evidence that the certificate had been backdated *for the purposes of determining whether the contract had been breached.* Of what, in light of this ruling, was the date in the certificate "conclusive proof"?

In *Conwest No. 2*, [1964] S.C.R. 20, 41 D.L.R. (2d) 198, the case came back to the Supreme Court of Canada for final decision. The majority held that the contract had been performed by the defendant. Mr. Justice Ritchie dissented, stating:

> the retroactive effect of the antedating of the charter ... might, after the company had been duly incorporated, have the effect of validating acts done by the embryo company, but in my view no such acts can have any validity as corporate acts until after the incorporation of the company on October 20th.

What is the policy inherent in the ruling of the S.C.C. majority? Of the dissent? With which is the *C.P.W. Valve* majority consistent? Are the two cases distinguishable?

The court in *C.P.W. Valve* considered s. 27 of the *Alberta Companies Act*, R.S.A. 1970, c. 60.

> 27. A certificate of incorporation given by the Registrar in respect of a company is conclusive proof that all the requirements of this Act in respect of registration and of matters precedent and incidental to incorporation have been complied with, and that the company is a company authorized to be registered and duly registered under this Act.

The Alberta legislation has been changed since the *C.P.W. Valve* ruling. The Alberta *Business Corporations Act*, R.S.A. 2000, c. B-9, s. 9(2) states:

> 9(2) A certificate of incorporation is conclusive proof for the purpose of this Act and for all other purposes …
>
> (*b*) that the corporation has been incorporated under this Act as of the date shown in the certificate of incorporation.

Would this change have affected the outcome of *C.P.W. Valve*?

According to Miller J. (*obiter*), in *Prim Investments Ltd. v. Madison Development Corp.*, [1982] A.J. No. 572, 20 B.L.R. 108 (Q.B.), "the problems raised by the *Letain* and *C.P.W. Valve* decisions … are no longer applicable in Alberta under the new Act and they may be quietly laid to rest". Do you agree?

Compare O.B.C.A., s. 7, which says:

> 7. A certificate of incorporation is conclusive proof that the corporation has been incorporated under this Act on the date set out in this certificate, except in a proceeding under s. 240 to cancel the certificate for cause.

Contrast C.B.C.A., M.C.A., S.B.C.A., s. 9; B.C.B.C.A., ss. 13 and 17; N.S.C.A., s. 24(2); and N.C.A., s. 15.

Incorporating statutes commonly authorize the "Director" or "Registrar" to issue a certificate of incorporation dated either on the date the documents were received or on whatever later date has been requested by the incorporator [see, *e.g.*, C.B.C.A., s. 262(3)]. Could a plaintiff in a case like *C.P.W. Valve* argue that a document dated as of some other date, backdated for example, is not a certificate of incorporation at all and is therefore conclusive proof of nothing? How would the date of incorporation be determined if that argument were to prevail? Would there be a corporation?

2. The Corporate Constitution: Minimum Requirements

An application to create a corporation must contain draft articles for that corporation. While incorporators have substantial freedom in structuring the corporate constitution, there are some restrictions. The C.B.C.A. is typical of the articles of incorporation jurisdictions. C.B.C.A., s. 6 requires that the name of the corporation, location of the head office, number of directors, details of the share structure and any restrictions on the business of the corporation must be set out in the articles. A.B.C.A., s. 6, M.C.A., s. 6, S.B.C.A., s. 6, O.B.C.A., s. 5, N.C.A., s. 15, and N.B.B.C.A., s. 4 are essentially the same. Compare B.C.B.C.A., ss. 11

and 12, which require the filing of similar "Notice of Articles" and "Articles". These are loosely based on the "Memorandum of Association" and "Articles of Association" required for English-model companies.

3. Continuance: Corporate Emigration and Immigration

Continuance is the procedure whereby a corporation incorporated in one jurisdiction emigrates and establishes a new home. This should not be confused with merely doing business in another jurisdiction. The effect of continuance is the same as if the corporation had been dissolved in its home jurisdiction and simultaneously reincorporated in another. There may be several reasons for such a move. The location of the corporation's business may have moved or the laws in another jurisdiction may better serve some aspect of the corporation's affairs. There might also be perceived to be some advantages to being federally or provincially incorporated.

A typical requirement (*e.g.*, C.B.C.A., s. 187(1)) is that a corporation seeking to immigrate be "so authorized by the laws of the jurisdiction where it is incorporated". Does this require an express authorization (such as that given by C.B.C.A., s. 188) or is the absence of a prohibition enough? If the absence of a prohibition is sufficient, what is the result if the equivalent of discontinuance (C.B.C.A., s. 188(7)) cannot be found in the incorporating jurisdiction's statute? How else can the result be achieved?

4. Amalgamation: Corporate Combination

The legal idea of amalgamation is much narrower than the corresponding business idea. Imagine that corporation A Ltd. has its eye on the business being carried on by corporation B Ltd. The two can be combined in various ways. The differences may have little practical effect if everything goes as everyone planned. Legally, however, the differences are radical, and can become very important if things go wrong. Consider the differences among the following possibilities:

(a) A Ltd. buys all of the business assets of B Ltd.;
(b) A Ltd. buys all of the shares of B Ltd.;
(c) C Ltd. buys all of the shares of A Ltd. and of B Ltd.;
(d) C Ltd. buys all of the business assets of A Ltd. and B Ltd.

None of these is an amalgamation in the legal sense. Under C.B.C.A., ss. 181 to 186 and corresponding provisions in other reformed statutes, two or more corporations "may amalgamate and continue as one corporation". The effect is that the old corporations cease to exist as separate entities; only one corporation remains. It is governed by its own set of articles, which must be sent to the Director as part of the process. The Director issues a certificate of amalgamation to complete the process.

B. THE CORPORATE NAME

The use of corporate names is regulated by the general law of trademarks, and also by the common law of "passing off". Apart from this, there are also provisions in the incorporating statutes imposing certain requirements for the names of corporations to which each statute applies.

All corporate statutes require that the corporate name include a word indicating that a corporation is being described. See, for example, C.B.C.A., s. 10(1), which stipulates variations on the words "corporation", "incorporated", and "limited". Corporate names must also be distinctive and not deceptive. (See, *e.g.*, C.B.C.A., s. 12(1).) The C.B.C.A. regulations prohibit false suggestions that the corporation has governmental association, professional connection, or operates a banking, financial intermediary or stock exchange business (Reg. 22) as well as restricting the use of certain listed phrases (Reg. 21). Regulation 23 prohibits the use of "obscene" names. Regulation 24 forbids the use of names that are too general, only descriptive of the goods or services provided, or primarily only the name of a person or a place. Regulations 18, 25-32 further clarify what is an acceptable name under s. 12(1) of the Act. To secure compliance with the Act and regulations, would-be incorporators are required to obtain a search result from a database containing all registered corporate names.

If a name is registered or refused registration by the Director there is a right of appeal under C.B.C.A., s. 246(*b*). To avoid these complications a corporation may have a number for a name (s. 11(2)). Under O.B.C.A., s. 8(1), (2) a number is automatically assigned upon incorporation and the corporation will be known by that number unless some other name is requested and approved. Note the directors' ability to change a number name to a verbal name without seeking the shareholder approval required which is required for any other name change: C.B.C.A., s. 173(3).

QUESTIONS

In *I. Browns Packaging Inc. v. Director of the Corporations Branch of the Department of Consumer and Corporate Affairs* (1982), 24 B.L.R. 44 (Que. S.C.), the question to be decided was whether the corporate name of the applicant "I. Browns Packaging Inc." was confusing or likely to be confused with the corporate name "Browns Bottle (Canada) Limited".

1.　What is the problem of incorporating a company whose proposed name is confusing or is likely to be confused with a corporate name already in existence?

2.　Are the two corporate names stated above confusing? To whom? What if "I. Browns Packaging Inc." manufactured brown paper bags while "Browns Bottle (Canada) Limited" was a new environmentally conscious recycling group? What if one was a packaging company and the other was a bottling company and both had majority shareholders with the surname "Brown"?

3.　What factors would you take into consideration to determine if a proposed corporate name is confusing or is likely to be confused with a corporate name already in existence?

4.　Who is being protected, and against what, by the public regulation of names at the incorporation stage? Who is bearing the cost? Does the general public have any more interest in what a new corporation is named than in what a mother calls her newborn baby?

5.　In answering the above questions, does it make a difference that there is no requirement that a corporation (or an individual) carry on business in its own name? See, on this point, *Heriteau v. W.D. Morris Realty*, [1943] O.R. 724, [1944] 1 D.L.R. 28 and *Albert E. Daniels Ltd. v. Sangster* (1976), 12 O.R. (2d) 512 (Co. Ct.). See also the rather complex reasons for judgment in *Reference re ss. 91 and 92 of the Constitution Act, 1867*, [1991] M.J. No. 190, 73 Man. R. (2d) 81, [1991] 4 W.W.R. 193, 80 D.L.R. (4th) 431 (C.A.), which considered the interaction of provincial attempts to regulate corporate names and business names with federal corporate law and trademark law. See also the Ontario *Business Names Act*, R.S.O. 1990, c. B.17.

For more theories on the regulation of corporate names, see *Canadian Motorways Ltd. v. Laidlaw Motorways Ltd.*, [1974] S.C.R. 675, 40 D.L.R. (3d) 52, 11 C.P.R. (2d) 1; *Re Menzies Gibson Ltd.*, [1955] O.W.N. 657, 1 D.L.R. (2d) 187 (H.C.); *Re F.P. Chapple Co.*, [1960] O.R. 531, 25 D.L.R. (2d) 706 (C.A.); *Re Cole's Sporting Goods Ltd.* (1965), 48 D.L.R. (2d) 47 (Ont. H.C.); *Re Office Overload Co. and Driver Overload Ltd.*, [1968] 1 O.R. 292, 39 Fox. Pat. C. 31, 54 C.P.R. 162 (H.C.); *Action Plumbing Ltd. v. Registrar of Companies*, [1976] A.J. No. 338, [1977] 1 W.W.R. 123 (C.A.); *Re Compro Ltd. and Combined Engineered Products Ltd.* (1974), 44 D.L.R. (3d) 21 (Ont. H.C.); *Unity Insurance Brokers (Windsor) Ltd. v. Unity Realty & Insurance Co.*, [2005] O.J. No. 1069, 3 B.L.R. (4th) 107 (S.C.J.).

C. PRE-INCORPORATION TRANSACTIONS

1. Introduction

WELLING, CORPORATE LAW IN CANADA: THE GOVERNING PRINCIPLES

(3rd ed., 2006), pp. 292-93 (Footnotes deleted.)

It is standard business practice to arrange for goods or services to be supplied between the time the idea of incorporation is conceived and the time of issue of the certificate of incorporation. Since a corporation does not come into existence until the date on the certificate of incorporation, it is impossible for a supplier to contract with the corporation prior to that time. Notwithstanding this legal impossibility, incorporators have made such arrangements in the past and will no doubt continue to do so. It is important then, to analyze the legal implications of any pre-incorporation transactions arranged on behalf of a corporation.

Pre-incorporation *transactions* is more apt than pre-incorporation *contracts*. A contract is a legally binding agreement between two persons. Whether an agreement concluded prior to the existence of a corporation constitutes a contract is a question of law. Merely labelling an agreement a contract does not make it so. When two parties agree what will happen following the creation of a third person — the corporation — the first question to be analyzed is whether those two parties or the corporation were intended to incur legal obligations. The analysis involves elementary points of contract law. Those elementary points have been obscured by judicial and academic disinclination to apply simple legal principles. ...

In any pre-incorporation transaction situation there will be two active parties. "A", usually an individual involved in the incorporation process, purports to act on behalf of the future corporation. "O", an outsider who is not involved in the incorporation process, intends to buy from or sell to the future corporation. The third party, the future corporation, is as yet only a figment of the parties' imagination.

2. Common Law Position

A contract requires two parties. It is clear that before a corporation comes into existence it cannot be a party to a contract any more than an individual can be a party to a contract before she is born. Therefore even if A and O are in agreement that the contract is to be between O and the corporation, the attempt to create a contract will fail.

A contract also requires agreement to at least its fundamental terms. The question of who are the parties to a contract is fundamental. Thus, if one of A and O seeks to create a contract between O and the corporation, and the other seeks to create a contract between A and O, then A and O are not in agreement as to who will be the parties, and the attempt to create a contract fails due to lack of agreement.

The result is that if a contract is to be created through the interaction of A and O, it is they who must be the parties. There must be a common intention that A is to be personally liable on the contract.

A more difficult situation arises when both parties know the corporation does not exist. Again, whether there is a contract depends upon whether there was an intention to contract with A personally. This will depend on a difficult factual determination: each party is likely to allege a common intention that happens to coincide with that party's success in litigation, and the whole issue will tend to become somewhat confused. As the following material indicates, confused legal analysis follows more often than not.

KELNER v. BAXTER

(1866), L.R. 2 C.P. 174, 36 L.J.C.P. 94, 15 L.T. 213,
15 W.R. 278 (Eng. Common Pleas)

[The defendant operated a hotel and the plaintiff was a dealer in wines. The defendant decided to create a company and to turn the hotel business over to it. The plaintiff offered to sell wine to the defendant "on behalf of the proposed Gravesend Royal Alexandra Hotel Company, Limited". The defendant accepted the terms proposed by the plaintiff "on behalf of the Gravesend Royal Alexandra Hotel Company, Limited" omitting the word "proposed". Wine was supplied by the plaintiff and consumed. Incorporation followed and the company purported to "ratify" the agreement, but became insolvent before the plaintiff was paid.]

Erle C.J.: — A difficulty has arisen because the plaintiff had at the head of the paper addressed it to the plaintiffs, "on behalf of the proposed Gravesend Royal Alexandra Hotel Company, Limited", and the defendants have repeated those words after their signatures to the document; and the question is, whether this constitutes any ambiguity on the face of the agreement, or prevents the defendants from being bound by it. I agree that if the Gravesend Royal Alexandra Hotel Company had been an existing company at this time, the persons who signed the agreement would have signed as agents of the company. But, as there was no company in existence at the time, the agreement would be wholly inoperative unless it were held to be binding on the defendants personally. The cases referred to in the course of the argument fully bear out the proposition that, where a contract is signed by one who professes to be signing "as agent", but who has no principal existing at the time, and the contract would be altogether inoperative unless binding upon the person who signed it, he is bound thereby; and a stranger cannot by a subsequent ratification relieve him from that responsibility. When the company came afterwards into existence it was a totally new creature, having rights and obligations from that time, but no rights and obligations by reason of anything which might have been done before. It was once, indeed, thought that an inchoate liability might be incurred on behalf of a proposed company, which would become binding on it when subsequently formed: but that notion was manifestly contrary to the principles upon which the law of contract is founded. There must be two parties to a contract; and the rights and obligations which it creates cannot be transferred by one of them to a third person who was not in a condition to be bound by it at the time it was made. The history of this company makes this construction to my mind perfectly clear. It was no doubt the notion of all the parties that success was certain; but the plaintiff parted with his stock upon the faith of the defendants' engagement that the price agreed on should be paid on the day named. It cannot be supposed that he for a moment contemplated that the payment was to be contingent on the formation of the company by the 28th of February. The paper expresses in terms a contract to buy. And it is a cardinal rule that no oral evidence shall be admitted to shew an intention different from that which appears on the face of the writing. I come, therefore, to the conclusion that the defendants, having no principal who was bound originally, or who could become so by a subsequent ratification, were themselves bound, and that the oral evidence offered is not admissible to contradict the written contract.

Willes J.: — I am of the same opinion. Evidence was clearly inadmissible to shew that the parties contemplated that the liability on this contract should rest upon the company and not upon the persons contracting on behalf of the proposed company. The utmost it could amount to is, that both parties were satisfied at the time that all would go smoothly, and consequently that no liability would ensue to the defendants. The contract is, in substance this, — "I, the plaintiff, agree to sell to you, the defendants, on behalf of the Gravesend Royal Alexandra Hotel Company, my stock of wines"; and, "We, the defendants, have received your offer, and agree to and accept the terms proposed; and you shall be paid on the 28th of February next." Who is to pay? The company, if it should be formed. But, if the company should not be formed, who not made by the company, it must, if by anybody, be by the defendants. That brings one to consider whether the company could be legally liable. I apprehend the company could only become liable upon a new contract. It would require the assent of the plaintiff to discharge the defendants. Could the company become liable by a mere ratification? Clearly not. Ratification can only be by a person ascertained at the time of the act done. ...

... Both upon principle and upon authority, therefore, it seems to me that the company never could be liable upon this contract; and, as was put by my Lord, construing this document *ut res magis valeat quam pereat*, we must assume that the parties contemplated that the persons signing it would be personally liable. Putting in the words "on behalf of the Gravesend Royal Alexandra Hotel Company", would operate no more than if a person should contract for a quantity of corn "on behalf of my horses".

BLACK v. SMALLWOOD

(1966), 117 C.L.R. 52, 39 A.L.J.R. 405 (Aust. H.C.)

Barwick C.J., Kitto, Taylor and **Owen JJ.:** — On 22nd December, 1959, the appellants purported to enter into a contract for the sale of certain land at Inglebun to Western Suburbs Holdings Pty. Ltd. The contract incorporated the conditions of sale approved by the Real Estate Institute of New South Wales and was executed by the appellants as vendors and it bore the following subscription as the signature of the purchaser:

Western Suburbs Holdings Pty. Ltd.
Robert Smallwood
J. Cooper

It was subsequently found that Western Suburbs Holdings Pty. Ltd. had not at that time been incorporated but it is common ground that both the appellants and the respondents, Smallwood and Cooper, who subscribed the name Western Suburbs Holding Pty. Ltd. to the form of contract and added their own signatures as directors, believed that it had been and that the latter were directors of the company. Thereafter the appellants instituted a suit for specific performance against the respondents alleging that by a written contract made between the appellants as vendors and the respondents who "described themselves therein as 'Western Suburbs Holdings Pty. Ltd.'" agreed to purchase the subject land from the appellants. No attempt was made at the trial to make this allegation good but, without amendment, the case proceeded as one in which the appellants sought to impose a liability in accordance with the terms of the contract upon the respondents as agents contracting on behalf of a principal not yet in existence.

…

Kelner v. Baxter was cited as an authority for the proposition that there is a rule of law to the effect that where a person contracts on behalf of a nonexistent principal he is himself liable on the contract. But we find it impossible to extract any such proposition from the decision. In that case it appeared from the contract itself that the defendants had no principal; they had purported to enter into a contract on behalf of the "proposed Gravesend Royal Alexandra Hotel Company", and the fact that they had no principal was obvious to both parties. But it was not by reason of this fact alone that the defendants were held to be liable; the court proceeded to examine the written instrument in order to see if, in these circumstances, an intention should be imputed to the defendants to bind themselves personally, or, perhaps, to put it in another way, whether, the intention being sufficiently clear that a binding contract was intended, there was anything in the writing inconsistent with the conclusion that the defendants should be bound personally. The decision was that, in the circumstances, the writing disclosed an intention that the defendants should be bound. …

Windeyer J.: — I agree that this appeal must be dismissed. I have come to that conclusion without hesitation but with regret. The law requires it, but I do not think that it accords well with a belief that bargains should be kept.

If before the document sued upon was signed the registration of Western Suburbs Holdings Pty. Ltd. had been completed and it had emerged from the Registrar-General's office as a new-born entity in the law, no difficulty could have arisen. It could not then have been said that Smallwood and Cooper had contracted as agents on its behalf. It must have been said that it, not they, had made the contract. It, not they, would have been the purchaser entitled to a conveyance. Their putting the company's name to the document would have been purely in execution of its corporate act and their added signatures would have no more bound them personally to perform the contract than would the signatures of the directors or secretary of a company authenticating the affixing of its seal. There is a difference between a man's own acts and acts done for him by another man. The difficulty of the distinction in the case of a corporation is that a corporation must manifest its acts and intentions by the actions and declarations of human beings; and ambiguities and limitations of language make it difficult sometimes to express the distinction between acts done by a person as executant of the will of a corporation and acts done by a person as agent for a corporation, his principal. That the word "agent" is in each case apt to describe the actor helps to disguise their different legal characters.

I appreciate the force of what Walsh J. said in the Supreme Court concerning the narrow differences in language upon which the decision in *Newborne v. Sensolid (Great Britain) Ltd.*, [1954] 1 Q.B. 45, turned. But the distinction that differences in language reflect, sometimes not very clearly, is the distinction between the act of a man himself and acts done by another on his behalf. If in the case of a company the distinction is difficult to preserve, and may seem unreal, or merely verbal not conceptual, that is because the legal personality and capacity of the corporation are artificially created by law. ... [T]he document which the respondents signed does not purport to be a contract made by them as agents for the supposed company. They thought that the company existed and that they were in fact directors. It is therefore impossible to regard them as having used the name of the company as a mere pseudonym or firm name or as having intended to incur a personal liability. The reason for the formation of the company may have been to ensure that they would not be personally liable. It is however suggested that, notwithstanding the form of the document, a personal obligation to perform the contract has been imposed upon them by law, because at the time they inserted the name of the company as purchaser there was no such company in existence.

[His Lordship here considered the wording of the agreement in *Kelner v. Baxter, supra,* and continued.] Their statement that they were buying on behalf of the proposed company was taken to mean, and could in the circumstances only mean, that they contracted to buy the goods with the intent and to the end that the company when formed might have the benefit of them. The words "on behalf of" do not necessarily imply agency in the relevant legal sense, any more than does the word "for" when a man says "I am buying this for" someone whom he names. The words cannot be regarded as indicative of agency for a principal when it is known to the user of the words that there is no principal in existence. The defendants in *Kelner v. Baxter* therefore contracted as principals. They were not substituted as principals. They were the principals. The contrast with this case is obvious. Here, instead of both parties knowing that the company was not in existence, they both, appellants and respondents, thought that it was. ...

NOTES

1. Not only is A not liable in contract where A and O mistakenly thought the corporation existed, but he is also not entitled to the benefits of the agreement. See *Newborne v. Sensolid (Great Britain) Ltd.*, [1954] 1 Q.B. 45, [1953] 1 All E.R. 708 (Eng. C.A.).

2. Ratification in the sense known to the common law of agency is impossible in these cases because the principal did not exist at the time of the agency's unauthorized act. It was once thought that there was a rule in Equity that a corporation could "adopt" as a contract a pre-incorporation agreement concluded on its behalf: see *Spillar v. Paris Skating Rink Co.* (1878), 7 Ch. D. 368. However, the courts have fairly consistently rejected the idea that a corporation might become bound by adopting such an agreement: *Re Empress Engineering Co.* (1880), 16 Ch. D. 125 (Eng. C.A.); *Natal*

Land and Colonization Co. v. Pauline Colliery Syndicate Ltd., [1904] A.C. 120 (J.C.P.C.); followed in *Nepetti Ltd. v. Oliver-Lee Ltd.* (1922), 52 O.L.R. 315, [1923] 3 D.L.R. 1100 (C.A.). Would such an equitable rule make sense? Analyze the effect of both rules in the situation where a corporation subsequently comes into existence, but is insolvent. What do the words "adoption" and "ratification" mean?

3.   Someone who falsely claims to have authority to act as an agent can be made liable for breach of warranty of authority. This cause of action does not appear to depend on establishing a contract between the plaintiff and the defendant. Strangely, though, damages are measured as though there was such a contract. O is not simply entitled to any loss suffered through the transaction. Rather, his damages will be measured by the position he would have been in if A had the authority that A claimed to have. Thus, if A's corporate principal is insolvent, O will likely get nothing, on the basis that even if A had authority, O's contractual rights against the principal would have been worthless. It follows that if A's principal does not exist, again O gets nothing: *Wickberg v. Shatsky* (1969), 4 D.L.R. (3d) 540 (B.C.S.C.).

Breach of warranty of authority can be proved even if A did not know that he lacked authority (*e.g.*, if he thought that the corporation existed). That is another reason that it is strange: the orthodox view is that damages cannot be collected for innocent misrepresentation. See generally S.M. Waddams, *The Law of Damages*, 3rd ed. (Toronto: Canada Law Book, 1997), pp. 279-84.

O could also sue A in fraudulent misrepresentation (deceit), which requires showing that A knowingly made a false statement, and that O relied on it and suffered a loss as a result. Negligence is also a possibility. In either case, O is entitled to be put in the position he would have been in if the misrepresentation had not been made, which appears to mean that O can recover any loss he has suffered. If A wants to allege that O suffered no loss because O would have behaved the same way even if the misrepresentation had not been made, then the onus of proof will lie on A: *Rainbow Industrial Caterers Ltd. v. C.N.R. Co.*, [1991] S.C.J. No. 67, [1991] 3 S.C.R. 3, 84 D.L.R. (4th) 291.

4.   O may also have rights based upon unjust enrichment. Where there is a transfer of wealth (money, goods or services) by mistake, there is, in general terms, a right of recovery. This includes transfers which were intended to be pursuant to a contract, where it turns out that there is no contract: see for example *Deglman v. Guaranty Trust Co. of Canada*, [1954] S.C.R. 725, [1954] 3 D.L.R. 785. Even if there was no mistake (for example, O knew there was no corporation), if the enrichment was transferred in anticipation of a contract that did not materialize, there is a right of recovery: *William Lacey (Hounslow) Ltd. v. Davis*, [1957] 1 W.L.R. 932 (Eng. Q.B.). On this basis, which does not depend in any way on contract or tort, O might have rights against A or the corporation (assuming it was formed). The question will be whether someone was enriched at O's expense, and if so, who. If there is a contract, however, generally there can be no recovery in unjust enrichment: the contract's distribution of rights and risks must be respected.

3. Attempts at Statutory Reform

Statutory reforms in this area have attempted to make two changes. First, the reformers tried to impose contractual liability on A in situations where there would be no contract at common law. Second, they tried to enable a corporation to "adopt" pre-incorporation transactions, making the corporation a party to the contract and excusing A.

The attempted reforms are flawed by legislative misuse of the term "contract". Section 21(1) of the O.B.C.A. is a typical example of the problem.

> 21(1) Except as provided in this section, a person who enters into an oral or written contract in the name of or on behalf of a corporation before it comes into existence is personally bound by the contract and is entitled to the benefits thereof.

Similar terminology is used in C.B.C.A., M.C.A., S.B.C.A., s. 14 and N.B.B.C.A., s. 12. The A.B.C.A., N.B.C.A. and Y.B.C.A. deal with pre-incorporation contracts in a manner that does not require this section.

As explained above, at common law there can only be "an oral or written contract" before incorporation if there is a contract between O and A. In such a case s. 21 is not needed to make A personally liable, although it might still serve its alternative function of allowing the corporation to adopt the contract. On the other hand, if at common law there is no contract between O and A, s. 21(1) does not seem to create one. The courts, however, disagree.

SZECKET v. HUANG

[1998] O.J. No. 5197, 168 D.L.R. (4th) 402 (C.A.)

[H approached S with a proposal to develop and market technology developed by S in Taiwan. The agreement that was eventually signed purported to be between, *inter alia*, the individual S, and H "acting on behalf of a company to be formed". The transaction was never completed, and the proposed company was never formed. S sued for breach of contract. H denied personal liability. The trial judge found that there was a common law contract between S and H, and applied s. 21(1) of the O.B.C.A. to hold H personally liable. H appealed.]

The Court (at 412): — ... In this appeal, all the evidence pointed to only one conclusion – that the respondents and Mr. Huang knew, and, indeed, intended, that Mr. Huang, and his associates, were contracting on behalf of a company to be incorporated. As Borins J.A. concluded in his analysis of the law pertaining to pre-incorporation contracts in the *Sherwood* case, in a situation like this where the company is not incorporated and the contract is not performed, liability for breach of the pre-incorporation contract depends on the application of s. 21, which was enacted to replace the common law.

There [is] no need ... to undertake the two-stage analysis suggested by *Westcom* and first determine whether it was the intention of the parties to the pre-incorporation contract that Mr. Huang incur personal liability before determining the ultimate issue of his liability through the application of s. 21(1). This represented one of the problems arising from the common law of pre-incorporation contracts, which the legislature intended to remedy by the enactment of s. 21. As we have stated, personal liability of the promoter is established by s. 21(1) and prevails unless either contracted out of pursuant to s. 21(4), or displaced by the adoption of the contract by the company subsequent to its incorporation pursuant to s. 21(2). Indeed, on its facts this is a simple and straightforward case, which clearly attracts the application of s. 21(1).

...

Appeal dismissed.

1394918 ONTARIO LTD. v. 1310210 ONTARIO INC.

[2002] O.J. No. 18, 57 O.R. (3d) 607 (C.A.)

[D Co agreed to sell property in land to "R in trust for a company to be incorporated and not in his personal capacity". The agreement was to become "null and void" if the purchaser did not complete the transaction within 120 days, and 119 days after the agreement was signed, D Co asserted the agreement was null and void. Two weeks later R's solicitor sent a letter claiming damages for unlawful repudiation. After another two weeks P Co was incorporated and R quickly attempted to assign his rights under the contract.]

Carthy J.A.: ... [it is] clear that s. 21 was intended to replace the common law. As such, that section should be read on its own terms and in an interpretative context of the purpose it was intended to fulfil. The statutory scheme for pre-incorporation contracts throws off the confusion of the common law and shouldn't be thwarted to that end by concern, for instance, that a common law contract requires two parties with co-existent liabilities. If s. 21 calls for liability absent those features, then those liabilities must flow and the "contract" referred to must be treated as a statutory creation.

Commercial business concerns inform s. 21. The section is clearly directed at meeting the needs of a party who wishes, and has negotiated for, liability to be assumed by an as-yet-unincorporated corporation. In the circumstances described in s. 21(1), the promoter is personally bound by the contract and entitled to its benefits. Either party can sue on the other's breach.

NOTES AND QUESTIONS

Prior to *1394918 Ontario Ltd. v. 1310210 Ontario Inc.*, courts did not find that s. 21(1) created a statutory contract and continued to apply the common law distinction between *Black v. Smallwood* and *Kelner v. Baxter*. See *Westcom Radio Group Ltd. v. MacIsaac* [1989] O.J. No. 1902, 70 O.R. (2d) 591 (Div. Ct.). Note that the courts have explicitly said that they are ignoring obvious language problems with the language of s. 21(1) when interpreting s. 21(1) in the manner seen in *1394918 Ontario*. See *1080409 Ontario Ltd. v. Hunter*, [2000] O.J. No. 2603, 50 O.R. (3d) 145 at 155 (S.C.J.).

How does one apply O.B.C.A., s. 21(1) without first determining whether the parties created a contract? What conditions must be satisfied for the creation of this nebulous "contract" that is a "statutory creation"? Suppose A kicks B in the shin while saying, "I am about to create a corporation": are A and B parties to a pre-incorporation contract? Does s. 21(1) apply?

Does O need to know that the corporation doesn't exist at the time the statutory contract is made? Is there any requirement for A to have communicated that the corporation does not yet exist at the time of agreement?

Must either party have an intention to create a corporation at the time the "contract" is signed? In *Mexam Corp. v. Coffee, Tea*, [2001] O.J. No. 3535 (S.C.J.) Master Haberman gave s. 21 a much broader purpose than to reform the confusing law regarding pre-incorporation transactions, saying:

> while the Ontario *Business Corporations Act* does not expressly deal with the situation of an incorrect name being inserted into a contract, section 21(1) is, in my view, applicable by analogy. That section provides that a party who enters into a

contract on behalf of a corporation before it comes into existence is personally bound by the agreement and entitled to benefits under it. The section does not appear to require that a corporation be eventually formed. The purpose of the section is, in large part, to ensure that parties do not escape their contractual obligations by contracting in the name of non-existent entities ... Thus, even in a case where the court was prepared to state that there was no intent to mislead, s. 21 of the O.B.C.A. was applied to render the signatory to the contract personally responsible for the debt of the non-existent corporation.

Is there any justification for this judicial activism? See also *Pelliccione v. John F. Hughes Contracting and Development Co.*, [2005] O.J. No. 4132 (S.C.J.). Examine *1080409 Ontario Ltd. v. Hunter*, [2000] O.J. No. 2603, 50 O.R. (3d) 145 at paras. 9, 13 and 34-5 (S.C.J.) to see the roots that lead to this misinterpretation.

C.B.C.A., s. 14(1) was nearly identical to O.B.C.A., s. 21(1) (except that it excluded oral contracts) until 2001, when the following five italicized words were added.

14(1) Subject to this section, a person who enters into, *or purports to enter into,* a written contract in the name of or on behalf of a corporation before it comes into existence is personally bound by the contract and is entitled to the benefits thereof.

Does the addition of this phrase change the interpretation of the section?

Apart from the terminological problem, there is also the question whether this provision could be enacted by the federal Parliament. It is hard to see how Parliament can be legislating in relation to "incorporation of companies other than with provincial objects" when the wording is not directly related to the incorporation process and applies only where no corporation exists. What if no corporation is ever set up?

Can even a provincial provision worded like O.B.C.A., s. 21 apply where no corporation is ever set up? Is anything done "in the name of or on behalf of" something which never comes into existence? Is anything done "before" a proposed being comes into existence if no such being ever comes into existence?

Note the statutory definition of "corporation". Where no corporation is ever set up, does the applicability of a particular statute depend on which jurisdiction a corporation was intended to be created in? Can the legislation of one jurisdiction apply if a corporation is set up in another? See *Rover International Ltd. v. Cannon Film Sales*, [1987] 3 All E.R. 986 (Eng. Ch. D.), var'd [1989] 1 W.L.R. 912, [1989] 3 All E.R. 423 (C.A.), which answered this question in the negative. Does the different wording of A.B.C.A. s. 15(1) solve this problem?

(1) This section applies unless the person referred to in subsection (2) [that is, A] and all parties to the contract referred to in that subsection

(a) believe that the body corporate exists and is incorporated under, or

(b) intend that the body corporate is to be incorporated under the laws of a jurisdiction other than Alberta.

A.B.C.A., s. 15, B.C.B.C.A., s. 20 and Y.B.C.A., s. 17 take a different approach to the personal liability of A. Rather than making A "bound by the contract and entitled to the benefits thereof", these sections deem A to warrant to O that the corporation will be formed and that it will adopt the contract within a reasonable time. They also say that A will be liable to O if the warranty is breached, and that the measure of damages will be the same as if the corporation had existed but had given no authority to A and had refused to ratify the contract. How does this approach differ from that in the O.B.C.A.? Does this wording solve the problem (mentioned above) of the way damages are assessed for breach of warranty of authority?

Note also these sections provide expressly for an unjust enrichment-like liability of a corporation that receives a benefit under a pre-incorporation transaction, but fails to adopt the transaction within a reasonable time. It is not clear that this adds anything to the common law of unjust enrichment; indeed it is more restrictive, since it does not provide for any unjust enrichment liability of O or A.

Provisions like O.B.C.A., s. 21 do not take account of the use of so-called "shelf corporations". These corporations are created by lawyers, but do not carry on business. When a client wants a new corporation, the lawyer transfers the shares of an existing "shelf corporation" to the client, as a quick alternative to creating a new corporation. Can s. 21 apply where all of the "pre-incorporation" transactions take place while the corporation is in existence, but before the client has picked it off the lawyer's shelf? Does it matter if the client intended to create a new corporation, and only used a shelf corporation at the suggestion of a lawyer? Can the corporation use the common law agency concept of ratification in this situation?

The attempted reform of pre-incorporation transactions continues with s. 21(4) of the O.B.C.A. It allows A to avoid liability in any event if the contract so specifies.

> (4) If expressly so provided in the oral or written contract referred to in subsection (1), a person who purported to act in the name of or on behalf of the corporation before it came into existence is not in any event bound by the contract or entitled to the benefits thereof.

What must the contract expressly provide in order for A to rely on this provision?

The Ontario Court of Appeal dealt with O.B.C.A., s. 21(4) in *Szecket v. Huang*, *supra*. During negotiations leading to the final agreement, S had proposed that H and his associates personally guarantee the benefits S was to receive under the contract, and this was included in a draft version of the agreement. However, H opposed this provision, and it did not appear in the final agreement. H pointed to the removal of the guarantee provision as an expression of his clear intention not to assume personal liability. The Ontario Court of Appeal found s. 21(4) to be clear and unambiguous, requiring an express provision limiting the liability of a person entering a pre-incorporation contract to be included within the agreement. As there was no such provision in this case, H was unable to rely on s. 21(4) to avoid liability under the contract.

A similar result was reached in *Landmark Inns of Canada Ltd. v. Horeak* (1982), Sask. R. 30, [1982] W.W.R. 377 (Q.B.), where Maurice J. said, in relation to s. 14(4) of the C.B.C.A.: "To relieve a person of personal responsibility, the contract must contain an express provision that a person who enters into a written contract in the name of a company before it comes into existence is not personally bound by the contract".

What happens to the contract prior to incorporation? This was discussed in *1394918 Ontario Ltd. v. 1310210 Ontario Inc.*, [2002] O.J. No. 18, 57 O.R. (3d) 607 (C.A.) where the court found that,

[p]rior to incorporation and adoption, [A] is not personally bound or entitled to benefits of the contract. He might be described as a functionary, performing such duties as assuring that any necessary inspections of property or title are pursued, that deadlines are met, and defaults avoided which might excuse the third party from the obligations. At the same time, the corporation does not exist or has not adopted the contract and thus is not bound by it or entitled to its benefits. There is an entity called a "contract" under the statute, but no one is entitled to sue for its breach. That is not to say that ongoing obligations can be ignored. I would term this a nascent contract, its enforceability being suspended.

NOTES

1.   The same issue was dealt with in *Phonogram Ltd. v. Lane*, [1981] 3 W.L.R. 736, a decision of the English Court of Appeal. On the question of contracting out of personal liability, Lord Denning said the following:

> The words "subject to any agreement to the contrary" mean … "unless otherwise agreed". If there was an express agreement that the man who was signing was not to be liable, the section would not apply. But, unless there is a clear exclusion of personal liability, section 9(2) should be given its full effect. It means that in all cases such as the present, where a person purports to contract on behalf of a company not yet formed, then however he expresses his signature he himself is personally liable on the contract.

The relevant legislation in this case was s. 9(2) of the *European Communities Act, 1972* (c. 68), which made A personally liable "subject to any agreement to the contrary". The Act was passed as part of the legislative package by which the U.K. joined the European Economic Community (now the European Union). Regarding the broader question of how this reasoning serves the objectives underlying attempts to "harmonize" English and European principles within the European Union, see Green, "Security of Transaction After Phonogram" (1984), 47 Mod. L. Rev. 671. Note that since the *Companies Act, 1989* (c. 40), the relevant provision is s. 36C of the *Companies Act, 1985* (c. 6).

2.   Is O required to do anything in cases where s. 21(4) applies because there is an express provision that A is not personally bound? Neither side has responsibilities or is entitled to benefits and there is no requirement for anyone to ever incorporate the corporation contemplated at the time the contract was signed. Nor is there a requirement that any corporation ever adopt the contract. If the parties are unknown and there is no certainty that anyone will *ever* have any obligations or right to benefits, what is the purpose of this "statutory contract"?

3.   What if pre-incorporation agreements, containing clauses expressly excluding the personal liability of A, are concluded with suppliers in Saskatchewan, Louisiana and Zambia, following which (i) no corporation is incorporated, or (ii) a corporation is incorporated under the C.B.C.A., but soon becomes bankrupt?

     (a)   Can A rely on the clause?

     (b)   Can O rely on the clause?

     (c)   Would the fact that the incorporating statute was one of the provincial variations on the C.B.C.A. approach make any difference?

Finally, the corporation may adopt the contract under s. 21(2) of the O.B.C.A.:

(2)   A corporation may, within a reasonable time after it comes into existence, by any action or conduct signifying its intention to be bound thereby, adopt an oral or written contract made before it came into existence in its name or on its behalf, and upon such adoption

> (*a*)   the corporation is bound by the contract and is entitled to the benefits thereof as if the corporation had been in existence at the date of the contract and had been a party thereto; and

> (*b*)   a person who purported to act in the name of or on behalf of the corporation ceases, except as provided in subsection (3), to be bound by or entitled to the benefits of the contract.

1394918 ONTARIO LTD. v. 1310210 ONTARIO INC.

[2002] O.J. No. 18, 57 O.R. (3d) 607 (C.A.)

[The facts of this case are summarized above.]

Carthy J.A.: — ... By the very terms of s. 21(4), Stern had no entitlement to the benefits of the contract and thus had nothing to assign.

The entitlement of the corporation must depend upon its adoption of the contract, if there was anything left to adopt. I am satisfied that the institution of the action was an indication of intention to adopt the contract and it remains to determine if the agreement had life at the time the action was commenced.

The appellants take the position that there can be no adoption under s. 21(2) following the letter of March 1, 2000 accepting the repudiation and thus terminating the contract. Because s. 21 gives little guidance on the question of whether accepted repudiation terminates the contract, I think it useful to look to the common law on this point.

[The court then reviewed British and Canadian decisions and academic commentary discussing if a contract continues to exist after repudiation. The court determined that] the position in Canada is that contractual obligations continue to exist after accepted repudiation. ... [A]ccepted repudiation "terminates" the contract, the context reveals that only future obligations under the contract are extinguished. Accrued obligations under the contract continue to exist, at least in the form of a secondary obligation to pay damages. To the extent that there remain in existence contractual obligations, it cannot be said that the contract ceases to exist.

...

Further, and returning from the common law to this statutory "contract", s. 21(2)(a) provides that the corporation is entitled to all the benefits as if it had been in existence at the date of the contract. The common law authorities cited above did not have before them this new breed of legislated "contract". There were two parties to those contracts and the aggrieved party could always sue for damages, whatever the significance of termination might be. In the instant case, if the purchaser had been in existence at the outset, or at any time before March 1, 2000, it could have sued for damages. The company would be denied "all the benefits of the contract" if disentitled to sue in these circumstances.

One curious feature of s. 21 deserves mention. The issues in this case arose because of the long time span between execution of the agreement and adoption by the corporation by the institution of this action. The legislation requires adoption by the company "within a reasonable time after it comes into existence" rather than a reasonable time after execution of the agreement. It is difficult to see a rationale for this provision but protection can presumably be provided by a suitably worded condition in the agreement.

Some of the difficulties encountered in applying of O.B.C.A. s. 21 to shelf corporations arose in *Sherwood Design Services Inc. v. 872935 Ontario Ltd.*, [1998] O.J. No. 1611, 39 O.R. (3d) 576 (C.A.). An agreement was reached to sell the assets of the plaintiff corporation. The memorandum of agreement was signed by the individual defendants "in trust for a corporation to be incorporated". The lawyer acting for the defendants indicated to the plaintiff that the corporate defendant, one of his law firm's "shelf corporations", was the corporation that would complete the purchase. The corporate defendant, 872935 Ontario Ltd., had been incorporated after the agreement was signed by a partner at the law firm, who was its first and sole director. No shares of the corporation had been issued, therefore there were no shareholders.

The next transaction, to issue shares of the corporation to the individual defendants, was never completed. Shares of the corporate defendant were subsequently issued to other clients of the defendants' lawyers. The majority of the Ontario Court of Appeal (Borins J.A. dissenting) ruled that the corporate defendant had adopted the contract. Accordingly, the corporation was held liable for breach of the agreement, notwithstanding the fact that it had never been controlled by anyone involved in, nor was it even aware of, the transaction.

The main issue in *Sherwood* was what constituted "any action or conduct signifying its [the corporation's] intention to be bound" by the pre-incorporation transaction. The majority held that, as there is no specified manner of adoption, there is no need to impose any stringent formality. As a result, the letter from the lawyer to the plaintiff was sufficient to indicate an intention on the part of the corporation. As Abella J.A. (as she then was) said at p. 581:

> The provision allows a corporation, "by *any* action or conduct signifying its intention to be bound thereby", to adopt a contract made before the corporation came into existence. There is nothing in the language of the section to suggest a requirement of formal documentation before any such intention can be extracted.

Justice Borins, in a lengthy dissent, put more emphasis on the need for the action or conduct to be that of the *corporation*. He would have found that the letter, which was sent by a lawyer who was not a director of the corporation, but only a representative of the individual defendants who were intended to become directors of the corporation in the future, was not a corporate act. As a result, there was no action or conduct to which s. 21(2) could apply, and therefore the corporation could not be liable under the contract.

PROBLEMS

1. The wording of s. 14(2) of the C.B.C.A. is almost identical to the wording of the O.B.C.A., s. 21(2). Assume that s. 14 of the C.B.C.A.

   (a) does, or

(b)   does not

cover the no-contract situation found in *Black v. Smallwood.* Summarize the constitutional bases upon which s. 14(2)(*a*) and (*b*) could have been enacted and could be attacked.

2.   Does the judgment in *1394918 Ontario Ltd. v. 1310210 Ontario Inc.* give A and the corporation the ability to unilaterally decide if the terms of the contract will ever be enforceable? Does this accord with principles of contract law? Does it seem fair? Would any person knowledgeable about this section choose to be O in this type of transaction?

3.   Based on the holding in *Sherwood Design Services*, the act or conduct that signifies the intention of the corporation to adopt the contract need not involve communication with O. This could easily result in O's breaching the contract because O has no idea for whom to perform acts specified in the contract. What would the courts do in this scenario? For examples of how innocuous the act triggering adoption can be, see *Design Home Associates v. Raviv*, [2004] O.J. No. 1710, 44 B.L.R. (3d) 124 (S.C.J.); *Winfull Supplies (Canada) Ltd. v. Goritsas*, [2003] O.J. No. 5402 (S.C.J.). For an example of when the courts have not been able to find a corporate act that signifies an intention to adopt a contract see *Vinpat Construction Ltd. v. Henze Holdings Inc.*, [2002] O.J. No. 2664, 18 C.L.R. (3d) 307 (S.C.J.). All three cases have similar facts yet different holdings. Can they be reconciled?

4.   If a pre-incorporation agreement is concluded and a corporation is subsequently incorporated under the C.B.C.A., how does one determine whether that is the corporation "in the name of or on behalf of" whom the agreement was set up? What if two corporations were set up? Consider this scenario: A enters into a written agreement "in the name of or on behalf of a corporation before it comes into existence". As a result, he finds himself arguably liable on the contract under s. 14(1). Then he decides that he has made a bad deal, and so he incorporates a C.B.C.A. corporation which has $1 in assets, and causes it to adopt the contract. Is A off the hook? In *Landmark Inns of Canada Ltd. v. Horeak*, [1982] S.J. No. 20, 18 Sask. R. 30, [1982] 2 W.W.R. 377, the Saskatchewan Court of Queen's Bench was able to avoid facing this issue because the individual had breached the contract before the adoption.

5.   Do you think s. 14(3) is able to deal with the problems in the previous two questions?

> (3) Subject to subsection (4), whether or not a written contract made before the coming into existence of a corporation is adopted by the corporation, a party to the contract may apply to a court for an order respecting the nature and extent of the obligations and liability under the contract of the corporation and the person who entered into, or purported to enter into, the contract in the name of or on behalf of the corporation. On the application, the court may make any order it thinks fit.

In what circumstances would a court exercise its discretion to issue an order under s. 14(3)? In *Banque Commerciale Italienne du Canada c. Almanza*, [1998] A.Q. No. 2701, Cohen J. of the Quebec Superior Court suggested that s. 14(3) is intended to address situations where an individual behaves in a manner that is almost fraudulent, entering a contract for his or her personal benefit alone, and only having a corporation adopt it in an attempt to avoid liability.

CHAPTER 7

CORPORATE MANAGEMENT

A. MANAGEMENT'S ROLE: THEORY AND PRACTICE

Every corporation must have a board of directors. Most also have officers. The position of director tends to be defined in every corporations statute, whereas the statutory coverage of officers tends to be somewhat haphazard. Understanding the roles and obligations of both is critical to understanding how corporations work. This is not a simple task, partially because the common law overestimated the directors' role and tended to ignore corporate officers.

The word "management" is not a term of art with a fixed definition. Sometimes (as in the title of this chapter) it means the whole managerial group, directors and officers. Sometimes (as in the extract below from Mace's *Directors: Myth and Reality*) it is used to refer to officers *as opposed* to directors. The context usually reveals the intended sense.

1. The Governing Principles

WELLING, CORPORATE LAW IN CANADA: THE GOVERNING PRINCIPLES

(3rd ed., 2006), pp. 322-23

Legal theory personifies the economic enterprise within which corporate managers work. This makes directors and officers responsible for the funds contributed by shareholders and creditors without making them directly responsible to the contributors, as a matter of legal obligation. The creation of a corporate legal person, the rise of a professional managerial class, and the popularization of corporate shares as investment property rather than licences to participate in business all contributed to a subtle, yet critical shift in how businesses were run during the 20th century.

Berle and Means illustrated the change by isolating three functions performed by groups of individuals in any economic pursuit:

(a) holding proprietary interests in the enterprise;
(b) exercising power over the enterprise; and
(c) acting with respect to the enterprise.

They pointed out that before the industrial revolution all three functions would likely co-exist in one individual or family. Later, during the 19th century, it would be common to find (a) and (b) coexisting in a classic capitalist, while (c) would often be carried out by a hired manager. During the 20th century (a) and (b) became separated as shareholders lost all practical power over large corporations and became passive investors. Those who managed the enterprise on a daily basis increasingly wielded real power. The result was a separation of power and property. Power over the enterprise and the role of acting with respect to it shifted to a new class of professional managers, without any necessary capital investment on their part. Those who had been viewed as proprietors under the classical theory became passive participants with little practical power. The law, rooted in pre-Marxian assumptions about the relationship between property and power, never fully adjusted to the new reality. One result is that the practical roles of shareholders and managers in a typical corporation today are different from the roles they play in legal theory.

2. Myth and Reality

MACE, DIRECTORS: MYTH AND REALITY

(Harvard Business School, 1971), pp. 185-90

I found that boards of directors of most large and medium-sized companies do not establish objectives, strategies, and policies, however defined. These roles are performed by company managements. Presidents and outside directors generally agreed that only management should have these responsibilities.

The determination of a company's objectives, strategies, and directions requires considerable study of the organization's strengths and weaknesses and its place in the competitive environment, careful, time-consuming, penetrating analysis of market opportunities, and a matching of the organizational capacities to meet and serve the changing requirements of the market. And the market, for more and more companies includes opportunities abroad, thus adding another complicating dimension of analysis. The typical outside director does not have time to make the kinds of studies needed to establish company objectives and strategies. At most he can approve positions taken by management, and the approval is based on scanty facts and not time-consuming analysis.

...

A second classical role ascribed to boards of directors is that of asking discerning questions — inside and outside the board meetings. Again it was found that directors do not, in fact, do this. Board meetings are not regarded as proper forums for discussions arising out of questions asked by board members. *It is felt that board meetings are not intended as debating societies.*

Many board members cited their lack of understanding of the problems and the implications of topics that are presented to the board by the president, and to avoid "looking like idiots" they refrain from questions or comments.

A third classical role usually regarded as a responsibility of the board of directors is the selection of the president... But in most cases the decision as to who should succeed the president is made by the president himself.

Boards or directors were found to serve in an advisory role in the selection of a new president — in their capacity as a sort of corporate conscience. The process of electing a new president requires a vote by the board, and the president observes the amenities of corporate good manners by discussing his choice with individual members prior to the meeting. Rarely does a board of directors reject a candidate for the presidency who is recommended by the president.

NOTES AND QUESTIONS

1. Among the many changes in the corporate environment that have occurred since the writings of Mace and of Berle and Means, two may be particularly noted. They relate primarily to corporations whose shares are publicly traded. The first is the rise, especially since the early 1980s, of "mergers and acquisitions". If a corporation is being poorly managed, the market price of its shares may be at a level below what it would be if the same business and assets were being better managed. "Corporate raiders" began to seek out such poorly managed firms in order to take them over and eventually to resell either the shares, or the assets of the corporation, at a profit. Of course mergers and acquisitions have always occurred in corporate law, but in the last two or three decades they have evolved from being an occasional and extraordinary occurrence to the point that they are now a full time activity for many business people and lawyers. The other development is the rise of the "institutional shareholder." This refers to an entity that holds enough shares in a large corporation that its voting power cannot be ignored by management. Typical examples are pension funds and mutual funds. These funds hold enormous amounts of wealth, managed for the benefit of employees or other investors. In some ways, institutional shareholders represent a return from myth to reality of the idea of shareholder control, because their holdings may be large enough to give them a significant voice in the way corporate decisions are made. Moreover, institutional shareholders cannot simply ignore their shareholder rights (*e.g.*, voting rights) as an individual shareholder would be free to do; an institutional shareholder holds those rights as trustee for the benefit of beneficiaries (*e.g.*, in the case of a pension fund, employees), and so must deploy them in the best interests of those beneficiaries. See generally J.G. McIntosh, "Institutional Shareholders and Corporate Governance in Canada" (1996), 26 C.B.L.J. 145.

2. The problem identified by Berle and Means, the split between property and power, has been addressed by many legal academics. Those using economic analysis have typically characterized the problem as one of "agency costs". (See, for example, F.H. Easterbrook and D. Fischel, *The Economic Structure of Corporate Law* (Cambridge: Harvard University Press, 1991).) Managers are not, legally speaking, agents of shareholders. If managers act as agents, they are agents of the corporation. For example, if an officer negotiates a contract on behalf of the corporation, the officer acts as the corporation's legal agent. A director might also negotiate a contract on behalf of the corporation. In this role, the director is not actually acting as a director in the sense that the director is not exercising the functions assigned to directors by the corporate constitution. Whether or not the director has been formally appointed as an officer, a director in this example is, like the officer in the previous example, acting as an agent of the corporation. But when directors are acting as directors, they are not acting as agents of the corporation. An agent is under the direction and control of a principal, but directors acting as such are in the opposite situation: they are the corporate brain, deciding what the corporation shall do. (Are directors, acting as directors, agents of the shareholders in contractarian jurisdictions?)

Although managers are not legally agents of the shareholders, the idea of "agency costs" is based on a non-legal sense of agency. Managers are agents of shareholders in the sense that they are the people whom shareholders (as investors) expect to look after their investment and make it grow. If the manager of a business is also the owner, then of course the manager (as owner) will bear the costs of sub-optimal management. If management and ownership of a business are divided, then the costs of sub-optimal management by the agent are not borne by the agent but rather by the owner. One might then think that the agent's incentive to manage optimally is less than if that person were also the owner; the costs to the owner so arising are called agency costs. The legal rules governing managers, discussed in this chapter, address this problem by creating legal liabilities for sub-optimal management. Economic analysts, responding to Berle and Means, have identified other mechanisms that may control agency costs.

For example, poor management may lead to the loss of a manager's job, or it might trigger a hostile takeover; these prospects may go some way towards changing a manager's incentives and so reducing agency costs. The effectiveness of these market disciplines, of course, depends (like any market mechanism) on a substrate of legal rules; in this case, the legal rules that govern the appointment and removal of managers, and the standards that govern their management. The prospect of a takeover concerns a manager precisely because it is the shareholders of a corporation who elect the directors.

3.   Mace showed that while in theory the directors control the officers, the reality is often the reverse. Attempts to re-align reality with theory, with the goal of ensuring that managers act in the best interests of shareholders, are often gathered under the rubric of "corporate governance". This has increasingly attracted the attention of academics, business people, and shareholders (especially institutional shareholders).

Principles of good corporate governance sometimes appear as rules of corporate law; one example is the fiduciary obligation that a manager owes to the corporation. They may, however, also appear in other forms. For example, in 1999 the Organization for Economic Co-operation and Development, comprising representatives of 29 countries, adopted the *OECD Principles of Corporate Governance*. These were adopted, with some amplifications, by the International Corporate Governance Network, which was created in 1995 largely through the efforts of institutional shareholders. These principles and guidelines have no legal force but as standards shift, corporations may feel obliged to comply.

Another manifestation of such principles may be in the rules of stock exchanges or securities commissions. A stock exchange may impose some requirement on corporations that wish their shares to be "listed" on that exchange. The requirement may then become a *de facto* rule for those corporations whose shares are publicly traded. The same can apply to requirements imposed by securities commissions. In these cases, the rules only govern corporations whose securities are publicly traded.

4.   In 1994, a committee of the Toronto Stock Exchange, chaired by Peter J. Dey, Q.C., published a report called "Where Were the Directors?" which listed 14 recommendations as "best practice guidelines" for corporations listed on the T.S.E. They were not mandatory, but listed corporations were required to make annual disclosure of their level of compliance. In 1999 a successor committee published a report called "Five Years to the *Dey*" [*sic*], which evaluated compliance with the 14 recommendations. Later still, a Joint Committee on Corporate Governance was created by the Toronto Stock Exchange, the Candian Venture Exchange, and the Canadian Institute of Chartered Accountants. This committee reported June 2001. Its recommendations also proceeded on the basis of guidelines, rather than binding rules, along with mandatory disclosure as to levels of compliance by publicly traded corporations.

Most of this work was then overshadowed by dramatic developments in the U.S., where a series of high-profile corporate failures brought the issue of corporate governance to the forefront of public consciousness. The case of Enron is probably the most notorious. This was a large U.S. corporation that was, in some sense, in the energy business. It had over 20,000 employees and in 2000 it claimed revenues of over $100 billion. The retirement savings of most of Enron's employees were invested in Enron shares. In 2001 the corporation became bankrupt and it was revealed to have had no real business at all. It was, effectively, an enormous accounting fraud. The value of the shares fell to zero, wiping out most of the value of employee pensions. Senior executives of Enron are facing criminal proceedings in 2006. One reaction to this and other high-profile scandals was legislation in the U.S. called the *Sarbanes-Oxley Act* of 2002. It reformed the rules for auditing of corporate accounts, and required senior management to take personal responsibility for the accuracy of these accounts. Canadian securities regulators responded by adopting, in 2004, some similar rules as mandatory for publicly listed corporations. These require personal certification by management of financial reports, and an independent and "financially literate" audit committee of the board of directors. In 2005, securities regulators also adopted rules similar to those adopted earlier by the Toronto Stock Exchange, requiring the disclosure by listed corporations of their degree of compliance with various governance principles. For example, National Policy 58-201 provides:

3.1 The board should have a majority of independent directors.

3.2 The chair of the board should be an independent director. Where this is not appropriate, an independent director should be appointed to act as "lead director". However, either an independent chair or an independent lead director should act as the effective leader of the board and ensure that the board's agenda will enable it to successfully carry out its duties.

These principles are not mandatory, but there is mandatory reporting under National Instrument 58-101. It requires disclosure of the answers to a series of questions such as these:

1. Board of Directors —

(a) Disclose the identity of directors who are independent.

(b) Disclose the identity of directors who are not independent, and describe the basis for that determination.

(c) Disclose whether or not a majority of directors are independent. If a majority of directors are not independent, describe what the board of directors (the board) does to facilitate its exercise of independent judgement in carrying out its responsibilities.

...

(e) Disclose whether or not the independent directors hold regularly scheduled meetings at which non-independent directors and members of management are not in attendance. If the independent directors hold such meetings, disclose the number of meetings held since the beginning of the issuer's most recently completed financial year. If the independent directors do not hold such meetings, describe what the board does to facilitate open and candid discussion among its independent directors.

(f) Disclose whether or not the chair of the board is an independent director. If the board has a chair or lead director who is an independent director, disclose the identity of the independent chair or lead director, and describe his or her role and responsibilities. If the board has neither a chair that is independent nor a lead director that is independent, describe what the board does to provide leadership for its independent directors.

(g) Disclose the attendance record of each director for all board meetings held since the beginning of the issuer's most recently completed financial year.

The goal is to try to ensure that there is some independent oversight of the officers.

5.   The readings above note that while officers often have more management power than directors, legal analysis has historically paid much more attention to the position of

directors. The reasons for this are fairly straightforward. In legal analysis, an officer is an employee. He or she is a very senior employee, of course, and the law now recognizes that an officer has such a degree of power over the corporation that it is appropriate to impose many of the same obligations on officers as have traditionally been imposed on directors. But the legal relationship between the corporation and an officer (such as the President) is a master-servant or employer-employee relationship. A related observation is that there is no legal requirement that a corporation have officers, or indeed that it have any employees. But a corporation needs directors (or at least one director). A director is not an employee of a corporation. The corporation is a legal person, but on its own it cannot make decisions. Somebody needs to decide how it will behave. That is the role of the directors. A useful analogy might be a natural person who lacks capacity to make decisions about his property. Assume that a group of people is designated to make those decisions for the incapacitated person. They are not employees, but administrators. This is why the law has always seen the need to provide particular regulation of their positions and their obligations, whereas the officers could largely be regulated by the ordinary law of employment. And indeed, it is the directors who decide whether there will be officers, and if so who they will be and what will be their duties (C.B.C.A., s. 121). In other words, the fundamental theoretical difference between directors and officers is this: the corporation as employer tells officers what to do; the directors are the ones who decide how the corporation behaves.

One complication is that the same person can be both a director and an officer. And of course she could be a shareholder as well. This is common in corporate law and requires us to make an effort to differentiate the various capacities in which such a person acts. As a shareholder, she can vote for the election of directors. As an officer, she may have a contract entitling her to a salary. As a director, she decides who the corporation hires as its officers. The potential for interesting disputes is obvious; by the end of this chapter you will have the tools to analyze these disputes.

3. Source of Management Power

(a) Directors

Most Canadian jurisdictions have the same basic starting point: directors are responsible for the management of corporate affairs. There are, however, variations on the theme.

Canada Business Corporations Act, s. 102(1):

Subject to any unanimous shareholder agreement, the directors shall manage, or supervise the management of, the business and affairs of a corporation.

Quebec *Companies Act*, s. 123.72:

The affairs of a company shall be managed by a board of one or more directors.

British Columbia *Business Corporations Act*, s. 136(1):

The directors of a company must, subject to this Act, the regulations and the memorandum and articles of the company, manage or supervise the management of the business and affairs of the company.

It is unanimously conceded that these provisions do not impose upon the board an obligation to supervise the minute details of daily corporate management.

However, it is agreed by all that the board of directors has a legal duty to, at least, establish long range corporate objectives and policies, to map out broad corporate strategies, and to provide competent managerial personnel to carry them out from day to day.

Under the reformed statutes directors are required to manage, or supervise the management of, the "business and affairs" of the corporation. Note that "affairs" is a defined term in most of these statutes. Why do you think the B.C. wording is so different? The original view under the contractarian model was that the "shareholders in general meeting" were the "company". The board of directors, collectively and individually, were seen as the agents of the shareholder group: see *Isle of Wight Ry. v. Tahourdin* (1883), 25 Ch. Div. 320 (C.A.). Two related developments made this theory unworkable. One was *Salomon v. Salomon*, [1897] A.C. 22 (H.L.), whereby the contractarian model company finally became recognized as a person separate from the shareholders. The other was a series of decisions whose cumulative effect made it unrealistic to analyze the board of directors under simple agency rules. After *Quinn & Axtens Ltd. v. Salmon*, [1909] 1 Ch. 311 (C.A.); aff'd [1909] A.C. 442 (H.L.), articles granting managerial powers to the board of directors were consistently interpreted as giving the directors broad, almost dictatorial powers that were shielded from shareholder review. Directors, like politicians, remained theoretically accountable at the polls when re-election time rolled around but their managerial decisions were not subject to shareholder review. Thus, where contractarian model articles contain a general assignment of managerial power to the board of directors, as appears to be almost universal practice, the effect is now similar to that under the C.B.C.A. and related statutes: shortly stated, the shareholders as a group have only those powers specifically given to them; all other managerial matters fall to the jurisdiction of the board of directors.

It remains true, however, that in the contractarian model all directors' powers are held by delegation from shareholders. Shareholders therefore retain any powers that are not within the delegation: see *Canadian Jorex Ltd. v. 477749 Alberta Ltd.* (1991), 85 Alta. L.R. (2d) 313, 117 A.R. 222 (C.A.), reproduced in Chapter 3. Consider also the English rule that if the board of directors cannot or will not act (for example, a voting deadlock) their power passes by default to the general meeting of shareholders: *Barron v. Potter*, [1914] 1 Ch. 895. Presumably, this means that the shareholders could temporarily manage by majority vote. This rule is clearly not applicable under statutes like the C.B.C.A. Do you see why? Do you think the rule would apply in British Columbia? In Nova Scotia?

Note the words "or supervise the management of" in the federal and B.C. statutes, which presumably are designed to make it clear that the directors may delegate day-to-day management to the officers.

(b) Officers

Under reformed statutes, officers acquire their managerial powers by delegation from the directors.

Canada Business Corporations Act, s. 121:

Subject to the articles, the by-laws or any unanimous shareholder agreement,

    (a)   the directors may designate the offices of the corporation, appoint as officers persons of full capacity, specify their duties and delegate to them powers to manage the business and affairs of the corporation, except powers to do anything referred to in subsection 115(3);

(b) a director may be appointed to any office of the corporation; and

(c) two or more offices of the corporation may be held by the same person.

The Dey Committee recommended:

12. The board of directors, together with the CEO, should develop position descriptions for the board and for the CEO, involving the definition of the limits to management's responsibilities. In addition, the board should approve or develop the corporate objectives which the CEO is responsible for meeting.

"Five Years to the *Dey*" found:

Just under two-thirds of corporate boards set or approve objectives for the CEO. While this is a clear majority, it may be lower than expected. Less frequent is board involvement in approving the position description for the CEO. Position descriptions for various board roles are drafted in only about one in five cases.

B. MANAGEMENT POSITIONS

Many details concerning becoming and ceasing to be a corporate manager are collected under this heading. Note particularly the continuing orientation, even in the newer statutes, toward directors rather than officers. Would it make sense to simply define the position of "manager" and subject all managers to the same legal standards?

1. Qualifications

(a) Minimum Standards

Most Canadian corporate statutes enact minimal standards for corporate directors. Typical requirements are that a candidate be 18 years of age, not incapacitated, and not a bankrupt (see, *e.g.*, C.B.C.A., s. 105(1), O.B.C.A., s. 118(1), Q.C.A., s. 123.73). Most statutes require that a majority of the board of directors be resident Canadians. Why do you think this should be? Would the absence of such a requirement be a factor in choosing the jurisdiction of incorporation?

The extract from Mace, above, discussed the problem that the directors' theoretical power to run the corporation is often subservient, in reality, to control by officers. In an attempt to ensure the board of directors some independence from day-to-day management, it is often thought to be appropriate that in the case of large corporations whose shares are widely held, at least some directors are "independent" or "non-executive" directors, who have no other role in the corporation. Corporate law as such may impose a minimal requirement of some independent directors for publicly trading corporations: see C.B.C.A., s. 102(2), O.B.C.A., s. 115(3). On the other hand, as was mentioned above, the securities regulators state that as a matter of principle, the majority of the board should be independent; non-compliance is permitted, but must be publicly disclosed.

There are generally no statutory minimum qualifications for corporate officers, although C.B.C.A., s. 121(1) requires that they be of full capacity. B.C.B.C.A.,

s. 141(3), by cross-reference to the qualifications for directors, imposes the same qualification requirements on officers.

It used to be standard practice to require corporate directors to hold at least one share. With some provincial exceptions, this requirement has been dropped, though it may be found in some corporate constitutions. The requirement never applied to officers.

Can a corporation be a director? An officer?

(b) Defects

One would think that a failure to meet the minimum qualifications would preclude the election of a person as director. However, there are complications. First, the attempted election may result in the unqualified person being "held out ... as a director" or listed in a notice to the Director, thus invoking protection for outsiders under sections like C.B.C.A., s. 18. Second, acts performed after the election may be effective even within the corporate hierarchy under sections like C.B.C.A., s. 116: "An act of a director or officer is valid notwithstanding an irregularity in his election or appointment or a defect in his qualifications". Just how far one can rely on such sections is dealt with in two contrasting cases.

MORRIS v. KANSSEN

[1946] A.C. 459, [1946] 1 All E.R. 586 (H.L.)

[Cromie and Kanssen were the only two shareholders and directors of a company. Cromie, with his ally Strelitz, wanted to oust Kanssen. C. and S. falsely claimed that at a directors' meeting at which C., S. and K. were present, S. was appointed a director. This meeting never occurred. Then C. and S. purported to issue shares to C. and S. Next there was a shareholders' meeting at which S.'s appointment as director was confirmed; but this was with the votes attached to the shares which C. and S. had purported to issue as directors. S. went on to act as a director for some time. When K. brought proceedings, his position was that the purported issue of shares by C. and S. was of no effect, and that S.'s appointment had no legal basis. C. and S. sought to validate S.'s acts through a section stating: "The acts of a director or manager shall be valid notwithstanding any defect that may afterwards be discovered in his appointment or qualification."]

Lord Simonds (with whom the other judges agreed): — There is, as it appears to me, a vital distinction between (a) an appointment in which there is a defect or, in other words, a defective appointment, and (b) no appointment at all. In the first case it is implied that some act is done which purports to be an appointment but is by reason of some defect inadequate for the purpose; in the second case there is not a defect, there is no act at all. The section does not say that the acts of a person acting as a director shall be valid notwithstanding that it is afterwards discovered that he was not appointed a director. Even if it did, it might well be contended that at least a purported appointment was postulated. But it does not do so, and it would, I think, be doing violence to plain language to construe the section as covering a case in which there has been no genuine attempt to appoint at all. These observations apply equally where the term of office of a director has expired, but he nevertheless continues to act as a director, and where the office has been from the outset usurped without the colour of authority. ...

The point may be summed up by saying that the section and the article [in the same terms, in the articles of association], being designed as machinery to avoid questions being raised as to the validity of transactions where there has been a slip in the appointment of a director, cannot be utilized for the purpose of ignoring or overriding the substantive provisions relating to such appointment.

OLIVER v. ELLIOTT

(1960), 23 D.L.R. (2d) 486, 30 W.W 641 (Alta. S.C.)

[A formal meeting was held on 20 March 1959 to retire and replace four of five corporate directors, the board being statutorily empowered to fill "casual vacancies". Rather than observing the common ritual whereby each incumbent resigned and was replaced by a new appointee, the incumbents all resigned together and their replacements (Elliott, Johnston, Hefflick and Begbie) purported to take over. At a later meeting on 23 March 1959, Elliott and Johnston decided to resign and the remaining three directors purported to fill the vacancies with two further appointees, Seeple and Rilling. On 3 November 1959 an interlocutory injunction was granted by Riley J., enjoining all six from acting as directors until further order. An identical section to that in the previous case was involved.]

Egbert J.: — The directors did not see fit to follow the well-known and commonly used method whereby when a number of directors are retiring and are to be replaced, each retiring directors retires individually and is replaced individually so that at all times a competent body in excess of a quorum is left to appoint each new director.

It seems to me that in adopting the method they did, the directors placed themselves on the horns of a dilemma. Either the retiring directors ceased to be directors the moment their resignations were tendered, in which event they were no longer directors, and were not competent to vote on the appointment of new directors; or they continued to be directors until their resignations were completed by their retirement from the meeting in which event, by the appointment of four additional directors, they increased the membership of the Board to nine, which was contrary to [the articles of association, which limited the Board to seven directors, and a resolution of the previous annual meeting, which limited the Board to five]. In other words there was no power in the Board elected at the annual meeting to increase its membership, and any attempted exercise of such power was completely ineffective.

It is really immaterial on which of these horns the directors become impaled, but in my view the first of these alternatives sets forth the correct situation, i.e., the retiring directors ceased to be directors immediately upon the tender of their resignations … .

… We are not dealing here with acts done by a director or by directors irregularly appointed; we are dealing with the question of whether or not certain directors were regularly appointed. There is a distinction between validating the appointment of directors, and validating the acts of improperly appointed directors, and the curative sections relate only to the latter of these. I am of the opinion for the reasons stated above, that the defendants Elliott, Johnston, Hefflick and Begbie never did become regularly appointed directors of the company.

They did, however, become *de facto* directors of the company, and two of them at least have acted in that capacity until the interim injunctions gratned by Riley J. That they did so brings us to a consideration of the meeting of March

23rd. ... Seeple and Rilling became directors by virtue of the appointment of a Board of Directors, of which two of the three remaining directors were not actually directors for the reasons I have stated above. The question at once arises — was a quorum of directors in existence, and were the appointments of Seeple and Rilling valid by reason of the curative section of the statute, and the curative provision of the articles of association [which was in the same terms]? The four persons who were supposed to be appointed directors at the meeting of March 20th, were not strangers or volunteers or intruders — they did not walk in without excuse and say "we are directors of the company". There can be no doubt that the intention of the meetings of March 20th was to appoint them directors ... . They did not become directors simply because there was a defect in their appointment. That being so, until effective proceedings were taken to prevent them acting as directors, their acts were, in my view, governed by the curative sections of the statute ... . In other words the acts of the directors at the meeting of March 23rd, including the appointment of two new directors, were valid and effective, despite the defects in the appointment of some of the existing directors.

Accordingly, I find that Seeple and Rilling were properly and effectively appointed directors ... . The injunctions granted by my brother Riley will be continued against the defendants Hefflick and Begbie so long as they are not properly appointed or elected directors ... but will be voided as against the defendants Elliott, Johnston, Seeple and Rilling.

NOTES AND QUESTIONS

1. Do you agree that "there is a vital distinction between (a) an appointment in which there is a defect or, in other words, a defective appointment, and (b) no appointment at all"? How do you tell one from the other? Do you agree that "there is a distinction between validating the appointment of directors, and validating the acts of improperly appointed directors"?

2. Note O.B.C.A., s. 115(4): "Where all of the directors have resigned or have been removed by the shareholders without replacement, any person who manages or supervises the management of the business and affairs of the corporation shall be deemed to be a director for the purposes of this Act." Would this have helped in *Morris*?

3. Compare the *Civil Code of Quebec*, art. 328:

   The acts of a director or senior officer may not be annulled on the sole ground that he was disqualified or that his designation was irregular.

4. C.B.C.A., s. 116 draws no distinction between election or appointment irregularities, and defects in qualifications. Should it make any difference if a qualification defect exists when the appointment or election occurs, as opposed to a defect arising after appointment or election? Note that s. 108(1)(c) provides that a director ceases to hold office when he becomes disqualified under s. 105(1). In *Olympia Interiors Ltd. v. Canada*, [1992] 2 C.T.C. 197 (F.C.T.D.) the sole shareholder and officer of a corporation became bankrupt and so ceased to be a director. Nevertheless, she commenced an action in the name of the corporation. A motion to dismiss the action as a nullity by the defendant because of the defect in her appointment was dismissed.

2. Elections and Appointments

(a) Number of Positions

Canadian statutes normally require only one director, leaving the corporate constitution to specify more or to set maximum and minimum numbers. At least three directors are usually required for corporations "offering securities to the public": see C.B.C.A., s. 102(2), O.B.C.A., s. 115(2), Q.C.A., s. 123.72. There are generally no statutory provisions concerning numbers of officers, although Q.C.A., s. 89(4) requires an office of president.

(b) Procedure

Most statutes require that "first directors" be named in the application for incorporation. They hold office until the first shareholders' meeting when they or others are elected on the basis of one vote per share, unless the corporate constitution provides otherwise. Although the process of shareholder voting is described in more detail in the next chapter, we will here note a few points that particularly relate to the election of directors. Election to staggered terms of office is the norm in Canada; the statute may limit the term (C.B.C.A., s. 106(3): maximum three years; s. 106(5): default term is one year; but see s. 106(6)). Subsequent elections will take place as required by the applicable statute and corporate constitution, or where vacancies have occurred.

It is common to enact sections designed to enhance shareholder participation in the process of nominating and electing directors. This is no doubt motivated by a general acceptance of the accuracy of the comments in *Directors: Myth and Reality*, set out earlier: a passive electorate quickly becomes a rubber stamp for managerial nepotism. Examples of such sections are C.B.C.A., s. 137(4), O.B.C.A., s. 99(4). Is it possible for a shareholder to nominate candidates "from the floor" at the shareholders' meeting as well? Such a procedure was accepted without discussion in *Canadian Express Ltd. v. Blair*, [1989] O.J. No. 1619, 46 B.L.R. 92 (H.C.J.), appeal quashed, [1991] O.J. No. 2176, 6 O.R. (3d) 212 (Div. Ct.).

Finally, the corporate constitution may permit class directors or cumulative voting. The former reserves one or more positions on the board for directors elected solely by a particular class of shareholders. Once elected, are the legal obligations imposed on these directors any different from those of other members of the board? The A.B.C.A. unusually provides for creditor or employee directors (s. 106(9)); see A.B.C.A., s. 122(4), which is set out in Chapter 3, Section B.2.c, page 95. Employee representation occurs on a much larger scale in some other legal systems, such as that of Germany: see, *e.g.*, T. J. André, "Some Reflections on German Corporate Governance: A Glimpse at German Supervisory Boards" (1996), 70 Tulane L. Rev. 1819.

Cumulative voting is another way of substituting proportional representation for strict majority rule. If each share has one vote for each position on the board, those who hold 51 per cent of the shares can elect 100 per cent of the directors by, at worst, a 51 per cent – 49 per cent split on each position. Cumulative voting allows each shareholder to cumulate all the votes attached to her shares in a multi-director election, and divide them as she sees fit among the candidates. The effect is to give minority shareholders who know what they are doing the opportunity to concentrate their votes and elect some candidates, rather than casting futile votes for a losing candidate at each position. Examples of sections authorizing cumulative voting are C.B.C.A., s. 107, O.B.C.A., s. 120 and N.B.B.C.A., s. 65 (which requires it).

The appointment of officers is generally subject to much less regulation, since, in theory, they are merely senior employees. The board of directors may designate corporate "offices" and then fill them: see, *e.g.*, C.B.C.A., s. 121, O.B.C.A., s. 133; B.C.B.C.A., s. 141.

The Dey Committee recommended:

4. The board of directors of every corporation should appoint a committee of directors composed exclusively of outside, i.e. non-management directors, a majority of whom are unrelated directors, with the responsibility for proposing to the full board new nominees to the board and for assessing directors.

5. Every board of directors should implement a process to be carried out by the nominating committee or other appropriate committee for assessing the effectiveness of the board as a whole and of committees of the board and for assessing the contribution of each individual director.

6. Every corporation, as an integral element of the process for appointing new directors, should provide an orientation and education program for new recruits to the board.

"Five Years to the *Dey*" found:

TSE guidelines provide that nominees to the board be proposed through a committee composed exclusively of non-management directors, a majority of whom are unrelated. A minority of boards have adopted this recommendation. In 40% of cases, the Chair chooses the nominee and seeks board approval. Only one third of boards have separate nominating committees. In the remaining cases, either the board as a whole operates as the nominating committee or some other process is followed. ...

Fewer than 20% of companies have any formal process for assessing board effectiveness–although almost all companies have ad hoc procedures or plans to adopt a more formal approach. Similarly, fewer than 20% have a process to assess the contribution of individual members. These findings reflect a recurrent theme of the study: most boards have been slow to formalize roles, policies, and evaluation methods. One CEO observed: *"Directors have 'spotted' the issue of director assessment, but it will take a few years for them to grapple with this."* ...

Only a quarter of corporate boards have a formal orientation process for new directors. Most expect new directors to learn on the job. In about half the cases, directors visit company operations to gain a better understanding of the business. These visits may be ad hoc or be part of a formal process. Only in rare cases (4%), does the company pay for seminars and other director education programs.

The survey asked about term limits and mandatory retirement ages. Four in ten companies have mandatory retirement ages, and one in ten has term limits for director appointments.

National Policy 58-201 tracks the recommendations of the Dey Committee, and National Instrument 58-101 requires disclosure as to compliance.

(c) Casual Vacancies

A quorum of the board of directors is usually statutorily empowered to fill vacancies occurring on the board through resignation, disqualification or death. The statute may contemplate, however, that the articles will give this power to the shareholders; and the statute may give it to the shareholders where there is not a quorum of directors: see, *e.g.*, C.B.C.A., s. 111(4), O.B.C.A., s. 124(5); *cf.* B.C.B.C.A., s. 134, allowing an inquorate board to act for this limited purpose.

(d) Removal

Canadian statutes provide a power for shareholders to remove directors, with some care taken to prevent this from being weakened by the corporate constitution: see, *e.g.*, C.B.C.A., ss. 6(4), 109; O.B.C.A., ss. 6(5), 122(1); compare B.C.B.C.A., s. 128(3). Special rules are included to deal with directors elected through cumulative or class voting. There may also be breach of contract implications. Where a director has a separate contract for services (usually because he or she is also an officer of some kind), the corporation will not be able to excuse a breach of this contract merely because the shareholders have voted the director out of office. Whether the contract has been breached may involve the issue whether the contract had an implied term requiring that the director maintain his elected position in order to enforce his contractual rights. For conflicting factual analyses on this point, see *Shuttleworth v. Cox Bros. & Co. (Maidenhead) Ltd.*, [1927] 2 K.B. 9 (C.A.) and *Shindler v. Northern Raincoat Co.*, [1960] 2 All E.R. 239 (Ch. D.).

It is not uncommon to find attempts to draft corporate constitutions that entrench directors. In *Bushell v. Faith*, [1970] A.C. 1099, the House of Lords held that it was permissible for a contractarian company to have a provision in its articles of association that on a resolution to remove a director from office, any shares held by that director carried three votes per share. This was so even in the face of a provision in the statute that said that notwithstanding anything in the articles, a director could be removed by an ordinary resolution. The House decided that the three-votes-per-share rule was not incompatible with the statute, and the three votes per share had to be counted in deciding whether or not an ordinary resolution had been passed. Does C.B.C.A., s. 6(4) change this? Or is the result different due to a fundamental difference in the source of power in a C.B.C.A. corporation? Recall the material in Chapter 3, Section C.2.b.

Officers will normally have service contracts and, if removed from office, may have actions for wrongful dismissal.

3. Money

(a) Salaries

The corporate constitution will ordinarily prescribe how much directors are to be paid. If it does not, the statute may permit the directors themselves to set the amount: C.B.C.A., s. 125; O.B.C.A., 137; Q.C.A., 123.75. If there is no such power, or if it has not been exercised, they are entitled to nothing: *Bray v. Ford*, [1896] A.C. 44 (H.L.); *Roray v. Howe Sound Mills & Logging Co.* (1915), 22 D.L.R. 855 (B.C.C.A.); *Guinness plc v. Saunders*, [1990] 2 A.C. 663 (H.L.). Officers, on the other hand, are probably entitled to be paid on a restitutionary basis where the board of directors or a contract has not fixed a salary. It has been held that such a claim was available where the plaintiff had worked as a managing director, but it later turned out that his contract (and his appointment as a director) was a nullity: *Craven-Ellis v. Canons Ltd.*, [1936] 2 K.B. 406 (C.A.).

What is the reason for the distinction between directors and officers on this point? The standard explanation is that a director, like a trustee, is not entitled to any remuneration except as expressly provided under the corporate constitution (or the trust deed) because of the fiduciary character of his or her position. The fiduciary obligation of loyalty (which is discussed in detail below, Section D) does not allow profit from the fiduciary position except as expressly provided. Now that officers are also recognized as owing fiduciary obligations, it may be harder to justify treating them differently. On the other hand, it remains true that it is the directors who set the level of remuneration, for themselves and for officers, so the potential or apparent conflict between self-interest and duty is more serious for directors.

The Dey Committee recommended:

> 8. The board of directors should review the adequacy and form of the compensation of directors and ensure the compensation realistically reflects the responsibilities and risk involved in being an effective director.

"Five Years to the *Dey*" found:

> The guideline leans toward a remuneration level that reflects a high degree of responsibility and expected commitment. If directors are paid a token amount, the authors of the TSE report observed, there may be a tendency to think the job is not important.

> Most respondents to the survey believe that the components of their current director compensation are appropriate. That said, more than 29% of respondents believe stock options should play a greater role in director compensation.

(b) Indemnification and Insurance

Indemnification against expenses incurred has always been viewed differently from remuneration for services rendered. Indemnification of corporate managers against expenses incurred in their managerial activities is generally covered by statute. The prevalent statutory technique is to specify those circumstances in which a corporation must indemnify its managers and those in which indemnification is permissible. In other circumstances, it may be inferred, indemnification is prohibited: see, *e.g.*, C.B.C.A., s. 124, O.B.C.A., s. 136; see the more thorough provisions of B.C.B.C.A., ss. 159-164. Generally, indemnity will not be permitted where a director or officer was acting in breach of his statutory obligation to act honestly and in what he perceived at the time to be the corporation's best interests. See generally B. Welling, "Indemnification Agreements in Canadian Corporate Law," [1994-95] Meredith Lectures 339. In *Blair v. Consolidated Enfield Corp.*, [1995] S.C.J. No. 29, [1995] 4 S.C.R. 5, 128 D.L.R. (4th) 73, Blair was ousted as a director following a legal dispute in which costs were awarded against him. Having lost the status of director, he applied to the corporation for indemnity under O.B.C.A., s. 136(1), but the corporation refused. In this litigation it was held that he was entitled to be indemnified, even though s. 136(1) says that the corporation "may" indemnify. A corporate by-law on indemnity used the word "shall", but Iacobucci J., for the court, seemed to say that nothing turned on this (see especially paras. 34-35).

It is also common for corporations to buy insurance policies to protect managers from liability risks. Generally, the statutes permit liability insurance, excepting the case of liabilities arising from a manager's breach of her statutory obligation to act honestly and in what she perceived at the time to be the corporation's best interests: see, *e.g.*, C.B.C.A., s. 124(4), O.B.C.A., s. 136(4), N.B.B.C.A., s. 81(4); see also G.B. Maughan, Q.C., "Directors' and Officers' Insurance Demystified," [1994-95] Meredith Lectures 299. Why might a manager prefer to have an insurance policy rather than an indemnity agreement with the corporation?

C. MANAGERS' LEGAL OBLIGATIONS

1. The Governing Principles

WELLING, CORPORATE LAW IN CANADA: THE GOVERNING PRINCIPLES

(3rd ed., 2006), p. 350

Directors and officers, who collectively make up corporate management, are individually constrained by statutory standards of behaviour. Some of the standards came from the common law: they have traditionally been labelled "legal" duties. Others were derived from general principles of Equity and were imposed by chancery judges: they have traditionally been known as "equitable" duties. A third group of standards, less general in nature, were statutorily created to deal with particular problems not covered by the legal and equitable rules.

Canadian corporate reforms during the last quarter of the 20th century swept all three kinds of rules into a more organized, statute-based code of minimum standards. That made the labels "legal duties" and "equitable duties" anachronistic. Nevertheless, they remind us where the rules came from and tell us where to look for analogies outside corporate law. I have kept the labels for those reasons.

2. The Standard of Care, Diligence and Skill

Section 122(1)(*b*) of the C.B.C.A. reads:

> 122. (1) Every director and officer of a corporation in exercising their powers and discharging their duties shall: ...
>
> (*b*) exercise the care, diligence and skill that a reasonably prudent person would exercise in comparable circumstances.

SOPER v. CANADA

[1997] F.C.J. No. 881, [1998] 1 F.C. 124, 149 D.L.R. (4th) 297 (C.A.)

[A corporation had gone bankrupt. Every employer is required to make deductions in respect of income tax from the money it pays to employees, and to remit these deductions to the Receiver General of Canada. The corporation had not done this. Under the *Income Tax Act*, s. 227.1(1), a corporation *and its directors* are made liable for failure to deduct and remit. Under s. 227.1(3), however, the director can avoid liability if he or she "exercised the degree of care, diligence and skill to prevent the failure that a reasonably prudent person would have exercised in comparable circumstances". In other words, the standard of care imposed by this provision is the same as that imposed by C.B.C.A., s. 122(1)(*b*). Soper was a director of the bankrupt corporation and the Crown sought to make him liable. **Robertson J.A.**, with whom **Linden J.A.** agreed, traced the history of the standard of care in corporate law continued as follows.]

The second proposition that I wish to discuss is the following: a director need not exhibit in the performance of his or her duties a greater degree of skill and care than may reasonably be expected from a person of his or her knowledge and experience. Thus, the standard of care is partly objective (the standard of the reasonable person), and partly subjective in that the reasonable person is judged on the basis that he or she has the knowledge and experience of the particular individual. It is a hybrid "objective subjective standard". ...

Third, a director is not obliged to give continuous attention to the affairs of the company, nor is he or she even bound to attend all meetings of the board. However when, in the circumstances, it is reasonably possible to attend such meetings, a director ought to do so. Subsequent English cases, though, went to more of an extreme, permitting a director to avoid liability despite having missed all board meetings for a period of several years: see *e.g. Re Denham & Co.* (1883), 25 Ch.D. 752 (C.A.); see also *Re Cardiff Savings Bank, Marquis of Bute's Case*, [1892] 2 Ch. 100. Notwithstanding such authorities, it would be silly to pretend that the common law would stand still and permit directors to adhere to a standard of total passivity and irresponsibility. At the risk of getting ahead of myself, it should be noted here that the law today can scarcely be said to embrace the principle that the less a director does or knows or cares, the less likely it is that he or she will be held liable. Further to this point, the statutory standard of care will surely be interpreted and applied in a manner which encourages responsibility. Accordingly, the director who acts irresponsibly, for example, by failing to attend all board meetings now does so at his own peril: see *McCandless (M.W.) v. Canada*, [1995] 2 C.T.C. 2111 (T.C.C.). That being said, the matter of director passivity will have to be reevaluated in light of the statutory standard discussed below. ...

In my opinion, it is not surprising that federal legislation has retained the subjective element of the common law standard of care for directors. Even the law of tort adjusts its objective standard of the reasonable person downward so as to account, for example, for the age, experience and intelligence of children. The standard may also be adjusted upward, as it is for professionals ... The reasonable person standard is thus hardly inflexible. It adjusts to the circumstances and to the individual qualities of the actor. This is all the more true in the context of federal company or taxation law where that standard, at least as it applies to directors' duties, is explicitly modified by the phrase "in comparable circumstances." ...

This is a convenient place to summarize my findings in respect of subsection 227.1(3) of the *Income Tax Act*. The standard of care laid down in subsection 227.1(3) of the Act is inherently flexible. Rather than treating directors as a homogeneous group of professionals whose conduct is governed by a single, unchanging standard, that provision embraces a subjective element which takes into account the personal knowledge and background of the director, as well as his or her corporate circumstances in the form of, inter alia, the company's organization, resources, customs and conduct. Thus, for example, more is expected of individuals with superior qualifications (*e.g.* experienced businesspersons).

The standard of care set out in subsection 227.1(3) of the Act is, therefore, not purely objective. Nor is it purely subjective. It is not enough for a director to say he or she did his or her best, for that is an invocation of the purely subjective standard. Equally clear is that honesty is not enough. However, the standard is not a professional one. Nor is it the negligence law standard that governs these cases. Rather, the Act contains both objective elements–embodied in the reasonable person language–and subjective elements–inherent in individual considerations like "skill" and the idea of "comparable circumstances". Accordingly, the standard can be properly described as "objective subjective".

[Soper was held to be liable. **Marceau J.A.** agreed for different reasons.]

The decision in *Soper* was addressed by the Supreme Court of Canada when it discussed the legal duties of directors in the following decision.

PEOPLES DEPARTMENT STORES INC. (TRUSTEE OF) v. WISE

[2004] S.C.J. No. 64, [2004] 3 S.C.R. 461, 244 D.L.R. (4th) 564

The judgment of the Court was delivered by
Major and Deschamps JJ.: —

I. Introduction

The principal question raised by this appeal is whether directors of a corporation owe a fiduciary duty to the corporation's creditors comparable to the statutory duty owed to the corporation. For the reasons that follow, we conclude that directors owe a duty of care to creditors, but that duty does not rise to a fiduciary duty. We agree with the disposition of the Quebec Court of Appeal. The appeal is therefore dismissed.

As a result of the demise in the mid-1990s of two major retail chains in eastern Canada, Wise Stores Inc. ("Wise") and its wholly-owned subsidiary, Peoples Department Stores Inc. ("Peoples"), the indebtedness of a number of Peoples' creditors went unsatisfied. In the wake of the failure of the two chains, Caron Bélanger Ernst & Young Inc., Peoples' trustee in bankruptcy ("trustee"), brought an action against the directors of Peoples. To address the trustee's claims, the extent of the duties imposed by s. 122(1) of the *Canada Business Corporations Act*, R.S.C. 1985, c. C-44 ("CBCA"), upon directors with respect to creditors must be determined; we must also identify the purpose and reach of s. 100 of the *Bankruptcy and Insolvency Act*, R.S.C. 1985, c. B-3 ("BIA") [the discussion of the BIA issue is omitted].

In our view, it has not been established that the directors of Peoples violated either the fiduciary duty or the duty of care imposed by s. 122(1) of the CBCA. As for the trustee's submission regarding s. 100 of the BIA, we agree with the Court of Appeal that the consideration received in the impugned transactions was not "conspicuously" less than fair market value. The BIA claim fails on that basis.

II. Background

[Wise acquired the shares of Peoples from Marks and Spencer Canada Inc. ("M & S") for $22 million. $5 million was paid on closing and the remainder was to be paid over eight years. The brothers Lionel, Ralph and Harold Wise were majority shareholders, officers and directors of Wise, and the only directors of Peoples. Because of contractual promises required by M & S as part of the share sale contract, Peoples could not be amalgamated with Wise until the purchase price had been fully paid.]

Following the acquisition, Wise had attempted to rationalize its operations by consolidating the overlapping corporate functions of Wise and Peoples, and operating as a group. The consolidation of the administration, accounting, advertising and purchasing departments of the two corporations was completed by the fall of 1993. As a consequence of the changes, many of Wise's employees worked for both firms but were paid solely by Wise. The evidence at trial was that because of the tax losses carried-forward by Peoples, it was advantageous for the group to have more expenses incurred by Wise, which, if the group was profitable as a whole, would increase its after-tax profits. Almost from the outset, the joint operation of Wise and Peoples did not function smoothly. Instead of the expected synergies, the consolidation resulted in dissonance.

After the acquisition, the total number of buyers for the two companies was nearly halved. The procurement policy at that point required buyers to deal simultaneously with suppliers on behalf of both Peoples and Wise. For the buyers, this nearly doubled their administrative work. Separate invoices were required for purchases made on behalf of Wise and Peoples. These invoices had to be separately entered into the system, tracked and paid.

Inventory, too, was separately recorded and tracked in the system. However, the inventory of each company was handled and stored, often unsegregated, in shared warehouse facilities. The main warehouse for Peoples, on Cousens Street in Ville St-Laurent, was maintained for and used by both firms. The Cousens warehouse saw considerable activity, as it was the central distribution hub for both chains. The facility was open 18 hours a day and employed 150 people on two shifts who handled a total of approximately 30,000 cartons daily through 20 loading docks. It was abuzz with activity.

Before long, the parallel bookkeeping combined with the shared warehousing arrangements caused serious problems for both Wise and Peoples. The actual situation in the warehouse often did not mirror the reported state of the inventory in the system. The goods of one company were often inextricably commingled and confused with the goods of the other. As a result, the inventory records of both companies were increasingly incorrect. A physical inventory count was conducted to try to rectify the situation, to little avail. Both Wise and Peoples stores experienced numerous shipping disruptions and delays. The situation, already unsustainable, was worsening.

In October 1993, Lionel Wise consulted David Clément, Wise's (and, after the acquisition, Peoples') vice-president of administration and finance, in an attempt to find a solution. In January 1994, Clément recommended and the three Wise brothers agreed that they would implement a joint inventory procurement policy ("new policy") whereby the two firms would divide responsibility for purchasing. Peoples would make all purchases from North American suppliers and Wise would, in turn, make all purchases from overseas suppliers. Peoples would then transfer to Wise what it had purchased for Wise, charging Wise accordingly, and vice versa. The new policy was implemented on February 1, 1994. It was this arrangement that was later criticized by certain creditors and by the trial judge.

Approximately 82 percent of the total inventory of Wise and Peoples was purchased from North American suppliers, which inevitably meant that Peoples would be extending a significant trade credit to Wise. The new policy was known to the directors, but was neither formally implemented in writing nor approved by a board meeting or resolution.

On April 27, 1994, Lionel Wise outlined the details of the new policy at a meeting of Wise's audit committee. A partner of Coopers & Lybrand was M & S's representative on Wise's board of directors and a member of the audit committee. He attended the April 27th meeting and raised no objection to the new policy when it was introduced.

By June 1994, financial statements prepared to reflect the financial position of Peoples as of April 30, 1994 revealed that Wise owed more than $18 million to Peoples. Approximately $14 million of this amount resulted from a notional transfer of inventory that was cancelled following the period's end. M & S was concerned about the situation and started an investigation, as a result of which M & S insisted that the new procurement policy be rescinded. Wise agreed to M & S's demand but took the position that the former procurement policy could not be reinstated immediately. An agreement was executed on September 27, 1994, effective July 21, 1994, and it provided that the new policy would be abandoned as of January 31, 1995. The agreement also specified that the inventory and records of the two companies would be kept separate, and that the amount owed to Peoples by Wise would not exceed $3 million.

Another result of the negotiations was that M & S accepted an increase in the amount of the TD Bank's priority to $15 million and a new repayment schedule for the balance of the purchase price owed to M & S. The parties agreed to revise the schedule to provide for 37 monthly payments beginning in July 1995. Each of the Wise brothers also provided a personal guarantee of $500,000 in favour of M & S.

In September 1994, in light of the fragile financial condition of the companies and the competitiveness of the retail market, the TD Bank announced its intention to cease doing business with Wise and Peoples as of the end of December 1994. Following negotiations, however, the bank extended its financial support until the end of July 1995. The Wise brothers promised to extend personal guarantees in favour of the TD Bank, but this did not occur.

In December 1994, three days after the Wise brothers presented financial statements showing disappointing results for Peoples in its third fiscal quarter, M & S initiated bankruptcy proceedings against both Wise and Peoples. A notice of intention to make a proposal was filed on behalf of Peoples the same day. Nonetheless, Peoples later consented to the petition by M & S, and both Wise and Peoples were declared bankrupt on January 13, 1995, effective December 9, 1994. The same day, M & S released each of the Wise brothers from their personal guarantees. M & S apparently preferred to proceed with an uncontested petition in bankruptcy rather than attempting to collect on the personal guarantees.

The assets of Wise and Peoples were sufficient to cover in full the outstanding debt owed to the TD Bank, satisfy the entire balance of the purchase price owed to M & S, and discharge almost all the landlords' lease claims. The bulk of the unsatisfied claims were those of trade creditors.

Following the bankruptcy, Peoples' trustee filed a petition against the Wise brothers. In the petition, the trustee claimed that they had favoured the interests of Wise over Peoples to the detriment of Peoples' creditors, in breach of their duties as directors under s. 122(1) of the CBCA. ...

III. Analysis

At the outset, it should be acknowledged that according to art. 300 C.C.Q. and s. 8.1 of the *Interpretation Act*, R.S.C. 1985, c. I-21, the civil law serves as a supplementary source of law to federal legislation such as the CBCA. Since the CBCA does not entitle creditors to sue directors directly for breach of their duties, it is appropriate to have recourse to the C.C.Q. to determine how rights grounded in a federal statute should be addressed in Quebec, and more specifically how s. 122(1) of the CBCA can be harmonized with the principles of civil liability: see R. Crête and S. Rousseau, *Droit des sociétés par actions: principes fondamentaux* (2002), at p. 58.

This case came before our Court on the issue of whether directors owe a duty to creditors. The creditors did not bring a derivative action or an oppression remedy application under the CBCA. Instead, the trustee, representing the interests of the creditors, sued the directors for an alleged breach of the duties imposed by s. 122(1) of the CBCA. The standing of the trustee to sue was not questioned.

The primary role of directors is described in s. 102(1) of the CBCA:

102. (1) Subject to any unanimous shareholder agreement, the directors shall manage, or supervise the management of, the business and affairs of a corporation.

As for officers, s. 121 of the CBCA provides that their powers are delegated to them by the directors:

121. Subject to the articles, the by-laws or any unanimous shareholder agreement,

    (*a*) the directors may designate the offices of the corporation, appoint as officers persons of full capacity, specify their duties and delegate to them powers to manage the business and affairs of the corporation, except powers to do anything referred to in subsection 115(3);

    (*b*) a director may be appointed to any office of the corporation; and

    (*c*) two or more offices of the corporation may be held by the same person.

Although the shareholders are commonly said to own the corporation, in the absence of a unanimous shareholder agreement to the contrary, s. 102 of the CBCA provides that it is not the shareholders, but the directors elected by the shareholders, who are responsible for managing it. This clear demarcation between the respective roles of shareholders and directors long predates the 1975 enactment of the CBCA: see *Automatic Self-Cleansing Filter Syndicate Co. v. Cuninghame*, [1906] 2 Ch. 34 (C.A.); see also art. 311 C.C.Q.

Section 122(1) of the CBCA establishes two distinct duties to be discharged by directors and officers in managing, or supervising the management of, the corporation:

122. (1) Every director and officer of a corporation in exercising their powers and discharging their duties shall (*a*) act honestly and in good faith with a view to the best interests of the corporation; and

(*b*) exercise the care, diligence and skill that a reasonably prudent person would exercise in comparable circumstances.

The first duty has been referred to in this case as the "fiduciary duty". It is better described as the "duty of loyalty". We will use the expression "statutory fiduciary duty" for purposes of clarity when referring to the duty under the CBCA. This duty requires directors and officers to act honestly and in good faith with a view to the best interests of the corporation. The second duty is commonly referred to as the "duty of care". Generally speaking, it imposes a legal obligation upon directors and officers to be diligent in supervising and managing the corporation's affairs.

The trial judge did not apply or consider separately the two duties imposed on directors by s. 122(1). As the Court of Appeal observed, the trial judge appears to have confused the two duties. They are, in fact, distinct and are designed to secure different ends. For that reason, they will be addressed separately in these reasons.

[The court next addressed the fiduciary duty. This is extracted later in the chapter.]

B. The Statutory Duty of Care: Section 122(1)(b) of the CBCA

As mentioned above, the CBCA does not provide for a direct remedy for creditors against directors for breach of their duties and the C.C.Q. is used as suppletive law.

In Quebec, directors have been held liable to creditors in respect of either contractual or extra-contractual obligations. Contractual liability arises where the director personally guarantees a contractual obligation of the company. Liability also arises where the director personally acts in a manner that triggers his or her extra-contractual liability. See P. Martel, "Le 'voile corporatif' — l'attitude des tribunaux face à l'article 317 du Code civil du Québec" (1998), 58 *R. du* B. 95, at pp. 135-36; *Brasserie Labatt ltée v. Lanoue*, [1999] Q.J. No. 1108 (QL) (C.A.), *per* Forget J.A., at para. 29. It is clear that the Wise brothers cannot be held contractually liable as they did not guarantee the debts at issue here. Extra-contractual liability is the remaining possibility.

To determine the applicability of extra-contractual liability in this appeal, it is necessary to refer to art. 1457 C.C.Q. [this is the basic provision governing the law of extracontractual wrongs in Quebec]:

> Every person has a duty to abide by the rules of conduct which lie upon him, according to the circumstances, usage or law, so as not to cause injury to another.
>
> Where he is endowed with reason and fails in this duty, he is responsible for any injury he causes to another person by such fault and is liable to reparation for the injury, whether it be bodily, moral or material in nature.
>
> He is also liable, in certain cases, to reparation for injury caused to another by the act or fault of another person or by the act of things in his custody. [Emphasis added.]

Three elements of art. 1457 C.C.Q. are relevant to the integration of the director's duty of care into the principles of extra-contractual liability: who has the duty ("every person"), to whom is the duty owed ("another") and what breach will trigger liability ("rules of conduct"). It is clear that directors and officers come within the expression "every person". It is equally clear that the word "another" can include the creditors. The reach of art. 1457 C.C.Q. is broad and it has been given an open and inclusive meaning. See *Regent Taxi & Transport Co. v. Congrégation des Petits Frères de Marie*, [1929] S.C.R. 650, *per* Anglin C.J., at p. 655 (rev'd on other grounds, [1932] 2 D.L.R. 70 (P.C.)):

> ... to narrow the *prima facie* scope of art. 1053 C.C. [now art. 1457] is highly dangerous and would necessarily result in most meritorious claims being rejected; many a wrong would be without a remedy.

This liberal interpretation was also affirmed and treated as settled by this Court in *Lister v. McAnulty*, [1944] S.C.R. 317, and *Hôpital Notre-Dame de l'Espérance v. Laurent*, [1978] 1 S.C.R. 605.

This interpretation can be harmoniously integrated with the wording of the CBCA. Indeed, unlike the statement of the fiduciary duty in s. 122(1)(*a*) of the CBCA, which specifies that directors and officers must act with a view to the best interests of the corporation, the statement of the duty of care in s. 122(1)(*b*) of the CBCA does not specifically refer to an identifiable party as the beneficiary of the duty. Instead, it provides that "[e]very director and officer of a corporation in exercising their powers and discharging their duties shall ... exercise the care, diligence and skill that a reasonably prudent person would exercise in comparable circumstances." Thus, the identity of the beneficiary of the duty of care is much more open-ended, and it appears obvious that it must include creditors. This result is clearly consistent with the civil law interpretation of the word "another". Therefore, if breach of the standard of care, causation and damages are established, creditors can resort to art. 1457 to have their rights vindicated. The only issue thus remaining is the determination of the "rules of conduct" likely to trigger extracontractual liability. On this issue, art. 1457 is explicit.

The first paragraph of art. 1457 does not set the standard of conduct. Instead, it incorporates by reference s. 122(1)(*b*) of the CBCA. The statutory duty of care is a "duty to abide by [a] rul[e] of conduct which lie[s] upon [them], according to the ... law, so as not to cause injury to another". Thus, for the purpose of determining whether the Wise brothers can be held liable, only the CBCA is relevant. It is therefore necessary to outline the requirements of the duty of care embodied in s. 122(1)(*b*) of the CBCA.

That directors must satisfy a duty of care is a long-standing principle of the common law, although the duty of care has been reinforced by statute to become more demanding. Among the earliest English cases establishing the duty of care were *Dovey v. Cory*, [1901] A.C. 477 (H.L.); *In re Brazilian Rubber Plantations and Estates, Ltd.*, [1911] 1 Ch. 425; and *In re City Equitable Fire Insurance Co.*, [1925] 1 Ch. 407 (C.A.). In substance, these cases held that the standard of care was a reasonably relaxed, subjective standard. The common law required directors to avoid being grossly negligent with respect to the affairs of the corporation and judged them according to their own personal skills, knowledge, abilities and capacities. See McGuinness, *supra*, at p. 776: "Given the history of the case law in this area, and the prevailing standards of competence displayed in commerce generally, it is quite clear that directors were not expected at common law to have any particular business skill or judgment."

The 1971 report entitled *Proposals for a New Business Corporations Law for Canada* (1971) ("Dickerson Report") culminated the work of a committee headed by R. W. V. Dickerson which had been appointed by the federal government to study the need for new federal business corporations legislation. This report preceded the enactment of the CBCA by four years and influenced the eventual structure of the CBCA.

The standard recommended by the Dickerson Report was objective, requiring directors and officers to meet the standard of a "reasonably prudent person" (vol. II, at. p. 74):

9.19

(1) Every director and officer of a corporation in exercising his powers and discharging his duties shall ...

   (b)   exercise the care, diligence and skill of a reasonably prudent person.

The report described how this proposed duty of care differed from the prevailing common law duty of care (vol. I, at p. 83):

242. The formulation of the duty of care, diligence and skill owed by directors represents an attempt to upgrade the standard presently required of them. The principal change here is that whereas at present the law seems to be that a director is only required to demonstrate the degree of care, skill and diligence that could reasonably be expected from him, having regard to his knowledge and experience — *Re City Equitable Fire Insurance Co.*, [1925] Ch. 425 — under s. 9.19(1)(b) he is required to conform to the standard of a reasonably prudent man. <u>Recent experience has demonstrated how low the prevailing legal standard of care for directors is, and we have sought to raise it significantly.</u> We are aware of the argument that raising the standard of conduct for directors may deter people from accepting directorships. The truth of that argument has not been demonstrated and we think it is specious. The duty of care imposed by s. 9.19(1)(b) is exactly the same as that which the common law imposes on every professional person, for example, and there is no evidence that this has dried up the supply of lawyers, accountants, architects, surgeons or anyone else. It is in any event cold comfort to a shareholder to know that there is a steady supply of marginally competent people available under present law to manage his investment. [Emphasis added.]

The statutory duty of care in s. 122(1)(*b*) of the CBCA emulates but does not replicate the language proposed by the Dickerson Report. The main difference is that the enacted version includes the words "in comparable circumstances", which modifies the statutory standard by requiring the context in which a given decision was made to be taken into account. This is not the introduction of a subjective element relating to the competence of the director, but rather the introduction of a contextual element into the statutory standard of care. It is clear that s. 122(1)(*b*) requires more of directors and officers than the traditional common law duty of care outlined in, for example, *Re City Equitable Fire Insurance, supra*. It is clear that s. 122(1)(*b*) requires more of directors and officers than the traditional common law duty of care outlined in, for example, *Re City Equitable Fire Insurance, supra*.

The standard of care embodied in s. 122(1)(*b*) of the CBCA was described by Robertson J.A. of the Federal Court of Appeal in *Soper v. Canada*, [1998] 1 F.C. 124, at para. 41, as being "objective subjective". Although that case concerned the interpretation of a provision of the *Income Tax Act*, it is relevant here because the language of the provision establishing the standard of care was identical to that of s. 122(1)(*b*) of the CBCA. With respect, we feel that Robertson J.A.'s characterization of the standard as an "objective subjective" one could lead to confusion. We prefer to describe it as an objective standard. To say that the standard is objective makes it clear that the factual aspects of the circumstances surrounding the actions of the director or officer are important in the case of the

s. 122(1)(*b*) duty of care, as opposed to the subjective motivation of the director or officer, which is the central focus of the statutory fiduciary duty of s. 122(1)(*a*) of the CBCA.

The contextual approach dictated by s. 122(1)(*b*) of the CBCA not only emphasizes the primary facts but also permits prevailing socio-economic conditions to be taken into consideration. The emergence of stricter standards puts pressure on corporations to improve the quality of board decisions. The establishment of good corporate governance rules should be a shield that protects directors from allegations that they have breached their duty of care. However, even with good corporate governance rules, directors' decisions can still be open to criticism from outsiders. Canadian courts, like their counterparts in the United States, the United Kingdom, Australia and New Zealand, have tended to take an approach with respect to the enforcement of the duty of care that respects the fact that directors and officers often have business expertise that courts do not. Many decisions made in the course of business, although ultimately unsuccessful, are reasonable and defensible at the time they are made. Business decisions must sometimes be made, with high stakes and under considerable time pressure, in circumstances in which detailed information is not available. It might be tempting for some to see unsuccessful business decisions as unreasonable or imprudent in light of information that becomes available *ex post facto*. Because of this risk of hindsight bias, Canadian courts have developed a rule of deference to business decisions called the "business judgment rule", adopting the American name for the rule.

In *Maple Leaf Foods Inc. v. Schneider Corp.* (1998), 42 O.R. (3d) 177 (C.A.), Weiler J.A. stated, at p. 192:

> The law as it has evolved in Ontario and Delaware has the common requirements that the court must be satisfied that the directors have acted reasonably and fairly. <u>The court looks to see that the directors made a *reasonable* decision not a perfect decision. Provided the decision taken is within a range of reasonableness, the court ought not to substitute its opinion for that of the board even though subsequent events may have cast doubt on the board's determination.</u> As long as the directors have selected one of several reasonable alternatives, deference is accorded to the board's decision. This formulation of deference to the decision of the Board is known as the "business judgment rule". The fact that alternative transactions were rejected by the directors is irrelevant unless it can be shown that a particular alternative was definitely available and clearly more beneficial to the company than the chosen transaction. [Underlining added; italics in original; references omitted.]

In order for a plaintiff to succeed in challenging a business decision he or she has to establish that the directors acted (i) in breach of the duty of care and (ii) in a way that caused injury to the plaintiff: W. T. Allen, J. B. Jacobs and L. E. Strine, Jr., "Function Over Form: A Reassessment of Standards of Review in Delaware Corporation Law" (2001), 26 *Del. J. Corp. L.* 859, at p. 892.

Directors and officers will not be held to be in breach of the duty of care under s. 122(1)(*b*) of the CBCA if they act prudently and on a reasonably informed basis. The decisions they make must be reasonable business decisions in light of all the circumstances about which the directors or officers knew or ought to have known. In determining whether directors have acted in a manner that breached the duty of care, it is worth repeating that perfection is not demanded. Courts are ill-suited and should be reluctant to second-guess the application of business expertise to the considerations that are involved in corporate decision making, but they are capable, on the facts of any case, of determining whether an appropriate degree of prudence and diligence was brought to bear in reaching what is claimed to be a reasonable business decision at the time it was made.

The trustee alleges that the Wise brothers breached their duty of care under s. 122(1)(*b*) of the CBCA by implementing the new procurement policy to the detriment of Peoples' creditors. After considering all the evidence, we agree with the Court of Appeal that the implementation of the new policy was a reasonable business decision that was made with a view to rectifying a serious and urgent business problem in circumstances in which no solution may have been possible. The trial judge's conclusion that the new policy led inexorably to Peoples' failure and bankruptcy was factually incorrect and constituted a palpable and overriding error.

In fact, as noted by Pelletier J.A., there were many factors other than the new policy that contributed more directly to Peoples' bankruptcy. Peoples had lost $10 million annually while being operated by M & S. Wise, which was only marginally profitable and solvent with annual sales of $100 million (versus $160 million for Peoples), had hoped to improve the performance of its new acquisition. Given that the transaction was a fully leveraged buyout, for Wise and Peoples to succeed, Peoples' performance needed to improve dramatically. Unfortunately for both Wise and Peoples, the retail market in eastern Canada had become very competitive in the early 1990s, and this trend continued with the arrival of Wal-Mart in 1994. At paras. 152 and 154 QL, Pelletier J.A. stated:

> [TRANSLATION] In reality, it was that particularly unfavourable financial situation in which the two corporations found themselves that caused their downfall, and it was M. & S. that, to protect its own interests, sounded the charge in December, rightly or wrongly judging that Peoples Inc.'s situation would only worsen over time. It is crystal-clear that the bankruptcy occurred at the most propitious time for M. & S.'s interests, when inventories were high and suppliers were unpaid. In fact, M. & S. recovered the entire balance due on the selling price and almost all of the other debts it was owed. ...
>
> ... the trial judge did not take into account the fact that the brothers derived no direct benefit from the transaction impugned, that they acted in good faith and that their true intention was to find a solution to the serious inventory management problem that each of the two corporations was facing. Because of an assessment error, he also ignored the fact that Peoples Inc. received a sizable consideration for the goods it delivered to Wise. Lastly, I note that the act for which the brothers were found liable, i.e. the adoption of a new joint inventory procurement policy, is not as serious as the trial judge made it out to be and that, in opposition to his view, the act was also not the true cause of the bankruptcy of Peoples Inc. [Emphasis added.]

The Wise brothers treated the implementation of the new policy as a decision made in the ordinary course of business and, while no formal agreement evidenced the arrangement, a monthly record was made of the inventory transfers. Although this may appear to be a loose business practice, by the autumn of 1993, Wise had already consolidated several aspects of the operations of the two companies. Legally they were two separate entities. However, the financial fate of the two companies had become intertwined. In these circumstances, there was little or no economic incentive for the Wise brothers to jeopardize the interests of Peoples in favour of the interests of Wise. In fact, given the tax losses that Peoples had carried forward, the companies had every incentive to keep Peoples profitable in order to reduce their combined tax liabilities.

Arguably, the Wise brothers could have been more precise in pursuing a resolution to the intractable inventory management problems, having regard to all the troublesome circumstances involved at the time the new policy was implemented. But we, like the Court of Appeal, are not satisfied that the adoption of the new policy breached the duty of care under s. 122(1)(*b*) of the CBCA. The directors cannot be held liable for a breach of their duty of care in respect of the creditors of Peoples.

The Court of Appeal relied on two additional provisions of the CBCA that in its view could rescue the Wise brothers from a finding that they breached the duty of care: ss. 44(2) and 123(4).

[Section 44 has now been repealed. Section 123 has been amended as the court notes in what follows.]

When faced with the serious inventory management problem, the Wise brothers sought the advice of the vice-president of finance, David Clément. The Wise brothers claimed as an additional argument that in adopting the solution proposed by Clément, they were relying in good faith on the judgment of a person whose profession lent credibility to his statement, in accordance with the defence provided for in s. 123(4)(*b*) (now s. 123(5)) of the CBCA. The Court of Appeal accepted the argument. We disagree.

The reality that directors cannot be experts in all aspects of the corporations they manage or supervise shows the relevancy of a provision such as s. 123(4)(*b*). At the relevant time, the text of s. 123(4) read:

> **123.** (4) A director is not liable under section 118, 119 or 122 if he relies in good faith on
>
> (*a*) financial statements of the corporation represented to him by an officer of the corporation or in a written report of the auditor of the corporation fairly to reflect the financial condition of the corporation; or
>
> (*b*) a report of a lawyer, accountant, engineer, appraiser or other person whose profession lends credibility to a statement made by him.

Although Clément did have a bachelor's degree in commerce and 15 years of experience in administration and finance with Wise, this experience does not correspond to the level of professionalism required to allow the directors to rely on his advice as a bar to a suit under the duty of care. The named professional groups in s. 123(4)(*b*) were lawyers, accountants, engineers, and appraisers. Clément was not an accountant, was not subject to the regulatory overview of any professional organization and did not carry independent insurance coverage for professional negligence. The title of vice-president of finance should not automatically lead to a conclusion that Clément was a person "whose profession lends credibility to a statement made by him". It is noteworthy that the word "profession" is used, not "position". Clément was simply a non-professional employee of Wise. His judgment on the appropriateness of the solution to the inventory management problem must be regarded in that light. Although we might accept for the sake of argument that Clément was better equipped and positioned than the Wise brothers to devise a plan to solve the inventory management problems, this is not enough. Therefore, in our opinion, the Wise brothers cannot successfully invoke the defence provided by s. 123(4)(*b*) of the CBCA but must rely on the other defences raised.

. . .

NOTES AND QUESTIONS

1. One of the most striking things in this decision is the holding (in paras. 56-57) that the duty in s. 122(1)(*b*) was owed by the directors to the creditors of the corporation. Usually the assumption is that the duty is owed only to the corporation itself. Of course, any successful claim made by the corporation for breach of the duty will mean that the corporation has more assets, and this will help to ensure that creditors get paid. But the court held that the creditors could directly enforce the duty against the directors.

    It must, however, be carefully observed that this particular part of the holding is based on the civil law of Quebec. In that legal tradition, there is less reluctance than in the common law to find duties of care that extend to pure economic loss. For example, in *Hercules Managements Ltd. v. Ernst & Young*, [1997] S.C.J. No. 51, [1997] 2 S.C.R. 165, 146 D.L.R. (4th) 577, the Supreme Court of Canada held that in the common law, the auditor of a corporation generally does not owe a duty of care to the shareholders of the corporation, in respect of financial loss (through the fall in value of shares) that might be caused to shareholders by a careless audit. On the other hand, *Houle v. Canadian National Bank*, [1990] S.C.J. No. 120, [1990] 3 S.C.R. 122, 74 D.L.R. (4th) 577 was a case under Quebec law. The corporation borrowed money from the bank, and the bank held a security interest over the corporation's assets. The bank breached its contract with the corporation by liquidating the corporation's assets without giving reasonable notice. The Supreme Court also held that the bank was liable to former shareholders of the corporation, who had suffered financial loss through the fall in value of their shares. This liability was based on art. 1053 of the old Civil Code of Lower Canada, the general article on negligence liability which was the predecessor of art. 1457 of the current Civil Code of Quebec, mentioned in *Wise*.

    Do you think the holdings in *Houle* and *Wise* are inconsistent with the principle of corporate personality? Or do they simply reflect a wider scope, in civil law, for duties to take care not to cause pure economic loss?

2. The court made reference to the "business judgment rule" which comes from U.S. cases. The idea behind this "rule" is that the court will not second-guess business judgments, as long as they are made in an informed way (and in accordance with fiduciary obligations). It is really just a statement of the principle of curial deference to managerial decisions, which only makes sense since the court has no authority to make such decisions. It is not clear that it adds much to the statement that managers have duties of care, skill and diligence, and duties of loyalty, and certain other duties.

    The rule was discussed in *Smith v. Van Gorkom*, 488 A.2d 858 (Del. 1985), although the holding there that the directors were liable caused consternation among directors and their advisors, and led Delaware and other states to amend their corporate law statutes to permit corporate constitutions to contain limitations of directors' liability for lapses of diligence. In Canada, such limitations are allowed in private trust deeds, to protect trustees from liability for breach of their duties of care. Industry Canada issued a Discussion Paper on directors' liabilities in November 1995, in which it recommended that there should be no mandatory or optional cap on such liabilities in the C.B.C.A. To the contrary, note s. 122(3):

    > Subject to subsection 146(5), no provision in a contract, the articles, the by-laws or a resolution relieves a director or officer from the duty to act in accordance with this Act or the regulations or relieves him from liability for a breach thereof.

Of course, as we noted earlier in this chapter, insurance and indemnification are permissible in Canada.

3. The general deference of courts to managers' business judgments is sometimes said to yield a paradox: in a negligence action, a judge might review in great detail the process by which a car was designed and manufactured, and apply a legal judgment as to whether reasonable care was taken in such things as the design and materials chosen; but in judging whether the managers of the manufacturing corporation fulfilled their legal duties to the corporation, the same judge will not second-guess their business choices. One way to understand this paradox is to see that a duty is a requirement to do, or not to do, something; and, that it is associated with a standard of care that must be taken in that regard. The general duty of care in negligence is a duty not to cause harm to people or their property (in some situations, there is a further duty not to cause pure economic loss). If you have caused harm to people to whom the duty was owed, or their property, we ask whether you nonetheless met the duty by taking reasonable care. In other words, the duty is not to cause harm by failing to take reasonable care. The cases extracted above are concerned with elucidating the standard of care that goes with a manager's "legal" duty. But is it a duty not to cause harm? If not, what is it?

4. Compare the standard in art. 322, first paragraph, of the Civil Code of Quebec:

A director shall act with prudence and diligence.

5. In modern corporate law, a director is not expected to have all the skills necessary to oversee all aspects of the corporate operation. It is usual for directors to consult others in an area beyond their expertise: admitting that you have no knowledge in a certain area and consulting someone who does is a diligent exercise of power. A director is entitled to rely on advice received from professionals, provided that there was no blatant evidence that the information received was inaccurate or misleading. In *Peoples Department Stores*, the Court set out the earlier C.B.C.A. provision, which was amended in 2001. Industry Canada issued a Discussion Paper on directors' liabilities in November 1995. Among other questions, this raised the issue whether the defence provided by s. 123(4) was wide enough; it only applied in the specific cases it mentioned, namely good faith reliance on particular kinds of information provided by particular classes of persons. It was amended in order to provide a more general "due diligence" defence to the liabilities in ss. 118-119. You will see that under the current provision, s. 123(4) provides a defence to breaches of ss. 118, 119 and 122(2). Does it have the effect of applying the *standard* of care in s. 122(1)(*b*) to all of the *duties* in the C.B.C.A.? Section 123(5) provides a defence to breaches of the duties of care and loyalty set out in s. 122(1). (Is not any breach of s. 122(1) also a breach of s. 122(2)? Why is s. 123 drafted this way?)

The Supreme Court of Canada noted the use of the word "profession" in what is now s. 123(5)(*b*) (it is also in s. 123(4)(*b*)) and indicated that this word should be interpreted quite literally. Note carefully the wording of your provincial statute. Although s. 123(4) is not mentioned in s. 124, which governs indemnification of directors in certain situations, may the director use reliance on legal advice to establish the good faith prerequisite for indemnification set out in s. 124? See *Blair v. Consolidated Enfield Corp.*, [1995] S.C.J. No. 29, [1995] 4 S.C.R. 5, 128 D.L.R. (4th) 73.

3. Insider Trading Rules

Corporate managers are subject to stringent rules about "insider trading": that is, trading in the securities of their corporation while they know information that is not generally available in the marketplace. Insider trading, however, goes well beyond the subject of corporate management.

The rules about insider trading have evolved and become stricter over the last century. In their modern form, they do not prohibit a manager from trading the shares of his or her own corporation; the prohibition is against trading with the benefit of non-public information. The rules usually require insiders (as defined) of a corporation to declare publicly all trading that they do in the corporation's securities. They prohibit trading on the basis of non-public information. This prohibition extends beyond directors and officers. It can also include various employees, affiliates and associates of the corporation, and those who have acquired non-public information from any of these people. The mere transfer of non-public information ("tipping") is itself also prohibited. These prohibitions are backed up by civil and penal consequences. In provincial law, the regulation is found in the provincial Securities Acts. At the federal level, where there is no Securities Act, the C.B.C.A. has some provisions in Part XI. This Part used to be more extensive, but a number of provisions were repealed in 2001. Persons involved with a C.B.C.A. corporation whose shares are publicly traded will be subject to one or more of the provincial securities acts, and this is why the federal Parliament has partially withdrawn from the field. Note, however, the provisions in the *Criminal Code* governing insider trading and tipping that came into force 15 September, 2004 (see s. 382.1, enacted by S.C. 2004, c. 3, s. 4, and note the "whistle-blower protection" in s. 425.1 that came into force at the same time, enacted by S.C. 2004, c. 3, s. 6).

4. Miscellaneous Statutory Duties

WELLING, CORPORATE LAW IN CANADA: THE GOVERNING PRINCIPLES

(3rd ed., 2006), pp. 397-98 (Footnotes deleted.)

In addition to the foregoing categories of statutorily imposed "legal" obligations, the Canadian statutes fix several particular obligations on corporate managers. They defy categorization.

In some circumstances, a director who votes for or consents to a resolution contrary to certain sections in the statute will be personally liable to the corporation. Some of these sections prevent a corporation from purchasing or redeeming its own securities, paying out dividends or making certain kinds of loans or guarantees if there are reasonable grounds for believing that the requirements of various financial tests will not be satisfied. Directors may also be liable where insufficient property is given as consideration for shares, excessive commissions are paid for the sale of shares or other corporate managers are improperly indemnified for legal costs, charges or expenses. Directors may become liable in some jurisdictions, regardless of their consent or voting records, for the wages of employees of the corporation. As well, individual directors and officers have duties to furnish information to the corporation's auditor, and to notify the auditor of any errors they know of in a financial statement.

There are other duties imposed upon the directors collectively rather than individually. These include duties to call a special meeting of the shareholders if there is no quorum of directors, and to correct errors in financial statements.

In sum, corporate directors and officers become subject to a myriad of legal obligations upon taking office in most Canadian jurisdictions. The trend toward legislated standards has made these obligations generally clearer and enables lawyers to better advise their clients by reference to the particular statute.

NOTES

1. In the C.B.C.A., for the individual liabilities of directors discussed in this extract, see ss. 118-119, referring in the case of s. 118 to prohibitions in other sections. For examples of the collective obligations of the board, see ss. 111(2); 158; 170-171.

2. Note that the liabilities in s. 118 turn on whether a director consented to the relevant resolution. This may mean that a director who does not agree with a resolution needs to be careful that this is recorded in the minutes. See s. 123. In the case of unpaid wages under s. 119, liabilities cease to accrue (and the limitation period starts to run) when directors resign (ss. 119(1), (3)). Does this create a perverse incentive? See R. Daniels, "Must Boards Go Overboard?" (1995), 24 C.B.L.J. 229. Note also that in *Barrette v. Crabtree Estate*, [1993] S.C.J. No. 37, [1993] 1 S.C.R. 1027, the Supreme Court of Canada held that s. 119 does not make a director liable on a judgment which an employee has obtained against the corporation for wrongful dismissal; and compare A.B.C.A., s. 119(2), which further restricts director liability.

3. The liabilities in s. 118 arise out of voting for or consenting to a resolution that is inconsistent with some other section; in many cases, the other section requires some financial test to be applied in order to determine whether the action is lawful. In this regard, it is important to remember s. 123(4).

4. Industry Canada issued a Discussion Paper on directors' liabilities in November 1995. Among other questions, this raised the issue of whether it was appropriate for directors' liability for wages to be in the C.B.C.A., or whether such a provision more properly belonged in the *Bankruptcy and Insolvency Act*, R.S.C. 1985, c. B-3 (B.I.A.). The B.I.A. interacts with the C.B.C.A. on this question, but of course the B.I.A. also applies to insolvent corporations incorporated under provincial law. It always gave some priority to employee wage claims (s. 136), but this was by no means absolute; for one thing, it came after the claims of secured creditors. If a corporation makes a proposal with its creditors to avoid bankruptcy, the proposal may provide for directors to avoid personal liability (s. 50(13)), but the required court approval for the proposal may not be granted unless certain employee wage claims are satisfied (s. 60(1.3)). After years of argument, the area of employee wage claims was finally reformed comprehensively in late 2005. This legislation has received Royal Assent but has not yet been proclaimed in force. It will establish the Wage Earner Protection Plan, under which a certain level of unpaid wages will be paid automatically by the Plan when an employer is bankrupt. The legislation will add to the B.I.A. ss. 81.3-81.6, which raise claims for unpaid wages and underfunded pensions to the level of secured claims in bankruptcy. Where a wage earner is paid under the Plan, the federal crown will be subrogated to that person's B.I.A. claim against the employer. Also added to the B.I.A. will be s. 60(1.5), under which a proposal to avoid bankruptcy cannot be approved unless it provides for certain payments into underfunded employee pensions.

5. Note also that managers may find themselves made liable by other statutes, such as those dealing with the protection of the environment: see *R. v. Bata Industries Ltd.*, [1992] O.J. No. 236, 9 O.R. (3d) 329 (Gen. Div.).

6.   The Dey Committee recommended an overall review of managers' potential personal liabilities. However, "Five Years to the *Dey*" reported, in the context of recruitment of new directors:

> Speculation sometimes arises that liability risk and restrained compensation will reduce the attraction of board appointments to those whose services might be most in demand. The survey results do not support this hypothesis. Respondents were asked to select statements that described difficulties their boards may have encountered while recruiting new directors. The largest group of responses dealt with the scarcity of acceptable candidates, or the fact that desirable candidates held too many directorships. Much less frequent were beliefs that compensation levels or liability concerns were deterring candidates.

D. MANAGERS' FIDUCIARY OBLIGATIONS

1. The Nature and Source of the Obligation

Directors have long been held to owe fiduciary obligations to their corporations. The fiduciary duty evolved from trust law, which requires trustees to act in the best interests of the trust beneficiaries. In England in the early nineteenth century, the trust was the main business organization. When registered companies took over this position, it was obvious that the power and influence that directors, by virtue of their positions, held over the corporate entity was exactly parallel to the power and influence that a trustee holds over the trust property. The duties of loyalty were therefore applied by analogy.

Somewhat belatedly, it has been recognized that corporate officers owe the same fiduciary duties. This change began as a judicial development, in *Canadian Aero Services Ltd. v. O'Malley*, [1974] S.C.R. 592, 40 D.L.R. (3d) 371, but it has since been legislated in most Canadian jurisdictions. Indeed, we now have a largely statutory regime to curb management's temptations, a regime which has as a major advantage the ability to carve into manageable portions what was before a loose statement of principle. But the general principle still lurks in the background and colours judicial analysis. Like many other obligations derived from the field of Equity, the scope of managers' fiduciary duties is much misunderstood.

L. SEALY, "FIDUCIARY RELATIONSHIPS"

[1962] Camb. L.J. 69 (Footnotes deleted.)

Today, the word "fiduciary" is still sometimes used in an indefinite and descriptive sense, so that it embraces all trust-like situations including the trust itself, but it is more precisely used, in contrast with trusts proper, in reference to those situations which are in some respects trust-like but are not, strictly speaking, trusts. The law of trusts is well recognised as a separate branch of the law, with its own textbooks and its own rules and principles, now highly developed. The law of fiduciary relationships will not, in general, be found in those textbooks, but the rules and principles governing these relationships are — in essence and in origin — the same as those of the law of trusts. This point was made by Fry J. in *Ex p. Dale & Co.* [(1879), 11 Ch.D. 772, at 778]; he said:

What is a fiduciary relationship? It is one in respect of which if a wrong arise, the same remedy exists against the wrongdoer on behalf of the principal as would exist against a trustee on behalf of the cestui que trust.

Fry, J.'s definition emphasises the essential quality of all fiduciary relationships: every remedy which can be sought against a fiduciary is one which might be sought against a trustee on the same grounds. But it is really not a definition at all: although it describes a common feature, it does not teach us to recognize a fiduciary relationship when we meet one. Still less does it assist us when we are faced with a particular relationship and asked the practical question: does a certain principle of the law of trust and trustee apply? John is my agent and is therefore, on good authority, in a fiduciary position towards me. Does this mean that he must not mix with his own money the sums which he holds on my account? Is there a presumption of undue influence if I make him a gift? Is he disqualified from becoming the lessee of land formerly held by me, after I have failed to secure a renewal of the lease for myself? Do all the trust principles apply to this fiduciary situation? When we examine the authorities, we learn — perhaps with some surprise — that this is not so. The word "fiduciary", we find, is not definitive of a single class of relationships to which a fixed set of rules and principles apply. Each equitable remedy is available only in a limited number of fiduciary situations; and the mere statement that John is in a fiduciary relationship towards me means no more than that in some respects his position is trustee-like; it does not warrant the inference that any particular fiduciary principle or remedy can be applied.

Fletcher Moulton L.J. once warned against what he called "the danger of trusting to verbal formulae" in this way. After illustrating a number of fiduciary situations and describing the ways in which the courts had interfered to grant relief in these cases, he said [*Re Coomber*, [1911] 1 Ch. 723 (C.A.), p. 729]:

> Thereupon in some minds there arises the idea that if there is any fiduciary relation whatever any of these types of interference is warranted by it. They conclude that every kind of fiduciary relation justifies every kind of interference. Of course that is absurd. The nature of fiduciary relation must be such that it justifies the interference.

It is obvious that we cannot proceed any further in our search for a general definition of fiduciary relationships. We must define them class by class, and find out the rule or rules which govern each class. In this task, we receive little help from the cases, or even the textbooks. The judges in most cases have been more ready to find that the type of fiduciary situation upon which their decision depends does or does not exist, than to say what, for that purpose, amounts to such a fiduciary position. Indeed, in very few cases has there been anything more than a ruling that the situation is or is not "fiduciary", without regard to the warning of Fletcher Moulton L.J. that this is not taking the inquiry far enough. In order to know whether a particular rule of equity is applicable we must know whether the situation is "fiduciary" in the appropriate special sense.

NOTES

1. The *source* of the fiduciary obligations of directors was Equity's concern with the degree of power the board of directors exercised over the destiny of the corporate person. With the recognition of corporations as legal persons separate from the shareholder collective, it became clear that directors could not properly be described

as trustees, who hold property "on trust" for someone else; the corporate person, not the directors, held the corporate property. However, corporate directors have always been understood as owing fiduciary obligations, and with the recognition of the corporation as a legal person, it followed that these obligations were owed to the corporate person, not individually or collectively to the shareholders.

2. As the extract from Sealy shows, the *content* of the obligation was derived by analogy from the obligations of trustees. The content, as regards corporate managers, is further elucidated in the following decision of the Supreme Court of Canada.

PEOPLES DEPARTMENT STORES INC. (TRUSTEE OF) v. WISE

[2004] S.C.J. No. 64, [2004] 3 S.C.R. 461, 244 D.L.R. (4th) 564

The judgment of the Court was delivered by
Major and Deschamps JJ.: —
[The facts are set out in the extract above, pp. 313-15.]

Section 122(1) of the CBCA establishes two distinct duties to be discharged by directors and officers in managing, or supervising the management of, the corporation ...

The first duty has been referred to in this case as the "fiduciary duty". It is better described as the "duty of loyalty". We will use the expression "statutory fiduciary duty" for purposes of clarity when referring to the duty under the CBCA. This duty requires directors and officers to act honestly and in good faith with a view to the best interests of the corporation. The second duty is commonly referred to as the "duty of care". Generally speaking, it imposes a legal obligation upon directors and officers to be diligent in supervising and managing the corporation's affairs.

The trial judge did not apply or consider separately the two duties imposed on directors by s. 122(1). As the Court of Appeal observed, the trial judge appears to have confused the two duties. They are, in fact, distinct and are designed to secure different ends. For that reason, they will be addressed separately in these reasons.

A. The Statutory Fiduciary Duty: Section 122(1)(a) of the CBCA

Considerable power over the deployment and management of financial, human, and material resources is vested in the directors and officers of corporations. For the directors of CBCA corporations, this power originates in s. 102 of the Act. For officers, this power comes from the powers delegated to them by the directors. In deciding to invest in, lend to or otherwise deal with a corporation, shareholders and creditors transfer control over their assets to the corporation, and hence to the directors and officers, in the expectation that the directors and officers will use the corporation's resources to make reasonable business decisions that are to the corporation's advantage.

The statutory fiduciary duty requires directors and officers to act honestly and in good faith *vis-à-vis* the corporation. They must respect the trust and confidence that have been reposed in them to manage the assets of the corporation in pursuit of the realization of the objects of the corporation. They must avoid conflicts of interest with the corporation. They must avoid abusing their position to gain personal benefit. They must maintain the confidentiality of information they acquire by virtue of their position. Directors and officers must serve the corporation selflessly, honestly and loyally: see K. P. McGuinness, *The Law and Practice of Canadian Business Corporations* (1999), at p. 715.

The common law concept of fiduciary duty was considered in *K.L.B. v. British Columbia*, [2003] 2 S.C.R. 403, 2003 SCC 51. In that case, which involved the relationship between the government and foster children, a majority of this Court agreed with McLachlin C.J. who stated, at paras. 40-41 and 49:

> Fiduciary duties arise in a number of different contexts, including express trusts, relationships marked by discretionary power and trust, and the special responsibilities of the Crown in dealing with aboriginal interests. ...
>
> What ... might the content of the fiduciary duty be if it is understood ... as a private law duty arising simply from the relationship of discretionary power and trust between the Superintendent and the foster children? In *Lac Minerals Ltd. v. International Corona Resources Ltd.*, [1989] 2 S.C.R. 574, at pp. 646-47, La Forest J. noted that there are certain common threads running through fiduciary duties that arise from relationships marked by discretionary power and trust, such as loyalty and "the avoidance of a conflict of duty and interest and a duty not to profit at the expense of the beneficiary". However, he also noted that "[t]he obligation imposed may vary in its specific substance depending on the relationship" (p. 646). ...
>
> ... concern for the best interests of the child informs the parental fiduciary relationship, as La Forest J. noted in *M. (K.) v. M. (H.)*, *supra*, at p. 65. But the duty imposed is to act loyally, and not to put one's own or others' interests ahead of the child's in a manner that abuses the child's trust. ... The parent who exercises undue influence over the child in economic matters for his own gain has put his own interests ahead of the child's, in a manner that abuses the child's trust in him. The same may be said of the parent who uses a child for his sexual gratification or a parent who, wanting to avoid trouble for herself and her household, turns a blind eye to the abuse of a child by her spouse. The parent need not, as the Court of Appeal suggested in the case at bar, be consciously motivated by a desire for profit or personal advantage; nor does it have to be her own interests, rather than those of a third party, that she puts ahead of the child's. It is rather a question of disloyalty — of putting someone's interests ahead of the child's in a manner that abuses the child's trust. Negligence, even aggravated negligence, will not ground parental fiduciary liability unless it is associated with breach of trust in this sense. [Emphasis added.]

The issue to be considered here is the "specific substance" of the fiduciary duty based on the relationship of directors to corporations under the CBCA.

It is settled law that the fiduciary duty owed by directors and officers imposes strict obligations: see *Canadian Aero Service Ltd. v. O'Malley*, [1974] S.C.R. 592, at pp. 609-10, *per* Laskin J. (as he then was), where it was decided that directors and officers may even have to account to the corporation for profits they make that do not come at the corporation's expense:

> The reaping of a profit by a person at a company's expense while a director thereof is, of course, an adequate ground upon which to hold the director accountable. Yet there may be situations where a profit must be disgorged, although not gained at the expense of the company, on the ground that a director must not be allowed to use his position as such to make a profit even if it was not open to the company, as for example, by reason of legal disability, to participate in the transaction. An analogous situation, albeit not involving a director, existed for all practical purposes in the case of *Phipps v. Boardman* [[1967] 2 A.C. 46], which also supports the view that liability to account does not depend on proof of an actual conflict of duty and self-interest. Another, quite recent, illustration of a liability to

account where the company itself had failed to obtain a business contract and hence could not be regarded as having been deprived of a business opportunity is *Industrial Development Consultants Ltd. v. Cooley* [[1972] 2 All E.R. 162], a judgment of a Court of first instance. There, the managing director, who was allowed to resign his position on a false assertion of ill health, subsequently got the contract for himself. That case is thus also illustrative of the situation where a director's resignation is prompted by a decision to obtain for himself the business contract denied to his company and where he does obtain it without disclosing his intention. [Emphasis added.]

A compelling argument for making directors accountable for profits made as a result of their position, though not at the corporation's expense, is presented by J. Brock, "The Propriety of Profitmaking: Fiduciary Duty and Unjust Enrichment" (2000), 58 *U.T. Fac. L. Rev.* 185, at pp. 204-5.

However, it is not required that directors and officers in all cases avoid personal gain as a direct or indirect result of their honest and good faith supervision or management of the corporation. In many cases the interests of directors and officers will innocently and genuinely coincide with those of the corporation. If directors and officers are also shareholders, as is often the case, their lot will automatically improve as the corporation's financial condition improves. Another example is the compensation that directors and officers usually draw from the corporations they serve. This benefit, though paid by the corporation, does not, if reasonable, ordinarily place them in breach of their fiduciary duty. Therefore, all the circumstances may be scrutinized to determine whether the directors and officers have acted honestly and in good faith with a view to the best interests of the corporation.

In our opinion, the trial judge's determination that there was no fraud or dishonesty in the Wise brothers' attempts to solve the mounting inventory problems of Peoples and Wise stands in the way of a finding that they breached their fiduciary duty. Greenberg J. stated:

> We hasten to add that in the present case, the Wise Brothers derived no direct personal benefit from the new domestic inventory procurement policy, albeit that, as the controlling shareholders of Wise Stores, there was an indirect benefit to them. Moreover, as was conceded by the other parties herein, in deciding to implement the new domestic inventory procurement policy, there was no dishonesty or fraud on their part.

((1998), 23 C.B.R. (4th) 200, at para. 183).
The Court of Appeal relied heavily on this finding by the trial judge, as do we. At para. 83 QL, Pelletier J.A. stated that:

> [TRANSLATION] In regard to fiduciary duty, I would like to point out that the brothers were driven solely by the wish to resolve the problem of inventory procurement affecting both the operations of Peoples Inc. and those of Wise. [This is a] motivation that is in line with the pursuit of the interests of the corporation within the meaning of paragraph 122(1)(a) C.B.C.A. and that does not expose them to any justified criticism.

As explained above, there is no doubt that both Peoples and Wise were struggling with a serious inventory management problem. The Wise brothers considered the problem and implemented a policy they hoped would solve it. In the absence of evidence of a personal interest or improper purpose in the new policy, and in light of the evidence of a desire to make both Wise and Peoples "better" corporations, we find that the directors did not breach their fiduciary duty under s. 122(1)(*a*) of the CBCA. See *820099 Ontario Inc. v. Harold E. Ballard Ltd.*, (1991), 3 B.L.R. (2d) 123 (Ont. Ct. (Gen. Div.)) (aff'd (1991), 3 B.L.R. (2d) 113 (Ont. Div. Ct.)), in which Farley J., at p. 171, correctly observes that in resolving a conflict between majority and minority shareholders, it is safe for directors and officers to act to make the corporation a "better corporation".

This appeal does not relate to the non-statutory duty directors owe to shareholders. It is concerned only with the statutory duties owed under the CBCA. Insofar as the statutory fiduciary duty is concerned, it is clear that the phrase the "best interests of the corporation" should be read not simply as the "best interests of the shareholders". From an economic perspective, the "best interests of the corporation" means the maximization of the value of the corporation: see E. M. Iacobucci, "Directors' Duties in Insolvency: Clarifying What Is at Stake" (2003), 39 *Can. Bus. L.J.* 398, at pp. 400-1. However, the courts have long recognized that various other factors may be relevant in determining what directors should consider in soundly managing with a view to the best interests of the corporation. For example, in *Teck Corp. v. Millar* (1972), 33 D.L.R. (3d) 288 (B.C.S.C.), Berger J. stated, at p. 314:

> A classical theory that once was unchallengeable must yield to the facts of modern life. In fact, of course, it has. If today the directors of a company were to consider the interests of its employees no one would argue that in doing so they were not acting *bona fide* in the interests of the company itself. Similarly, if the directors were to consider the consequences to the community of any policy that the company intended to pursue, and were deflected in their commitment to that policy as a result, it could not be said that they had not considered *bona fide* the interests of the shareholders.
>
> I appreciate that it would be a breach of their duty for directors to disregard entirely the interests of a company's shareholders in order to confer a benefit on its employees: *Parke v. Daily News Ltd.*, [1962] Ch. 927. But if they observe a decent respect for other interests lying beyond those of the company's shareholders in the strict sense, that will not, in my view, leave directors open to the charge that they have failed in their fiduciary duty to the company.

The case of *Re Olympia & York Enterprises Ltd. and Hiram Walker Resources Ltd.*, (1986), 59 O.R. (2d) 254 (Div. Ct.), approved, at p. 271, the decision in *Teck*, *supra*. We accept as an accurate statement of law that in determining whether they are acting with a view to the best interests of the corporation it may be legitimate, given all the circumstances of a given case, for the board of directors to consider, *inter alia*, the interests of shareholders, employees, suppliers, creditors, consumers, governments and the environment.

The various shifts in interests that naturally occur as a corporation's fortunes rise and fall do not, however, affect the content of the fiduciary duty under s. 122(1)(*a*) of the CBCA. At all times, directors and officers owe their fiduciary obligation to the corporation. The interests of the corporation are not to be confused with the interests of the creditors or those of any other stakeholders.

The interests of shareholders, those of the creditors and those of the corporation may and will be consistent with each other if the corporation is profitable and well capitalized and has strong prospects. However, this can change if the corporation starts to struggle financially. The residual rights of the shareholders will generally become worthless if a corporation is declared bankrupt. Upon bankruptcy, the directors of the corporation transfer control to a trustee, who administers the corporation's assets for the benefit of creditors.

Short of bankruptcy, as the corporation approaches what has been described as the "vicinity of insolvency", the residual claims of shareholders will be nearly exhausted. While shareholders might well prefer that the directors pursue high-risk alternatives with a high potential payoff to maximize the shareholders' expected residual claim, creditors in the same circumstances might prefer that the directors steer a safer course so as to maximize the value of their claims against the assets of the corporation.

The directors' fiduciary duty does not change when a corporation is in the nebulous "vicinity of insolvency". That phrase has not been defined; moreover, it is incapable of definition and has no legal meaning. What it is obviously intended to convey is a deterioration in the corporation's financial stability. In assessing the actions of directors it is evident that any honest and good faith attempt to redress the corporation's financial problems will, if successful, both retain value for shareholders and improve the position of creditors. If unsuccessful, it will not qualify as a breach of the statutory fiduciary duty.

For a discussion of the shifting interests and incentives of shareholders and creditors, see W. D. Gray, "*Peoples v. Wise* and *Dylex*: Identifying Stakeholder Interests upon or near Corporate Insolvency — Stasis or Pragmatism?" (2003), 39 *Can. Bus. L.J.* 242, at p. 257; E. M. Iacobucci and K. E. Davis, "Reconciling Derivative Claims and the Oppression Remedy" (2000), 12 *S.C.L.R.* (2d) 87, at p. 114. In resolving these competing interests, it is incumbent upon the directors to act honestly and in good faith with a view to the best interests of the corporation. In using their skills for the benefit of the corporation when it is in troubled waters financially, the directors must be careful to attempt to act in its best interests by creating a "better" corporation, and not to favour the interests of any one group of stakeholders. If the stakeholders cannot avail themselves of the statutory fiduciary duty (the duty of loyalty, *supra*) to sue the directors for failing to take care of their interests, they have other means at their disposal.

The Canadian legal landscape with respect to stakeholders is unique. Creditors are only one set of stakeholders, but their interests are protected in a number of ways. Some are specific, as in the case of amalgamation: s. 185 of the CBCA. Others cover a broad range of situations. The oppression remedy of s. 241(2)(*c*) of the CBCA and the similar provisions of provincial legislation regarding corporations grant the broadest rights to creditors of any common law jurisdiction: see D. Thomson, "Directors, Creditors and Insolvency: A Fiduciary Duty or a Duty Not to Oppress?" (2000), 58 *U.T. Fac. L. Rev.* 31, at p. 48. One commentator describes the oppression remedy as "the broadest, most comprehensive and most open-ended shareholder remedy in the common law world": S. M. Beck, "Minority Shareholders' Rights in the 1980s", in *Corporate Law in the 80s* (1982), 311, at p. 312. While Beck was concerned with shareholder remedies, his observation applies equally to those of creditors.

The fact that creditors' interests increase in relevancy as a corporation's finances deteriorate is apt to be relevant to, *inter alia*, the exercise of discretion by a court in granting standing to a party as a "complainant" under s. 238(*d*) of the CBCA as a "proper person" to bring a derivative action in the name of the corporation under ss. 239 and 240 of the CBCA, or to bring an oppression remedy claim under s. 241 of the CBCA.

Section 241(2)(*c*) authorizes a court to grant a remedy if

(*c*)   the powers of the directors of the corporation or any of its affiliates are or have been exercised in a manner

that is oppressive or unfairly prejudicial to or that unfairly disregards the interests of any security holder, creditor, director or officer . ...

A person applying for the oppression remedy must, in the court's opinion, fall within the definition of "complainant" found in s. 238 of the CBCA:

(*a*)   a registered holder or beneficial owner, and a former registered holder or beneficial owner, of a security of a corporation or any of its affiliates,

(*b*)   a director or an officer or a former director or officer of a corporation or any of its affiliates,

(*c*)   the Director, or

(*d*)   any other person who, in the discretion of a court, is a proper person to make an application under this Part.

Creditors, who are not security holders within the meaning of para. (*a*), may therefore apply for the oppression remedy under para. (*d*) by asking a court to exercise its discretion and grant them status as a "complainant".

Section 241 of the CBCA provides a possible mechanism for creditors to protect their interests from the prejudicial conduct of directors. In our view, the availability of such a broad oppression remedy undermines any perceived need to extend the fiduciary duty imposed on directors by s. 122(1)(*a*) of the CBCA to include creditors.

...

In light of the availability both of the oppression remedy and of an action based on the duty of care, which will be discussed below, stakeholders have viable remedies at their disposal. There is no need to read the interests of creditors into the duty set out in s. 122(1)(*a*) of the CBCA. Moreover, in the circumstances of this case, the Wise brothers did not breach the statutory fiduciary duty owed to the corporation.

NOTES AND QUESTIONS

1.   The fiduciary obligation is an obligation of loyalty or selflessness; the fiduciary must put the interests of his or her beneficiary ahead of the fiduciary's own interests. As the C.B.C.A. says, the fiduciary must act "with a view to the best interests of the corporation". This is easy enough to say, but the practical consequences are somewhat difficult to work out. In the part of *Peoples* extracted earlier, at para. 63, the Court said that the "subjective motivation of the director or officer" is "the central focus of the statutory fiduciary duty". In para. 35, the Court begins by saying more or less exactly what the statute says, that the "statutory fiduciary duty requires directors and officers to act honestly and in good faith *vis-à-vis* the corporation". Note how the Court goes on to say, "They must avoid conflicts of interest with the corporation. They must avoid abusing their position to gain personal benefit. They must maintain the confidentiality of information they acquire by virtue of their position". These additional requirements are based on centuries of cases arising in the contexts of trusts.

Adding a bit more detail, we can observe that a fiduciary may not put himself or herself in a position in which his or her own interests might conflict with the duty of loyalty to the beneficiary (unless the beneficiary has authorized the situation, with full information). This is often called the "no-conflict" rule, and the term "conflict of interest" is used as a short form of the full expression, "conflict of self-interest and duty". In fact, the fiduciary is not even allowed to put himself or herself in a position where duty to one beneficiary conflicts with duty to another beneficiary (see *Canson Enterprises Ltd. v. Boughton & Co.*, [1991] 3 S.C.R. 534, 85 D.L.R. (4th) 129). Furthermore, a fiduciary may not derive an unauthorized profit from his or her position. It is controversial whether the "no-conflict" and "no-profit" principles are separate principles, or whether one collapses into the other. The two principles are sometimes called *prophylactic* rules because they are designed to *prevent* fiduciaries from being in situations where they might not act in the best interests of their beneficiaries.

The implications of the "no-profit" rule for managers' remuneration have already been mentioned (above, p. 309). The wider implications of the "no-conflict" rule for corporate fiduciaries are discussed later in this chapter.

2. A related principle of trust law is that a trustee is constrained in his or her ability to deal, in a personal capacity, with the beneficiaries or with the trust property. There is a "self-dealing" rule that renders voidable, at the instance of trust beneficiaries, any transaction in which the trustee buys trust property or sells property to the trust. For example, a trustee holds an estate in land in trust; the trustee purports to buy it for personal use, so that the trustee now holds the estate, not in trust, but for personal benefit; conversely, the trustee now holds the purchase price as trust property. This sale clearly creates a conflict of interest and duty: the trustee's self-interest is in buying the property for as little as possible, while the trustee's duty to the trust beneficiaries is to sell it for as much as possible. As a result, this transaction is voidable by the trust beneficiaries, unless, before or after the sale, the beneficiaries consented to it, with full knowledge of the material facts. There is also said to be a "fair dealing" rule that applies to the slightly different case in which the trustee purports to buy, not the trust property, but the interest of a beneficiary in the trust. There is some discussion as to whether there are really two rules or only one. In corporate law, the same problem manifests itself when a director or an officer purports to make a contract with the corporation to which he or she owes a duty of loyalty. This issue is addressed in the next section of this chapter.

3. If the core fiduciary duty is to act in what one perceives to be the best interests of one's beneficiary, the no-conflict and no-profit rules create something of a paradox. The reason is that if a fiduciary violates one of those rules (say, by being in a conflict of interest and duty), then a liability will arise, *even if* the fiduciary was acting in what he or she perceived to be the best interests of the beneficiary. The cases, in both trust law and corporate law, make this quite clear. For an analysis of the relationship between the core fiduciary duties and the prophylactic rules, see L. Smith, "The Motive, Not the Deed" in in J. Getzler, ed., *Rationalizing Property, Equity and Trusts: Essays in Honour of Edward Burn* (London: Butterworths, 2003) at p. 53. Smith argues that the core duty of loyalty is to act with the right motive; usually, to act in what the fiduciary perceives to be the best interests of the beneficiary. The prophylactic rules can then be analyzed as protecting the beneficiary from the burden of proving an improper motive. The fiduciary must not only act with the proper motive; he or she must be seen so to act, and so the fiduciary is forbidden to be in situations of conflicting motivational pressure.

4. Being an officer of a corporation is a full-time job. It is a senior employment position with the corporation. On the other hand, being a director is not supposed to be a full-time job. It is common to be a director of more than one corporation, and then perhaps

to be an officer of one of them as well. We say that a fiduciary must act in what he or she perceives to be the best interests of his or her beneficiary; but this does not mean that the fiduciary is not allowed ever to act in his or her own interests, or to act in the interests of some other person. The fiduciary duty of loyalty requires a manager to act in a certain way in a managerial role; but it does *not* say how much work the manager is required to put in. In the case of an officer, the express or implied terms of the contract of employment will be the most important determinants of this. For a director who is not an officer, the question of how much action is required is primarily determined by the duty of care, skill and diligence. "Diligence," in particular, connotes a duty to act.

5. It is now clear that not every breach of duty by a fiduciary is a breach of fiduciary duty. Carelessness or lack of diligence, for example, are not the same as disloyalty. This was accepted in *LAC Minerals Ltd. v. International Corona Ltd.*, [1989] S.C.J. No. 83, [1989] 2 S.C.R. 574, 61 D.L.R. (4th) 14, and confirmed in *Peoples*.

6. Corporate directors have been held to be fiduciaries for many years. The courts were somewhat slow to catch on to the fact that corporate officers often had equal or greater powers, in fact if not in law. By 1974, however, the Supreme Court of Canada extended the fiduciary obligation to "senior officers". In *Canadian Aero Services Ltd. v. O'Malley*, [1974] S.C.R. 592, 40 D.L.R. (3d) 371, Laskin J. noted (at D.L.R. p. 381):

> I am unable to appreciate the basis upon which the Ontario Court of Appeal concluded that O'Malley and Zarzycki were mere employees, that is servants of Canaero rather than agents. Although they were subject to supervision..., their positions as senior officers... charged them with initiatives and with responsibilities far removed from the obedient role of servants. It follows that O'Malley and Zarzycki stood in a fiduciary relationship to Canaero.

The implications of this ruling will be appreciated upon reading the fuller exposition of the *Canaero* case set out later in this chapter. For the moment, it is sufficient to note how the duty arose from the power relationship, not simply from the formalistic job title.

7. More broadly, Canadian law now recognizes fiduciary obligations in two ways. There are some relationships, such as trustee-beneficiary, solicitor-client, director-corporation, and officer-corporation, in which the fiduciary relationship arises automatically. Even where a relationship is not in one of these categories, it may nonetheless be characterized as a fiduciary relationship, on the basis of the particular incidents of the relationship. When exactly this is appropriate is a difficult issue. The Supreme Court of Canada's most recent attempt to clarify this is in *Hodgkinson v. Simms*, [1994] S.C.J. No. 84, [1994] 3 S.C.R. 377, 117 D.L.R. (4th) 161, discussed in (1995) 74 Can. Bar Rev. 714. The issue often comes up in cases of misfiring joint ventures: *LAC Minerals Ltd. v. International Corona Resources Ltd.*, [1989] S.C.J. No. 83, [1989] 2 S.C.R. 574, 61 D.L.R. (4th) 14; *Visagie v. TVX Gold Inc.*, [2000] O.J. No. 1992, 49 O.R. (3d) 198, 187 D.L.R. (4th) 193 (C.A.); but it also frequently arises in non-commercial settings: *Norberg v. Wynrib*, [1992] S.C.J. No. 60, [1992] 2 S.C.R. 226, 92 D.L.R. (4th) 449; *M. v. M.*, [1992] S.C.J. NO. 85, [1992] 3 S.C.R. 6, 96 D.L.R. (4th) 289. In *Brant Investments Ltd. v. Keeprite Inc.*, [1991] O.J. No. 683, 3 O.R. (3d) 289, 80 D.L.R. (4th) 161 (C.A.) it was held that majority shareholders do not owe a fiduciary duty to minority shareholders.

8. *Peoples* is part of a line of cases addressing the question *to whom* managers owe their fiduciary duties. The case rejected the argument that the duty is owed to creditors when the corporation is "in the vicinity of insolvency," an argument that based on the

assumption that the duty is usually owed to shareholders. The Court rejected the assumption, affirming the traditional view that the duty is owed to the corporation, whether it is solvent or not. The effect of this is that other parties (such as creditors) do not have the right to sue for breach of fiduciary duty (although they may well be able to use the oppression remedy, as the court noted).

This, however, raises a further issue. The fiduciary duty is only owed to the corporation, and it is a duty to act in what the manager thinks is the best interests of the corporation. The further issue is: what considerations may the manager take into account in deciding what is in the best interests of the corporation? Although the duty is not owed directly to shareholders, employees, or creditors, may managers take their interests into account? Most everyone would agree that shareholder interests may be taken into account; indeed, most would argue that they must be. Some writers have argued that *only* the interests of shareholders should be taken into account, since in economic (not legal) terms, they are the owners of the corporate enterprise. See, for example, the ambitiously titled article by H. Hansmann and R. Kraakman, "The End of History for Corporate Law" (2001), 89 Georgetown L.J. 439.

The Supreme Court said in *Peoples*, at para. 42: "We accept as an accurate statement of law that in determining whether they are acting with a view to the best interests of the corporation it may be legitimate, given all the circumstances of a given case, for the board of directors to consider, *inter alia*, the interests of shareholders, employees, suppliers, creditors, consumers, governments and the environment". This leaves managers with much more latitude as to the factors they may consider when deciding what *they* think is in the best interests of the corporation. Recall the cases and discussion in Chapter 4, section E, on Corporate Purpose, and see also R.O. Kuras, "Corporate Social Responsibility: A Canada-U.S. Comparative Analysis" (2002), 28 Man. L.J. 303.

9.   Although the duty of loyalty is not owed to creditors, they are protected in insolvency situations in other ways. Provincial law relating to voidable preferences and voidable conveyances, and federal law as to voidable transactions under the *Bankruptcy and Insolvency Act*, allows certain transactions to be set aside if they harm the interests of creditors. What should be done with directors who disregard the interests of creditors? In Quebec, art. 329 of the Civil Code of Quebec provides:

> The court, on the application of an interested person, may prohibit a person from holding office as a director of a legal person if the person has been found guilty of an indictable offence involving fraud or dishonesty in a matter related to legal persons, or who has repeatedly violated the Acts relating to legal persons or failed to fulfil his obligations as a director.

In England and Wales, not only can directors be disqualified under the *Company Directors Disqualification Act 1986*, but under the *Insolvency Act 1986*, s. 214, a director can be liable to the corporation for "wrongful trading" if the director allowed the corporation to continue in business when he or she "knew or ought to have concluded that there was no reasonable prospect that the company would avoid going into insolvent liquidation". Liability is avoided if the director "took every step with a view to minimising the potential loss to the company's creditors as ... he ought to have taken". In the more serious case where the director (or even a non-director) was party to the carrying on of business "with intent to defraud creditors", there is both a civil liability to the corporation (*Insolvency Act 1986*, s. 213) and a penal offence that can lead to imprisonment (*Companies Act 1985*, s. 458). Are such provisions needed to protect creditors?

10. There are several ways a legal analyst could interpret the requirement that a manager act "with a view to the best interests of the corporation". Consider the following propositions regarding *how one determines* what is in the corporation's best interests:

   (i) "The corporation" is, for this purpose, to be identified with the shareholder collective, which then creates a sub-issue concerning the extent to which majority rule is to be allowed to prevail over minority protection.

   (ii) The corporation is its own person and, in considering its best interests, the accumulated votes and opinions of individual shareholders are irrelevant.

   (iii) The corporation is its own person and, in considering its best interests, one must/may take into account the accumulated views of various groups of individuals such as the shareholders, the employees, members of the community and, in the case of exporting corporations, the government and people of Canada.

   Now consider these propositions regarding *who determines* what is in the corporation's best interests:

   (i) The best interests of the corporation are to be objectively determined in light of all the evidence available to the judge at the time of trial.

   (ii) The best interests of the corporation are to be assessed in terms of what a reasonably prudent person would have done on the facts that the particular manager had at the time he or she acted.

   (iii) The best interests of the corporation are to be subjectively assessed by the manager whose function it is to manage corporate affairs. As long as that person takes into account those factors that must be taken into account, and does not take into account any factors that must not be taken into account, the decision is not reviewable by the court.

   Which, if any, of the above propositions do you think can be supported as a general approach? Which is most consistent with *Peoples?*

11. In *Peoples*, at para. 50, the Court indicated that an ordinary creditor is not within the terms of C.B.C.A., s. 238(*a*) and would have to invoke the discretion of the court under s. 238(*d*) in order to be a "complainant". Check the definitions of "security" and "debt obligation" in the C.B.C.A. and see whether you agree.

12. Most of the cases in this chapter are about whether corporate fiduciaries must give up *gains* that they have allegedly made in breach of their fiduciary duties of loyalty. We can notice that if a breach of these duties causes a *loss,* as in a case of improper transfer of corporate funds to a third party, the manager is obliged to compensate the corporation (*Re Lands Allotment Co.*, [1894] 1 Ch. 616 (C.A.); *Bishopsgate Investment Management Ltd. (in liquidation) v. Maxwell (No. 2)*, [1994] 1 All E.R. 261 (C.A.)). Here there is an overlap with managers' "legal" duties, which may also be violated in such a case; but the fiduciary duty may be stricter than the "legal" duties.

   Note also that if a fiduciary enters a legal transaction in breach of the duty of loyalty, the beneficiary can demand that the transaction be set aside, in addition to demanding compensation for loss or disgorgement of gain. In the corporate context, this could allow the avoidance of a self-dealing contract between the manager and the corporation. It might also allow the avoidance of a contract (or an issue of shares) between the corporation and some other party, if that party knew or ought to have known that the contract was being made through a breach of duty by a corporate manager. The agreement may be voidable in equity (due to the breach of the fiduciary duty) even though it might have been enforceable at common law (as a matter of the law of agency). If, however, the third party contracted in good faith with the corporation, and neither knew nor ought to have known of any breach of fiduciary duty by the corporation's managers, the contract will not be voidable and the beneficiary of the fiduciary duty will be confined to a claim against the fiduciary for loss or gain. See P. Watts, "Authority and Mismotivation" (2005), 121 L.Q.R. 4, criticizing *Criterion Properties plc v. Stratford UK Properties LLC*, [2004] 1 W.L.R. 1846 (H.L.).

13. For a detailed theoretical analysis of the fiduciary obligation, see L. Rotman, *Fiduciary Law* (Toronto: Carswell, 2005).

2. Judicial Review of the Exercise of Managerial Powers

Directors and officers have many powers. They may not, however, use them for any purpose they wish. If you gave your friend power of attorney over your bank account while you went off to Uzbekistan, you would rightly hope that there would be some recourse if the friend used the power to extract money to feed his habit of wagering on greyhound races.

There are two ways to understand the fact that the exercise of a power is reviewable based on the purpose for which it was exercised. One finds the limitation within the power, as a matter of construction. Clearly, if you give someone a power to deposit money into your bank account, she cannot withdraw money from it. One could understand legal powers to be implicitly limited as to the purposes for which they may be used. In other words, if a power was given for a particular purpose, it cannot be exercised for some other purpose and any attempt to do so will be legally ineffective. This implies that one could, at least in principle, make a list of proper purposes and a list of improper purposes. It would never be permissible to use the power for a purpose on the "impermissible" list. The other way to understand the principle that allows the evaluation of purposes would be to find the limitation in the fiduciary obligation owed by corporate managers (as well as trustees and others, including agents holding powers of attorney). On this view, whether or not the power has been effectively exercised requires an examination of the motives for which it was used. If it was used in what the fiduciary thought was the best interest of the corporation, it is effective; otherwise, not. This implies that in some cases it would be permissible to use the power for some purpose, and in other cases it would be impermissible to use the power for the same purpose.

Is there any difference between these theories? Are they mutually exclusive as explanations? In the cases that follow, the question is whether directors may issue shares in order to thwart a takeover bid by diluting the voting power of existing shareholders.

HOGG v. CRAMPHORN LTD.

[1967] Ch. 254, [1966] 3 All E.R. 420, [1966] 3 W.L.R. 995 (Ch. D.)

[Cramphorn Ltd. was faced with a takeover bid. Colonel Cramphorn, the chairman and managing director, took the view that such a takeover was disadvantageous as the company's business would be altered and the employees would be "unsettled".

An employees' trust was set up and it was proposed to issue shares to the trustee in order to maintain corporate control in friendly hands. A minority shareholder sought to prevent the share issue scheme. The articles said, "The shares shall be under the control of the directors, who may allot or otherwise dispose of the same to such persons, on such terms and conditions, and at such times as the directors think fit."]

Buckley J.: — ... Accepting as I do that the board acted in good faith and that they believed that the establishment of a trust would benefit the company, and that avoidance of the acquisition of control by Mr. Baxter would also benefit the company, I must still remember that an essential element of the scheme, and indeed its primary purpose, was to ensure control of the company by the directors and those whom they could confidently regard as their supporters. Was such a manipulation of the voting position a legitimate act on the part of the directors?

Somewhat similar questions have been considered in the well-known cases of *Punt v. Symons & Co. Ltd.,* [1903] 2 Ch. 506, and *Piercy v. S. Mills & Co. Ltd.,* [1920] 1 Ch. 77. In *Punt v. Symons & Co. Ltd.* the directors had issued shares with the object of creating a sufficient majority to enable them to pass a special resolution depriving other shareholders of special rights conferred on them by the company's articles. In *Piercy v. S. Mills & Co. Ltd.* the directors had issued shares with the object of creating a sufficient majority to enable them to resist the election of three additional directors, whose appointment would have put the two existing directors in a minority on the board. In each case the directors were held to have acted improperly. In *Punt v. Symons & Co. Ltd.* Byrne J. said:

> A power of the kind exercised by the directors in this case, is one which must be exercised for the benefit of the company: primarily it is given them for the purposes of enabling them to raise capital when required for the purposes of the company. There may be occasions when the directors may fairly and properly issue shares in the case of a company constituted like the present for other reasons. For instance, it would not be at all an unreasonable thing to create a sufficient number of shareholders to enable statutory powers to be exercised; but when I find a limited issue of shares to persons who are obviously meant and intended to secure the necessary statutory majority in a particular interest, I do not think that is a fair and bona fide exercise of the power.

In *Piercy v. S. Mills & Co. Ltd.*, Peterson J., after citing *Fraser v. Whalley* (1864), 2 H. & M. 10 and *Punt v. Symons & Co. Ltd.* said:

> The basis of both cases is, as I understand, that directors are not entitled to use their powers of issuing shares merely for the purpose of maintaining their control or the control of themselves and their friends over the affairs of the company, or merely for the purpose of defeating the wishes of the existing majority of shareholders. That is, however, exactly what has happened in the present case. With the merits of the dispute as between the directors and the plaintiff I have no concern whatever. The plaintiff and his friends held a majority of the shares of the company, and they were entitled, so long as that majority remained, to have their views prevail in accordance with the regulations of the company; and it was not, in my opinion, open to the directors, for the purpose of converting a minority into a majority, and solely for the purpose of defeating the wishes of the existing majority, to issue the shares which are in dispute in the present action.

With those observations I respectfully agree. Unless a majority in a company is acting oppressively towards the minority, this court should not and will not itself interfere with the exercise by the majority of its constitutional rights or embark upon an inquiry into the respective merits of the views held or policies favoured by the majority and the minority. Nor will this court permit directors to exercise powers, which have been delegated to them by the company in circumstances which put the directors in a fiduciary position when exercising those powers, in such a way as to interfere with the exercise by the majority of its constitutional rights; and in a case of this kind also, in my judgment, the court should not investigate the rival merits of the views or policies of the parties. Thus in *Fraser v. Whalley* Page Wood V.-C. said: "I say nothing on the question whether the policy advocated by the directors, or that which I am told is to be pursued by Savin, is the more for the interest of the company," and in *Piercy v. S. Mills & Co. Ltd.*, Peterson J. said that he had no concern whatever with the merits of the dispute. It is not, in my judgment, open to the directors in such a case to say, "We genuinely believe that what we seek to prevent the majority from doing will harm the company and therefore our act in arming ourselves or our party with sufficient shares to outvote the majority is a conscientious exercise of our powers under the articles, which should not be interfered with."

Such a belief, even if well founded, would be irrelevant. A majority of shareholders in general meeting is entitled to pursue what course it chooses within the company's powers, however wrong-headed it may appear to others, provided the majority do not unfairly oppress other members of the company. These considerations lead me to the conclusion that the issue of the 5,707 shares, with the special voting rights which the directors purported to attach to them, could not be justified by the view that the directors genuinely believed that it would benefit the company if they could command a majority of the votes in general meetings. The fact that, as I have held, the directors were mistaken in thinking that they could attach to these shares more than one vote each is irrelevant. The power to issue shares was a fiduciary power and if, as I think, it was exercised for an improper motive, the issue of these shares is liable to be set aside. ...

In these circumstances I propose to stand the action over for a specific period to enable the directors, if so advised, to convene a general meeting to consider such resolutions as may be submitted to it. I will consider what order I should make in the light of the proceedings at any such meeting. Mr. Goulding will undertake that at any such meeting the trustees will not vote in respect of the 5,707 shares, but I do not think there is any need for me to disenfranchise any other shares from voting at the meeting.

NOTES AND QUESTIONS

1. Did Buckley J. find that the purported share issue was void or voidable? Does this tell us anything about whether the share issue was (a) not permitted by the power or (b) permitted by the power but made in breach of the duty of loyalty?

2. See also *Bamford v. Bamford*, [1970] Ch. 212, [1969] 2 W.L.R. 1107, [1969] 1 All E.R. 969 (C.A.), in which it was assumed for the purposes of litigation that shares had been issued for the same kind of "improper motive" (i.e. retention of control) as in *Hogg v. Cramphorn*. It was held that this made the issue voidable, not void, and it was up to the corporation (acting, under this English legislation, in respect of this decision, through its shareholders) to decide whether to avoid the issue or not.

3. Did Buckley J. decide that the purpose was outside the purpose of the power, or that the directors could not issue the shares because they would breach their fiduciary

obligations? If the only limitation was that the directors not issue shares in such a way as to breach their fiduciary obligation to the corporation, how was what they did a breach of that duty? Does the following case answer any of these questions?

TECK CORP. v. MILLAR

(1972), 33 D.L.R. (3d) 288, [1973] 2 W.W.R. 385 (B.C.S.C.)

[Afton Mines Ltd. was a junior mining company which had several mining properties ripe for development. Two major corporations, the plaintiff ("Teck") and Canadian Exploration Ltd. ("Canex") were interested. The defendant Millar and his fellow directors of Afton were confident that the best interests of Afton would be served by concluding a long term development agreement with Canex, a major shareholder, Placer Development Ltd. ("Placer"), a large, international mining corporation. However, Teck had been buying shares of Afton Mines Ltd. on the Vancouver Stock Exchange and had, by late May 1972, attained a majority position. The defendants purported to conclude a contract with Canex for both the development of the mining properties and the issue to Canex of a sufficient number of Afton Mines Ltd. shares to frustrate the takeover by Teck. Teck sought a declaration that the directors had acted for an improper purpose and that, therefore, the shares could not be issued.]

Berger J.: — ...Now the whole case for the plaintiff is that the defendant directors were actuated by an improper motive, and that Canex knew it. That is the footing on which the case had proceeded.

There is no dispute that the directors had the power to manage the affairs of the company. Afton's articles of association contain the following provision regarding the powers and duties of the directors:

> The management of the business of the Company shall be vested in the directors, and the directors may exercise all such powers and do all such acts and things as the Company is, by its memorandum of association or otherwise, authorized to exercise and do, and are not hereby or by statute directed or required to be exercised or done by the Company in general meeting, but subject nevertheless to the provisions of the "Companies Act" and of these regulations, and to any regulations not being inconsistent with these regulations from time to time made by the Company in general meeting; PROVIDED that no such regulation shall invalidate any prior act of the directors which would have been valid if such regulation had not been made.

There is no dispute that under the articles of association the directors had the power to enter into the contract here, and no dispute that they had the power to allot shares pursuant to such a contract. The case alleged against them is that they were actuated by an improper purpose in the exercise of their powers. ...

Teck had the right, however, like any other shareholder, to challenge the exercise of any power by the directors on the ground that such power was being exercised for an improper purpose. This is not an allegation that the directors acted *ultra vires*, it is rather an allegation of abuse of power: Gower, *Principles of Modern Company Law*, 3rd ed. (1969), at p. 524.

The cases decided in the United Kingdom make it plain that directors, in the exercise of their powers, must act in what they bona fide consider to be the best interests of the company. If they issue shares to retain control for themselves, that is an improper purpose: *Fraser v. Whalley* (1864), 2 H. & M. 10, 71 E.R. 361; *Punt v. Symons & Co. Ltd.*, [1903] 2 Ch. 506; *Piercy v. S. Mills & Co. Ltd.*, [1920] 1 Ch. 77. The cases decided in Canada proceed on the same footing: *Madden et al.*

v. Dimond (1905), 12 B.C.R. 80 (Full Court); *Bonisteel v. Collis Leather Co. Ltd.*
(1919), 45 O.L.R. 195 (Ont. High Court); *Smith et al. v. Hanson Tire & Supply
Co. Ltd.*, [1927] 3 D.L.R. 786, 21 S.L.R. 621, [1927] 2 W.W.R. 529 (Sask. C.A.).

Now counsel for Teck does not accuse the defendant directors of a crass desire
merely to retain their directorships and their control of the company. Teck
acknowledges that the directors may well have considered it to be in the best
interests of the company that Teck's majority should be defeated. Even so, Teck
says, the purpose was not one countenanced by the law. Teck relies upon *Hogg v.
Cramphorn Ltd.*, [1967] Ch. 254, [1966] 3 W.L.R. 995, [1966] 3 All E.R. 420. In
that case the directors of Cramphorn Ltd. established a trust for the benefit of the
company's employees and allotted shares to the trust, nominating themselves as
trustees to enable them to purchase the shares, Buckley, J. (as he then was), found
that the directors had done so to ensure that a Mr. Baxter, who was seeking to
acquire control of the company, could not achieve a majority. Buckley, J., was
persuaded that the directors had acted in good faith, believing they were serving
the best interests of the company.

... Thus Buckley, J., takes the view that the directors have no right to exercise
their power to issue shares, in order to defeat an attempt to secure control of the
company; even if they consider that in doing so they are acting in the company's
best interests.

Counsel for Teck says the reasoning in *Hogg v. Cramphorn Ltd.*, *supra*, is
applicable in the case at bar. He says the defendant directors believed Teck would
use its dominant position to compel Afton to give Teck the ultimate deal. They
believed that under Teck's management the property would not be developed as
profitably as it would under Placer's management. They also believed that the
value of Afton's shares, including their own, would decline, under Teck's
management. Therefore, the argument goes, the defendant directors entered into
the contract with Canex so that shares would be allotted under the contract to
defeat Teck's majority. The case then is on all fours with *Hogg v. Cramphorn Ltd.*

Counsel for Teck says that *Hogg v. Cramphorn Ltd.* offers an elaboration of the
rule that directors may not issue shares for an improper purpose. If their purpose is
merely to retain control, that is improper. So much may be taken for granted.
Counsel then goes on to say that *Hogg v. Cramphorn Ltd.* lays it down that an
allotment of shares, and any transaction connected with it, made for the purpose of
defeating an attempt to secure a majority is improper, even if the directors
genuinely consider that it would be deleterious to the company if those seeking a
majority were to obtain control.

This, it seems to me, raises an issue of profound importance in company law.
Lord Greene, M.R., expressed the general rule in this way in *Re Smith & Fawcett,
Ltd.*, [1942] Ch. 304 at p. 306, [1942] 1 All E.R. 542: "They [the directors] must
exercise their discretion bona fide in what they consider — not what a court may
consider — is in the interests of the company, and not for any collateral purpose."
Yet, if *Hogg v. Cramphorn Ltd.*, *supra*, is right, directors may not allot shares to
frustrate an attempt to obtain control of the company, even if they believe that it is
in the best interests of the company to do so. This is inconsistent with the law as
laid down in *Re Smith & Fawcett Ltd.* How can it be said that directors have the
right to consider the interests of the company, and to exercise their powers
accordingly, but that there is an exception when it comes to the power to issue
shares, and that in the exercise of such power the directors cannot in any
circumstances issue shares to defeat an attempt to gain control of the company? It
seems to me that is what *Hogg v. Cramphorn Ltd.* says. If the general rule is to be

infringed here, will it not be infringed elsewhere? If the directors, even when they believe they are serving the best interests of the company, cannot issue shares to defeat an attempt to obtain control, then presumably they cannot exercise any other of their powers to defeat the claims of the majority or, for that matter, to deprive the majority of the advantages of control. I do not think the power to issue shares can be segregated, on the basis that the rule in *Hogg v. Cramphorn Ltd.* applies only in a case of an allotment of shares.

Neither can it be distinguished on the footing that the power to issue shares affects the rights of the shareholders in some way that the exercise of other powers does not. The Court's jurisdiction to intervene is founded on the theory that if the directors' purpose is not to serve the interest of the company, but to serve their own interest or that of their friends or of a particular group of shareholders, they can be said to have abused their power. The impropriety lies in the directors' purpose. If their purpose is not to serve the company's interest, then it is an improper purpose. Impropriety depends upon proof that the directors were actuated by a collateral purpose, it does not depend upon the nature of any shareholders' rights that may be affected by the exercise of the directors' powers.

Should *Hogg v. Cramphorn Ltd.* be followed? Counsel for Teck says that in *Bamford v. Bamford*, [1970] Ch. 212, the English Court of Appeal approved *Hogg v. Cramphorn Ltd.* Indeed the headnote says that *Hogg v. Cramphorn Ltd.* is approved. However, an examination of the judgments of the three Judges who sat on the case indicates that only Harman, L.J., referred to *Hogg v. Cramphorn Ltd.* I suppose it may be said that he approved it. But there was nothing in the judgment of Russell, L.J. (who delivered a reasoned judgment), about *Hogg v. Cramphorn Ltd.* Karminski, L.J., simply agreed and added nothing. In any event, the *ratio decidendi* of *Bamford v. Bamford* relates to quite a different point. There, allegedly improper acts of the directors were afterwards ratified by a meeting of the shareholders. The issue was whether the shareholders could waive the defect when the directors wrongly exercised one of their powers from an improper motive. The Court of Appeal held they could.

In Canada there is authority on both sides of the question: in *Bonisteel v. Collis Leather Co. Ltd.* (1919), 45 O.L.R. 195, Rose, J., anticipated *Hogg v. Cramphorn Ltd.* He said at p. 199:

> Upon the evidence there is no doubt at all that the purpose of the defendant directors in all that they did was to deprive the plaintiff of the controlling position which he had acquired. No doubt they thought that it was not in the best interest of the company that he should control its affairs, and, in that sense, they acted in good faith and in what they believed to be the best interest of the company; but, nevertheless, I think that what they attempted to do was exactly what *Martin v. Gibson* (1907), 15 O.L.R. 623, shews that directors have no right to do: they were making a one-sided allotment of stock with a view to the control of the voting power...

On the other hand, Harvey, C.J.A., in *Spooner v. Spooner Oils Ltd.*, [1936] 2 D.L.R. 634 at pp. 635-6, [1936] 1 W.W.R. 561, said quite the opposite:

> The cases cited and relied on by the plaintiff on this branch of the case merely establish that when an issue of shares by the directors for the purpose of giving control cannot be deemed to be intended to be in the interest of the shareholders generally but on the contrary appears to be intended to accomplish some other purpose, then it constitutes a breach of trust on the part of the directors who occupy a fiduciary position in which they must act bona fide for the interests of the general body of shareholders. It is simply an instance of the acts of the directors being at

variance with this duty. There is nothing in the authorities cited that would stand in the way of ... giving someone control of the company if the directors honestly believed on reasonable grounds that it was for the interest of the company that should be done.

The classical theory is that the directors' duty is to the company. The company's shareholders are the company: Boyd, C., in *Martin v. Gibson* (1907), 15 O.L.R. 623, and therefore no interests outside those of the shareholders can legitimately be considered by the directors. But even accepting that, what comes within the definition of the interests of the shareholders? By what standards are the shareholders' interests to be measured?

In defining the fiduciary duties of directors, the law ought to take into account the fact that the corporation provides the legal framework for the development of resources and the generation of wealth in the private sector of the Canadian economy: Bull, J.A., in *Peso Silver Mines Ltd. v. Cropper* (1966), 56 D.L.R. (2d) 117 at pp. 154-5, 54 W.W.R. 329 (B.C.C.A.); affirmed 58 D.L.R. (2d) 1, [1966] S.C.R. 673, 56 W.W.R. 641.

> ... the corporation has become almost the unit of organization of our economic life. Whether for good or ill, the stubborn fact is that in our present system the corporation carries on the bulk of production and transportation, is the chief employer of both labour and capital, pays a large part of our taxes, and is an economic institution of such magnitude and importance that there is no present substitute for it except the State itself.

Jackson, J. in *State Tax Commission v. Aldrich* (1942), 316 U.S. 174 at p. 192.

A classical theory that once was unchallengeable must yield to the facts of modern life. In fact, of course, it has. If today the directors of a company were to consider the interests of its employees no one would argue that in doing so they were not acting bona fide in the interests of the company itself. Similarly, if the directors were to consider the consequences to the community of any policy that the company intended to pursue, and were deflected in their commitment to that policy as a result, it could not be said that they had not considered bona fide the interests of the shareholders.

I appreciate that it would be a breach of their duty for directors to disregard entirely the interests of a company's shareholders in order to confer a benefit on its employees: *Parke v. Daily News Ltd.*, [1962] Ch. 927. But if they observe a decent respect for other interests lying beyond those of the company's shareholders in the strict sense, that will not, in my view, leave directors open to the charge that they have failed in their fiduciary duty to the company. In this regard, I cannot accept the view expressed by Professor E.E. Palmer in *Studies in Canadian Company Law*, c. 12, "Directors Power and Duties", pp. 371-2.

So how wide a latitude ought the directors to have? If a group is seeking to obtain control, must the directors ignore them? Or are they entitled to consider the consequences of such a group taking over? In *Savoy Corp. Ltd. v. Development Underwriting Ltd.* (1963), N.S.W.R. 138 at p. 147, Jacobs, J., said:

> It would seem to me to be unreal in the light of the structure of modern companies and of modern business life to take the view that directors should in no way concern themselves with the infiltration of the company by persons or groups which they bona fide consider not to be seeking the best interests of the company.

My own view is that the directors ought to be allowed to consider who is seeking control and why. If they believe that there will be substantial damage to the company's interests if the company is taken over, then the exercise of their powers to defeat those seeking a majority will not necessarily be categorized as improper.

I do not think it is sound to limit the directors' exercise of their powers to the extent required by *Hogg v. Cramphorn Ltd.*, [1967] Ch. 254, [1966] 3 W.L.R. 995, [1966] 3 All E.R. 420. But the limits of their authority must be clearly defined. It would be altogether a mistake if the law, in seeking to adapt itself to the reality of corporate struggles, were to allow the directors any opportunity of achieving an advantage for themselves at the expense of the shareholders. The thrust of companies legislation has brought us a long way since *Percival v. Wright*, [1902] 2 Ch. 421.

If the directors have the right to consider the consequences of a takeover, and to exercise their powers to meet it, if they do so bona fide in the interests of the company, how is the Court to determine their purpose? In every case the directors will insist their whole purpose was to serve the company's interest. And no doubt in most cases it will not be difficult for the directors to persuade themselves that it is in the company's best interests that they should remain in office. Something more than a mere assertion of good faith is required.

How can the Court go about determining whether the directors have abused their powers in a given case? How are the Courts to know, in an appropriate case, that the directors were genuinely concerned about the company and not merely pursuing their own selfish interests? Well, a similar task has been attempted in cases of conspiracy to injure. There the question is whether the primary object of those alleged to have acted in combination is to promote their own interests or to damage the interests of others: *Crofter Hand Woven Harris Tweed Co. v. Veitch*, [1942] A.C. 435.

I think the Courts should apply the general rule in this way: The directors must act in good faith. Then there must be reasonable grounds for their belief. If they say that they believe there will be substantial damage to the company's interests, then there must be reasonable grounds for that belief. If there are not, that will justify a finding that the directors were actuated by an improper purpose. ...

I think that Millar's position is one that can be understood. He was considering bringing the project through to the completion of feasibility, and he told all of the majors that approached him that he intended to. ...

The plaintiff relies on Millar's statement, made at Kamloops on May 27th, that Price was running around trying to dilute Teck down. I accept the evidence that Millar made the statement. It reveals he was aware that Teck was concerned that if Afton signed a contract providing for the issuance of shares, Teck's position would be jeopardized. It shows that Millar was well aware that Teck's whole purpose would be frustrated if further shares were issued pursuant to a contract. But does that mean that was Millar's purpose, to dilute Teck's share interest? Or was his purpose to sign a contract that he considered to be in the best interests of the company? Millar, after all, said he did not think he approved of what Price was doing and then he laughed. I do not think this establishes any Machiavellian intent on Millar's part. ... Does it show that Millar was primarily actuated by a desire to frustrate Teck's attempt to gain control? Millar gave evidence that he was by that time resigned to Teck obtaining control. He did not think he could prevent that. Indeed he could not. Teck did obtain its majority. It now controls the company. I do not think the evidence shows that Millar was willing to make any deal so long as it would lead to the issuance of shares in sufficient numbers to frustrate Teck. ...

So it is necessary, then, to disentangle the directors' primary motive or purpose from subsidiary ones. I do not think it is necessary to distinguish motive, purpose or object. The question is, what was it the directors had uppermost in their minds?

The plaintiff's case comes down to this: Counsel says that Millar and Price were wary of Teck, that they were afraid once Teck got control, the possibility of a deal with Placer would be gone, that Teck might very well force a disadvantageous contract upon Afton, that the mining property would not be developed as profitably as they thought it would be under Placer's management. So, he says — and this is the key to the plaintiff's case — the directors made the contract with Placer, their purpose being to secure the issuance of the shares to Canex, and the defeat of Teck's majority position. ...

I find their object was to obtain the best agreement they could while they were still in control. Their purpose in that sense was to defeat Teck. But, not to defeat Teck's attempt to obtain control, rather it was to foreclose Teck's opportunity of obtaining for itself the ultimate deal. That was, as I view the law, no improper purpose. In seeking to prevent Teck obtaining the contract, the defendant directors were honestly pursuing what they thought was the best policy for the company. ...

Now Teck, of course, was a shareholder. And it is said that it was no part of Millar's purpose to protect Teck's interests. I think it is fair to say that Millar's primary purpose was to make the most advantageous deal he could for Afton. That is as far as the Court ought to go in seeking to analyze his motivation. And, in my view, in trying to make the best deal he could for Afton. Millar was acting in the best interests of the general body of shareholders, including Teck, because once Teck's interest in acquiring control is put to one side, its interest, like that of the other shareholders, was in seeing Afton make the best deal available. I find Millar's purpose was to serve that interest.

The defendant directors were elected to exercise their best judgment. They were not agents bound to accede to the directions of the majority of the shareholders. Their mandate continued so long as they remained in office. They were in no sense a lame duck board. So they acted in what they conceived to be the best interests of the shareholders, and signed a contract which they knew the largest shareholder, holding a majority of the shares, did not want them to sign. They had the right in law to do that. When a company elects its board of directors and entrusts them with the power to manage the company, the directors are entitled to manage it. But they must not exercise their powers for an extraneous purpose. That is a breach of their duty. At the same time, the shareholders have no right to alter the terms of the directors' mandate except by amendment of the articles or by replacing the directors themselves.

The purpose of the directors in their negotiations with Placer was from the beginning a legitimate one. The purpose was to make a favourable deal for Afton. That purpose continued throughout. Did it become an improper purpose because Teck acquired large shareholdings? Did it become an improper purpose because the directors made a deal with Canex knowing that they had to before Teck acquired the power to stop them? I think on the evidence the answer must be no.

The onus of proof is on the plaintiff: see *Australian Metropolitan Life v. Ure* (1923), A.L.J.R. 199 at p. 219, Isaacs, J. Applying what I conceive to be the proper test for determining whether the defendant directors acted in good faith within the meaning of *Re Smith & Fawcett, Ltd.*, [1942] Ch. 304, the plaintiff has failed to show the directors had no reasonable grounds for believing that a takeover by Teck would cause substantial damage to the interests of Afton and its shareholders. Indeed, I am satisfied that it has been affirmatively shown that the directors did have reasonable grounds for such belief.

I find here that the directors had a sufficient knowledge of Teck's reputation, its technical and managerial capacity, and its previous experience, to consider the consequences of a takeover. They decided to make a deal with Placer while they still had the power to do so. They wanted to see the company's principal asset, its copper property, developed efficiently and profitably. They believed, and they had reasonable grounds for such belief, that the property would not be developed efficiently and profitably for the benefit of the shareholders, if Teck got control of it.

If I am wrong in rejecting *Hogg v. Cramphorn Ltd.*, [1967] Ch. 254, [1966] 3 W.L.R. 955, [1966] 3 All E.R. 420, it is not applicable here in any event. In *Hogg v. Cramphorn Ltd.* the primary purpose of the directors was to frustrate an attempt to obtain control of the company. In the case at bar the primary purpose of the directors was to make the best contract they could for Afton. I find that the primary purpose of the directors was to serve the best interests of the company. Their primary purpose was to see that the ultimate deal the company made was a deal with Placer, not Teck. They were not motivated by a desire to retain control of the company. They may have thought the issuance of shares under the contract with Canex would enable them, if they had Canex's support, to regain control from Teck. If they did, that was a subsidiary purpose. On any view of the law, therefore, no allegation of improper purpose can be sustained against the defendant directors. ...

[Teck withdrew a proposed appeal in this case in consideration of the assignment to Teck, for four million dollars, of Canex's rights under the contract with Afton Mines, Ltd.]

NOTES AND QUESTIONS

1. Was Berger J. applying the "proper purpose" doctrine or was he saying that the directors have an obligation to exercise their powers in the best interest of the corporation? Does the fact that the directors were thwarting the desires of the incumbent shareholder majority have any relevance to either proper purpose or the best interest of the corporation? Is it possible to distinguish a primary purpose from purposes that are not primary?

2. Why must the directors have reasonable grounds for their belief that they were acting in the corporate best interests? Is this really a legal requirement or is it merely a suggestion that judges, being human, are unlikely to believe stories that stray too far from their own biases and cultural norms? See *Olson v. Phoenix Industrial Supply Ltd.*, [1984] M.J. No. 113, 9 D.L.R. (4th) 451 (C.A.) at p. 455:

    The onus was upon [the plaintiff] to prove that the directors did not act in good faith. He has failed to do so. The evidence is overwhelming that the directors believed that their actions... were in the best interests of the company ... and that there were reasonable grounds for their belief.

3. Most Canadian jurisdictions now have sections like C.B.C.A., s. 25(1), saying:

    Subject to the articles, the by-laws and any unanimous shareholder agreement and to section 28 [a special section dealing with pre-emptive rights if provided in the articles], shares may be issued at such times and to such persons and for such consideration as the directors may determine.

In assessing the limits on the scope of this particular power, which judicial analysis do you find more helpful? Does C.B.C.A., s. 122(1)(*a*) (or any equivalent provincial section) influence your decision?

4.   The same issue came up in a New South Wales case, *Howard Smith Ltd. v. Ampol Petroleum Ltd.*, [1974] A.C. 821, [1974] 1 All E.R. 1125 (P.C.). Ampol made a takeover bid which was resisted by the target company's management. After Ampol had acquired 55 per cent of the outstanding shares, a sufficient number of shares were issued to reduce Ampol's holding to a minority position. Once again, the only relevant article of association was functionally identical to C.B.C.A., s. 25(1), yet the judges invalidated the share issue. Lord Wilberforce said, for the Board (at p. 835 [A.C.]):

> ... it is, in their Lordships' opinion, too narrow an approach to say that the only valid purpose for which shares may be issued is to raise capital for the company. The discretion is not in terms limited in this way: the law should not impose such a limitation on directors' powers. To define in advance exact limits beyond which directors must not pass is, in their Lordships' view, impossible. This clearly cannot be done by enumeration, since the variety of situations facing directors of different types of company in different situations cannot be anticipated. ...
>
> It is necessary to start with a consideration of the power whose exercise is in question, in this case a power to issue shares. Having ascertained, on a fair view, the nature of this power, and having defined as can best be done in the light of modern conditions the, or some, limits within which it may be exercised, it is then necessary for the court, if a particular exercise of it is challenged, to examine the substantial purpose for which it was exercised, and to reach a conclusion whether that purpose was proper or not. In doing so it will necessarily give credit to the bona fide opinion of the directors, if such is found to exist, and will respect their judgment as to matters of management; having done this, the ultimate conclusion has to be as to the side of a fairly broad line on which the case falls.

So far, so good. He continued (at p. 837 [A.C.]):

> The constitution of a limited company normally provides for directors, with powers of management, and shareholders, with defined voting powers having power to appoint the directors, and to take, in general meeting, by majority vote, decisions on matters not reserved for management. Just as it is established that directors, within their management powers, may take decisions against the wishes of the majority of shareholders, and indeed that the majority of shareholders cannot control them in the exercise of these powers while they remain in office (*Automatic Self Cleaning Filter Syndicate Co. Ltd. v. Cunninghame*, [1906] 2 Ch. 34 (Eng. C.A.)), so it must be unconstitutional for directors to use their fiduciary powers over the shares in the company purely for the purpose of destroying an existing majority, or creating a new majority which did not previously exist. To do so is to interfere with that element of the company's constitution which is separate from and set against their powers.

Does this seem correct to you?

5.   The cases above all deal with the directors' power to issue shares in the context of a battle for control. We shall return to takeover bids later in this chapter, but for the role of directors in planning strategies to deal with take over bids generally see F. Iacobucci,

"Planning and Implementing Defences to takeover Bids: The Director's Role" (1981), 5 C.B.L.J. 131; F.H Easterbrook and D.R. Fischel, "The Proper Role of a Target's Management in Responding to a Tender Offer" (1982), 94 Harv. L.R. 1161. Meanwhile, it should be stressed that the same principles apply when interpreting any specifically limited power in the hands of corporate managers. Is every power held by directors limited in respect to purpose? In *Lee Panavision Ltd. v. Lee Lighting Ltd.*, [1992] B.C.L.C. 22 (Eng. C.A.), the directors proposed to renew a long-term management contract between the company and another company when the directors knew that they were about to be deposed by the shareholders. How would this be resolved under *Teck?* Dillon L.J. said:

> To my mind the crucial question is whether, in the circumstances trenchantly summarised by the judge, it was within the directors' powers at all to commit Lee Lighting to the second management agreement, however much they may have thought it in that company's best interests, as well as Panavision's, to thwart the intention of the 100 per cent shareholders. ... The function of the directors is to manage, but the appointment of the directors who are to do the managing is constitutionally a function of the shareholders in general meeting. Therefore it must have been unconstitutional for the directors, knowing ... that the shareholders were proposing as soon as they could to exercise their constiutional right to appoint new directors, to take all managerial powers away from any new directors who might be appointed by committing Lee Lighting to the second management agreement and giving exclusive managerial power to Panavision over the possibly crucial period until the end of April 1992.

Is this logic sound? By the time you reach the end of this chapter, see if you can come up with a better explanation for the non-enforceability of such an agreement.

6. Is it possible to examine the validity of any board decision (or perhaps any corporate decision) by the following process? First, we must determine whether the board had the legal power to make the decision under the corporate constitution; if the answer is "no," the decision is a nullity. If the answer is "yes," one then asks whether the decision was made loyally; if the answer is "no," the decision is voidable, and if the answer is "yes," it is fully effective. See *Zapata Corp. v. Maldonado*, 430 A.2d 779 (Del. 1981); *Unocal Corp. v. Mesa Petroleum*, 493 A.2d 946 (Del. 1985); *Moran v. Household International Inc.*, 500 A.2d 1346 (Del. 1985). See also S. Worthington, "Corporate Governance: Remedying and Ratifying Directors' Breaches" (2000), 116 L.Q.R. 683, at p. 643, adding the question that is logically prior to both of those: did the corporation have capacity to do the act? This is usually a non-issue in Canada.

3. Conflict of Interest and Duty: Interests in Corporate Contracts

A corporate body can only act by agents, and it is, of course, the duty of those agents so to act as best to promote the interests of the corporation whose affairs they are conducting. Such an agent has duties to discharge of a fiduciary character towards his principal, and it is a rule of universal application that no one having such duties to discharge shall be allowed to enter into engagements in which he has or can have a personal interest conflicting or which possibly may conflict with the interests of those whom he is bound to protect. So strictly is this principle adhered to that no question is allowed to be raised as to the fairness or unfairness of a contract so entered into. It obviously is, or may be, impossible to demonstrate how far in any particular case the terms of such a contract have been the best for the *cestui que trust* [the beneficiary] which it was impossible to obtain. It may sometimes happen that the terms on which a trustee has dealt or attempted to deal with the estate or interests of those for whom he is a trustee have been as good as could have been obtained from any other person; they may even at the time have been better. But still so inflexible is the rule that no inquiry on that subject is permitted... [*Aberdeen Railway Co. v. Blaikie Bros.* (1854), 1 Macq. 461, [1843-60] All E.R. Rep 249 at pp. 252-53 (Scot. H.L.), *per* Lord Cranworth L.C.].

This broad statement of the no-conflict rule illustrates not only the traditional strictness of the rule, but also its paradox. In order to protect the duty to act in the beneficiary's best interests, we forbid conflicts; and if there is a conflict, the fiduciary is not even allowed to try to prove that he was, in fact, acting in the best interests of the beneficiary. The prophylactic rule is stricter than the underlying duty that it seeks to protect. Some scholars question the traditional strictness of the rule, arguing that it is partly founded on difficulties of proof that may no longer exist: J. Langbein, "Questioning the Trust Law Duty of Loyalty: Sole Interest or Best Interest?" (2005), 114 Yale L.J. 929.

The no-conflict rule is inevitably triggered where a corporation's manager is somehow involved on the other side of a contract that the corporation has made. In such a case, there must always be a question whether the manager will bargain to the full extent of his abilities on the corporation's behalf. There is at least the appearance or the possibility of a conflict between self-interest and duty to the corporation. The traditional solution is simple: such contracts are voidable by the corporation, absent corporate authorization to deal notwithstanding the conflict, given with full and frank disclosure by the fiduciary. However, early misconceptions about the nature of corporate personality muddied the waters. The following case illustrates the problem and facilitates understanding of the Canadian statutory reforms.

NORTH-WEST TRANSPORTATION CO. v. BEATTY

(1887), 12 App. Cas. 589 (Ont. J.C.P.C.)

Sir Richard Baggally: — The action, in which this appeal has been brought, was commenced on the 31st of May, 1883, in the Chancery Division of the High Court of Justice of Ontario. The plaintiff here, Henry Beatty, is a shareholder in the North-West Transportation Company, Limited, and he sues on behalf of himself and all other shareholders in the company, except those who are defendants. The defendants are the company and five shareholders, who, at the commencement of the action, were the directors of the company. The claim in the action is to set aside a sale made to the company by James Hughes Beatty, one of the directors, of a steamer called the United Empire, of which previously to such sale he was sole owner.

The general principles applicable to cases of this kind are well established. Unless some provision to the contrary is to be found in the charter or other instrument by which the company is incorporated, the resolution of a majority of the shareholders, duly convened, upon any question with which the company is legally competent to deal, is binding upon the minority, and consequently upon the company, and every shareholder has a perfect right to vote upon any such question, although he may have a personal interest in the subject-matter opposed to, or different from, the general or particular interests of the company.

On the other hand, a director of a company is precluded from dealing, on behalf of the company, with himself, and from entering into engagements in which he has a personal interest conflicting, or which possibly may conflict, with the interests of those whom he is bound by fiduciary duty to protect; and this rule is as applicable to the case of one of several directors as to a managing or sole director. Any such dealing or engagement may, however, be affirmed or adopted by the company, provided such affirmance or adoption is not brought about by unfair or improper means, and is not illegal or fraudulent or oppressive towards those shareholders who oppose it. ...

At a meeting of the directors held on the 10th of February, 1883, and at which all the directors except the defendant William Beatty were present, it was resolved that a by-law, which was read to the meeting, for the purchase of the United Empire should pass. It is unnecessary to refer in detail to the terms in which this by-law was expressed; it is sufficient to state that, after reciting an agreement between the company and the defendant James Hughes Beatty, that the company should buy and the defendant should sell the steamer United Empire for the sum of $125,000, to be in part paid in cash and in part secured, as therein mentioned, it was enacted that the company should purchase the steamer from the defendant upon those terms, with various directions for giving effect to the terms of the contract.

The agreement recited in the by-law was executed at the same meeting.

At a meeting of shareholders, held, as arranged, on the 16th of February, 1883, the by-law which had been enacted by the directors was read by the secretary, and, after being modified in its terms, with respect to the price, was adopted by a majority of votes.

The United Empire, on her completion, was delivered to the company, and has ever since been employed in the ordinary business of the company.

It is proved by uncontradicted evidence, and is indeed now substantially admitted, that at the date of the purchase the acquisition of another steamer to supply the place of the Asia was essential to the efficient conduct of the company's business; that the United Empire was well adapted for that purpose; that it was not within the power of the company to acquire any other steamer equally well adapted for its business; and that the price agreed to be paid for the steamer was not excessive or unreasonable.

Had there been no material facts in the case other than those above stated, there would have been, in the opinion of their Lordships, no reason for setting aside the sale of the steamer; it would have been immaterial to consider whether the contract for the purchase of the United Empire should be regarded as one entered into by the directors and confirmed by the shareholders, or as one entirely emanating from the shareholders; in either view of the case, the transaction was one which, if carried out in a regular way, was within the powers of the company; in the former view, any defect arising from the fiduciary relationship of the defendant James Hughes Beatty to the company would be remedied by the resolution of the shareholders, on the 16th of February, and, in the latter, the fact of the defendant being a director would not deprive him of his right to vote, as a shareholder, in support of any resolution which he might deem favourable to his own interests.

There is, however, a further element for consideration, arising out of the following facts, which have been relied upon in the arguments on behalf of the plaintiff, as evidencing that the resolution of the 16th of February was brought about by unfair and improper means.

[At the shareholder meeting of 16 February, the by-law was approved by the shareholders by a vote of 306 to 289. Of the 306 votes in favour, 291 were cast by J.H. Beatty.]

It is clear upon the authorities that the contract entered into by the directors on the 10th of February could not have been enforced against the company at the instance of the defendant J.H. Beatty, but it is equally clear that it was within the competency of the shareholders at the meeting of the 16th to adopt or reject it. In form and in terms they adopted it by a majority of votes, and vote of the majority must prevail, unless the adoption was brought about by unfair or improper means.

The only unfairness or impropriety which, consistently with the admitted and established facts, could be suggested, arises out of the fact that the defendant J.H. Beatty possessed a voting power as a shareholder which enabled him, and those who thought with him, to adopt the by-law and thereby either to ratify and adopt a voidable contract, into which he, as a director, and his co-directors had entered, or to make a similar contract, which latter seems to have been what was intended to be done by the resolution passed on the 7th of February.

But the construction of the company enabled the defendant J. H. Beatty to acquire this voting power; there was no limit upon the number of shares which a shareholder might hold, and for every share so held he was entitled to a vote, the charter itself recognised the defendant as a holder of 200 shares, one-third of the aggregate number; he had a perfect right to acquire further shares, and to exercise his voting power in such a manner as to secure the election of directors whose views upon policy agreed with his own, and to support those views at any shareholders' meeting; the acquisition of the United Empire was a pure question of policy, as to which it might be expected that there would be differences of opinion, and upon which the voice of the majority ought to prevail; to reject the votes of the defendant upon the question of the adoption of the by-law would be to give effect to the views of the minority and to disregard those of the majority.

The judges of the Supreme Court appear to have regarded the exercise by the defendant J.H. Beatty of his voting power as of so oppressive a character as to invalidate the adoption of the by-law; their Lordships are unable to adopt this view; in their opinion the defendant was acting within his rights in voting as he did, though they agree with the Chief Justice in the views expressed by him in the Court of Appeal, that the matter might have been conducted in a manner less likely to give rise to objection.

Their Lordships will humbly advise Her Majesty to allow the appeal; to discharge the order of the Supreme Court of Canada; and to dismiss the appeal to that Court with costs; the respondent must bear the costs of the present appeal.

NOTES AND QUESTIONS

1. The Judicial Committee accepted that the breach of duty could be forgiven by majority vote of the shareholders. Do you agree? To whom was the fiduciary obligation owed? Did that person wish to "ratify" the breach? How would one ascertain if that person wanted to, or had done so? This notion of "ratification" is not as straightforward as the Judicial Committee made it seem. The concept is dealt with in detail below, in Section D.7.

2. In *Burland v. Earle*, [1902] A.C. 83 (Ont. J.C.P.C.), a director and officer acquired certain assets and then immediately sold them to the corporation at a substantial personal profit. The Ontario Court of Appeal ((1900), 27 O.A.R. 540) ordered him to account for the profit, saying that only a *unanimous* shareholder vote, following full disclosure, would have allowed him to keep it (at p. 561). The Judicial Committee held that because Burland had not been commissioned by the company to buy the assets for the company, he could do what he wanted with them. This seems to miss the point, that it was the sale to the corporation that created the problem. As to that, the Judicial Committee seemed to hold (at p. 99) that while the corporation might

have demanded that the contract be avoided, it could not affirm the contract and still demand that Burland account for his profit. Although the case is often cited for certain general propositions, the holding as to Burland's profit must now be considered out of date. It is inconsistent with the other cases in this area. In *Canada Safeway Ltd. v. Thompson*, [1951] 3 D.L.R. 295 (B.C.S.C.), the Court preferred the Ontario Court of Appeal's decision in *Burland* to that of the Judicial Committee.

3. In *Holder v. Holder*, [1968] Ch. 353, [1968] 1 All E.R. 665 (C.A.), the propriety of the defendant executor's purchase of one of the deceased's assets, a fee simple in a farm, was questioned. As executor, he was a trustee of the property and owed a fiduciary obligation to the beneficiaries. On the facts of the case, it was clear that he had acquired all his knowledge about the farm by virtue of occupying it as a tenant, and not because of his position as executor. Additionally, it was clear that the beneficiaries did not depend upon him to protect their interest in the farm. Citing particularly the latter point, the Court of Appeal held that the principal reason for the strict rule, the potential for abuse of power, did not exist in this situation and that, therefore, the rule should not be applied. Alternatively, if there was a breach, the court held that the beneficiaries had acquiesced in it. Could the same have been said if there had been an independent board decision in *North-West Transportation v. Beatty*? Could the corporation have upheld the contract, but effectively lowered the selling price to Mr. Beatty's cost by requiring him to account for his profit?

Canadian statutory reform of this unsatisfactory situation began in the 1970s and is now common. It has proceeded on the basis that conflict of interest situations are inevitable and that the real problem is what to do about the voidable contracts that result from them. The usual solution is to legislate a routine procedure by which individuals and groups within the corporate organization can dispose of the problem in most situations. The appropriate procedure is prescribed by C.B.C.A. and A.B.C.A., s. 120, S.B.C.A. and M.C.A., s. 115, B.C.B.C.A., ss. 147-153, and O.B.C.A., s. 132(7). See also Civil Code of Québec, arts. 325-326.

Section 120 of the C.B.C.A. requires a director or officer who is a party to a material or proposed contract or transaction to disclose the nature and extent of his interest as soon as possible and to refrain from voting on any resolution to approve the contract. Subsection (7) provides that such contracts become non-voidable, and the conflicted director is not accountable, so long as disclosure was made appropriately, the (non-conflicted) directors approved the transaction, *and* it was reasonable and fair. Even if subs. (7) is not satisfied, the recently-added subs. (7.1) allows shareholder approval by a special resolution, again subject to the requirement of fairness and reasonableness. If any part of s. 120 has not been complied with, then under subs. (8) the Court, on an application by the corporation or a shareholder, may set aside the contract on terms that it thinks fit. This is a minority protection remedy that is specific to conflict of interest transactions.

In a situation identical to *North-West Transportation v. Beatty*, could the contract be rendered non-voidable under the C.B.C.A.? What about under your provincial statute? If not, what additional steps would have been necessary?

Note the statutory requirement that the contract be "reasonable and fair to the corporation". Normally the fairness or otherwise of the contracts a corporation makes is purely a matter for the corporation. Think about the consequences of this: assume that all of the steps mandated by s. 120 have been followed to the letter, and every director and every shareholder approves. Does a person who buys one share have standing under s.-s. (8) to argue that the contract should be set aside because it was fair but unreasonable (or reasonable but unfair) at the time it was made?

Note that only "material" contracts or transactions are covered by the statutory procedure. What does "material" mean? What about a non-material contract: is it non-voidable by statutory inference?

The C.B.C.A. and many provincial statutes provide that if the contract is made non-voidable it is also the case that the fiduciary is not accountable for any profit made on the contract. This also appears to be the law under the Civil Code of Quebec, arts. 325-326. Is it possible, under those statutes, for the corporation to uphold the contract, but require an accounting? What is the situation under the other reformed statutes, such as the M.C.A.?

NOTES AND QUESTIONS

1. Did you notice that a director *can* vote on certain contracts in which he or she has an interest in those situations governed by C.B.C.A., s. 120(5)? What could be the justification for s. 120(5)(*a*)?

2. We have seen that C.B.C.A., s. 120 and related provisions are built on the idea of disclosure. It is a general principle that a director may solve a problem of conflict of interest and duty by getting the informed consent to the conflict of the person to whom the fiduciary duty is owed. Where there is a statutory provision like s. 120, it may regulate disclosure, but in other situations (like those discussed in the next section) the general equitable principles govern. In *Gray v. New Augarita Porcupine Mines*, [1952] 3 D.L.R. 1, the Judicial Committee of the Privy Council had this to say about the details that must be revealed if disclosure is to occur.

    > There is no precise formula that will determine the extent of detail that is called for when a director declares his interest or the nature of his interest. Rightly understood, the two things mean the same. The amount of detail required must depend in each case upon the nature of the contract or arrangement proposed and the context in which it arises. It can rarely be enough for a director to say "I must remind you that I am interested" and to leave it at that, unless there is some special provision in a company's articles that makes such a general warning sufficient. His declaration must make his colleagues "fully informed of the real state of things" (see *Imperial Mercantile Credit Assn. v. Coleman* (1873), L.R. 6 H.L. 189 at p. 201, per Lord Chelmsford). If it is material to their judgment that they should know not merely that he has an interest, but what it is and how far it goes, then he must see to it that they are informed (see Lord Cairns in the same case at p. 205) [per Lord Radcliffe at p. 14].

    Note also that disclosure which will make the contract non-voidable does not relieve the manager of his or her ongoing fiduciary obligations: see *Levy-Russel Ltd. v. Tecmotiv Inc.*, [1994] O.J. No. 650, 13 B.L.R. (2d) 1 (H.C.).

4. Corporate Opportunities

Conflicts can arise in situations other than those covered in the previous situation. A director or officer who profits out of a conflict between self-interest and fiduciary duty to the corporation is liable to give up those profits. When is there a conflict? Recall the wide statement of the fiduciary's obligation in *Aberdeen Railway Co. v. Blaikie Brothers* (1854), 1 Macq. 461, [1843-60] All E.R. Rep 249

(Scot. H.L.), above at p. 349-50; a similar statement, and an attempt to justify the rule, is that of Lord Herschell in *Bray v. Ford*, [1896] A.C. 44 at p. 51 (H.L.). The context is that a governor of a college was also employed as its solicitor, and charged his usual scale of fees for that work.

> It is an inflexible rule of the court of equity that a person in a fiduciary position, such as the plaintiff's, is not, unless otherwise expressly provided, entitled to make a profit; he is not allowed to put himself in a position where his interests and duty conflict. It does not appear to me that this rule is, as has been said, founded upon principles of morality. I regard it rather as based on the consideration that, human nature being what it is, there is danger, in such circumstances, of the person holding a fiduciary position being swayed by interest rather than by duty, and thus prejudicing those whom he was bound to protect. It has, therefore, been deemed expedient to lay down this positive rule. But I am satisfied that it might be departed from in many cases, without any breach of morality, without any wrong being inflicted, and without any consciousness of wrong-doing. Indeed, it is obvious that it might sometimes be to the advantage of the beneficiaries that their trustee should act for them professionally rather than a stranger, even though the trustee were paid for his services.

This clearly covers the case of managers who are interested in corporate contracts, but the principle can cover other situations as well. For example, in *Cook v. Deeks*, [1916] 1 A.C. 554 (Ont. J.C.P.C.), a corporation had four shareholders and the same four men were its directors. The corporation's business was railway construction for the C.P.R. There was a falling-out between one of the four men, who later became the plaintiff, and the other three, who became the defendants. The defendants decided to exclude the plaintiff from further railway construction profits. They accelerated the work on an expiring contract between the corporation and the C.P.R. in order to stand well with the C.P.R. when the next contract was tendered, knowing that efficient work in the past had gained the corporation C.P.R. contracts even when it had not submitted the lowest tender. They negotiated with C.P.R. for the next contract exactly as they had in the past, but when the contract was offered the defendants proposed that they carry out the contract through a new corporation, Dominion Construction Company. C.P.R. agreed, thus excluding the corporation from the contract. No doubt influenced by cases like *North-West Transportation Co. v. Beatty*, the defendants held a shareholder meeting of the corporation at which it was resolved that the corporation had no interest in the contract that had been awarded to the Dominion Construction Company. Even so, the plaintiff's action was successful.

The Judicial Committee, speaking through Lord Buckmaster L.C., first held that the defendants breached their fiduciary duties to the corporation. It said (at p. 563):

> It is quite right to point out the importance of avoiding the establishment of rules as to directors' duties which would impose upon them burdens so heavy and responsibilities so great that men of good position would hesitate to accept the office. But, on the other hand, men who assume the complete control of a company's business must remember that they are not at liberty to sacrifice the interests which they are bound to protect, and, while ostensibly acting for the company, divert in their own favour business which should properly belong to the company they represent.

> Their Lordships think that, in the circumstances, the defendants T.R. Hinds and G.S. and G.M. Deeks were guilty of a distinct breach of duty in the course they took

to secure the contract, and that they cannot retain the benefit of such contract for themselves, but must be regarded as holding it on behalf of the company.

This is a clear and obvious conflict of interest situation, but not one in which the directors made any kind of contract with their own corporation. Rather, they intercepted an opportunity that they should have got for their corporation, and instead got it for themselves. (In fact, they got it for the Dominion Construction Co., but that was in their own self-interest, and in any event, as we shall see, the law is just as stern in the case of disloyalty for the benefit of a third party as it is the case of disloyalty for one's own benefit.)

The Board had a little more trouble with the effect of the shareholder vote, given their own decision in *North-West Transportation Co. v. Beatty*. They distinguished that case by saying that it was a case of contracting with the corporation, while *Cook v. Deeks* was effectively a case of misappropriation of an asset of the company. This was a stretch: the new contract was an opportunity, not an asset in the usual sense. But the result was that the defendants had to account to the corporation for all the profit they had made.

We saw in the last section that modern statutes have specific regulation for the kind of conflict that arises where the manager makes a contract with his own corporation. Usually, the kind of conflict we are now concerned with — the misappropriation of opportunities — is not specifically regulated in the statute. See, however, B.C.B.C.A., s. 53; Civil Code of Quebec, art. 324, paragraph 2.

The breach of duty in *Cook v. Deeks* was rather heavy handed and obvious. The following case illustrates a more difficult situations in which, nonetheless, a conflict was found.

REGAL (HASTINGS) LTD. v. GULLIVER

[1942] 1 All E.R. 378, [1967] 2 A.C. 134 (H.L.)

[Regal (Hastings) Ltd. ("Regal") was in the cinema business in Hastings. In order to take advantage of opportunities arising in this business, Regal decided (through its Board of Directors) to form a subsidiary ("Amalgamated") for the purpose of acquiring certain cinema leases. The Regal directors decided that Regal would subscribe £2,000 for 2,000 shares of Amalgamated; this was all that Regal could afford, but the original plan was that Regal would be the only shareholder of Amalgamated. However, the lessor of the cinema leases was concerned about the risk of Amalgamated's insolvency. It was suggested that the directors of Regal could provide personal guarantees of Amalgamated's liability; they did not wish to do so, and of course they had no obligation to do so. The lessor agreed that if Amalgamated had £5,000 in paid-up capital, it would be satisfied. In order that the plan should go ahead, four of the five Regal directors agreed to invest their own money; they would take 500 Amalgamated shares each, at £1 per share, as would Garton, Regal's solicitor. Gulliver, the chairman of Regal, took no shares personally, but he persuaded two companies and one individual to take, among them, the remaining 500 shares of Amalgamated. In this way, £5,000 was raised to acquire shares in Amalgamated; it was duly formed and it acquired the leases, which were valuable. Soon after, the shareholders of Regal and Amalgamated wanted to sell their investments. The shares of both Regal and Amalgamated were sold to common purchasers. The shares of Amalgamated that were not held by Regal were sold for almost £4 each. The new shareholders of Regal subsequently elected a new board of directors for Regal. These new directors then resolved to have Regal bring this action for breach of fiduciary duty against the former directors of Regal and Garton, the solicitor. It was assumed throughout that the directors acted in the best interests of the company.]

Lord Russell of Killowen: — [at p. 386] The leading case of *Keech v. Sandford* (1726), Sel. Cas. Ch. 61, is an illustration of the strictness of this rule of equity in this regard, and of how far the rule is independent of these outside considerations. A lease of the profits of a market had been devised to a trustee for the benefit of an infant. A renewal on behalf of the infant was refused. It was absolutely unobtainable. The trustee, finding that it was impossible to get a renewal for the benefit of the infant, took a lease for his own benefit. Though his duty to obtain it for the infant was incapable of performance, nevertheless he was ordered to assign the lease to the infant, upon the bare ground that, if a trustee on the refusal to renew might have a lease for himself, few renewals would be made for the benefit of cestuis que trust. Lord King, L.C., said, at p. 62:

> This may seem hard, that the trustee is the only person of all mankind who might not have the lease; but it is very proper that the rule should be strictly pursued, and not in the least relaxed....

One other case in equity may be referred to in this connection, viz., *Ex p. James* (1803), 8 Ves. 337, (2), decided by Lord Eldon, L.C. That was a case of a purchase of a bankrupt's estate by the solicitor to the commission, and Lord Eldon, L.C., refers to the doctrine thus, at p. 345:

> The doctrine as to purchases by trustees, assignees, and persons having a confidential character, stands much more upon general principles than upon the circumstances of any individual case. It rests upon this: that the purchase is not permitted in any case however honest the circumstances; the general interests of justice requiring it to be destroyed in every instance; as no court is equal to the examination and ascertainment of the truth in much the greater number of cases.

Let me now consider whether the essential matters, which the plaintiff must prove, have been established in the present case. As to the profit being in fact made there can be no doubt. The shares were acquired at par and were sold three weeks later at a profit of £2 16s. 1d. per share. Did such of the first five respondents as acquired these very profitable shares acquire them by reason and in course of their office of directors of Regal? In my opinion, when the facts are examined and appreciated, the answer can only be that they did. The actual allotment no doubt had to be made by themselves and Garton (or some of them) in their capacity as directors of Amalgamated; but this was merely an executive act, necessitated by the alteration of the scheme for the acquisition of the lease of the two cinemas for the sole benefit of Regal and its shareholders through Regal's shareholding in Amalgamated. That scheme could only be altered by or with the consent of the Regal board. ...

My Lords, I have no hesitation in coming to the conclusion, upon the facts of this case, that these shares, when acquired by the directors, were acquired by reason, and only by reason of the fact that they were directors of Regal, and in the course of their execution of that office. ...

In the result, I am of opinion that the directors standing in a fiduciary relationship to Regal in regard to the exercise of their powers as directors, and having obtained these shares by reason and only by reason of the fact that they were directors of Regal and in the course of the execution of that office, are accountable for the profits which they have made out of them. The equitable rule laid down in *Keech v. Sandford* and *Ex p. James* and similar authorities applies to them in full force. It was contended that these cases were distinguishable by reason of the fact that it was impossible for Regal to get the shares owing to lack of funds, and that the directors in taking the shares were really acting as members of the public. I cannot accept this argument. It was impossible for the cestuis que trust in *Keech v. Sandford* to obtain the lease, nevertheless the trustee was accountable. The suggestion that the directors were applying simply as members of the public is a travesty of the facts. They could, had they wished, have protected themselves by a resolution (either antecedent or subsequent) of the Regal shareholders in general meeting. In default of such approval, the liability to account must remain. The result is that, in my opinion, each of the respondents Bobby, Griffiths, Bassett and Bentley is liable to account for the profit which he made on the sale of his 500 shares in Amalgamated.

The case of the respondent Gulliver, however, requires some further consideration, for he has raised a separate and distinct answer to the claim. He says: "I never promised to subscribe for shares in Amalgamated. I never did so subscribe. I only promised to find others who would be willing to subscribe. I only found others who did subscribe. The shares were theirs. They were never mine. They received the profit. I received none of it." If these are the true facts, his answer seems complete. The evidence in my opinion establishes his contention. ...

Gulliver accordingly made no profit for which he is accountable. As regards Gulliver, this appeal should, in my opinion, be dismissed.

There remains to consider the case of Garton. It stands on a different footing from the other respondents in that he was not a director of Regal. He was Regal's legal advisor; but, in my opinion, he has a short but effective answer to the plaintiff's claim. He was requested by the Regal directors to apply for 500 shares. They arranged that they themselves should each be responsible for £500 of the Amalgamated capital, and they appealed, by their chairman, to Garton to subscribe the balance of £500 which was required to make up the £3,000. In law his action, which has resulted in a profit, was taken at the request of Regal, and I know of no principle of authority which would justify a decision that a solicitor must account for profit resulting from a transaction which he has entered into on his behalf, not merely with the consent, but at the request of his client.

One final observation I desire to make. In his judgment Lord Greene, M.R., stated that a decision adverse to the directors in the present case involved the proposition that, if directors bona fide decide not to invest their company's funds in some proposed investment, a director who thereafter embarks his own money therein is accountable for any profits which he may derive therefrom. As to this, I can only say that to my mind the facts of this hypothetical case bear but little resemblance to the story with which we have had to deal.

...

Lord Porter: — My Lords, I have had an opportunity of reading the speech which has been delivered by my noble and learned friend, Lord Russell of Killowen, and had we not been differing from the view of the Court of Appeal I should not desire to add to what he has said. As we are reversing the judgment of both the court of first instance and the Court of Appeal I desire, out of respect for the opinions expressed in them, to state in the briefest possible compass the grounds for the view which I hold.

My Lords, I am conscious of certain possibilities which are involved in the conclusion which all your Lordships have reached. The action is brought by the

Regal company. Technically, of course, the fact than an unlooked for advantage may be gained by the shareholders of that company is immaterial to the question at issue. The company and its shareholders are separate entities.

...

One cannot help remembering; however, that in fact the shares have been purchased by a financial group who were willing to acquire those of the Regal and the Amalgamated at a certain price. As a result of your Lordships' decision that group will, I think, receive in one hand part of the sum which has been paid by the other. For the shares in Amalgamated they paid £3 16s. 1d. per share, yet part of that sum may be returned to the group, though not necessarily to the individual shareholders by reason of the enhancement in value of the shares in Regal — an enhancement brought about as a result of the receipt by the company of the profit made by some of its former directors on the sale of Amalgamated shares. This, it seems, may be an unexpected windfall, but whether it be so or not, the principle that a person occupying a fiduciary relationship shall not make a profit by reason thereof is of such vital importance that the possible consequence in the present case is in fact as it is in law an immaterial consideration.

...

That the shares were obtained by the defendants by reason of their position as directors of Regal is, I think, plain. The original proposition, when the formation of the subsidiary company was suggested, was that the whole of the shares should be issued to the Regal company, partly for cash and partly for services rendered, and this proposition was discussed and accepted at board meetings of that company. It was only afterwards when the necessity for finding £5,000 cash arose, that the issue to any one other than the company was considered, and then the directors turned to themselves. "There is no doubt it was only because they were directors and solicitor respectively of the plaintiff company that this stroke of fortune came their way," says Wrottesley, J., and I agree with his observation.

In these circumstances, it is to my mind immaterial that the directors saw no way of raising the money save from amongst themselves and from the solicitor to the company, or, indeed, that the money could in fact have been raised in no other way. The legal proposition may, I think, be broadly stated by saying that one occupying a position of trust must not make a profit which he can acquire only by use of his fiduciary position, or, if he does, he must account for the profit so made. For this proposition the cases of *Keech v. Sandford* and *Ex p. James* are sufficient authority. Wrottesley, J., and the members of the Court of Appeal appear to have adopted a narrower outlook with which, with all respect, I find myself unable to agree. Wrottesley, J., said:

> In order to succeed the plaintiff company must show that the defendants both ought to have caused and could have caused the plaintiff company to subscribe for these shares and that the neglect to do so caused a loss to the plaintiff company.

In the Court of Appeal, Lord Greene, M.R., said:

> It must be shown that in the circumstances of the case it was the duty of the directors to obtain these shares for their company ... The position of the Regal company would have been very much strengthened by having all these shares in the two companies in the same hands with the possibility of one control. That being so, the only way in which these directors could secure that benefit for their company was by putting up the money themselves. Once that decision is held to be a bona fide one,

and fraud drops out of the case, it seems to me here is only one conclusion, namely, that the appeal must be dismissed with costs.

To treat the problem in this way is, in my view, to look at it as involving a claim for negligence or misfeasance and to neglect the wider aspect. Directors, no doubt, are not trustees, but they occupy a fiduciary position towards the company whose board they form. Their liability in this respect does not depend upon breach of duty but upon the proposition that a director must not make a profit out of property acquired by reason of his relationship to the company of which he is director. It matters not that he could not have acquired the property of the company itself — the profit which he makes is the company's, even though the property by means of which he made it was not and could not have been acquired on its behalf. Adopting the words of Lord Eldon, L.C., in *Ex p. James* at p. 345:

> ... the general interests of justice require it to be destroyed in every instance; as no court is equal to the examination and ascertainment of the truth in much the greater number of cases.

[Separate, concurring reasons for judgment were delivered by **Viscount Sankey**, **Lord MacMillan** and **Lord Wright**].

NOTES

1. The reasoning in *Regal* was expressly adopted in a Nova Scotia case by the Supreme Court of Canada: *Zwicker v. Stanbury*, [1953] 2 S.C.R. 438, [1954] 1 D.L.R. 257. Contrast the English Court of Appeal's refusal to apply the rule to an executor in *Holder v. Holder*, [1968] Ch. 353, noted above at p. 353, on the ground that no real conflict of interest was involved. *Holder* was decided before the publication of the House of Lords' decision in *Boardman v. Phipps*, [1967] 2 A.C. 46, [1966] 3 All E.R. 721 (H.L.) and may be of doubtful authority in the light of that judgment. In *Boardman*, trustees held shares in a company that was not prospering. The trustees did not have the power to acquire more shares of the company. Boardman, the solicitor to the trustees, and one of the trust beneficiaries, Tom Phipps, took it upon themselves to take control of the company, by buying shares with their own money. With the knowledge of the trustees, they acquired information by purporting to act on behalf of the trustees, and they succeeded in taking control of the company and turning its fortunes around. This resulted in a profit to the trust beneficiaries, since the value of the shares held by the trust rose greatly; but Boardman and Tom Phipps also profited as shareholders. Another beneficiary sued for a declaration that their profits must be handed over to the trustees for the trust beneficiaries. It was held in the House of Lords that both were fiduciaries, and, by a 3-2 majority, that they had put themselves in a conflict of interest and duty, and must give up the profit they had derived. They were, however, allowed a kind of counterclaim for the effort they had invested which had benefited the trust beneficiaries. This can be understood as a response preventing unjust enrichment.

2. More recently, in *Guinness plc v. Saunders*, [1990] 2 A.C. 663 (H.L.), Guinness was trying to take control of another company. A committee of the board of directors of Guinness purported to authorize a payment of £5.2 million one director's services in connection with the takeover. The bid was successful and the money was paid; Guinness then brought these proceedings to recover it, and succeeded. The House of Lords held that on a correct interpretation of the corporate constitution, there was no authority in the committee to authorize the payment. The director could not have any claim in unjust enrichment; *Boardman* was held not to apply in this regard, since granting an allowance would contradict the corporate constitution.

PESO SILVER MINES LTD. v. CROPPER

[1966] S.C.R. 673, 58 D.L.R. (2d) 1, 56 W.W.R. 641

[The plaintiff, a British Columbia company, was offered a speculative mining property by one Dickson. Dickson had offered the property to the plaintiff at the suggestion of a geologist, Dr. Aho. The defendant was managing director of the plaintiff. The board of directors considered Dickson's offer and rejected it. Subsequently, the defendant became involved in a group who purchased Dickson's claims. The control of plaintiff company changed hands and the plaintiff sought to acquire the defendant's interest in the now profitable mine at his cost.]

Cartwright J. (for the Court): — [at p. 677, citing Bull J.A. in the Court below]

> It was common ground, and so found by the learned trial Judge, that this decision rejecting the acquisition was an honest and considered decision of the appellant's board of directors as a whole and done in the best of faith and solely in the interest of the appellant, and not from any personal or ulterior motive on the part of any director, including the respondent.

During the time that the respondent was an officer of the appellant there were between 200 and 300 mining properties offered to it; it was usual for it to receive two or three of such offers a week.

After the appellant had rejected Dickson's offer and the matter had passed out of the respondent's mind, Dr. Aho came to the respondent and suggested the possibility of a group being formed to acquire Dickson's claims. After some discussion it was agreed that Dr. Aho, Walker, Verity and the respondent would take up these claims and they did so, each contributing an equal amount to finance the purchase.

The appellant submits that the shares ... are property obtained by him as a result of his position as a director of the appellant, without the approval of the latter's shareholders, and that equity imposes upon him an obligation to account to the appellant for that property which is unaffected by the circumstances that he acted throughout in good faith, that the appellant had decided for sound business reasons not to acquire the property and had suffered no loss by reason of the respondent's actions.

[**Cartwright J.** here cited various passages from the *Regal* case, *supra*, concluding with the following quote from Lord Russell of Killowen]:

> In the result, I am of opinion that the directors standing in a fiduciary relationship to Regal in regard to the exercise of their powers as directors, and having obtained these shares by reason and only by reason of the fact that they were directors of Regal and in the course of the execution of that office, are accountable for the profits which they have made out of them.

In *Midcon Oil and Gas Ltd. v. New British Dominion Oil Co. Ltd.*, 12 D.L.R. (2d) at pp. 726-7, Locke J., giving the judgment of the majority of this Court quoted this passage and said it summarized the ground on which the judgment of the House of Lords proceeded. The difference of opinion in this Court was not as to the principles of law stated in Regal but as to whether the facts of the case fell within those principles.

On the facts of the case at bar I find it impossible to say that the respondent obtained the interests he holds...by reason of the fact that he was a director of the appellant and in the course of the execution of that office.

When Dickson, at Dr. Aho's suggestion, offered his claims to the appellant it was the duty of the respondent as director to take part in the decision of the board as to whether that offer should be accepted or rejected. At that point he stood in a fiduciary relationship to the appellant. There are affirmative findings of fact that he and his co-directors acted in good faith, solely in the interests of the appellant and with sound business reasons in rejecting the offer. There is no suggestion in the evidence that the offer to the appellant was accompanied by any confidential information unavailable to any prospective purchaser or that the respondent as director had access to any such information by reason of his office. When, later, Dr. Aho approached the appellant, it was not in his capacity as a director of the appellant, but as an individual member of the public whom Dr. Aho was seeking to interest as a co-adventurer.

In [*Regal*], Lord Russell of Killowen concluded his reasons, at p. 391, with the following paragraph:

> In his judgment [in the Court of Appeal], Lord Greene, M.R., stated that a decision adverse to the directors in the present case involved the proposition that, if directors bona fide decide not to invest their company's funds in some proposed investment, a director who thereafter embarks his own money therein is accountable for any profits which he may derive therefrom. As to this, I can only say that to my mind the facts of this hypothetical case bear but little resemblance to the story with which we have had to deal.

If the members of the House of Lords in Regal had been of the view that in the hypothetical case stated by Lord Greene the director would have been liable to account to the company, the elaborate examination of the facts contained in the speech of Lord Russell of Killowen would have been unnecessary.

The facts of the case at bar appear to me in all material respects identical with those in the hypothetical case stated by Lord Greene and I share the view which he expressed that in such circumstances the director is under no liability. I agree with the conclusion of the learned trial Judge and of the majority of the Court of Appeal that this action fails.

NOTES AND QUESTIONS

1. Would Cropper have been liable if he had not been so forgetful? What if he had remembered, but Dr. Aho had not? What if he had forgotten Dickson's offer to the company, but Dr. Aho had remembered, and had approached Cropper only because he knew Cropper through his position as a director of Peso Silver Mines Ltd.?

2. Cropper would surely have been in breach if he had appropriated the opportunity the first time, when it was presented to him in his capacity as a director of the plaintiff. Why was he not in breach the second time? Was it because he had forgotten about the first approach? Or was it because the second offer was made to him in his personal capacity? Or were both of these things essential?

3. What was the role of the plaintiff's refusal? Does the refusal of an opportunity amount to informed consent for a fiduciary to take it up for his or her own benefit? If some members of a joint venture (holding equal shares in a corporation) refuse to take the necessary steps to realize the opportunity, can the remaining partners walk away from the deadlock and realize the opportunity by using a second corporation? See *Hoffman Products Ltd. v. Karr*, [1989] O.J. No. 2280, 70 O.R. (2d) 789 (H.C.); aff'd (1990), 71 O.R. (2d) 734n.

INDUSTRIAL DEVELOPMENT CONSULTANTS LTD. v. COOLEY

[1972] 1 W.L.R. 443, [1972] 2 All E.R. 162 (Eng., Birmingham Assizes)

[The defendant, an architect of considerable distinction, was employed as managing director of the plaintiff company. He attempted to negotiate contracts on behalf of the plaintiff company with the Eastern Gas Board, but was unsuccessful because the Gas Board disliked plaintiff's corporate setup. Subsequently, a new deputy-chairman of the Gas Board, Mr. Smettom, was appointed. Mr. Smettom began negotiating with the defendant for certain Gas Board contracts and he made it clear that the Gas Board was interested only in contracting with the defendant in his personal capacity. The defendant resigned his position, alleging ill-health, and contracted with the Gas Board. The plaintiff sought an accounting of profits for breach of fiduciary duty.]

Roskill J. (orally): — ... There can be no doubt that the defendant got this Eastern Gas Board contract for himself and got it as a result of work which he did whilst still the plaintiffs' managing director. It is, of course, right to say that the contract for that work was not concluded until after he had left the plaintiffs. That work, as I have already said, was work which the plaintiffs would very much have liked to have had and, indeed, was in substance the same work as they had unsuccessfully tried to get in 1968.

There are a number of other points with which it may be convenient to deal in rather summary form. It is only fair to the defendant to say that the negotiations for the Eastern Gas Board work were initiated in the first instance by Mr. Smettom and not by himself. At the time when Mr. Smettom first approached the defendant at the end of May 1969, Mr. Smettom did know that the plaintiffs had been interested in the previous proposals and had failed to get the work. He learned that the defendant was still with the plaintiffs as their managing director and was not then in private practice. It is important to realize that by the time when the defendant and Mr. Smettom met on 13th June the defendant was desperately anxious to obtain this business for himself if he could succeed in doing so. He then learned, first, that the Eastern Gas Board were coming back, if I may use the phrase, into the market and were considering building these depots, and, secondly, that Mr. Smettom regarded the implementation of this project as urgent and, thirdly, in round and general terms, the sort of capital sum which would be involved.

All those matters vitally concerned the plaintiffs. At that time the defendant was still their managing director. He was still their managing director not only at the time when he met Mr. Smettom on 13th June but when he prepared the documents over the ensuing weekend, sending them off on 17th June so as to get this work for himself. ...

It is plain that at the meeting of 13th June the defendant became possessed of knowledge and information which was not possessed by his employers, the plaintiffs, knowledge which the plaintiff would have wished to possess. When the defendant saw Mr. Hicks [managing director of the parent of the plaintiff] on 16th June he did so in order to obtain his freedom as quickly as possible. ... Unless the defendant could be free in time to enable him to meet Mr. Smettom's programme requirements both for Letchworth and the rest, it seems plain that Mr. Smettom would not in any event have given the defendant the job ultimately offered in the letter of 6th August. ...

...

When one looks at the letters of 17th June and the associated documents, there is disclosed the plainest conflict of interest between the defendant as potential architect or project manager of the Eastern Gas Board and as managing director of the plaintiffs. Finally I ought to say that I am sure Mr. Hicks would not have agreed to give the defendant the carte blanche release claimed by the defendant if he had known the full facts about the Eastern Gas Board project. I am also satisfied that Mr. Hicks never made the agreement with the defendant which the defendant alleges. It is against this background that I turn to consider the difficult questions of law involved.

Mr. Davies, for the defendant, has forcefully described the cause of action for an account which is relied on in this case as misconceived. His admirable argument ran thus: true some directors are in a fiduciary relationship with their companies but when the defendant saw Mr. Smettom on 13th June Mr. Smettom made it plain that he was consulting the defendant not as managing director of the plaintiffs, but in a private capacity. Therefore, what the defendant did on 13th June and thereafter was not done qua managing director of the plaintiffs. The information he received was not received qua managing director of the plaintiffs. On the contrary the information was given and received in a purely private capacity. There was thus no breach of any duty, even the barest contractual duty in failing to pass that information on to the plaintiffs. Still less was there any breach of any fiduciary duty because, having regard to the fact this information was received by the defendant in his private capacity, there could be no fiduciary obligation to pass on this information to Mr. Hicks or to his employers generally. The argument continued that, that being the position, the defendant did not and could not have got this valuable Eastern Gas Board work by virtue of his position as managing director of the plaintiffs. Indeed, the converse of that was true because the defendant could never have got work so long as he was their managing director. Therefore, none of the requirements indicated in some of the cases which have been referred to, notably *Regal (Hastings) Ltd. v. Gulliver*, have been satisfied.

Further, it was said that under no circumstances would the plaintiffs have ever got this work because of Mr. Smettom's and Mr. Lacey's objections in principle to the setup, if I may use that phrase, not only of the plaintiffs but of the IDC Group as a whole. Thus, the argument continued, there is no duty to account. The whole action is completely misconceived. If there be any claim here at all it must lie in damages but a claim for relief by way of an account cannot succeed.

Mr. Davies summarised his argument in this way. Any duty which might otherwise have been owed to the plaintiffs by the defendant was eliminated by the nature of Mr. Smettom's approach which was from the outset a private approach. He pointed out that contracts in this connection fell into two different classes, first, contracts with a company in which the director is interested — in relation to those Mr. Davies said there was what he described as an inherent and inevitable conflict of interest and, therefore, there was a duty to disclose and a consequential liability in the event of a failure to disclose — and, secondly, contracts with a third party with which alone he submitted the court was concerned in this case. The relevant contract was not, as he put it, a contract with the plaintiffs at all. It was a contract with a third party and being with a third party there was no inherent conflict between interest and duty unless it could be said that this contract was equally available to the plaintiffs as his employers. As it was a contract which was not available to the plaintiffs and with a third party there could be no duty to account.

[**Roskill J.,** here quoted from previous cases and in particular from the judgment of Lord Upjohn in *Boardman v. Phipps*, [1967] 2 A.C. 46 (Eng. H.L.).]

...

I should have added that Lord Upjohn's speech was a dissenting speech. I do not, however, detect any difference in principle between the speeches of their five Lordships but merely a difference in the application of the facts to principles which were not in dispute. Later Lord Upjohn stated four propositions as follows:

1. The facts and circumstances must be carefully examined to see whether in fact a purported agent and even a confidential agent is in a fiduciary relationship to his principal. It does not necessarily follow that he is in such a position. ...

2. Once it is established that there is such a relationship, that relationship must be examined to see what duties are thereby imposed on the agent, to see what is the scope and ambit of the duties charged on him.

3. Having defined the scope of those duties one must see whether he has committed some breach thereof by placing himself within the scope and ambit of those duties in a position where his duty and interest may possibly conflict. It is only at this stage that any question of accountability arises.

4. Finally, having established accountability it only goes so far as to render the agent accountable for profits made within the scope and ambit of his duty.

I think that Mr. Brown [counsel for the plaintiff] was right when he said in his reply that that is the basic rule from which all else has been founded. Certainly Viscount Sankey in the *Regal* case so stated it and Lord Cranworth's well-known statement [in *Aberdeen Railway Co. v. Blaikie Bros.* (1854), 1 Macq. 461, [1843-60] All E.R. Rep 249 (Scot. H.L.)] has been repeated in innumerable cases of the highest authority.

Therefore, the starting point for consideration of the present case is the application of the facts of this case to the propositions stated by Lord Upjohn, bearing in mind, as Lord Upjohn said in the passage I have quoted that the application of "this great principle" may be infinitely variable. It is the principle which is important and there is no limit, I venture to think, to the cases to which that principle can be applied, always provided that in applying the principle, the court does not go outside the well established limits of the principle.

The first matter that has to be considered is whether or not the defendant was in a fiduciary relationship with his principals, the plaintiffs. Mr. Davies argued that he was not because he received this information which was communicated to him privately. With respect, I think that argument is wrong. The defendant had one capacity and one capacity only in which he was carrying on business at that time. That capacity was as managing director of the plaintiffs. Information which came to him while he was managing director and which was of concern to the plaintiffs and was relevant for the plaintiffs to know, was information which it was his duty to pass on to the plaintiffs because between himself and the plaintiffs a fiduciary relationship existed as defined in the passage I have quoted from *Buckley on the Companies Acts* and, indeed, in the speech of Lord Cranworth L.C.

It seems to me plain that throughout the whole of May, June and July 1969 the defendant was in a fiduciary relationship with the plaintiffs. From the time he embarked on his course of dealing with the Eastern Gas Board, irrespective of anything which he did or he said to Mr. Hicks, he embarked on a deliberate policy and course of conduct which put his personal interest as a potential contracting party with the Eastern Gas Board in direct conflict with his pre-existing and continuing duty as managing director of the plaintiffs. That is something which for over 200 years the courts have forbidden.

Does accountability arise? It is said: "Well, even if there were that conflict of duty and interest, nonetheless, this was a contract with a third party in which the plaintiffs never could have had any interest because they would have never got it." That argument has been forcefully put before me by Mr. Davies.

The remarkable position then arises that if one applies the equitable doctrine on which the plaintiffs rely to oblige the defendant to account, they will receive a benefit which on Mr. Smettom's evidence at least it is unlikely they would have got for themselves had the defendant complied with his duty to them. On the other hand, if the defendant is not required to account he will have made a large profit as a result of having deliberately put himself into a position in which his duty to the plaintiffs who were employing him and his personal interests conflicted. I leave out of account the fact that he dishonestly tricked Mr. Hicks into releasing him on 16th June although Mr. Brown urged that that was another reason why equity must compel him to disgorge his profit. It is said that the plaintiffs' only remedy is to sue for damages either for breach of contract or maybe for fraudulent misrepresentation. Mr. Brown has been at pains to disclaim any intention to claim damages for breach of contract save on one basis only and he has disclaimed specifically any claim for damages for fraudulent misrepresentation. Therefore, if the plaintiffs succeed they will get a profit which they probably would not have got for themselves had the defendant fulfilled his duty. If the defendant is allowed to keep that profit he will have got something which he was able to get solely by reason of his breach of fiduciary duty to the plaintiffs.

When one looks at the way the cases have gone over the centuries it is plain that the question whether or not the benefit would have been obtained but for the breach of trust has always been treated as irrelevant. I mentioned *Keech v. Sandford* a few moments ago and this fact will also be found emphasised if one looks at some of the speeches in *Regal (Hastings) Ltd. v. Gulliver* although it is true as was pointed out to me, that if one looks at some of the language used in the speeches in *Regal* such phrases as "he must account for any benefit which he obtains in the course of and owing to his directorship" will be found.

In one sense the benefit in this case did not arise because of the defendant's directorship; indeed, the defendant would not have got this work had he remained a director. However, one must, as Lord Upjohn pointed out, look at the passages in the speeches in *Regal* having regard to the facts of that case to which those passages and those statements were directed. I think Mr. Brown was right when he said that it is the basic principle which matters. It is an overriding principle of equity that a man must not be allowed to put himself in a position in which his fiduciary duty and his interests conflict. The variety of cases where that can happen is infinite. The fact there has not previously been a case precisely of this nature with precisely similar facts before the courts is of no import. The facts of this case are, I think, exceptional and I hope unusual. They seem to me plainly to come within this principle.

I think, although perhaps the expression is not entirely precise, Mr. Brown put the point well when he said that what the defendant did in May, June and July was to substitute himself as an individual for the company of which he was managing director and to which he owed a fiduciary duty. It is on the ground which I have stated that I rest my conclusion in this case. Perhaps it is permissible to say that I have less reluctance in reaching that conclusion on the application of this basic principle of equity since I know that what happened was enabled to happen because a release was obtained by the defendant from a binding contractual obligation by the dishonest and untrue misrepresentations which were made to Mr. Hicks on 16th June. In my judgment, therefore, an order for an account will be issued because the defendant made and will make his profit as a result of having allowed his interests and his duty to conflict.

I would only add that if I am wrong on this central question Mr. Brown did in the alternative advance a claim for damages — this was the only claim for damages advanced — for the plaintiffs' loss of the opportunity to get this contract. I mentioned earlier in this judgment the fact that Mr. Lacy and Mr. Smettom both said they would not — I think I can put it as high as this — have employed the plaintiffs because of their objection to this type of organization. Therefore it cannot be said that it is anything like certain that the plaintiffs would ever have got this contract. I accept both those witnesses as witnesses of truth. On the other hand, there was always the possibility of the plaintiffs persuading the Eastern Gas Board to change their minds; and ironically enough, it would have been the defendant's duty to try and persuade them to change their minds. It is a curious position under which he whose duty it would have been to seek to persuade them to change their minds should now say that the plaintiffs suffered no loss because he would never have succeeded in persuading them to change their mind.

In the circumstances while I do not put the chance of their being shifted from the stand they adopted very high, nonetheless, the opportunity was there and could not be taken because the plaintiffs never knew about it owing to the defendant's conduct. I do not put the chance very high. I cannot rate it, as I am dealing with liability only, at a greater than ten per cent chance. If I am wrong in making an order for account I should have given the plaintiffs as damages whatever would represent a ten per cent chance.

Judgment for the plaintiff.

NOTES AND QUESTIONS

1. Do you think this decision is consistent with *Cropper*? If so, what is the difference in the facts that justifies the different result? If not, which decision do you think is the better one? For a criticism of *Cropper*, see L. Smith, "The Motive, Not the Deed" in J. Getzler, ed., *Rationalizing Property, Equity and Trusts: Essays in Honour of Edward Burn* (London: Butterworths, 2003), at p. 53.

   On the reasoning of *Cooley*, what should Cropper have done when the opportunity was offered to him personally, *assuming it had never been offered* to the corporation?

2. Cooley's resignation did not help him. Nor did it help the defendants in the next case, which extended the fiduciary duty from directors to officers. This extension is now enshrined in the legislation, as we have seen.

CANADIAN AERO SERVICES LTD. v. O'MALLEY

[1974] S.C.R. 592, 40 D.L.R. (3d) 371

[Canadian Aero Service Ltd. ("Canaero") was interested in securing a contract involving aerial photography and topographical mapping in Guyana, through an external aid programme of the Canadian government. Promotional work for

Canaero with the Guyana authorities was done personally by defendant O'Malley, the president, while the technical work was done by defendant Zarzycki, an executive vice-president. Until their resignations, both defendants worked exclusively to promote Canaero for the contract. Both became discontented with certain limitations placed on their general authority within Canaero by Canaero's parent corporation and both were apprehensive that they might lose their positions if Canaero should fail to get some of the contracts they were pursuing on its behalf. They decided to incorporate Terra Surveys Limited to pursue the same type of business as Canaero was involved in. O'Malley became president and Zarzycki became executive vice-president. Shortly after incorporating Terra Surveys Limited, both defendants resigned from Canaero. Within four days of their resignations, and before the resignations were formally acknowledged by Canaero, five corporations were invited to bid on the Guyana project. Canaero and Terra Surveys Limited were among the five. Terra Surveys Limited was awarded the contract, partially on the ground that its proposal "covered the operation in much greater detail than might normally be expected".]

Laskin J. (for the Court): — This appeal arises out of a claim by the plaintiff-appellant (hereinafter referred to as Canaero) that the defendants had improperly taken the fruits of a corporate opportunity in which Canaero had a prior and continuing interest. The allegation against the defendants O'Malley and Zarzycki is that while directors or officers of Canaero they had devoted effort and planning in respect of the particular corporate opportunity as representatives of Canaero, but had subsequently wrongfully taken the benefit thereof in breach of a fiduciary duty to Canaero,... the defendant Terra Surveys Limited was joined as the vehicle through which the individual defendants in fact obtained the benefit for which Canaero had been negotiating.

...

There are four issues that arise for consideration on the facts so far recited. There is, first, the determination of the relationship of O'Malley and Zarzycki to Canaero. Secondly, there is the duty or duties, if any, owed by them to Canaero by reason of the ascertained relationship. Thirdly, there is the question whether there has been any breach of duty, if any is owing, by reason of the conduct of O'Malley and Zarzycki in acting through Terra to secure the contract for the Guyana project; and, fourthly, there is the question of liability for breach of duty if established.

Like Grant J., the trial judge, I do not think it matters whether O'Malley and Zarzycki were properly appointed as directors of Canaero or whether they did or did not act as directors. What is not in doubt is that they acted respectively as president and executive vice-president of Canaero for about two years prior to their resignations. To paraphrase the findings of the trial Judge in this respect, they acted in those positions and their remuneration and responsibilities verified their status as senior officers of Canaero. They were "top management" and not mere employees whose duty to their employer, unless enlarged by contract, consisted only of respect for trade secrets and for confidentiality of customer lists. Theirs was a larger, more exacting duty which, unless modified by statute or by contract (and there is nothing of this sort here), was similar to that owed to a corporate employer by its directors. I adopt what is said on this point by Gower, *Principles of Modern Company Law*, 3rd ed. (1969), at p. 518 as follows:

... these duties, except in so far as they depend on statutory provisions expressly limited to directors, are not so restricted but apply equally to any officials of the company who are authorised to act on its behalf and in particular to those acting in a managerial capacity.

The distinction taken between agents and servants of an employer is apt here, and I am unable to appreciate the basis upon which the Ontario Court of Appeal concluded that O'Malley and Zarzycki were mere employees, that is servants of Canaero rather than agents. Although they were subject to supervision of the officers of the controlling company, their positions as senior officers of a subsidiary, which was a working organization, charged them with initiatives and with responsibilities far removed from the obedient role of servants.

It follows that O'Malley and Zarzycki stood in a fiduciary relationship to Canaero, which in its generality betokens loyalty, good faith and avoidance of a conflict of duty and self-interest. Descending from the generality, the fiduciary relationship goes at least this far: a director or a senior officer like O'Malley or Zarzycki is precluded from obtaining for himself, either secretly or without the approval of the company (which would have to be properly manifested upon full disclosure of the facts), any property or business advantage either belonging to the company or for which it has been negotiating; and especially is this so where the director or officer is a participant in the negotiations on behalf of the company.

An examination of the case law in this Court and in the Courts of other like jurisdictions on the fiduciary duties of directors and senior officers shows the pervasiveness of a strict ethic in this area of the law. In my opinion, this ethic disqualifies a director or senior officer from usurping for himself or diverting to another person or company with whom or with which he is associated a maturing business opportunity which his company is actively pursuing; he is also precluded from so acting even after his resignation where the resignation may fairly be said to have been prompted or influenced by a wish to acquire for himself the opportunity sought by the company, or where it was his position with the company rather than a fresh initiative that led him to the opportunity which he later acquired.

It is this fiduciary duty which is invoked by the appellant in this case and which is resisted by the respondents on the grounds that the duty as formulated is not nor should be part of our law and that, in any event, the facts of the present case do not fall within its scope....

[**Laskin J.** then quoted passages from the *Regal* case, *supra*.]

I need not pause to consider whether on the facts in *Regal (Hastings) Ltd. v. Gulliver* the equitable principle was overzealously applied; see, for example, Gower, *op. cit.*, at pp. 535-7. What I would observe is that the principle, or, indeed principles, as stated, grew out of older cases concerned with fiduciaries other than directors or managing officers of a modern corporation, and I do not therefore regard them as providing a rigid measure whose literal terms must be met in assessing succeeding cases. In my opinion, neither the conflict test, referred to by Viscount Sankey, nor the test of accountability for profits acquired by reason only of being directors and in the course of execution of the office, reflected in the passage quoted from Lord Russell of Killowen, should be considered as the exclusive touchstones of liability. In this, as in other branches of the law, new fact situations may require a reformulation of existing principle to maintain its vigour in the new setting.

The reaping of a profit by a person at a company's expense while a director thereof is, of course, an adequate ground upon which to hold the director accountable. Yet there may be situations where a profit must be disgorged, although not gained at the expense of the company, on the ground that a director must not be allowed to use his position as such to make a profit even if it was not open to the company, as for example, by reason of legal disability, to participate in the transaction. An analogous situation, albeit not involving a director, existed for all practical purposes in the case of *Boardman et al. v. Phipps*, [1967] 2 A.C. 46 which also supports the view that liability to account does not depend on proof of an actual conflict of duty and self-interest. Another, quite recent illustration of a liability to account where the company itself had failed to obtain a business contract and hence could not be regarded as having been deprived of a business opportunity is *Industrial Development Consultants Ltd. v. Cooley*, [1972] 2 All E.R. 162, a judgment of a Court of first instance. There, the managing director, who was allowed to resign his position on a false assertion of ill health, subsequently got the contract for himself. That case is thus also illustrative of the situation where a director's resignation is prompted by a decision to obtain for himself the business contract denied to his company and where he does obtain it without disclosing his intention.

What these decisions indicate is an updating of the equitable principle whose roots lie in the general standards that I have already mentioned, namely, loyalty, good faith and avoidance of a conflict of duty and self-interest. Strict application against directors and senior management officials is simply recognition of the degree of control which their positions give them in corporate operations, a control which rises above day to day accountability to owning shareholders and which comes under some scrutiny only at annual general or at special meetings. It is a necessary supplement, in the public interest, of statutory regulation and accountability which themselves are, at one and the same time, an acknowledgment of the importance of the corporation in the life of the community and of the need to compel obedience by it and by its promoters, directors and managers to norms of exemplary behaviour.

...

A useful examination of the approach to corporate opportunity in American decisions is that found in *Burg v. Horn* (1967), 380 F. 2d 897, a majority decision of the Second Circuit Court of Appeals applying New York law in a diversity suit. What was involved in that case was not the usurpation of an opportunity which the particular company was pursuing, but the more far-reaching question whether a director was obliged to offer to the company, before taking them for himself, opportunities in its line of business of which he rather than the company became aware and which he pursued. The facts, briefly, were that directors of a company, operating low rental housing, who were known to their co-director plaintiff to have unrelated interests and also interests, acquired earlier, in other like companies, acquired a number of low rental properties which they did not offer to the company of which they and the plaintiff were co-directors. These properties had not been sought by the company nor did the defendants learn of them through the company. In denying liability, the majority expressed New York law to require a determination in each case, by considering the relationship between director and company, whether a duty to offer the company all opportunities within its line of business was fairly to be implied. The dissenting Judge saw the case as one where, in the absence of a contrary understanding between the parties, the defendants were under a fiduciary obligation to offer the properties to the company before buying them for themselves.

That the rigorous standard of behaviour enforced against directors and executives may survive their tenure of such offices was indicated as early as *Ex p.*

James (1803), 8 Ves. Jun. 337, 32 E.R. 385, where Lord Eldon, speaking of the fiduciary in that case who was a solicitor purchasing at a sale, said (at p. 352, pp. 390-1 E.R.):

> With respect to the question now put, whether I will permit Jones to give up the office of solicitor, and to bid, I cannot give that permission. If the principle is right, that the solicitor cannot buy, it would lead to all the mischief of acting up to the point of the sale, getting all the information that may be useful to him, then discharging himself from the character of solicitor, and buying the property. ...On the other hand I do not deny that those interested in the question may give the permission.

The same principle, although applied in a master-servant case in respect of the use to his own advantage of confidential information acquired by the respondent while employed by the appellant, was recognized by this Court in *Pre-Cam Exploration Development Ltd. v. McTavish*, [1966] S.C.R. 551, 57 D.L.R. (2d) 557.

The trial Judge appeared to treat this question differently in quoting a passage from *Raines v. Toney* (1958), 313 S.W. 2d 802, a judgment of the Supreme Court of Arkansas, at p. 809. The passage is in the following words:

> It is, however, a common occurrence for corporate fiduciaries to resign and form a competing enterprise. Unless restricted by contract, this may be done with complete immunity because freedom of employment and encouragement of competition generally dictate that such persons can leave their corporation at any time and go into a competing business. They cannot while still corporate fiduciaries set up a competitive enterprise...or resign and take with them the key personnel of their corporations for the purposes of operating their own competitive enterprise... But they can, while still employed, notify their corporation's customers of their intention to resign and subsequently go into business for themselves, and accept business from them when offered to them...But they can use in their own enterprise the experience and knowledge they gained while working for their corporation...They can solicit the customers of their former corporation for business unless the customer list is itself confidential.

Prior to quoting from *Raines v. Toney*, Grant, J., had referred to and rejected a submission of the appellant that [61 C.P.R., at p. 39]: "... as long as the defendants came upon the profit making possibility inherent in the Guyana contract in the course of and by reason of occupying their positions as directors and senior officers of Canaero...the strict equitable rule must be applied against them". *Albert A. Volk Co. v. Fleschner Bros. Inc.* (1945), 60 N.Y.S. 2d 244, had been cited in support of the submission. The trial Judge's position on this point was put by him as follows [61 C.P.R., at p. 39]:

> I do not interpret the decision above quoted as indicating that the mere fact of learning of the contract or even doing extensive work and preparation in attempts to secure the same for the plaintiff while they were still in their offices for it, of itself prevents them after severing relations with their employer, from seeking to acquire it for themselves. It is not the coming upon or learning of the proposed contract while directors that establishes liability, but rather obtaining the same because of such fiduciary position and in the course of their duties as such. I would think that when directors or senior officers leave the employ of the company they must not use confidential information which they have acquired in such employment for the purpose of assisting them in getting such a contract for themselves. Such information so acquired by them would remain an asset of their principal even after they had left their employment.

In so far as the trial Judge, founding himself upon what Lord Russell of Killowen said in *Regal (Hastings) Ltd. v. Gulliver*, would limit the liability of director or senior officers to the case where they obtained a contract "in the course of their duties as such", I regard his position as too narrowly conceived. *Raines v. Toney* does not support the trial Judge's view, as is evident from the assertion of the Supreme Court of Arkansas that the fiduciary duty of a director or officer does not terminate upon resignation and that it cannot be renounced at will by the termination of employment: see also *Mile-O-Mo Fishing Club Inc. v. Noble* (1965), 210 N.E. 2d 12. The passage quoted by Grant, J., from *Raines v. Toney* was directed to a different point, namely, that of a right to compete with one's former employer unless restricted by contract.

The view taken by the trial Judge, and affirmed by the Court of Appeal (which quoted the same passage from the reasons of Lord Russell of Killowen in *Regal (Hastings) Ltd. v. Gulliver*), tended to obscure the difference between the survival of fiduciary duty after resignation and the right to use non-confidential information acquired in the course of employment and as a result of experience. I do not see that either the question of the confidentiality of the in formation acquired by O'Malley and Zarzycki in the course of their work for Canaero on the Guyana project or the question of copyright is relevant to the enforcement against them of a fiduciary duty. The fact that breach of confidence or violation of copyright may itself afford a ground of relief does not make either one a necessary ingredient of a successful claim for breach of fiduciary duty. ...

In my opinion, the fiduciary duty upon O'Malley and Zarzycki, if it survived their departure from Canaero, would be reduced to an absurdity if it could be evaded merely because the Guyana project had been varied in some details when it became the subject of invited proposals, or merely because Zarzycki met the variations by appropriate changes in what he prepared for Canaero in 1965, and what he proposed for Terra in 1966. I do not regard it as necessary to look for substantial resemblances. Their presence would be a factor to be considered on the issue of breach of fiduciary duty but they are not a sine qua non. The cardinal fact is that the one project, the same project which Zarzycki had pursued for Canaero, was the subject of his Terra proposal. It was that business opportunity, in line with its general pursuits, which Canaero sought through O'Malley and Zarzycki. There is no suggestion that there had been such a change of objective as to make the project for which proposals were invited from Canaero, Terra and others a different one from that which Canaero had been developing with a view to obtaining the contract for itself.

Again, whether or not Terra was incorporated for the purpose of intercepting the contract for the Guyana project is not central to the issue of breach of fiduciary duty. Honesty of purpose is no more a defence in that respect than it would be in respect of personal interception of the contract by O'Malley and Zarzycki. This is fundamental in the enforcement of fiduciary duty where the fiduciaries are acting against the interests of their principal. Then it is urged that Canaero could not in any event have obtained the contract, and that O'Malley and Zarzycki left Canaero as an ultimate response to their dissatisfaction with that company and with the restrictions that they were under in managing it. There was, however, no certain knowledge at the time O'Malley and Zarzycki resigned that the Guyana project was beyond Canaero's grasp. Canaero had not abandoned its hope of capturing it, even if Wells was of opinion, expressed during his luncheon with O'Malley and Zarzycki on August 6, 1966, that it would not get a foreign aid contract from the Canadian Government. Although it was contended that O'Malley and Zarzycki did not know of the imminence of the approval of the Guyana project, their ready run for it, when it was approved at about the time of their resignations and at a time when they knew of Canaero's continuing interest, are factors to be considered in deciding whether they were still under a fiduciary duty not to seek to procure for themselves or for their newly-formed company the business opportunity which they had nurtured for Canaero.

Counsel for O'Malley and Zarzycki relied upon the judgment of this Court in *Peso Silver Mines Ltd. v. Cropper*, [1966] S.C.R. 673, 58 D.L.R. (2d) 1, as representing an affirmation of what was said in *Regal (Hastings) Ltd. v. Gulliver* respecting the circumscription of liability to circumstances where the directors or senior officers had obtained the challenged benefit by reason only of the fact that they held those positions and in the course of execution of those offices. In urging this, he did not deny that leaving to capitalize on their positions would not necessarily immunize them, but he submitted that in the present case there was no special knowledge or information obtained from Canaero during their service with that company upon which O'Malley and Zarzycki had relied in reaching for the Guyana project on behalf of Terra.

There is a considerable gulf between the *Peso* case and the present one on the facts as found in each and on the issues that they respectively raise. In *Peso*, there was a finding of good faith in the rejection by its directors of an offer of mining claims because of its strained finances. The subsequent acquisition of those claims by the managing director and his associates, albeit without seeking shareholder approval, was held to be proper because the company's interest in them ceased. There is some analogy to *Burg v. Horn* because there was evidence that Peso had received many offers of mining properties and, as in *Burg v. Horn*, the acquisition of the particular claims out of which the litigation arose could not be said to be essential to the success of the company. Whether evidence was overlooked in Peso which would have led to the result reached in *Regal (Hastings) Ltd. v. Gulliver* (see the examination by Beck, "The Saga of Peso Silver Mines: Corporate Opportunity Reconsidered" (1971), 49 Can. Bar Rev. 80 at p. 101) has no bearing on the proper disposition of the present case. What is before this Court is not a situation where various opportunities were offered to a company which was open to all of them but rather a case where it had devoted itself to originating and bringing to fruition a particular business deal which was ultimately captured by former senior officers who had been in charge of the matter for the company. Since Canaero had been invited to make a proposal on the Guyana project, there is no basis for contending that it could not, in any event, have obtained the contract or that there was any unwillingness to deal with it.

It is a mistake, in my opinion, to seek to encase the principle stated and applied in Peso, by adoption from *Regal (Hastings) Ltd. v. Gulliver*, in the straight-jacket of special knowledge acquired while acting as directors or senior officers, let alone limiting it to benefits acquired by reason of and during the holding of those offices. As in other cases in this developing branch of the law, the particular facts may determine the shape of the principle of decision without setting fixed limits to it. So it is in the present case. Accepting the facts found by the trial Judge, I find no obstructing considerations to the conclusion that O'Malley and Zarzycki continued, after their resignations, to be under a fiduciary duty to respect Canaero's priority, as against them and their instrument Terra, in seeking to capture the contract for the Guyana project. They entered the lists in the heat of the maturation of the project, known to them to be under active Government consideration when they resigned from Canaero and when they proposed to bid on behalf of Terra.

In holding that on the facts found by the trial Judge, there was a breach of fiduciary duty by O'Malley and Zarzycki which survived their resignations I am not to be taken as laying down any rule of liability to be read as if it were a statute. The general standards of loyalty, good faith and avoidance of a conflict of duty and self-interest to which the conduct of a director or senior officer must conform, must be tested in each case by many factors which it would be reckless to attempt to enumerate exhaustively. Among them are the factor of position or office held, the nature of the corporate opportunity, its ripeness, its specificness and the director's or managerial officer's relation to it, the amount of knowledge possessed, the circumstances in which it was obtained and whether it was special or, indeed, even private, the factor of time in the continuation of fiduciary duty where the alleged breach occurs after termination of the relationship with the company, and the circumstances under which the relationship was terminated, that is whether by retirement or resignation or discharge.

There remains the question of the appropriate relief against O'Malley and Zarzycki, and against Terra through which they acted in breach of fiduciary duty. In fixing the damages at $125,000, the trial Judge based himself on a claim for damages related only to the loss of the contract for the Guyana project, this being the extent of Canaero's claim as he understood it. No claim for a different amount or for relief on a different basis as, for example, to hold Terra as constructive trustee for Canaero in respect of the execution of the Guyana contract, was made in this court. Counsel for the respondents, although conceding that there was evidence of Terra's likely profit from the Guyana contract, emphasized the trial Judge's finding that Canaero could not have obtained the contract itself in view of its association with Spartan Air Services Limited in the submission of a proposal. It was his submission that there was no evidence that that proposal would have been accepted if Terra's had been rejected and, in any event, there was no evidence of Canaero's likely share of the profit.

Liability of O'Malley and Zarzycki for breach of fiduciary duty does not depend upon proof by Canaero that, but for their intervention it would have obtained the Guyana contract; nor is it a condition of recovery of damages that Canaero establish what its profit would have been or what it has lost by failing to realize the corporate opportunity in question. It is entitled to compel the faithless fiduciaries to answer for their default according to their gain. Whether the damages awarded here be viewed as an accounting of profits or, what amounts to the same thing, as based on unjust enrichment, I would not interfere with the quantum. The appeal is, accordingly, allowed...and judgment should be entered against them for $125,000. The appellant should have its costs against them throughout. ...

NOTES AND QUESTIONS

1. It is now clear that there can be liability for misuse of confidential information, whether or not the defendant is a fiduciary: *LAC Minerals Ltd. v. International Corona Resources Ltd.*, [1989] S.C.J. No. 83, [1989] 2 S.C.R. 574, 61 D.L.R. (4th) 14; *Cadbury Schweppes Inc. v. FBI Foods Ltd.*, [1999] S.C.J. No. 6, [1999] 1 S.C.R. 142, 167 D.L.R. (4th) 577.

2. The imposition of a fiduciary duty on the managers of a corporation may well restrict the business opportunities of those managers who leave the employ of the corporation and who wish to establish competing businesses. In one sense the imposition of a fiduciary obligation runs counter to legal principles governing "non-competition" clauses, which need to be carefully drafted to avoid being declared void as operating in "restraint of trade". Consider how far the Court should go in imposing the fiduciary obligation. In *R.W. Hamilton Ltd. v. Aeroquip Corp.* (1988), 40 B.L.R. 79 (Ont. H.C.) the Court refused to extend the duty to a manager who formed a competing corporation when the manager had very limited powers. The Court said at p. 86:

> An officer or manager will not be saddled with a fiduciary duty under *Canadian Aero Services* unless the position he occupies contains the power and the ability to direct and guide the affairs of the company. A title may or may not match reality per se. It is superficial and as such of little interest or assistance to the Court. The job content is what the trial Judge must define in light of all the evidence and of all reasonable inferences derived from it. A judgment call thereupon follows in the nature of a finding of facts as to whether the defendant was an *agent* or an *employee*.

Several cases following *Canaero* illustrate that difficulty. In *Quantum Management Services v. Hann*, [1989] O.J. No. 542, 69 O.R. (2d) 26 (H.C.) top employees in a personnel placement business left to form their own business and drew on the clients of the plaintiff. A fiduciary obligation was imposed on the employees. See also *Alberts v. Mountjoy* (1977), 16 O.R. (2d) 682 (H.C.). Conversely, no fiduciary obligation was placed on a "national sales and marketing manager" in *Dialadex Communications v. Crammond*, [1987] O.J. No. 88, 57 O.R. (2d) 746 (H.C.).

Even if there is a fiduciary obligation, the resigning fiduciary is not forbidden forever from setting up a competing business. Based on *Canaero Services*, what is it that the resigning fiduciary cannot do?

3. In *Island Export Finance Ltd. v. Umunna*, [1986] B.C.L.C. 460 (Eng. Ch. D.), the defendant was the managing director of the plaintiff. In 1976 he secured a contract by which the plaintiff sold mailboxes to the government of Cameroon. The plaintiff was hoping to get further such orders, but had no assurance that they would be forthcoming. The next year the defendant resigned, as the judge found for unrelated reasons. He formed a new company (now also a defendant) and secured another order for mail boxes from Cameroon; at this time the plaintiff was not actively seeking such business. The plaintiff sued for breach of fiduciary duty. Hutchison J. rejected the claim. After referring to *Canaero*, he said:

> Furthermore, counsel [for the defendants] submits that there is no authority for the proposition that the fiduciary duty of agents or trustees continues after their office has terminated. While in a sense this may be correct, if it is intended to mean that immediately on termination an agent or trustee is completely unfettered in the use he may make of information acquired during his period of office, it seems to me to be self-evidently wrong.

> It appears to me, if I may say so with respect, that the judges in the *Canaero* case were absolutely right to conclude that on the facts of that case there was a breach of fiduciary duty by the defendants: and that in so holding they were consistently applying the principles laid down in the line of authorities of which *Regal (Hastings) Ltd. v. Gulliver* is an example. I do, however, question whether in stating the principle (40 D.L.R. (3d) 371 at 382) they do not put the matter somewhat too widely in the last three lines of the passage I have cited. The words in question are: '... or where it was his position with the company

> rather than a fresh initiative that led him to the opportunity which he later acquired.'

It is to be noted that this passage begins with the word 'or', and that it would seem that the phrase 'that led him to the opportunity which he later acquired' has been deliberately chosen rather than the phrase 'that led him to acquire the opportunity'. Thus, it seems to me that, literally construed, this last part of the formulation could justify holding former directors accountable for profits wherever information acquired by them as such led them to the source from which they subsequently, perhaps as the result of prolonged fresh initiative, acquired business. If it is intended to mean that, it is far more widely stated than the facts of the case require: but I do not believe that that is what was intended.

After citing another passage from *Canaero*, he went on:

> In this context counsel for the defendants rightly stresses the fundamental principles relating to contracts in restraint of trade. It would, it seems to me, be surprising to find that directors alone, because of the fiduciary nature of their relationship with the company, were restrained from exploiting after they had ceased to be such any opportunity of which they had acquired knowledge while directors. Directors, no less than employees, acquire a general fund of knowledge and expertise in the course of their work, and it is plainly in the public interest that they should be free to exploit it in a new position. It is one thing to hold them accountable when, in the graphic words of Laskin J. (at 391), 'they entered the lists in the heat of the maturation of the project, known to them to be under active Government consideration when they resigned from Canaero and when they proposed to bid on behalf of Terra'; but it is an altogether different thing to hold former directors accountable whenever they exploit for their own or a new employer's benefit information which, while they may have come by it solely because of their position as directors of the plaintiff company, in truth forms part of their general fund of knowledge and their stock-in-trade.

> It is, in my judgment, unnecessary in the present case that I should attempt definitively to state the limits of the rule as to accountability of directors. Since it is not necessary, it would be presumptuous of me to make the attempt. I return to the formulation of counsel for the plaintiff. It appears to me that, on the basis of the findings I have made, the plaintiff's claim fails for a variety of reasons. I would summarise them as follows: (a) The hope of obtaining further orders for postal caller boxes could not in any realistic sense be said to be 'a maturing business opportunity'. (b) Neither when Mr. Umunna resigned nor when he succeeded in obtaining the two June 1977 orders was tbe plaintiff actively pursuing the matter. (c) It cannot in any true sense be said that, at the time he resigned, Mr. Umunna had in contemplation the exploitation of the Cameroons postal box business. As I have already indicated, the highest that it can be put is that, if asked, he would undoubtedly have replied that that was a potential source of business which he might be minded to pursue. It was certainly not his motive for resigning, and it cannot possibly be said that his resignation was 'prompted or influenced by a wish to acquire for himself the opportunity sought by the company'.

Hutchison J. also rejected a claim that the defendant had misused confidential information.

4.   In *Balston Ltd. v. Headline Filters Ltd.*, [1990] Fleet Street Reports 385 (Ch. D.) a long-time director of the plaintiff company decided to resign and start his own business. Before he had decided what business he would pursue, he learned that the plaintiff was going to stop supplying filters to a customer. He started a business

supplying those filters. Falconer J. held that he was not liable; he said the following at p. 412:

> In my judgment an intention by a director of a company to set up business in competition with the company after his directorship has ceased is not to be regarded as a conflicting interest within the context of the principle, having regard to the rules of public policy as to restraint of trade, nor is the taking of any preliminary steps to investigate or forward that intention so long as there is no actual competitive activity, such as, for instance, competitive tendering or actual trading, while he remains a director.

5.   How are the courts to draw the limits around what corporate fiduciaries can and cannot do? On the one hand, as we have said, it is *not* the case that a director must spend 24 hours per day trying to advance the interests of the corporation. In other words, a director *is* allowed to be self-interested, to some extent. Directors can have a good night's sleep, and can even undertake profitable outside activities, whether they be employment with another corporation, or other directorships. The fiduciary obligation does not forbid all self-interested action. It forbids conflicts between self-interest and fiduciary duty, but the fiduciary obligation does not say *how much* the fiduciary must do *for the benefit of the corporation*. Other duties, however, may have a lot to say about that. Think first of the case of a director who is also an officer of the corporation; he or she is a full-time employee and the employment relationship creates positive duties towards the corporation. Is that a fair description of Mr. Cooley in *I.D.C. v. Cooley*? He had a *contractual* duty (not arising from his directorship) to further the interests of his employer. Hence, even if the opportunity came to him personally, he was bound *contractually* to try to use it for the benefit of his corporate employer. And since he was a fiduciary, he was also forbidden to be in a conflict of interest and duty; the breach of contract thus became a breach of the duty of loyalty. But what if a director was only a director? Surely the positive duties to benefit the corporation would be less; if the director took up an opportunity that he or she came upon privately, without the use of any information acquired in the course of acting as a director, this might be just as lawful as other self-interested acts which a director is allowed to engage in. In *Canaero* the Court mentioned *Burg v. Horn* (1967), 380 F.2d 897, in which directors of Darand Corp. acquired buildings that the corporation might have been interested in. They were allowed to keep them. The majority noted (at p. 900):

> Had the Horns been full-time employees of Darand with no prior real estate ventures of their own, New York law might well uphold a finding that they were subject to such an implied duty. But as they spent most of their time in unrelated produce and real estate enterprises and already owned corporations holding similar properties when Darand was formed, as plaintiff knew, we agree with Judge Dooling that a duty to offer Darand all such properties coming to their attention cannot be implied absent some further evidence of an agreement or understanding to that effect.

D.D. PRENTICE AND J. PAYNE,
THE CORPORATE OPPORTUNITY DOCTRINE

(2004), 120 Law Q. Rev. 198

Painting with a broad brush, the corporate opportunity doctrine proscribes a director from diverting to his own advantage a commercial opportunity that could have been exploited by his company. As Arden L.J. stated when giving leave to appeal in *Bhullar v. Bhullar*, [2002] EWCA Civ 1509, there is no clear test to determine what constitutes a corporate opportunity particularly "in an owner-managed company ... where the information [which is the alleged corporate opportunity] is obtained on a private occasion and without use of company property" (at [14]). An answer was given to some of these difficulties in *Bhullar v. Bhullar*, [2003] 2 B.C.L.C. 241.

Two sides of a family, referred to in the judgment as M's family and S's family, owned Bhullar Bros. Ltd. M's family had two directors on the board (the M directors), S's family had three (the S directors). One of the objects of the company was to acquire property for investment. Relations between the two sides broke down and the M directors informed the S directors in 1998 that in their view the two sides should go their separate ways and therefore no further properties should be acquired by the company. However, it took a further three years for the division of the company's assets to take place. In the meantime, in 1999 two of the S directors saw that a "sold" sign had appeared on the building contiguous to the company's major premises. They discovered this information in their own time, simply by observing the "sold" sign and then persuading the vendor to sell to them. They purchased the building in the name of a company (Silvercrest) owned and controlled by them personally. The M faction petitioned for relief under s. 459 of the Companies Act 1985 alleging unfair prejudice in the purchase of the building by Silvercrest. In deciding whether or not there was unfair prejudice the court had to determine whether the opportunity to acquire the building was a corporate opportunity vested in Bhullar Bros Ltd. The court at first instance, affirmed on appeal, held that the opportunity to acquire the property was a corporate opportunity.

Prior to *Bhullar* two distinct tests of a corporate opportunity had emerged, both developed in first instance decisions. The "maturing business opportunity" test provides that directors are disqualified from obtaining for themselves, or diverting to another with whom they are associated, a maturing business opportunity which the company is actively pursuing (see Hutchinson J. in *Island Export Finance Ltd v. Umunna*, [1986] B.C.L.C. 460, borrowing from the Canadian case of *Canadian Aero Service v. O'Malley*, [1974] S.C.R. 592). This test is unsatisfactory in that it is the directors themselves who ultimately determine whether or not the company will actively pursue an opportunity, and thus fails to provide an adequate incentive for directors to further the interests of the company. By comparison, the stricter "line of business" test provides that a director may come under a positive duty to make a business opportunity available to his company if it is in the company's line of business or if the director has been given responsibility to seek out particular opportunities for the company and the opportunity concerned is of such a nature as to fall within the scope of that remit (see Roskill J. in *Industrial Development Consultants Ltd v. Cooley*, [1972] 1 W.L.R. 443).

The Court of Appeal in *Bhullar* rejected the maturing business opportunity test. It was argued for the appellants that the company was not negotiating for or interested in acquiring the property at the time of the acquisition and that the property was obtained by the S directors in their private capacity. Jonathan Parker L.J., giving the judgment of the court, reasoned that these factors did not preclude liability on the part of a director. The relevant consideration was not whether the director had dealt improperly with the company's property, but whether by taking up the opportunity the director would be putting himself in a "position where his interest and duty conflict" (*Bray v. Ford*, [1896] A.C. 44 at p. 51 per Lord Herschell). This includes not just actual conflict but also circumstances in which "the reasonable man looking at the relevant facts and circumstances of the particular case would think that there was a real sensible possibility of conflict" (*Boardman v. Phipps*, [1967] 2 A.C. 46 at p. 124 per Lord Upjohn). Importantly, this approach is unconcerned with the issue of whether the director made a profit, although this may have a bearing on the remedy awarded to the company. Rather, the breach of duty arises from the failure to pass relevant information to the company: "the existence of the opportunity was information which it was relevant for the Company to know, and it follows that the appellants were under a duty to communicate it to the Company" (at [41]).

The judgment in *Bhullar* adopts a strict, status-based approach to the issue of what constitutes a corporate opportunity. The directors in *Bhullar* did not come across this opportunity when performing their functions as directors, they were literally mere passers by. Liability attached to them merely because they were directors of the company: the directors had "at the material time, one capacity and one capacity only in which they were carrying on business, namely as directors of the Company" [at 41]. This is a rigorous test. A way to assess its rigours is to examine a range of possible defences that could be raised by directors alleged to have appropriated a corporate opportunity.

Bona fides

The S directors in *Bhullar* did not attempt to rely on the bona fides of their actions as this does not affect the classification of the opportunity as "corporate" and in corporate fiduciary law it is not normally a relevant consideration in determining whether there has been a breach of duty: *Regal (Hastings) Ltd v. Gulliver*, [1967] 2 A.C. 134n).

Source of information

The information in *Bhullar* was "private" in the sense that the information did not come to the directors in the discharge of their duties as directors as, for example, it did in Regal Hastings. The court in *Bhullar* did not consider this to be a defence.

Rejection

A company's board of directors may reject a particular opportunity. The rejection could take one of two forms. The rejection may be ex ante, that is, a decision not to pursue a particular type of business. *Bhullar* indicates that this will not be a defence: "whether the Company could or would have taken that opportunity, had it been aware of it, is not to the point" (at [41]). To decide otherwise would be to relax unacceptably the disincentive effects of the corporate opportunity proscription. The S directors could have informed the M directors of the opportunity and sought to persuade them to reverse their decision of May 1998. As Roskill J. pointed out in *Industrial Development Consultants Ltd v. Cooley*, it would be odd if "he whose duty it would have been to seek them to change their mind should now say that the plaintiffs suffered no loss because he would never have succeeded in persuading them to change their mind" ([1972] 1 W.L.R. 443 at p.454).

The rejection may be ex post, as, for example, occurred in *Queensland Mines Ltd v. Hudson* (1978), 52 A.L.J.R. 379. In that case the Privy Council held that on the facts this defence was effective in that the rejection had been by an independent board, but the concept of what constitutes independence was not elaborated upon. It is submitted that at least in English law, since the persons who reject are the persons who may benefit from the rejection, this defence is not available (cf. *Regal (Hastings) Ltd v. Gulliver*, above). A more objective test would be to preclude a director from taking up the opportunity if he was involved in the rejection decision. However, even where such a criterion of disinterest is satisfied there is a risk that other directors may be unduly influenced by the fact that the person taking up the opportunity is a fellow director. The test of disinterestedness would be particularly difficult to apply in the context of family structured companies. For example, the application of such a test in a *Salomon v. Salomon & Co. Ltd*, [1897] A.C. 22 type of company raises intractable problems and is unworkable.

Commercial impossibility

It may be that the company simply lacked the resources to exploit the opportunity. This was rejected, rightly it is submitted, as a defence by the House of Lords in *Regal Hastings* and is also implicitly rejected in the judgment of Jonathan Parker L.J. in *Bhullar* (at [41], quoted above). The difficulties here are similar to those relating to ex ante rejection. As the directors are the persons who have to seek to overcome the company's commercial inability and who will benefit if they fail to do so, the conflict is obvious if the directors can appropriate the opportunity.

Third party unwillingness to deal

The opportunity may involve a third party who is unwilling to deal with the company. This is not a defence, again for the good reason that it is the directors who would have to persuade the third party to deal (*Industrial Development Consultants Ltd v. Cooley*, above).

Resignation

A director's power to resign is not a fiduciary power but if he exercises it to enable him to appropriate a business opportunity he will have to account (*CMS Dolphin Ltd v. Simonet*, [2001] 2 B.C.L.C. 704). Resignation is not a defence.

There is a niggling incompleteness about *Bhullar*. Although Jonathan Parker L.J. rejects the maturing business opportunity test he does not articulate a clear definition of what does constitute a corporate opportunity. On the facts in *Bhullar*, the test is probably that the opportunity must be one that falls within the company's line of business and that this has to be expansively interpreted to cover not only what the company is interested in, but what it could be interested in. It would be in keeping with the approach in *Bhullar* to treat anything of economic value to the company as potentially within the company's line of business, and therefore a corporate opportunity. ...

NOTES AND QUESTIONS

1.   If the directors in *Bhullar* were only directors (which is not clear from the judgments), does the holding imply that directors, even if they are not also employees like Mr.

Cooley, must offer every business opportunity they come across to their corporation? Is that going too far?

2.   Do the rules applied in corporate opportunity cases seem too harsh? Bear in mind the principle of informed consent. In each case, if the fiduciary had obtained the fully informed consent of the corporation in advance, he would have been able to keep the gain. Why do you think this was not done?

3.   For a detailed analysis of corporate opportunity cases, see L. Rotman, *Fiduciary Law* (Toronto: Carswell, 2005), pp. 434-58.

5. Conflict of Duty and Duty

In principle, the rule against a conflict of duty and duty is just as strict as the rule against conflict of self-interest and duty. A lawyer cannot act for both sides in the same dispute, as duties to the two sides conflict.

It is common for the same person to be a director of more than one corporation. This will create duties of loyalty to both. If the corporations do not compete in any sense, this should not create any perception of conflict. In an old English case, *London and Mashonaland Exploration Co. Ltd. v. New Mashonaland Exploration Co.*, [1891] W.N. 165 (Ch. D.), a director was allowed to stay on the boards of two companies in direct competition. This case is now considered to be out of date. It was doubted in *In Plus Group Ltd. v. Pyke*, [2002] 2 B.C.L.C. 201 (Eng. C.A.). In the note by Prentice and Payne extracted immediately above, the authors say (at p. 202), "In the light of *Bhullar* a director simply could not carry on a competing business with his company unless there was consent."

In the area of corporate opportunities, the presence of another corporation is often just a distraction that should not make any difference to the analysis. If the director could take up an opportunity on his or her own, it can be taken up via another corporation in which the director has an interest. If the director cannot take up the opportunity, the use of another corporation will not save the director from liability, even though he or she can now say that a duty of loyalty is owed to the second corporation. This was illustrated as far back as *Cook v. Deeks* and *Regal (Hastings) Ltd. v. Gulliver*; in both cases, the opportunity was taken up by a corporation of which the disloyal directors were shareholders. A more recent example was *Levy-Russel Ltd. v. Tecmotiv Inc.*, [1994] O.J. No. 650, 13 B.L.R. (2d) 1 (H.C.). In that case, Lane J. discussed the director whom "everyone knows" is on the board to represent a certain interest. For example, if half of the shares of a corporation are held by family A, and the other half by family B, it may be that some of the directors are understood to be the "family A" directors and others, the "family B" directors. Alternatively, a corporate constitution may provide that one or more directors are to be elected exclusively by the shareholders of a particular class of shares. This kind of director is sometimes called a "nominee", in the sense that he or she is named by a particular constituency, and one might be tempted to think he or she is answerable only to that constituency. Justice Lane reviewed the authorities and concluded that a nominee director is not accorded an attenuated standard of loyalty to the corporation. A director is a director of the corporation and must act in what he or she considers its best interests. Compare the case of a Member of Parliament. You may have noticed that between elections, it is customary for an M.P. to remove all evidence of party affiliation from the constituency office. Why? Although the M.P. is usually elected under a particular party's banner, nonetheless, once elected, that M.P. represents *all* constituents, not just those who voted for him or her. Note A.B.C.A., s. 122(4), which is set out above at page 95. If shareholders take over director's powers under a unanimous shareholders agreement, does a different rule apply? The common law said no; see C.B.C.A., s. 146(6), added in 2001.

The principle of informed consent also applies to conflicts of duty and duty. The fiduciary is allowed to be in the conflict if he or she obtains the fully informed consent, in advance, of both of the parties to whom the duty is owed. In some cases this may be impossible, if the provision of some information to one of them would be a breach of duty to the other. The equitable principle is not relaxed in this situation; there is always a way out, because the fiduciary can always resign from one or both of the conflicting offices. Directors often do not like being presented with this option, but this is a consequence of the strictness of the duty of loyalty.

6. Ownership, Obligation and Opportunity

In the Western legal tradition, the difference between property and obligation, between owning and owing, is fundamental. If I own a watch and lend it to you, it is still my watch. If you give possession of it to a third party, I will have some right to recover possession of the watch or its ownership value from that third party, and if you become bankrupt, I will not be affected so long as I can find the watch. Contrast the case in which you only owe me an obligation. It might be an obligation to make me the owner of a watch, if we have an agreement to buy and sell a watch; or it might just be an obligation to pay money. If you owe me $50, I have a claim against you, but not to any particular asset or any particular $50. In general, I cannot stop you giving your property away to others, nor will I have a claim against them if you do (although there is a limit in the case in which you are trying to hide assets from your creditors). If you go bankrupt, I will be one of many creditors who will get little or nothing.

The distinction between ownership and obligation features in various ways in the cases on fiduciary obligations. In *Cook v. Deeks*, the Judicial Committee distinguished *North-West Transportation Co. v. Beatty* on this basis, saying that "ratification" by shareholders was not permissible in a case in which the breach of fiduciary obligation involved the taking of corporate property. But what was the "property" in *Cook v. Deeks*? Is there any reason why the rules relating to ratification (which are discussed in the next section of this chapter) should be different depending on whether or not the breach consisted of a property taking?

The question of whether or not something is property has arisen in another context. Sometimes, on the difficult question of whether the defendant has actually breached a fiduciary obligation, judges are more comfortable in so characterizing the situation if they can somehow view the case as one in which property has been misappropriated. This is why some of the judges in *Boardman v. Phipps*, [1967] 2 A.C. 46, [1966] 3 All E.R. 721 (H.L.) said that the information used by Boardman was trust property. The Supreme Court of Canada rejected this approach to information in *Cadbury Schweppes Inc. v. FBI Foods Ltd.*, [1999] S.C.J. No. 6, [1999] 1 S.C.R. 142, 167 D.L.R. (4th) 577. Similarly, some cases and articles in corporate law show a parallel urge to characterize what was taken as property, when they say that a director has "misappropriated" an opportunity that "belonged" to the corporation. The more recent evolution fiduciary liability, however, should have reduced the need to blur the line between ownership and obligation, or between property (rights that are held) and opportunity (possibilities of profit); it is now clear that a breach of fiduciary obligation is not dependent on a misappropriation of property. In other words, as cases like *Canaero* show, one can say that in relation to an opportunity, a fiduciary has obligations to his principal; one does not have to focus on any property held by the principal. Does characterizing the opportunity as a form of property add anything to the analysis?

Assume that a corporation has issued 100 shares each and the corporation has assets worth $100. You might think the shares are worth $1 each. Now consider how much you would pay for (a) a block of 51 shares; (b) a block of 49 shares? Block (a) would give you total control over the election of directors and any other votes requiring only an ordinary resolution. To the extent that a person would pay more than $51 for those $51 shares, this is called a "control premium". Is "control" a form of property that somehow exists separately from the 51 shares? To whom does the control premium belong?

PERLMAN v. FELDMANN

219 F.2d 173 (U.S. Court of Appeals, 2nd Circuit, 1955)

[The defendant was the dominant stockholder and chairman and president of a steel sheet manufacturing corporation. Steel was in short supply at a time when the defendant sold his stock to Wilport Co., a corporation whose shares were held by various end users of steel sheets. The purpose of the share transfer was to ensure the users a continuing supply of steel during the shortage caused by the Korean War. The minority brought an action seeking to recover the premium paid for the stock. The action was a "derivative action", meaning that the minority shareholders claimed that they were asserting a right that belonged, not to them personally, but to the corporation.]

Clark C.J.: — ... Plaintiffs contend that the consideration paid for the stock included compensation for the sale of a corporate asset, a power held in trust for the corporation by Feldmann as its fiduciary. This power was the ability to control the allocation of the corporate product in a time of short supply, through control of the board of directors; and it was effectively transferred in this sale by having Feldmann procure the resignation of his own board and the election of Wilport's nominees immediately upon consummation of the sale.

The present action represents the consolidation of three pending stockholders' actions in which yet another stockholder has been permitted to intervene. Jurisdiction below was based upon the diverse citizenship of the parties. (Plaintiffs argue here, as they did in the court below, that in the situation here disclosed the vendors must account to the non-participating minority stockholders for that share of their profit which is attributable to the sale of the corporate power.) Judge Hincks denied the validity of the premise, holding that the rights involved in the sale were only those normally incident to the possession of a controlling block of shares, with which a dominant stockholder, in the absence of fraud or foreseeable looting, was entitled to deal according to his own best interests. Furthermore, he held that plaintiffs had failed to satisfy their burden of proving that the sales price was not a fair price for the stock per se. Plaintiffs appeal from these rulings of law which resulted in the dismissal of their complaint. ...

Both as director and as dominant stockholder, Feldmann stood in a fiduciary relationship to the corporation and to the minority stockholders as beneficiaries thereof. ... In *Schemmel v. Hill* (1930), 169 N.E. 678 (Ind.), at pp. 682, 683,

McMahan, J., said: "Directors of a corporation are its agents, and they are governed by the rules of law applicable to other agents, and, as between themselves and their principal, the rules relating to honesty and fair dealing in the management of the affairs of their principal are applicable. They must not, in any degree allow their official conduct to be swayed by their private interest, which must yield to official duty. ... In a transaction between a director and his corporation, where he acts for himself and his principal at the same time in a matter connected with the relation between them, it is presumed, where he is thus potential on both sides of the contract, that self-interest will overcome his fidelity to his principal, to his own benefit and to his principal's hurt." And the judge added: "Absolute and most scrupulous good faith is the very essence of a director's obligation to his corporation. The first principal duty arising from his official relation is to act in all things of trust wholly for the benefit of his corporation."

In Indiana, then, as elsewhere, the responsibility of the fiduciary is not limited to a proper regard for the tangible balance sheet assets of the corporation, but includes the dedication of his uncorrupted business judgment for the sole benefit of the corporation, in any dealings which may adversely affect it. ... Although the Indiana case is particularly relevant to Feldmann as a director, the same rule should apply to his fiduciary duties as majority stockholder, for in that capacity he chooses and controls the directors, and thus is held to have assumed their liability. ... This, therefore, is the standard to which Feldmann was by law required to conform in his activities here under scrutiny.

It is true, as defendants have been at pains to point out, that this is not the ordinary case of breach of fiduciary duty. We have here no fraud, no misuse of confidential information, no outright looting of a helpless corporation. But on the other hand we do not find compliance with that high standard which we have just stated and which we and other courts have come to expect and demand of corporate fiduciaries. In the often-quoted words of Judge Cardozo: "Many forms of conduct permissible in a workaday world for those acting at arm's length, are forbidden to those bound by fiduciary ties. A trustee is held to something stricter than the morals of the market place. Not honesty alone, but the punctilio of an honour the most sensitive, is then the standard of behaviour. As to this there has developed a tradition that is unbending and inveterate. Uncompromising rigidity has been the attitude of courts of equity when petitioned to undermine the rule of undivided loyalty by the 'disintegrating erosion of particular exceptions'." The actions of defendants in siphoning off for personal gains corporate advantages to be derived from a favourable market situation do not betoken the necessary undivided loyalty owed by the fiduciary to the principal.

The corporate opportunities of whose misappropriation the minority stockholders complain need not have been an absolute certainty in order to support his action against Feldmann. If there was possibility of corporate gain, they are entitled to recover. ...

This rationale is equally appropriate to a consideration of the benefits which Newport might have derived from the steel shortage. In the past Newport had used and profited by its market leverage by operation of what the industry had come to call the "Feldmann Plan". This consisted of securing interest-free advances from prospective purchasers of steel in return for firm commitments to them from future production. The funds thus acquired were used to finance improvements in existing plants and to acquire new installations. In the summer of 1950 Newport had been negotiating for cold-rolling facilities which it needed for a more fully integrated operation and a more marketable product, and Feldmann plan funds might well have been used toward this end.

Further, as plaintiffs alternatively suggest, Newport might have used the period of short supply to build up patronage in the geographical area in which it could compete profitably even when steel was more abundant. Either of these opportunities was Newport's, to be used to its advantage only. Only if defendants had been able to negate completely any possibility of gain by Newport could they have prevailed. It is true that a trial court finding states:

> Whether or not, in August, 1950, Newport's position was such that it could have entered into "Feldmann Plan" type transactions to procure funds and financing for the further expansion and integration of its steel facilities and whether such expansion would have been desirable for Newport, the evidence does not show.

This, however, cannot avail the defendants, who — contrary to the ruling below — had the burden of proof on this issue, since fiduciaries always have the burden of proof in establishing the fairness of their dealings with trust property. ...

We do not mean to suggest that a majority stockholder cannot dispose of his controlling block of stock to outsiders without having to account to his corporation for profits or even never do this with impunity when the buyer is an interested customer, actual or potential, for the corporation's product. But when the sale necessarily results in a sacrifice of this element of corporate good will and consequent unusual profit to the fiduciary who has caused the sacrifice, he should account for his gains. So in a time of market shortage, where a call on a corporation's product commands an unusually large premium, in one form or another, we think it sound law that a fiduciary may not appropriate to himself the value of his premium. Such personal gain at the expense of his co-venturers seems particularly reprehensible when made by the trusted president and director of his company. In this case the violation of duty seems to be all the clearer because of this triple role in which Feldmann appears, though we are unwilling to say, and are not to be understood as saying, that we should accept a lesser obligation for any of his roles alone.

Hence to the extent that the price received by Feldmann and his co-defendants included such a bonus, he is accountable to the minority stockholders who sue here. ... And plaintiffs, as they contend, are entitled to a recovery in their own right, instead of in right of the corporation (as in the usual derivative actions), since neither Wilport nor their successors in interest should share in any judgment which may be rendered. ... Defendants cannot well object to this form of recovery, since the only alternative, recovery for the corporation as a whole, would subject them to a greater total liability.

The case will therefore be remanded to the district court for a determination of the question expressly left open below, namely, the value of defendants' stock without the appurtenant control over the corporation's output of steel. We reiterate that on this issue, as on all others relating to a breach of fiduciary duty, the burden of proof must rest on the defendants. ... Judgment should go to these plaintiffs and those whom they represent for any premium value so shown to the extent of their respective stock interests. ...

Swan C.J. (dissenting): —

... The power to control the management of a corporation, that is, to elect directors to manage its affairs, is an inseparable incident to the ownership of a majority of its stock, or sometimes, as in the present instance, to the ownership of enough shares, less than a majority, to control an election. Concededly a majority or dominant shareholder is ordinarily privileged to sell his stock at the best price obtainable from the purchaser. In so doing he acts on his own behalf, not as an agent of the corporation. ...

My brothers say that "the consideration paid for the stock included compensation for the sale of a corporate asset", which they describe as "the ability to control the allocation of the corporate product in a time of short supply, through control of the board of directors; and it was effectively transferred in this sale by having Feldmann procure the resignation of his own board and the election of Wilport's nominees immediately upon consummation of the sale." The implications of this are not clear to me. ... For reasons already stated, in my opinion Feldmann was not proved to be under any fiduciary duty as a stockholder not to sell the stock he controlled.

Feldmann was also a director of Newport. Perhaps the quoted statement means that as a director he violated his fiduciary duty in voting to elect Wilport's nominees to fill the vacancies created by the resignations of the former directors of Newport. As a director Feldmann was under a fiduciary duty to use an honest judgment in acting on the corporation's behalf. A director is privileged to resign, but so long as he remains a director he must be faithful to his fiduciary duties and must not make a personal gain from performing them. Consequently, if the price paid for Feldmann's stock included a payment for voting to elect the new directors, he must account to the corporation for such payment, even though he honestly believed that the men he voted to elect were well qualified to serve as directors. He can not take pay for performing his fiduciary duty. There is no suggestion that he did do so ...

The final conclusion of my brothers is that the plaintiffs are entitled to recover in their own right instead of in the right of the corporation. This appears to be completely inconsistent with the theory advanced at the outset of the opinion, namely, that the price of the stock 'included compensation for the sale of a corporate asset.' If a corporate asset was sold, surely the corporation should recover the compensation received for it by the defendants. Moreover, if the plaintiffs were suing in their own right, Newport was not a proper party. ...

NOTES AND QUESTIONS

1. In *Farnham v. Fingold*, [1972] 3 O.R. 688, 29 D.L.R. (3d) 279 (H.C.), minority shareholders wanted to bring a class action against majority shareholders to share in a control premium that the majority had obtained. They were asserting individual rights, not corporate rights. The defendant moved to have the action struck out as disclosing no cause of action. Justice Morand dismissed the motion to strike, saying that while there is no automatic fiduciary duty owed by majority shareholders to minority shareholders, the case should be allowed to go to trial to permit the plaintiffs to try to prove a fiduciary relationship arising out of the particular facts. The Court of Appeal allowed an appeal ([1973] 2 O.R. 132, 33 D.L.R. (3d) 156), finding that the action as pleaded was asserting corporate rights; such derivative or representative actions can only be brought with the leave of the court.

2. In *Peoples Department Stores Inc. v. Wise*, [2004] S.C.J. No. 64, [2004] 3 S.C.R. 461, 244 D.L.R. (4th) 564 the Supreme Court of Canada clarified that directors' fiduciary duties are owed not to shareholders but to the corporation. In *Brant Investments Ltd. v. Keeprite Inc.*, [1991] O.J. No. 683, 3 O.R. (3d) 289, 80 D.L.R. (4th) 161 (C.A.) it was held that majority shareholders do not automatically owe a fiduciary duty to

minority shareholders. In what circumstances do you think a shareholder should be held to owe such a duty to another shareholder?

The distinction between property and obligation also arises after a gainful breach of fiduciary obligation has been established, when the legal effect of the breach is in issue. Assume that a director makes a gain in breach of duty. The traditional language has it that the director is "accountable" for the gain. This implies that the director is obliged to render an account to show the amount of the gain, and then to hand over the total. It refers to an obligation. On the other hand, many of the cases (such as *Keech v. Sandford* (1726), Sel. Cas. Ch. 61 and *Boardman v. Phipps*, [1967] 2 A.C. 46, [1966] 3 All E.R. 721 (Eng. H.L.)) have said that the director holds the gain on "constructive trust" for the corporation. This refers to a trust arising by operation of law. The effect is that the plaintiff has an ownership right in the gain. This protects the plaintiff if the defendant is bankrupt or makes a transfer to a third party; but the bankruptcy protection comes at the expense of other creditors of the defendant.

In *Lister v. Stubbs* (1890), 45 Ch.D. 1 (Eng. C.A.), the defendant was an agent and so a fiduciary of the plaintiff. He took bribes from third parties. The question was whether he held the bribes on trust for the plaintiff, or was only accountable. The context of the dispute was that a plaintiff asserting ownership of an asset held by the defendant may be able to get a pre-trial injunction to prevent a transfer of that asset, but if a plaintiff is merely asserting an obligation, such an injunction is much harder to get. The court held that Stubbs was only accountable. This holding was apparently approved by the Supreme Court of Canada in *Aetna Financial Services Ltd. v. Feigelman*, [1985] S.C.J. No. 1, [1985] 1 S.C.R. 2, 15 D.L.R. (4th) 161. In *Attorney General for Hong Kong v. Reid*, [1994] A.C. 324, [1994] 1 All E.R. 1 (J.C.P.C., N.Z.), the Judicial Committee of the Privy Council held that *Lister* was wrongly decided and that a bribe taken in breach of fiduciary obligation was held on constructive trust for the person to whom the obligation was owed.

The issue arose in *Soulos v. Korkontzilas*, [1997] S.C.J. No. 52, [1997] 2 S.C.R. 217, 146 D.L.R. (4th) 214, discussed (1997), 76 Can. Bar Rev. 539, which was another case of breach of fiduciary obligation by an agent. The defendant did not take a bribe, but he bought an estate in land for himself that, as the plaintiff's agent, he should have procured for the plaintiff. This dispute was therefore similar to the typical corporate law breach of fiduciary obligation. The Court held that a trust is appropriate if certain conditions are satisfied (unfortunately without reference to either *Lister* or *Reid*). Justice McLachlin, as she then was, for the majority, said at para. 45:

> Extrapolating from the cases where courts of equity have imposed constructive trusts for wrongful conduct, and from a discussion of the criteria considered in an essay by Roy Goode, "Property and Unjust Enrichment", in Andrew Burrows, ed., Essays on the Law of Restitution (1991), I would identify four conditions which generally should be satisfied:
>
> (1) The defendant must have been under an equitable obligation, that is, an obligation of the type that courts of equity have enforced, in relation to the activities giving rise to the assets in his hands;
>
> (2) The assets in the hands of the defendant must be shown to have resulted from deemed or actual agency activities of the defendant in breach of his equitable obligation to the plaintiff;

(3)   The plaintiff must show a legitimate reason for seeking a proprietary remedy, either personal or related to the need to ensure that others like the defendant remain faithful to their duties and;

(4)   There must be no factors which would render imposition of a constructive trust unjust in all the circumstances of the case; *e.g.*, the interests of intervening creditors must be protected.

A "deemed agency gain" refers to a gain that the defendant was under a duty to make, if he or she made it all, on behalf of the plaintiff. The introduction of this test would seem to mean that corporate fiduciaries will generally (subject to the rather open-ended fourth requirement) hold gains on constructive trust for the corporation.

This kind of constructive trust remains rather controversial; many commentators take the view that *Lister* was right, and that a breach of obligation does not generate ownership of the resulting gain. This controversial constructive trust can be contrasted with the much clearer case of misappropriation of corporate property. Property taken from the corporation by a fiduciary, of course, still belongs to the corporation. Moreover, if the fiduciary generates profits or proceeds with the misappropriated asset, these will be held on trust for the corporation. This is not so much a principle of corporate law or even fiduciary law, but rather is part of the way in which property behaves in the common law system: see L. Smith, *The Law of Tracing* (Oxford: Clarendon Press, 1997); *Foskett v. McKeown*, [2001] 1 A.C. 102, [2000] 2 W.L.R. 1299, [2000] 3 All E.R. 97 (Eng. H.L.). The much clearer availability of the trust where the plaintiff starts with a "proprietary base" (see P. Birks, *An Introduction to the Law of Restitution*, rev. ed. (Oxford: Clarendon Press, 1989), at pp. 378-84) provides another motivation for judges to blur the line between property and obligation, as discussed above.

Note, however, that the civil law of Quebec would admit neither the possibility of a trust arising in response to a breach of fiduciary or any other duty, nor a trust of the traceable proceeds of misappropriated property. Civilian systems, as a general rule, are more careful to distinguish property and obligation than is the common law, influenced as the latter is by the practise of the Chancery court.

7. "Ratification": Red Tape or Red Herring

It has long been a corporate tradition for the annual general meeting of shareholders to approve a formalistic motion to forgive ("ratify") any breaches of duty the corporate management may have accidentally committed in the past year. It seems relevant to distinguish this sense of "ratification" from that which is known to the common law of agency. There, ratification means a principal's decision to authorize an act that was done by his agent, on the principal's behalf, but without authority. The legal effect is to cure retroactively the want of authority. In this common law sense, there can be no ratification in advance; the concept is simply inapplicable in such a case. Moreover, it is not possible to ratify, in this sense, unless the act was done by the agent *as agent* on behalf of the principal (*Keighley, Maxsted & Co. v. Durant*, [1901] A.C. 240 (H.L.), apparently approved in *Crampsey v. Deveney*, [1969] S.C.R. 267, 2 D.L.R. (3d) 161).

The sense of ratification which is relevant in the context of a breach of fiduciary duty is one which comes from equity. It effectively means "forgiveness". Just as what would otherwise be a breach can be authorized in advance by the beneficiary of the fiduciary duty, so too it can be forgiven after the fact (see generally *Re Pauling's Settlement*, [1961] 3 All E.R. 713 (Eng. Ch. D.), aff'd [1964] Ch. 303, [1963] 3 All E.R. 1 (Eng. C.A.), foll'd *Holder v. Holder*, [1968] Ch. 353, [1968] 1 All E.R. 665 (Eng. C.A.)). Indeed, unlike in the common law agency sense, even advance approval is sometimes called "ratification". In either case, ratification is only effective if done with full information. This concept, differently from the common law agency idea of ratification, can apply whether or not the fiduciary purported to act on behalf of the beneficiary. It also shows a difference from common law reasoning in another respect. If a defendant has committed a common law wrong, say a tort of battery, and the victim, with full information, forgives the defendant, it is not clear that there is any effect on the plaintiff's legal rights. A release, like any other contract, requires consideration or a seal. But claims for breaches of equitable obligations, it seems, can be released without consideration. (In such a case, can the person who decided to forgive and forget change its mind and decide to sue? If not, why not?)

Clearly the relevant sense, in the context of the shareholders' motion to "ratify" any breaches of directors' duties, is the equitable sense. (What implications does this have for any purported ratification of a breach of the duty of care, skill and diligence?) What is the effect of the passage of such a motion? Many older cases assume that such a motion is effective. Recall *North-West Transportation Co. v. Beatty* (1887), 12 App. Cas. 589 (Ont. J.C.P.C.), extracted and discussed earlier in this chapter, and *Cook v. Deeks*, [1916] 1 A.C. 554 (Ont. J.C.P.C.), discussed earlier in this chapter, which found it necessary to distinguish *Beatty* on this point. In *Regal (Hastings) Ltd. v. Gulliver*, Lord Russell of Killowen said that the directors "could, had they wished, have protected themselves by a resolution (either antecedent or subsequent) of the Regal shareholders in general meeting". In *Bamford v. Bamford*, [1970] Ch. 212, [1969] 2 W.L.R. 1107, [1969] 1 All E.R. 969 (C.A.), Harman L.J. said (at p. 237-38 [Ch.]):

> It is trite law, I had thought, that if directors do acts, as they do every day, especially in private companies, which, perhaps because there is no quorum, or because their appointment was defective, or because sometimes there are no directors properly appointed at all, or because they are actuated by improper motives, they go on doing for years, carrying on the business of the company in the way in which, if properly constituted, they should carry it on, and then they find that everything has been so to speak wrongly done because it was not done by a proper board, such directors can, by making a full and frank disclosure and calling together the general body of the shareholders, obtain absolution and forgiveness of their sins; and provided the acts are not *ultra vires* the company as a whole everything will go on as if it had been done all right from the beginning. I cannot believe that that is not a commonplace of company law. It is done every day. Of course, if the majority of the general meeting will not forgive and approve, the directors must pay for it.

Do these cases reflect a prehistoric (*i.e.*, pre-*Salomon*) failure to distinguish between the corporation and the shareholders? See S. Worthington, "Corporate Governance: Remedying and Ratifying Directors' Breaches" (2000), 116 L.Q.R. 683, at pp. 653-54. Or do they attempt to reflect the underlying economic reality of investment in the corporate form?

While most would accept that according to general principle it should be possible to ratify and so extinguish a manager's breach of fiduciary obligation, the great unanswered question is how this can properly be done. The fiduciary obligation is owed to the corporate entity. How can it be decided whether a shareholder vote on this issue represents a corporate decision to forgive? If there is a breach of a director's duty, there is a claim, and that claim is an asset of the corporation. Who is competent to decide that the corporation will give away this asset? Does the answer depend on the type of corporate constitution?

In most corporations an amendment to the constitution must be effected by a special majority, usually two-thirds or three-quarters of the shareholders. What would be the result of a vote by 51 per cent of the shareholders voted to authorize in advance a breach of the corporate constitution? Do you find it ironic that the legal consequences of such a breach might be avoided by majority "ratification"? In *Bamford, supra*, it was specifically held that only an ordinary resolution is required. In *Burland v. Earle* (1900), 27 O.A.R. 540, the Ontario Court of Appeal indicated (at p. 561) that shareholder approval of a disloyal profit required unanimous consent. On appeal to the Judicial Committee of the Privy Council ([1902] A.C. 83 (Ont. J.C.P.C.)) the point did not arise.

If a shareholder vote could be effective as a corporate decision, can the breaching director vote if he holds shares, as he did in *Beatty*? Is it possible to accept that shareholders do not owe fiduciary duties, and yet still argue that the shareholder voting power is subject to a "proper purposes" doctrine? See S. Worthington, above, at pp. 646-51, 672-73.

Although it is not a case about ratification, this issue can be brought into focus by a recent case with a high profile in Canada: *Hollinger International Inc. v. Black*, 844 A.2d 1022 (Del. Ch. 2004); aff'd 872 A.2d 559 (Del. 2005). Conrad Black, a former Canadian but now an Englishman, was the controlling shareholder of Hollinger Inc., an O.B.C.A. corporation, via two levels of intermediate holding corporations. Hollinger Inc. was the controlling shareholder of Hollinger International, a Delaware corporation whose shares were publicly traded. Black was the Chief Executive Officer of Hollinger International and chairman of its board, but he was in an ongoing dispute with the other members of the board regarding past transactions. He agreed to resign as C.E.O. and to assist in the implementation of an agreed strategic process, involving the sale of major assets. He then contracted with another party to sell to that party a controlling interest in Hollinger Inc., which would give the outsider control of Hollinger International and frustrate the strategic process that Black had promised to foster. The other directors of Hollinger International tried to resist. Hollinger Inc. then purported to change the by-laws of Hollinger International, so as to require (among other things) unanimity for important board decisions. Unlike in Canadian law, the Delaware General Corporation Law, 8 Del. Code §109, provides that by-laws can be adopted, amended or repealed by shareholder vote. If the by-law amendments were valid, they would have given Black a veto over all important decisions, since he was still chairman of the board of Hollinger International. Chancellor Strine held that Hollinger Inc. had the legal power to change the by-laws of Hollinger International, but it could not use that power inequitably. The by-law amendments were held to be invalid, although there was no holding that Hollinger Inc. owed a duty of loyalty. Does this holding support an argument that even shareholder powers are reviewable as to the motivation behind them? Is there another way of explaining Hollinger Inc.'s inability to use its by-law amendment power?

Under an English-model corporate constitution a manager's breach of fiduciary obligation would initially seem to be a violation of the terms of the corporate constitution. The reason is that the power to manage is found there, not in the corporate statute. Any shareholder would thus seem to have standing to sue the corporation to compel specific performance of the corporate constitution, because it is a contract between each shareholder and the corporation (see Chapter 3). This would allow an indirect attack on the defaulting fiduciary (although if that fiduciary is also a shareholder, it would seem that he could be sued directly on the contract). A vote of other shareholders to "ratify" hardly seems relevant. Again, however, the English courts confused the shareholder collective with the corporate entity. Under the "rule in *Foss v. Harbottle*" (1843), 2 Hare 461 (approved in *Hercules Managements Ltd. v. Ernst & Young*, [1997] S.C.J. No. 51, [1997] 2 S.C.R. 165, 146 D.L.R. (4th) 577), shareholders are not generally allowed to complain of wrongs done to the corporation. That in itself seems right, but in the English model it ignores the fact that shareholders should be able to sue on the constitutional contract to which they are parties. This is ameliorated somewhat by the recognition of an uncertain number of exceptions to the rule, by which the judges seem to have taken the thoroughly illogical step of converting the shareholder's contractual action into a direct standing to pursue the corporate right of action. They have compounded their error by making this action subject, at least some of the time, to majority disapproval via "ratification".

In the letters patent system, the individual has no contractual right to have the corporate constitution enforced. Somehow, perhaps due to the English-model orientation and education of the Judicial Committee, the letters patent shareholder got standing to pursue the corporate right of action in such cases *North-West Transportation Co. v. Beatty*, *Burland v. Earle*, [1902] A.C. 83, and *Cook v. Deeks*. Somehow, this too became subject to the will of the majority. See generally S.M. Beck, "The Shareholders' Derivative Action" (1974), 52 Can. Bar Rev. 159.

In most Canadian jurisdictions an individual shareholder has no *right* to bring this kind of corporate action. Instead, a shareholder may apply for specific judicial permission to bring a statutory representative action: C.B.C.A., s. 239; A.B.C.A., s. 240; S.B.C.A., M.C.A., B.C.B.C.A., s. 232; O.B.C.A., s. 246; N.B.B.C.A., s. 164; N.L.C.A., s. 369; N.S.C.A., Third Schedule, s. 4; compare Civil Code of Quebec, art. 316. The judge has complete discretion whether to grant or refuse permission. If permission is granted, the shareholder sues as a representative capacity, on behalf of the corporation. In *Farnham v. Fingold*, [1973] 2 O.R. 132, 33 D.L.R. (3d) 156, the Ontario Court of Appeal said that s. 99 of the original O.B.C.A., which was the forerunner of the current statutory representative action section:

> embraces all causes of action under any statute or in law or in equity that a shareholder may sue for or on behalf of a corporation. All forms of derivative actions purporting to be brought on behalf of and for the benefit of the corporation come within its terms.

In other words, the "common law" governing derivative actions is displaced by the statutory regulation. The modern statutes also add an important remedy called the oppression remedy, and we will see later in this chapter that this is also sometimes used to rectify breaches of directors' duties. Statutory representative actions, and the oppression remedy, are covered in detail in Chapter 9. For present purposes, it is noteworthy that the statutes also say that a statutory representative action, or an oppression claim,

> ... shall not be stayed or dismissed by reason only that it is shown that an alleged breach of a right or duty owed to the corporation ... has been or may be approved by the shareholders ... but evidence of approval by the shareholders may be taken into account by the court in making an order ...[C.B.C.A., s. 242].

How do you think that majority "ratification" would affect the outcome of a statutory representative action brought on the facts of *Cook v. Deeks*? Of *Regal*?

Of *Canaero*? Of *North-West Transportation v. Beatty*? In regard to the last case, remember C.B.C.A., s. 120(7.1).

Remember that *Regal* and *Canaero* were corporate, not shareholder actions. Under one of the above statutes, do you think that would make a difference?

Is "ratification" dead?

8. Takeover Bids and Directors' Fiduciary Obligations

A takeover bid is an offer to purchase or otherwise acquire sufficient shares of the target corporation so as to gain control of it. Generally this is done with the belief that the corporation is not being well managed. Assume that the shares are trading in the market at $10. The offeror probably believes that the shares are or could be worth more than that. In other words, it believes that for some reason, the market's valuation does not reflect the corporation's potential. Usually, this belief is based partly or wholly on the idea that if the management were operating differently, the corporation would be making more money. All else being equal, this would increase the value of the shares. The bidder may therefore be willing to pay more per share than the market valuation before the bid; in this example, the bidder might offer $12. Hence the common attempt to describe takeover bids as efforts to "unlock shareholder value". On an economic analysis, real and potential takeover bids are an important discipline for management to manage well.

If the basis of a takeover bid is typically an understanding that the management is performing sub-optimally, it is easy to understand why managers are often hostile to such bids. Where management is not in favour of a bid, it is usually called a hostile bid. If, however, the bidder is offering a price above recent market valuations, management may feel the need to present some alternative to shareholders, other than an assurance that the board is doing its best, to induce shareholders to resist the offer. One solution is for management to find another potential bidder, perhaps willing to offer more. This counter-bid would probably be a friendly bid. Offers may be all in cash, but are often in a mixture of cash and shares in the offeror corporation; there may also be various conditions attached to an offer. These considerations may make it more difficult to evaluate rival bids. Note that one response to a takeover is an "issuer bid," in which the target offers to buy back its own shares. Such shares are then cancelled (C.B.C.A., 39(6)).

Takeover bids are heavily regulated, mostly by provincial securities law. The C.B.C.A. used to have its own regulation in Part XVII, but much of this was repealed in 2001 on the basis that publicly traded C.B.C.A. corporations are subject to provincial securities law. Note, however, the remaining rules in Parts XVI and XVII. Takeover regulation is supposed to strike a balance among the interests of the offeror, the target, and the shareholders of the target corporation, whose shares the offeror is trying to buy. The board of the target corporation needs information to assess the bid, and time to decide whether or not to recommend it to shareholders. The shareholders also need information, both from the offeror and the board of the target corporation, to make an informed choice; and time in which to make it. There is also a sense that all of the shareholders need to be treated equally (contrary to the normal rules of the marketplace, which allow a buyer to purchase shares without any obligation to make a similar offer to others). The equality is in terms of the price offered, and also the number of shares bought, if the bid is for less than 100 per cent of the shares and it is oversubscribed (*e.g.*, a bid for 50 per cent of the shares, and 60 per cent of the shares are tendered by shareholders). All of this regulation needs to be done without precluding the ability of offerors to move quickly and respond to changing markets.

Provincial securities law defines a takeover bid as an offer to acquire sufficient shares that would allow the offeror to have 20 per cent of a class of shares that are voting shares, or that allow participation in assets on a winding up. Closely held corporations (fewer than 50 shareholders) are exempt. The bid is sent in a prescribed form to shareholders and directors of the target (or "offeree") corporation, and to the securities regulator. The board of the target then sends its own "circular", that is, a document in which it recommends acceptance or rejection of the offer. (Why should the directors of the corporation be obliged to give advice to shareholders as to whether the shareholders should accept someone else's offer to buy the shares?) Shareholders who wish to accept the offer tender their shares to the offeror, although they may then withdraw them for at least 10 days, and longer if the offeror does not take them up; often the offer specifies that shares will not be taken up unless some minimum number have been tendered. All of these steps are subject to minimum and maximum time limits. If the offer is for less than all the shares, it may be oversubscribed, in which case the offeror must take up shares from each shareholder who tendered, proportionately to the number tendered. The C.B.C.A. has provisions on "going private" (ss. 193, 206): if an offeror succeeds in getting 90 per cent of the shares in a class, it can force the remainder to sell at an agreed or assessed value. Since 2001, it also has the converse rule in s. 206.1, allowing the minority in such a case to force the offeror to buy their shares. See O.B.C.A., ss. 188-189. Other provincial statutes have the "going private" rule but may not have the converse rule.

As mentioned above, commonly management are hostile to a takeover. They may adopt some measures to foil the bid. Does any defensive response by the directors of the target corporation indicate that they are motivated by self-interest and not by the best interests of the corporation? What if the motive behind the takeover is to break up the corporation and sell its prime assets at favourable prices? Are the managers of the target *always* in a conflict of self-interest and duty? Does this mean all their acts are voidable? Are officers (and directors who are also officers) in a greater conflict than "independent directors", who do not have any other position with the corporation than their directorships? All of these questions should be kept in mind when reading the remainder of this section.

While the defensive response of directors to takeover bids is but one of many decisions directors make, the inherent conflict of interest that directors face in such a case places in stark relief two fundamental principles of corporate law. The courts are properly reluctant to interfere with business decisions made by managers. At the same time they have the authority to supervise actions of management, as to skill and as to loyalty. On one side of the scale lie the directors' skill, expertise and knowledge. On the other is the potential that the directors may further their own economic interest at the expense of the corporation, the shareholders, or both.

Two popular defensive responses by directors of the target corporation are the issuance of more shares (so as to make control more difficult to obtain) and the use of "poison pill" plans. The former has already been encountered and the latter will be discussed later in this section. Section D.2 of this chapter examined the British courts' use of the "proper purpose" doctrine to limit the directors' ability to issue new shares as a response to a takeover bid. We have also seen the Canadian response in *Teck Corp. v. Millar, supra*, where Berger J. rejected the "proper purpose" doctrine and determined that the directors had to act in the best interests of the corporation, *i.e.*, had to meet their fiduciary obligations to the corporation. Our present concern is to explore other implications of the directors' fiduciary obligations to the corporation when a takeover bid is underway. A subsidiary question is whether the directors owe any fiduciary obligation to shareholders in this context.

OLYMPIA & YORK ENTERPRISES LTD. v. HIRAM WALKER RESOURCES LTD.

(1986), 59 O.R. (2d) 254 (H.C.J.)

[Gulf Canada sought to acquire a majority of the shares of Hiram Walker Resources Ltd., offering $32 per share for 39 per cent of the shares. The directors of Hiram Walker adopted a complicated defensive strategy involving a deal with Allied Lyons plc. Allied bought the liquor division of Hiram Walker, which amounted to 40 per cent of the business assets of Hiram Walker, for $2.6 billion. The directors created a new corporation, Fingas, which issued shares to Hiram Walker, so that Hiram Walker held 49 per cent of the voting shares of Fingas. Hiram Walker paid for the shares with the proceeds of the sale of the liquor division. Fingas used the money so acquired to offer $40 per share for 48 per cent of the shares of Hiram Walker. The plaintiff, the parent of Gulf, tried to get an injunction to stop the sale of the liquor division to Allied, arguing that the Hiram Walker directors were breaching their fiduciary obligations in making the sale, since they were using corporate assets of Hiram Walker to entrench themselves in management.]

Montgomery J.: — In *Howard Smith Ltd. v. Ampol Petroleum Ltd. et al.*, [1974] A.C. 821 (P.C.), on appeal from the Supreme Court of New South Wales, Ampol and an associate had 55 per cent and wanted to make an offer for the balance of Millers. The directors of Millers did not want to be taken over so they issued shares to Howard Smith and effectively gave Smith a large voting percentage. Smith and Ampol then pursued competing takeover bids. The Privy Council held that, although the directors acted honestly and had power to make the allotment, to alter a majority shareholding was to use the directors' fiduciary powers over the shares of the company for the purpose of destroying an existing majority and that because the directors' primary objective for the allotment of the shares was to alter the majority shareholders, the directors had improperly exercised their powers and the allotment was invalid. At p. 835:

> In their Lordships' opinion it is necessary to start with a consideration of the power whose exercise is in question, in this case a power to issue shares. Having ascertained, on a fair view, the nature of this power, and having defined as can best be done in light of modern conditions the, or some, limits within which it may be exercised, it is then necessary for the court, if a particular exercise of it is challenged, to examine the substantial purpose for which it was exercised, and to reach a conclusion whether that purpose was proper or not. In doing so it will necessarily give credit to the bona fide opinion of the directors, if such is found to exist, and will respect their judgment as to matters of management; having done this, the ultimate conclusion has to be as to the side of a fairly broad line on which the case falls.

And at p. 837:

The purpose found by the judge is simply and solely to dilute the majority voting power held by Ampol and Bulkships so as to enable a then minority of shareholders to sell their shares more advantageously. So far as authority goes an issue of shares purely for the purpose of creating voting power has repeatedly been condemned. ... Just as it is established that directors, within their management powers, may take decisions against the wishes of the majority of shareholders, and indeed that the majority of shareholders cannot control them in the exercise of these powers while they remain in office (*Automatic Self-Cleansing Filter Syndicate Co. Ltd. v. Cunninghame*, [1906] 2 Ch. 34), so it must be unconstitutional for directors to use their fiduciary powers over the shares in the company *purely* for the purpose of destroying an existing majority, or creating a new majority which did not previously exist. (emphasis added by Montgomery J.)

In *Howard Smith* the Privy Council referred with approval to the decision of Mr. Justice Berger of the British Columbia High Court in *Teck Corp. Ltd. v. Millar* (1972), 33 D.L.R. (3d) 288, [1973] 2 W.W.R. 385. [**Montgomery J.** discussed Teck and quoted from the judgment.]

The U.S. Court of Appeals, Second Circuit, looked at the defensive techniques of the target company in *Norlin Corp. v. Rooney*, 744 F.2d 255, [1984] Fed. Sec. L. Rep. ¶ 91,565. A target company transferred newly issued stock to a wholly-owned subsidiary and a newly created stock option plan. This defensive strategy was enjoined on a finding that the stock transfer was part of a management entrenchment effort, and as such was *prima facie* evidence of the board's self-interest such that would defeat the wide latitude given directors by the business judgment rule.

Norlin's directors had been warned by their financial advisers that, absent shareholder approval, the stock transaction violated the rules of the New York Stock Exchange. Hiram Walker's directors were advised by their financial advisers that the defensive strategy was in the best interests of shareholders. In *Norlin* at p. 98,867, the following is stated:

A board member's obligation to a corporation and its shareholders has two prongs, generally characterized as the duty of care and the duty of loyalty. The duty of care refers to the responsibility of a corporate fiduciary to exercise, in the performance of his tasks, the care that a reasonably prudent person in a similar position would use under similar circumstances. See NYBCL s. 717. In evaluating a manager's compliance with the duty of care, New York courts adhere to the business judgment rule, which "bars judicial inquiry into actions of corporate directors taken in good faith and in the exercise of honest judgment in the lawful and legitimate furtherance of corporate purposes". *Auerbach v. Bennett*, 47 N.Y. 2d 619, 629, 419 N.Y.S. 2d 920, 926 (1979).

The second restriction traditionally imposed, the duty of loyalty, derives from the prohibition against self-dealing that inheres in the fiduciary relationship. See *Pepper v. Litton*, 308 U.S. 295, 306-07 (1939). Once a prima facie showing is made that directors have a self-interest in a particular corporate transaction, the burden shifts to them to demonstrate that the transaction is fair and serves the best interests of the corporation and its shareholders. [citations omitted.]

As Judge Kearse made clear in those cases, however, the business judgment rule governs only where the directors are not shown to have a self-interest in the transaction at issue. *Treadway*, 638 F. 2d at 382. Once self-dealing or bad faith is demonstrated, the duty of loyalty supersedes the duty of care, and the burden shifts to the directors to "prove that the transaction was fair and reasonable to the corporation."

And at ¶ 98,868:

We reject the view, propounded by Norlin, that it concludes that an actual or anticipated takeover attempt is not in the best interests of the company, a board of directors may take any action necessary to forestall acquisitive moves. The business judgment rule does indeed require the board to analyze carefully any perceived threat to the corporation, and to act appropriately when it decides that the interests of the company and its shareholders might be jeopardized.

The applicants contend that it is improper to have the board continue in control for even a day to analyze its options.

I now address issue No. 1.

Issue No. 1

Did Hiram Walker directors propose to buy back shares of Hiram Walker with corporate assets for the purpose of entrenching themselves in the management of Hiram Walker? Did the directors act in good faith?

I am satisfied on the basis of the affidavits of Mr. Downing and Mr. Lambert that the sole purpose of the conduct of the directors of Hiram Walker was to maximize the position of all their shareholders after Gulf's takeover bid. It is idle speculation and complete hearsay for Mr. Cohen to attempt to attribute motives to the directors of Hiram Walker. As a question of fact I am satisfied that the directors acted prudently, properly, reasonably and fairly upon the advice of their legal and financial advisers and resorting to the opinions of management and their collective store of business acumen. Mr. Laskin argued that while the board of Hiram Walker has a discretion to carry on a certain type of conduct, there is a line beyond which it may not go. He contended that the board had gone too far. I am satisfied that the board did not cross that line. It was a legitimate objective for the directors to ensure that as much as possible of all economic value go to *all* shareholders and not just to these shareholders. I also find as a fact that that was the sole and primary objective of the directors. These factual findings distinguish the *Howard Smith* case, *supra*. There, the court found the primary object of the allotment of shares was to alter the majority shareholdings.

In *Teck v. Millar*, *supra*, Berger J. held the directors were not in breach of their fiduciary duty to the company if they acted in good faith, on what they believed on reasonable and probable grounds, to be in the best interests of the company. I have found that Hiram Walker's directors did that. It matters not when the directors act in the best interests of the company and in good faith that they also benefit as a result. I find that there was no attempt at management entrenchment by the directors of Hiram Walker. In *Norlin*, the board failed to consider the caution of their advisers that what they proposed to do contravened stock exchange rules. Hiram Walker directors considered and acted upon the advice of their experts. Hiram Walker directors sought independent advice about the adequacy of the Gulf offer. They had only 18 days to act because of the terms of the Gulf offer. I hasten to say that the 18-day period was not Gulf's choice; that falls within purview of the exchange regulations. Hiram Walker's board found the intrinsic value of the company was not being recognized by those people who trade in the stock exchange. They found that while the market was trading at $28 a share and Gulf was offering $32, the real value of the shares was between $40 and $43 a share. What options did the directors have? If they did nothing, it would be a breach of duty to shareholders. It would be apparent to them that because of the premium over market, sufficient shares might be acquired for Gulf to buy control of the company at an unreasonably low price. Then the vast majority of shareholders would be denied the right to benefit from the real value of the company in which they held shares. No one can assail their advice to shareholders to reject the Gulf bid.

As Mr. Thomson argued, this is a battle over money. Gulf and I.P.L. want the company and its assets at the cheapest possible price. The board wants the shareholders to get more. How then could they achieve that single purpose? They decided to sell the distilled-spirits business at a price over premium — indeed, at the true value for the benefit of all shareholders. If, as Mr. Laskin wanted, an issuer bid had been the vehicle, control would pass to Gulf at no cost. This is so because shares that are acquired on an issuer bid are cancelled by the company. If the Fingas offer is foreclosed by this court, all shareholders will be denied the opportunity to sell their shares for $40 a share.

Mr. Sexton's complaint is that it is not fair when the company's money issued to better the offer of an outsider. What is not fair is for all shareholders to be compelled to take less than proper value for their shares. I.P.L. would be happy with $40 a share if it were here in its capacity as a shareholder. I.P.L. feels prejudiced because I.P.L. wants the bargain that is in sight and does not want the directors to keep it from I.P.L. and provide it to all shareholders. The same may be said of Olympia & York. There is no obligation, as the applicants would like, to force the directors to use an issuer bid as opposed to a third-party bid. It is clear from Mr. Fatt's affidavit that the third-party approach will save $300 million in tax to Hiram Walker.

I agree that the law in Ontario is as stated by Berger J. in *Teck, supra,* at pp. 330-1:

> The purpose of the directors in their negotiations with Placer was from the beginning a legitimate one. The purpose was to make a favourable deal for Afton. That purpose continued throughout. ...

> The onus of proof is on the plaintiff. ... In the case at bar the primary purpose of the directors was to make the best contract they could for Afton. I find that the primary purpose of the directors was to serve the best interests of the company. Their primary purpose was to see that the ultimate deal the company made was a deal with Placer, not Teck. They were not motivated by a desire to retain control of the company.

It is the directors' duty to take all reasonable steps to maximize value for all shareholders. I am satisfied they have done that.

In *First City Financial Corp. Ltd. v. Genstar Corp.* (1981), 33 O.R. (2d) 631 at p. 646, 125 D.L.R. (3d) 303 at p. 319, 15 B.L.R. 60, Reid J. said:

> The right and indeed the obligation of directors to take steps that they honestly and reasonably believe are in the interests of the company and its shareholders in a takeover contest or in respect of a takeover bid, is perfectly clear and unchallenged. An illustration of that is *Teck Corp. Ltd. v. Millar et al.* (1972), 33 D.L.R. (3d) 288, [1973] 2 W.W.R. 385.

I find that the applicants have failed in their attack upon the conduct of the Board.

[The remainder of the judgment is omitted. An appeal to the Divisional Court, (59 O.R. (2d) 281) was dismissed.]

NOTES AND QUESTIONS

1. Justice Montgomery referred to the directors as having a duty to the shareholders. Do you think he meant a duty to the corporation?

2. In *Revlon Inc. v. MacAndrews & Forbes Holdings Inc.*, 506 A.2d 173 (Del. 1986), Revlon Inc. was the target of a takeover bid by Pantry Pride Inc. The Delaware Court of Chancery accepted that defensive measures can be acceptable in the face of a takeover, as long as the board of the target meets its duties of care and of loyalty. The court held, however (at p. 182):

    > However, when Pantry Pride increased its offer to $50 per share, and then to $53, it became apparent to all that the break-up of the company [Revlon] was inevitable. The Revlon board's authorization permitting management to negotiate a merger or buyout with a third party was a recognition that the company was for sale. The duty of the board had thus changed from the preservation of Revlon as a corporate entity to the maximization of the company's value at a sale for the stockholders' benefit. This significantly altered the board's responsibilities. ... It no longer faced threats to corporate policy and effectiveness, or to the stockholders' interests, from a grossly inadequate bid. The whole question of defensive measures became moot. The directors' role changed from defenders of the corporate bastion to auctioneers charged with getting the best price for the stockholders at a sale of the company.

    Do you think this reasoning is sound? Do you think a director's job description includes becoming an auctioneer? Is a corporation (as opposed to its shares, or its assets) ever "for sale"? Should directors' behaviour differ as between the cases where (a) someone is trying to buy the corporation's assets from the corporation (b) someone is trying to buy the shareholders' shares from the shareholders? Justice Blair seemed to accept the holding in *Revlon* in *CW Shareholdings Inc. v. WIC Western International Communications Ltd.*, [1998] O.J. No. 1886, 39 O.R. (3d) 755, 160 D.L.R. (4th) 131 (Gen. Div.). However, in *Maple Leaf Foods Inc. v. Schneider Corp.*, [1998] O.J. No. 4142, 42 O.R. (3d) 177 (C.A.), which was cited with approval in *Peoples Department Stores Inc. v. Wise*, [2004] S.C.J. No. 64, [2004] 3 S.C.R. 461, 244 D.L.R. (4th) 564, Weiler J.A. said, for the Court:

    > The decision in *Revlon* ... stands for the proposition that if a company is up for sale, the directors have an obligation to conduct an auction of the company's shares. *Revlon* is not the law in Ontario. In Ontario, an auction need not be held every time there is a change in control of a company.

    > An auction is merely one way to prevent the conflicts of interest that may arise when there is a change of control by requiring that directors act in a neutral manner toward a number of bidders ... The more recent *Paramount* decision in the United States, [*Paramount Communications v. QVC Network Inc.*, 637 A.2d 34 (Del. 1994)] at pp. 43-45 has recast the obligation of directors when there is a bid for change of control as an obligation to seek the best value reasonably available to shareholders in the circumstances. This is a more flexible standard, which recognizes that the particular circumstances are important in determining the best transaction available, and that a board is not limited to considering only the amount of cash or consideration involved as would be the case with an auction: *Paramount, supra*, at p. 44. There is no single blueprint that directors must follow. Although the decision in *Paramount* and the other decisions of the courts in Delaware to which I have referred are not the law of Ontario, they can, however, offer some guidance.

820099 ONTARIO INC. v. HAROLD E. BALLARD LTD.

[1991] O.J. No. 1082, 3 B.L.R. (2d) 113 (Gen. Div.)

[This judgment set aside certain transactions involving Harold Ballard, Harold E. Ballard Limited and Maple Leaf Gardens Limited. We need not explore the complex and troubled history of the Ballard family and Harold Ballard's corporate holdings other than to note that part of the transactions impugned involved the issuance of shares to Harold Ballard in the face of an actual or perceived takeover threat.]

Farley J.: — In the context of an actual or perceived takeover threat, Canadian law appears to have a number of variations as to the duties of directors. (However, it does not seem that these tests should be restricted to this area alone.) There is the "proper purpose" test (see *Bonisteel v. Collis Leather Co.* (1919), 45 O.L.R. 195 (H.C.); *Hogg v. Cramphorn Ltd.*, [1967] Ch. 254, [1966] 3 All E.R. 420) with the courts ruling that directors may not issue shares for the purpose of affecting control of the corporation even where they were acting bona fide in the best interests of the corporation. Then there is the "bona fide in the best interests of the corporation" test (see *Teck Corp. v. Millar* (1972), [1973] 2 W.W.R. 385, 33 D.L.R. (3d) 288 (B.C.S.C.) where Berger J. felt that the onus was on the plaintiff to prove either that the directors' purpose was not to serve the best interests of the corporation or that there was a lack of reasonable grounds for the directors' decision). Richard J. in *Exco Corp. v. Nova Scotia Savings & Loan Co.* (1987), 35 B.L.R. 149, 78 N.S.R. (2d) 91, 193 A.P.R. 91 (T.D.) in citing at p. 256 [B.L.R.] that in the jurisprudence dealing with directors' fiduciary duties there was a "morass of conflicts and inconsistencies. However, if there is any principle which can be synthesized out of the cases it is that the Courts are reluctant to condone, let alone approve, any action which appears unfair, unjust or motivated by self-interest to the detriment of other legitimate interests" may have created a third test. He stated at p. 261 [B.L.R.]:

> Even the test laid out by Berger J., in the *Teck* case requires further refinement if it [is] to be applied generally. When exercising their power to issue shares from treasury the directors must be able to show that the considerations upon which the decision to issue was based are consistent only with the best interests of the company and inconsistent with any other interests. This burden ought to be on the directors once a treasury share issue has been challenged. I am of the view that such a test is consistent with the fiduciary nature of the director's duty, in fact, it may be just another way of stating that duty.

It seems to me that the *Exco* test may be unduly harsh in that it might inhibit reasonable business decisions. It also appears somewhat logically inconsistent in that it cuts off one's nose to spite one's face. The dominant or overwhelming basis on which a decision may be made could be in the very best interests of the corporation, yet *Exco* would prohibit that decision if there were also a minor premise which could be consistent with another interest.

In *Teck* Berger J. discussed at p. 312 [D.L.R.] the responsibility of directors to serve the interests of the corporation. He concluded that if their purpose was not to serve the corporation's interest (but rather to serve their own interest or that of their friends or of a particular group), then it would be an improper purpose. He felt that impropriety depended on proof that the directors were actuated by a collateral purpose. [**Farley J.** quoted at length from *Teck*, ending with **Berger J.**'s statement, "The question is, what was it the directors had uppermost in their minds?"]

This conclusion however does not seem to impart the necessary objectivity that s. 134 OBCA requires. I think it would have been better expressed as "The question is, what was it the directors had uppermost in their minds *after a reasonable analysis of the situation*". (See *Olson v. Argus Industrial Supply Ltd.*, 26 B.L.R. 183, [1984] 4 W.W.R. 498, (*sub nom. Olson v. Phoenix Industrial Supply Ltd.*) 27 Man. R. (2d) 205, 9 D.L.R. (4th) 451 (C.A.) which commented favourably on *Teck*, especially at p. 506 [W.W.R.] to the same effect.)

Montgomery J. in *Olympia & York Enterprises Ltd. v. Hiram Walker Resources Ltd.* (1986), 59 O.R. (2d) 254 at 255, 37 D.L.R. (4th) 193 at 194 (H.C.), affirmed (1986), 59 O.R. (2d) 254, 37 D.L.R. (4th) 193 (Div. Ct.), discussed Berger J.'s reasoning in *Teck* on the question that if the directors' primary purpose was to act in the best interests of the corporation, they were acting in good faith even though they benefited as a result. He found that there was no attempt to entrench management. [**Farley J.** quoted again from *Teck*.]

I cannot but think that directors in exercising their duty of care towards the corporation must consider the shareholders generally — not only the shareholders with the votes, but also shareholders (common and preferred). In the case of HEBL, the directors had to consider the interests of not only Harold Sr. but also the Ballard children. Harold Sr.'s voting control had to be considered in the sense that the directors should not consider issuing more voting shares to swamp this voting control. On the other hand, the Ballard children were the common shareholders with a substantial equity. They would be entitled with the continued good fortune of increased value of HEBL (through MLGL's prosperity) to enjoy an increase in their common equity (or suffer, if there were a reversal of fortunes). Harold Sr. got rid of Mary-Elizabeth by buying her out; with the assistance of Crump and Giffin, Harold Sr. got HEBL to buy out Junior. Neither Mary-Elizabeth nor Junior have complained of their deals. While I assume that they are content, I would think that with the strained relationships and the manoeuvring going on, it might not have been beyond the realm of possibilities that either may have complained that, in effect, they were forced out at an undervalue. Finally, there was only William as a common shareholder. He was never consulted. Was he considered? It seems only to the extent of offering him Junior's deal later. This offer did not seem to have a firm financial underpinning. While it is not legally necessary for the directors to consult a shareholder, ordinarily it would be prudent to do so when the directors are contemplating major transactions that will affect the position of a very material minority shareholder. (They may not wish to if they were concerned that the shareholder deal with the information in some way inimical to the corporation.) The directors would at least benefit from a first-hand view of what that particular shareholder feels his interests are. Whether they have those views or not, the directors are required by s. 247 OBCA to avoid injuring in some unfair or oppressive way those interests.

The transactions complained of were major ones involving substantial amounts of money or key voting power in certain circumstances. One would normally think that in such circumstances proper valuations would have been the watch word. They were not, although I can think of no logical or practical reason why they were not. One would also normally think that there would be some well thought out, reasonable explanation of how these transactions would benefit HEBL. I was disappointed to see the scrambling that appears to have gone on in attempting to justify much of these transactions, most of which would seem to be after-the-fact rationalization. It may well be that the directors were in a big rush because they perceived that if they didn't take action right away, some opportunity may slip away. But did they really ask from whom it would slip? Would it have slipped from HEBL or from Harold Sr.? An easy litmus test to that question is that in a similar situation if there were two shareholders in effect, one a controlling preferred shareholder and the other a common shareholder with substantial amount of equity attributable to him, would one not expect the directors to consider both shareholders (and even possibly consult both as to their views).

If Harold Sr. as a HEBL shareholder or his advisors were to have given advice to the HEBL directors (including himself), it ought to have been to consider the corporation and its shareholders as a whole. If HEBL or its advisors were to have similarly given advice, it ought to have been the same. Given the present situation, the HEBL directors must give recognition that the present shareholders of HEBL are the trust and William. (If the trust documentation is silent, then it does not appear to me that they can listen to Harold Sr.'s ghost for advice as to the trust.) Given that the trustees of the trust are also at present directors of HEBL, they must recognize that they are wearing different hats as to these different functions.

It is also clear that s. 134 OBCA is separate and distinct from s. 247 OBCA. That is, a director may, after a proper analysis, act in good faith in what he considers to be the best interests of the corporation; if he does so he will not run afoul of s. 134. However, the result of such action may be such that it oppresses or unfairly deals with the interests of a shareholder; in which case s. 247 comes into play. (See *Palmer v. Carling O'Keefe Breweries of Canada Ltd.* (1989), 41 B.L.R. 128, 67 O.R. (2d) 161, 56 D.L.R. (4th) 128, 32 O.A.C. 113 (Div. Ct.) at pp. 142-143 [B.L.R.].)

...

[The Ontario Divisional Court dismissed an appeal (3 B.L.R. (2d) 122).]

NOTES AND QUESTIONS

1. Was Farley J. saying that the directors have a fiduciary duty to the shareholders in the context of a takeover threat, or was he saying that in determining what are the best interests of the corporation, shareholder interests must be considered?

2. In *Exco Corp. v. Nova Scotia Savings & Loan Co.*, [1987] N.S.J. No. 56, 78 N.S.R. (2d) 91, 35 B.L.R. 149 (S.C.T.D.), Exco made a tender offer to gain control of Nova Scotia Savings and Loan. Exco already held 49 per cent of N.S.S. & L.'s common stock. To thwart the bid, the directors of the target sought to find a friendly bidder (often called a "white knight"). Halifax Developments Holdings Ltd. agreed to play that role once the directors of the target issued it and others enough shares to dilute Exco's holdings to 34 per cent.

Richard J. held that the shares had been issued for an improper purpose, *i.e.*, the sole purpose of the issuance was to dilute Exco's holdings. He stated at pp. 261-62 (B.L.R.).:

Even the test laid out by Berger J. in the *Teck* requires further refinement if it [is] to be applied generally. When exercising their power to issue shares from treasury the directors must be able to show that the considerations upon which the decision to issue was based are consistent only with the best interests of the company and inconsistent with any other interests. This burden ought to be on the directors once a treasury share issue has been challenged.

...

In relating the facts of this case to the law respecting the duty of directors in issuing treasury shares I find that NSS&L directors made a one-sided allotment of shares for the purpose of "watering down" the commanding share equity position of the so-called EXCO group. The NSS&L directors used their rather substantial power for a wrong purpose, i.e., a purpose which was not demonstrably in the best interests of the company. They used their power to support one group in a takeover, a group which the directors had sought out and which was "not unfriendly" to those directors. What the directors did in this case is more consistent with a finding of self-interest than with bona fide company interest. Or, to put it more in the context of the test which I previously set out, what the directors did was not inconsistent with self-interest. In so doing they breached their fiduciary duty to the general body of the shareholders.

(A "treasury share issue" means the original issue of new shares.) Is it possible for any board of directors to meet this test? Do directors owe a fiduciary duty to the shareholders? Should one draw a distinction between "inside" directors (those directors who are also officers and members of management) and "outside" directors (those who are not)? How does one establish the motive of a group of individuals as opposed to the motive of each individual?

3.   The U.S. courts, when faced with a challenge to the judgment of directors, have applied the so-called business judgment rule. That rule presumes that if the directors acted on an informed basis, in good faith and with an honest belief that their decision was in the best interest of the corporation, and in the absence of any disqualifying self-interest, their decision should not be reviewable by the court (see *Aronson v. Lewis*, 473 A.2d 805 (Del. 1984)). In the context of a takeover bid the Delaware Court said that the directors must not act "solely or primarily out of a desire to perpetuate themselves in office" (see *Unocal Corp. v. Mesa Petroleum*, 493 A.2d 946 (Del. 1985)).

Is this test different from the one enunciated by Richard J. in *Exco, supra*?

The second type of defence mechanism is the use of a "poison pill" plan. The analysis of the directors' fiduciary obligations does not differ significantly. A "poison pill" is some policy that is designed foil a takeover bid. For example, the directors may permit existing shareholders (except the acquiring shareholder) to obtain additional shares below market value through the use of a "rights" agreement (the right to acquire additional shares based on the number of existing shares held). If the plan is successful the party seeking to take over control will have to acquire more shares at a high cost, and the mere existence of the plan is designed to discourage takeover attempts.

It is called a "poison pill" because the bidder gets "poisoned" in attempting to devour the target. The target management who put the plan in place, however, must be acting in what they consider to be the best interests of the target corporation. They often prefer to call a poison pill a "shareholder rights plan" or "shareholder rights agreement". Since the plan usually involves the right to acquire shares, it is within the authority of the directors, who have the power to determine whether shares shall be issued, and if so on what terms.

Several American courts have examined "poison pill" plans. In *Moran v. Household International Inc.*, 500 A.2d 1346 (Del. 1985) the Court found that the directors had reasonable grounds to believe that Household was vulnerable to a takeover and a break-up of the corporation, and upheld the poison pill plan which gave the shareholders the right to purchase $200 worth of the acquiror's stock for $100. The majority of directors were "outside" directors and the plan was challenged before any hostile takeover was on the horizon. In these circumstances the Court was prepared to apply the business judgment rule.

However, even if the original creation of the plan may be justified, its implementation may be successfully challenged if the operation of the plan limits the directors in obtaining the best price possible for shares held by shareholders, in circumstances where it is inevitable that the company is to be broken up (*Revlon Inc. v. MacAndrews & Forbes Holdings Inc.*, 506 A.2d 173 (Del. 1986)).

The Saskatchewan Court of Appeal reviewed "poison pill" plans under Canadian legislation.

347883 ALBERTA LTD. v. PRODUCERS PIPELINES INC.

[1991] S.J. No. 222, 3 B.L.R. (2d) 237 (C.A.)

[The respondent P.P.I. was a public company with fewer than 200 shareholders. In 1990, another corporation became interested in acquiring all of the outstanding shares of P.P.I.

The directors of P.P.I. then implemented a shareholder's rights agreement whereby each shareholder would receive 10 shares for $75 if any person acquired more than 10 per cent of the shares of P.P.I. between certain dates. The acquirer would not receive this right and thus its shares would be greatly diluted. The rights would not be triggered by a "permitted" bid, one that met certain conditions. The rights agreement was to expire on December 27, 1990, unless ratified by the shareholders.

The appellant, a wholly owned subsidiary of the outside corporation, became a shareholder in P.P.I. Under the rights agreement the appellant could not make a permitted bid.

In December 1990, the directors amended the rights agreement to extend the expiry date and to require unanimous director approval of the terms of any takeover bid.

In December 1990, the directors called a shareholders' meeting to approve an issuer bid by P.P.I. to purchase up to 33 per cent of its outstanding shares. In February 1991, the shareholders' meeting was held and the issuer bid was approved. The rights agreement was not submitted for approval.

In March 1991, the appellant applied to have the rights agreement and issuer bid set aside under s. 234 of the S.B.C.A. (equivalent to C.B.C.A., s. 241). Its application was dismissed. On appeal, its appeal was allowed; the issuer bid was set aside.]

Sherstobitoff J.A. [with whom **Tallis J.A.** concurred]: —

The Issues

The appellant's grounds of appeal are that the directors of P.P.I. acted unlawfully (1) in failing to obtain shareholder approval of the S.R.A., although two shareholders' meetings were held after its implementation, (2) in amending the S.R.A. to provide that the directors must unanimously approve any takeover bid before it could be put to the shareholders as a permitted bid under the amended

S.R.A., (3) in entering into the S.R.A. when it discriminated against the appellant shareholder, and (4) in failing to act in the best interests of the corporation because it could not be demonstrated that there was any valid business purpose for the issuer bid and that the effect of it would be to entrench the board of directors and give them control of a majority of the shares in the corporation.

For its part, aside from the above issues, the respondent questioned the right of this appellant to relief under s. 234 for two reasons: (1) it purchased its shares in P.P.I. after the S.R.A. was in place and thus voluntarily "bought in to any oppression" that might exist, and (2) its purpose in bringing the application was to permit it to make a takeover bid, something unrelated to the rights conferred by ownership of the shares.

Poison Pills in Canada

The poison pill was developed in the United States as a defence to coercive takeover bids. It has begun to appear more frequently in Canada and has been subjected to critical analysis in Coleman, "Poison Pills in Canada" (1988), 15 Can. Bus. L.J. 1, and Jeffrey G. MacIntosh, "The Poison Pill: A Noxious Nostrum for Canadian Shareholders" (1988-89), 15 Can. Bus. L.J. 276. The poison pill in this case conforms with the typical poison pill described by Mr. Coleman at pp. 1 and 2:

How Pills Work

A typical poison pill plan works as follows: A corporation distributes rights to acquire common shares. The rights trade with the common shares and have a life of 10 years but their "strike price" is sufficiently high (say, $100 compared to a $25 market price) to make them worthless. The rights carry no vote and are redeemable at a nominal amount by the board of directors before the poison pill provision is triggered and, in some cases, for a short period after the poison pill is triggered (to allow the board to negotiate an acceptable deal).

A first generation poison pill, such as that considered by the Delaware Supreme Court in *Moran v. Household International Inc.*, 500 A.2d 1346 (1985) is triggered upon the acquisition by a third party of 20 per cent or more of the corporation's common shares or upon a takeover bid being made for 30 per cent or more of the common shares. At that point, the rights separate from the common shares to which they were formerly attached, trade separately from them and become exercisable.

Upon the further occurrence of a defined "merger event", the rights "flip-over" allowing the rights holders to purchase shares of the acquiror or the merged entity at half price. This is achievable only where a contract is entered into between the target and the acquiring company (such as a merger or sale of assets).

Should the acquiring company attempt to avoid the "flip-over" for instance by engaging in defined "self-dealing" transactions which do not require a contract between the acquiring company and the target, then the rights holders, other than the acquiring company, are entitled to purchase stock of the target at half price (the "flip-in").

In transactions where there is no merger event or self-dealing, there is no flip-over or flip-in. Accordingly, what has evolved is a second generation Pill in which a percentage-based flip-in feature is added. This provision allows the rights holders, other than the acquiror of a specified percentage (say, 20 per cent), of the target's stock, to purchase shares in the target at a 50 per cent discount upon the accumulation by the acquiror of the specified percentage (*i.e.*, no self-dealing is required). Poison pill plans which include the percentage-based flip-in feature are now common because they give the Board an opportunity to negotiate an acceptable acquisition with a hostile acquiror which treats shareholders fairly and equally (i.e., the Board can redeem the Pill if a deal meeting these criteria is struck).

The two competing overall views of the function and purpose of poison pills are best summarized in Mr. MacIntosh's article at pp. 278-281:

(1) Shareholder Interest Hypothesis

The germ of this explanation is that a hostile acquiror is able to employ coercive tactics that effectively force target shareholders to tender into a low bid, even though shareholders as a group would prefer to hold out for more. The poison pill is the antidote to this coercion. By making an acquisition prohibitively expensive without the co-operation of management, the pill enables management to, in effect, act as a bargaining agent for shareholders. So empowered, management may either defeat a bid that is too low, force the acquiror to make a more generous offer, or shop the company around for a better bid. Alternatively, management may use the breathing space accorded them by the pill to put together a competing proposal, like a "self-tender" (issuer bid), recapitalization, divestiture of assets or the like resulting in greater value for the target shareholders. In this way, shareholders will receive "full and fair value" for their shares.

(2) The Management Entrenchment Hypothesis

When a successful hostile takeover bid occurs, the end result may be, and often is, loss of employment for the incumbent managers. This creates a potent conflict of interest for target managers, who may be more tempted to preserve their jobs at all costs than to act in the best interests of shareholders. Thus, the power given target management by the pill may be used abusively, rather than beneficially, to deter or thwart hostile bids and preserve managerial tenure. Because takeover bids usually result in the payment of large premiums to target shareholders, foreclosing a bid will result in a loss of potential takeover premiums with a corresponding diminution in share values. Moreover, incumbent managers will be insulated from the market for corporate control; shareholders may therefore find themselves stuck with inefficient managers, resulting in further losses in share volume [Footnotes omitted].

The coercive tactics which the poison pill was intended to counteract are two-tier bids, street sweeps and greenmail. They are described by Mr. Coleman at p. 3 and Mr. MacIntosh at pp. 279-280. However, in Canada, these tactics are limited by securities laws designed to protect shareholders in cases of takeover bids. Such legislation was first enacted in Ontario and in Saskatchewan is Pt. XVI of the *Securities Act, 1988*, S.S. 1988-89, c. S-42.2. This Part includes rules:

(i) requiring that identical consideration be paid to all shareholders in connection with the bid (s. 106);

(ii) integrating prebid purchases made within 90 days prior to a formal offer by requiring that the subsequent offer be made at a consideration at least equal to the consideration paid in connection with the prebid purchases (s. 103(6));

(iii) restricting market acquisitions during the course of a bid (s. 103(2));

(iv) prohibiting postbid acquisitions for a period of 20 days following the expiration of a bid (s. 103(7));

(v) restricting private agreement acquisitions at a premium to the market price (ss. 103(2), (6), (7), 104 and 106);

(vi) regulating certain private business (ss. 110, 111).

The effect of these provisions is to prohibit, or at least render less effective, coercive tactics available to corporate raiders in the United States. As a result, Canadian securities regulators have generally taken the position that poison pills are unnecessary in Canada.

This is reflected in National Policy No. 38, published by the Canadian Securities Administrators, which says, in part, as follows:

> 2. The primary objective of takeover bid legislation is the protection of the bona fide interest of the shareholders of the target company. A secondary objective is to provide a regulatory framework within which takeover bids may proceed in an open and even-handed environment. The rules should favour neither the offeror nor the management of the target company, but should leave the shareholders of the offeree company free to make a fully informed decision. The administrators are concerned that certain defensive measures taken by management may have the effect of denying to shareholders the ability to make such a decision and of frustrating an open takeover bid process.

> ...

> 5. The administrators consider that unrestricted auctions produce the most desirable results in takeover bids and is reluctant to intervene in contested bids. However, the administrators will take appropriate action where they become aware of defensive tactics that will likely result in shareholders being deprived of the ability to respond to a takeover bid or to a competing bid.

> 6. The administrators appreciate that defensive tactics, including those that may consist of some of the actions listed in paragraph 4, may be taken by a board of directors in genuine search of a better offer. It is only those tactics that are likely to deny or severely bid or a competing bid, that may result in action by the administrators.

The National Policy also makes the point that prior shareholder approval of corporate action against apprehended or actual takeover bids would, in appropriate cases, allay concerns over shareholders' rights.

> ...

Part XVI of the *Securities Act, 1988*, also places certain duties on the directors of a corporation in respect of which a takeover bid has been made. [**Sherstobitoff J.A.** quoted from the Act's s. 108, setting out the directors' obligations to produce a circular.]

This background as to adoption of poison pills, as created in the United States, and imported into Canada, and the policy behind the takeover bid provisions in the provincial *Securities Acts* in Canada is important to this case. One of the fundamental issues in this case is the extent to which the policy considerations behind the securities legislation should influence the court's interpretation of (a) the powers of directors to act, in respect of actual or apprehended takeover bids, with or without the approval of shareholders (b) the duties of the directors to act in the best interests of the corporation, including the shareholders, and (c) the right of shareholders to decide the disposition of their shares and the terms of disposition.

Powers and duties of directors in respect of issue of shares: the proper purpose test

The effectiveness of the poison pill generally, and the S.R.A. in this case, is based on the power of the directors to issue new shares and rights to purchase new shares at a discount to real value (ss. 25 and 29, the *Business Corporations Act*). The appellant's argument is that this power was used for an improper purpose.

The powers and duties of the directors are set out in ss. 97(1) and 117(1) of the *Business Corporations Act* ...

Although the duties of the directors are stated to be to the corporation, the authorities say that the corporation cannot be considered as an entity separate from its shareholders. The directors must act in the best interests of the corporation and all of its shareholders. In *Martin v. Gibson* (1907), 15 O.L.R. 623 Boyd c. said [p. 632]:

> Now, the persons to be considered and to be benefitted are the whole body of shareholders — not the majority, who may for ordinary purposes control affairs — but the majority plus the minority — all in fact who, being shareholders, constitute the very substance (so to speak) of the incorporated body.

Evershed M.R. said in *Greenhalgh v. Arderne Cinemas*, [1951] Ch. 286 at 291, [1950] 2 All E.R. 1120 (C.A.):

> ... the phrase, "the company as a whole" does not (at any rate in such a case as the present) mean the company as a commercial entity, distinct from the corporators: it means the corporators as a general body.

There are limits to the powers of directors to issue shares to defeat a takeover bid. [**Sherstobitoff J.A.** quoted from *Howard Smith Ltd. v. Ampol Petroleum Ltd.*, [1974] A.C. 821, [1974] 1 All E.R. 1126 (P.C.), discussed above, Section D.2.] See also *Hogg v. Cramphorn Ltd.* (1963), [1967] Ch. 254, [1966] 3 All E.R. 420.

On the surface, *Teck Corp. v. Millar* (1972), [1973] 2 W.W.R. 385, 33 D.L.R. (3d) 288 (B.C.S.C.), presents a different point of view on this issue. Berger J. held that it was within the proper purposes of the directors to consider who is attempting to take over the company, and whether this would be in the best interest of the company as a whole. If it was not, then it would be appropriate for the directors to take action with the purpose of defeating such a takeover notwithstanding that they acted contrary to the wishes of the majority shareholders. He said at p. 315 [D.L.R.]:

> My own view is that the directors ought to be allowed to consider who is seeking control and why. If they believe that there will be substantial damage to the company's interests if the company is taken over, then the exercise of their powers to defeat those seeking a majority will not necessarily be categorized as improper.

However, as Richard J. points out in *Exco Corp. v. Nova Scotia Savings & Loan Co.* (1987), 35 B.L.R. 149 at 259, 78 N.S.R. (2d) 91, 193 A.P.R. 91 (T.D.), *Teck* could have been decided on a much narrower footing. In *Teck*, the company over which control was sought was a small company with a mining interest it wished to develop. The normal practice in the industry was for such a small company to find a major mining company to participate in the development. It was customary in such a venture for the major mining partner to acquire a significant shareholding in the minor company. Thus, the question of the allotment of shares in *Teck* was inextricably bound up in a question of business judgment concerning the ordinary course of the affairs of the business. This factor placed the decision properly within the purview of the directors. Indeed, Lord Wilberforce spoke of *Teck* with approval in *Howard Smith* (at p. 1135) on this basis.

[**Sherstobitoff J.A.** quoted from *Teck*, from *Exco Corp. v. Nova Scotia Savings & Loan Co.*, and from *Olympia & York v. Hiram Walker Resources Ltd.*]

The tests adopted by Berger J. in *Teck* and by Richard J. in *Exco*, while stated in a different way, do not conflict with the business judgment rule developed in the United States. Although different states have developed different rules, some of the more notable jurisdictions in corporate law have developed a business judgment rule. It recognizes that, in a takeover situation, the directors will often be in a conflict of interest situation, and, in implementing a poison pill defence strategy, the directors must be able to establish that (a) in good faith they perceived a threat to the corporation, (b) they acted after proper investigation, and (c) the means adopted to oppose the takeover were reasonable in relationship to the threat posted: *Unocal Corp. v. Mesa Petroleum Co.*, 493 A.2d 946 (Del. 1985) and *Desert Partners Ltd. Partnership v. USG Corp.*, 686 F. Supp. 1289 (N.D. Ill. 1988).

The tests developed in *Teck* and *Exco*, and in the American authorities above referred to, contain relevant considerations. They also extend considerable deference to bona fide business judgments of the directors. However, they do not go far enough to determine this case. They give no principles for determining whether or not the defensive strategy was reasonable in relationship to the threat posed. They do not deal with the principle that shareholders have the right to determine to whom and at what price they will sell their shares as stated in *Howard Smith Ltd.* They fail to consider the effect of the takeover provisions in the provincial securities legislation.

In respect of the latter, National Policy No. 38 of the Canadian Securities Administrators referred to earlier in this judgment accurately reflects the policy considerations behind that legislation and must have a substantial impact in any review of defensive tactics against takeovers. Just as the provisions were intended to prevent abusive, coercive or unfair tactics by persons making takeover bids, they were equally intended to limit the powers of directors to use defensive tactics which might also be abusive, coercive or unfair to shareholders, or tactics which unnecessarily deprive the shareholders of the right to decide to whom and at what price they will sell their shares. Section 108 of the *Securities Act, 1988*, indicates that the primary role of the directors in respect of a takeover bid is to advise the shareholders, rather than to decide the issue for them. As noted in the policy statement, the primary objective of the legislation is to protect the bona fide interests of the shareholders of the target company and to permit takeover bids to proceed in an open and even-handed environment. Unrestricted auctions produce the most desirable results in takeover bids. Accordingly, defensive measures should not deny to the shareholders the ability to make a decision, and if follows that, whenever possible, prior shareholder approval of defensive tactics should be obtained. There may be circumstances where it is impractical or impossible to obtain prior shareholder approval, such as lack of time, but in such instances, delaying measures will usually suffice to give the directors time to find alternatives. The ultimate decision must be left with the shareholders, whether by subsequent ratification of the poison pill, or by presentation to them of the competing offers or other alternatives to the takeover bid, together with the takeover bid itself.

In summary, when a corporation is faced with susceptibility to a takeover bid or an actual takeover bid, the directors must exercise their powers in accordance with their overriding duty to act bona fide and in the best interests of the corporation even though they may find themselves, through no fault of their own, in a conflict of interest situation. If, after investigation, they determine that action is necessary to advance the best interests of the company, they may act, but the onus will be on them to show that their acts were reasonable in relation to the threat posed and were directed to the benefit of the corporation and its shareholders as a whole, and not for an improper purpose such as entrenchment of the directors.

Since the shareholders have the right to decide to whom and at what price they will sell their shares, defensive action must interfere as little as possible with that right. Accordingly, any defensive action should be put to the shareholders for prior approval where possible, or for subsequent ratification if not possible. There may be circumstances where neither is possible, but that was not so in this case. Defensive tactics that result in shareholders being deprived of the ability to respond to a takeover bid or to a competing bid are unacceptable.

Conclusion as to proper purpose

In applying the above criteria to the facts of this case, the most important issue is whether the directors, in adopting the defensive tactics culminating in the issuer bid, met the onus upon them to show that they acted in the best interests of the corporation as a whole, and whether their actions were reasonable in relation to the threat posed. There was no direct evidence from the directors as to their purpose in implementing their defensive strategy. The evidence from which the court must draw its inferences may be summarized as follows.

From the point of view of the directors, the stated purpose of the S.R.A. in documents circulated to the shareholders was to give the directors time to assess any takeover offer and to consider alternatives. Later, after amendment of the S.R.A., the purpose was stated to be "to protect shareholders from an unfair, abusive, or coercive takeover bid." The circular accompanying the issuer bid to shareholders stated as follows:

2. Purpose of the Offer

The directors believe that the Corporation's prospects in the medium to long term are excellent. The Corporation is not, however, widely known in the capital markets nor are its Shares listed for trading on any stock exchange. Although the Shares trade in the over-the-counter market, because of the small number of shareholders and the nature of the shareholdings, trading in the Shares is extremely limited and the trading value of the Shares is not reasonably ascertainable. Accordingly, the opportunity for shareholders to realize on their investment is limited and the directors believe that the price available to shareholders for their Shares does not adequately reflect their value. The directors believe that the purchase by the Corporation of up to 560,000 Shares at a price of $21.50 a Share represents a worthwhile investment and is an appropriate use of the Corporation's funds while providing the Corporation's shareholders with an opportunity to sell a portion of their Shares at a favourable price.

...

It is fair to infer that the board of directors saw the proposed bid of Saskoil in August to be too low and that, in response, it implemented the S.R.A. to give it until December 27, 1990, when the agreement would expire, to consider alternatives. In view of the subsequent valuation of the shares at $19 to 21.50 per share, the concern of the directors was clearly justified and their actions to this point were reasonable, except in one respect. They did not put the S.R.A. to the shareholders for ratification at the meeting in October 1990. It was said that this was done because the S.R.A. would lapse, by its own terms, on December 27. However, that proved not to be the case.

It was the extension and amendment of the S.R.A., which was outlined in a management information circular accompanying the notice of special general meeting of the shareholders scheduled for February 25, 1991, which was the real cause for complaint. The circular stated as follows:

> In order to protect shareholders from an unfair, abusive or coercive takeover bid, on December 15, 1990, the Board of Directors amended the Rights plan to extend its operation until February 28, 1991. The Rights plan was also amended to provide that a permitted bid can now only be made with the prior approval with the Board of Directors even if it is in all cash bid for all the common shares of the Corporation. The Rights plan will terminate on February 28, 1991.

Later, the S.R.A. was again extended to April 15, 1991, a date after which the issuer bid would be completed.

The purpose of the extended and amended S.R.A., in conjunction with the issuer bid, was, at this point, unequivocal. The terms of a permitted takeover bid were, all cash, for all shares, and only with the unanimous approval of the board of directors. There was agreement among the directors that approval would not be given at a price less than $25 a share, a price 25 per cent above the appraised value. These terms were so onerous that any takeover bid was effectively prohibited.

At the same time as the shareholders were deprived of the right to consider any takeover bid, they were forced to consider authorization of the issuer bid. The effect of these tactics was coercion of the shareholders for the reasons stated in Mr. Ludke's affidavit. In view of the lack of liquidity, due to lack of market for the shares, those shareholders who wanted to realize anything approaching the appraised value of a portion of their shares had no choice but to tender to the issuer bid. While the result would be liquidation of an uncertain number of their shares at appraised value, they would be left with a substantial number of the shares which, if saleable at all, would be saleable at a substantially lesser value. A shareholder seeking some liquidity, with the knowledge that takeover bids were effectively prohibited, would have no choice but to authorize the issuer bid and to tender to it. For these reasons, no weight can be given to the shareholder vote authorizing the issuer bid.

The purpose of the defensive action is apparent: effective prohibition of the appellant's proposed takeover bid or any other takeover bid, until after the shareholders were forced to consider authorization of and tender to the issuer bid. The result was to deprive the shareholders of any alternative to the issuer bid except to hold their shares which, if marketable, would no doubt continue to trade at a value substantially less than appraised value. The fact that the S.R.A. was not put to the shareholders for ratification either prior to, or simultaneous with, the issuer bid confirms the view that the purpose of the directors was to force the issuer bid on the shareholders without the choice of any possible alternative such as the appellant's proposed takeover bid or any other takeover bid.

These actions were in interference with the shareholders' rights to determine the disposition of their shares. That raises the question of whether acting without shareholder approval of the S.R.A. was necessary in the circumstances. No reason was advanced by the directors for failure to put the matter to the shareholders. The only interference which can be drawn from that is that the directors wished to make the decision themselves in order to ensure their continued control of the company. They thus acted for an improper purpose.

There are a number of other reasons which support a conclusion that the defensive action was neither reasonable in proportion to the threat posed, nor taken in the best interests of the company, but was taken with a view to further entrenching the directors group: (a) the board of directors made no effort to show that a takeover by Saskoil would be harmful to the corporation except that the proposed offer at $16 to $18 per share was below the appraised value of the shares; (b) they made no effort to negotiate with Saskoil to increase the amount offered per share; (c) they did not seek any competitive bids (except their own issuer bid) although the material indicated that a couple of other parties had indicated an interest in making a takeover offer; (d) they made no effort to establish, through evidence, that tender of shares to the issuer bid would ultimately result in a better value to the shareholders for all of their shares than a takeover bid, even at a price of $16 to $18 per share; (e) they agreed among themselves that they would not permit a bid under the S.R.A. at less than $25 per share, some 25 per cent above appraised value; (f) they offered no valid business reason, from the point of view of the company, for the issuer bid, the completion of which would further entrench the directors at the expense of a substantial increase in the indebtedness of the company.

None of these things point to any effort to increase or maximize the value of the shares, or to obtain the best possible offer for them. They point to one objective, and one objective only: the prohibition of any takeover bid until after completion of the issuer bid, the result of which would be that the directors group would control a majority of the shares, thus making the company impregnable to any takeover bid unacceptable to the board.

In fairness to the directors, it was assumed by all parties, and accepted by the court, that the board of directors acted bona fide and in the belief that the future of the company was such that the shareholders would be better off maintaining the corporation as it was, rather than letting it be taken over by Saskoil.

However, as noted above, the directors did not meet the onus upon them to show that their actions were necessarily in the best interests of the company. Furthermore, a decision of that nature was one to be taken by the shareholders, and the directors were not, in the circumstances, entitled to deprive them of the right to make that decision.

...

The actions taken by the directors in this case amounted to telling Saskoil that it would not, under any circumstances, permit itself to be taken over. We agree with the following comment by Mr. Coleman in his article at p. 6:

> Some U.S. securities lawyers have suggested that so long as they act in good faith and on reasonable grounds, boards of directors can just say no to a potential acquiror whose price the board believes to be inadequate. In such a case, it is argued, directors should be able to resist pressure to withdraw poison pill defences and they do not have to seek higher bidders or recapitalize to boost short term value. Because it is reminiscent of the "just say no" anti-drug campaign, this approach has been termed the "Nancy Reagan defence".

> Does a Board breach its fiduciary duty by refusing to negotiate with a potential acquiror to remove the coercive and inadequate aspects of an offer? A Board may decide not to bargain over the terms of an offer because doing so conveys a message to the market that (a) the company is for sale when, in fact, it is not; and (b) the

initial offer by the bidder is "in the ballpark" when, again, it is not. However, it can be expected that the courts will conclude that a "just say no" response to a cash takeover bid for all shares does not justify keeping a Pill in place indefinitely if shareholders are prevented from responding to the bid.

The S.R.A. is objectionable in three other respects. First, as found by the trial judge, it may, in certain circumstances, required the directors to act contrary to the rule that the directors cannot, without the consent of the shareholders, fetter their future discretion: L.C.B. Gower *et al., Gower's Principles of Modern Company Law*, 4th ed. (London: Sweet & Maxwell, 1979, p. 582; *Ringuet v. Bergeron*, [1960] S.C.R. 672, 24 D.L.R. (2d) 449. Second, it may, in certain circumstances, require the directors to act contrary to s. 108 of the *Securities Act, 1988*, quoted above, which imposes certain duties upon the directors when a takeover bid is made, including the duty to send a directors' circular to every person affected within 10 days of a takeover bid. Third, its extension beyond December 27, 1990, violated the terms of the S.R.A. itself, which provided that it would expire on December 27, 1990, if not previously ratified by the shareholders of the corporation.

. . .

Section 234, Business Corporations Act

This application is brought under s. 234 of the *Business Corporations Act* ...

. . .

This judgment has determined that the appellant's right to determine disposition of its shares was violated by the directors acting beyond their powers. Such action was unfairly prejudicial to the appellant and entitles the court to grant relief under s. 234.

. . .

Remedy

P.P.I. suggested that an appropriate remedy, if oppression were found, would be to require the respondent to buy the appellant's shares. It further argued that any order setting aside the issuer bid might be unfairly prejudicial to those shareholders who had tendered to it and had expected to receive the proceeds of the sale.

We are fully aware of the breadth of s. 234 and the problem of balancing the rights of an individual shareholder in conflict with the rights of the company as a whole, or with the rights of all of the other shareholders.

This case poses no such problem in that a remedy is available which will give the shareholders, as a whole, the right to determine the issue themselves. The remedy is to set aside the S.R.A. and to extend the closing date of the issuer bid from March 28, 1991, to 45 days after the date of this judgment. All other dates under the issuer bid are extended accordingly. Otherwise, all terms remain the same. This will permit the appellant, or any other person interested, to make a takeover bid and will give all shareholders a choice between the issuer bid (if the respondent chooses not to withdraw it) and any takeover bid. The parties are to agree on the form of the formal judgment before it is issued and, failing agreement, application may be made to the court for further directions.

The appellant will have its costs of this application under double col. V.

Since this judgment was written, we have had the opportunity to read the judgment of the Chief Justice in draft form, as well as an article, just published, by Jeffrey G. MacIntosh, "The Oppression Remedy: Personal or Derivative?" (1991), 70 Can. Bar Rev. 29. Both raise the question of whether these proceedings were in the nature of derivative proceedings (concerning alleged harm to the corporation as a whole) rather than personal proceedings (concerning alleged harm to the appellant as an individual shareholder), and if the former, whether the appellant should have proceeded under s. 232 of the *Business Corporations Act*, rather than s. 234. Mr. MacIntosh makes the point that these are issues of some complexity and difficulty in view of the ambiguity of the statutory provisions, and the division of judicial opinion. These issues were not (and could not be) considered in this judgment because they were not raised by the respondent in its notice of appeal, factum or argument. This judgment should not, therefore, be taken to have pronounced on these issues except to the extent that the appellant, on the facts of this particular case, was entitled, in the absence of any challenge to the procedural propriety of proceeding under s. 234 rather than s. 232, to relief of the nature given in this case, under s. 234.

NOTES AND QUESTIONS

1. Chief Justice Bayda dissented, in part on the ground that the plaintiff could not challenge the validity of the poison pill using the oppression remedy. The oppression remedy would only allow a complainant to argue that he or she had suffered oppression or unfair prejudice from some corporate conduct that was valid as such. This is what the majority judgment is addressing in the last paragraph. If managerial conduct is disloyal, this primarily creates a claim by the corporation. Can it also generate a claim by an individual under the oppression remedy?

2. The majority judgment mentions National Policy No. 38 of the Canadian Securities Administrators. This has now been replaced by National Policy 62-202, which provides in part:

    > The Canadian securities regulatory authorities recognize that takeover bids play an important role in the economy by acting as a discipline on corporate management and as a means of reallocating economic resources to their best uses. In considering the merits of a takeover bid, there is a possibility that the interests of management of the target company will differ from those of its shareholders. …

    > The Canadian securities regulatory authorities have determined that it is inappropriate to specify a code of conduct for directors of a target company, in addition to the fiduciary standard required by corporate law. Any fixed code of conduct runs the risk of containing provisions that might be insufficient in some cases and excessive in others. However, the Canadian securities regulatory authorities wish to advise participants in the capital markets that they are prepared to examine target company tactics in specific cases to determine whether they are abusive of shareholder rights. Prior shareholder approval of corporate action would, in appropriate cases, allay such concerns.

3. Issuer bids, like the one in *347883 Alberta Ltd. v. Producers Pipelines Inc.*, [1991] S.J. No. 222, 80 D.L.R. (4th) 359 (C.A.) are thought to create particular conflict problems. The Ontario Securities Commission has a Rule 61-501 on *Insider Bids, Issuer Bids, Going Private Transactions and Related Party Transactions*. Where it applies, it requires the formal valuation by an outside valuer of the securities in issue.

Related party transactions (like the structure used in *Olympia & York, supra*) require shareholder approval by a "majority of the minority": each shareholder class must approve the transaction, with votes controlled by management not being counted.

4.   The judgment mentions that there are many kinds of poison pills. A new breed was reported in the *Globe and Mail*, 4 December 2000, page B1. It was reported that a large publicly traded corporation makes a practice of having legal work done by all of the large law firms. The goal is that in the event of a takeover bid, the corporation would be able to disqualify any of those large firms from acting for the offeror, on the basis of prior acquisition by the lawyers of confidential information. For an example of such a disqualification in a recent takeover bid, see *Chapters Inc. v. Davies, Ward & Beck L.L.P.*, [2001] O.J. No. 206, 52 O.R. (3d) 566 (C.A.).

5.   Can directors even comment on the adequacy of a takeover bid, either for or against, without violating their fiduciary obligation? They are fiduciaries and they have an obvious conflict between their self-interest (staying incumbent) and the interests of the corporation (maximum profitability). Aren't they obliged to announce their conflict and refrain from participating in any decisions on the issue giving rise to the conflict of interest?

Directors of a target corporation are required by securities law to issue a prospectus. The Ontario *Securities Act*, R.S.O. 1990, c. S.5, s. 99(2), provides:

The board of directors shall include in a directors' circular either a recommendation to accept or to reject a takeover bid and the reasons for their recommendation, or a statement that they are unable to make or are not making a recommendation and if no recommendation is made, the reasons for not making a recommendation.

One way in which target boards try to deal with situations that seem to raise particular problems of conflict of interest and duty is via the "independent committee". The committee is a subset of the board, made up of directors who are "independent" or "non-executive" directors: that is, directors with no other roles in the corporation. Such committees may be used, for example, to set the pay of directors and officers, and they are often used when a response to existing or future takeover bids is being formulated.

Obviously, the "independence" of the committee will be a relevant issue when the directors rely on the committee's recommendation, and that reliance is subsequently challenged in court. But if the independence of the committee is enough to remove the taint of any conflict of interest, its recommendations are more likely to be accepted by a court as a business decision properly belonging to the board. Rule 61-501 of the Ontario Securities Commission requires the use of independent committees in certain situations, and provides its own definition. Corporate governance guidelines or rules, like those discussed at the beginning of this chapter, always provide their own definitions of independence.

Can a truly independent review be conducted within the corporation when in practice the members of the committee are appointed by the incumbent management and their tenure may be dependent on future support? See *Dynamics Corp. of America v. CTS Corp.*, 805 F.2d 705 (7th Cir. 1986).

When faced with a decision made in accordance with the recommendation of an independent committee, is the court's role more akin to an appeal court hearing an appeal from a trial decision, or to a court reviewing the decision of an administrative tribunal? If the latter, the court would limit itself to procedural issues such as the independence of the committee, the adequacy of its investigation and its use of expert advice; if the former, the court would simply treat the recommendation as only evidence before it, much like an expert's opinion.

The next case reviews the role of the independent committee.

BRANT INVESTMENTS LTD. v. KEEPRITE INC.

[1991] O.J. No. 683, 3 O.R. (3d) 289, 80 D.L.R. (4th) 161 (C.A.)

[KeepRite was a C.B.C.A. corporation that made and sold air conditioning equipment. Inter-City Gas ("I.C.G."), a Manitoba corporation had a subsidiary, Inter-City Manufacturing ("I.C.M."). They made heating equipment. In 1981, I.C.G. acquired 64 per cent of KeepRite shares and transferred them to I.C.M. In March 1983, KeepRite purchased $20 million of assets from two corporations that were subsidiaries of I.C.M. The purchase was made pursuant to a recommendation of an independent committee of the board of KeepRite, and was financed by an issue of rights to existing shareholders. The rights offering required an amendment to the articles of KeepRite which was passed by special resolution in April 1983.

The plaintiffs, who were minority shareholders of KeepRite, brought an oppression action under C.B.C.A., s. 234 (now s. 241). They also argued that the majority shareholders of KeepRite owed fiduciary obligations to them. The action was dismissed and the plaintiffs appealed.]

McKinlay J.A. (for the Court): —

...

It is clear that none of the foregoing authorities imposes a fiduciary duty on majority shareholders or directors in favour of minority shareholders. The case that comes closest to doing so is the *Goldex Mines* case [*Goldex Mines Ltd. v. Revill* (1974), 7 O.R. (2d) 216, 54 D.L.R. (3d) 672 (C.A.)], which was decided prior to the coming into force of the C.B.C.A. in December of 1975, and involved facts which, if they arose at the present time, would appropriately lead to an application under s. 234 of the C.B.C.A. or its counterpart, s. 247(2) [now s. 248(2)] of the Ontario *Business Corporations Act, 1982*, S.O. 1982, c. 4 (the "O.B.C.A."). The enactment of these provisions has rendered any argument for a broadening of the categories of fiduciary relationships in the corporate context unnecessary and, in my view, inappropriate.

It must be recalled that in dealing with s. 234, the impugned acts, the results of the impugned acts, the protected groups, and the powers of the court to grant remedies are all extremely broad. To import the concept of breach of fiduciary duty into that statutory provisions would not only complicate its interpretation and application, but could be inimical to the statutory fiduciary duty imposed upon directors in s. 117(1) (now s. 122(1)) of the C.B.C.A. That provision required that

117. (1) Every director and officer of a corporation in exercising his powers and discharging his duties shall

(a) act honestly and in good faith *with a view to the best interests of the corporation*; (Emphasis added by **McKinlay J.A.**)

Acting in the best interests of the corporation could, in some circumstances, require that a director or officer act other than in the best interests of one of the groups protected under s. 234. To impose upon directors and officers a fiduciary duty to the corporation as well as to individual groups of shareholders of the corporation could place directors in a position of irreconcilable conflict, particularly in situations where the corporation is faced with adverse economic conditions.

Courts impose fiduciary duties only in situations where someone stands in a particular position of trust by virtue of an agreement or as a result of the circumstances and relationship of the parties. In an application under s. 234, evidence of any relevant agreement between the parties and evidence of the circumstances of their relationship would appropriately be adduced to assist in determining whether the facts of the case warrant a remedy. Because the statutory scheme of s. 234 is so broadly formulated, the evidence necessary to establish a breach of fiduciary duty would be subsumed in the broader range of evidence which would be appropriately adduced on an application under the section.

In any event, on the facts of this case, I do not consider that the respondents, the board of directors of KeepRite, or the members of the independent committee owed a fiduciary duty to the appellants.

. . .

Independent committee

The appellants attack the role of the independent committee on the basis, first, that it was not in fact independent, and second, that the advice given by the committee to the directors of KeepRite was not in the best interests of the company and its shareholders.

With respect to the make-up of the committee, the evidence discloses that all of its members were outside members of the board of KeepRite. None was an officer or director of ICG. The three-member committee comprised H. Purdy Crawford and John Edison, both solicitors, and Ross Hanbury, a former partner of Wood, Gundy. Mr. Crawford became involved with KeepRite in the winter of 1979 when the Odette Group retained him and the law firm in which he was a senior partner in connection with the possible acquisition of KeepRite. That group eventually became owners of approximately 50 per cent of the shares of KeepRite. It was at the request of the Odette Group that Mr. Crawford became in director of KeepRite. His first encounter with ICG was at the time of its failed takeover bid for KeepRite. He continued as a member of the board after ICG acquired its interest in KeepRite in 1981. Mr. Edison had acted as legal adviser to the founder of KeepRite from its inception, and had also acted for the company over a number of years. He was a long-term member of the KeepRite board. Mr. Hanbury had been involved with KeepRite since the 1960s, when Wood, Gundy was involved in a public offering of KeepRite shares. There is no evidence of any involvement with ICG by any of these individuals.

The trial judge found as a fact that the members of the committee were truly independent in the sense that they "felt at all times free to deal with the impugned transaction upon its merits" (at p. 34). There was more than adequate evidence to substantiate such a finding.

That, of course, does not end the matter, since the appellants allege that the advice given by the committee to KeepRite was not in the best interests of KeepRite and its shareholders. With respect to those issues, the learned trial judge made the following findings, at p. 34:

I conclude and find that the members of the committee were fully aware that the transaction was not at arm's length and that the function of the committee was to assure that the impugned transaction be fair to the minority shareholders as well as in the best interests of KeepRite as a whole. I likewise conclude and find that the advice which it gave was independent advice and had not been in any way dictated or predetermined.

The real complaint of the appellants on this appeal is that, rather than making his own assessment of the value of KeepRite of the transaction, the learned trial judge relied on the decision of the independent committee that the transaction was of value to KeepRite because of the synergies and economics of scale involved. The appellants argue that, although reliance on investigations carried out by such a committee may be appropriate in some cases, it is not appropriate in this case where, they argue, the committee itself did not adequately assess the benefits of the transaction to KeepRite. The appellants criticize the work of the independent committee on the following bases:

(a) the committee did not consider whether there were alternative transactions open to KeepRite;

(b) the committee approved the transaction based upon assurances that certain "synergistic" benefits could be achieved by combining the businesses — they were aware of the need for a strategic plan to realize these benefits but proceeded without obtain one;

(c) the committee never received a final report from the consultants retained to review management's assumptions concerning the anticipated synergies; and

(d) the committee did not commission a valuation of the Inter-City businesses on a going concern basis.

[The Court then examined the arguments and evidence in detail, under each of these headings; most of the detail is omitted in this extract.]

(a) *Possible alternative transactions*

The appellants argue that there were a number of alternative transactions available to KeepRite which were not considered by the independent committee, and they points specifically to three. ...

...

It is clear from the evidence that the independent committee did consider some alternative possibilities for solving KeepRite's problems. It did so, however, in the context of a concrete proposal for the purchase of assets from the ICG companies. The evaluation of that proposal was the purpose for which the committee was struck. I agree with the words of the trial judge where he stated at pp. 35-6:

> There is nothing inherently wrong in a parent company making such a proposal to a subsidiary. Any difficulty arises because the transaction, if carried forward, will not be at arm's length. It was because of the aspect of the transaction, and to protect against the vices which may be involved, that the Independent Committee was called into existence. In my view, the committee was not thereupon called to make a wide-ranging search for alternatives, or in other words, to determine whether the proposal which had been made was the best possible solution to the problem. Its function was to determine whether the *proposed* transaction was fair and reasonable and of benefit to KeepRite and its shareholders.

(b) *Strategic plan*

The appellants argue that, although the independent committee was aware of the need for a strategic plan to realize the synergistic benefits of the transaction, they proceeded without obtaining such a plan. ...

...

It is clear from the evidence that KeepRite did have a plan to realize the proposed benefits of the transaction, which was reviewed by the independent committee. There does not appear to have been a minutely detailed plan setting out projected day-by-day actions to be followed after closing of the transaction, but no one suggests that such a detailed plan was necessary, or even desirable.

(c) *Consultants' report*

The independent committee retained the firm of Crosbie, Armitage as consultants to assess the benefits of the proposed transaction to KeepRite. Crosbie, Armitage did in fact make an assessment of the anticipated synergistic benefits of the transaction. ...

...

The learned trial judge considered it completely appropriate that the assumptions on which the report were based were developed by senior operating personnel of KeepRite and ICG, along with personnel of Crosbie, Armitage. I agree. Those individuals were not only the persons who had access to and familiarity with the relevant information, but many of them were also the officers who would be implementing the integrated business plan after the completion of the transaction. There was no suggestion that any of the information presented was inaccurate or misleading.

(d) *Valuation of the Inter-City business on a going concern basis*

...

Since KeepRite was purchasing assets for the purpose of combining the two operations, the committee did not consider a going-concern valuation to be necessary.

The trial judge was satisfied that the independent committee was aware of its mandate, was at all times conscious that this was not an arm's length transaction, and appropriately carried out its function of assessing the benefits of the transaction to KeepRite. He was completely satisfied on the evidence that the committee carried out its function in an appropriate and independent manner. I see no reason whatever to doubt the correctness of that finding. Neither the evidence nor the argument persuades me that his findings were anything other than appropriate.

(e) *Business judgment and the oppression remedy*

The appellants argue strongly that since the enactment of s. 234 (now s. 241) of the C.B.C.A., it is no longer appropriate for a trial judge to delegate to directors of a corporation, or to a committee such as that established in this case, judgment as to the fairness of conduct complained of by dissenting shareholders. This is particularly important, they argue, because the persons to whom that judgment is delegated are the very persons whose conduct is under scrutiny. They argue that the trial judge in this case erred in his approach to the exercise of his jurisdiction under s. 234, when he stated, at pp. 37-8:

> ... the court ought not to usurp the function of the board of directors in managing the company, nor should it eliminate or supplant the legitimate exercise of control by the majority...Business decisions, honestly made, should not be subjected to microscopic examination.

This, they argue, indicates that the trial judge declined to exercise independent judgment with respect to the fairness of essential aspects of the impugned transaction. Such a submission is, in my view, patently unfounded. The portion of the trial judge's reasons quoted above should be placed in context. The relevant portion of the reasons is quoted below [at pp. 37-8]:

> The jurisdiction is one which must be exercised with care. On the one hand the minority shareholder must be protected from unfair treatment; that is the clearly expressed intent of the section. On the other hand the court ought not to usurp the function of the board of directors in managing the company, nor should it eliminate or supplant the legitimate exercise of control by the majority. In *Re Bright Pine Mills Pty, Ltd.* [1969] V.R. 1002 (Supreme Court of Victoria), analogous legislation to s. 234 was under consideration. At p. 1011 O'Bryan J., writing for the full court, says:
>
> > It is true to say, however, that it was not intended ... to give jurisdiction to the Court (a jurisdiction the courts have always been loath to assume) to interfere with the internal management of a company by directors who in the exercise of the powers conferred upon them by the memorandum and articles of association are acting honestly and without any purpose of advancing the interests of themselves or others of their choice at the expense of the company or contrary to the interests of other shareholders.
>
> Although the statute there under consideration was confined to "oppression", I consider the *caveat* there expressed to apply with equal force to the wider language of s. 234. Business decisions, honestly made, should not be subjected to microscopic examination. There should be no interference simply because a decision is unpopular with the minority.

There can be no doubt that on an application under s. 234 the trial judge is required to consider the nature of the impugned acts and the method in which they were carried out. That does not mean that the trial judge should substitute his own business judgment for that of managers, directors, or a committee such as the one involved in assessing this transaction. Indeed, it would generally be impossible for him to do so, regardless of the amount of evidence before him. He is dealing with the matter at a different time and place; it is unlikely that he will have the background knowledge and expertise of the individuals involved; he could have little or no knowledge of the background and skills of the persons who would be carrying out any proposed plan; and it is unlikely that he would have any knowledge of the specialized market in which the corporation operated. In short, he does not know enough to make the business decision required. That does not mean that he is not well equipped to make an objective assessment of the very factors which s. 234 requires him to assess. Those factors have been discussed in some detail earlier in these reasons.

It is important to note that the learned trial judge did not say that business decisions honestly made should not be subjected to examination. What he said was that they should not be subjected to *microscopic* examination. In spite of those words, the learned trial judge did not in fact scrutinize, in a very detailed and careful manner, the nature of the transaction in this case and the manner in which it was executed. Having carefully reviewed the major aspects of the appellants' criticisms of the transaction, he cam to the conclusion that it in no way, either substantively or procedurally, offended the provisions of s. 234. Having carefully reviewed all of the exhibits and transcribed evidence to which we were referred, I have no hesitation in agreeing with the correctness of his assessment. ...

NOTES AND QUESTIONS

1. What is the effect of the recommendation of the independent committee on the Court? Compelling, persuasive, conclusive? The Court said that a trial judge should not "substitute his own business judgment for that of managers, directors, or a committee such as the one involved in assessing this transaction". Is this consistent with the way in which the Court of Appeal evaluated the evidence?

2. For the positive effect of an independent committee when defending an oppression action, see *General Accident Assurance Co. of Canada v. Lornex Mining Corp.*, [1988] O.J. No. 2009, 66 O.R. (2d) 783 (H.C.). For the negative effect when no independent committee was established, see *Palmer v. Carling O'Keefe Breweries of Canada Ltd.*, [1989] O.J. No. 32, 67 O.R. (2d) 161 (Div. Ct.). *Maple Leaf Foods Inc. v. Schneider Corp.*, [1998] O.J. No. 4142, 42 O.R. (3d) 177 (C.A.) involved an attempted takeover of Schneider Corp. by Maple Leaf Foods Inc. Schneider's shares were publicly traded, but the Schneider family retained control of the corporation. Schneider's board created a special committee of independent directors, none of whom were members of the Schneider family. The family members told the special committee that the only offer they would accept was one from Smithfield Foods Inc. On the advice of the committee, the board of Schneiders took certain steps (including the suspension of a shareholder rights plan) that allowed control to be sold by the Schneider family members to Smithfield. Maple Leaf alleged that the conduct of the board was improper, using the oppression remedy as the vehicle for its claim. The Court of Appeal held that the committee was properly independent, and adopted a fair process in the takeover battle. The advice it gave was reasonable at the time and fair to the non-family shareholders, and the board was justified in following that advice. The claim was dismissed.

3. Although the details of the "oppression remedy" will be set out later, in Chapter 9, we can note here that it is clearly possible to satisfy the requirements for relief under that remedy, without necessarily establishing a breach of fiduciary obligation or any other unlawful act. Following on from cases like *347883 Alberta Ltd. v. P.P.I. Inc.* and *Brant Investments Ltd. v. Keeprite*, can we expect that in the future, all claims that used to be pleaded as breaches of the duty of loyalty (or even the duty of care) owed to the corporation will henceforth be pleaded simply under the oppression remedy? One reason to think this will not happen is that while a shareholder must obtain the leave of the court in order to cause the corporation to sue a director (*e.g.*, C.B.C.A., s. 239), he or she can assume that if such leave is granted, the corporation will bear the costs and the risks of the lawsuit, rather than the shareholder (C.B.C.A., s. 240). See E. M. Iacobucci and K. E. Davis, "Reconciling Derivative Claims and the Oppression Remedy" (2000), 12 S.C.L.R. (2d) 87, reprinted in L. Smith, ed., *Ruled by Law: Essays in Memory of Mr. Justice John Sopinka* (Toronto: LexisNexis Butterworths, 2003), p. 87.

CHAPTER 8

MAJORITY RULE

A. INTRODUCTION

If majority rule is a solution, what is the problem? The problem is action by a collective. Robinson Crusoe, alone on his island, did not need a principle of majority rule. But when a group of people has to make a *collective* decision, majority rule is *one* possible solution to how that decision can be made. We will see in this chapter that while it is the usual solution in corporate law, it is not the only one. Sometimes a special majority of two-thirds is required, and in some cases a decision can only be made unanimously.

The corporate constitution is likely to include at least two groups that are required to make collective decisions. One is the board of directors, which makes decisions regarding the business and affairs of the corporation. The other is the shareholder collective, which elects the directors and makes certain other decisions as well. In both cases, the usual principle is that the majority rules. One big difference is that in a meeting of the board of directors, each director gets one vote; in a meeting of shareholders, each voting share gets one vote.

You should bear in mind that division of powers statutes usually contemplate the possibility of a unanimous shareholder agreement (U.S.A.), which changes the constitutional arrangements by transferring management powers and duties from the directors to the shareholders. These were discussed in Chapter 3. Much as in a partnership, the U.S.A. will lay down its own rules for governance. With the recent enactment of C.B.C.A., s. 146(6), it appears that shareholders acquiring management powers under a U.S.A. can contractually bind themselves in advance to act in a way that would otherwise be a breach of the fiduciary duty of loyalty owed to the corporation. But although a U.S.A. may dramatically change the normal rules of the corporate constitution, the requirement of unanimity for the effectiveness of a U.S.A. is itself an important form of minority protection. Contrast the contractarian approach in B.C.B.C.A., s. 137: management powers, and hence liabilities, can be transferred to shareholders, or anyone else, via an amendment to the articles, which requires only a special resolution.

Those who are entitled to participate in a collective decision governed by the principle of majority rule are implicitly protected by certain procedural safeguards. The requirement that the decision be made in a *meeting* is one such safeguard: it provides a formal framework for the decision, and allows opposing voices to be heard. Imagine that there are five directors on a board of directors. Three of them acting together will be able to pass whatever resolutions they wish. It does not, however, follow that those three can simply send, from time to time, notices to the other directors, telling them what decisions have been made by the board. Another procedural safeguard is the right to *notice* of a meeting; your right to vote would not be worth much if you were not told about the meetings at which it could be exercised.

In *Barron v. Potter*, [1914] 1 Ch. 895 (Eng.), the director Mr. Potter alleged that he had participated in a directors' meeting while running alongside a taxicab that was carrying the director Canon Barron, as the latter ignored Potter's shouting and urged the driver to speed away from Paddington station. Justice Warrington said:

> ... there was no directors' meeting at all for the reason that Canon Baron to the knowledge of Mr. Potter insisted all along that he would not attend any directors' meeting with Mr. Potter or discuss the affairs of the company with him, and it is not enough that one of two directors should say "this is a directors' meeting" while the other says it is not. Of course, if the directors are willing to hold a meeting they may do so under any circumstances, but one of them cannot be made to attend the board or to convert a casual meeting into a board meeting...

The word "meeting" would seem to import a requirement that at least two people be present. It has been held that one person cannot "meet" unless so authorized in the statute or corporate constitution: *Re Primary Distributors Ltd.* (1954), 11 W.W.R. 449, [1954] 2 D.L.R. 438 (B.C.S.C.); *Re London Flats Ltd.*, [1969] 2 All E.R. 744, [1969] 1 W.L.R. 711 (Eng. Ch.). Would it be impossible to hold the statutorily required annual general meeting if the corporation had only one shareholder and the statute did not contemplate one-person meetings? Since business corporations started as collective enterprises (remember the meaning of the word "company" in this connection), the idea of a one-shareholder corporation was historically impossible, but most statutes have now reversed this rule as we will see.

The idea of a meeting also imports a requirement of a common purpose; two strangers sitting together on a park bench does not amount to a meeting. This serves to inhibit those who convene one type of meeting and attempt, despite some minority's protests, to convert it into another type. Thus, in a corporation where all the shareholders are directors and all attend a directors' meeting, a shareholders' meeting cannot be casually convened at the close of business unless all consent: see *Re Empress Engineering Works Ltd.*, [1920] 1 Ch. 466 (Eng. C.A.).

B. DIRECTORS

The C.B.C.A. and other statutes lay out some ground rules for directors' meetings, but they may be varied by the corporate constitution. See for example C.B.C.A., ss. 114, 117. The by-laws usually add detail to the statute. The board must generally act in the setting of a meeting, with a quorum present, following notice to the directors. A director may participate by telephone, if the by-laws permit and the other directors consent (s. 114(9)). A decision may be made without a meeting, but only if the decision is in writing and unanimous (s. 117). Where the corporation has only one director, he or she can act unilaterally, either on the basis of unanimity (s. 117) or on the basis that he or she "may constitute a meeting" (s. 114(8)) and may waive any notice requirements (s. 114(6)). If the statute has rules regarding the residency of directors (*e.g.*, C.B.C.A., ss. 105(3)-(4); O.B.C.A., s. 118(3)), these will usually have an impact on the rules for directors' meetings (*e.g.*, C.B.C.A., s. 114(3); O.B.C.A., s. 126(6)). There may also be rules about the location of directors' meetings (O.B.C.A., s. 126(1)-(2)).

C. SHAREHOLDERS

1. Shareholder Meetings

(a) Kinds of Meetings

Canadian corporate law statutes give various powers to the shareholders, and they usually stipulate whether such powers are to be exercised at an "annual meeting" or at a "special meeting". For example, the C.B.C.A. provides:

106. (3) ... shareholders of a corporation shall, by ordinary resolution at the first meeting of shareholders and at each succeeding annual meeting at which an election of directors is required, elect directors to hold office for a term expiring not later than the close of the third annual meeting of shareholders following the election.

109. (1) ... the shareholders of a corporation may by ordinary resolution at a special meeting remove any director or directors from office.

As you may find in reading cases, in English parlance the annual meeting is called an "ordinary meeting" and a special meeting is called an "extraordinary meeting". The main items of ordinary business for the annual meeting are (i) election of directors, (ii) shareholder approval of by-laws (C.B.C.A., s. 103(2)); (iii) disclosure by the directors to the shareholders of the corporation's financial position (C.B.C.A., s. 155); and (iv) appointment of the auditor (C.B.C.A., s. 162).

When a special meeting is needed, it may be called at the same time and place as the following annual meeting, but if it is urgent, it can be held on its own.

(b) Notice Requirements

The obvious issues here are to whom must notice be given, timing of the notice, and the adequacy of the information contained in the notice.

Strangely, it is not absolutely clear who is entitled to receive notice of shareholders' meetings. Those shareholders who will have a vote on matters to be dealt with at the meeting clearly must be notified, and so too must directors and the auditor: C.B.C.A., s. 135(1), A.B.C.A., s. 134(1), M.C.A., S.B.C.A., s. 129(1), O.B.C.A., s. 96(1), B.C.B.C.A., s. 169, N.B.B.C.A., s. 87(1); see also *Garvie v. Axmith*, [1962] O.R. 65, 31 D.L.R. (2d) 65 (Ont. H.C.), extracted below. But what about non-voting shareholders? As we will see in more detail in Chapter 10, there must be some shareholders who can vote, and so if there is only one class of shares, they are voting shares. But it is quite common for corporations to have more than one class of shares, with some classes being non-voting. With shares of this kind, the shareholder accepts that he or she has no say in the election of directors, the approval of by-laws, and so on. Can the following judicial comment be interpreted to support a requirement that all shareholders be notified so they can make up their own minds whether to attend and make a speech?

Although, no doubt, the directors held proxies for the meetings of July 3 and 18, 1906, enough to carry their propositions, and though it is highly probable that at any other meeting dealing with a like subject, or any other subject affecting the company, the directors will again hold proxies enough to countervail any opposition, yet it is impossible to predict that, when the shareholders have had an opportunity of considering the objections of the plaintiffs and others to the new regulations, they will not revolt and vote against the directors. It is because they may do this, while on the other hand, they may for reasons satisfactory to themselves, which no one has a right to examine, support the directors and pass the new regulations, that it is dangerous and wrong to interfere with their liberty of action.

(Justice Kekewich in *Normandy v. Ind, Coope & Co. Ltd.*, [1908] 1 Ch. 84, 109 (Eng. Ch.)).

The case dealt with adequacy of notice, but the underlying principle may be applicable to the question whether non-voting shareholders must be notified of shareholders' meetings.

A question may arise as to which of a transferor or transferee of shares is the appropriate person to receive notice of and attend the meeting. If there were no rules peculiar to corporate law on the point, what would be the property law result? Note the advantage of having a "record date" on which the identity of those who must be notified of the next meeting is ascertained from the corporate records: see, *e.g.*, C.B.C.A., s. 134. For the position of transferees, see C.B.C.A., s. 138(2) and (3). Most shares in publicly traded corporations are now held through indirect holding systems in which the registered shareholder may be a "depository" that holds large numbers of shares on behalf of clients that are financial services providers; in turn, those financial services providers hold their interests in the shares on behalf of the investors. Under this system, the investors never become registered shareholders. Through securities regulation (notably National Instruments 54-101 and 54-102), a system is in place that allows investors who are not registered shareholders to elect to receive some or all of the information that must be sent to shareholders.

Timing is another important feature of the notice requirement. The applicable statute usually sets both a minimum and maximum number of days notice for a meeting: see, *e.g.*, C.B.C.A., s. 135(1), referring the timing to the regulations (see *Canada Business Corporations Regulations, 2001*, SOR/2001-512, s. 44). What is the rule where no such limits are prescribed in the statute or corporation constitution?

Adequacy of notice is a difficult point on which to legislate because the great variety of detail to be covered among the various types of corporations makes general rules difficult to formulate. The following case provides some guidance.

GARVIE v. AXMITH

(1961), 31 D.L.R. (2d) 65, [1962] O.R. 65 (H.C.)

[The directors of the defendant corporation gave notice of a special general meeting of shareholders to approve (a) an agreement by the corporation to purchase the assets and undertaking of a second corporation and (b) an application for supplementary letters patent to permit refinancing of the defendant corporation under a new name. Some shareholders received no notice of the meeting. The plaintiff applied to the court for an injunction and a declaration that the resolutions the shareholders attempted to pass were invalid on the grounds, inter alia, that there had not been proper and adequate notice. Only that part of the judgment dealing with notice is reproduced here.]

Spence J.: — ... In *Pacific Coast Coal Mines Ltd. v. Arbuthnot*, 36 D.L.R. 564 at pp. 5712, [1917] A.C. 607 at p. 618, Viscount Haldane said:

Their Lordships are of opinion that to render the notice a compliance with the Act under which it was given it ought to have told the shareholders, including those who gave proxies, more than it did. It ought to have put them in a position in which each of them could have judged for himself whether he would consent, not only to buying out the shares of directors, but to releasing possible claims against them. Now, this is just what it did not do, and therefore, quite apart from the fact that the meeting was held in half an hour from the time the Act passed and before the shareholders could have had a proper opportunity of learning the particulars of what the legislature had authorized, their Lordships are of opinion that the notice was bad, and that what was done was consequently ultra vires.

In *Re Nat'l Grocers Ltd.*, [1938] 3 D.L.R. at p. 116, O.R. at p. 154, Roach, J. (as he then was), said:

No doubt such a prospect would be enticing to a common shareholder, but it seems to me that the directors might well have included with this circular a statement showing briefly the financial progress of the company, or, at least, sufficient information to enable the common shareholder to appreciate the full and complete result of the adoption of the plan.

Roach, J., then follows with a citation from *Re Dorman Long & Co.*, [1934] Ch. 635, where Maugham, J. (as he then was), at p. 665 said:

If no explanatory circular is sent, he [a shareholder] may be quite unable to understand or form an opinion as to which way he should vote in the matter without attending the meeting... The practice being to send out an explanatory circular in such a case, it is, in my opinion, the duty of the Court very carefully to scrutinize the circular when the matters involved are matters of considerable difficulty and doubt.

In *Re N. Slater Co.*, [1947] 2 D.L.R. 311 at pp. 3134 O.W.N. 226 at p. 227, LeBel, J. (as he then was), said:

It seems to me that a shareholder is entitled to such information as will permit him to reach his own decision and that his understanding of the proposed scheme is not assisted by such generalizations as are contained in Mr. Cooper's letter. The directors should have included in the material sent out a statement which reflected, at least briefly, the financial position of the company so that a shareholder might come to the conclusion as to the respective values of the two classes of shares. Without such information, it was, in my opinion, impossible for any shareholder, particularly a holder of common shares, to exercise any intelligent judgment as to the value of the shares of either class.

Similarly, in this case I believe I have illustrated that without an adequate explanation including a statement of what, in fact, was the evidence of Messrs. Markle, Bartley and Mitchell given at the trial, it was impossible for any Rockwin shareholder to come to any intelligent conclusion as to whether he should favour or oppose the transaction, and that is the right of each shareholder and a right which he must have accorded to him in the notice of the special general meeting sent to him. It is not, in my opinion, a sufficient answer to say either that the plaintiff Garvie was given that information in his two attendances upon Mr. Axmith, or that other shareholders could have had that information had they in turn attended Mr. Axmith. The shareholders might well be any place on the American continent, or overseas, and the shareholders should be able to sit down with the material and come to an intelligent conclusion. As the Courts did in the various cases to which I have last referred, I have come to the conclusion that this failure to give proper and adequate notice of what the transaction involved, is fatal to the defendant.

Therefore, for these reasons the injunction granted by the Honourable Mr. Justice Aylen on June 20, 1961, should be made permanent. The plaintiff is entitled to a declaration that the resolutions which purported to be passed by the shareholders of the defendant company on June 5, 1961, which authorized an application for letters patent and approved the agreement dated May 11, 1961, are invalid. This submission of the matter to another special general meeting of shareholders of Rockwin Mines Limited, with proper notice of what was actually involved, if the directors of that company should deem that step appropriate.

The plaintiff is entitled to his costs.

Judgment for the plaintiff.

NOTES

See also: *Re Hampshire Land Co.*, [1896] 2 Ch. 743; *Ballie v. Oriental Telephone & Electric Co.*, [1915] 1 Ch. 503 (C.A.); *Wood v. PanAmerican Investments Ltd.* (1961), 28 D.L.R. (2d) 703 (B.C.S.C.); *Rudkin v. B.C. Automobile Assn.*, [1969] B.C.J. No. 39, 70 W.W.R. 649 (B.C.S.C.); and *Bayshore Inv. Ltd. v. Endako Mines Ltd.*, [1971] B.C.J. No. 317, [1971] 2 W.W.R. 622 (B.C.S.C.).

The two basic aspects of the notice principle, namely, the requirement that every matter to be acted upon at the meeting be properly identified and the requirement that all matters to be acted on must be sufficiently described to permit shareholders to form a reasoned judgment, are also set out in the provisions governing proxies contained in the various provincial corporate and securities statutes. Proxies will be discussed below.

(c) Location of Meetings

The general rule is that shareholders' meetings must be held within the jurisdiction of incorporation, but exceptions may be allowed if the articles contemplate it or there is unanimous consent: C.B.C.A., s. 132, A.B.C.A., s. 131, M.C.A., S.B.C.A., s. 126, N.B.B.C.A., s. 84; but see O.B.C.A., s. 93. The Ontario provision was changed, perhaps in the light of the following case, which was decided under the old s. 105.

RE UPPER CANADA RESOURCES LTD. AND MINISTER OF CONSUMER AND COMMERCIAL RELATIONS

(1978), 20 O.R. (2d) 100 (H.C.)

Southey J. (orally): — This is an application by Upper Canada Resources Limited under s. 194(5) of the *Business Corporations Act*, R.S.O. 1970, c. 53, as amended, for an order approving a scheme prescribing details of an arrangement dated February 1, 1978, between the applicant and its common shareholders, as subsequently amended at the annual general meeting of shareholders held on March 27, 1978.

Under the arrangement, the issued and outstanding shares of the applicant, consisting of 5,826,677 commons shares with a par value of $1 each, were to be converted into a new class of no par value shares to be designated "Class A Special Shares" on the basis of one Class A Special Share for 10 common shares. The Class A Special Shares carried one vote per share and were entitled to a cumulative preferential dividend on $2.50 per share. The Class A Special Shares were redeemable at the option of the applicant and the shareholder could call for their redemption after 12 years at a price of $35 per share together with any unpaid cumulative dividends.

The Class A Special Shares were convertible, except in the case of United States shareholders, into nonvoting shares of Turbo Resources Limited or, in the case of all shareholders, could be converted into 10 no par value common shares of the applicant. The latter provision, in my view, is of considerable importance in assessing the fairness of the scheme because it meant that any shareholder who did not regard the other options under the arrangement as being in his best interest could, by accepting the new no par value commons shares, leave himself in substantially the same position with respect to his holding in the equity of the applicant as he had been in before the arrangement was carried out.

The scheme was brought before the shareholders of the applicant at a meeting held in Calgary, Alberta, on March 27, 1978. The scheme was approved at that meeting by 94.6% of the votes cast. There were 3,039,749 shares of the applicant represented in person or by proxy at the meeting. Fifty-eight shareholders present in person or represented by proxy holding 160,425 shares, voted against approving the arrangement.

The Minister of Consumer and Commercial Relations was given notice of the application before me in accordance with s. 194(6) of the *Business Corporations Act* as were the dissentient shareholders. No dissentient shareholders appeared before me, but the Minister was represented by counsel and opposed the approval of the scheme.

The opposition of the Minister was not based on any view that the scheme was unfair, but arose out of the fact that the holding of the shareholders' meeting in Calgary was in contravention of s. 105 of the *Business Corporations Act*. Section 105 reads as follows:

105.(1) Subject to subsections (2) and (3), the meetings of the shareholders shall be held at the place where the head office of the corporation is located.

(2) Where the bylaws of the corporation so provide, the meetings of the shareholders may be held at any place within Ontario.

(3) Where the articles of the corporation so provide, the meetings of the shareholders may be held at one or more places outside Ontario specified therein.

The applicant was incorporated by letters patent dated April 4, 1929, in which it was provided that the head office was to be situated at Toronto. The letters patent authorized the company to hold meetings of its shareholders at any place other than the head office either within or without the Province of Ontario. Because of that provision in the letters patent, it was lawful for the corporation to hold shareholders' meetings outside Ontario prior to the coming into force of the *Business Corporations Act* on January 1, 1971.

Section 272 [am. 1971, Vol. 2, c. 26, s. 45; 1972, c. 138, s. 60] of the *Business Corporations Act* provides that any provision in the letters patent of a corporation that was valid immediately before the Act came into force, but which contravenes the Act, with certain exceptions, continues to be valid and in effect until January 1, 1975. The purpose of s. 272 obviously, was to give corporations time to change their letters patent or articles and bylaws in order to meet the provisions of the new statute.

At a shareholders' meeting in April, 1977, the shareholders of the applicant by bylaw authorized the holding of meetings outside Ontario, but no steps were taken to amend the letters patent or articles. The result is that they continue to authorize simply the holding of meetings outside Ontario without specifying the places outside Ontario where those meetings can be held as required by s. 105(3).

The position taken on behalf of the Minister is that the applicant has not complied with the provisions of the *Business Corporations Act* in the procedures followed in obtaining the approval of the shareholders to the scheme, and that the Court ought not to approve the scheme for that reason.

Section 194(2), providing for submission of the scheme to the shareholders, reads as follows:

> 194(2) The corporation shall submit the scheme to the shareholders, or to the class of them affected, as the case may be, at a meeting duly called by the corporation for the purpose of considering the scheme.

I have emphasized the word "duly" because, in my view, it indicates that the Legislature intended that a corporation must follow strictly the provisions of the statute in attempting to bring into force an arrangement under ss. 193 and 194 of the *Business Corporations Act*.

This view is supported by the leading case on the matter, *Re Dairy Corp. of Canada Ltd.*, [1934] O.R. 436 at p. 439, [1934] 3 D.L.R. 347, in which Mr. Justice Middleton described the duty of a Judge hearing an application such as the present in the following terms:

> Upon this motion I think it is incumbent upon the Judge to ascertain if all statutory requirements which are in the nature of conditions precedent have been strictly complied with and I think the Judge also is called upon to determine whether anything has been done or purported to have been done which is not authorized by this Statute. Beyond this there is, I think, the duty imposed upon the Court to criticize the scheme and ascertain whether it is in truth fair and reasonable.

There is much force in the submissions ably advanced by Mr. Roland on behalf of the applicant to the effect that the place of the meeting is unlikely to have any substantial result on the outcome of the vote of shareholders at the meeting. He pointed out that the shareholders had been informed in 1977 at the time the by-laws were changed to authorize meetings outside Ontario that the intention was to hold meetings in the future in Calgary. The general offices of the applicant were moved from Ontario to Calgary during the last year.

I accept without question that the applicant was acting in good faith in believing that it had the right to hold the meeting in Calgary and was not attempting to hold a meeting at a place impossible or inconvenient for the shareholders to attend, nor was the applicant, in my view, acting in a fraudulent or oppressive manner.

There is every indication that the scheme would have been approved by substantially the same majority if the meeting had been held in Toronto and that that will be the case if I refuse to approve the scheme and the applicant proceeds with a meeting in Toronto in compliance with the Ontario statute. Although the evidence indicated that that probably would have been the result, there is no way in which I can be sure that that would have been the result. If the meeting had been held in Toronto, it might have been possible for persons to attend who could have persuade other shareholders in attendance that the arrangement was not one which should be approved. Such shareholders would then be dissentients; would be entitled to notice of the proceedings before me, and might have had some submissions to make on the question of fairness. To act on the suggestion that it would make no difference whether the meeting were held in Calgary or in Toronto would involve accepting, to a large extent, the view that any shareholders' meeting is but a formality and that the proceedings and discussions at such meetings are of little consequence. While that may often be the case, it is a fundamental underlying assumption of our corporation law that meetings of shareholders may be of significance, even where one shareholder or group of shareholders owns a predominant proportion of the shares.

In my view, the applicant has failed unintentionally to comply with the provisions of the *Business Corporations Act* respecting the approval of a scheme. The meeting was not duly called as required by the Act and, applying the rules suggested by Mr. Justice Middleton, I must find that the applicant has done something that it was not authorized by statute to do.

For these reasons, I feel that I have no alternative but to dismiss the motion and an order will go to that effect.

Motion dismissed.

(d) Voting at a Meeting

How do shareholders vote at a meeting? In principle, by raising their hands: C.B.C.A., s. 141(1). However, any shareholder may demand a ballot, with one vote per share, and the corporation's articles may eliminate the show of hands. Voting can also be electronic (specifically contemplated by C.B.C.A., s. 141; under other statutes, the corporate constitution can probably authorize this).

We describe holders of voting shares as having a "right to vote" and consider the vote to be one of the most important attributes of a voting share, since each vote is an element of control, however indirect, over the corporation. Some English cases are not so clear about this.

MacDOUGALL v. GARDINER

(1875) 1 Ch.D. 13 (Eng. C.A.)

[The articles of association provided that on the request of five shareholders a poll vote (counting shares rather than hands) had to be taken on a resolution. A special meeting of shareholders was called to discuss the removal of a director, Colonel Gardiner. Before any other resolution had been voted upon, a resolution for adjournment of the meeting was proposed, and it was carried by a show of hands. The chairman refused a request for a poll vote, even though it was made by the requisite number of shareholders, on the grounds that this provision did not apply to adjournment motions. If the chairman had taken the vote by poll the motion for adjournment would have been defeated. The plaintiff, a shareholder, filed a bill on behalf of himself and all other shareholders against the directors asking for a declaration that the chairman's conduct was unlawful and requesting an injunction prohibiting the directors from concluding a proposed transaction. The plaintiff alleged, *inter alia*, that the majority of the shareholders were opposed to the transaction, but would be frustrated by the chairman's refusal to poll the meeting. Vice-Chancellor Malins overruled the defendant Gardiner's demurrer, that is, an argument that the plaintiff's claim had no legal foundation. By the time the appeal reached the Court of Appeal the offending chairman had been removed and the plaintiff appointed a director.]

James L.J.: — ... I cannot conceive that there is any equity on the part of a shareholder, on behalf of himself and the minority, to say, "True it is that the majority have a right to determine everything connected with the management of the company, but then we have a right — and every individual has a right — to have a meeting held in strict form in accordance with the articles." Has a particular individual the right to have it for the purpose of using his power of eloquence to induce the others to listen to him and to take his view? That is an equity which I have never yet heard of in this court, and I have never known it insisted upon before; that is to say, that this court is to entertain a bill for the purpose of enabling one particular member of the company to have an opportunity of expressing his opinions viva voce at a meeting of the shareholders. If so, I do not know why we should not go further, and say, not only must the meeting be held, but the shareholders must stay there to listen to him and to be convinced by him. The truth is, that is only part of the machinery and means by which the internal management is carried on. The whole question comes back to a question of internal management ... From the first opening of this case before us, I have never had any doubt in my own mind that this was a bill which, if it was to be sustained at all, could only be sustained by the company. ...

Mellish L.J.: — I am of the same opinion. I think it is a matter of considerable importance to determine this question, whether a suit ought to be brought in the name of the company or in the name of one of the shareholders on behalf of the others. It is not at all a technical question, but it may make a very serious difference in the management of the affairs of the company. The difference is this: — Looking to the nature of these companies, looking at the way in which their articles are formed, and that they are not all lawyers who attend these meetings, nothing can be more likely than that there should be something more or less irregular done at them — some directors may have been irregularly appointed, some directors as irregularly turned out, or something or other may have been done which ought not to have been done according to the proper construction of the articles. Now, if that gives a right to every member of the company to file a bill to have the question decided, then if there happens to be one cantankerous member, or one member who loves litigation, everything of this kind will be litigated; whereas, if the bill must be filed in the name of the company, then, unless there is a majority who really wish for litigation, the litigation will not go on. Therefore, holding that such suits must be brought in the name of the company does certainly greatly tend to stop litigation.

In my opinion, if the thing complained of is a thing which in substance the majority of the company are entitled to do, or if something has been done irregularly which the majority of the company are entitled to do regularly, or if something has been done illegally which the majority of the company are entitled to do legally, there can be no use in having a litigation about it, the ultimate end of which is only that a meeting has to be called, and then ultimately the majority gets its wishes. Is it not better that the rule should be adhered to that if it is a thing which the majority are the masters of, the majority in substance shall be entitled to have their will followed? If it is a matter of that nature, it only comes to this, that the majority are the only persons who can complain that a thing which they are entitled to do has been done irregularly; and that, as I understand it, is what has been decided by the cases of *Mozley v. Alston* (1847), 1 Ph. 790, and *Foss v. Harbottle* (1843), 2 Hare 461. In my opinion that is the rule that is to be maintained. Of course if the majority are abusing their powers, and are depriving the minority of their rights, that is an entirely different thing, and there the minority are entitled to come before this court to maintain their rights; but if what is complained of is simply that something which the majority are entitled to do has been done or undone irregularly, then I think it is quite right that nobody should have a right to set that aside, or to institute a suit in Chancery about it, except the company itself.

[The concurring judgment of **Baggally J.A.** is omitted.]

PENDER v. LUSHINGTON

(1877), 6 Ch. D. 70 (Eng. Ch.)

[The articles of association of the Direct United States Cable Co. Ltd. provided that members shall have "one vote for every complete number of ten shares, with the limit that no shareholder shall be entitled to more than a hundred votes in all". The articles also provided that the company was not to be affected by notice of any trust relating to the shares held by any member. At an extraordinary general meeting the chairman refused to register the votes cast by certain shareholders in question who had merely obtained their shares for the purpose of increasing the voting power of the transferor. This was found to be in violation of the articles, on the ground that the chairman was not entitled to look behind the share register to ascertain who was a member. But this brought up the question of who was entitled to sue.]

Jessel M.R.: — ... In all cases of this kind, where men exercise their rights of property, they exercise their rights from some motive adequate or inadequate, and I have always considered the law to be that those who have the rights of property are entitled to exercise them, whatever their motives may be for such exercise that is as regards a court of law as distinguished from a court of morality or conscience, if such a court exists. I put to Mr. Harrison, as a crucial test, whether, if a landlord had six tenants whose rent was in arrear, and three of them voted in a way he approved of for a member of Parliament, and three did not, the court could restrain the landlord from distraining on the three who did not, because he did not at the same time distrain on the three who did. He admitted at once that whatever the motive might be, even if it could be proved that the landlord had distrained on them for that reason, that I could not prevent him from distraining because they had not paid their rent. I cannot deprive him of his property, although he may not make use of that right of property in a way I might altogether approve. That is really the question, because if these shareholders have a right of property, then I think all the arguments which have been addressed to me as to the motives which induced them to exercise it are entirely beside the question. ...

I now come to the subordinate question ... namely, whether you have the right plaintiffs here. The plaintiffs may be described as three, though there are really two. There is, first Mr. Pender himself, on behalf of himself; next, as the representative of the class of shareholders who voted with him, whose votes I hold to have been improperly rejected, and next, there is the Direct United States Cable Company. It is said that the company ought not to have been made plaintiffs.

[**Jessel M.R.** then considered the consequences of ordering the company's name removed and decided the case mainly on that point.]

I think I ought not on this summons to take away the name of the company, but to let the summons stand over, leaving either party to call a meeting to decide whether the company's name is to be used or not. In the meantime, whether this is an action in the name of the shareholders or in the name of the company, in either case I think there should be an injunction. ...

But there is another ground on which the action may be maintained. This is an action by Mr. Pender for himself. He is a member of the company, and whether he voted with the majority or the minority he is entitled to have his vote recorded — an individual right in respect of which he has a right to sue. That has nothing to do with the question like that raised in *Foss v. Harbottle* and that line of cases. He has a right to say, "Whether I vote in the majority or minority, you shall record my vote, as that is a right of property belonging to my interest in this company, and if you refuse to record my vote I will institute legal proceedings against you to compel you." What is the answer to such an action? It seems to me it can be maintained as a matter of substance, and that there is no technical difficulty in maintaining it. ...

NOTE

The leading textbook on company law in the U.K. is P.L. Davies, *Gower and Davies' Principles of Modern Company Law*, 7th ed. (London: Sweet & Maxwell, 2003), where the author says at pp. 450-51 that these two cases are "ultimately irreconcilable" and that each of them "has spawned a line of equally irreconcilable authorities". In the English model, the articles are a contract among the shareholders and the corporation, and denial of the right to vote in accordance with the articles is a violation of the shareholder's personal rights. In Gower and Davies' view, the effective protection of the procedural voting entitlements is "basic to any satisfactory system of company law".

More pithily, Welling says (*Corporate Law in Canada: The Governing Principles*, 3rd ed., at p. 485), "The result in *MacDougall v. Gardiner* is absurd." It appears, however, that it has not been overruled in England.

(e) Proxy Voting

There is a long history of management sending out "forms of proxy" along with notices of meeting. A form of proxy allows a shareholder to authorize someone else to cast his or her votes. One might think that proxies would empower shareholders. The difficulty under the common law was that management might not send out enough information with the notice to allow the shareholder to understand fully the matters to be voted upon. Moreover, the forms sent out typically named, as the proxy, a member of the corporation's management, or someone under management's direction. Following the "Kimber Report" in Ontario in 1965, proxies for publicly traded corporations are now closely regulated. For federal corporations, see C.B.C.A., Part XIII; at the provincial level, the regulation has been via secondary legislation under the provincial Securities Acts.

These rules require management to solicit proxies, and to provide detailed information about the matters to be voted upon. It remains permissible to name a member of management as the default holder of the proxy, but the form of proxy must state that the shareholder is at liberty to name someone else. Interestingly, one rule that has survived since the Kimber Report (see paragraph 6.14(a) of the Report) is that the election of directors and the appointment of the auditor, which one might consider to be fundamental shareholder concerns, are understood to be routine matters. The consequence is that for those matters, the form of proxy does not need to give the shareholder the option to vote *against* management's proposals on those issues, although that option must be given in respect of all other matters. For the election of directors and the appointment of the auditor, the form need only give the options (i) to vote in favour, and (ii) to withhold the vote. This is how the forms are routinely printed. Assume that management proposes a candidate for election as a director; that 300 votes are cast using forms of proxy; there are 100 votes in favour and 200 votes "withheld". Outside of cumulative voting systems, a director must be elected by an ordinary resolution (C.B.C.A., s. 106(3)). An ordinary resolution is defined in the C.B.C.A., s. 2(1) as "... a resolution passed by a majority of the votes cast by the shareholders who voted in respect of that resolution". Was the candidate elected? Were the withheld votes "cast" at all? A shareholder receiving this kind of form of proxy can vote *against* the resolution only by attending the meeting, or by creating his or her own form of proxy (making sure that it complies with the corporate constitution).

A related issue is that management typically proposes a "slate" of directors. If there are three vacancies on the board, three candidates are proposed together on the form of proxy. In relation to all three, the shareholder can vote in favour or withhold his or her vote. It is not possible to vote in favour of two but against one (or even to vote in favour of two and withhold any vote regarding one). Both the practice of proposing slates, and of using "for or withhold" forms, have recently been targeted by advocates for better corporate governance practices.

(f) Shareholder Initiatives

Once general managerial power is vested in the board of directors, the shareholder majority cannot directly dictate management policy. Obviously anyone, including the shareholders, can submit petitions to the board, asking that management action be taken. However, petitions from minority shareholders are likely to be ignored while, especially in large corporations, petitions from significant numbers of shareholders are difficult and costly to organize. There has been some statutory recognition that such petitions often promote better corporate management and should be facilitated. What the modern statutes contemplate is a system by which shareholders can place items on the agenda of a shareholders meeting; this includes the circulation in advance of information about the initiative, at the expense of the corporation. In the C.B.C.A. these initiatives are called "proposals" and they are governed by s. 137. This provision was recently substantially amended. In one sense, it was made less accessible to shareholders: under s. 137(1.1), a minimum number of shares is required to activate the section, and these must have been held for a minimum period of time. The current minima are set out in the *Canada Business Corporations Regulations, 2001*, SOR/2001-512, s. 46. It is not necessary for a single person to hold the minimum number of shares, so long as there is a group in support that together meets the threshold. The power to nominate a director is regulated separately in s. 137(4), with a statutory 5 per cent minimum required. In another sense, s. 137 has been made more accessible to shareholders. This was via a change in the wording of s. 137(5), which allows management to decline to circulate the proposal and its supporting documentation in various situations. The wording of the old provision allowed management a wider range of discretion to decline the proposal; compare, for example, M.C.A., s. 131(5), which retains the previous wording. See also A.B.C.A., s. 136, S.B.C.A., s. 131, N.B.B.C.A., s. 89, O.B.C.A., s. 99, B.C.B.C.A., ss. 187-191; Q.C.A., ss. 98.1-98.12 (not proclaimed in force). For an example of management disqualifation of a proposal, see *Re Variety Corp. and Jesuit Fathers of Upper Canada* (1987), 60 O.R. (2d) 640 (C.A.).

Even if the proposal is eligible, do these provisions include the right to put the shareholder's proposal to a vote at the general meeting? Even if the proposal is put to a vote and accepted by a majority, what would follow from that? Is the answer different if the vote is one that creates a new by-law (C.B.C.A., s. 103(5)) or amends the articles of incorporation (C.B.C.A., s. 175(1))? Changes to by-laws and the articles are addressed in more detail below.

Suppose a shareholder proposal that was circulated by management turned out to contain libellous statements concerning some person. Is someone in the corporate management liable to that person in tort? Is the corporation? Does it make a difference if the allegation of defamation is based on the sending of the proposal to a shareholder outside the incorporating jurisdiction?

2. Ordinary Business: Annual Meetings

The statute requires the directors to call annual meetings, with some flexibility as to timing (*e.g.*, C.B.C.A., s. 133). If the directors default in calling the meeting, it may be called by the shareholders or the court (C.B.C.A., ss. 143-144). It also provides the requirements for giving notice of the meeting. As with directors, there is a quorum requirement (C.B.C.A., s. 139), which however is routinely lowered by the by-laws. Again as with directors, the meeting can be avoided in favour of a written resolution, but only if it is unanimous (C.B.C.A., s. 142). If there is only one shareholder, he or she constitutes a meeting (C.B.C.A., 139(4)). Meetings may be electronic (*e.g.*, C.B.C.A., s. 132(5)).

Generally, whatever shareholders must decide is decided by a simple majority ("ordinary resolution": see the definition of this term in s. 2 of the statute). We will see, however, that there are many exceptions. One example is B.C.B.C.A., s. 182(2), which allows deferral or waiver of the annual meeting, but only if there is a *unanimous* resolution to that effect.

(a) Election of Directors

The shareholders' power to elect directors by simple majority vote derives from the statute in most Canadian jurisdictions: see, *e.g.*, C.B.C.A., s. 106(3).

The ordinary system for electing directors can create problems. Assume that in a corporation with 100 shares and 1 vote per share, 51 shares are held by faction A and 49 are held by faction B. The two factions have opposing views on how to manage the corporation. Three directors are to be elected. The candidates are A1, A2, and A3 (from faction A) and B1, B2, and B3 (from faction B). Who will be the three directors after the election? The result is obvious unless strict majority rule is modified. There are three common modifications: cumulative voting, class directors, and voting contracts.

Cumulative voting is optional under most statutes — *e.g.*, C.B.C.A., s. 107, A.B.C.A., s. 107, S.B.C.A., M.C.A., s. 102, O.B.C.A., s. 120 — but compulsory in New Brunswick (s. 65(1)). Where it is optional, however, it is rarely adopted. It is one example of a mitigation of the results of strict majority rule. Under cumulative voting, a shareholder gets a number of votes equal to the product of (i) the number of voting shares he or she holds, and (ii) the number of vacancies on the board that must be filled. The shareholder may divide his or her votes among different candidates, or cumulate them and cast them all for one candidate. This system requires that there be a fixed number of directors, and that they be elected to one-year terms. It also requires that all candidates are voted upon together; the candidates who receive the fewest votes are eliminated until the number of candidates remaining is equal to the number of positions to be filled. In this system, there are no votes *against* candidates, only votes *for*. What would be the outcome of the above election under cumulative voting? There are six candidates for three positions; Faction A would have 153 votes, and Faction B, 147 votes. How many votes must Faction A cast in favour of a candidate to be sure that the candidate will be elected?

Class directors are directors elected by the votes of only one class of shares. The theory is that different classes of shares will appeal to and be acquired by different types of people whose views will, without class voting, be under-represented on a majority elected board. C.B.C.A., s. 111(3) is an example of a section authorizing such a rule. What are the legal rules binding a director elected by a particular class of shareholders? See A.B.C.A., s. 122(4), set out on p. 95.

Voting contracts among shareholders are common in small corporations. Such contracts have long been regarded as enforceable: see, *e.g.*, *Ringuet v. Bergeron*, [1960] S.C.R. 672, 24 D.L.R. (2d) 449 (S.C.C.). Why, then, does the C.B.C.A. have s. 145.1?

> A written agreement between two or more shareholders may provide that in exercising voting rights the shares held by them shall be voted as therein provided.

Does this section make unwritten voting contracts unenforceable? Does it make written agreements enforceable even if they are not contracts? A voting agreement among shareholders who are also directors is severable and illegal to the extent that it attempts to affect the casting of votes on the board of directors. The reason is that each director owes an individual fiduciary obligation to the corporation to make management decisions that appear to be in the corporate best interest at the time of the decision. As a result, a director is not permitted to "fetter his discretion" by an earlier contractual promise: see *Motherwell v. Schoof*, [1949] 2 W.W.R. 529 (Alta. S.C.); *McQuade v. Stoneham*, 189 N.E. 234 (N.Y.C.A., 1934); and *Ringuet v. Bergeron*, above. Compare the situation under unanimous shareholder agreements after the enactment of C.B.C.A., s. 146(6).

In the context of the election of directors, what is the significance of a provision like C.B.C.A., s. 145?

> (1) A corporation or a shareholder or director may apply to a court to determine any controversy with respect to an election or appointment of a director or auditor of the corporation.

> (2) On an application under this section, the court may make any order it thinks fit including, without limiting the generality of the foregoing ... [a list of specific examples of possible judicial orders].

Is majority rule the law in Canadian business corporations, or is it merely a practice adopted by such a large portion of the populace that, like wearing neckties or eyeliner, it has become a traditional, though not legally mandated, aspect of business life? Does s. 145 authorize a court to disregard a majority vote in favour of a director? If so, on what grounds? If not, what does subs. (2) mean?

(b) Approval of By-laws

In almost all types of corporate constitution, the by-laws are designed to be the part of the constitution that is most easily modified. Typically, the directors have the power to create or amend by-laws, but that change is effective only until the next shareholder meeting. At that time, the change must be approved by the shareholders in order for it to continue in effect. See C.B.C.A., s. 103. By ss. 103(5) and 137 (discussed above), a shareholder who holds enough shares may be able to propose his or her own by-law.

(c) Financial Disclosure

At annual meetings, the directors must report to the shareholders on the corporation's financial position (C.B.C.A., s. 155). This is not something that requires a vote, although this disclosure includes the auditor's report, and the auditor is appointed directly by the shareholders.

(d) Appointment of Auditor

Shareholders are supposed to be protected against management disloyalty and incompetence by the legal duties described in Chapter 7. Another protection for shareholders is the auditor. This person — more likely a firm of accountants — is appointed directly by the shareholders (*e.g.*, C.B.C.A., s. 162). The idea is that the auditor provides an independent verification of the financial information being presented by the directors. The expense of having an auditor can be waived, but only with the unanimous consent of all shareholders, including those not normally entitled to vote (C.B.C.A., 163(3)). The auditor cannot be waived if the shares of the corporation are publicly traded. This rare requirement of unanimous consent (as opposed to majority rule) underlines the protective role of the auditor.

There are, however, some difficulties with this theoretical position. Although the legal power to appoint the auditor lies with the shareholders, it is the directors who propose an auditor for the approval of the shareholders. In a large corporation, the voting process becomes a rubber-stamp, just as with the election of directors, who are also proposed by the incumbent board. Moreover, the auditor's effectiveness may be impugned, or appear to be impugned, if the auditor is not seen as independent of the directors. Provisions like C.B.C.A., s. 161 aim to ensure this independence, but problems can remain. A typical one is that the auditor may provide other services to the corporation, such as management consulting advice; and these other services may be much more lucrative for the auditor than the auditing of the annual reports to shareholders. In this case, it may appear that the auditor has an interest in retaining the favour of the directors, in relation to the possibility of future consulting opportunities. This creates a conflict between that interest and the auditor's duty to shareholders. In the U.S., the *Sarbanes-Oxley Act* of 2002 was passed in the wake of high-profile corporate collapses, some of which were thought to be exacerbated by auditors who were not sufficiently independent of management. Among many other changes, the Act prohibits auditors from performing other services. In Canada the same concerns have issued in new standards in the accounting profession and the creation of the

Canadian Public Accountability Board, which oversees auditors of publicly traded corporations.

Another reason why the auditor's protection for shareholders may be illusory is illustrated by *Hercules Managements Ltd. v. Ernst & Young*, [1997] S.C.J. No. 57, [1997] 2 S.C.R. 165, 146 D.L.R. (4th) 577. That case held that an auditor does not in general owe a duty of care in respect of the audit directly to any shareholder, but rather only to the corporation. If the auditor is careless, it is the corporation that must sue in negligence. But does careless auditing cause any loss to the corporation? Assume a corporation with 100 shares of a single class. They trade at $1 each, meaning that the market values the corporate assets at $100. Then it is discovered that the financial statements have been misleading, and the audit that should have uncovered this was done carelessly. The shares drop in value to 50 cents each. At least some shareholders may have bought or retained their shares in reliance on the audited accounts. According to *Hercules Managements*, only the corporation can sue in negligence. But what loss has the corporation suffered? See M. Percival, "After *Caparo* — Liability in Business Transactions Revisited" (1991), 54 M.L.R. 739.

There are situations, however, in which auditors may be held liable to investors (see for example *Haig v. Bamford*, [1977] 1 S.C.R. 466, not overruled in *Hercules*). If the auditors are made liable along with some other defendants, perhaps the corporation's management, the common law provides for "joint and several liability" which means that each tortfeasor can be liable to the plaintiff for the full loss, regardless of his or her own degree of responsibility. So if the management were responsible to the extent of 95 per cent, and the auditor to the extent of 5 per cent, the corporation could recover the full amount from the auditor, which would have a claim against management for contribution. This pushes the risk of insolvency of one defendant on to the other defendant(s) so that it need not be borne by the plaintiff. The same concept exists in the civil law of Quebec, where it is known as solidary liability. Large firms of accountants are usually solvent and usually have professional liability insurance.

Note, however, C.B.C.A., Part XIX.1 (ss. 237.1-237.9), added in 2001, which changes this rule in many cases (s. 237.3) for C.B.C.A. corporations. What are the principles that could have led to this legislation? Which industry do you think lobbied for it? Does Parliament have the power to pass such a law?

3. Extraordinary Business: Special Meetings

Directors can call special meetings: C.B.C.A., s. 133(2). Shareholders can too, although only shareholders who meet some minimum threshold of shareholding (C.B.C.A., s. 143(1): at least 5 per cent of the voting shares; Q.C.A., s. 99: 10 per cent). This can represent a huge amount of capital in the case of a large corporation. The statute attempts to balance the interests of shareholders in having their voices heard, against the expense and inconvenience that is occasioned by a special meeting (remember that not only must a venue be found and paid for, but notice must be given to all shareholders, and the time involved in the meeting is lost to what might be more productive activities).

There is a wide range of extraordinary business that can lead to the calling of a special meeting. Some of the items discussed below (such as removing a director before his or her term is up) can only be resolved at a special meeting. In the case of other items, it may be that they can be addressed in an annual meeting as well as at a special meeting. For example, shareholder approval of a corporate contract in which a director has a material interest can be addressed under the O.B.C.A. only at a special meeting (s. 132(8)(*a*)), but under the C.B.C.A. at any meeting (s. 120(7.1)(*a*)). These items are noted here because they are not in the ordinary course of business that arises at an annual meeting, but the statute must be consulted for details as to whether they can in fact be dealt with at an annual meeting.

(a) Removal of Directors

In some U.S. jurisdictions, directors elected for a term cannot be removed until the term expires. This is not the case in Canada, where the statutes provide for the possibility of democratic recall (C.B.C.A., A.B.C.A., s. 109, S.B.C.A., M.C.A., s. 104, N.B.B.C.A., s. 67(1), O.B.C.A., s. 122(1); B.C.B.C.A., s. 128(3), where the default rule is a special majority rather than a simple majority). This would obviously cause problems if the rule were unqualified, as directors elected to office by either cumulative voting or class election could be immediately dismissed by a majority vote. Each statute prevents this by varying the voting rules on removal in the case of cumulative voting or class directors.

A second method of entrenching incumbent directors is by contract. What is the effect of a contract that warrants a specific time on the board in a situation where the appropriate majority wishes to remove the director?

A third entrenchment method is by changing the voting rules for resolutions to remove directors. This was discussed in Chapter 3, where we noted that it is more likely to be effective in a contractarian jurisdiction than in a division of powers jurisdiction.

Suppose the corporate constitution said that a majority was a sufficient quorum for a shareholders' meeting except in a takeover bid situation, where any meeting convened to remove the incumbent directors required a 75 per cent majority quorum. Could such a constitutional provision succeed in protecting against removal? Would it make any difference how many shares the directors held? How could the majority get around this rule?

(b) Shareholder Approval of Conflict-of-Interest Contracts

As we noticed in Chapter 7, there is statutory regulation of the problem that arises where a director or officer has an interest in a "material contract" made by the corporation. This is a classic situation of a conflict of interest and duty. The statute provides for a system of disclosure and recusal (non-participation in the corporate decision) by the conflicted manager, in order to make the contract non-voidable and to allow the manager to keep any resultant gain. By an amendment (S.C. 2001, c. 14, s. 48), the C.B.C.A. (s. 120(7.1)) now deals with the case where such a contract has been made but the system for disclosure and recusal was not properly followed. It requires disclosure to shareholders of the manager's interest, and approval of the contract by a special resolution of the shareholders. No doubt influenced by *North-West Transportation Co. v. Beatty* (1887), 12 App. Cas. 589 (J.C.P.C., Ont.), s. 120(7.1) adds a substantive requirement that the contract was "reasonable and fair" to the corporation when it was approved by shareholders, a standard that must also be met even if disclosure was properly made (s. 120(7)(*c*)). See also A.B.C.A., s. 120(8.1), O.B.C.A., s. 132(8). B.C.B.C.A., s. 149(1) lacks a "reasonable and fair" provision; so too does S.B.C.A., s. 115(8.1), but it requires *unanimous* shareholder approval. N.B.B.C.A., s. 77(9) also lacks the "reasonable and fair" provision, and only requires an ordinary resolution, but allows only "disinterested" shareholders to vote. Note also M.C.A., s. 115(5), providing for shareholder approval in a different context. N.L.C.A., s. 200 allows shareholder approval by an ordinary resolution in place of director approval; the contract must be "reasonable and fair"; but the section only applies where disclosure was properly made. It seems that in Newfoundland and Labrador, as in Manitoba, if proper disclosure is not made in advance, the contract can only be saved by an order of the court.

(c) Constitutional Amendments

The by-laws, as we have seen, are the part of the corporate constitution that is the easiest to amend. The directors can make or amend by-laws, subject to the approval of a simple majority of voting shares.

Changes to the most permanent corporate documents — the articles of incorporation, or memorandum and articles of association in an English-model jurisdiction — are more difficult to make. We have, however, made the process easier: the original English-model rule was that the memorandum of association could not be amended (see *English Companies Act*, 1862, 25 & 26 Vict. c. 89, s. 12), requiring those who wanted a different corporate constitution to go through the messy processes of inducing the corporation to suicide followed by the birth of a replacement corporation. The letters patent system required that supplementary letters patent be applied for, following the adoption of a special resolution of the shareholders: see P.E.I.C.A., ss. 17-19.

The reformed Canadian statutes permit constitutional amendments to be made by routine, internal procedures followed by public registration of the amended documents. However, a number of safeguards that change the ordinary simple principle of majority rule are imposed. Why is it deliberately made difficult to amend the corporate constitution? Assume you invested $1,000 in shares of a corporation that ran a paper-making business and one day, the other shareholders told you that they proposed to abandon paper-making and redirect the corporation's efforts to a new business in web site design (with a new slate of directors if need be). Would you say, "ah well, majority rules", or would the fact that you never intended to invest in web site design give you some ground for a grievance? What if you were the only holder of Class B shares in a corporation, and you learned of a plan by the more numerous holders of Class A shares to amend the articles so that all Class B shares were to be eliminated with no compensation?

As usual, the C.B.C.A. can be used as a model of the reformed statutes, although the appropriate statute must always be checked for particular variations. Section 173(1) of the C.B.C.A. sets out, at great length, the basic rule for constitutional amendments. Does it effectively read as follows?

> (1) Subject to sections 176 [class veto] and 177 [subsequent registration with the Director], the articles of a corporation may by special resolution be amended to
>
> ...
>
> (*o*) add, change or remove any ... provision that is permitted by this Act to be set out in the articles.

What do you think is the purpose of the remaining subsections?

The first amendment to the simple principle of majority rule is the requirement of a special resolution for such amendments. Is it possible to set up the corporate constitution to preclude a constitutional amendment unless 90 per cent of the shareholders cast their votes in favour of the proposal? Could the articles state that on a proposal to amend the articles each share carries either one "yes" vote or 10 "no" votes? Could they additionally state that that any shareholder who did not vote was to be counted as casting ten votes against the proposal?

Section 174 deals with the amendment the articles to restrict shareholding by non-residents; what is the justification for such constraints?

Section 175 contemplates that a proposal to amend the articles may come from a shareholder using the proposal mechanism in s. 137, which was discussed above.

Section 176 deals with the case where the proposed amendment has some particular effect on a particular class of shares. Here we see further amendments to the ordinary principles of majority rule. First, the vote must be held class by class, and the required special resolution must be passed by each affected class (s. 176(6)). Second, an affected class gets a vote even if shares in that class are normally non-voting shares (s. 176(5)). This prevents the holders of voting shares from expropriating the investments of the holders of non-voting shares.

Note the other "fundamental changes" in ss. 181-186.1 (amalgamation, that is turning two or more corporations into one) and s. 188 (continuance, that is moving from the C.B.C.A. to another "home statute"). These fundamental changes involve amendment of the corporate constitution. The procedures are spelled out in detail. Note that in each case, the basic principles of majority rule are modified by requiring a special resolution, by allowing non-voting shares to vote, and in some cases by requiring a class vote. Section 187 covers the "import" version of continuance: a corporation incorporated under another statute becomes a C.B.C.A. corporation. Here the protection needs to be found in the "home" statute which the corporation is "leaving". Sections 191 and 192 deal with "reorganizations" and "arrangements": these take place under the supervision of the court and shareholder approval is not an issue.

On the completion of any amendment to the articles, the amendment must be filed with the Director, because articles are public documents. The amendment is then made effective when the Director issues either a "certificate of amendment" (s. 178) or, where cumulative amendments are collected in "restated articles" (s. 180), a "restated certificate of incorporation" (s. 180(3)). See also ss. 185(4) and 186 (amalgamation), s. 187(3) and (6) (import continuance), s. 188(7) (export continuance), s. 191(4)-(6) (reorganization), s. 192(5)-(7) (arrangement).

Despite all of the procedural protections around fundamental changes, it remains possible that one will be approved against the wishes of some disaffected shareholders. A special resolution does not require unanimity. Even in this case, there is one more layer of protection: dissenting shareholders may force the corporation to buy their shares and so opt out of the newly constituted corporation (see C.B.C.A., s. 190). This remedy is the subject of fuller analysis in Chapter 9.

(d) Fundamental Change without Constitutional Amendment

Some fundamental changes can be made without any amendment to the articles. Return to our earlier example: you invested $1,000 in shares of a corporation that ran a paper-making business and one day, the other shareholders told you that they proposed to abandon paper-making and redirect the corporation's efforts to a new business in web site design. Assume that the directors are in favour of the plan, or, if need be, the majority shareholders are able to elect a new slate of directors who are in favour. In the old days, this would have required a constitutional amendment, because the corporate constitution probably stated what were the "objects" of the corporation. Today, the articles rarely restrict the business that the corporation can conduct. A decision to sell the whole business of the corporation and to move off in a completely new direction is, in one sense, purely a business decision, and so it belongs to the directors. In legal terms, it may involve nothing more than a couple of sale contracts, albeit large ones: a sale by the corporation of the assets of the old business, and a purchase of the assets of the new business. However, shareholders usually buy shares based on some idea that the corporation is engaged in some particular business, not that the directors are free to do absolutely anything they want.

The compromise is found in C.B.C.A., s. 189(3): a sale, lease or exchange of all or substantially all of the property of a corporation is treated as a fundamental change, even though in legal terms it is just a contract or two with no amendment to the corporate constitution. This transaction triggers the same protections as a constitutional amendment: special resolutions are required, non-voting shares are allowed to vote, and class votes are required where there is a particular effect on a class. Moreover, this kind of transaction, even if approved, triggers the right of dissenters to require the corporation to buy their shares (C.B.C.A., s. 190(1)(e)). An equivalent provision is found in all division of powers statutes. See also B.C.B.C.A., s. 301 (lacking class votes and enfranchisement of non-voting shares) and P.E.I.C.A., s. 15(1)(m) (which requires a special majority but lacks the other protection devices).

For a discussion of when s. 189(3) is triggered, see M. Gannage, "Sale of Substantially All the Assets of a Corporation" (2000), 33 C.B.L.J. 264. Note also the litigation in *Hollinger Inc. v. Hollinger International Inc.*, 858 A.2d 342 (Del. Ch. 2004), examining the scope of the equivalent provision in Delaware law.

(e) Corporate Suicide

The ultimate power the majority may exercise over the corporate person is to compel its suicide. Corporate suicide, usually catalogued under esoteric labels like "winding up", "dissolution" and "liquidation" is a complex topic, in part because the federal field of Bankruptcy and Insolvency (*Constitution Act, 1867*, s. 91(22)) overlaps with the provisions of the applicable provincial or federal incorporating statute. It is possible, though unusual, for the shareholders of a corporation to decide to wind it up even though it is solvent. This rather melancholy possibility is covered in provisions like C.B.C.A., s. 211, which requires special resolutions of each class of shares, and allows non-voting shares to vote. Subsequent sections cover dissolution at the instance of the Director and under the supervision of the court.

D. ARE THERE LEGAL RESTRICTIONS ON HOW SHAREHOLDERS VOTE?

Canadian and English corporate law entered the twentieth century in a curiously unprincipled state. The fundamental principles of corporate personality and majority rule in areas of shareholder competence were firmly established; but the judiciary seemed unable to see the corporate person as the economic entity, and judges repeatedly contradicted themselves by treating the majority of the shareholders as if they were the corporation. The result was chaotic and unpredictable litigation. No better example of this confusion can be found than the English judges' attempts to forge an unlegislated minority bill of rights by positing restrictions on how shareholders could vote, particularly when faced with amendments to the corporate constitution.

ALLEN v. GOLD REEFS OF WEST AFRICA, LTD.

[1900] 1 Ch. 656, [1900-1903] All E.R. Rep. 746 (Eng. C.A.)

[The defendant was incorporated in 1895 under the English *Companies Acts* 1862 to 1890. In those days, corporate shares were often issued for less than their full price; for example, a £2 share might be issued for £1. In such a case, the company could make a "call" on shareholders for any part of the unpaid capital. The registered articles of association, after setting forth the liability of shareholders for calls and to forfeiture of shares for nonpayment of calls, provided: "that the company shall have a first and paramount lien for all debts, obligations and liabilities of any member to or towards the company upon all shares (not being fully paid) held by such member." One Zuccani held both fully paid and partly paid shares. Calls were made on Zuccani from time to time and he adopted the practice of paying up some of his shares in full and then transferring them to others free of all lien, while leaving other shares in arrears of call. On his death he held fully paid shares and partly paid shares on which he was in arrears of call and interest on calls.

An extraordinary meeting of shareholders was called for the purpose of passing a special resolution to alter the lien article (above) by omitting the words "not being fully paid", thereby extending the company's lien to fully paid as well as unpaid shares. Zuccani's executors sought a declaration that the defendant had no lien on the fully paid shares.]

Lindley M.R.: — ... The articles of a company prescribe the regulations binding on its members: Companies Act, 1862, s. 14. They have the effect of a contract (see s. 16); but the exact nature of this contract is even now very difficult to define. Be its nature what it may, the company is empowered by the statute to alter the regulations contained in its articles from time to time by special resolutions (ss. 50 and 51); and any regulation or article purporting to deprive the company of this power is invalid on the ground that it is contrary to the statute: *Walker v. London Tramways Co.* (1879), 12 Ch. D. 705.

The power thus conferred on companies to alter the regulations contained in their articles is limited only by the provisions contained in the statute and the conditions contained in the company's memorandum of association. Wide, however, as the language of s. 50 is, the power conferred by it must, like all other powers, be exercised subject to those general principle of law and equity which are applicable to all powers conferred on majorities and enabling them to bind minorities. It must be exercised, not only in the manner required by law, but also bona fide for the benefit of the company as a whole, and it must not be exceeded. These conditions are always implied, and are seldom, if ever, expressed. But if they are complied with I can discover no ground for judicially putting any other restrictions on the power conferred by the section than those contained in it. How shares shall be transferred, and whether the company shall have any lien on them, are clearly matters of regulation properly prescribed by a company's articles of association. ...

[On the facts of this case it was determined that the alteration of the articles was perfectly legitimate.]

The possibility of minority protection through invalidation of majority votes was subsequently considered in *Brown v. British Abrasive Wheel Co.*, [1919] 1 Ch. 290 (Eng. Ch.), in which the court invalidated an amendment to the articles of association that would have allowed the majority shareholders to force the minority to sell their shares to the majority. It was also addressed in *Sidebottom v. Kershaw Leese & Co.*, [1920] 1 Ch. 154 (Eng. C.A.), in which the Court upheld as valid an amendment that allowed the directors of the corporation to force a shareholder to sell his shares, if that shareholder was engaged in a business that competed with the corporation. These decisions came to be considered in *Dafen Tinplate Co. Ltd. v. Llanelly Steel Co. (1907) Ltd.*, [1920] 2 Ch. 124 (Eng. Ch.). In that case, the plaintiff was a shareholder in the defendant corporation. When the defendant was originally formed, for the purpose of manufacturing steel bars, its shares were offered to tinplate manufacturers who were the major purchasers of the defendant's product. There was an understanding among the initial shareholders that they would purchase their requirements of steel bars from the defendant. The plaintiff obtained control of a corporation that manufactured steel bars and it no longer continued its custom with the defendant. The defendant purported to alter its articles of association in order to be able to compel a shareholder to transfer his shares at a fair value to be determined by the board of directors.

The question was whether this alteration of the articles, approved by a special majority of the shareholders, was effective. Justice Peterson held that it was not. He said (pp. 140-142):

It has been suggested that the only question in such a case as this is whether the shareholders bona fide or honestly believed that the alteration was for the benefit of the company. But this is not, in my view, the true meaning of the words of Lindley, M.R. or of the judgment in *Sidebottom's Case*. The question is whether in fact the alteration is genuinely for the benefit of the company. ...

The question of fact then which I have to consider is whether the alteration of the articles which enables the majority of the shareholders to compel any shareholder to transfer his shares, can properly be said to be for the benefit of the company. It may be for the benefit of the majority of the shareholders to acquire the shares of the minority, but how can it be said to be for the benefit of the company that any shareholder, against whom no charge of acting to the detriment of the company can be urged, and who is in every respect a desirable member of the company, and for whose expropriation there is no reason except the will of the majority, should be forced to transfer his shares to the majority or to anyone else? Such a provision might in some circumstances be very prejudicial to the company's interest. For instance, on an issue of new capital, the knowledge that he might be expropriated as soon as his capital was on the point of producing profitable results might well exercise a deterrent influence on a man was invited to take shares in the company. ... In my view it cannot be said that a power on the part of the majority to expropriate any shareholder they may think proper at their will and pleasure is for the benefit of the company as a whole. To say that such an unrestricted and unlimited power of expropriation is for the benefit of the company appears to me to be confusing the interests of the majority with the benefit of the company as a whole. In my opinion the power which, in this case, has been conferred upon the majority of the shareholders by the alteration of the articles of association in this case is too wide and is not such a power as can be assumed by the majority. The power of compulsory acquisition by the majority of shares which the owner does not desire to sell is not lightly to be assumed whenever it pleases the majority to do so. The shareholder is entitled to say non haec in foedera veni; and while on the authorities as they stand at present it is possible to alter the articles in such a way as to confer this power, if it can be shown that the power is for the benefit of the company as a whole, I am of opinion that such a power cannot be supported if it is not established that the power is bona fide or genuinely for the company's benefit.

Later, in *Shuttleworth v. Cox Brothers & Co. (Maidenhead) Ltd.*, [1927] 2 K.B. 9 (Eng. C.A.), the articles were amended to add a provision that a director must resign if requested to do so in writing by all the other directors. This amendment was passed by a special majority of shareholders, but its validity was challenged by the director who was sought to be removed. The amendment was upheld. Bankes L.J. said (at p. 19):

> I cannot agree with what seems to have been the view of Peterson J. in *Dafen Tinplate Co. v. Llanelly Steel Co.*, that whenever the Court and the shareholders may differ in opinion upon what is for the benefit of the company, the view of the Court must prevail. In the present case it seems to me impossible to say that the action of these defendants was either incapable of being for the benefit of the company or such that no reasonable men could consider it for the benefit of the company.

Scrutton L.J. also disapproved of *Dafen Tinplate*, saying (at p. 22): "To adopt that view would be to make the Court the manager of the affairs of innumerable companies instead of the shareholders themselves." And Atkin L.J. said (at pp. 26-27):

> It is not matter of law for the Court whether or not a particular alteration is for the benefit of the company, nor is it the business of a judge to review the decision of every company in the country on these questions. ... In my view the question is solely for the shareholders acting in good faith. The circumstances may be such as to lead to one conclusion only, that the majority of the shareholders are acting so oppressively that they cannot be acting in good faith; or, to put it in another way, it may be that their decision must be one which could be taken by persons acting in good faith with a view to the benefit of the company. But these are matters outside and apart from the question, Does this or that tribunal consider, in the light of events which have happened, that the alteration was or was not for the benefit of the company? With great respect to a very learned judge I cannot agree with the judgment of Peterson J. to the contrary on this point.

The courts could not seem to decide whether to let the shareholders make decisions, however unpalatable, or whether those decisions were subject to the court's oversight. The whole line of cases was addressed by the English Court of Appeal in the following case.

GREENHALGH v. ARDERNE CINEMAS LTD.

[1951] Ch. 286, [1950] 2 All E.R. 1120 (Eng. C.A.)

[The original articles of the company precluded share transfers to outsiders so long as an existing shareholder was willing to buy the shares in question at fair value. An amendment to this article was passed by a special resolution. The amended article would permit transfers to outsiders if approved by a simple majority of the shareholders. The plaintiff sought judicial invalidation of the amendment to the articles.]

Evershed M.R.: — The burden of the case is that the resolution was not passed bona fide and in the interests of the company as a whole, and there are, as Mr. Jennings has urged, two distinct approaches.

The first line of attack is this, and it is one to which, he complains, Roxburgh, J., paid no regard: this is a special resolution, and, on authority, Mr. Jennings say, the validity of a special resolution depends upon the fact that those who passed it did so in good faith and for the benefit of the company as a whole. The cases to which Mr. Jennings referred are *Sidebottom v. Kershaw, Leese & Co. Ld.*, Peterson, J.'s decision in *Dafen Tinplate Co. Ld. v. Llanelly Steel Co. (1907). Ld.*, and, finally, *Shuttleworth v. Cox Brothers & Co. (Maidenhead) Ld.* Certain principles, I think, can be safely stated as emerging from those authorities. In the first place, I think it is now plain that "bona fide for the benefit of the company as a whole" means not two things but one thing. It means that the shareholder must proceed upon what, in his honest opinion, is for the benefit of the company as a whole. The second thing is that the phrase, "the company as a whole", does not (at any rate in such a case as the present) mean the company as a commercial entity, distinct from the corporators: it means the corporators as a general body. That is to say, the case may be taken of an individual hypothetical member and it may be asked whether what is proposed is, in the honest opinion of those who voted in its favour, for that person's benefit.

I think that the matter can, in practice, be more accurately and precisely stated by looking at the converse and by saying that a special resolution of this kind would be liable to be impeached if the effect of it were to discriminate between the majority shareholders and the minority shareholders, so as to give to the former an advantage of which the latter were deprived. When the cases are examined in which the resolution has been successfully attacked, it is on that ground. It is therefore not necessary to require that persons voting for a special resolution should, so to speak, dissociate themselves altogether from their own prospects and consider whether what is thought to be for the benefit of the company as a going concern [*sic*]. If, as commonly happens, an outside person makes an offer to buy all the shares, prima facie, if the corporators think it is a fair offer and vote in favour of the resolution, it is no ground for impeaching the resolution that they are considering their own position as individuals. [In the end, the English Court of Appeal ruled against the plaintiff.]

NOTES AND QUESTIONS

Corporate shares are property. The voting right is part of that property. What standard do these cases set for shareholder voting on a resolution to amend the corporate constitution?

Legal powers, including powers of control over a corporation, are often held for the benefit of another person. A parent's power to consent to medical treatment on behalf of his or her child is an example a power held in this way. Another example is found in the powers of directors to manage the business of the corporation: these powers are held for the benefit of the corporation. When powers are held by one person for the benefit of another, it is typical to attach duties (duties of loyalty and care: see Chapter 7) to the exercise of those powers.

At the opposite extreme, legal powers may be held entirely for one's own benefit. If I hold a season ticket for a professional sports team, at the end of the season I might have a power to renew for another season. I do not owe anyone any duties as regards that power. I can ignore it or use it capriciously.

Is there a middle ground, in which one can use (or choose not to use) a power for one's own benefit, but at the same time, one is constrained to some extent in relation to how the power can be exercised? Take the example of voting in a federal election. Are voters required to vote fairly, or may they vote capriciously (for example, for the tallest candidate)? On the other hand, even you are allowed to vote capriciously, does it follow that you are allowed (for example) to sell your vote to the highest bidder? See *Canada Elections Act*, S.C. 2000, c. 9, s. 481.

Do these English cases try to put the shareholder voting power into this middle ground? Can we define the constraint with sufficient precision? Consider the following *obiter dictum* from *Goldex Mines Ltd. v. Revill* (1974), 7 O.R. (2d) 216, 54 D.L.R. (3d) 672 (Ont. C.A.):

> The principle that the majority governs in corporate affairs is fundamental to corporation law, but its corollary is also important — that the majority must act fairly and honestly. Fairness is the touchstone of equitable justice, and when the test of fairness is not met, the equitable jurisdiction of the Court can be invoked to prevent or remedy the injustice which misrepresentation or other dishonesty has caused.

Does this strike you as a sensitive balancing of interests, or a hopelessly vague aspiration?

What was missing in the English statute and in the Canadian statutes prior to the 1970s was a statutory bill of rights for minority shareholders. Most Canadian jurisdictions have now enacted precisely that. We have seen above that a number of safeguards are in place to protect minority shareholders, especially when fundamental changes are proposed. We will see in the next chapter that the minority bill of rights goes further. It allows any action or inaction of a corporation, or its insiders, to be reviewed by a judge against a open-ended standard of fairness, usually structured by the idea of the reasonable expectations of the parties. Does the presence of this new bill of rights validate the struggles of courts to define the constraints on shareholder voting, or does it render those cases irrelevant? Or both?

CHAPTER 9

MINORITY PROTECTION

A. THE REFORMED STATUTE RESPONSE

1. Introduction

Each of the reformed Canadian statutes has enacted what amounts to a bill of rights for minority shareholders. Perhaps a bill of *remedies* would be a more accurate description. The most striking feature of the minority protection devices is the degree to which they are causing Canadian corporate law to diverge from the paths laid down by English and American judges.

WELLING, CORPORATE LAW IN CANADA: THE GOVERNING PRINCIPLES

(3rd ed., 2006), p. 538

The common law courts, under both contractarian and letters patent corporate statutes, failed to find any principled approaches to the problem of minority shareholder protection. Canadian legislatures have created some. They began about 1970, and much of their reform has been directed toward codifying in the statutes *procedural remedies*, designed to protect the individual shareholder from the twin oppressors of managerial power and majority rule. Remedy, not right, was clearly the legislative technique and was, I suggest, philosophically, the better way to go. The procedural remedies are dealt with, one by one, after a brief overview of the role of judicial discretion in Canadian corporate statutes.

2. STANDING

One of the most elementary rules in our legal system is that one person can not sue on the basis of an injury suffered by someone else. Only the injured party has standing to complain, absent a statutory rule to the contrary.

Section 238 of the C.B.C.A. provides:

> 238. In this Part,
>
> "action" means an action under this Act;
>
> "complainant" means
>
> > (*a*) a registered holder or beneficial owner, and a former registered holder or beneficial owner, of a security of a corporation or any of its affiliates,
> >
> > (*b*) a director or an officer or a former director or officer of a corporation or any of its affiliates,

(*c*)   the Director, or

(*d*)   any other person who, in the discretion of a court, is a proper person to make an application under this Part.

There are identical or similar definitions of "complainant" in most provincial statutes: see, for example, O.B.C.A., s. 245. Complainant is defined somewhat less broadly in British Columbia: see B.C.B.C.A., ss. 228(1), 232.

Any "complainant" has standing to seek leave to commence a statutory representative action under the C.B.C.A. and similar statutes. The complainant need not be a shareholder, although minority shareholders are clearly enough the primary objects of the statutory protections.

FIRST EDMONTON PLACE LTD. v. 315888 ALBERTA LTD.

[1988] A.J. No. 511, 60 Alta. L.R. (2d) 122 (Q.B.)

McDonald J.:— This is an application by a lessor pursuant to the remedy provisions contained in the *Business Corporations Act*, Stats. Alta. 1981 c.B-15. That statute is commonly known as the "Alberta *Business Corporations Act*" and will be referred to henceforth as the "ABCA". The applicant seeks relief for losses it has suffered which were, in its submission, due to the actions of the respondent numbered company and the three individual respondents who were and are its directors. The issues raise fundamental principles of corporate law and require consideration of the scope and purpose of the new remedies provided for by the ABCA and not previously available in the law of Alberta. These are (1) an action to right a wrong done to the corporation where the directors of the corporation will not sue to right the wrong (commonly called a "derivative action"), and (2) a remedy which may be sought by minority shareholders and others where there has been oppression or unfair prejudice to or that unfairly disregards the interests of any security holder, creditor, director or officer of the corporation.

. . .

[The] two remedies sought are in the nature of permission to bring an action. Consequently it will be borne in mind throughout these reasons for judgment that what is being considered now is not whether on the evidence the damages sought in each proposed action should be awarded, but whether the applicant qualifies for an order granting leave to bring each action.

The applicant is a corporation which constructed an office building in Edmonton. The three individual respondents were lawyers in practice in Edmonton. Two of them are still in practice in Edmonton and one is now a resident in British Columbia. I shall refer to the applicant as "First Edmonton Place", and to the three individual respondents as "the three lawyers". The three lawyers practised in association with each other. The corporate respondent. which was named as lessee in a lease entered into with First Edmonton Place, was a "shelf company". That is, it was a numbered company which had already been incorporated by the three lawyers for an undefined purpose. According to the affidavit of the property manager of the applicant, one of the lawyers told him that the company was to be used as their management company. They were its sole shareholders and directors. The corporate respondent had no assets. As a result of the negotiations, a lease agreement for a term of 10 years commencing December 1, 1984, was entered into between the numbered company and First Edmonton

Place commercial Centre Ltd., the predecessor entitled to the applicant, as lessor. As the present applicant stands in the shoes of the original lessor, and has a very similar name, I shall not distinguish between the original lessor and the present applicant, and I shall refer to them interchangeably as "First Edmonton Place".

As an inducement to enter into the lease, First Edmonton Place granted the corporate respondent an 18 months rent-free period, a leasehold improvement allowance of $115,900.00 and a cash payment of $140,126.00. The three lawyers occupied the premises without entering into a written lease with the numbered company. One of them, in an affidavit, has stated that the law firm occupied the premises "as a monthly sub-tenant" of the numbered company. They did so for the entire rent-free period and for three months beyond it, that is, until September 27, 1986. The numbered company paid rent for the three months after the expiry of the rent-free period. The three lawyers vacated the premises on the date mentioned, and no further rent was ever paid by the numbered company to First Edmonton Place.

Some time following the payment of the cash of $140,126.00, those funds were paid out by the numbered company to the three lawyers. ...

... [T]he two forms of benefit which First Edmonton Place says were received by the three lawyers, and as to which First Edmonton Place claims to be entitled to a remedy, are the benefit of free occupancy of the business premises by the three lawyers for a period of 18 months, and their taking from the numbered corporation the amount which had been paid to it as a cash inducement.

First Edmonton Place submits that the actions of the three lawyers as directors of the numbered corporation, (a) in causing the corporation to allow their law firm to occupy the premises with no lease, written or unwritten, and without requiring rent to be paid during the rent-free period, and (b) causing the corporation to pay out the proceeds of the cash inducement to themselves, and constituted deliberate breaches of their obligations as directors of the numbered corporation. As a result, First Edmonton Place seeks alternative forms of relief under secs. 232 (statutory representative action) and 234 (oppression) of the ABCA. ...

In order to obtain leave to bring an action under either of these sections, the applicant must be found to be a "complainant" as defined in s. 231. ... First Edmonton Place can satisfy this requirement only if it can come within s. 231(b) (i) or (iii).

Is the applicant a "complainant" within the meaning of s. 231(b)(i)?

It will be recalled that s. 231(b)(i) defines a "complainant" as "a registered holder or beneficial owner, or a former registered holder or beneficial owner, of a security of a corporation or any of its affiliates". ...

This plain meaning reflects the meaning of "bonds, debentures and notes" in the world of corporate financing. In *Securities Law and Practice* (Vol. 1. 1984) by V.P. Alboini, bonds and debentures are stated to be the "traditional debt instruments issued by corporations" while notes are "issued by any issuer including individuals" (at pp. 0-33, 0-34).

Is the applicant a "complainant" under s. 231(b)(iii)?

Under s. 231(b)(iii), a person may be a "complainant" if he is a person "who, in the discretion of the court, is a proper person to make an application under this Part".

This is not so much a definition as a grant to the court of a broad power to do justice and equity in the circumstances of a particular case, where a person, who otherwise would not be a "complainant", ought to be permitted to bring an action under either s. 232 or s. 234 to right a wrong done to the corporation which would not otherwise be righted, or to obtain compensation himself or itself where his or its interests have suffered from oppression by the majority controlling the corporation or have been unfairly prejudiced or unfairly disregarded, and the applicant is a "security holder, creditor, director or officer".

... [T]he circumstances in which a person who is not a security holder (as I have interpreted that phrase), or a director or officer should be recognized as "a proper person to make an application" must show that justice and equity clearly dictate such a result.

In the case of a creditor who claims to be a "proper person" to make a s. 232 application, in my view the criterion to be applied would be whether, even if the applicant did not come within s. 231(b)(i) or (ii), he or it would nevertheless be a person who could reasonably be entrusted with the responsibility of advancing the interests of the corporation by seeking a remedy to right the wrong allegedly done to the corporation. The applicant would not have to be a security holder (as I have defined that notion), director or officer of the corporation. The applicant could be a creditor. The applicant might even be a person who at the time of the act or conduct complained of was not a creditor but was a person toward whom the corporation might have a contingent liability. No good purpose would be served in saying more than that now.

I turn now to an application by a person who claims to be a "proper person" to make an application under s. 234. As in the case of an application made under s. 232, an applicant for leave to bring an action under s. 234 does not have to be a security holder, director or officer. The applicant could be a creditor, or even a person toward whom the corporation had only a contingent liability at the time of the act or conduct complained of. However, it is important to note that he would not be held to be a "proper person" to make the application under s. 234 unless he satisfied the court that there was some evidence of oppression or unfair prejudice or unfair disregard for the interests of a security holder, creditor, director or officer.

Having said that, assuming that the applicant was a creditor of the corporation at the time of the act or conduct complained of, what criterion should be applied in determining whether the applicant is "a proper person" to make the application? Once again, in my view, the applicant must show that in the circumstances of the case justice and equity require him or it to be given an opportunity to have the claim tried.

There are two circumstances in which justice and equity would entitle a creditor to be regarded as "a proper person". (There may be other circumstances; these two are not intended to exhaust the possibilities.) The first is if the act or conduct of the directors or management of the corporation, which is complained of, constituted using the corporation as a vehicle for committing a fraud upon the applicant. (In the present case there is no evidence suggesting such fraud, although there is some evidence of the directors having used the money paid as a cash inducement for their own personal investment purposes, and that ... may constitute fraud against the corporation ...

Second, the court might hold that the applicant is a "proper person to make an application" for an order under s. 234 if the act or conduct of the directors or management of the corporation, which is complained of, constituted a breach of the underlying expectation of the applicant arising from the circumstances in which the applicant's relationship with the corporation arose. For example, where the applicant is a creditor of the corporation, did the circumstances, which gave rise to the granting of credit, include some element which prevented the creditor from taking adequate steps when he or it entered into the agreement, to protect his or its interests against the occurrence of which he or it now complains? Did the creditor entertain an expectation that, assuming fair dealing, its chances of repayment would not be frustrated by the kind of conduct which subsequently was engaged in by the management of the corporation? Assuming that the evidence established the existence of such an expectation, the next question would be whether that expectation was, objectively, a reasonable one.

Thus, in the present case, an inquiry would properly be directed at trial toward whether the lessor, First Edmonton Place, at the time of entering into the lease, consciously and intentionally decided to contract only with the numbered company, and not to obtain personal guarantees from the three lawyers. A further proper inquiry would be into whether the lessor entered into the lease fully aware that it was not protecting itself against the possibility that the corporation might pay out the cash advance to the lawyers, leaving no other assets in the corporation, and that the corporation might permit the lawyers to occupy the space without entering into a sub-lease either for ten years or for any lesser period. In the absence of evidence establishing at least a *prima facie* case that an injustice would be done to the lessor or that there would be inequity if the lessor were not allowed to bring its action and go to trial, leave to bring the action ought not to be granted. There is, in the present case, no evidence showing that there was an expectation on the part of the lessor that the lessee corporation would retain the funds in its hands for any set period of time or any time at all. Nor is there any evidence that there was an expectation that the lessee corporation would grant a lease for a term of ten years or any other set term beyond the rent-free period, to the law firm or any other person or persons. It is true that the lease contemplated the possibility that the corporation would enter into a lease with the lawyers, for it specified that the lessee could do so. That falls far short of evidencing the existence of an expectation that there would be a lease for the entire ten-year period or for any set term longer than the rent-free period and less than ten years. Nor does the evidence establish any inequality of bargaining power between First Edmonton Place on the one hand and the three lawyers and their corporation on the other, at the time the lease was being negotiated. If there were some circumstances evidencing such inequality of bargaining power, the result might be different.

It is not without significance that the ABCA does provide specific remedies to creditors where, for example, money is paid out of the corporation and the solvency test has not been passed, or where a director contravenes other parts of the act (such as secs. 113(5), (6) and 240). ...

In these provisions, creditors are specifically mentioned as persons entitled to apply to the Court for remedies. While these sections do not preclude creditors from applying for other remedies (such as those provided for by secs. 232 and 234), the Legislature has singled out cases in which creditors generally are specifically entitled to protection.

In reaching my conclusion as to the interpretation of the phrase "proper person", I have not found it necessary to rely upon the reasoning of Wallace J. in *Re MacRae and Daon Development Corp.* (1984) 10 D.L.R. (4th) 216 (B.C.S.C.). ... The question [in *Daon*] ... would not have arisen in Alberta as the definition of complainant in s. 231(b)(i) of the ABCA, unlike the British Columbia provisions, includes any security holder, and would therefore include a debenture holder. However Wallace J. did make some general comments concerning the interpretation of a "proper person" which may be of assistance in the present case. At p. 225 he said:

> I consider the history of derivative actions and the wording of the section requires that the category be composed of those persons who have a direct financial interest in how the company is being managed and are in a position — somewhat analogous to minority shareholders — where they have no legal right to influence or change what they see to be abuses of management or conduct contrary to the company's interest.

The Court denied the application on behalf of the debenture holder "whose only interest in the management of the company is the general and indirect one of wishing to see the company prosper ...". Under the ABCA the debenture holder would have come within the definition of "complainant" in s. 231(b)(i). It might be thought that the statements of Wallace J. would nevertheless be relevant in deciding upon the proper approach to be taken to the definition of a "proper person" in s. 231(b)(iii) of the ABCA; that is, it might be contended that the phrase "proper person" in the ABCA ought not to be expanded to include a creditor who had no "direct financial interest" in the corporation. Thus, in the present case, it would be argued, the lessor would not be a "proper person" because it did not invest money directly in the corporation, i.e., did not hold any shares in the corporation. However, in my view that argument, based on [*Daon*], ought not to influence the interpretation of s. 231(b)(iii) of the ABCA, for the very fact that the Legislature of Alberta has chosen, in s. 231(b)(i), to extend the scope of complainants to include debenture holders (by virtue of using the phrase "a security"), indicates that the ABCA was intended to give protection to persons who have not directly invested money in the corporation and are not shareholders in the corporation. Nor, with respect, is assistance provided by the observation of Wallace J., at p. 224, that the "Legislature intended that the person making the application must have some particular legitimate interest in the matter in which the affairs of the company are managed". Without presuming to comment on what a "legitimate interest" would be in British Columbia, it need only be said that the Legislature of Alberta appears to have considered that the registered holder or beneficial owner of a mortgage or debenture creating a charge has a sufficient financial interest in the corporation to justify protection being afforded expressly to such a person.

In deciding who is a "proper person", and whether justice and equity require a particular applicant to be recognized as a "proper person", it is appropriate to bear in mind the purposes of the statutory actions provided for in secs. 232 and 234. To the extent that these actions were intended to protect minority shareholders, Professor Bruce Welling, in *Corporate Law in Canada*, stated at p. 504:

> A statutory representative action is the minority shareholder's sword to the majority's twin shields of corporate personality and majority rule.

In addition to protecting minority shareholders, the actions provided for by secs. 232 and 234 serve the more general purpose of ensuring managerial accountability. That purpose encompasses protection of the rights of not only minority shareholders but also creditors and even the public in general. It is obvious that by permitting s. 232 and s. 234 actions to be brought by persons other than shareholders, the Legislature intended that the abuse of majority corporate power be capable of remedial action at the invocation of persons other than shareholders.

[The applicant was held to be a proper person to make an application to proceed with a statutory representative action, insofar a fraud may have been committed on the corporation, but not an oppression remedy, since the applicant was not a creditor at the time of the act or conduct complained of.]

NOTES

In *R. v. Sands Motor Hotel Ltd.*, [1984] S.J. No. 56, [1985] 1 W.W.R. 59 (Q.B.) the Crown, which was claiming taxes owing, was held to be a complainant under S.B.C.A., s. 231(*b*) for purposes of bringing an "oppression" remedy. In *Canadian Opera Co. v. 670800 Ontario Inc.*, [1989] O.J. No. 1307, 69 O.R. (2d) 532 (H.C.); affd, [1990] O.J. No. 2270, 75 O.R. (2d) 720 (Gen. Div.), the Ontario court granted status to a creditor of the corporation. See also *Sidaplex-Plastic Suppliers Inc. v. Elta Group Inc.*, [1995] O.J. No. 4048, 131 D.L.R. (4th) 399 (Gen. Div. [Commercial List]), var'd, [1998] O.J. No. 2910, 40 O.R. (3d) 563, (C.A.).

If the statute is designed to create remedies for minority shareholders, can majority shareholders claim standing as complainants? See *Cairney v. Golden Key Holdings (No. 1)*, [1987] B.C.J. No. 1151, 40 B.L.R. 263 (S.C.); *Gandalman Investments Inc. v. Fogle* (1985), 52 O.R. (2d) 614, 22 D.L.R. (4th) 638 (H.C.).

If someone has paid for shares by way of promissory note, or has only partially paid for the shares, can he or she still qualify as a complainant shareholder? See C.B.C.A., s. 25(3) and (5). What if the failure to pay resulted from inadvertence? See *Dunham v. Apollo Tours Ltd.* (1978), 20 O.R. (2d) 3 (H.C.).

Although former shareholders are complainants under s. 238, in *Michalak v. Biotech Electronics Ltd.*, [1986] Q.J. No. 1882, 35 B.L.R. 1 (S.C.), the court held that the conduct alleged to be oppressive must exist when the application is heard. If the shareholder has sold his or her shares to the corporation he or she no longer has a sufficient interest to complain of oppression. Does this reasoning make sense?

Can a person who becomes a shareholder after the conduct complained of has occurred, and with full knowledge of that conduct, qualify as a complainant? In *Richardson Greenshields of Canada Ltd. v. Kalmacoff*, [1995] O.J. No. 941, 22 O.R. (3d) 577, the Court of Appeal had to confront this question under a provision of the *Trust and Loan Companies Act*, S.C. 1991, c. 45, s. 2, which defined complainant in language almost identical to s. 238 of the C.B.C.A. Robins J.A., delivering the judgment of the court, stated at pp. 583-84:

The term "complainant" is defined in s. 2 of the Act as follows:

"complainant", in relation to a company or any matter concerning a company, means

    (*a*) a registered holder or beneficial owner, and a former registered holder or beneficial owner, of a security of a company or any of its affiliates,

    (*b*) a director or an officer, or a former director or officer, of a company or any of its affiliates, or

    (*c*) any other person who, in the discretion of a court, is a proper person to make an application under section 339, 343 or 537;

Justice Farley was of the view that Richardson Greenshields did not qualify under para. (*a*) of this definition section and, therefore, in so far as this clause is concerned, failed to meet the threshold requirement entitling it to proceed under s. 339. Relying on his decision in *Royal Trust Corp. of Canada v. Hordo* (1993), 10 B.L.R. (2d) 86 (Ont. H.C.), he concluded that in a derivative action, as in an oppression action, "persons who acquire shares after the fact which were the subject of the complaint were known should not be treated as a complainant".

The respondents do not seek to support this conclusion. They acknowledge, properly, in my opinion, that the appellant is a complainant for the purposes of s. 339. Although its shares were acquired after the roll-down had been announced and for the express purpose of launching a derivative action, it is now common ground that this does not in itself preclude the appellant from being a complainant. The Act does not impose a condition of ownership contemporaneous with the acts complained of and, in any event, it may be noted that the breaches complained of are of an ongoing nature. It is sufficient that Richardson Greenshields is "a registered holder ... of a security of [the] company" at the time it brings the application. As such, it meets the requirements of cl. (*a*). It follows that the judge erred in restricting the term "complainant" to persons who were shareholders at the time the facts which gave rise to the complaint occurred and in holding that the appellant did not have the necessary status by virtue of cl. (*a*) of the defining section to invoke s. 339.

Do you agree? Did the applicant simply purchase the right to a lawsuit when it bought its shares? Do the concepts of maintenance and champerty have any application to these facts?

The Director (the civil servant who administers the statute) is authorized as *parens patriae* to institute actions and to compromise them: *Sparling v. Southam Inc.*, [1988] O.J. No. 1745, 66 O.R. (2d) 225 (H.C.); *Sparling v. Royal Trustco Ltd.* (1984), 6 D.L.R. (4th) 682 (Ont. C.A.); aff'd [1986] S.C.J. No. 64, [1986] 2 S.C.R. 537.

Can the corporation itself be a "proper person" under s. 238(*d*) as a complainant when it seeks an oppression remedy against a former director? For cases that suggest that it is possible for the corporation to be a complainant, see *Gainers Inc. v. Pocklington*, [1992] A.J. No. 603, 7 B.L.R. (2d) 87 (Q.B.); *Calmont Leasing Ltd. v. Kredl*, [1993] A.J. No. 569, [1993] 7 W.W.R. 428 (Q.B.), var'd [1995] A.J. No. 475, [1995] 8 W.W.R. 179 (C.A.).

Can an employee who is also a director, shareholder and officer of the corporation rely on his or her dismissal as an act of oppression and use the oppression remedy to recover damages for wrongful dismissal? See *Naneff v. Con-Crete Holdings Ltd.*, [1993] O.J. No. 1756, 11 B.L.R. (2d) 218 (Gen. Div.); var'd, [1994] O.J. No. 1811, 19 O.R. (3d) 691 (Div. Ct.); var'd [1995] O.J. No. 1377, 23 O.R. (3d) 481 (C.A.).

B. STATUTORY REPRESENTATIVE ACTIONS

1. Introduction

Several Canadian jurisdictions have enacted sections authorizing various individuals to bring representative actions on behalf of corporations. Under most such sections, the right given is to appear in court and to invoke the discretion of a judge.

Before delving into the statutes, it is imperative that the meaning of judicial discretion be understood. A statutory grant of discretion permits a judge to reach his decision unhampered by ironclad legal rules. The judge is expected to make use of wisdom, though not necessarily of legal precedent. Because of a judge's previous experience, it is ordinarily expected that he or she will be guided by usage or by general legal principles. On the legal control of the exercise of discretion, see *Roncarelli v. Duplessis*, [1959] S.C.R. 121, 16 D.L.R. (2d) 689, *per* Rand J., or any textbook in the field of administrative law.

The C.B.C.A. is set out here as a model of the reformed statutes, but in any particular case the applicable statute must be analyzed for differences in detail.

239(1) Subject to subsection (2), a complainant may apply to a court for leave to bring an action in the name and on behalf of a corporation or any of its subsidiaries, or intervene in an action to which any such body corporate is a party, for the purpose of prosecuting, defending or discontinuing the action on behalf of the body corporate.

(2) No action may be brought and no intervention in an action may be made under subsection (1) unless the court is satisfied that

(*a*) the complainant has given notice to the directors of the corporation or its subsidiary of the complainant's intention to apply to the court under subsection (1) not less than fourteen days before bringing the application, or as otherwise ordered by the court, if the directors of the corporation or its subsidiary do not bring, diligently prosecute or defend or discontinue the action;

(*b*) the complainant is acting in good faith; and

(*c*) it appears to be in the interests of the corporation or its subsidiary that the action be brought, prosecuted, defended or discontinued.

240. In connection with an action brought or intervened in under section 239, the court may at any time make any order it thinks fit including, without limiting the generality of the foregoing,

(*a*) an order authorizing the complainant or any other person to control the conduct of the action;

(*b*) an order giving directions for the conduct of the action;

(*c*) an order directing that any amount adjudged payable by a defendant in the action shall be paid, in whole or in part, directly to former and present security holders of the corporation or its subsidiary instead of to the corporation or its subsidiary; and

(*d*) an order requiring the corporation or its subsidiary to pay reasonable legal fees incurred by the complainant in connection with the action.

You will note that in the descriptive words attached to s. 239 the action is referred to as a "derivative action". Whence the derivation? What do you think "derivative" means?

None of these sections uses the word "derivative," although it is commonly found in the descriptive highlights and has been wholeheartedly adopted by writers and judges.

This usage tends to cause confusion, primarily because the term is used in American corporate law to describe a common law action brought by a shareholder (contrast the broader "complainant" in the statutory definition) to redress a wrong done to the corporation, but which is construed as also violating the rights the shareholder "derived" through the corporate entity. A well developed, if somewhat complex jurisprudence on this type of common law action has developed in American courts. The term has recently been introduced to English corporate law, though with mixed success: see *Wallersteiner v. Moir*, [1974] 3 All E.R. 217, [1974] 1 W.L.R. 991 (Eng. C.A.); *Prudential Assurance Co. v. Newman Industries Ltd. (No. 2)*, [1982] 1 All E.R. 354, [1982] 2 W.L.R. 31 (Eng. C.A.); *Estmanco (Kilner House) Ltd. v. Greater London Council*, [1982] 1 All E.R. 437, [1982] 1 W.L.R. 2 (Eng. Ch.). The problem there, of course, is twofold: first, there is ample English precedent, some of which has been encountered throughout the preceding chapters, denying minority shareholders standing where the right of action belongs to the corporate entity, and very little rational explanation of why, in some other cases, minority shareholders' actions have been allowed to proceed; second, it is not at all clear how a right is "derived" through another person. In any event, it is clear that the term is now used in America and England to describe a common law right of minority shareholders. Section 239 of the C.B.C.A., by contrast, looks at first glance rather more like a litigious right vested in a statutorily created guardian *ad litem*.

Does the enactment of sections like C.B.C.A., s. 239 entail that no common law "derivative" actions remain in Canada? In *Shield Development Co. v. Snyder*, [1976] 3 W.W.R. 44 (B.C.S.C.), it was held that the B.C. statute abrogated any such common law actions. As McKay J. explained (at p. 52):

> The legislation does not expressly prohibit the bringing of a common law derivative action but, in my view, such an action is prohibited by necessary implication. I am unable to see how the two remedies can exist side by side without creating confusion to an intolerable degree. As was stated in a recent article in the Canadian Bar Review:
>
> > "On balance, it is clear that the section was intended to be a Code for the expansion and control of the derivative suit. To allow both judicial controls and unfettered access to the Courts would only lead to confusion. A more orderly development of the law would result from one point of access to a derivative action and would allow for a body of experience and precedent to be built up to guide shareholders": Stanley Beck "The Shareholders Derivative Action" (1974), 52 Can. Bar Rev. 159.

NOTES

Do you agree with this finding regarding the exclusivity of the statutory representative action? What would be the result if this were not the rule? Would a judge then have discretion to deny standing to a minority shareholder who proved, through undistinguishable precedent, a common law "derivative" right to sue?

Contrast situations in which an actor might coincidentally violate separate obligations owed directly to two persons — rather like a bus driver running down two individuals in one accident. In such situations the injury suffered by one is in no sense "derived" through the other merely because the two victims happen to be in a corporation-shareholder relationship. It is, however, the responsibility of the plaintiffs to identify the separate causes of action, as noted in the following cases.

FARNHAM v. FINGOLD

[1973] 2 O.R. 132, 33 D.L.R. (3d) 156 (C.A.)

Jessup J.A.: — This is an appeal from the order of Morand, J., dismissing, *inter alia*, three motions of various of the defendants to strike out the statement of claim on the grounds that the claims therein set forth disclose no reasonable cause of action and that the plaintiff has no status to maintain the claims in a class action. The appellants ask for an order dismissing the plaintiff's action without prejudice to the plaintiff's right to commence a fresh and properly constituted action, alternatively for an order striking out the statement of claim with leave to amend the writ of summons and to deliver a fresh statement of claim, and, alternatively for an order striking out specific paragraphs of the statement of claim.

The judgment of Morand, J., is reported in [1972] 3 O.R. 688, 29 D.L.R. (3d) 279, and it sets forth the facts alleged to give rise to the action and its nature so that it is unnecessary to repeat them. The prayer for relief reads:

37. The plaintiff therefore claims:

   (a) damages in the amount of $25 million against the defendants for conspiracy to injure the plaintiff and other shareholders and former shareholders of Slater Steel Industries Limited;

   (b) damages in the amount of $25 million as against the defendants J. Paul Fingold, David B. Fingold, Ralph W. Cooper, Harvey Fingold, Marvin Gerstein, Sidney Fingold, Fobasco Limited, for breach of their fiduciary duty as directors and/or officers and/or insiders of Slater Steel Industries Limited to the plaintiff and other shareholders of Slater Steel Industries Limited in the sale of shares of Slater Steel Industries Limited to Stanton Pipes Limited;

   (c) damages in the amount of $25 million against all the defendants for breach of the provisions of The Securities Act and The Business Corporations Act of Ontario in the sale of shares of Slater Steel Industries Limited to Stanton Pipes Limited;

   (d) damages in the amount of $25 million against the defendant Stanton Pipes Limited for inducing a breach by the other defendants of their fiduciary duties to the shareholders of Slater Steel Industries Limited and breach of The Securities Act and The Business Corporations Act of Ontario, in the sale of shares of Slater Steel Industries Limited to Stanton Pipes Limited;

   (e) a declaration that the controlling shareholders hold any premium obtained upon the sale of their shares in Slater Steel Industries Limited to Stanton Pipers Limited over the market price of those shares for the benefit of Slater Steel Industries Limited and/or its general shareholders and/or the vendors of such shares to them;

   (f) an accounting of all sums paid to be paid by Stanton Pipes Limited to the other defendants except Slater Steel Industries Limited and McDonald Currie & Co. on account of the sale of shares of Slater Steel Industries Limited to Stanton Pipes Limited by such defendants, a reference to the Master at Toronto for the taking of such accounting and directions for the payment of any sums as may have been or may be received by such defendants;

(g) damages in the amount of $25 million against the defendants Henderson and Morris;

(h) an interlocutory and permanent injunction restraining the defendants and each of them from entering into or completing any sale of shares or purported sale of shares of Slater Steel Industries Limited to Stanton Pipes Limited;

(i) his costs of this action;

(j) such further and other relief as to this Court may seem just.

The claims made in the statement of claim are completely novel. Their success may depend on the trial Court applying or extending the principle followed in *Perlman v. Feldmann* (1955), 219 F. 2d 173, and *Brown v. Halbert* (1969), 76 Cal. Rptr. 781, or on the trial Court holding that a breach of the provisions of Part IX of the *Securities Act*, R.S.O. 1970, c. 426, constitutes an actionable civil wrong. As I appreciate the appellants' argument, they do not now challenge Morand, J.'s decision that the difficult questions of law raised by the novelty of the plaintiff's claims should not be determined in interlocutory proceedings, and their attack on the form of the action and the statement of claim is confined to matters not specifically dealt with in the judgment below.

. . .

Certain parts of the statement of claim in particular all or parts of paras. 22, 23, 29, 32, 34, 36 and 37E are concerned with rights, duties or obligations owed to the defendant Slater Steel Industries Limited or with damage alleged to be suffered by that corporation as a result of the actions of the other defendants. Such matters are properly the subject of a derivative action rather than a class action. Morand, J., said it was "crucial" to distinguish between the two types of action, but found this action to be entirely a class action. I respectfully disagree.

Section 99 of the *Business Corporations Act*, R.S.O. 1970, c. 53, provides in part;

> 99(1) Subject to subsection 2, a shareholder of a corporation may maintain an action in a representative capacity for himself and all other shareholders of the corporation suing for and on behalf of the corporation to enforce any right, duty or obligation owed to the corporation under this Act or under any other statute or rule of law or equity that could be enforced by the corporation itself, or to obtain damages for any breach of any such right, duty or obligation.
>
> (2) An action under subsection 1 shall not be commenced until the shareholder has obtained an order of the court permitting the shareholder to commence the action.

. . .

It was also argued that in so far as the plaintiff's cause of action is founded upon s. 113 of the *Securities Act* and s. 150 of the *Business Corporations Act* it cannot be maintained because the loss claimed is not "direct loss" within the meaning of those sections. I agree with Morand, J., that this is not a question that should be decided in interlocutory proceedings.

Besides those mentioned, the statement of claim is prejudicial or embarrassing in the following respects:

(1) Special damages and not the conspiracy is the gist of an action for conspiracy and the special damages of each member of the class should be pleaded. As I understand the respondent's argument, those special damages will be pleaded as the *pro rata* share of each member of the class of the gross premium I have mentioned.

(2) The class on behalf of which the action is maintained is not clearly and specifically defined and facts are not alleged to show the plaintiff is a member of that class. As I understand the respondent's factum, the class comprises all shareholders and former shareholders of Slater Steel Industries Limited who were shareholders at the time of the sale of control to Stanton Pipes Limited. I see no antagonism between the interests of the members of such a class but it should be so defined in the statement of claim.

(3) Paragraphs 34 and 35 are embarrassing in that they do not allege facts but rather possible future wrongs.

(4) Paragraphs 37(b) to (e) both inclusive are evidently alternative claims and should be pleaded as such. Moreover, the plaintiff's claim is not for 25 million dollars but rather for whatever is shown to be the amount of the gross premium I have mentioned.

In the result, I would allow the appeal with costs her and below, set aside the order of Morand, J., and in its place direct an order:

A. Dismissing the action with costs against the defendants Morris and Henderson in so far as the action against them is based on the allegations of fact made in para. 30 of the statement of claim, without prejudice to the right to commence a separate action against such defendants;

B. Dismissing the action with costs against all defendants in so far as the action is derivative in nature, without prejudice to the right to commence such separate action for which leave may be granted in the future under s. 99(2) of the *Business Corporations Act*;

C. Striking out the statement of claim with liberty to amend the writ of summons and deliver a fresh amended statement of claim within 20 days.

Appeal allowed.

GOLDEX MINES LTD. v. REVILL

(1974), 7 O.R. (2d) 216, 54 D.L.R. (3d) 672 (C.A.)

[This was the fifth time in the courts for two warring factions of shareholders of Probe Mines Ltd. Various misdeeds by directors and defendant shareholders were alleged, but it was not clearly specified in the writ whether the duties alleged to have been breached were owed to the shareholders or to the corporation. The plaintiffs had not sought permission to bring a representative action on behalf of the corporation.]

By the Court: — With the foregoing questions dealt with, there remains the real and important issue: does Goldex have the right to maintain this (second) action without first obtaining the leave of the Court under s. 99 of the Act [the original O.B.C.A.]?

In broad terms the issue is whether the Divisional Court was right in its conclusion. We think the issue can be confined in narrower terms. It is this: Where the same acts of directors or of shareholders cause damage to the company and also to shareholders or a class of them, is a shareholder's cause of action for the wrong done to him derivative?

It is well to draw attention to the appropriate terminology which should be employed. The point is well taken by Professor Stanley M. Beck in his thorough and useful article "The Shareholders' Derivative Action", 52 Can. Bar Rev. 159 (1974) (see pp. 185-6). Where a legal wrong is done to shareholders by directors or other shareholders, the injured shareholders suffer a personal wrong, and may seek redress for it in a personal action. That personal action may be by one shareholder alone, or (as will usually be the case) by a class action in which he sues on behalf of himself and all other shareholders in the same interest (usually, all other shareholders save the wrongdoers). Such a class action is nevertheless a personal action.

A derivative action, on the other hand, is one in which the wrong is done to the company. It is always a class action, brought in representative form, thereby binding all the shareholders. This was so at common law, as s. 99 recognizes (see Beck, op. cit., at p. 185).

The distinction, therefore, as Professor Beck points out, is not between a class action and a derivative action, but between a personal action (whether or not a class action) and a derivative action. The action here is a class action. No one suggest that on that ground alone it is open to objection. The objection is that it is derivative, and cannot be brought without leave.

In *Farnham v. Fingold, supra,* this Court was not required, on the facts of that case, to consider a situation where the same wrongful act is both a wrong to the company and a wrong to each individual shareholder. In one sense every injury to a company is indirectly an injury to its shareholders. On the other hand, if one applies the test: "Is this wrongful act one in respect of which the company could sue?", a shareholder who is personally and directly injured must surely be entitled to say, as a matter of logic, "the company cannot sue for my injury; it can only sue for its own".

These distinctions have been considered in several American cases, usually in States where a shareholder bringing a derivative action may be required to put up security for costs. Some of these cases are discussed by Professor Beck, op. cit. It has not been necessary in Ontario heretofore to draw such a fine dividing line, but the enactment of s. 99 makes some distinction essential, because leave of the Court is required for all those parts of a claim that are derivative. (Once leave is obtained, personal and derivative claims may be joined, subject to the Rules, i.e., if the claims arise out of the same transaction or occurrence.)

It would not be difficult to reach the conclusion that a shareholder's action is personal where one group of shareholders, by their own non-representative activities (i.e., not as directors) acts in such a way as to deprive another group of shareholders of their rights, where those rights are derived from the letters patent (or articles of incorporation), the company's by-laws, or from statutory provisions enacted for the protection of shareholders as such. The more difficult case arises where the directors, whose shareholdings are controlling or merely substantial, for a collateral purpose of their own, cause the company to act in a manner that deprives a group of shareholders of their rights (Beck, op. cit., at p. 174). To cause the company to act to serve personal objectives of the directors would clearly be a breach of the directors' fiduciary duty to the company. Beck suggests that it is also a breach of the directors' fiduciary duty to shareholders as a whole — also asserts that this principle has been indicated (if not always clearly expressed) in the decided cases.

The line of demarcation between a derivative action and a personal action was discussed by Traynor, C.J., in *Jones v. H.F. Ahmanson & Co. et al.* (1969), 460 Pac. Rep. 2d 464 at p. 470 et seq., 81 Cal. Rptr. 592. The argument that the directors, officers and controlling shareholders owe a duty only to the corporation was rejected. The plaintiff was held entitled to bring her action without complying with s. 7616 of the California Financial code, requiring a prior determination by a commissioner that a proposed derivative action complied with certain statutory prerequisites.

One phrase used in the judgment of Traynor, C.J., requires comment. At pp. 470-1, referring to *Shaw v. Empire Savings & Loan Ass'n*, 186 Cal. App. 2d 401 at p. 407, he said:

> ... the court [in *Shaw*] noted the "well established general rule that a stockholder of a corporation has no personal or individual right of action against third persons, including the corporation's officers and directors, for a wrong or injury to the corporation which results in the destruction or depreciation of the value of his stock, since the wrong thus suffered by the stockholder is merely incidental to the wrong suffered by the corporation and affects all stockholders alike." From this the court reasoned that a minority shareholder could not maintain an individual action unless he could demonstrate the injury to him as somehow different from that suffered by other minority shareholders. In so concluding the court erred. The individual wrong necessary to support a suit by a shareholder need not be unique to that plaintiff. The same injury may affect a substantial number of shareholders. If the injury is not incidental to an injury to the corporation, an individual cause of action exists.

What limitation on the general principle is intended by the words in the last sentence: "... not incidental to an injury to the corporation"?

In the context of the whole judgment, we believe Traynor, C.J., meant by this phrase: "... not arising simply because the corporation itself has been damaged, and as a consequence of the damage to it, its shareholders have been injured".

In *Charlebois et al. v. Bienvenue et al.*, [1967] 2 O.R. 635 at p. 644, 64 D.L.R. (2d) 683 at p. 692, Fraser, J., held that the holding of an annual meeting and election of directors after the sending out of a misleading information circular by the directors was a breach of the directors' fiduciary duty to the company. We hold that such an act is also a breach of duty to the other shareholders. If the directors of a company choose, or are compelled by statute, to send information to shareholders, those shareholders have a right to expect that the information sent to them is fairly presented, reasonable accurate, and not misleading.

The proposition that a shareholder is entitled to adequate information from which he can form an intelligent judgment on the matters he is entitled to vote on was enunciated by Spence, J., in *Garvie v. Axmith et al.*, [1962] O.R. 65 at pp. 82-7, 31 D.L.R. (2d) 65 at pp. 82-7. It was supported by quotations of opinion by Roach, J., in *Re National Grocers Co. Ltd.*, [1938] O.R. 142 at p. 154, [1938] 3 D.L.R. 106 at p. 116, and LeBel, J., in *Re N. Slater Co. Ltd.*, [1947] O.W.N. 226 at p. 227, [1947] 2 D.L.R. 311 at pp. 313-4, 28 C.B.R. 31. We accept the proposition and hold that it is not confined to cases under s. 33 of the *Corporations Act*, R.S.O. 1960, c. 71 (special resolutions; see now s. 189(2) of the Act).

Examples of statutory directions respecting the sending of information to shareholders are found in ss. 106(1)(*a*), 115 to 120, 134(5)(*b*), 169, 184 and 194(2) and (3) of the Act. Section 256 provides that every person who makes or assists in making a statement in any document required by or for the purposes of the act or the Regulations that, at the time and in the light of the circumstances under which it was made, is false or misleading in respect of any material fact or that omits to state a material fact the omission which makes the statement false or misleading, is guilty of an offence.

It has long been the law that minority shareholders can sue, even where there is a clear wrong to the company, where there has been "an oppressive and unjust exercise of the powers of the majority shareholders for the promotion of an advantage to themselves to the peculiar detriment of the minority": *Henderson v. Strang et al.* (1919), 60 S.C.R. 201 at p. 202, 54 D.L.R. 674 at p. 675, [1920] 1 W.W.R. 982 followed in *Grau v. Yellowknife Gold Mines Ltd. et al. (No. 1)*, [1974] O.R. 928 at p. 963, [1948] 1 D.L.R. 473 at p. 498. With the legislative trend obviously towards greater protection of shareholders by seeing that they receive certain information, truthfully and fairly presented, we see no difficulty in holding that shareholders are injured if they do not receive it, apart altogether from any breach of duty owed to the company itself. Where information is sent to shareholders that is untrue or misleading, the duty to shareholders is breached, whether the senders were required by statute to send out that class of information, or whether they simply chose to do so.

The principle that the majority governs in corporate affairs is fundamental to corporation law, but its corollary is also important — that the majority must act fairly and honestly. Fairness is the touchstone of equitable justice, and when the test of fairness is not met, the equitable jurisdiction of the Court can be invoked to prevent or remedy the injustice which misrepresentation or other dishonesty has caused. The category of cases in which fiduciary duties and obligations arise is not a closed one: *Laskin v. Bache & Co. Inc.*, [1972] 1 O.R. 465 at p. 472, 23 D.L.R. (3d) 385 at p. 392.

Turning to the way the plaintiff's case is pleaded in the extensive endorsement on the writ, set out in full in the reasons of Hughes, J., there is no clear allegation anywhere personally. On the contrary — as Hughes, J., pointed out: [1973] 3 O.R. at p. 885, 38 D.L.R. (3d) at p. 529 — cls. E, G and I all give grounds for the injunctions sought therein, and in each case the concluding ground is that "the Defendant Directors are in breach of their fiduciary duty to Probe" (giving reasons for the allegation). The grounds are expressed cumulatively and not in the alternative. Thus, on their face, these three clauses assert claims to relief which are founded on a breach of duty to Probe and which Probe itself could assert.

Clause E(1) asserts that the defendants

> ... circulated to all shareholders of the corporation a communication dated the 29th day of September, 1972 which was calculated to result in the procurement of proxies in favour of the personal defendants and the withholding of provides in favour of the plaintiff, thereby effecting a solicitation without appendixing thereto or delivering as a separate document accompanying such solicitation an information circular as prescribed by section 118 of the Business Corporations Act ...

If this passage stood alone, it could be interpreted as a pleading of wrongful acts causing damage to the plaintiff and other shareholders, and thus disclosing a cause of action which we have earlier said is not derivative, and which is therefore outside s. 99.

Similarly, cl. E(2) alleges that the information circular dated October 5, 1972, approved by the defendant directors and sent out with the notice calling the annual meeting of Probe for October 31, 1972, in conjunction with a solicitation of proxies by the defendant directors, was false and misleading in three respects. This subcl. (2), while not framed as an allegation of wrongful acts causing damage to the plaintiff and other shareholders, as shareholders, could also be interpreted as meaning that in substance.

The allegations with respect to the annual report of Probe to its shareholders dated September 25, 1972, pose more difficult problems. They occur:

(1) in Clause C. of the endorsement, claiming that the resolution of the directors approving the annual report is a nullity;

(2) in Clause D., claiming that all proxies obtained by the defendant directors "in response to the solicitation of proxies accompanies by the information Circular ... and the Annual Report ... " are null and void;

(3) in Clause E(3), which, in support of the claim for an injunction restraining the personal defendants from voting their proxies, alleges that the Annual Report is false and misleading.

There is also an oblique reference to the annual report in cl. L, which seeks to prevent the defendant directors from engaging in any renewed solicitation of proxies "until a corrected and complete Information Circular and annual Report are provided to shareholders".

While the preparation, approval and circulation to shareholders of a "false and misleading" annual report is undoubtedly a wrong to the company, the circulation of such a report to shareholders, accompanied by a solicitation on behalf of the directors of the shareholders' proxies, is in our view also a wrong to shareholders as such, affecting their own personal rights. An action attacking such a report, seeking a declaration or an injunction, or both, is not derivative, and leave of the Court to bring it is not required.

The allegations in the endorsement respecting the Mountain Gypsum agreement with Probe, as now framed, all raise causes of action which are really Probe's, although the carrying out of them could affect shareholders of Probe and possibly solidify or change the control of Probe's shares. This portion of the claim, referred to in cls. E(2)(a), (3), (4), F, G, H, I and K, is in substance derivative. The same applies to the underwriting agreement of June 21, 1972, with W.D. Latimer Co. Ltd. which is tied to cl. E(2)(b) and (C).

The trouble with the endorsement is that it disclosed no attempt to differentiate between claims personal to shareholders and claims which are derivative. As already indicated, the subclauses of claims E and G intermingle "grounds" that are clearly derivative in nature with some that are not. We do not think it is our function to suggest a redraft of the endorsement so as to bring it into conformity with the principles enunciated herein.

The Divisional Court decided that all the claims made were derivative, and set aside the writ and the interlocutory orders made on the basis of it. We have concluded that the facts set out in the material would support an endorsement making some claims for relief that are personal and not derivative, if properly pleaded, but they are inextricably woven into the derivative claims, in the present endorsement.

We considered whether it would be appropriate merely to strike out the endorsement on the writ, with leave to amend, rather than strike out the writ itself, as the Divisional Court did. We have decided against doing so, for two reasons. No limitation period is involved, and a new writ can be issued. In addition, the plaintiff may decide to apply for leave under s. 99, and if it obtains leave, it can add to the derivative claims thus permitted such personal claims as it sees fit (subject, of course, to the Rules).

The Divisional Court was asked to grant leave nunc pro tunc under s. 99(2), if it concluded that the claims made were derivative. It declined to do so: [1973] 3 O.R. at pp. 886-7, 38 D.L.R. (3d) at pp. 530-1. The same request was made to this Court. We agree with the reasons for refusing leave given by the Divisional Court, which apply with even greater force to the application for leave made to us. We refuse leave also.

NOTES

The *Goldex* case clearly shows the necessity of carefully drawing up the writ. It also stands as authority for the joinder of representative and personal actions. However, the court rambled on at great length, albeit *obiter*, making some extremely confusing statements regarding various duties owed to the minority by both directors and by majority shareholders. Does the case establish a fiduciary relationship in Ontario between directors and shareholders? Does the court refer to any alleged wrongs of a personal nature which could not have been handled in the simple manner contemplated by a division of powers statute — here, by a compliance order? See Section C, "Compliance and Restraining Orders", below. *Goldex* contains many dangerous statements which, as they come from the Court of Appeal, will inevitably be picked up and cited in support of further extensions of fiduciary duties.

The question of shareholders' personal causes of action outside the statutory framework will be further dealt with after all the statute-based minority protection devices are examined.

The discussion of whether a cause of action is properly framed as a statutory representative action or an oppression remedy, a matter of significance in *Goldex*, will be revisited later in this chapter in the excerpt from *Hercules Managements Ltd. v. Ernst & Young*, [1997] S.C.J. No. 51, [1997] 2 S.C.R. 165, 146 D.L.R. (4th) 577.

2. Prerequisite Steps

We have already discussed the importance of standing at the beginning of this chapter. Our present concern is to examine the prerequisite steps that a complainant with standing must take in order to have the complaint heard.

No "complainant" will have standing to bring a statutory representative action unless four prerequisites are satisfied. The C.B.C.A. sets them out as follows:

239(2) ...

(a) the complainant has given notice to the directors of the corporation or its subsidiary of the complainant's intention to apply to the court under subsection (1) not less than fourteen days before bringing the application, or as otherwise ordered by the court, ...

(b) the complainant is acting in good faith ...

(c) it appears to be in the interests of the corporation ... that the action be brought. ...

...

240. In connection with an action brought ... under section 239, the court may at any time make any order it thinks fit including ...

(a) an order authorizing the complainant or any other person to control the conduct of the action ...

Failure to give notice to the directors (so as to permit them to take action in the corporate name) will be fatal to the application: *Covia Canada Partnership Corp. v. PWA Corp.*, [1993] O.J. No. 1757, 105 D.L.R. (4th) 60 (Gen. Div.); aff'd, [1993] O.J. No. 1793, 106 D.L.R. (4th) 608 (C.A.).

The courts are not likely to require much formality in the notice requirement, as this next case indicates.

ARMSTRONG v. GARDNER

(1978), 20 O.R. (2d) 648 (H.C.)

[For more than 25 years, the sole business operation of Elsley's Frosted Foods Limited ("the corporation") has been as a landlord to a Royal Bank branch in Oakville, Ontario. One Seward wanted to buy and develop estates in land in the area. Various offers to purchase the corporation's estate were declined, following which corporations controlled by Seward acquired a majority of the corporation's shares.]

Cory J. [having summarized the above facts]: — It is not necessary to review in detail the series of shareholders' meetings which followed. ...

The result of the actions of the directors of the Elsley company, confirmed by the majority of the shareholders, is that the sole asset of the company is very substantially encumbered. The proceeds have been placed in a company without assets over which the Elsley company has no control whatsoever. There does not appear to be any likelihood of any capital appreciation occurring to the Elsley company. This application should be considered in light of that background.

It is the position of the counsel for the respondent that the application is in the nature of an originating motion, and that the Court ought not to act upon the affidavit material based upon information and belief.

Section 99(3) of the *Business Corporations Act*, R.S.O. 1970, c. 53, sets out the basis upon which application for an order to commence an action is to be brought and reads as follows:

99.(3) A shareholder may, upon at least seven days notice to the corporation, apply to the court for an order referred to in subsection 2, and, if the court is satisfied that,

(a) the shareholder was a shareholder of the corporation at the time of the transaction or other event giving rise to the cause of action;

(b) the shareholder has made reasonable efforts to cause the corporation to commence or prosecute diligently the action on its own behalf; and

(c) the shareholder is acting in good faith and it is prima facie in the interests of the corporation or its shareholders that the action be commenced.

the court may make the order upon such terms as the court thinks fit, except that the order shall not require the shareholder to give security for costs.

The problems that awaited a minority shareholder prior to the passage of the Act have been done away with. It would seem that the scheme and intent of the legislation was to permit an action to be brought so long as the requirements of s. 99(3) were complied with.

An application to bring an action such as this must in a great many situations be dependent on information and belief of others that has been related to the deponent. Almost invariably minority shareholders will be in such a disadvantageous position that they will not be able to obtain first-hand evidence and information upon which to found their motion. To deny an application on that ground would, in my opinion, fly in the face of both the provisions and intent of the *Business Corporations Act*.

It may be that this application ought not to be considered an originating motion. By analogy it most closely resembles an application under the former Rules of Practice for leave to commence an action out of the jurisdiction. The affidavits used on such applications were also of necessity often based on information and belief but were accepted, for such applications were not considered to be originating motions. In my opinion, this is not an originating motion. It is in nature an interlocutory application brought pursuant to the provisions of the *Business Corporations Act* and ought not to be refused solely because the affidavit in support is based in part upon information and belief.

It is further submitted on behalf of the respondents that the applicant has not complied with section 99(3)(b) in that no reasonable efforts were made to cause the corporation to commence or prosecute diligently the proposed action. There is material which indicates that in July of 1977 the solicitor for the minority shareholders wrote to Mr. Gardner suggesting that action be taken with regard to the $250,000 mortgage and to prevent the investment of the mortgage proceeds in a Mid Oak company, that is a Seward interest corporation. The reply from Mr. Gardner dated the next day was not particularly helpful. A further letter was sent on July 11th, and the reply from Mr. Gardner dated July 14th confirmed the acquisition of the shares in Mid Oak Investments Limited. It must be remembered that although the letters requesting action were not framed with great particularity as to the cause of action to be brought, they were directed to a solicitor. I think that there was a sufficient demand made to bring an appropriate action by the two letters sent on behalf of the minority shareholders to satisfy the provisions of s. 99(3)(b). I do not think that this section of the *Business Corporations Act* ought to be construed in an unduly technical or restricted manner.

...

In my opinion, the facts are overwhelming in their support of the applicant's position. The test by which I should be governed in such applications has been laid down in the decision of O'Leary J., in *Re Marc-Jay Investments Inc. and Levy et al.* (1974), 5 O.R. (2d) 235, 50 D.L.R. (3d) 45. It is clear that I am not to try the action on the hearing of this application. Rather, if I come to the conclusion that the applicant is acting in good faith, has complied with the requirements of s. 99, that the action does not appear to be frivolous or vexatious and could reasonably succeed and that it is in the interests of the shareholders, then leave to bring the action should be granted. In my opinion, all the requirements of that test have been complied with. ...

Any detriment to the proposed defendants occasioned by the institution of the action can be compensated by way of costs. I have, therefore, determined that the application should be granted and leave given to the applicants to commence the action. The costs of this application [are] to be reserved to the trial Judge.

Application allowed.

NOTES

A similar view of the notice requirement was expressed in *Bellman v. Western Approaches Ltd.*, [1981] B.C.J. No. 1548, 33 B.C.L.R. 45, 53, 130 D.L.R. (3d) 193 (C.A.), where Nemetz C.J.B.C. said: "Failure to specify each and every cause of action in a notice does not, in my opinion, invalidate the notice as a whole." It is clear, however, that notice must be given, as there would be no point in authorizing someone to bring a representative action on behalf of another unless at least some attempt had been made to ascertain whether the other person might want to sue. See, to this effect *MacRae v. Daon Development Corp.*, [1984] B.C.J. No. 2945, 26 B.L.R. 38 at 45 (S.C.).

In *Olympia & York Enterprises Ltd. v. Hiram Walker Resources Ltd.* (1986), 59 O.R. (2d) 254 (Div. Ct.) failure to give notice, together with failure to meet other prerequisites led to the dismissal of the complaint. However, Montgomery J. said at p. 274, "... If notice only was missing, I might conclude otherwise ... ".

"Good faith," the second prerequisite, probably does not mean much. In *Bellman v. Western Approaches Ltd*, Nemetz C.J.B.C. made the following comments:

[The directors] argued where the relief requested in both [statutory representative and personal] actions is substantially the same, that is evidence of a lack of good faith since it is vexatious to seek the same relief in two actions. However, after examining the relief sought in each action, I conclude that the relief is not the same. Damages for breach of fiduciary duty are not available in the personal action, nor have such damages in that action been sought. Damages are being sought in the derivative action. That distinction, among others, is sufficient to justify the initiation of the derivative action under this heading.

For another look at the concept of "good faith," see *Groeneveld v. Groeneveld Brothers Holdings Ltd.*, [1998] A.J. No. 973, 229 A.R. 288 (Q.B.).

Some suggest that the "good faith" requirement can be invoked to disallow "strike suits," a term used to categorize minority shareholders' actions brought in an attempt to profit from the nuisance value of forcing the directors to appear and defend the action. Would not the fourth prerequisite, as well as the requirement for judicial supervision of out-of-court settlements, discussed below, adequately inhibit such profit-seeking complainants?

In *Richardson Greenshields of Canada Ltd. v. Kalmacoff*, [1995] O.J. No. 941, 22 O.R. (3d) 577 (C.A.) the Court of Appeal said at pp. 586-87:

In my opinion, the extent of Richardson Greenshields' stake, monetary or otherwise, in the outcome of these proceedings is of little weight in deciding whether it has met the good faith test applicable to the present circumstances. This case is not at all akin to a strike or bounty action. Although the appellant purchased shares for the purpose of bringing these proceedings, it is by definition a complainant, and stands, vis-à-vis the company, in the same position as any other person who fits within the definition of "complainant". The issues involved are of a continuing nature, and it seems to me apparent that the appellant is in a better position than most shareholders to pursue the complaint. Indeed, I see no advantage in requiring that the action be brought by another shareholder, as suggested by the judge hearing the application. I think it significant that the appellant has had a long-standing commercial connection with this class of shares and is familiar with the matters in dispute. It acknowledges that it has clients who purchased shares on its recommendation, and, it can be inferred from the shareholders' vote, that it voices the views of a substantial number of the preferred shareholders. Whether it is motivated by altruism, as the motions court judge suggested, or by self-interest, as the respondents suggest, is beside the point. Assuming, as I suppose, it is the latter, self-interest is hardly a stranger to the security or investment business. Whatever the reason, there are legitimate legal questions raised here that call for judicial resolution. The fact that this shareholder is prepared to assume the costs and undergo the risks of carriage of an action intended to prevent the board from following a course of action that may be *ultra vires* and in breach of shareholders' rights does not provide a proper basis for impugning its *bona fides*. In my opinion, there is no valid reason for concluding that the good faith condition specified in s. 339(2)(*b*) has not been satisfied.

...

The third prerequisite — that bringing the action appears to be in the corporate interest — raises some interesting points.

This latter point is contemplated in the following case.

BELLMAN v. WESTERN APPROACHES LTD.

[1981] B.C.J. No. 1548, 33 B.C.L.R. 45, 130 D.L.R. (3d) 193 (C.A.)

[Minority shareholders, by letters to a C.B.C.A. corporation, alleged that some of the directors had breached their fiduciary duties. They asked that the corporation sue the directors. The board asked a law firm and an accounting firm to investigate the allegations. This resulted in an opinion from the law firm that there was no evidence to support the allegations. The minority shareholders sought leave to bring a statutory representative action.]

Nemetz C.J.B.C. [having stated the facts, noted that judicial permission to bring the action had been granted in the lower court, and commented on the other prerequisites, he now considered the question of the interests of the corporation]: — In my view this is the key section for consideration in this case. The section does not say that the Court must be satisfied that it is in the interests of the corporation. It says that no action may be brought unless the Court is satisfied that it appears to be in the interests of the corporation to bring the suit. I take that to mean that what is sufficient at this stage is that an arguable case be shown to subsist. This is quite different from the rules established at common law. ...

...

How is a Court to exercise its discretion in coming to a determination that it is satisfied that "it appears to be in the interests of the corporation" to allow the derivative action to be brought? The discretion is a wide one. However, despite its breadth, nowhere does Parliament say, nor, in my opinion, was it intended, that the logic of the common law in cases of this kind be disregarded. One must first look to the decision of the directors who, having been given reasonable notice by a complainant in good faith, decide not to assert a corporate right of action. In this case they refused. Can it be said that this refusal was given impartially? It was submitted that the resolution not to sue was passed by four independent directors since the Duke group and Asper did not vote. It was also submitted that the decision of these "independent" directors was based upon the reports of their accountants and outside lawyers and that in any event they could reasonably conclude that the disadvantages to the company outweighed the advantages. How do I conclude that these four directors were not independent? Messrs. Miroy, Dewar, Shier and Atkinson were nominated by the Investors Group on January 16, 1980, at a time when the Duke group held a majority of the investors' shares. More important is the effect upon their independence of cls. 3.03 and 3.04 of the guarantor's agreement where the borrowers covenanted to use their powers as directors to assert control over the directors nominated by the investor's group to act and vote in ways favourable to the lender.

It is also curious that the instructions of the directors to the investigators, i.e., Price Waterhouse, were limited to certain periods of time in respect only of legal expenses, expenses charged to the company and contra account settlements. Since the legal opinion of January 15, 1981, was based on this limited report it can hardly be said to have been conclusive of the substantive issues raised by the complainants, namely, the breach of fiduciary duty.

Considering the whole of the evidence before the Chambers Judge, she could have come to the conclusion that at the time when they came to the decision not to sue, the directors did stand in a dual relation which prevented them from exercising an unprejudiced judgment. While it is true that a quantifiable loss was not proven, nevertheless, it was sufficient to have adumbrated a potential loss resulting from the covenant in the guarantor's agreement requiring the borrowers to pay a fee to the guarantor in the event that they were not able to cause the company to go public. Since the fee was based on gross revenue, it might place the directors in a position of conflict in deciding whether it is in their best interest to keep revenues down in order to reduce the potential fee or to maximize revenues in the interest of all the shareholders. However, this would be a matter for the trial Court to consider. It is sufficient that it appears to be in the interest of the company that the action be brought.

I would accordingly, dismiss the appeal.

Appeal dismissed.

NOTES

Do you agree? What judicial view of corporate personality underlies this reasoning?

In *Primex Investments Ltd. v. Northwest Sports Enterprises Ltd.*, [1995] B.C.J. No. 2262, 13 B.C.L.R. (3d) 300 (S.C.); var'd, [1996] B.C.J. No. 2309, 26 B.C.L.R. (3d) 357 (C.A.), *Bellman's* findings that (a) the granting of leave to commence a statutory representative action does not require a determination that the matters in question are in the best interests of the company, but simply must appear to be in the interests of the company, and (b) that there is no need for the applicant to demonstrate the likelihood of success of the action were affirmed.

Does a single shareholder have standing to bring a statutory representative action if all the other shareholders oppose the action? What view of corporate personality underlies your reasoning? See *Feld v. Glick* (1975), 8 O.R. (2d) 7, 56 D.L.R. (3d) 649 (H.C.). Compare the comments (*obiter*) of Montgomery J. in *Olympia & York Enterprises Ltd. v. Hiram Walker Resources Ltd.* (1986), 59 O.R. (2d) 254 (Div. Ct.), to the effect that it would be a fatal flaw not to have the shareholders represented, and since no party can represent all of the shareholders in a hostile takeover bid, a representative action should not be permitted. Does this reasoning make sense? Does it ignore the concept of corporate identity?

Do persons granted leave to commence a statutory representative action owe a fiduciary duty to the corporation on whose behalf the action was brought? If so, how may this duty be fulfilled? See *Discovery Enterprises Inc. v. Ebco Industries Ltd.*, [1998] B.C.J. No. 2674, 58 B.C.L.R. (3d) 105 (C.A.).

3. The "Independent Committee"

A common defensive tactic in American corporate practice is to have the board of directors establish a committee from among its members to investigate whether the corporation should take legal action as requested by the complainant. The report of the committee, assuming that it concludes action should not be taken, can be used to demonstrate that it does not appear in the interest of the corporation to take action, *i.e.*, to convince the court that the complainant has not met a condition precedent to the action. However, if the representative action is permitted, the report may also be used as a substantive defence.

We have already considered the role of the independent committee when considering the fiduciary obligation of directors in Chapter 7. Re-read the extract from *Brant Investments Ltd. v. KeepRite Inc.*, [1991] O.J. No. 683, 3 O.R. (3d) 289, 1 B.L.R. (2d) 225 (C.A.) in that chapter. For different judicial views of the evidentiary value of the committee's reports in American jurisprudence, see *Auerbach v. Bennett*, 393 N.E.2d 994 (N.Y.C.A. 1979); *Zapata Corporation v. Maldonado*, 430 A.2d 779 (Del. 1981).

Recall that most Canadian jurisdictions have sections similar to C.B.C.A., s. 242(1), which notes that majority shareholder approval is not conclusive against the minority's request to bring a statutory representative action. Is the negative opinion of a directors' committee more or less persuasive than a shareholder vote? For some further views on the judicial role in such disputes, see Buckley, "Ratification and the Derivative Action Under the Ontario Business Corporations Act" (1976), 22 McGill L.J. 167.

4. Conduct of the Action

Once the complainant has satisfied the prerequisites and obtained judicial permission to proceed, one would anticipate that the action would be conducted as if the corporation itself were the active plaintiff. Oddly, this is not the way it works. Some of the reasons are formalistic, but some are not, and some of the latter are difficult to understand. The C.B.C.A. provisions will again serve to illustrate the points.

> 240. In connection with an action brought or intervened in under section 239, the court may at any time make any order it thinks fit including, without limiting the generality of the foregoing,
>
> > (a) an order authorizing the complainant or any other person to control the conduct of the action;
> >
> > (b) an order giving directors for the conduct of the action;
> >
> > (c) an order directing that any amount adjudged payable by a defendant in the action shall be paid, in whole or in part, directly to former and present security holders of the corporation or its subsidiary instead of to the corporation or its subsidiary;
> >
> > (d) an order requiring the corporation or its subsidiary to pay reasonable legal fees incurred by the complainant in connection with the action.

...

242(2) An application made or an action brought or intervened in under this Part shall not be stayed, discontinued, settled, or dismissed for want of prosecution without the approval of the court given upon such terms as the court thinks fit and, if the court determines that the interests of any complainant may be substantially affected by such stay, discontinuance, settlement or dismissal, the court may order any party to the application or action to give notice to the complainant.

(3) A complainant is not required to give security for costs in any application made or action brought or intervened in under this Part.

(4) In an application made or an action brought or intervened in under this Part, the court may at any time order the corporation or its subsidiary to pay to the complainant interim costs, including legal fees and disbursements, but the complainant may be held accountable for such interim costs upon final disposition of the application or action.

What do you think would be the result in a typical statutory representative action if, once judicial permission to proceed had been obtained, the complainant were free to discontinue the action without judicial approval? What do you think happens in a typical statutory representative action after judicial permission to proceed has been obtained? Are your answers to these two questions different?

Why do you think the judge is empowered to give directions for the conduct of the action (C.B.C.A., s. 240(*b*))? What types of orders are likely to be given?

Why, under C.B.C.A., s. 240(*c*), is the judge empowered to have amounts paid to "former and present security holders"? Do you approve of this provision and, if so, on what basis?

Consider a typical statutory representative action in which a minority shareholder has obtained judicial permission to proceed in an action for breach of fiduciary duty by the board of directors. Can the judge order that the directors pay the complainant or the corporation the amount claimed even if no breach of fiduciary duty is demonstrated? If you think the answer is no, re-read C.B.C.A., s. 240.

You will recall that the case of *Burland v. Earle*, [1902] A.C. 83 (Ont. J.C.P.C.) kept cropping up in both English and Canadian decisions concerning minority complaints throughout this book. *Burland v. Earle* was important not so much for what was decided, but for the judicial attitude it set out. Lord Davey's statement of principle was really an attitudinal bias which underlay the common law of corporations:

> It is an elementary principle of the law relating to joint stock companies that the court will not interfere with the internal management of companies acting within their powers, and in fact has no jurisdiction to do so. Again, it is clear law that in order to redress a wrong done to the company or to recover moneys or damages alleged to be due to the company, the action should prima facie be brought by the company itself.

Do you think any portions of Lord Davey's "elementary principle" remain in Canadian corporate law? Reconsider that question after each of the remaining minority protection devices has been covered.

C. COMPLIANCE AND RESTRAINING ORDERS

The statute, the articles and by-laws, and unanimous shareholder agreements are the basic constitutional documents setting out the rules by which the corporation is to be governed. As has been seen throughout this book, enforcing compliance with these rules has not been a simple matter in our corporate law. Sections like C.B.C.A., s. 247 offer a new approach.

> 247. If a corporation or any director, officer, employee, agent, auditor, trustee, receiver, receiver-manager or liquidator of a corporation does not comply with this Act, the regulations, articles, by-laws, or a unanimous shareholder agreement, a complainant or a creditor of the corporation may, in addition to any other right they have, apply to a court for an order directing any such person to comply with, or restraining any such person from acting in breach of, any provisions thereof, and upon such application the court may so order and make any further order it thinks fit.

CALERON PROPERTIES LTD. v. 510207 ALBERTA LTD.

[2000] A.J. No. 1237, [2001] 3 W.W.R. 323, 9 B.L.R. (3d) 218 (Q.B.)

McIntyre J.: —

I. INTRODUCTION

The Class "A" and Class "B" shareholders of 510207 Alberta Ltd. (the "Corporation") battle over the last asset of the Corporation, 4.51 acres of land. The Corporation's management intends to donate the land to a church. The market value of the land is $835,000. Two of the directors of the Corporation are members of the church. Some shareholders object. I am case management judge.

Caleron Properties Ltd., the Class "B" shareholder, ("Caleron") applies pursuant to s. 240 of the Alberta Business Corporations Act, S.A. 1981, c. B-15 (the "ABCA") for an order directing certain directors of the Corporation, and anyone acting in their stead, to comply with the by-laws of the Corporation as amended and with the ABCA.

II. FACTS

The relevant facts are not in dispute. The Corporation was incorporated under the laws of Alberta on November 15, 1991. The two original shareholders were Namo Management Ltd. ("Namo"), controlled by Ed Oman, and Caleron, controlled by Ron Slater. Initially, Namo held 51,000 Class "A" Shares and Caleron held 51,000 Class "B" Shares. Additional shares were later sold to other persons pursuant to a Private Placement Memorandum (the "Memorandum") executed on June 9, 1993 by Oman as President, and by Slater as Chief Executive Officer and Chief Financial Officer of the Corporation.

The Memorandum stated that Class "A" shareholders would be entitled to elect four directors of the Corporation and Class "B" shareholders would be entitled to elect one director. The articles of the Corporation were amended on June 8, 1993 to reflect these entitlements. The articles have always provided that all matters at meetings of the Board of Directors will be decided by majority vote.

Following further amendments to the Corporation's articles, Caleron became the sole Class "B" shareholder. Caleron currently holds 150,000 Class "B" Common Shares, while various other persons hold a total of 344,000 Class "A" Common Shares.

An Annual and Special Meeting of the Shareholders of the Corporation (the "Meeting") was held on December 13, 1999 and continued on January 12, 2000. At the Meeting, a Shareholder Resolution proposing amendments to the Corporation's by-laws was presented by later and was passed by a majority of 59.4% of the shareholders.

The amendments are: 1) directors' meetings require 10 business days notice in writing, 2) directors must attend directors' meetings in person, 3) directors' meetings must be held at the registered office of the Corporation, 4) the presence of Slater and any two other directors at a directors' meeting constitutes quorum for the transaction of business, and 5) Slater is appointed signing authority, either alone or in concert with another person, with respect to documents and instruments executed by the Corporation.

After the Meeting, two directors' meetings of the Corporation were held on February 3 and 24, 2000 (the "Directors' Meetings"). Neither of these meetings were attended by Slater. The Directors' Meetings were called with less than 10 business days notice and were held at a place other than the Corporation's registered office. The business conducted at those meetings consisted of appointing new directors to fill vacancies left by those who had resigned, appointing Michael Smith as counsel, appointing Bill Ferguson to direct counsel for the Corporation, and appointing persons other than Slater as signing authority for the Corporation.

The struggle between these "A" and "B" shareholders is not new to this Court. Power J., in an unreported decision dated 30 November 1998, allowed an earlier application by Caleron to force compliance pursuant to s. 240 of the ABCA. This decision will be discussed below.

III. POSITION OF THE APPLICANT

Caleron submits that majority rule is the overarching principle guiding the governance of corporations, and that the will of the majority of the shareholders binds the Corporation and all of its members. It argues that though the directors are responsible for a corporation's management, their powers are nevertheless subject to the corporate constitution and the decisions of the shareholders as expressed at a general meeting.

In applying this principle to the case at bar, Caleron asserts that the majority of the Corporation's shareholders have spoken at the Meeting by duly passing the by-law amendments in accordance with the ABCA, the Corporation's articles, and with recent rulings of this Court impacting the Meeting's process. As such, Caleron argues that the by-law amendments are effective and binding on the directors.

Caleron contends that the Directors' Meetings held after the passage of the by-law amendments have no legal validity and that the directors' resolutions passed at those meetings are of no force and effect, because those meetings were convened in violation of valid amendments to the Corporation's by-laws. In particular, Caleron argues that counsel for the Corporation in this matter was not effectively retained, as a duly passed Directors' Resolution at a validly constituted directors' meeting is required to appoint counsel to conduct litigation on behalf of a corporation.

IV. POSITION OF THE RESPONDENT

The Respondent Corporation argues that responsibility for the management of a corporation's business affairs is vested with the directors and that there is no provision in the ABCA which gives shareholders the authority to manage and control a corporation, whether or not they act as a majority. The Respondent maintains that the control shareholders may exert over the management of a corporation's affairs is limited to their right to elect the Board of Directors.

The Respondent further argues that a corporation's by-laws are subordinate to its Articles of Incorporation and to the ABCA, and that the by-law amendments in question are invalid because they have the effect of amending the articles of the Corporation by altering the rights privileges, restrictions or conditions attaching to the Class "A" and Class "B" Shares. The Respondent maintains that the Articles of Incorporation can only be amended pursuant to the provisions of the articles themselves and the paramount provisions of the ABCA.

The Respondent asserts that the Corporation's articles clearly intend that a majority of the Board of Directors is to have the authority to manage the Corporation, and that the Class "A" shareholders are to have the right to elect a controlling majority of that Board. The Respondent further submits that the by-law amendments are a colourable attempt to give the Class "B" shareholders the right to block any action by the Board of Directors and thereby remove the Class "A" shareholders' rights intended in the articles. In support of this proposition, the Respondent draws particular attention to the provision requiring the attendance of Slater at directors' meetings in order to constitute quorum.

Accordingly, the Respondent's position is that the Board of Directors may disregard the by-law amendments with impunity. Furthermore, it submits that this Court has no jurisdiction to order the directors to comply with them.

V. ISSUES

The issues raised by this application are as follows:

1. Whether the Court has jurisdiction to rule on the validity of the by-law amendments and to order compliance with them if the Court finds the by-law amendments to be valid.
2. Whether the by-law amendments passed by a majority of shareholders at the Meeting are valid and binding on the Corporation and its Board of Directors.

VI. ANALYSIS

A. Jurisdiction of the Court

The remedy sought by Caleron is pursuant to s. 240 of the ABCA. That section provides:

> 240 If a corporation or any shareholder, director, officer, employee, agent, auditor, trustee, receiver-manager or liquidator of a corporation contravenes this Act, the regulations, the articles or by-laws or a unanimous shareholder agreement, a complainant or a creditor of the corporation may, in addition to any other right he has, apply to the Court for an order directing that person to comply with, or restraining that person from contravening any of those things, and on the application the Court may so order and make any further order it thinks fit.

Section 240 provides, *inter alia*, broad discretion to the Court to order compliance with the by-laws of a corporation. Moreover, the section specifically enumerates corporations and directors as persons who may be subject to such orders. However, there is little case law interpreting the meaning and scope of s. 240 and similar statutory provisions of other jurisdictions.

In *Re Goldhar and Quebec Manitou Mines Ltd.* (1976), 61 D.L.R. (3d) 612 (Ont. Div. Ct.), [not cited by counsel] the Court addressed the scope of s. 261(1) of the *Business Corporations Act*, R.S.O. 1970, c. 53 (the "OBCA"), a provision similar to Alberta's s. 240. In that case, the applicant shareholders sought an order under s. 261(1) requiring the corporation's directors to comply with s. 144 of the OBCA, which stipulated that the directors and officers of a corporation shall act honestly, in good faith and in the best interests of the corporation.

Reid J., for the Court, dismissed the application on two grounds. He first held that s. 261 was not intended to deal with the complexities of fact and law involved in an inquiry into whether a director's duty under s. 144 has been breached. At p. 615 he states:

> The difficulty of passing judgment on the honesty and good faith of directors in respect of decisions made sometimes of necessity hurriedly in sophisticated and complicated factual settings, or upon the credibility of witnesses when the directors as well as the witnesses are revealed only through affidavits and transcripts, needs no illustration. Suffice to say that these questions may be difficult enough to weigh fairly even after a full trial where the appearance and demeanour of witnesses has been experienced, and the testimony of directors tested against pre-trial discovery.

Reid J. further states at p. 615 that the Court was inclined to agree with the Respondent's proposition that s. 261 "should be confined to the rectification of simple 'mechanical' omissions of a type that lend themselves to summary disposition." He did not attempt to define "mechanical omissions", but rather adopted the examples suggested by the Respondent, i.e. failure to furnish a list of shareholders, to send proxies or information circulars to shareholders prior to a meeting, or to file an insider's report.

With respect to the second ground, Reid J. held that s. 261 was limited to the enforcement of personal rights, as opposed to derivative rights, and that the rights asserted by the applicants were more properly characterized as derivative since s. 144 states the obligations owed by directors to a corporation. He further found that shareholders could only enforce s. 144 rights through s. 99, a provision dealing specifically with derivative actions (the oppression remedy was not available under the OBCA when *Goldhar* was decided). Reid J. was concerned that a broad interpretation of s. 261 would permit an applicant to circumvent the leave requirement in s. 99.

Goldhar has been criticized for its narrow approach to the application of the statutory restraining and compliance order. D.H. Peterson, *Shareholder Remedies in Canada* (Markam: Butterworths, 2000), asserts that the Court's second ground cannot be supported in law. At para. 10.16 he states: "[T]he restraining and compliance order expressly provides that it is available in addition to any other right, suggesting that a characterization of the breach as personal or derivative is unnecessary." Also, R.L. Campbell, in "Summary Enforcement of Directors' Duties: *Re Goldhar and Quebec Manitou Mines Ltd.*" (1978), 2 C.B.L.J 92 at 96 suggests that the proper test for s. 261 is whether there has been non-compliance with any statutory provision, rather than whether the applicant's rights are direct or derivative.

B. Welling, *Corporate Law in Canada — The Governing Principles*, 2nd ed. (Toronto: Butterworths, 1991), notes at p. 52ff that statutes such the OBCA and ABCA are based on the statutory division of powers model, that is, they impose a division of powers between the two main power groups, directors and shareholders. He further points out that this model is entirely separate and distinct from the out-moded English memorandum and articles of association or contractarian model, in that it is status and remedy oriented, whereas the latter is contract and rights oriented. At p. 54 the author describes the statutory division of powers model in the following terms:

> The corporate constitution is not a contract among the participating individuals. A person wishing to preclude or redress a breach of the statute or the corporate constitution is not called upon to show some personal "right" concerning the point. The constitutional model is designed to give him two chances:
>
> (a) he can attempt to persuade the majority to his point of view;
>
> (b) he is given an extensive list of statutory remedies to which he has access because of his status, not because of any personal "rights" he may be able to identify.

With respect to the compliance and restraining order remedy in particular, B. Welling states at pp. 59-60:

> This statutory remedy provides shareholder access to judicial discretion whenever a breach of the corporate constitution occurs, without regard to the seriousness of the alleged breach.
>
> The minority remedies are about standing, not about substantive rights. The compliance and restraining order section is typical of shareholder remedies under the reformed Canadian statutes and is, radically different from minority remedies under the English-model, contractarian statutes.
>
> Failure to appreciate the distinction, or to recognize the type of statute involved, can lead to the misapplication of some anomalous distinctions from contractarian-model cases.

In other words, the type of "right" referred to in s. 240 is the right to access the discretion of the Court, as opposed to the right to a remedy per se. B. Welling strongly criticized Reid J.'s reasoning in *Goldhar* for failing to recognize such distinction. At p. 552 he states that had Reid J. applied the correct model, he would have dismissed the application on the basis of his statutory grant of discretion, because the compliance and restraining order sections are the place for judicial discretion. B. Welling's analysis, in my view, makes good sense.

In *Hill v. Silmil Explorations*, [1978] O.J. No. 93 (Ont. H.C.), Griffiths J. rejected the notion of restricting restraining and compliance orders to the enforcement of mechanical omissions. In that case, the applicants sought a compliance order alleging, inter alia, that an information circular issued by the management of a mining company did not comply with the OBCA. The Respondents relied on *Goldhar* in arguing that many of the applicants' allegations could not properly be regarded as simple mechanical omissions. Griffiths J. reserved judgment as to whether all the remedies requested were within the jurisdiction conferred by s. 261, but commented at para. 11:

> Although Reid, J., in delivering the reasons for judgment in the *Goldhar* case said at p. 743 of the report that the Court was "inclined to agree" with the respondent's argument that s. 261 should be "confined to the rectification of simple mechanical omissions" of the type then enumerated, this was in my view *obiter*

dicta. The case was really decided on the basis that the applicants in seeking a declaration that officers of the corporation had failed to comply with s. 144 of the Act, were asserting a derivative right to remedy a wrong alleged to have been done by the directors to the company and a derivative claim does not lie under s. 261. While the *obiter dicta* is of the strongest persuasive value, it seems to me that the jurisdiction of the Court under s. 261 would be too narrowly cast if it was restricted to applications to enforce simple mechanical omissions by the corporation or its directors or officers.

I am not certain that the statement of Reid J. cited by Griffiths J. is *obiter dicta*. Nevertheless, based on the plain meaning of s. 240 in the context of the ABCA as a whole, I can see no justification for restricting its application to the rectification of simple mechanical omissions. Furthermore, because the right conferred on a complainant by s. 240 is in addition to any other right the complainant may have, I can see no justification for restricting its application based on whatever other standing that person may have. A complainant is not precluded from relying on s. 240 merely because that complainant may have concurrent standing pursuant to other sections of the ABCA. Indeed, as D.H. Peterson comments at para. 10.14, "[t]o strictly require that the wrongdoing be remedied through the traditional remedies, such as the oppression remedy and derivative and personal actions, can be overkill in many cases."

Of course, the complexities of fact and law involved in a given case may well militate against a summary disposition of the matter. That is not to say difficult issues of fact and law cannot be treated under s. 240; it is ultimately within the discretion of the Justice in Chambers to determine whether there is sufficient evidence upon which to grant summary relief. However, this judicial discretion must not be confused with a lack of judicial jurisdiction. The result in *Goldhar* would appear to be correct, given that the Court was faced with an elaborate set of disputed facts and a novel question of law, indicating the need for a full trial. But the application would have been more properly dismissed, in my view, based on the judicial discretion conferred by s. 261, rather than on any perceived lack of jurisdiction under that provision.

In contrast to the circumstances in *Goldhar*, the facts in the present application are not in dispute, nor are they particularly complicated. Unlike *Goldhar*, the Applicant does not ask the Court to order compliance with a broad and nebulous section of the ABCA, but rather seeks compliance with certain amendments to the Corporation's by-laws. The amendments in question were passed by due process, they are procedural or "mechanical" in nature, and they stipulate clearly-defined rights and obligations. It is not difficult to determine if they have been breached. Indeed, the Respondent does not deny its non-compliance with them. If the validity of the by-law amendments were not in issue, this Court would certainly have jurisdiction under s. 240 to enforce compliance with them, even if Reid J.'s narrow interpretation of the section were to be applied.

However, in the present case, the validity of the by-law amendments has been squarely raised by both parties. The remaining question then, is whether the issue of the amendments' validity can be effectively resolved by summary process under s. 240 of the ABCA. It would seem logical that when a Court is deciding whether to exercise its discretion to enforce a corporation's by-laws or articles, an inquiry into their legality will at times be a necessary part of the process. On this point, D.H. Peterson at para. 10.10 states:

As a preliminary matter, the obligations underlying the statutory restraining and compliance order must be determined. The provisions of the Act and the Regulation are, of course, expressly stated; in the case of articles, by-laws, and unanimous shareholder agreements, however, it may be necessary to determine whether such documents exist and, if so, whether they comply with the legal requirements. In each case the document in question, the relevant provisions of the Act, and the common law must be reviewed.

Therefore, a determination of the validity of the by-laws in the present case would necessarily involve interpreting the Corporation's articles and by-law amendments to determine if the amendments are *ultra vires* the articles, interpreting the provisions of the ABCA pertaining to articles and by-laws, as well as reviewing the common law in this area.

Legal issues of comparable complexity have been addressed by the courts in response to other applications for compliance and restraining orders. For instance, in *Fidelity Management & Research Co. v. Gulf Canada Resources Ltd.* (1996), 27 B.L.R. (2d) 135 (Ont. Gen. Div.), the applicants sought an order pursuant to s. 247 of the Canada Business Corporations Act (the "CBCA"), a provision substantially similar to Alberta's s. 240, requiring Gulfs directors to comply with that corporation's articles. The articles in question pertained to the payment of dividends and dividend arrears with respect to Gulf's senior preference shares. Gulf countered that the directors' discretion to declare dividends was not restricted by the articles. The Court engaged in a detailed analysis of Gulf's articles before interpreting them in favour of the respondent corporation.

Another example is *Caleron Properties Ltd. v. 510207 Alberta Ltd.* (30 November 1998), Calgary 9801-14606 (Alta. Q.B.), an unreported decision of Power J. of this Court, with the same parties represented in the present application. There, the Corporation's management proposed to donate certain lands to a Church without the prior approval of the shareholders. Caleron brought a s. 240 application, requesting an order directing management to comply with s. 183 of the ABCA. Power J. analysed the transaction and interpreted s. 183 in determining that the transaction constituted a disposition of all or substantially all of the assets of the Corporation, other than in the ordinary course of business, and thus required a special resolution of all of the shareholders. In granting the order, Power J. noted at p. 52 that "[s]ection 240 gives the court broad discretion to grant orders to ensure compliance with the Articles of a corporation or the provisions of the Act." I agree with this holding.

It should further be noted that Griffiths J. in *Hill* made the following comment at para. 12:

> In my respectful view a shareholder under the authority of s. 261 is entitled to have the court examine an information circular to determine whether the information therein contained meets the requirements of the Act, even though such a determination will involve consideration of complex issues of fact and law.

Finally on this point, it has long been established that a superior court of record derives a broad general jurisdiction from its nature as a court of law. This jurisdiction is affirmed in the *Judicature Act*, R.S.A. 1980, c. J-1. Section 8 of that statute provides the following:

> 8 The Court in the exercise of its jurisdiction in every proceeding pending before it has power to grant and shall grant, either absolutely or on any reasonable terms and conditions that seem just to the Court, all remedies whatsoever to which any of

the parties thereto may appear to be entitled in respect of any and every legal or equitable claim properly brought forward by them in the proceeding, so that as far as possible all matters in controversy between the parties can be completely determined and all multiplicity of legal proceedings concerning those matters avoided.

In *80 Wellesley St. East Ltd. v. Fundy Bay Builders Ltd.*, [1972] 2 O.R. 280 Brooke J.A. for the Ontario Court of Appeal makes the following statement at p. 282:

As a superior Court of general jurisdiction, the Supreme Court of Ontario has all of the powers that are necessary to do justice between the parties. Except where provided specifically to the contrary, the Court's jurisdiction is unlimited and unrestricted in substantive law in civil matters.

The learned Justice then quoted with approval from *Re Michie Estate and City of Toronto et al.*, [1968] 1 O.R. 266 at 268, in which Stark J. observed:

It appears clear that the Supreme Court of Ontario has broad universal jurisdiction over all matters of substantive law unless the Legislature divests from this universal jurisdiction by legislation in unequivocal terms. The rule of law relating to the jurisdiction of superior Courts was laid down at least as early as 1667 in the case of *Peacock v. Bell and Kendall* (1667), 1 Wms. Saund. 73 at p. 74, 85 E.R. 84.

There are no unequivocal terms divesting this Court of its universal jurisdiction to rule on the validity of a corporation's by-laws, either in s. 240 or in any other section of the ABCA.

Based on the foregoing analysis, I conclude that this Court has the jurisdiction to rule on the validity of the by-law amendments and order compliance with them if it finds the by-law amendments to be valid.

B. Validity of the by-law amendments

The Respondent's argument that the only control shareholders have over the management of a corporation's affairs is their right to elect the board of directors, understates the expanded role of shareholders as a result of legislative reforms dating from the 1970s. The ABCA is modelled on the CBCA, which in turn was developed from a comprehensive report by R. Dickerson *et al.*, entitled *Proposals for a New Business Corporations Law for Canada* (Ottawa: Information Canada, 1971), better known as the Dickerson Report. This report propounded the innovative statutory division of powers model for corporate constitutions, and set out the respective powers of directors and shareholders. ...

... [S]hareholders have the power to amend by-laws, and that such amendments are effective upon their confirmation by ordinary resolution of the shareholders at a shareholders' meeting. On this point, D.H. Peterson states at para. 14.26:

A shareholder proposal to make, amend or repeal a by-law represents an assault on this statutory division of power. If upon presentation to the shareholders the by-law is approved by ordinary resolution, the by-law comes into force thereby circumventing the input of the directors altogether.

The rationale for conferring these powers on shareholders is found at para. 195 in vol. 1 of the Dickerson Report itself, as quoted by D.H. Peterson at para. 14.26:

Section [105] accordingly confers power upon shareholders not merely to sanction by-law changes proposed by the directors — subsection (2) — but also to initiate changes in the corporate structure: subsection (5)...In the result, this scheme recognizes the realities of corporate management by placing residual control of internal government where it belongs — with the shareholders — but giving the directors power to administer the corporation from day to day.

As to the general powers of shareholders, K.P. McGuinness, *The Law and Practice of Canadian Business Corporations* (Toronto: Butterworths, 1999), makes the following observations at pp. 911-12:

> [T]he OBCA and the CBCA have rejected the common law approach towards shareholder management, and the old common law position has now been substantially abrogated by statute in the case of business corporations. It may now be stated with some confidence that Canada — on paper, at least — has one of the most "democratic" corporate law regimes of any of the world's major industrial states (in the sense that it is responsive to shareholders holding a majority of voting shares). Under both the OBCA and the CBCA there are a number of different routes by which the shareholders can exercise control over the conduct of the business and affairs of the corporation ...

The obligations of directors and officers with respect to by-laws are clear from s. 117(2) of the ABCA, which states:

> 117(2) Every director and officer of a corporation shall comply with this Act, the regulations, articles, by-laws and any unanimous shareholder agreement.

The duty under this provision does not vary, regardless of whether the by-laws are initiated by directors or by shareholders. However, the Respondent argues such duty does not apply to by-laws that have the effect of amending the articles. It contends that the shareholders must not be permitted to circumvent the procedures prescribed by the ABCA for changing the articles, by passing by-laws that are ultra vices. Such procedures relevant to the present case are found in the following provisions of the ABCA:

> 169(1) Subject to subsection (2), a director or a shareholder who is entitled to vote at an annual meeting of shareholders may, in accordance with section 131, make a proposal to amend the articles .

> ...

> 170(1) The holders of shares of a class or, subject to subsection (2), of a series are entitled to vote separately as a class or series on a proposal to amend the articles to...

> (c) add, change or remove the rights, privileges, restrictions or conditions attached to the shares of that class...

> (4) A proposed amendment to the articles referred to in subsection (1) is adopted when the holders of the shares of each class or series entitled to vote separately on the amendment as a class or series have approved the amendment by special resolution.

Based on these provisions, the Respondent reasons that the proposed by-law amendments are ineffective because they were not approved by special resolutions of both the Class A and Class B shareholders, voting as separate classes.

The ABCA provides little guidance as to the vices of by-laws, and so it is necessary to consult the common law in this regard. It is trite law that a corporation's by-laws derive their authority from the articles, similar to regulations under a statute. K.P. McGuinness states the principle in the following terms at p. 123:

> The by-laws of a corporation are subordinate to the articles in the sense that the by-laws cannot confer powers that are excluded by or not conferred under the articles. If there is any inconsistency between the two, the articles will prevail and any purported alteration of the articles made by way of by-law is void to the extent of the inconsistency.

See also: *Ashbury v. Watson* (1885), 30 Ch. D. 376 (C.A.); *Re Good & Jacob Y. Shantz & Son Co.* (1910), 21 O.R. 153; aff'd 23 O.L.R. 554 (C.A.).

Counsel for the parties provided no case law to assist in the determination of whether the by-law amendments in the present case are in fact *ultra vices* the articles of the Corporation. Indeed, there appear to be no Canadian cases sufficiently similar on their facts to provide guidance on the question. However, the issue has been addressed more extensively in the U.S. courts and the facts of one U.S. case in particular are analogous to the essential facts of the present application.

In *I.P. Phillips and D.J. Buchler v. Insituform of North America Inc., et al.,* [1987] DE-QL 719, the Court of Chancery of Delaware ruled on the validity of certain amendments made to the by-laws of Insituform of North America Inc. ("INA"). The common stock of INA was divided into two classes having equal rights, powers and privileges, except that Class B shareholders were entitled to elect two thirds of the Board of Directors, while Class A shareholders were entitled to elect one third. The Class B shares passed into receivership as a result of some complex litigation, and the Board of Directors responded, *inter alia*, by passing the following by-law amendments: 1) quorum of the board is present only when the two directors elected by the Class A shareholders (the "A directors") are present, 2) the board may act only with the concurrence of a majority of the two A directors, and 3) the A directors and the Chairman of the Board constitute an executive committee, with power to call director and shareholder meetings.

The Court found the combined effect of the by-law amendments to be *ultra vires* the Certificate of Incorporation, and in its discretion, nullified them by reinstating the by-laws as they existed prior to those amendments. At para. 61, the Court states:

> [A] realistic evaluation leads to the conclusion that a fundamental shift in the allocation of power between the A shareholders and the B shareholders has taken place and that that new arrangement is inconsistent with what would have been the reasonable understanding of the effect of the provisions of the certificate.
>
> Moreover, consideration of these amendments must take into account the fact that these by-laws were adopted as a second line of defense against the exercise of power ...by the B shareholders. They were designed to equip the A class of stock with an effective veto over future board action.

In reaching its decision, the Court rejected the argument that the right to elect a majority of the board should not be equated with the right to control the board's action or the corporation; the duty of directors is to act in the best interests of the corporation, and they owe no special duty to the class electing them. The gist of this argument would appear to be that altering the power structure within the board of directors does not have the effect of altering shareholder rights. Such argument is even less persuasive in Alberta, given s. 117(4) of the ABCA, which states:

(4) In determining whether a particular transaction or course of action is in the best interests of the corporation, a director, if he is elected or appointed by the holders of a class or series of shares or by employees or creditors or a class of employees or creditors, may give special, but not exclusive, consideration to the interests of those who elected or appointed him.

As with Insituform, the by-law amendments in the present case assigning sole signing authority to Slater and requiring his presence at board meetings to constitute quorum, effectively give the director elected by the minority shareholders a veto power over future board action. Moreover, as with Insituform, there is nothing in the Corporation's articles conferring such a power on directors elected by the minority class of shareholders. The potency of such a power should not be understated, because its exercise can potentially paralyze the Corporation to its detriment (see *Paul T. Smith v. Atlantic Properties Inc.*, [1981] MA-QL 592 (Mass. Ct. App.), where a minority shareholder in a closely held corporation repeatedly exercised his veto power to prevent the corporation from declaring dividends, resulting in serious tax penalties).

The by-law amendments with respect to quorum and signing authority purport to confer powers that are not conferred under the articles of the Corporation. Furthermore, they have the effect of altering the rights and privileges allocated to the two classes of shareholders by the articles. Such alterations are not legal unless they are made in compliance with the procedures prescribed by s. 170 of the ABCA. Therefore, I find the by-law amendments with respect to quorum and signing authority to be *ultra vires* the articles and in violation of the ABCA, and declare them to be void and of no force and effect. In so ruling, I do not intervene lightly in the exercise of the shareholders' power to amend by-laws. However, equity requires the Court to intervene in the internal governance of a corporation when a clear case is made out for doing so. I find this to be such a case.

With respect to the other by-law amendments, however, I do not find them to be of the same kind or quality as those dealing with quorum and signing authority. The provisions requiring that 10 days written notice of directors' meetings be given, that directors must attend directors' meetings in person, and that directors' meetings be held at the registered office of the Corporation, do not have the effect of altering shareholder rights or the Corporation's structure of governance. They are not inconsistent with the Corporation's articles. However, if I am wrong, there is certainly no clear case made out in this regard that would warrant striking them down.

Thus, the question is raised as to whether the offending amendments may be severed from the balance of the by-law. K.P. McGuinness summarizes the general principles regarding severance at p. 129:

> Where there is a partial inconsistency between a by-law and applicable statute, it may be possible to sever the offending part of the by-law from the balance, so as to permit the balance to continue in force. In order for an offending provision to be severed from the by-law, the offending portion of the text must be capable of deletion in a single stroke, while leaving the rest of the text intelligible. The court will not re-write the by-law, for if it does, no severance is possible. More specifically, in deciding whether a particular provision is severable it is necessary to decide whether that provision deals with a distinct matter from the balance of the by-law, or whether it is one and entire with the balance of the bylaw — in which case it is not possible to sever.

See also, *Warren v. Superior Engravers Ltd.*, [1941] 1 D.L.R. 323 at 327 (Ont. C.A.).

The offending amendments in the present case deal with matters that are distinct and discreet in nature, and which are not integral to the by-law as a whole. Their deletion would not in any way affect the intelligibility of the remaining text. I therefore find the amendments with respect to quorum and signing authority to be severable from the balance of the by-law, and declare them so severed.

With respect to the other amendments passed by the shareholders at the Meeting, I am guided by two considerations. First, by-laws are void only to the extent that they are inconsistent with the articles or are in violation of the ABCA. Second, the legitimate exercise of shareholder power under the ABCA to amend by-laws is to be respected and endorsed. Therefore, I find the amendments with respect to notice, place, and attendance of directors' meetings to be valid and binding on the Corporation and its Board of Directors, and order the Corporation and its Board of Directors to comply with these amendments and to be restrained from contravening them. I further find that the two Directors' Meetings held on February 3 and 24, 2000, were not properly constituted, in that they violated the provisions of the Corporation's by-laws with respect to notice and place of such meetings. I therefore declare them to be a nullity and any business transacted at those meetings is of no force and effect.

VII. CONCLUSION

I direct all directors of the Corporation, and anyone acing in their stead, to comply with the by-laws of the Corporation that I have ruled to be in force and effect. Costs may be spoken to.

NOTES

Note that while evidence of shareholder approval is not decisive, judicial approval is required to discontinue the action, and security for costs cannot be required (C.B.C.A., s. 242). Section 248 of the C.B.C.A. says that "the application may be made in a summary manner". What does this mean? Note the constitutional problem.

Can the compliance and restraining order section be invoked to enforce compliance with a unanimous shareholder agreement? How, and against whom? What would you recommend to a shareholder who was setting up a unanimous shareholder agreement and wanted to ensure the section could be applied? See *Duha Printers (Western) Ltd. v. R.*, [1998] S.C.J. No. 41, [1998] 1 S.C.R. 795.

Why is this remedy made available to "a complainant or a creditor"?

How does the compliance and restraining order differ in effect from the statutory contract of the English-model corporate constitution? Which do you prefer?

D. THE OPPRESSION REMEDY

1. Introduction

Most Canadian jurisdictions have followed the C.B.C.A. lead and enacted an "oppression" remedy. There is a relatively large volume of cases in Canada since the statutory change. One reason for the volume is lack of theory: the remedy is relatively new to Canada. Moreover, precedent is not particularly helpful: the remedy is invoked in a wide variety of circumstances and judges are statutorily empowered to do whatever they want in each case.

The provisions of the C.B.C.A. are indicative of the scope of the oppression remedy in Canada. Its provisions read as follows:

241(1) A complainant may apply to a court for an order under this section.

(2) If, on application under subsection (1), the court is satisfied that in respect of a corporation or any of its affiliates

(*a*)   any act or omission of the corporation or any of its affiliates effects a result,

(*b*)   the business or affairs of the corporation or any of its affiliates are or have been carried on or conducted in a manner, or

(*c*)   the powers of the directors of the corporation or any of its affiliates are or have been exercised in a manner

that is oppressive or unfairly prejudicial to or that unfairly disregards the interests of any security holder, creditor, director or officer, the court may make an order to rectify the matters complained of.

(3) In connection with an application under this section, the court may make any interim or final order it thinks fit including, without limiting the generality of the foregoing, [sub-paras (*a*) – (*n*) set out specific orders a judge might want to issue].

(4) If an order made under this section directs amendment of the articles or by-laws of a corporation,

(*a*)   the directors shall forthwith comply with subsection 191(4); and

(*b*)   no other amendment to the articles or by-laws shall be made without the consent of the court, until a court otherwise orders.

(5) A shareholder is not entitled to dissent under section 190 if an amendment to the articles is effected under this section.

(6) A corporation shall not make a payment to a shareholder under paragraph (3)(*f*) or (*g*) if there are reasonable grounds for believing that

(*a*)   the corporation is or would after that payment be unable to pay its liabilities as they become due; or

(*b*)   the realizable value of the corporation's assets would thereby be less than the aggregate of its liabilities.

(7) An applicant under this section may apply in the alternative for an order under section 214.

The oppression remedy will be invoked most often when the complainant has all of the equities and few if any legalities on his side. Does the extract from the C.B.C.A. reproduced above support this statement?

2. The Meaning of Oppression

While the statutory remedy of oppression has been entrenched in various Canadian corporate law statutes, it has been left to the courts to determine the *indicia* of oppression, including who must be oppressed to trigger the remedy.

(a) Defining the Standard

WESTFAIR FOODS LTD. v. WATT

[1991] A.J. No. 321, 5 B.L.R. (2d) 160 (C.A.)

[The appellant corporation had two classes of shares. The class A non-voting shares were entitled to a fixed preferential dividend of $2 per share and were entitled to share in surplus assets, including retained earnings, upon liquidation. For many years the appellant had paid the fixed dividend and retained a substantial part of its earnings. In 1985 it changed its policy and after paying the fixed dividend it paid all its net annual earnings to the single common shareholder. At trial the court concluded that the new policy was oppressive in that it disregarded the interests of the class A shareholders to share in future expansion.]

Kerans J.A. (in dismissing the appeal, at pp. 165-69): — I turn then to the substantial rights conferred by the provision. Obviously, they turn on effect not intent. Equally obviously, they govern all the activities of the corporation. The rights conferred upon shareholders are that they, at any time and in any way during their relationship with the company, are to be insulated from anything oppressive, unfairly prejudicial or that unfairly disregards their interests. For the relations among shareholders, this is a major modification of majority rule.

In my view, the provisions were and remain a compendious way for Parliament to say to the courts that the classes mentioned in the Act are to be treated *fairly* in the sense of *justly* by corporations. For example, both parties cite and rely on *Ebrahimi v. Wesbourne Galleries*, [1973] A.C. 360, [1972] 2 W.L.R. 1289, [1972] 2 All E.R. 492 (H.L.). Lord Wilberforce there said at p. 500: "there is room in company law for recognition of the fact that behind it, or amongst it, there are individuals, with rights, expectations and obligations inter se which are not necessarily submerged in the company structure".

I agree with a similar sentiment by McDonald J. in *First Edmonton Place Ltd. v. 315888 Alta. Ltd.* (1988), 60 Alta. L.R. (2d) 122, 40 B.L.R. 28 (Q.B.), at p. 148 (Alta. L.R.).

I cannot put elastic adjectives like "unfair", "oppressive" or "prejudicial" into watertight compartments. In my view, this repetition of overlapping ideas is only an expression of anxiety by Parliament that one or the other might be given a restrictive meaning. I am grateful for the history in the *First Edmonton Place* case. Recent changes adding words like "unfairly disregard" reflect just that concern. See Dickerson, Proposals for a New Business Corporations Law for Canada (Ottawa: Information Canada, 1971), p. 163, where the mischief was reported to be "the self-imposed judicial qualifications that have limited the application ... and ... cast considerable doubt upon the effectiveness of the original provisions."

The irony is that too much repetition encourages rather than eliminates narrowing arguments. For example, in Peterson *Shareholder Remedies in Canada* (Toronto: Butterworths, 1989), para. 18.60, the author contends that "unfairly disregards" implies *some* "disregarding" is fair! I reject that kind of parsing. The original words, like the new additions, command the courts to exercise their duty "broadly and liberally", as this court has already said about the nearly identical Alberta law in *Keho Holdings Ltd. v. Noble* (1987), 52 Alta. L.R. (2d) 195, 38 D.L.R. (4th) 368, 78 A.R. 131 (C.A.).

Having concluded that the words charge the courts to impose the obligation of fairness on the parties, I must admit that the admonition offers little guidance to the public, and Parliament has left elucidation to us. I have elsewhere said that I take this sort of indirection as legislative delegation: see *Transalta Utilities Corp. v. Alta. (Public Utilities Bd.)* (1986), 43 Alta. L.R. (2d) 171, 21 Admin. L.R. 1, 68 A.R. 171 (C.A.), at p. 180 (Alta. L.R.).

We fail in that duty of elucidation, I think, if we merely say "this is fair" or "that is not fair" without ever explaining why we think this or that is fair. Thus I, and I dare say others, am not much helped by cases and comments that simply announce that I am to enforce "fair play" or "fair dealing": see, for example, Dickerson, op. cit., para. 48.

On the other hand, I do not understand that the delegation of this duty permits a judge to impose personal standards of fairness. Let me illustrate what is probably obvious by two extreme examples. A judge who firmly believes in the virtues of unrestricted private enterprise might say that fairness requires that people protect themselves to their best capacity, and that the courts not protect those who fail to protect themselves. On the other hand, a judge who firmly believes that private property is a trust held for the benefit of society as a whole might say that what is fair is what best benefits society.

The role of a judge in our society limits the impulses of both my mythical judges. We must not make rules unless we can tie them to values that seem to have gained wide acceptance. We do that largely by testing any proposed rule against other legal rules, which by long tradition seem accepted. In short we seek precedent, or we seek to argue from what we consider to be principles adopted in precedent. So, in *Keho*, this court relied upon precedent in other situations where courts were asked to decide what was "just and equitable."

I will not attempt to catalogue all the rules generated by the words in the statute. For example, the courts have imposed the duty on directors to protect the interests of all shareholders, not just those who elect them. I will later deal with that rule. The authorities also impose upon the majority interest the obligation not to use their electoral power to profit themselves at the expense of minority shareholders. The principal complaint here does not engage that rule. The complaint is not by a minority who has been outvoted. It is by an entire class of shares in competition with another class of shares.

It is said for the shareholders that yet another rule exists. This is that the directors must have due regard for, and deal fairly with, the "interests" of all shareholders. I have concern about overuse of the word *interests*. This example serves to express it: a thief is very interested in my watch, and will get it if he can. A law about fairness will not, however, show any respect for his interest. The real question is whether the law should accept his obvious interest in financial gain as, in all the circumstances, one that *deserves* protection. I do not accept that all ambition to acquire property deserves protection. I do accept that our tradition is that a *hope* for profit, as opposed to a mere *desire*, sometimes deserves protection.

One deserving case is where the person to whom the profit will go has *nourished* that hope. The company and the shareholders entered voluntarily, not by duty or chance, into a relationship. Our guides are the rules in other contexts, such as contract law, equity, and partnership law, where the courts have also considered just rules to govern voluntary relationships. In very general terms, one clear principle that emerges is that we regulate voluntary relationships by regard to the expectations raised in the mind of a party *by the word or deed of the other*, and which the first party ordinarily would realize it was encouraging by its words and deeds. This is what we call reasonable expectations, or expectations deserving of protection. Regard for them is a constant theme, albeit variously expressed, running through the cases on this section or its like elsewhere. I emphasize that *all* the words and deeds of the parties are relevant to an assessment of reasonable expectations, not necessarily only those consigned to paper, and not necessarily only those made when the relationship first arose.

I do not for a moment suggest that that analysis about expectations deserving protection is the sole basis for rules under the statute. I think, for example, of totally unforeseen windfalls or calamities. This is not such a case, but I dare say that even in those cases the expectations of the parties are a sound starting point. And the test will always be helpful in cases where mere interests collide.

The test then is always facts-specific, and cases decided on other facts offer only a limited guide. Unfortunately, no other reported case offers the same facts as this. …

NOTES AND QUESTIONS

Ultimately, the court found that certain procedural matters amounted to oppression and upheld the order for the corporation to purchase the class A shares.

Does this case define the standard to be applied or does it opt for a general "unfairness" standard? How does it compare to the case below?

DELUCE HOLDINGS INC. v. AIR CANADA

[1992] O.J. No. 2382, 98 D.L.R. (4th) 509 (Gen. Div.)

R.A. Blair J.: — There are competing "stay" motions before me. They raise interesting questions concerning the interplay between the broad "oppression" remedy made available to minority shareholders by statute and the very clear "arbitration" direction set by the legislature in the *Arbitration Act, 1991*, S.O. 1991, c. 17. In what circumstances, if at all, may "oppressive" conduct operate to undermine what would otherwise be a contractually arbitrable issue, enforceable by that mechanism in accordance with the provisions of the *Arbitration Act, 1991*, and justify the postponement of the arbitration procedure pending determination of the threshold "oppression" issue?

Background and overview

Air Canada and Deluce Holdings Inc. ("Deluceco") are indirectly the 75% and 25% shareholders, respectively, in Air Ontario Inc. Their interests are held through a numbered company, 152160 Canada Inc. ("the holding company"). Air Ontario Inc. ("Air Ontario") is a regional airline operating out of London, Ontario. It serves as a "connector" airline, feeding passengers into the overall Air Canada network.

Air Canada acquired its controlling interest in Air Ontario in 1986 when, in a complicated transaction, it bought the controlling interest of the members of the

Deluce family in Air Ontario Limited and Austin Airways, and the minority interest of other shareholders in Air Ontario Limited. Air Ontario Limited and Austin Airways were subsequently merged to form Air Ontario Inc.

Air Canada has seven "nominees" on the Air Ontario board of directors; Deluceco has three.

At the outset of the relationship the plan and the arrangement seemed straightforward. The members of the Deluce family — William Deluce, in particular — would be responsible for the management and operations of Air Ontario, and Air Canada would maintain its distance from the day-to-day operations of the regional airline. Subsequently, however, Air Canada's views on the suitability of this type of relationship between it and its regional connector changed.

In April, 1991, Air Canada decided to acquire 100% ownership of its connectors. The issue of whether or not it acted legitimately in carrying out this quite legitimate corporate objective, lies at the heart of these proceedings.

A unanimous shareholders agreement ("the Agreement") governs the relationship between Air Canada and Deluceco as shareholders in the holding company which owns Air Ontario Inc. One of the provisions in the Agreement gives Air Canada the option to acquire the Deluceco interest upon the termination of employment of the last of Stanley Deluce (the father) and William Deluce by Air Ontario or the holding company. Another calls for arbitration in the event of a dispute over the value of the shares. It is the triggering of this latter provision which is the subject-matter of the "oppression" action that has been commenced on behalf of Deluceco.

In February, 1989, the two-year employment contract of Stanley Deluce as chairman of Air Ontario came to an end and was not renewed. He was replaced as chairman by Roger Linder, a retiring Air Canada executive. In October, 1991, the employment of William Deluce was terminated.

Deluceco alleges that Air Canada improperly exercised its majority control of the board of directors of the holding company to terminate Mr. Deluce's employment as vice-chairman and C.E.O. of Air Ontario, and that it did so for the sole purpose of enabling it to buy out the Deluceco minority interest in the holding company, and thus in Air Ontario. This was done, so the argument goes, as part of Air Canada's corporate strategy to acquire 100% control of the regional air carriers associated with it and, accordingly, to be able to deal with them without the constraints imposed by the bother of minority shareholders.

Deluceco says this conduct is "oppressive" — using that term in the broad manner by which the remedy granted under s. 241 of the Canada *Business Corporations Act*, R.S.C. 1985, c. C-44 ("the C.B.C.A.") is commonly referred — and that the purported exercise of the arbitration clause is therefore of no force and effect. In other words, so the submission goes, the action calls into question the very underpinning of the arbitration proceeding, and the arbitration should not be allowed to go ahead.

Air Canada says, on the other hand, that under the provisions of the Agreement, Air Canada is entitled, "upon the termination of" the employment of Bill Deluce, to exercise its call on the minority shares of Deluceco. If there is no agreement as to the price for the shares, the agreement requires the issue of the fair market of those shares to be arbitrated. The terms of the Agreement are clear, Air Canada argues, and the dispute which the parties have thus agreed to submit to arbitration must go to arbitration by virtue of the provisions of the *Arbitration Act, 1991*.

Therefore, submits Air Canada, the arbitration must be allowed to proceed and Deluceco's action and application must be stayed, at least to the extent that they purport to deal with matters that the parties have agreed to submit to arbitration. For Deluceco, of course, the proposed solution is completely the reverse.

...

Central to a resolution of these competing claims is an analysis of the circumstances leading up to the termination of the employment of William Deluce by the Air Ontario board of directors in October, 1991.

...

[**Justice Blair** set out some details of the clash in management styles, and continued.]

While I have no reason to doubt their belief in this regard, expressed now, I none the less have some difficulty in concluding, on the materials before me, that the factors outlined above were the motivating ones at the time of the termination. Only a trial, whenever that takes place, can thresh these matters out adequately, and I therefore confine my remarks in this regard to what is necessary to explain the reasons prompting me to come to this conclusion.

A review of some of the chronology is a helpful starting point.

[**Justice Blair** set out the details of what happened between the spring and fall of 1991. Of particular note are the minutes of a board meeting of May 21, 1991, reproduced immediately below.]

What was said regarding Mr. Deluce, as reflected in the minutes of that board meeting, is instructive. I note the following:

> Roger Linder expressed the appreciation of the Board *for the excellent stewardship provided by William Deluce* as President and Chief Executive Officer of the Company. Mr. Linder confirmed that William Deluce *had done a superb job in directing the Company throughout his tenure* as President and expressed the thanks of the Board for his efforts.

(Emphasis added.)

Not to be outdone, Mr. Aleong,

> ... advised the Board that he was *very impressed with the professional and pragmatic approach* taken by William Deluce in managing the Company.

(Emphasis added.)

...

Two meetings of the Air Ontario board followed in which the final coup de grace was administered and the groundwork laid for the triggering of Air Canada's option to purchase the Deluceco interest in Air Ontario. Again, the minutes of the meetings provide an instructive reflection of what went on. Mr. Aleong has deposed that "the reasons for termination are as set out in the Minutes" (Aleong affidavit, para. 95). Two "reasons" only were advanced. Neither of them relate to any of the concerns apparently harboured in a growing fashion over the years by Air Canada's representatives about Mr. Deluce's management style or the performance of Air Ontario and its management.

The first reason was that Mr. Deluce's employment was too costly and that, while his employment contract was to expire in February, 1992, Mr. Aleong preferred that any costs associated with the termination of Mr. Deluce be taken in

1991. When it was pointed out to him that the same result could be achieved by accruing the cost in 1991, however, he acknowledged that such was the case.

The second reason was that Mr. Deluce had a conflict of interest as an officer of both Air Ontario and Deluceco. This conflict, however, had existed with everyone's knowledge since the inception of Air Canada's acquisition of its 75% interest and, indeed, was built into the shareholder relationship.

Given the realities of what was going on at the time between these parties and the realities of Air Canada's pending implementation of its changed corporate objective, one might be forgiven a certain scepticism about accepting the foregoing two reasons as those which lay behind the termination of Mr. Deluce's employment. One might also be forgiven a similar doubt about the notion that Air Canada's concerns regarding Mr. Deluce's management style, regarding his expenses, regarding Air Ontario's performance, and regarding the Dryden crash were what triggered this action by the Air Ontario board at the instance of Air Canada's nominees.

In this respect, Mr. Aleong is reported in the minutes of the October 21st meeting as having advised as follows:

> Conrad Aleong advised the meeting that anything he had to say in support of a Resolution he proposed to make with respect to William S. Deluce had nothing to do with Mr. Deluce personally *and, in particular, nothing to do with the performance of William S. Deluce in his capacity as an officer and director of the Company.* Mr. Aleong stated that he had the highest regard for Mr. Deluce.

(Emphasis added.)

Mr. Aleong attempts to explain the language in the minutes of these two meetings and the May meeting as nothing more than "the normal good things [one says] about people when they're leaving a company or when they are being relieved of a position". He said that he and Mr. Linder were being careful not to criticize Mr. Deluce's performance because Air Canada and Deluceco were entering into negotiations and he did not want any negative comments to affect those negotiations.

I find this hard to accept, in view of the clear and unequivocal language which the minutes reflect. It is readily apparent why the Air Canada representatives would not want to offend Mr. Deluce, if at all possible, in the face of pending negotiations. None the less, if Mr. Deluce's management performance and the financial and safety performance of Air Ontario under his stewardship were as uppermost in the minds of Mr. Aleong and the other Air Canada board representatives as counsel have submitted, I am sure that less categorically positive testimony to Mr. Deluce could have been crafted and still have met the requirements of corporate niceties.

One need look no further than Air Canada's own internal documentation regarding its connector restructuring plan for further confirmation of what appears to be the effective motivation for the termination of Mr. Deluce's employment. The proposal itself, prepared by Mr. Aleong and others and presented to the Air Canada executive in November, 1990, speaks of "the shared view at Air Canada … that today's 'separate companies' approach is financially inefficient", and of "a growing view that the connectors are not effectively serving AC's interest". The phraseology "as an instrument of the parent" is used frequently in relation to Air Canada's plans for the connectors, both in this document and in others.

With regard to Air Ontario, the plan for effecting this corporate objective is set out succinctly in one of the transparencies used by the Air Canada planners in explaining the proposal. Entitled "Connector Restructuring", and under the heading "Corporate Ownership", it said:

— There are provisions in the shareholders and employment agreements to achieve minority interest buyouts.

— *Strategy for 152160 Canada Inc. (the holding company) would be to terminate Mr. Bill Deluce's employment contract, giving Air Canada the right to call Deluceco's 25% interest.*

— Contract cancellation cost approximately $400,000.

(Emphasis added.)

I have little difficulty in concluding, on the materials before me and for the purposes of these motions, therefore, that the operating motivation triggering the termination of Mr. Deluce's employment with Air Ontario was the foregoing strategy, designed to enable Air Canada to exercise its call on Deluceco's 25% interest in furtherance of its goal of acquiring 100% ownership of Air Ontario and the other regional connectors. Certainly, it was the primary motivation. Any consideration of the negatives of Mr. Deluce's management style and performance, or of the safety and performance concerns at Air Ontario, or of the interests of Air Ontario generally, were at best in the remote background.

There is no suggestion that Air Canada's changed corporate objective of acquiring 100% equity ownership of its regional airline and making the connectors "instruments of the parent" in order "to achieve an efficient, integrated, effective and profitable domestic feeder system ... all with uncompromising safety", was anything but a perfectly legitimate corporate objective.

Two questions arise out of what transpired, however. The first question is whether Air Canada was entitled to utilize its majority position on the Air Ontario board, as it seems to have done, for the predominant purpose of carrying out that objective or whether such conduct was "oppressive" of the minority. If the latter is the case, the second question is whether such "oppression" undercuts the apparent right of Air Ontario, on the face of the provisions of the unanimous shareholders agreement, to terminate Mr. Deluce for any reason, thus triggering Air Canada's call on the Deluceco shares.

The law

"Oppression"

In my view, the conduct of Air Canada and its nominee directors, as outlined above, could be found, after a trial, to constitute "oppression" of Deluceco's interests as a minority shareholder in Air Ontario. While the conduct may not constitute "oppression" in the classic sense of conduct which is "lacking in probity" or "burdensome, harsh and wrongful", it may none the less be conduct which is "unfairly prejudicial" to or which "unfairly disregards" the interests of Deluceco as a minority shareholder, contrary to s. 241 of the C.B.C.A. The authorities make it clear that this distinction exists and that the latter sort of conduct constitutes grounds which are "less rigorous" than oppression: see *Mason v. Intercity Properties Ltd.* (1987), 38 D.L.R. (4th) 681 at pp. 684-5, 67 B.L.R. 6,

59 O.R. (2d) 631 (C.A.), per Blair J.A.; *Re Jermyn Street Turkish Baths Ltd.*, [1971] 3 All E.R. 184 (C.A.).

...

Much was made in argument by counsel for Air Canada about the plain wording of the Agreement which says, simply, that "upon the termination of the employment" of Mr. Deluce, Air Canada's call upon the Deluceco shares becomes operative. No cause is required for termination by its terms. There are no qualifiers to the circumstances surrounding the termination which may lead to the exercise of the option. Parol evidence is not admissible, counsel submit, to alter or vary or add to the clear and unambiguous language of the Agreement.

Equally as much was made in argument by counsel for Deluceco about the nature of the relationship between Air Canada and Deluceco, as set out in the Agreement. While that relationship is not a partnership in law, counsel submitted that it is more than simply a relationship of employment coupled with an option on the part of Air Canada to purchase the Deluceco shares by bringing about the termination of that employment. The relationship is akin to a partnership, they argue, premised on the sort of mutual trust and confidence which characterizes such a relationship, and on a mutual expectation, as stated in their factum, that,

(a) both Air Canada and Deluceco would at all times act in good faith and with a view to the best interests of Air Ontario and [the holding company]; and,

(b) Air Ontario would be managed by William Stanley Deluce ("Bill Deluce") and other members of the Deluce family.

...

Counsel for Deluceco rely upon a number of provisions in the unanimous shareholders agreement to emphasize their characterization of the relationship, ...

Section 2.03 of the Agreement clearly states that the relationship is not that of agent or partner. It is equally clear from ... other provisions of the Agreement ... however, that the parties have bound themselves to act, and to cause their nominees to act, in good faith and in the best interests of Air Ontario, and with a view to facilitating the implementation of the Agreement. In addition, of course, a director has a statutory duty, under s. 122 of the C.B.C.A. to act in good faith and with a view to the best interests of the corporation.

I have considered the provisions of the unanimous shareholders agreement as a whole ... I have attempted, as I must, to ascertain the intentions of the parties from those provisions. I am satisfied, having done so, that it was not the intention of the parties to permit Air Canada to trigger its call on the Deluceco shares at will by causing its nominees on the Air Ontario board to terminate Mr. Deluce's employment for that predominant purpose.

In my opinion, only a termination effected for the purpose of promoting the best interests of Air Ontario — for whatever reason — can constitute a "termination" within the meaning of the Agreement such as to trigger Air Canada's right to call the Deluceco shares. Having regard to the terms of the Agreement, Deluceco had a reasonable expectation as shareholder, I believe, that, in the absence of the termination of Bill Deluce's employment for reasons having to do with interests of Air Ontario or even in the absence of the non-renewal of his employment contract for similar reasons, the management/ shareholder relationship between Air Canada and the members of the Deluce family would remain as envisaged in the Agreement.

Cases dealing with oppression remedy situations have emphasized the distinction between the strict "legal rights" of shareholders and their "interests". For instance, in *Westfair Foods Ltd. v. Watt* (1990), 48 B.L.R. 43, [1990] 4 W.W.R. 685, 73 Alta. L.R. (2d) 326 (Q.B.); affirmed 79 D.L.R. (4th) 48, 5 B.L.R. (2d) 160, [1991] 4 W.W.R. 695 (Alta. C.A.), Moore C.J.Q.B. stated at p. 59:

> An examination of the leading cases dealing with the C.B.C.A., and in particular s. 241, is worthwhile. In enacting s. 241, Parliament obviously intended that strict attention should be paid to the *interests* of all shareholders, not just the legal *rights* of shareholders.

(Emphasis in original.)

Mr. Justice Farley elaborated on this distinction in *820099 Ontario Inc. v. Harold E. Ballard Ltd.* (1991), 3 B.L.R. (2d) at p. 123, 25 A.C.W.S. (3d) 853 (Ont. Ct. (Gen. Div.)), by commenting on the connection between shareholder "interests" and shareholder "expectations". At pp. 185-6 he said:

> Shareholder interests would appear to be intertwined with shareholder expectations. It does not appear to me that the shareholder expectations which are to be considered are those that a shareholder has as his own individual "wish list". They must be expectations which could be said to have been (or ought to have been considered as) part of the compact of the shareholders. ...

Speaking for the Court of Appeal for Ontario in *Ferguson v. Imax Systems Corp.* (1983), 150 D.L.R. (3d) 718, 43 O.R. (2d) 128, 21 A.C.W.S. (2d) 443, Brooke J.A. stated at p. 727:

> But s. 234 [the predecessor to the present s. 241 of the C.B.C.A.] must not be regarded as being simply a codification of the common law. Today one looks to the section when considering the interests of the minority shareholders and the section should be interpreted broadly to carry out its purpose: see the *Interpretation Act*, R.S.C. 1970, c. I-23, s. 11. Accordingly, when dealing with a close corporation, the court may consider the relationship between the shareholders and not simply legal rights as such. In addition the court must consider the bona fides of the corporate transaction in question to determine whether the act of the corporation or directors effects a result which is oppressive or unfairly prejudicial to the minority shareholder. Counsel has referred us to a number of decisions. They establish primarily that each case turns on its own facts. What is oppressive or unfairly prejudicial in one case may not necessarily be so in the slightly different setting of another.

Under s. 122 of the C.B.C.A. directors have a duty, amongst other things, (a) to act honestly and in good faith with a view to the best interests of the corporation, and (b) to comply with any unanimous shareholders agreement. In considering whether or not the directors have complied with these obligations in a given situation more is required than a mere assertion of good faith on the part of the directors. There will almost always be a tension between the director's position as a director of the corporation in question and the director's position as a shareholder or the nominee of a shareholder. Where an issue arises, hindsight and after-the-fact rationalizations all too naturally make it easy for the directors to believe that they were, indeed, acting for the benefit of the corporation. As I have indicated, I have no doubt that Mr. Aleong and Mr. Linder now believe, genuinely, that they were doing so in these circumstances.

All of the facts must be considered, however. I agree with Farley J.'s conclusion in *Ballard*, *supra*, at p. 176, that when assessing the directors' conduct in relation to the s. 122 duty to act in good faith with a view to the best interests of the corporation, "[t]he question is, what was it the directors had uppermost in their minds after a reasonable analysis of the situation" (emphasis in original). I also agree with the view expressed at p. 178 of the same decision, that even if, after a proper analysis of the situation, the directors may be said to have acted in good faith, as required by s. 122 of the C.B.C.A., the result of such action may still be such that it "oppresses" the interests of the minority shareholder in a fashion which brings the "oppression remedy" section (s. 241) into play.

...

In *Ballard*, Farley J. summed up the directors' obligations in respect of these competing shareholder interests as follows, at pp. 171-2:

> It seems to me that while it would be appropriate for a director to consider the individual desires of one or more various shareholders (particularly his "appointing" shareholder) in order to come up with a plan for the operation of a corporation, it would be inappropriate for that director (or directors) to only consider the interests of certain shareholders and to either ignore the others or worse still act in a way detrimental to their interests. The safe way to avoid this problem is to have the directors act in the best interests of the corporation (and have the shareholders derive their benefit from a "better" corporation).

> It may well be that the corporate life of a nominee director who votes against the interest of his "appointing" shareholder will be neither happy nor long. However, the role that any director must play (whether or not a nominee director) is that he must act in the best interests of the corporation. If the interests of the corporation (and indirectly the interests of the shareholders as a whole) require that the director vote in a certain way, *it must be the way that he conscientiously believes after a reasonable review is the best for the corporation.*

(Emphasis added.)

As I have indicated, the evidence here strongly supports a conclusion that, in causing the Air Ontario board to terminate the employment of Mr. Deluce, the Air Canada nominees were acting to carry out an Air Canada agenda and made little, if any, analysis of what was in the best interests of Air Ontario. Whether, had they done so, such an analysis might have yielded sufficient reasons from Air Ontario's perspective to carry out the act of termination, is not the point. Not only was there no "reasonable analysis of the situation" from that perspective, the question which was uppermost in the minds of the directors was to effect Air Canada's newly developed corporate objective, it would appear.

I am satisfied that such conduct could be found, at law, to be unfairly prejudicial to and to have unfairly disregarded the interests of Deluceco as a minority shareholder, as those interests are set out in the unanimous shareholders agreement.

...

The court has a very broad discretionary power under the oppression remedy legislation to select a remedy appropriate to the situation at hand. Its mandate is to "make any interim or final order it thinks fit". This discretion must be exercised in accordance with judicial principles, of course, and within the overall parameters of corporate law. ... Courts are prepared to be creative and flexible in fashioning remedies to fit the case when called upon to apply this broad remedy.

...

... I have already concluded that Air Canada's conduct in these circumstances may be found to have been "oppressive" to Deluceco. It follows, in my view, that to allow Air Canada to take advantage of that oppression, in the meantime, and forge ahead with its plan to dislodge Deluceco from Air Ontario in accordance with Air Canada's impugned agenda may also be oppressive. It would, in any event, be "unjust".

...

If Deluceco is right in its contention regarding the "oppressive" nature of Air Canada's conduct, Deluceco is entitled to remain in its position as a shareholder while these matters are being resolved. It has rights in that capacity and ought not to be deprived of those rights at the whim of the alleged oppressor until the issue has been determined.

For all of these reasons I am satisfied that the proper disposition of the stay motions before me is to stay the arbitration proceeding that has been instituted by Air Canada and to allow the Deluceco action and application to proceed. ...

...

In the result, then, Deluceco's motion to stay the arbitration proceeding is allowed and Air Canada's motions to stay the Deluceco action and application are dismissed. ...

[A discussion of a motion to strike portions of the statement of claim is omitted.]

NOTES AND QUESTIONS

Several cases have attempted to establish standards for the application of the oppression remedy. Does the following statement of Blair J. in *Naneff v. Con-Crete Holdings Ltd.*, [1993] O.J. No. 1756, 11 B.L.R. (2d) 218 at 245 (Gen. Div.) assist in defining the standard?

I turn now to a brief review of the provisions of subs. 248(2) of the OBCA — the "oppression remedy" section, and some of the principles which have evolved in case law in relation to the remedy it provides. Subsection 248(2) reads as follows:

(2) Where, upon an application under subsection (1), the court is satisfied that in respect of a corporation or any of its affiliates,

    (*a*) any act or omission of the corporation or any of its affiliates effects or threatens to effect a result;

    (*b*) the business or affairs of the corporation or any of its affiliates are, have been or are threatened to be carried on or conducted in a manner; or

    (*c*) the powers of the directors of the corporation or any of its affiliates are, have been or are threatened to be exercised in a manner,

that is oppressive or unfairly prejudicial to or that unfairly disregards the interests of any security holder, creditor, director or officer of the corporation, the court may make an order to rectify the matters complained of.

The powers of the court when such a finding is made are very broad. Essentially, the court "may make any ... order it thinks fit," acting judicially as it must. In addition to this wide-sweeping jurisdiction, but without limiting their generality, there are 14 types of relief specifically listed. Citing the decision of Blair J.A. in *Mason v. Intercity Properties Ltd.*, [1987] O.J. No. 448, 59 O.R. (2d) 631 at 636 (C.A.), Farley J. made the following remark in *820099 Ontario Inc. v. Harold E. Ballard Ltd.*, [1991] O.J. No. 1082, 3 B.L.R. (2d) 113 at 181 (Div. Ct.):

> I too feel that s. 247(3) [now s. 248(3)] gives the court tremendous latitude. Subject to being concerned about the interfering as little as possible (see *Explo Syndicate v. Explo Inc.*, unreported, (June 29, 1989), Gravely L.J.S.C. (Ont. H.C.) and *Re Sabex Internationale Ltée* (1979), 6 B.L.R. 65 (Que. S.C.) *infra*), a judge should be able to use his [or her] ingenuity to effect the remedy most suitable to the situation.

Evidence of bad faith or want of probity is not essential to ground a finding of oppression: *Brant Investments Ltd. v. KeepRite Inc.*, [1991] O.J. No. 683, 3 O.R. (3d) 289 at 302-07 (C.A.).

A strong theme running through the authorities dealing with the oppression remedy is its emphasis on the protection of reasonable shareholders' expectations in the context of the shareholders' corporate relationship. Justice Farley dealt with this aspect of the remedy in *Ballard* as well. At p. 185 (B.L.R.) of his reasons he said:

> Shareholder interests would appear to be intertwined with shareholder expectations. It does not appear to me that the shareholder expectations which are to be considered are those that a shareholder has as his own individual "wish list." They must be expectations which could be said to have been (or ought to have been considered as) part of the compact of the shareholders. ...

Lord Wilberforce (in *Ebrahimi v. Westbourne Galleries Ltd.*, [1972] 2 All E.R. 492 (H.L.)) went on to enshrine shareholder expectations as the guiding principle of statute-based judicial intervention, saying:

> Acts which, in law, are valid exercises of powers conferred by the articles may nevertheless be entirely outside what can fairly be regarded as having been in the contemplation of the parties when they became members of the company.

Lord Wilberforce also made the following comments in *Ebrahimi* (at p. 499):

> My Lords, in my opinion these authorities represent a sound and rational development of the law which should be endorsed. The foundation of it all lies in the words "just and equitable" and, if there is any respect in which some of the cases may be open to criticism, it is that the courts may sometimes have been too timorous in giving them full force. The words are a recognition of the fact that a limited company is more than a mere judicial entity, with a personality in law of its own: that there is room in company law for recognition of the fact that behind it, or amongst it, there are individuals, with rights, expectations and obligations inter se which are not necessarily submerged in the company structure. That structure is defined by the Companies Act 1948 and by the articles of association by which shareholders agree to be bound. In most companies and in most contexts, this definition is sufficient and exhaustive, equally so whether the company is large or small. The "just and equitable" provision does not, as the respondents suggest, entitle one party to disregard the obligation he assumes by entering a company, nor the court to dispense him from it. It does, as equity always does, enable the court to

subject the exercise of legal rights to equitable considerations; considerations, that is, of a personal character arising between one individual and another, which may make it unjust, or inequitable, to insist on legal rights, or to exercise them in a particular way.

(Emphasis added.)

The decision of Blair J. in *Naneff* was varied in part by the Ontario Divisional Court (1994), 19 O.R. (3d) 691 and a further appeal to the Ontario Court of Appeal was allowed. The decision of the Court of Appeal is set out in Section D.3, "Remedies", below.

Other relevant assessments of the standard for oppression may be observed in *Arthur v. Signum Communications Ltd.*, [1991] O.J. No. 86 (Gen. Div.), (additional reasons, [1991] O.J. No. 1357, 2 C.P.C. (3d) 74 (Gen. Div.); aff'd [1993] O.J. No. 1928 (Div. Ct.)), where Austin J. set out a number of factors that indicate oppressive conduct:

> Amongst the indicia of conduct which runs afoul of s. 247 are the following:
>
> (i) lack of a valid corporate purpose for the transaction;
>
> (ii) failure on the part of the corporation and its controlling shareholders to take reasonable steps to simulate an arm's length transaction;
>
> (iii) lack of good faith on the part of the directors of the corporation;
>
> (iv) discrimination between shareholders with the effect of benefiting the majority shareholder to the exclusion or to the detriment of the minority shareholder;
>
> (v) lack of adequate and appropriate disclosure of material information to the minority shareholders; and
>
> (vi) a plan or design to eliminate the minority shareholder.

In *Krynen v. Bugg*, [2003] O.J. No. 1209, 64 O.R. (3d) 393 (S.C.J.), Killeen J. set out a useful summary of principles and guiding rules on the oppression remedy at 409-12:

> A useful starting point for any consideration of the oppression remedy and its ramifications may be found in Professor Welling's landmark treatise, *Corporate Law in Canada*, 2nd ed. (Toronto: Butterworths, 1991) where he says this about the purpose and philosophy behind the oppression principle and remedy:
>
> > Thwarted shareholder expectation is what the oppression remedy is all about. Each shareholder buys shares with certain expectations. Some of these are outlandish. But some of them, particularly in a small corporation with few shareholders, are quite reasonable expectations in the circumstances. It is not unusual for three or four individuals to go into business together with shared expectations of mutual profits, to use a corporate form as a convenient organizing vehicle, and to have a subsequent falling out. Individuals in such a situation are like the parties to a decaying marriage relationship: they cannot be expected to operate by friendly compromise in search of mutually satisfactory or "fair" settlements of the many routine disagreements that can arise. The corporate vehicle that was once a convenience now becomes a prison with rigid rules for bars, a frame of reference for bad-tempered dispute settlement. The rules in a corporate constitution, like all legalistic rules, can become practical tools for dictatorship of the majority and oppression of the minority.

When this occurs, some measure of disinterested judicial activism can be useful. As the situation will usually (though not always) arise in smaller corporations one assumes that the oppression remedy was essentially designed for these corporations, where legitimate shareholder expectations are highly likely to exist, are unlikely to be set out on paper, yet are, because of the parties involved, susceptible of objective proof in the usual legal manner. This, I suggest, is the place for the oppression remedy.

There has been a steady and coherent evolution of the case law under s. 248 of the BCA since its enactment in the 1970s, following upon the release of the famous Dickerson Report of 1971.

A summary of the leading principles and guiding rules which has come out of that case law would include the following:

(1) The overriding lodestar principle of oppression law is that, when determining whether there has been oppression of a shareholder, the court must determine what the reasonable expectations of that person were according to the arrangements which existed between the principals. The cases on this issue have been helpfully collected and reviewed by Farley J. in *820099 Ontario Inc. v. Harold E. Ballard Ltd.* (1991), 3 B.L.R. (2d) 123 (Ont. Gen. Div.) …

(2) The term "oppression" connotes an inequality of bargaining power while "unfairness" connotes an obligation to act equitably and impartially in the exercise of power and authority: *Alldrew Holdings Ltd. v. Nibro Holdings Ltd.* (1993), 16 O.R. (3d) 718 (Gen. Div.) at p. 732.

(3) The terms, "unfair prejudice to" and "unfair disregard of the interests of" require less rigorous tests than oppression. Where on the totality of the evidence the actions and conduct complained of go beyond mere inconvenience and lack of information, and the interests of the complainant have been unfairly disregarded, the complainant will be entitled to a remedy: *Mason v. Intercity Properties Ltd.* (1987), 59 O.R. (2d) 631, 38 D.L.R. (4th) 681 (C.A.) at p. 635 O.R.

(4) There is no requirement that bad faith must be shown before an order to rectify a complaint may be made in an oppression case: *Sidaplex-Plastic Suppliers Inc. v. Elta Group Inc.* (1998), 40 O.R. (3d) 563, 162 D.L.R. (4th) 367 (C.A.) at p. 567 O.R.; *Loveridge Holdings v. King-Pin Ltd.* (1991), 5 B.L.R. (2d) 195 (Ont. Gen. Div.) at p. 203.

(5) Where expectations are apparently reasonable on their face but where there is a contract dealing with these expectations, the reasonableness of these expectations cannot prevail over the contract.

(6) Reasonable expectations are not necessarily "static" or frozen expectations and may evolve or change as the principals adapt their arrangements from time to time: *820099 Ontario Inc. v. Harold Ballard Ltd.*, *supra*, at p. 191 B.L.R.

(7) The business and affairs of a corporation are managed by or under the direction of its board of directors. The "business judgment rule" operates to shield from court intervention business decisions which have been made honestly, prudently, in good faith and on reasonable grounds. In such cases, the board's decisions will not be subject to microscopic examination and the court will be reluctant to interfere with and usurp the board's function in managing the corporation: *C.W. Shareholdings Inc. v. WIC Western*

International Communications Ltd. (1998), 39 O.R. (3d) 755, 160 D.L.R. (4th) 131 (Gen. Div.) at para. 57, p. 774 O.R.; *Brant Investments Ltd. v. KeepRite Inc.* (1991), 3 O.R. (3d) 289, 80 D.L.R. (4th) 161 (C.A.) at pp. 320-21 O.R. A useful three-part test or approach has been suggested for the application of the business judgment rule:

(1) Was the impugned conduct outside the range of reasonable business judgment?

(2) Was the impugned conduct inconsistent with the reasonable expectations of the complainant?

(3) Did the impugned conduct cause prejudice to the complainant?

Main v. Delcan Group Inc. (1999), 47 B.L.R. (2d) 200 (Ont. S.C.J.) at para. 31.

The Ontario Court of Appeal has also considered the rule in *Pente Investment Management Ltd. v. Schneider Corp.* (1998), 42 O.R. (3d) 177, 44 B.L.R. (2d) 115 (C.A.) at para. 36, p. 192 O.R.:

> The law as it has evolved in Ontario and Delaware has the common requirements that the court must be satisfied that the directors have acted reasonably and fairly. The court looks to see that the directors made a reasonable decision not a perfect decision. Provided the decision taken is within a range of reasonableness, the court ought not to substitute its opinion for that of the board even though subsequent events may have cast doubt on the board's determination. As long as the directors have selected one of several reasonable alternatives, deference is accorded to the board's decision. ... This formulation of deference to the decision of the Board is known as the "business judgment rule". The fact that alternative transactions were rejected by the directors is irrelevant unless it can be shown that a particular alternative was definitely available and clearly more beneficial to the company than the chosen transaction ...

See, also, *Themadel Foundation v. Third Canadian General Investment Trust Ltd.* (1998), 38 O.R. (3d) 749 (C.A.) at p. 754.

(8) Actual or material loss is not a prerequisite to a finding either of oppression, unfair prejudice or unfair disregard of interest. The object of the remedies available under s. 248(3) is to prevent the continuation of the misconduct in question if it is established that a harm or detriment, in the sense of infringement of rights or privileges, will follow in the absence of restraining such misconduct. On this issue, the concept of detriment as a prerequisite to obtaining a remedy is similar to the concept inherent in a *quia timet* injunction — even if there is no material loss or damage at the time but reasonable grounds are established to apprehend the same occurring if there is no relief granted, the applicant for the *quia timet* remedy will be entitled to the relief sought. Thus, in establishing unfair disregard of the applicant's interests as a result of misconduct, there is no requirement that there be actual detriment or loss to the applicant: *Sahota v. Basra* (1999), 45 B.L.R. (2d) 143, 44 C.C.E.L. (2d) 114 (Ont. Gen. Div.) at para. 30.

(9) Wrongful dismissal, standing alone, will not justify a finding of oppression. It is only where the interests of the employee are closely intertwined with his interests as a shareholder, and where the dismissal is part of a pattern of conduct to exclude the complainant from participation in the corporation,

that the dismissal can be found to be an act of oppression: *Naneff v. Con-Crete Holdings Ltd.* (1993), 11 B.L.R. (2d) 218 (Ont. Gen. Div.) at para. 125; Koehner, "The Oppression Remedy: Reasonable Expectations" (1994) 73 Can. Bar Rev. 274 at p. 278.

RE FERGUSON AND IMAX SYSTEMS CORP.

(1983), 43 O.R. (2d) 128 (C.A.)

[The corporation, at the instigation of one of its majority shareholders, refused to pay dividends beyond the minimum rate on certain preference shares held by the divorced wife of the majority shareholder. The corporation proposed to redeem the preference shares that the wife held. She sought relief under s. 234 (now s. 241) of the C.B.C.A.]

Brooke J.A.: — ... The policy of the law to ensure just and equitable treatment of minorities can be traced back to early cases. ...

But s. 234 must not be regarded as being simply a codification of the common law. Today one looks to the section when considering the interests of the minority shareholders and the section should be interpreted broadly to carry out is purpose: see the *Interpretation Act*, R.S.C. 1970, c. I-23, s. 11. Accordingly, when dealing with a close corporation, the court may consider the relationship between the shareholders and not simply legal rights as such. In addition the court must consider the *bona fides* of the corporate transaction in question to determine whether the act of the corporation or directors effects a result which is oppressive or unfairly prejudicial to the minority shareholder. Counsel has referred us to a number of decisions. They establish primarily that each case turns on its own facts. What is oppressive or unfairly prejudicial in one case may not necessarily be so in the slightly different setting of another.

Here we have a small close corporation that was promoted and is still controlled by the same small related group of individuals. The appellant's part in that group and her work for the corporation is important. Further, the attempt to force her to sell her shares through non-payment of dividends was not simply the act of Mr. Ferguson, but was also the act of the others in the group including the present director, in concert with him. Having regard to the intention of that group to deny the appellant any participation in the growth of the company I think the resolution authorizing the change in the capital of the company is the culminating event in a lengthy course of oppressive and unfairly prejudicial conduct to the appellant. In my opinion the company has not acted *bona fides* in exercising its powers to amend. By the payment of moneys now as a capital payment, which moneys on the evidence ought to have been paid by way of dividends over the years the appellant's non-redeemable shares are now to be redeemed and those in control of the company will be rid of her. She is the only one so affected. All of the other class B shareholders hold an equal number of common shares personally or through their spouses. The appellant cannot be considered like someone who came to the company lately and took a minority position in one of several classes of stock. Like the Kroiters and the Kerrs, her investment must be regarded as being in the shares which she and her husband held. The agreements as to the disposition of family shares in the event of the death of the husband or the wife confirm that this was really a family venture not only in the case of the Fergusons but for each of the three couples. ...

NOTES AND QUESTIONS

Do the reasons for this judgment assist in defining the standard for oppression? Can any standard be defined? Does a "reasonable expectation" test help? Although the party alleging oppression bears the onus of proof (*Brant Investments Ltd. v. KeepRite Inc.*, [1991] O.J. No. 683, 3 O.R. (3d) 289, 80 D.L.R. (4th) 161 (C.A.)), certain conduct may *prima facie* suggest oppression. Indications of oppressive behaviour can include lack of corporate purpose for the impugned conduct, lack of good faith by directors and discriminatory conduct between shareholders, lack of adequate disclosure and the presence of non-arm's-length transactions (*Miller v. McNally*, [1991] O.J. No. 1772, 3 B.L.R. (2d) 102 (Gen. Div.). For a flagrant example of oppressive conduct see *PCM Construction Control Consultants v. Heeger*, [1989] A.J. No. 487, 67 Alta. L.R. (2d) 302, 44 B.L.R. 289 (Q.B.).

Can the violation of a unanimous shareholder agreement amount to oppression? See *Lyall v. 147250 Canada Ltd.*, [1993] B.C.J. No. 874, 12 B.L.R. (2d) 161 (C.A.). What about a situation where a corporation holds life insurance policies on the lives of its shareholders and does not use the proceeds of those policies to purchase the shares of a deceased shareholder from his personal holding company? See *Gordon Glaves Holdings Ltd. v. Care Corp. of Canada*, [2000] O.J. No. 1989, 48 O.R. (3d) 737 (C.A.). Oppressive conduct may even invade the relationship between spouses, as seen in *Baxter v. Baxter*, [2000] O.J. No. 1172, 7 R.F.L. (5th) 243 (Ont. S.C.J.). In that case, a wife caused the corporation, through which she and her former husband each operated a drive-in, to not renegotiate the lease on her former husband's drive-in, thereby depriving him of his livelihood. Her actions were found to be oppressive, with the result that she was forced to purchase her husband's shares.

May employees bring oppression claims against their employers? In *Joncas v. Spruce Falls Power & Paper Co.*, [2000] O.J. No. 1721, 48 O.R. (3d) 179, 6 B.L.R. (3d) 109 (S.C.J.), it was held that aggrieved employees on long-term disability who had expectations of sharing in the distribution of shares of a corporation as part of its reorganization, but who were excluded because of their disabled status, qualified as "complainants" under s. 245(*c*) of the O.B.C.A. However, because those same employees did not fall within the scope of protection under s. 245(2) — since they could not be classified as security holders, creditors, directors or officers — they were not entitled to an oppression remedy.

Can an application in respect of alleged oppression be brought in respect of a corporation whose shares are widely distributed among the general public? For affirmative responses to this query, see, for example, *AMCU Credit Union Inc. v. Olympia and York Developments Ltd.*, [1992] O.J. No. 1681, 7 B.L.R. (2d) 103 (Gen. Div.); *Brant Investments Ltd. v. KeepRite Inc.*, [1991] O.J. No. 683, 3 O.R. (3d) 289 (C.A.).

May a breach of fiduciary duty constitute oppression? Alternatively, may an oppressive action by a director amount to a breach of fiduciary duty? What are the differences between the two?

It is clear that while bad faith may be an indicium of oppression, a finding of bad faith is not a prerequisite to the success of the application (*Brant Investments Ltd. v. KeepRite Inc.*, [1991] O.J. No. 683, 3 O.R. (3d) 289 (C.A.). Nor does the complainant have to show that the respondents did anything dishonest or illegal or that they intended to oppress: *Loveridge Holdings Ltd. v. King-Pin Ltd.*, [1992] O.J. No. 47, 5 B.L.R. (2d) 195 (Gen. Div.).

Consider the following comments of Mason J. in *Such v. RW-LB Holdings Ltd.*, [1993] A.J. No. 1033, 11 B.L.R. (2d) 122 (Q.B.), at pp. 137-38, 143-44:

As previously stated, the statutory remedy was first introduced into the law by the U.K. *Companies Act, 1948*. Analysis of the jurisprudence of the statutory derivative action both in English and Canadian Courts has focused on two main themes. First, whether or not a threshold finding of lack of probity and fair dealing, i.e., bad faith, is required before a court may exercise the powers granted to redress the effect of the impugned action. Early development of the oppression remedy action determined that bad faith by definition had to underlie the impugned action as oppression was the only ground in s. 210 of the U.K. *Companies Act, 1948*. Following upon the introduction of the remedy the English courts defined "oppression" as involving "an element of lack of probity or fair dealing", "of being burdensome, harsh and wrongful." See *Elder v. Elder & Watson Ltd.*, [1952] S.C. 49 at 60, and *Scottish Co-operative Wholesale Society v. Meyer*, [1959] A.C. 324 at 342. With the additional grounds of conduct unfairly prejudicial or conduct amounting to unfair disregard, courts began to determine they need only find that the acts of the controlling majority shareholders had an unfair result for the protected interests, in most cases the minority shareholders.

These additional grounds permitted the development of the second related theme, the broadened scope of the action and the development of a less rigorous standard of proof. The Court's focus on unfair results and away from the requirement of bad faith, permitted the Courts to utilize a more objective approach to proof as opposed to the more subjective and more difficult proof essential to establish the state of mind for bad faith.

The burden of proof of unfair prejudice or disregard is less rigorous than the burden of proof of oppression because what is at issue is the unfair result not a state of mind. In a sense, these broader grounds have absorbed the oppression ground. Once established, the court is given very broad powers to redress that result. Here it is sufficient to quote from *Mason v. Intercity Properties Ltd.*, [1987] O.J. No. 448, 59 O.R. (2d) 631 (C.A.), *per* Blair J.A. (at p. 685):

> The present Act provides relief for minority shareholders without forcing the break-up of the company. Relief may be given to a minority shareholder upon proof of unfair prejudice to or disregard of his or her interests, *both of which are less rigorous grounds than oppression*. In *Re Ferguson and Imax Systems Corp.* (1983), 43 O.R. (2d) 128, 150 D.L.R. (3d) 718, Brooke J.A. said of an identically worded section in the *Canada Business Corporations Act*, 1974-75-76 (Can.), c. 33, that it "must not be regarded as being simply a codification of the common law". He declared that "the section should be interpreted broadly to carry out its purpose". He emphasized, as other judges have done in dealing with this and similar sections, the flexibility of the remedy and after referring to several decisions he said at p. 137 O.R., p. 727 D.L.R.: They establish primarily that each case turns on its own facts. What is oppressive or unfairly prejudicial in one case may not necessarily be so in the slightly different setting of another. *The Court has a broad discretion to make the "order it thinks fit"* including 14 types of relief listed in the clauses of s. 247(3).

(Emphasis added.)

While *Farnham v. Fingold*, [1973] 2 O.R. 132, 33 D.L.R. (3d) 156 (C.A.) and *Goldex Mines Ltd. v. Revill* (1974), 7 O.R. (2d) 216, 54 D.L.R. (3d) 672 (C.A.) illustrate the need to distinguish harm to a corporation, which is properly the subject of a statutory representative action, from harm to shareholders, or other "complainants", which may amount to oppressive conduct, it is sometimes difficult to distinguish between the two scenarios.

(b) Oppression vs. Statutory Representative Action

One of the earliest cases attempting to draw meaningful distinctions between the statutory representative action and the oppression remedy is *First Edmonton Place Ltd. v. 315888 Alberta Ltd.*, excerpted below. In reading the case, note the particular emphasis on the impact of the impugned actions, whether they create harm, and to whom that harm is directed.

FIRST EDMONTON PLACE LTD. v. 315888 ALBERTA LTD.

[1988] A.J. No. 511, 60 Alta. L.R. (2d) 122 (Q.B.)

[The facts are set out in the excerpt of the case, *supra*.]

McDonald J.: —

. . .

First Edmonton Place submits that the actions of the three lawyers as directors of the numbered corporation, (a) in causing the corporation to allow their law firm to occupy the premises with no lease, written or unwritten, and without requiring rent to be paid during the rent-free period, and (b) causing the corporation to pay out the proceeds of the cash inducement to themselves, and constituted deliberate breaches of their obligations as directors of the numbered corporation. As a result, First Edmonton Place seeks alternative forms of relief under secs. 232 (statutory representative action) and 234 (oppression) of the ABCA. ...

. . .

Underlying both actions as to which leave to commence the action is sought, are the scheme and purpose of the remedial sections of the ABCA. It is only in the light of understanding such scheme and purpose that it is possible to define the content and limits of the remedies, and, in the course of doing so, to define the word "complainant" as that word used in s. 231.

GENERAL POLICY OF THE NEW REMEDIES:

The general remedies available to those persons having interests in limited companies have been the subject of major reform in recent years. Major changes have occurred in the whole area of company law with the enactments of new Business Corporations Acts in several jurisdictions including the Canadian federal jurisdiction and the province of Alberta. In order to determine whether the remedies provided by secs. 232 or 234 of the ABCA are available to the present applicant, it may be of some assistance to examine the policy reasons that caused these remedies to be enacted.

In late 1967 the Government of Canada set up a task force under Dr. R.W.V. Dickerson to consider the philosophy, the substance, and the administration of the Canada *Corporations Act*. As the new remedy provisions of the ABCA were modelled after those which were enacted in the Canada Business Corporations ("CBCA") after 1967, an examination of the policies which resulted in the new remedies in the CBCA, will be useful in interpreting the analogous provisions in the ABCA. One of the objectives of the federal task force, as set out in the Detailed Background Paper for the New Canada Business Corporations Bill ... was to achieve a balance between those who have competing interests in the corporate structure. Recognition of the rights of creditors, minority shareholders and the public played a major role.

Prior to the statutory enactment of the remedy provisions, the rights of the minority shareholder as against those controlling a corporation were virtually non-existent, and the plight of creditors was worse yet. The courts adopted the general view that had been stated by Scrutton L.J. as follows:

> "It is not the business of the court to manage the affairs of the company. That is for the shareholders and directors."

(*Shuttleworth v. Cox Bros. and Co.* [1927] 2 K.B. 9, L.J., at p. 23). The concepts of majority rule, and of the corporate personality as distinct from its members, stood as major roadblocks to any suits to remedy mis-management of the corporation or to remedy wrongs done to minority shareholders.

The reforms were aimed at balancing the interests of all persons having interests in the corporation and, in doing so, the legislators have given the courts a "very broad discretion, applying general standards of fairness, to decide these cases on their merits" (R.W.V. Dickerson, et al., *Proposals for a New Business Corporations Law for Canada*, Volume 1 Commentary (Dickerson Report) at p. 162). ...

By framing the remedy provisions in very broad terms, the reformers have sought to do away with the restrictive approach that the courts had previously taken when judging the conduct or misconduct of corporate management. The old view that the management of the company was in the total discretion of its directors and shareholders has been replaced by an expansive view of the court's role in balancing the interests of shareholders (majority and minority), creditors, and the public in general.

The present applicant has sought relief under both ss. 232 and 234 of the ABCA. The Alberta Institute of Law Research and Reform, in its Report on Proposals for a New Alberta Business corporations Act (Volume 1, August 1980) at p. 144, had this to say with respect to the relationship between the derivative action (s. 232) and personal actions (s. 234):

> It seems to us that the essential point in proceedings under either CBCA s. 232 or 234 is that a person with an interest in a corporation is complaining about the abuse of power by someone who controls the machinery of the corporation. In legal form the wrongdoers in one case may be doing a wrong to the corporation; in another they may be causing the corporation to act in a way which is wrongful; and in a third they may be changing the corporation's constitution in a way which will give them an unfair advantage over the minority; but in substance they are wrongfully using the power of control. It may be that the remedy for a case in which directors who have done a wrong to the corporation and refuse to allow that corporation to sue them is to allow the complainant to bring an action against them in the corporation's name; that the remedy in another case may be an injunction to stop the company from acting in contravention of a restriction on the business which it is restricted from carrying on (probably supported by an injunction against the directors); and that the remedy in a third case may be an injunction to prevent shareholders from passing a resolution approving a sale of the corporation's property to themselves or an order deleting an amendment made by the shareholders to the articles of incorporation. In all those cases, however, the wrongdoers are doing something to the prejudice of the complainant's interest in the corporation, whether it prejudices his rights under the corporate constitution or affects the value of the corporation to which his rights apply. The crux of the matter is that the wrongdoers are abusing their power of control.

(emphasis added)

It has been held that relevant law reform material can be used to help determine the mischief at which legislation is directed (*Mazurenko v. Mazurenko* (1981) 124 D.L.R. (3d) 406 at p. 413 (Alta. C.A.)).

Section 232 - The Statutory Derivative Action

The enactment of the derivative action provisions resulted from the harsh consequences of the common law which essentially permitted the abuse by majority shareholders at the expense of the minority. ...

The derivative action was clearly meant to overcome the plight of minority shareholders in the face of majority rule.

Section 234 - Action for Oppression, Unfair Prejudice or Unfair Disregard of the Interests of a Security Holder, Creditor, Director or Officer.

This remedy, as it appears in s. 234 of the CBCA (and now in s. 234 of the ABCA) has been described as "the broadest, most comprehensive and most open-ended shareholder remedy in the common law world". (Stanley M. Beck, "Minority Shareholders' Rights in the 1980s", *in Law Society of Upper Canada Special Lectures 1982* "Corporate Law in the 80s", p. 311 at p. 312). It gives the court wide discretion to remedy virtually any corporate conduct that is unfair. In view of this, each case will depend largely on its facts; however, analysis of the policy underlying this remedy can provide some guidance to the court in exercising its discretion.

...

b. Policy

The introduction of a statutory remedy against oppression and unfair prejudice is a deliberate departure from the policy of judicial non-intervention in corporate affairs. Section 234 "casts the court in the role of an active `arbiter of business policy'" (Shapira, at p. 137). It is drawn in very broad terms and as remedial legislation should be given a liberal interpretation in favour of the complainant (*Abraham v. Inter Wide Investments* (1985) 30 D.L.R. (4th) 177 (Ont. S.C.) at 187); *Stech v. Davies* (1987) 53 Alta. L.R. (2d) 373 (Q.B.)). In *Keho Holdings v. Noble* (1987) 78 A.R. 131 (C.A.), Haddad, J.A. stated (at 136):

> I concur, without hesitation, that these sections ought to be broadly and liberally interpreted. A broad interpretation will reflect the intention of the legislation to ensure settlement of intra-corporate disputes on equitable principles as opposed to adherence to legal rights.

The addition of "unfairly prejudicial" and "unfairly disregards" to "oppressive" gives the court a broad basis upon which to apply notions of equity and fairness to the conduct of the directors and the majority. As Professor Shapira pointed out, at p. 145 of his article, the notion of "unfair prejudice" is "not merely a relaxation of the term oppression" and in "important respects it is its antithesis". Clearly, the addition of "unfairly prejudicial" and "unfairly disregards" puts the court in a position to judge the fairness of the actions of management (*Journet v. Superchef Industries* (1984) 29 B.L.R. 206 (Que. S.C.), at p. 223 per Gomery J.). ...

Section 234 provides a broad basis for liability with enormous potential for controlling corporate behaviour. As Professor Waldron said at p. 152, this new spirit of flexibility and fairness may be welcomed but some definition of its scope is vital. In *Vedova v. Garden House Inn* (1985) 29 B.L.R. 3 (Ontario S.C.). Anderson, J. held that the Ontario equivalent of s. 234 is available only to protect minorities against adverse treatment by the majority (at p. 240):

The relief available is to be determined by tests less stringent than those which traditionally had to be met in order to procure an order for winding up. But in my view they continue to be confined to protection of minorities. Specifically, they are not intended as a method of mediating between opposing groups of shareholders acting from a position of equality ... In the context of section 247, "oppressive" connotes an equality of power or authority ... "Unfair" connotes an obligation to act inequitably or impartially in the exercise of power or authority ... I find no such obligation where, as here, power and authority, in the legal sense, are equally divided, and are so divided by pre-existing arrangement.

In *Re Gandalman Investments & Fogle* (1985) 22 D.L.R. (4th) 638 (Ontario H.C.). at p. 640, Callon, J. interpreted the above quotation, not as stating that only minority shareholders can apply for an oppression remedy, but rather, that the relief is not available where power and authority are equally divided and that "oppressive" connotes an inequality of power or authority. In *H.J. Rai Ltd. v. Reid Point Marina Ltd.*, May 26, 1981, B.C.S.C., cited in *Brant Investments Ltd. v. Keeprite Inc.*, (1987) 37 B.L.R. 65 at p. 108, Skipp, J. stated that the legislation "was not intended to diminish but to temper the ordinary presumption of majority rule". In *Brant Investments v. Keeprite*, Anderson J. expressed the following concern (at p. 99):

The jurisdiction is one which must be exercised with care. On the one hand the minority shareholder must be protected from unfair treatment; that is the clearly expressed intent of the section. On the other hand the court ought not to usurp the function of the board of directors in managing the company, nor should it eliminate or supplant the legitimate exercise of control by the majority.

He went on to state (at p. 100):

Business decisions, honestly made, should not be subjected to microscopic examination. There should be no interference simply because a decision is unpopular with the minority.

There are almost no decisions on the availability of s. 234 to creditors. most applications under s. 234 are made by minority shareholders. With respect to the applicability of decisions involving minority shareholders to cases involving creditors, in *Bank of Montreal v. Dome Petroleum* (1987) 54 Alta. L.R. (2d) 289 (Q.B.), Forsyth, J. quoted the above statements of Anderson, J. in Brant Investments. He then commented (at p. 298):

While Mr. Justice Anderson in that decision was dealing with the rights of minority shareholders, I fully subscribe to those views and would adopt the same approach in dealing with the rights of creditors when it is alleged same are being unfairly dealt with in some fashion and relief is sought under s. 234.

In the *Dome Petroleum* case, the Bank of Montreal claimed that an arrangement agreement entered into by Dome and Amoco, coupled with certain confidentiality agreements, which effectively restricted any sale of Dome shares or assets for an indeterminate amount of time, unfairly prejudiced or unfairly disregarded the Bank of Montreal's position as a creditor. As the arrangement agreement could not go forward in the absence of the Bank of Montreal's consent, Forsyth, J. could not find any oppression, unfair prejudice or unfair disregard on the evidence before him. As such, he granted Dome Petroleum's application for summary dismissal of the application under s. 234.

Three cases merit discussion for their attempts to define the key terms of the legislation. In *Scottish Co-operative Wholesale Society v. Mayer* [1959] A.C. 324, at p. 342, Viscount Simmonds defined "oppressive" as "burdensome, harsh and wrongful". Numerous cases have subsequently quoted and adopted this definition (see *Re National Building Maintenance* [1971] 1 W.W.R. 9 (B.C.S.C.), at 21; *Re Cucci's Restaurant* (1985) 29 B.L.R. 3 (Alta. Q.B.) at 202). In *Diligenti v. R.W.M.D. Operations Kelowna* (1976) 1 B.C.L.R. 36 S.C., at 45, the court considered the meaning of "unfairly prejudicial". Fulton, J. ruled that in adding the words "unfairly prejudicial" to the statute, the legislature must have intended that the courts would give those words "an effect different from and going beyond that given to the word oppressive". Turning to the Oxford Dictionary, he found that "prejudicial" meant detrimental or damaging to the applicant's right or interest and "unfair" meant inequitable or unjust. He concluded that "the dictionary's definition supported the instinctive reactions that what is unjust and inequitable is obviously unfairly prejudicial" (at 46). Finally, In *Stech v. Davies, supra*, at p. 379, Egbert, J. defined "unfairly disregard" as "to unjustly or without cause, in the context of a. 234(2), pay no attention to, ignore or treat as of no importance the interests of security holders, creditors, directors or officers of a corporation."

In *Diligenti*, the applicant and the three individual respondents formed a partnership to enter into the restaurant business. They incorporated two companies for this purpose. Each individual was a director of and held one-quarter of the shares in the corporation. Subsequently. the respondents removed the applicant as director and took away his managerial responsibilities. In addition, they began paying management fees to another corporation in which the three individual Respondents were the sole shareholders. The applicant applied for relief under the oppression remedy. The British Columbia provision required that the acts complained of affect the applicant in his capacity as a shareholder. With respect to this requirement, Fulton, J. made the following remarks:

> I consider, however, that the new provision is not to be so narrowly interpreted or its effect so narrowly confined, for to do so would be to deal with it as though the word was still "oppressive". I consider that there are rights — equitable rights — attaching to the position of the applicant as shareholder in the circumstances present here, in respect of which he has been unfairly prejudiced, and in reaching this conclusion I rely upon and respectfully adopt the reasoning of Lord Wilberforce as distilled from a perusal of the whole of his judgment in the *Ebrahimi* case.

In *Ebrahimi v. Westbourne Galleries* [1972] 2 All E.R. 492, in the context of a petition for equitable winding up of a company, Lord Wilberforce stated (at p. 500):

> The words are a recognition of the fact that a limited company is more than a mere judicial entity, with a personality in law of its own: that there is room in company law for recognition of the fact that behind it, or amongst it, there are individuals, with rights, expectations and obligations inter se which are not necessarily submerged in the company structure ... It does, as equity always does, enable the court to subject the exercise of legal rights to equitable considerations; considerations. that is, of a personal character arising between one individual and another, which may make it unjust, or inequitable, to insist on legal rights, or to exercise them in a particular way.

Fulton, J. recognized that the same principles could be applied in determining whether the conduct complained of unfairly prejudiced the applicant's interests as a shareholder (at p. 51):

First, in circumstances such as exist here there are "rights, expectations and obligations inter se" which are not submerged in the company structure, and these rights are enjoyed by a member as part of his status as a shareholder in the company which has been formed to carry on the enterprise: amongst those rights are the rights to continue to participate in the direction of that company's affairs. Second, although his fellow members may be entitled as a matter of strict law to remove him as a director, for them to do so in fact is unjust and inequitable, and is a breach of equitable rights which he in fact possesses as a member. And third, although such breach may not "oppress" him in respect of his proprietary rights as a shareholder, such unjust and inequitable denial of his rights and expectation is undoubtedly "unfairly prejudicial" to him in his status as member.

. . .

[T]he basic formula for establishing unfair prejudice or unfair disregard of the interests of the creditor should reflect as a goal the desire to seek to balance protection of the creditor's interest against the policy of preserving freedom of action for management and the right of the corporation to deal with a creditor in a way that may be to the prejudice of the interests of the creditor or that may disregard those interests so long as the prejudice or disregard is not unfair.

The s. 234 remedy would be available if the act or conduct of the directors or management of the corporation which is complained of amounted to using the corporation as a vehicle for committing fraud upon a creditor. An example might be the directors of a corporation using it to obtain credit for the purchase of goods by means which if the credit were obtained by an individual would be fraudulent on the part of the individual.

Assuming the absence of fraud, in what other circumstances would a remedy under s. 234 be available? In deciding what is unfair, the history and nature of the corporation, the essential nature of the relationship between the corporation and the creditor, the type of rights affected and general commercial practice should all be material. More concretely, the test of unfair prejudice or unfair disregard should encompass the following considerations: the protection of the underlying expectation of a creditor in its arrangement with the corporation, the extent to which the acts complained of were unforeseeable or the creditor could reasonably have protected itself from such acts, and the detriment to the interests of the creditor. The elements of the formula and the list of considerations as I have stated them should not be regarded as exhaustive. Other elements and considerations may be relevant, based upon the facts of a particular case.

There is an emerging view in Australia that the test to be applied in interpreting a statutory provision such as s. 234 is whether "objectively in the eyes of a commercial bystander. there has been unfairness, namely conduct that is so unfair that reasonable directors who consider the matter would not have thought the decision fair": per Young J. in *Morgan v. 45 Flers Avenue Pty. Ltd.*, (1986) 10 A.C.L.R. 692 at p. 704 (S.C.N.S.W., Equity Div.). However, this test would still leave unarticulated the basis upon which unfairness or unreasonableness is to be determined. I suggest that, at least when it is a creditor who seeks the remedy, the tests I have enunciated will be more precise.

To adapt a statement by Professor Shapira (at p. 145) as to the objective of the remedy provided for by a remedy such as that provided by s. 234, the type of conduct against which s. 234 affords protection should be understood in terms of the impact of the conduct complained of upon the interests of the security holder, creditor, director or officer, not in terms of intention to damage such interests or to damage the corporation. ...

The oppression remedy also has provided relief where the affairs of the corporation were being conducted so as to cause a diminution of the corporation's assets. In *Jackman v. Jackets Enterprises* (1977) 4 B.C.L.R. 358 (S.C.). the corporation borrowed money on a mortgage, used half of this money to repay a lower interest debt to an associated corporation and lent the rest to that corporation. The majority shareholder fully owned the associated corporation. Notwithstanding the absence of fraud or appropriation of corporate property, the court found that these actions unfairly prejudiced the interests of the minority shareholder. In *Keho Holdings v. Noble* (1987) 78 A.R. 131 (C.A.), a majority shareholder who controlled the board of directors caused the corporation to borrow money and loan it, without obtaining security, to one of his own corporations and granted himself a stock option at a price below market value of the shares. Following *Jackman v. Jackets Enterprises*, Haddad, J.A. found these actions both oppressive and unfairly prejudicial.

...

In the present case it is clear that First Edmonton Place is in good faith in seeking the potential return of money paid out by the corporation, in order that the corporation will have assets with which to meet the action of First Edmonton against the corporation for breach of the lease. The proposed action to be brought under s. 232 is not designed to obtain a tactical advantage against the directors. If obtaining a tactical advantage against the directors were the motive, that might constitute lack of good faith (see *Vendova v. Garden House Inn Ltd.* (1985) 29 B.L.R. 3 (Ont. H.C.J.)).

...

... In the present case, there is uncertainty as to the way in which the signing bonus monies paid over by the corporation to the directors was used, but there is no doubt that they took the money. It appears to be in the interests of the corporation that it be determined at a trial whether their doing so constituted a wrong against the corporation.

...

In the present case, the duties of the directors would not change merely because the directors also happened to be the sole shareholders of the corporation. In *Sigurdson v. Fidelity Ins. Co.* (1977) 2 B.L.R. 1 at p. 22 (B.C.S.C.), McKenzie J., held that "the responsibility of the directors and officers of the corporation is to the corporation itself, whatever its composition at any moment as to number of corporators".

...

If an action were brought under s. 234 on the ground that the conduct of the directors was "oppressive or unfairly prejudicial to" or unfairly disregarded "the interests of any ... creditor...", was the lessor a "creditor" at the time of the conduct complained of?

The discussion of this issue is also relevant to the question whether the lessor can be regarded as a "complainant", for the definition of "complainant" contained in s. 231(b)(i) refers to "a security of a corporation", and the meaning of the word "security" includes "a debt obligation of a corporation". I have already held that it is only certain limited kinds of debt obligations, of which this lease is not one, which can qualify as a "security", but if I am wrong in my decision in that regard, it would be necessary to consider whether the lessor is a creditor.

Bearing that in mind, I turn to the requirement of s. 234(2) that, if leave to commence the action is to be granted, it must be shown that the conducts of the directors was oppressive or unfairly prejudicial to or unfairly disregarded the interests of, inter alia, a "creditor". The applicant must have had an interest as creditor at the time the acts complained of occurred ...

At the time of the acts complained of, there was not any rent yet due under the lease. The applicant contends that the lease obligations of the corporation were a present debt at the time of the acts complained of, citing *Re Hulbert & Mayer* (1916) 11 W.W.R. 380 (Alta S.C.). According to *Re Hulbert & Mayer*, the legal liability to pay rent is incurred at time the lease is created. Thus, at the time of the acts complained of, although the corporation did not owe any rent to the applicant, it did have an obligation to the applicant in respect of future rent. Notwithstanding this obligation, it may be that the applicant was not a creditor at the relevant time as its claim was for unliquidated damages. ...

In *Gardner v. Newton* (1916) 29 D.L.R. 276 (Man. K.B.), the issue was whether a landlord is a creditor in respect of rent which has not become due and payable. With respect to cases dealing with the general meaning of "creditor", Mathers, C.J.K.B. said, at p. 282:

> The above cases all deal with the definition of the words "debtor" and "creditor" in particular statutes. They show that in the absence of anything to indicate that a more comprehensive meaning was intended that which is ascribed to them in everyday usage is to be applied. In its largest sense "creditor" is one who has a right to require the fulfilment of an obligation or contract; but its general and almost universal meaning is a person to whom a debt is payable. Stroud, Judicial Dictionary.

As to the specific contention that a landlord is a creditor in respect of future rent by virtue of the covenant to pay rent, he stated, at p. 285:

> The very most [the landlord] would be entitled to do would be to prove for the present value of his claim. But how is that value to be arrived at even if the trust instruments made provision for assessing it? The premises might have been destroyed the next day or they may remain intact until the expiration of the lease. No tribunal, however wide its powers, could possibly name a sum which will certainly accrue to the plaintiff. It seems to me quite impossible to say that a man is a "creditor" even using the word in its largest sense, in respect of a sum of money not one penny of which may ever become payable.

... My conclusion is that the word "creditor" as it is used in s. 234 does not include a lessor in respect of rent which is not owing at the time of the acts complained of, and that therefore the applicant could not succeed in its claim in so far as it is based upon the lease.

Conclusion

In the case of the application under s. 232, the applicant was not a holder of a security or a "creditor" at the time of use of the cash inducement money by the three directors. However, there is some evidence that the cash inducement money was not used for purposes of the corporation and that its use might have been a fraud upon the corporation. If it was a fraud upon the corporation, and if the corporation were entitled to recover the money from the three directors, the applicant may have a genuine interest in advancing the claim to such recovery because the corporation might be liable in damages to the applicant. Therefore the applicant is in my opinion a proper person to make an application under s. 232 and should be granted leave to bring an action in the name and on behalf of the corporation in respect of the payment of the cash inducement money to or for the benefit of the three lawyers.

Moreover, as for the three lawyers, as directors of the corporation, permitting themselves as lawyers to occupy the leased premises without paying rent or entering into a lease, whether that conduct constituted a wrong to the corporation is a matter that should be tried. Once again, if there was a wrong, the applicant might ultimately stand to benefit from any recovery by the corporation. Therefore the applicant is in my opinion a proper person to make an application under s. 232 in regard to this head of claim and should be granted leave in the same action to advance a claim in the name and on behalf of the corporation in respect of the occupation of the premises by the directors for their own personal purposes and in respect of the failure of the directors to obtain from themselves personally (or their law firm) a sub-lease for the term of the lease.

...

Granting leave to bring the statutory derivative action under s. 232 does not in any way imply that on the basis of the evidence placed before me I am of the view that the action is likely to succeed. As to that, of course, I offer no opinion.

...

In the case of the application under s. 234, leave to bring an action in regard to either claim is denied because the applicant was not a creditor at the time of the act or conduct complained of.

Application granted in part.

NOTE

The *First Edmonton Place* case demonstrates that while it may not always be easy to ascertain whether one's facts support a statutory representative action or an oppression remedy, there is no substitute for a close examination of the particular facts and the impact of the impugned activity to make this determination. The Supreme Court of Canada has also provided some helpful guidelines for distinguishing between these two types of actions in *Hercules Managements Ltd. v. Ernst & Young*, excerpted below.

HERCULES MANAGEMENTS LTD. v. ERNST & YOUNG

[1997] S.C.J. No. 51, [1997] 2 S.C.R. 165, 146 D.L.R. (4th) 577

[Two companies, Northguard Acceptance Ltd. ("NGA") and Northguard Holdings Ltd. ("NGH") were engaged in the business of lending and investing money on the security of real property mortgages. The appellants, Hercules Managements and Max Freed, were shareholders in NGA. Ernst & Young was the long-standing auditor of both companies. In 1984, both NGA and NGH went into receivership. The appellants sought a determination that the audit reports prepared on behalf of NGA and NGH for 1980-82 by Ernst & Young were negligently prepared, as well as damages for financial losses stemming from their reliance on those reports.]

La Forest J. (for the court): — This appeal arises by way of motion for summary judgment. It concerns the issue of whether and when accountants who perform an audit of a corporation's financial statements owe a duty of care in tort to shareholders of the corporation who claim to have suffered losses in reliance on the audited statements. It also raises the question of whether certain types of claims against auditors may properly be brought by shareholders as individuals or whether they must be brought by the corporation in the form of a derivative action.

[Only the portion of the judgment concerned with who may bring the claims against the auditors is reproduced below.]

...

The claims of Hercules and Mr. Freed with respect to their 1982-83 investments can be addressed quickly. The essence of these claims must be that these two appellants relied on the respondents' reports in deciding whether or not to make further investments in the audited corporations. In other words, Hercules and Mr. Freed are claiming to have relied on the audited reports for the purpose of making personal investment decisions.

...

With respect to the claim concerning the loss in value of their existing shareholdings, the appellants make two submissions. First, they claim that they relied on the 1980-82 reports in monitoring the value of their equity and that, owing to the (allegedly) negligent preparation of those reports, they failed to extract it before the financial demise of NGA and NGH. Secondly, and somewhat more subtly, the appellants submit that they each relied on the auditors' reports in overseeing the management of NGA and NGH and that had those reports been accurate, the collapse of the corporations and the consequential loss in the value of their shareholdings could have been avoided.

...

... The essence of the appellants' submission here is that the shareholders would have supervised management differently had they known of the (alleged) inaccuracies in the 1980-82 reports, and that this difference in management would have averted the demise of the audited corporations and the consequent losses in existing equity suffered by the shareholders. At first glance, it might appear that the appellants' claim implicates a use of the audit reports which is commensurate with the purpose for which the reports were prepared, i.e., overseeing or supervising management. One might argue on this basis that a duty of care should be found to inhere because, in view of this compatibility between actual use and intended purpose, no indeterminacy arises. In my view, however, this line of reasoning suffers from a subtle but fundamental flaw.

As I have already explained, the purpose for which the audit reports were prepared in this case was the standard statutory one of allowing shareholders, <u>as a group</u>, to supervise management and to take decisions with respect to matters concerning the proper overall administration <u>of the corporations</u>. In other words, it was ... to permit the shareholders to exercise their role, <u>as a class</u>, of overseeing the <u>corporations'</u> affairs at their annual general meetings. The purpose of providing the auditors' reports to the appellants, then, may ultimately be said to have been a "collective" one; that is, it was aimed not at protecting the interests of individual shareholders but rather at enabling the shareholders, acting as a group, to safeguard the interests of the corporations themselves. On the appellants' argument, however, the purpose to which the 1980-82 reports were ostensibly put was not that of allowing the shareholders as a class to take decisions in respect of the overall running of the corporation, but rather to allow them, as <u>individuals</u>, to monitor management so as to oversee and protect their own personal investments. Indeed, the nature of the appellants' claims (i.e. personal tort claims) <u>requires</u> that they assert reliance on the auditors' reports *qua* individual shareholders if they are to recover any personal damages. In so far as it must concern the interests of each individual shareholder, then, the appellants' claim in this regard can really be no different from the other "investment purposes" discussed above, in respect of which the respondents owe no duty of care.

...

All the participants in this appeal — the appellants, the respondents, and the intervener — raised the issue of whether the appellants' claims in respect of the losses they suffered in their existing shareholdings through their alleged inability to oversee management of the corporations ought to have been brought as a derivative action ... rather than as a series of individual actions. The issue was also raised and discussed in the courts below. In my opinion, a derivative action — commenced, as required, by an application under s. 232 of the Manitoba *Corporations Act* — would have been the proper method of proceeding with respect to this claim. Indeed, I would regard this simply as a corollary of the idea that the audited reports are provided to the shareholders as a group in order to allow them to take collective (as opposed to individual) decisions. ...

... As I have already explained, the appellants allege that they were prevented from properly overseeing the management of the audited corporations because the respondents' audit reports painted a misleading picture of their financial state. They allege further that had they known the true situation, they would have intervened to avoid the eventuality of the corporations' going into receivership and the consequent loss of their equity. The difficulty with this submission, I have suggested, is that it fails to recognize that in supervising management, the shareholders must be seen to be *acting as a body* in respect of the corporation's interests rather than as individuals in respect of their own ends. In a manner of speaking, the shareholders assume what may be seen to be a "managerial role" when, as a collectivity, they oversee the activities of the directors and officers through resolutions adopted at shareholder meetings. In this capacity, they cannot properly be understood to be acting simply as individual holders of equity. Rather, their collective decisions are made in respect of the corporation itself. Any duty owed by auditors in respect of this aspect of the shareholders' functions, then, would be owed not to shareholders *qua* individuals, but rather to all shareholders as a group, acting in the interests of the corporation. And if the decisions taken by the collectivity of shareholders are in respect of the corporation's affairs, then the shareholders' reliance on negligently prepared audit reports in taking such decisions will result in a wrong to the corporation for which the shareholders cannot, as individuals, recover.

This line of reasoning finds support in Lord Bridge's comments in *Caparo*, *supra*, at p. 580:

> The shareholders of a company have a collective interest in the company's proper management and in so far as a negligent failure of the auditor to report accurately on the state of the company's finances deprives the shareholders of the opportunity to exercise their powers in general meeting to call the directors to book and to ensure that errors in management are corrected, the shareholders ought to be entitled to a remedy. But in practice no problem arises in this regard since the interest of the shareholders in the proper management of the company's affairs is indistinguishable from the interest of the company itself and any loss suffered by the shareholders ... will be recouped by a claim against the auditor in the name of the company, not by individual shareholders.

[Emphasis added.]

It is also reflected in the decision of Farley J. in *Roman I, supra*, the facts of which were similar to those of the case at bar. In that case, the plaintiff shareholders brought an action against the defendant auditors alleging, *inter alia*, that the defendant's audit reports were negligently prepared. That negligence, the shareholders contended, prevented them from properly overseeing management which, in turn, led to the winding up of the corporation and a loss to the shareholders of their equity therein. Farley J. discussed the rule in *Foss v. Harbottle* and concluded that it operated so as to preclude the shareholders from bringing personal actions based on an alleged inability to supervise the conduct of management.

One final point should be made here. Referring to the case of *Goldex Mines Ltd. v. Revill* (1974), 7 O.R. (2d) 216 (C.A.), the appellants submit that where a shareholder has been directly and individually harmed, that shareholder may have a personal cause of action even though the corporation may also have a separate and distinct cause of action. Nothing in the foregoing paragraphs should be understood to detract from this principle. In finding that claims in respect of losses stemming from an alleged inability to oversee or supervise management are really derivative and not personal in nature, I have found only that shareholders cannot raise individual claims in respect of a wrong done <u>to the corporation</u>. ... Where, however, a separate and distinct claim (say, in tort) can be raised with respect to a wrong done to a shareholder *qua* individual, a personal action may well lie, assuming that all the requisite elements of a cause of action can be made out.

...

Conclusion

In light of the foregoing, I would find that even though the respondents owed the appellants (*qua* individual claimants) a *prima facie* duty of care both with respect to the 1982-83 investments made in NGA and NGH by Hercules and Mr. Freed and with respect to the losses they incurred through the devaluation of their existing shareholdings, such *prima facie* duties are negated by policy considerations which are not obviated by the facts of the case. Indeed, to come to the opposite conclusion on these facts would be to expose auditors to the possibility of indeterminate liability, since such a finding would imply that auditors owe a duty of care to any known class of potential plaintiffs regardless of the purpose to which they put the auditors' reports. This would amount to an unacceptably broad expansion of the bounds of liability drawn by this Court in *Haig, supra*. With respect to the claim regarding the appellants' inability to oversee management properly, I would agree with the courts below that it ought to have been brought as a derivative action. On the basis of these considerations, I would find under Rule 20.03(1) of the Manitoba *Court of Queen's Bench Rules* that the appellants have failed to establish that their claims as alleged would have "a real chance of success". ...

Appeal dismissed with costs.

NOTE

From *Hercules Managements*, it may be seen that shareholders will be prevented from bringing personal claims for losses suffered as a result of a harm done to the corporation.

Where shareholder losses are incidental to a primary harm that is done to the corporation, the Supreme Court has established that the proper cause of action to redress the harm done is the statutory representative action.

In order to support a personal cause of action, such as an oppression remedy, a shareholder must demonstrate direct and individual harm suffered. Where, however, shareholders act in respect of a corporation's interests, such as in *Hercules Managements* where they collectively oversaw the activities of the directors and officers through resolutions adopted at shareholder meetings, they may not also be seen to be acting in their individual capacities as shareholders and, thus, will not be entitled to a personal remedy.

(c) Oppression vs. Fiduciary Duty

There are similarities between the oppression remedy and the implications of corporate fiduciary duties, which are discussed in Chapter 7. The vagueness of the standards to be imposed and the breadth of the measures of relief available are two of the more obvious commonalities between these two causes of action. In addition, neither requires the presence of bad faith, notwithstanding that the actions giving rise to a claim of oppression or breach of fiduciary duty are necessarily antagonistic to and may in fact exploit the interests of the adversely affected parties. Finally, both oppression and breach of fiduciary duty are activated upon certain forms of inequitable conduct or unfairness that are facilitated by the nature of the interaction between the parties. For this reason, it may be possible to use either in situations where complainants' interests are adversely affected by corporate activities.

One might, however, question why there are similarities between the oppression remedy and corporate fiduciary duties when the beneficiaries of the former are the parties aggrieved by the oppressive conduct whereas the beneficiaries of the latter are, for the most part, corporations rather than their shareholders. Does this suggest that the oppression remedy is not exclusively personal or that a breach of fiduciary duty owed to a corporation is not necessarily "derivative"? Are there circumstances in which an oppression remedy may be used while a claim of breach of fiduciary duty cannot or is one cause of action broader than the other? Are there advantages to using one cause of action over the other? These are but some of the questions that exist when contemplating the similarities and distinctions between the oppression remedy and corporate fiduciary duties.

The case of *Peoples Department Stores Inc. (Trustee of) v. Wise*, [2004] S.C.J. No. 64, [2004] 3 S.C.R. 461 contemplates the nature of the duties owed by directors of an insolvent corporation to creditors of the corporation and whether any such duties owed are more appropriately covered by the oppression remedy or a finding of breach of fiduciary duty. Refer to the excerpts from the *Peoples* case in Chapter 7, sections C.2 and D.1.

The *Peoples Department Store* case was the first case heard by the Supreme Court of Canada concerned with the fiduciary duties of corporate directors to creditors. For the reasons indicated in the judgment, the court thought the more appropriate method of relief in the circumstances was an oppression remedy. There are potential problems with this result, as the following commentary indicates.

ROTMAN, FIDUCIARY LAW

(2005), pp. 503-04, 517-19 (Footnotes deleted.)

... [T]he court's conclusion on the fiduciary duty issue [in *Peoples*] appears to be premised more upon the court's belief that fiduciary duties to creditors are unnecessary since creditors' interests may be accounted for by the statutory oppression remedy ... than whether the fiduciary concept properly applies to the facts in issue. As the court states:

> [s]ection 241 of the CBCA provides a possible mechanism for creditors to protect their interests from the prejudicial conduct of directors. In our view, the availability of such a broad oppression remedy undermines any perceived need to extend the fiduciary duty imposed on directors by s. 122(1)(a) of the CBCA to include creditors.

The claim in *Peoples* did not, however, rely upon the oppression remedy.

It is clear that this latter assertion underlying the Supreme Court's dismissal of the fiduciary duty claim in *Peoples* is incorrect and based on irrelevant considerations. It matters not a wit to the lawful determination of a plaintiff's claim whether that plaintiff had other causes of action available that were not pleaded; rather, what is relevant is simply whether the cause of action pleaded may be properly made out on the facts. This is clearly indicated by Viscount Haldane in *Nocton v. Lord Ashburton*:

> It did not matter that the client would have had a remedy in damages for breach of contract. Courts of Equity had jurisdiction to direct accounts to be taken, and in proper cases to order the solicitor to replace property improperly acquired from the client, or to make compensation if he had lost it by acting in breach of a duty which arose out of his confidential relationship to the man who had trusted him.

La Forest J. acknowledges this same idea in his own judgment in *M.(K.) v. M.(H.)*, where he expressly states that "a breach of fiduciary duty cannot be automatically overlooked in favour of concurrent common law claims." Similarly, in *Hodgkinson v. Simms*, Justice La Forest states that "the existence of a contract does not necessarily preclude the existence of fiduciary obligations between the parties ..." For these reasons, the Supreme Court's judgment in *Peoples* ought not be regarded as having a sound basis in law.

...

... [U]nlike in other jurisdictions, creditors in Canada need not resort to allegations of breach of fiduciary duty to resolve their claims of actions injurious to their interests, as the Supreme Court of Canada indicates in the *Peoples* case. This may help to explain why the issue of directors' and officers' fiduciary duties to creditors arose so much later in Canada than elsewhere. Canadian creditors have recourse to the statutory oppression remedy, of which section 241 of the *CBCA* is illustrative ... Creditors have been found to qualify as "complainants" under Canadian division of powers corporations statutes and thus able to seek an oppression remedy where corporate directors and officers act in a manner that is "oppressive or unfairly prejudicial to or that unfairly disregards [their] interests ..."

The oppression remedy has been described by Beck as "beyond question, the broadest, most comprehensive and most open-ended shareholder remedy in the common law world ... unprecedented in its scope." Further ... the range of remedies that may be imposed where oppression is found is wider than the relief available for a breach of fiduciary duty. Bringing an oppression claim as opposed to a claim based on breach of fiduciary duty also dispenses with issues pertaining to creditors' standing to bring an action against a corporation, alleviates the burden on plaintiffs of establishing a fiduciary relationship and its breach, and eliminates the need to demonstrate that the corporation was not a viable going concern at the time. Consequently, there are definite reasons for creditors to consider this course of action either in addition to or as an alternative to seeking relief based upon a breach of fiduciary duty.

NOTE

As Rotman indicates, there are definite advantages to bringing a claim based on oppression as opposed to one alleging a breach of fiduciary duty. There are, however, advantages to bringing a fiduciary duty claim as well. For example, fiduciary law's reverse onus requires a fiduciary who is demonstrated to have committed a *prima facie* breach of fiduciary duty to disprove or rebut the beneficiaries' allegations rather than requiring the aggrieved party to fully demonstrate the basis of the claim on a balance of probabilities, as would be the case with a claim of oppression. Claiming a breach of fiduciary duty also avails the claimant of the benefits associated with equitable versus common law rules of causation, which may be of assistance both in demonstrating the claim and in the breadth of the relief available. For these reasons, and others, it is incorrect to suggest that the law of fiduciary duty has been swallowed up by the oppression remedy. Each retains its appropriate place in the scheme of corporate law.

3. Remedies

Once oppression is established the court has a broad range of remedies. The section directs the court "to rectify the matters complained of," and the specifics set out in s. 241(3) of the C.B.C.A. suggest a broad range of judicial action. Given the wording of the section why are specific remedies enumerated?

The following cases demonstrate the attitude of some Canadian judges when called upon to exercise the extensive power they have been given.

NANEFF v. CON-CRETE HOLDINGS LTD.

[1995] O.J. No. 1377, 23 O.R. (3d) 481 (C.A.)

[Mr. Naneff built a successful business and controlled several corporations. In 1977, by means of an estate freeze he made his two sons, Alex and Boris, equal holders of all of the common shares of one corporation. However, he retained complete control through redeemable preference voting shares. Later both sons entered the business and worked effectively. However, in 1990, a family rupture occurred when the family became concerned over the lifestyle of Alex. It removed him as an officer of all of the corporations and excluded him from participation in and management of the business. His income from the business was virtually eliminated.]

Galligan J.A. (for the court): — ... This conduct, and other conduct by Mr. and Mrs. Naneff and Boris toward Alex after December 25, 1990, was found by Blair J. to be oppressive to Alex within the meaning of s. 248 of the O.B.C.A. No appeal is taken, nor could it successfully be taken, from that finding.

Before turning to a consideration of the remedies granted to Alex I think this review of the background should be completed by the following extract from the reasons for judgment given by Blair J. (at p. 251):

> The desire — understandable and genuine as it may be — to chastise and correct the actual and perceived failing of a son or brother in his personal life, is not a basis for ignoring the duties and obligations which the parent and sibling owe in their corporate capacities to the son and brother in his corporate capacity. In circumstances such as these, the strictures of the O.B.C.A. and of corporate law override the family desires. In their corporate capacity as directors they are required to act in good faith and in the best interests of the company, and not for some extraneous purpose ...

(References omitted.)

...

B. THE REMEDIES ORDERED BY BLAIR J.

The judgment at trial contained a number of specific remedies. The fundamental and most important remedy, contained in para. 9, was that the business, *i.e.*, those corporations which comprise it, be sold publicly as a going concern with each of or any combination of Mr. Naneff, Alex and Boris being entitled to purchase it. There were remedies contained in paras. 4 to 7 inclusive of the judgment which set aside certain changes in corporate structure and other corporate arrangements which were made after Alex was ejected. Those remedies were ordered in an effort to restore the corporate arrangements to the state which they were in at the time of Alex's ejection. One remedy ordered the payment to Alex of his outstanding shareholder's loans to two of the corporations together with interest. There were two other ancillary remedies which I will mention later. I propose to discuss those remedies and give my opinion with respect to their validity.

1. Public Sale of the Companies Forming the Business as a Going Concern

Before discussing the merits of the challenge to this remedy, I wish to make brief reference to the principles which guide an appellate court in its review of a remedy ordered under s. 248(3) of the O.B.C.A. Section 248(3) empowers a court upon a finding of oppression to make any order "it thinks fit". When that broad discretion is given to a court of first instance, the law is clear that an appellate court's power of review is quite limited. In *Mason v. Intercity Properties Ltd.* (1987), 59 O.R. (2d) 631 at p. 636, 38 D.L.R. (4th) 681 (C.A.), Blair J.A. set out the governing principle:

> The governing principle is that such a discretion must be exercised judicially and that an appellate court is only entitled to interfere where it has been established that the lower court has erred in principle or its decision is otherwise unjust.

I approach this issue, therefore, keeping in mind that this court can only interfere with the remedy if it concludes that there was an error in principle on the part of Blair J. or if the remedy in all of the circumstances is an unjust one. It cannot be interfered with, as Carruthers J. said (at p. 701) when giving the judgment of the Divisional Court, "simply because someone else might prefer a different way of going about things". With great deference to Blair J., who is a distinguished jurist with extensive commercial law experience, I regret to say that I have concluded, in the circumstances of this case, that the remedy of public sale of this business amounts to an error in principle and is unjust to Mr. Naneff.

At the outset I think it is important to keep in mind that this is not a normal commercial operation where partners make contributions and share the equity according to their contributions or where persons invest in a business by the purchase of shares. This is a family business where the dynamics of the relationship between the principals are very different from those between the principals in a normal commercial business. As the courts below have correctly held, the fact that this is a family business cannot oust the provisions of s. 248 of the O.B.C.A. Nevertheless, I am convinced that the fact that this is a family matter must be kept very much in mind when fashioning a remedy under s. 248(3) as it bears directly upon the reasonable expectations of the principals.

...

Thus, I think any remedy granted under s. 248(3) in this case had to be fashioned so that it was just, having regard to the considerations of a personal character which existed among Mr. Naneff, Alex and Boris.

The provisions of s. 248(3) give the court a very broad discretion in the manner in which it can fashion a remedy. Broad as that discretion is, however, it can only be exercised for a very specific purpose; that is, to rectify the oppression. This qualification is found in the wording of s. 248(2) which gives the court the power, if it finds oppression or certain other unfair conduct, to "make an order to *rectify the matters complained of*". Therefore, the result of the exercise of the discretion contained in s. 248(3) must be the rectification of the oppressive conduct. If it has some other result the remedy would be one which is not authorized by law. I agree with the opinion expressed by Professor J.G. MacIntosh in his paper "The Retrospectivity of the Oppression Remedy" (1987-88), 13 *Can. Bus. L.J.* 219 at p. 225:

> The private law character of the enactment strengthens the argument, for in seeking to redress equity between private parties the provision *does not seek to punish but to apply a measure of corrective justice.*

[Emphasis added.]

That opinion was referred to with approval by Glube C.J.T.D. in *Mathers v. Mathers* (1992), 113 N.S.R. (2d) 284 (N.S.T.D.) at p. 340, 309 A.P.R. 284, reversed on other grounds (1993), 123 N.S.R. (2d) 14, 340 A.P.R. 14 (C.A.).

My analysis of s. 248(2) indicates that there is another limit imposed by law upon the apparently unlimited discretionary powers contained in s. 248(3). Section 248(2) provides that when the court is satisfied that in respect of a corporation there is certain specified conduct "that is oppressive, or unfairly prejudicial to or that unfairly disregards the interest of *any security holder, creditor, director*, or *officer* of the corporation, the court may make an order to rectify the matters complained of" (emphasis added). The expression "security holder" includes a shareholder. Thus, the provision only deals with the interest of a shareholder, creditor, director or officer. It follows from a plain reading of the provision that any rectification of a matter complained of can only be made with respect to the person's interest as a shareholder, creditor, director or officer.

In *Stone v. Stonehurst Enterprises Ltd.* (1987), 80 N.B.R. (2d) 290, 202 A.P.R. 290 (Q.B.), Landry J. was called upon to interpret s. 166(2) of the New Brunswick Business Corporations Act, R.S.N.B. 1973, c. B-9.1, whose provisions are the same as s. 248(2) of the O.B.C.A. The company in question was a family company run as a family business. The company decided to sell its assets. A minority shareholder in his personal capacity wanted to buy the assets and bid for them. When the majority shareholder exercised her controlling interest and sold the assets to someone else, the minority shareholder attacked the transaction as being oppressive to him as a shareholder. Landry J. held that the Act protected a person's interest as a shareholder "as such". Basing his opinion on the judgment of Jenkins L.J. in *Re H.R. Harmer Ltd.*, [1958] 3 All E.R. 689 at p. 698, [1959] 1 W.L.R. 62 (C.A.), Landry J. said at p. 305:

> It must be remembered, and it is very important in this case, that it is only the interest of a shareholder as such ... that is protected by this section.
>
> The applicant must establish that his interest *as a shareholder* has been affected. He may of course have other interests, such as being a prospective purchaser of the assets of the company. But it is only the applicant's interest as a shareholder which we must be concerned with in applying s. 166.

[Emphasis in original.]

I agree with and adopt Landry J.'s analysis as a correct statement of the law. Persons who are shareholders, officers and directors of companies may have other personal interests which are intimately connected to a transaction. However, it is only their interests as shareholder, officer or director as such which are protected by s. 248 of the O.B.C.A. The provisions of that section cannot be used to protect or to advance directly or indirectly their other personal interests.

I conclude, therefore, that the discretionary powers in s. 248(3) O.B.C.A. must be exercised within two important limitations:

(i) they must only *rectify* oppressive conduct

(ii) they may protect only the person's interest as a shareholder, director or officer *as such*.

The law is clear that when determining whether there has been oppression of a minority shareholder, the court must determine what the reasonable expectations of that person were according to the arrangements which existed between the principals. The cases on this issue are collected and analyzed by Farley J. in *8220099 Ontario Inc. v. Harold E. Ballard Ltd.* (1991), 3 B.L.R. (2d) 113 at p. 123 (Ont. Gen. Div.), affirmed (1991), 3 B.L.R. (2d) 113 (Ont. Div. Ct.). I agree with his comment at pp. 185-86:

> Shareholder interests would appear to be intertwined with shareholder expectations. It does not appear to me that the shareholder expectations which are to be considered are those that a shareholder has as his own individual "wish list". They must be expectations which could be said to have been (or ought to have been considered as) part of the compact of the shareholders.

The determination of reasonable expectations will also, in my view, have an important bearing upon the decision as to what is a just remedy in a particular case.

The finding made by Blair J. that Alex expected ultimately to be an equal co-owner of the business with his brother cannot be challenged. However, it must be interpreted in the light of two other important and intertwined considerations. The first consideration is that Alex fully understood that until death or voluntary retirement his father retained ultimate control over the business even to the extent of deciding what dividends would be paid and what would be done with any of those dividends. The second consideration is that this was a family business which had been built by his father.

The importance of the first of those considerations is that Alex knew that until his father died or retired he could under no circumstances have any right to have or even to share absolute control of the business. Therefore, under no circumstances could Alex's reasonable expectations include the right to control the family business while his father was alive and active. The second consideration is important because, while Alex expected that his father would give him an equal share in the control of the business upon his death or retirement, that expectation was based upon his belief that his father would continue to be bountiful to him in the future. It should have been apparent to Alex that he could not expect that paternal bounty to continue if his father for good reason or bad no longer considered him to be a dutiful son. It would have been quite unrealistic of Alex to expect that his father would continue to be bountiful to him if his family ties were severed. Alex knew that the reason for his father giving him one-half of the equity in the family business was his father's desire for his sons to work with him in his business. He must also have known that it would be impossible for him, Mr. Naneff and Boris to work together in the business as a family if the family bonds ceased to exist. It is for those reasons that Alex's reasonable expectation must be looked at in the light of the family relationship.

It is my view that the first error in principle in this remedy is that it did more than simply rectify oppression. As I noted above, the O.B.C.A. authorizes a court to rectify oppressive conduct. I think the words of Farley J. in *Ballard, supra*, at p. 197 are very appropriate in this respect:

> The court should not interfere with the affairs of a corporation lightly. I think that where relief is justified to correct an oppressive type of situation, the surgery should be done with a scalpel, and not a battle axe. I would think that this principle would hold true even if the past conduct of the oppressor were found to be scandalous. *The job for the court is to even up the balance, not tip it in favour of the hurt party.* I note that in *Explo* [*Explo Syndicate v. Explo Inc.*, a decision of the Ontario High Court, released June 29, 1989], Gravely L.J.S.C. stated at p. 20:
>
>> In approaching a remedy the court, in my view, should interfere as little as possible and *only to the extent necessary to redress the unfairness.*
>
>   [Emphasis added.]

The order of Blair J. gave Alex something which he knew he could never have while his father was alive and active — the opportunity to obtain full control of the family business. A remedy that rectifies cannot be a remedy which gives a shareholder something that even he never could have reasonably expected.

Moreover, I am unable to view the remedy as anything other than a punitive one towards Mr. Naneff. There was never any doubt among the three men that Mr. Naneff would exercise ultimate control of the family business until he died or retired. Mr. Naneff solidified his right of complete control by the corporate arrangements he put in place at the time of the estate freeze and which he kept in place to the knowledge of his sons throughout the time that the three of them worked together. It is not the task of any court of law to judge the family dispute or to rule upon the justice of the expulsion of Alex from the family. However, I am unable to accept as anything other than punitive, a remedy which puts at risk the very condition upon which Mr. Naneff exercised his bounty in favour of his sons — his total control of the business during his active life. The O.B.C.A. authorizes a court to rectify oppression; it does not authorize the court to punish for it.

The second error in this remedy is that it attempts to protect Alex's interest in the family business as a son and family member, in addition to protecting his interest as a shareholder *as such*. As I mentioned above, it is my view that Alex's expectation of ultimately obtaining an equal share of the control of the business with Boris was based upon his expectation of being the continuing object of his father's bounty. That in turn depended upon him remaining in his father's favour and remaining in his father's eyes a member of the family. The remedy of public sale, which gives Alex the opportunity to buy the company, enables him to obtain that control while out of his father's favour. This appears to protect much more than his interest as a shareholder as such; it protects, indeed it advances, his interest as a son.

It is my view, therefore, that the remedy imposed in this case constituted an error in principle in that it did more than rectify oppression, and it did more than protect Alex's interest as a shareholder as such in the companies. As well as concluding that the remedy granted to Alex was wrong in principle it is my view that the remedy was unjust to Mr. Naneff. By the time of Alex's ouster from the business, Mr. Naneff had devoted almost 40 years of his life to creating, nurturing and building the business into a very significant enterprise. Instead of using profits from the business to acquire other personal assets, he used them to finance the growth and expansion of the business. There was never any doubt in the minds of his sons that their father gave them their equity positions upon the understanding that he would retain ultimate control as long as he wanted to exercise it. No one can disparage the productive and devoted work which Alex put into the business. But his nine years of contribution pales to almost insignificance when compared with that of his father's contribution.

The effect of the relief granted to Alex is to put Mr. Naneff in the position where he is just another person, equal to Alex, who is entitled to buy the business which he had himself founded and built from nothing. The remedy jeopardizes something which Alex knew was always to be his father's, the right to ultimate control of the business. The remedy gives to Alex the possibility of taking control of the business, something he knew he could never have during his father's lifetime. Having regard to the circumstances of this case this remedy, which jeopardizes the right which everyone knew belonged to Mr. Naneff and which gives Alex the opportunity to take away that right, strikes me as unjust.

At trial there were three possible fundamental remedies suggested to the trial judge. One of them was properly rejected out of hand. No more need be said about it. The alternative remedy to public sale of the business as a going concern was that Mr. Naneff and Boris acquire Alex's shares of the companies at fair market value, without minority discount. In my view that was the just remedy in this case. While I find that Mr. Naneff's oppressive conduct should not endanger his right to control the business, neither should he be able to take away what he had given to Alex, or to take away what Alex had contributed to the business. This remedy, together with certain of the other remedies ordered by Blair J., would have had the effect of fully compensating Alex for the value of the equity given to him by his father and for his own contributions to the business. The value of his shares would reflect the success of the business and Alex's contribution toward that success, as well as the value of the gift of equity which he had received from his father. When I discuss the remedy respecting the shareholders' loans, it will be seen that when the business was ordered to repay Alex the amounts of his loans, in fact he was receiving his share of the operating profits of the business over previous years.

This remedy would be just because it will put Alex, in so far as money can, in the position which he would have been in had he not been ejected. It would not give him an opportunity to which he had no reasonable expectation. It would not put at risk Mr. Naneff's right to ultimate control which Alex knew was a condition of his father's gift of equity. The remedy would protect Alex's interest as a shareholder as such.

It is my opinion that para. 9 of the trial judgment, which provides for the sale of the appellant companies on the open market as a going concern, cannot be sustained. In its place, I would order that the appellants acquire Alex's shares of the companies at fair market value fixed as of the date of his ouster, December 25, 1990. It is conceded on behalf of the appellants that it would not be fair to apply a minority discount to the market value of Alex's shares. I agree and would order that there be no minority discount when fixing the fair market value of his shares. Alex is also entitled to prejudgment interest on the value of his shares as provided in the *Courts of Justice Act*, R.S.O. 1990, c. C.43, from December 25, 1990.

In the event that the parties cannot agree upon the value of the shares or to having the value of them fixed in some other way, I would direct a new trial restricted to fixing the value of Alex's shares in the appellant companies as of December 25, 1990. In my view the costs of such a new trial ought to be in the discretion of the judge presiding at it.

NOTES AND QUESTIONS

Does the use of the "reasonable expectation" test assist the court in determining whether there has been oppression within the meaning of s. 241? In determining what remedy should be given? In determining how judicial discretion should be exercised? Is any other test needed?

If the reasonable expectation of shareholder test is used to determine judicial discretion, is it not then appropriate to enforce rigidly to their logical extremes the principles of corporate personality, managerial power and majority rule except to the extent that judicial discretion is actually invoked for minority protection?

E. CLASS VETO

No corporation is required to have more than one class of shares: most do. The division of shares into classes is an efficient way to package different types of participatory rights in corporate governance and to market these rights to investors. The underlying principles of the class structure are explored in the next chapter. For the moment, it will suffice to assume that shares can be divided into as many classes, with as many different participatory rights, as are specified in the corporate constitution.

Classes of shareholders may be seen as different minority groups, each of which will sometimes have views different from or opposed to the majority of shareholders of other classes. The class as a minority group is given, in certain, pre-determined situations, a class veto. The class then votes separately and can defeat proposals notwithstanding their overwhelming approval by other shareholders of other classes.

The process is simple and, unlike the other minority protection devices, generally operates without judicial intervention. The main legal issue is identification of situations that trigger the class veto.

The C.B.C.A. is typical:

176(1) The holder of shares of a class or, subject to subsection (4), of a series are, unless the articles otherwise provide in the case of an amendment referred to in paragraphs (*a*), (*b*) and (*e*), entitled to vote separately as a class or series upon a proposal to amend the articles to

(*a*) increase or decrease any maximum number of authorized shares of such class, or increase any maximum number of authorized shares of a class having rights or privileges equal or superior to the shares of such class;

(*b*) effect an exchange, reclassification or cancellation of all or part of the shares of such class;

(*c*) add, change or remove the rights, privileges, restrictions or conditions attached to the shares of such class and, without limiting the generality of the foregoing,

(i) remove or change prejudicially rights to accrued dividends or rights to cumulative dividends,

(ii) add, remove or change prejudicially redemption rights,

(iii) reduce or remove a dividend preference or a liquidation preference, or

(iv) add, remove or change prejudicially conversion privileges, options, voting, transfer or pre-emptive rights, or rights to acquire securities of a corporation, or sinking fund provisions;

(*d*) increase the rights or privileges of any class of shares having rights or privileges equal or superior to the shares of such class;

(*e*) create a new class of shares equal or superior to the shares of such class;

(*f*) make any class of shares having rights or privileges inferior to the shares of such class equal or superior to the shares of such class;

(*g*) effect an exchange or create a right of exchange of all or part of the shares of another class into the shares of such class; or

(*h*) constrain the issue, transfer or ownership of the shares of such class or change or remove such constraint.

(2) Subsection (1) does not apply in respect of a proposal to amend the articles to add a right or privilege for a holder to convert shares of a class or series into shares of another class or series that is subject to a constraint permitted under paragraph 174(1)(*c*) but is otherwise equal to the class or series first mentioned.

(3) For the purpose of paragraph (1)(*e*), a new class of shares, the issue, transfer or ownership of which is to be constrained by an amendment to the articles pursuant

to paragraph 174(1)(*c*), that is otherwise equal to an existing class of shares shall be deemed not to be equal to an existing class of shares.

(4) The holders of a series of shares of a class are entitled to vote separately as a series under subsection (1) only if such series is affected by an amendment in a manner different from other shares of the same class.

(5) Subsection (1) applies whether or not shares of a class or series otherwise carry the right to vote.

(6) A proposed amendment to the articles referred to in subsection (1) is adopted when the holders of the shares of each class or series entitled to vote separately thereon as a class or series have approved such amendment by a special resolution.

Note also s. 183(4) (class vote on amalgamations) and s. 189(6) (class vote on certain major property transfers).

There is obviously no point in memorizing sections of this nature. But an easily remembered technique may be useful. On any proposed amendment to the corporate constitution, a two-step mental checklist is likely the best way of determining whether a class veto will be triggered. Step 1 involves recitation of the various types of changes that might be described in the section. Step 2 involves reading the detailed provisions, but only if the proposed amendment fits one of the general descriptions recited at Step 1.

There are three types of change to the corporate constitution that might generate a class veto:

(1) proposals that particular rights of a class named in the proposal are to be varied;
(2) proposals that shuffle the hierarchy of classes;
(3) proposals dealing with "authorized" shares, redemptions, or new classes.

The first type is easy. C.B.C.A., s. 176(1)(*c*) clearly sets out those direct changes to class rights which trigger the class veto. This subsection is detailed and generally requires little interpretation. A further triggering device of this type is set out in C.B.C.A., s. 176(1)(*h*), though it was probably already covered in para. (*c*).

The second type is more complex, but it breaks down as follows. Any particular right — for example dividends, voting rights, the right to attend meetings — can be used to compare (*i.e.*, rank) various classes. Picking thus any right attached to any class, one can easily rank all other classes as having more, less, or the same degree of that right. A class veto will be generated by a proposal that will effect certain changes to these inter-class rankings. The section is worded to cover changes in the rankings through broadening existing gaps ((*d*)), leapfrogging ((*d*), (*f*)) or dilution ((*f*), (*g*)).

It will be noted that the wording seems prolix and there is substantial overlap among the subsections. The following case serves to illustrate the advantages of this legislative approach.

RE TREND MANAGEMENT LTD.

[1977] B.C.J. No. 30, 3 B.C.L.R. 186 (S.C.)

[The articles gave class A shareholders the right to elect one of three members of the board of directors. The remaining two directors were elected by class B shareholders. On other matters, the class B votes vastly outnumbered class A. The articles also stipulated that the company could not make purchases in excess of $10,000 unless all three directors approved. The class A shareholders sought a ruling that they could veto a proposal to change this article, invoking s. 247 of the B.C. *Companies Act*, which then read: "No right ... attached to any issued share shall be prejudiced or interfered with ... unless members holding shares of each class whose right ... is prejudiced or interfered with consent thereto by separate resolution requiring a majority of three-fourths of the issued shares of the class."]

Andrews J.: — [T]he respondents argue that the special resolution does not deprive the applicants of their vote, their right to elect a director and their entitlement to dividends. They never did have any assurance that their director would exercise his vote in accordance with their collective wishes and hence the function of a director could not be considered a right attached to the share.

I am persuaded by respondents' argument that it cannot be said in the circumstances at hand that any "right" or "special right" attached to the Class A shares has been affected by this resolution. It seems to me it might be argued that the "enjoyment" of the right has been affected to the extent that the director elected by the Class A shareholders no longer enjoys a veto but that, I repeat, is at most an abrogation of an "enjoyment", as opposed to the "right".

I, like counsel, have been unable to find Canadian authority for the proposition that there is a difference between varying or abrogating a right attached to the share and taking some action which affects the enjoyment of that right: see *Greenhalgh v. Arderne Cinemas Ltd.*, [1946] 1 All E.R. 512, where the effect of a proposed sub-division of shares was to deprive the plaintiff of voting control and where Lord Greene M.R. drew a distinction between being "affected as a matter of business" and "varied as a matter of law" [p. 518]. See also *Re Mackenzie & Co. Ltd.*, [1916] 2 Ch. 450 and *White v. Bristol Aeroplane Co.*, [1953] Ch. 65, [1953] 1 All E.R. 40.

In my view, the most the applicants can complain of is the enjoyment of their right being affected as a matter of business, but this does not bring into operation the protective provisions of s. 248 [*sic*] of the Act.

NOTES AND QUESTIONS

How do you think this case would have been decided under the C.B.C.A.? In *Greenhalgh v. Arderne Cinemas Ltd.*, [1951] Ch. 286, [1950] 2 All E.R. 1120 (Eng. C.A.), the section involved was essentially the same as the applicable section in *Re Trend Management*. How would *Greenhalgh* have been decided under the C.B.C.A.? Do you think either case would have gone to court under the C.B.C.A. wording?

The third type of proposal that might trigger a class veto is really a catch-all. C.B.C.A., s. 176(1)(*a*) deals only with proposals to vary a stipulated maximum number of "authorized" shares that cannot be exceeded by the corporation without constitutional amendment. Section 176(1)(*b*) deals with proposals to exchange, reclassify or cancel shares of the class. Section 176(1)(*e*) deals with proposals to create a new class of shares with equal or superior rights. Proposals covered by paras. (*a*), (*b*) and (*e*) generate a class veto only if the articles do not state otherwise, whereas the other types cannot be overridden. What about proposals covered by the wording of both one of these last three subsections and another of the first or second type; can the articles override the class veto provision in such a case?

Note the reference in the section to a series of shares. Series may be established within a class: see, for example, C.B.C.A., s. 27. Where the articles authorize the issue of shares in series, the statute permits the board of directors substantial flexibility in changing the corporate capital structure. Consider a proposal by the directors to issue a third series within a class already having two series issued. If the new series is to have superior rights to those attached to the previously issued series, do the first and second series holders have a veto? What does "amendment" mean in C.B.C.A., s. 176(1)?

F. APPRAISAL REMEDY

Shareholders who invest in corporate shares sometimes find that other shareholders have voted to change the corporate constitution. Some such changes are inconsequential. Some, however, may be viewed by those who voted against the change as radical and economically disadvantageous redirections of the capital they have invested. The obvious solution, once majority rule prevails, is to sell their shares and invest elsewhere. But a ready market for their shares does not always exist.

Most Canadian jurisdictions have enacted an "appraisal remedy" whereby dissenting minorities can sometimes force the corporation to buy their shares at either a mutually satisfactory or a judicially set "fair" price.

The events that give rise to the appraisal remedy are clearly identified in the statutes. In the C.B.C.A. these comprise:

(1) amalgamation with another corporation (s. 190(1)(c));
(2) major business changes, involving either imposition, variation or removal of restrictions on the business ("objects") or transfers of substantially all the corporate property (s. 190(1)(b) and (e));
(3) "emigration" to another jurisdiction (s. 190(1)(d));
(4) varying share provisions by either changing share issue or transfer provisions (s. 190(1)(a)) or affecting class rights in one of the ways set out under the "class veto" heading; and
(5) court supervised "arrangements" (see s. 192(4)(d)).

A brief review of these statutory provisions will indicate that it will not usually be controversial whether the appraisal remedy has been triggered.

There is likely to be more dispute as to whether the procedural steps have been followed. C.B.C.A., s. 190 sets out a detailed statutory process to be followed when invoking the remedy. The statutory technique was explained (and criticized) in the following case.

JEPSON v. CANADIAN SALT CO.

[1979] A.J. No. 481, [1979] 4 W.W.R. 35, 99 D.L.R. (3d) 513 (S.C.)

[An amalgamation proposal triggered the appraisal remedy under C.B.C.A., s. 184 (now s. 190).]

Laycraft J.: — This is an application in Chambers under Rule 220 of the Supreme Court Rules for the determination prior to trial of a number of preliminary points of law, under an agreed statement of facts. The dispute concerns the rights of dissident minority shareholders in an amalgamation of the defendant, Canadian Salt, with Morton Industries of Canada Ltd. ("MIC") carried out under the provisions of the *Canada Business Corporations Act*, 1974-75-76 (Can.), c. 33.

Prior to July 7, 1977, MIC, which is a wholly-owned subsidiary of Morton-Norwich Products Inc., a Delaware corporation, was the owner of approximately 80% of the issued shares of Canadian Salt. By a circular letter of that date, Canadian Salt advised its shareholders of an impending offer by MIC to the remaining minority shareholders for the purchase of their shares at $20 per share. The same circular advised that after making its take-over offer, MIC intended to implement an amalgamation between itself and Canadian Salt. By the terms of this amalgamation, Morton-Norwich would receive one common share of the amalgamated company for each share of MIC held by it; MIC would receive nothing for its shares of Canadian Salt and other shareholders would receive one $20 redeemable preferred share in the amalgamation company for each share of Canadian Salt. Since such an amalgamation may proceed under s. 177 of the *Canada Business Corporations Act* with the sanction of two-thirds of the votes at a shareholders' meeting, this amalgamation — and the $20 price for shares — seemed to be a foregone conclusion before the offer was made or the shareholders' meeting was held.

The plaintiffs, all members of the same family, immediately objected to the proposal. ...

The MIC offer affected 460,855 shares of Canadian Salt. In the result the owners of some 96% of these shares accepted the offer so that only 18,130 shares, including those owned by the plaintiffs, remained outstanding. Whether the owners accepted the offer because they felt it was advantageous for them or because they felt the result was inevitable cannot, of course, be known.

On September 26, 1977, notice was given of a Special General and Annual General Meeting of shareholders of Canadian Salt to be held on October 27, 1977, for the purpose of approving an amalgamation agreement between MIC and Canadian Salt. The agreement was in the terms earlier predicted.

On October 17, 1977, Richard Jepson as to 1,400 shares and Joanne G. Jepson as to 100 shares gave notice in two separate letters that they objected to the proposal. I shall consider the effect of these notices later in these reasons. The corporation acknowledged receipt of these notices of October 21, 1977.

At the meeting of October 27, 1977, the holders of 99.97 per cent of the shares represented at this meeting approved the proposed amalgamation. The Plaintiffs did not attend the meeting and did not file proxies. On November 11, 1977, the corporation issued the following notice:

November 11, 1977

TO THE HOLDERS OF COMMON SHARES OF THE CANADIAN SALT COMPANY LIMITED (as it existed prior to amalgamation).

Dear Sirs;

The September 15, 1977 Amalgamation Agreement between The Canadian Salt Company Limited (herein referred to as "Old Salt") and Morton Industries of Canada Ltd. has now been made fully effective by the issue of a Certificate and Articles of Amalgamation to the corporation resulting from the amalgamation which now bears the name "The Canadian Salt Company Limited" (herein referred to as "New Salt").

Under the terms of amalgamation you are to receive for each common share of Old Salt which is registered in your name, one preferred share of New Salt. Your preferred share certificate accompanies this letter. No continuing value attaches to the certificate or certificates you hold for shares of Old Salt. You need not return any certificates but should now treat them as worthless paper. Your share certificate for preferred shares of New Salt fully replaces your Old Salt certificate(s).

You will be receiving soon a notice of redemption of your New Salt preferred shares, which are redeemable at $20.00 per share.

Yours very truly,

THE CANADIAN SALT COMPANY LIMITED

On November 17, 1977, the plaintiffs responded:

Further to our letters of October 17, 1977, we the undersigned and Edith Maude Jepson (presently hospitalized) reject the sale of our common shares of Canadian Salt or exchange for callable preferred shares of the new amalgamated company.

Therefore, pursuant to Section 184 of the *Canada Business Corporations Act*, we request that the corporation submit a "written offer in an amount considered by the directors of the corporation to be a fair value thereof, accompanied by a statement showing how the value was determined".

...

The corporation then replied that the "time for dissenting under Section 184 of The *Canada Business Corporations Act* expired October 28 last. Your November 17 letter is beyond the delay afforded." The reference to "October 28" is not clear but it may be a mistaken reference to the date of the meeting. Further correspondence, containing some very forceful expressions of opinion then ensued before this action was commenced on January 25, 1978. The plaintiffs formally tendered their common shares of the old company to the transfer agent on February 28, 1978.

The relief claimed by the plaintiffs in this action is a declaration for the fair value of their shares, judgment for that value, and "general and punitive and exemplary damages" in an unspecified amount.

A number of questions have been posed for determination on this application. They may be considered, however, in four groups:

1. Did any or all of the letters from the plaintiffs prior to the meeting of October 27, 1977, constitute notice of dissent to the plan of amalgamation under s. 184 of the *Canadian Business Corporations Act*?
2. Did the plaintiffs send a valid notice under s. 184(7) of the Act?
3. Have the plaintiffs lost their right to claim under s. 184 of the Act by reason of their failure to tender their shares within the time limited by s. 184(8) of the Act?
4. Is this action a valid "application" under s. 184, commenced within the time limited by that section?

As was pointed out by Bouck, J., in *Neonex International Ltd. v. Kolasa et al.* (1978), 84 D.L.R. (3d) 446, [1978] 2 W.W.R. 593, the use of the amalgamation provisions of the *Canada Business Corporations Act* as a "force-out" mechanism against minority shareholders has made virtually redundant [by] the sections of the Act designed to cover the "force-out" situation. Section 199 of the Act provides a much more elaborate procedure to safeguard the minority than does s. 184, governing amalgamations. For example, the "force-out" procedure in s. 199 requires that the take-over offer be accepted by holders of 90% of the shares apart from those owned by the offeror, while an amalgamation may be achieved by a two-thirds majority without any requirement that the majority come from the independently held shares.

In this case holders of 96% of the independently held shares accepted the offer, so that MIC could have met the more stringent requirements of s. 199. It may be, however, that the shareholders accepted the offer because they had little or no choice but to accept it. When a $20 offer is combined with the promise of an amalgamation resulting in a $20 share which it is intended immediately to redeem, only a shareholder willing to involve himself in litigation has any choice. Moreover, many minority shareholders will not possess a sufficient degree of business sophistication or will not have available the expert advice needed to meet, as an equal, persons able to devise such take-over mechanisms. With respect, I agree completely with the view expressed by Bouck, J., that, where the amalgamation provisions are used as a "force-out" mechanism, the Court must be astute to protect the rights of minority shareholders, so far as it is possible to do, while giving effect to the clear provisions of the statute. At pp. 452-3 D.L.R., 600-1 W.W.R., in the *Neonex* case, Bouck, J., said:

> If a shareholder wants to acquire all other shares in the company by using the amalgamation sections rather than the forcing-out provisions then the law will be particularly concerned over the rights of the dissenters. Their property is being expropriated. It has always been the policy of the common law to protect the rights of the minority as against the abuse of an unreasonable majority. This is more so where an individual's property is being taken by the majority and it is claimed there has not been adequate compensation.

> If Parliament intended to deprive the minority of these common law rights then the law demands the statute say so in the most clear and unequivocal language. Otherwise, the common law will blossom through the cracks and crevices of the legislation and try to ensure that justice is done.

Section 184 of the *Canada Business Corporations Act* prescribes a remarkably rigid procedure which, moreover, seems to be slanted in favour of the amalgamated corporation and against a dissenting shareholder. In several places in s. 184 there is a requirement that specified notices, containing specified information, be sent within specially limited times. On the face of the sections, failure by the corporation to meet the requirements of the section has no particular penalty. On the other hand, failure by the shareholder to observe some provision of the section can result in the Draconian penalty of complete loss of his investment in the corporation. Indeed, in this case, it is urged by the corporation that that is the result.

I have reproduced the relevant portions of s. 184 as an appendix to these reasons. The procedures outlined in s. 184 may be summarized as follows:

1. At or before the meeting at which the amalgamation resolution is to be considered, the shareholder gives notice of dissent (s-s. (5)).
2. Subsection (6) requires the corporation to send to the shareholder within 10 days a notice that the amalgamation resolution has been passed.
3. The shareholder then has 20 days within which to send a notice containing his name and address, the number and value of such shares (s-s. (7)). That subsection contemplates that the corporation may not have sent the notice required by s-s. (6), in which event the 20 days starts running when the shareholder "learns that the resolution has been

adopted". After sending the notice under s-s. (7), a dissenting shareholder ceases to have any rights except the right to be paid fair value unless he withdraws his notice before the corporation makes an offer of fair value (s-s. (11)).

4. Within 30 days of sending the notice under s-s. (7) the shareholder must send his shares to the corporation or its transfer agent (s-s. (8)). If he does not, he has "no right to make a claim under this section". Since this failure would be subsequent to his notice under s-s. (7) by which his rights as shareholder have already terminated, it is arguable (and in this case the corporation so contends) that he has lost all his rights. He has ceased to be a shareholder and has left to him no mechanism by which he is able to have his day in Court so that it may be determined.

5. Subsection (12) then requires the corporation to send a notice to the shareholder containing a written offer of the amount considered by the directors to be fair value. Again, failure by the corporation to send this notice has no particular result and s-s. (15) expressly contemplates that the notice may not be sent.

6. By s-s. (15), if the corporation fails to make an offer or if the shareholder does not accept it, the corporation may within 50 days after the amalgamation is effective (which is the date the Director under the Act issues the certificate of amalgamation) apply to the Court to fix the fair value.

7. If the corporation does not apply to the Court under s-s. (15), then by s-s. (16), the shareholder has a further 20 days within which to make the application. The application may be made to the Court in the Province where the corporation has its registered office or in the Province where the shareholder resides, provided the corporation carries on business there. The sections does not expressly state what result follows if the shareholder fails to meet this limitation period. It is urged on behalf of the corporation in this case that the plaintiffs, having ceased to be shareholders, and having failed to bring the action on time, are therefore left with no means to have fair value determined. Presumably, therefore, if this contention is correct they have completely lost their investment in Canadian Salt.

I am left to wonder at the legislative policy which produced this procedural morass. Under earlier legislation a dissident shareholder could hamper or prevent the operation of the company by litigation challenging an amalgamation approved by the majority and it was undoubtedly thought desirable to prevent any such impasse in the corporation's activities. Under the new statute, however, the dissident shareholder cannot impede corporate operations. His right is converted to a simple right to be paid the fair value of the shares. Why it is thought necessary to prescribe a 20-day limitation period with an uncertain commencement for such a claim is not apparent in the statute. No power to relieve against the provision is expressly given to the Court.

The first question to be determined is whether the plaintiffs acquired the status of dissenting shareholders by their correspondence with the corporation prior to the meeting of October 27, 1977. In my opinion no particular form of objection is required so long as the shareholder makes clear, in writing, the essential fact that he does object to the proposal. It was argued on behalf of the company that the failure by the plaintiffs in their two letters of October 17, 1977, to make specific reference to the proposed resolution approving the amalgamation agreement was a fatal defect. One of the letters stated:

> As registered holder of 1,400 shares of Canadian Salt Company Limited I object to the price of $20 per share you offer or a preference share of $20. (Italics are mine.)

The other stated:

> Please be advised that I do not wish to sell my 100 shares in Canadian Salt for $20 per share, nor do I wish to be forced into this by issuance and immediate call of preferred shares.

In my view each of these letters makes it plain that the writer opposes the proposed amalgamation, even though there is also reference to the original offer. Thus, as at the date of the shareholders' meeting, the plaintiffs had acquired the status of dissenting shareholders under s. 184.

The corporation did not meet the time limit of 10 days for the notice specified by s-s. (6). Thus the shareholders' 20-day period for its notice was delayed in starting but, in any event, the plaintiffs responded within six days of the date of the notice.

Section 184(7) requires that the notice by the shareholder give to the company the name and address of the shareholder, the number and class of shares in respect of which he dissents and a demand for payment of the fair value of such shares. The notice sent by the plaintiffs on November 17, 1977, contains each requirement except the exact number of shares held by each, though that information was clearly possessed by the corporation in its own records. In any event, the notice of November 17, 1977, makes reference to the letters of October 17, 1977, in which Richard Jepson and Joanne Jepson (though not Edith Maude Jepson) specified the number of shares held by each. Again this reference to the information is, in my view, sufficient compliance with the section. I therefore hold that the plaintiffs, other than Edith Maude Jepson, did send a valid notice under s. 184(7) of the Act.

The third question is whether the plaintiffs have lost their rights because they did not tender their shares to the transfer agent within 30 days after sending their notice of November 17, 1977. The corporation urges that they have lost their rights even though its letter of November 11, 1977, informed shareholders that:

> No continuing value attached to the certificate or certificates you hold for shares of Old Salt. You need not return any such certificates but should now treat them as worthless paper.

In my view the language used in the notice of November 11, 1977, constituted a waiver by the corporation of its right to insist on the tender of the share certificates.

"Waiver" is defined by Hyndman, J., in *Crump et al. v. McNeill et al.*, [1919] 1 W.W.R. 52, 14 Alta. L.R. 206, where he says at p. 57:

> Waiver is defined as the act of waiving, or not insisting on some right, claim or privilege; a foregoing or giving up of some advantage, which but for such waiver, the party would have enjoyed; an election to dispense with something of value, the giving up, relinquishing, or surrendering some known right; and intentional relinquishment of a known right, or such conduct as warrants an inference of the relinquishment or waiver of such right; waiver involves both knowledge and intention. It is distinguishable from estoppel inasmuch as estoppel may arise where there is no intent to mislead; it depends upon what one himself intends to do;

estoppel depends rather upon what he caused his adversary to do; waiver involves the act and conduct of only one of the parties; estoppel involves the conduct of both. A waiver does not necessarily imply that one has been misled to his prejudice or into an altered position; an estoppel always involves this element.

This definition has been quoted in a number of other cases including *Ross v. Imperial Life Ass'ce Co.*, [1929] 1 D.L.R. 324, [1928] 3 W.W.R. 593, 23 Alta. L.R. 614; *Tanenbaum et al. v. Winston-Wright Ltd.* (1963), 39 D.L.R. (2d) 433 at p. 448, [1963] 2 O.R. 320 at p. 335 [affd 49 D.L.R. (2d) 386, [1965] 2 O.R. 1 (C.A.)]; and *Brunswick of Canada Ltd. v. Mountainview Bowl Ltd.* (1971), 21 D.L.R. (3d) 759 at p. 763, [1972] 1 W.W.R. 524 [affd 26 D.L.R. (3d) 640, [1972] 5 W.W.R. 366 (Alta. C.A.); affd 31 D.L.R. (3d) 128*n*, [1973] 2 W.W.R. 480 (S.C.C.)].

The notice by the corporation calling the meeting of October 27, 1977, at which the amalgamation was to be considered, shows clearly that it was aware of its rights. A copy of s. 184 of the *Canada Business Corporations Act* was attached to the notice. The corporation was aware that the plaintiffs were opposed to the proposal and that the procedures in s. 184 would therefore be followed. One of the procedures required was to give notice to the dissenting shareholders that the resolution had been passed. When the notice states that the certificates need not be returned and are "worthless paper" the corporation has thereby waived its right to insist on tender of them. Though the right to tender of the certificates is one prescribed by statute, it seems clearly to have been intended for the benefit of the corporation rather than the public generally and may therefore be waived: *Wilson v. McIntosh*, [1894] A.C. 129 at p. 133 (Judicial Committee).

The final question posed is whether this action is a valid "application" under s. 184 commenced within the time limited by that section. In my view no particular type of Court process is contemplated in the section by the words "apply" or "application". This is a statute enacted by the Parliament of Canada providing for recourse to the various provincial Courts. Those Courts have varying procedures. In Alberta, for instance, a solicitor might consider procedure by originating notice of motion though he could not know whether facts are in dispute when he commenced the action. The declaratory action seems to me to be an equally effective mode and is within the very general wording used by Parliament. I leave open, because it has not been raised in the preliminary questions of law, the issue whether a statutory cause of action under s. 184 may be combined with a claim for "general damages and punitive and exemplary damages".

The time limited by s. 184(16) for commencement of the application by the dissenting shareholder is "within a further ... twenty days" after the 50 days allotted to the corporation. That 50 days commences with the date that the amalgamation resolution became effective.

The dissenting shareholder is required by s. 184 to be remarkably alert. This case affords an example of what is required of him. Here the dissenter was required to find out when the Director issued the certificate of amalgamation. Then he was required to ascertain that the corporation had not, during the next 50 days, at some judicial centre either in the Province of Quebec or in the Province of Alberta, commenced some Court process which could be termed an "application" to have the fair value of the shares determined. Within the next 20 days and while his frantic search in Quebec and Alberta proceeded, his own action could be commenced.

While this remarkably short limitation period would lead to an assumption that some great degree of urgency exists, the application is simply to determine the amount of a money claim, for such claims the law often prescribes limitation periods up to six years in length.

Moreover, the section contemplates an action which, once commenced, will take considerable time to complete. The section requires that all dissenting shareholders, including all those who did not meet the 20-day deadline, are to be joined as parties to the action. Since those shareholders may come from every other Province and Territory in Canada, and will need to retain and instruct counsel, anyone familiar with the Court process will predict very long delays before the opening day of the trial.

In this case the notice of November 11, 1977, does not disclose the day on which the Director issued the certificate of amalgamation. It merely states that as of that date the certificate had been issued. Taking November 11th as the day of issue, 50 days expired on January 1, 1978. A "further twenty days" expired on Saturday, January 21, 1978, making the final day of the 20-day period January 23, 1978. This action was commenced on January 25, 1978.

I cannot believe that Parliament intended the absurd and onerous result for which the corporation contends. A 20-day limitation period is so short that it must have been intended not to commence until the dissenting shareholders became aware that the company had not made the application contemplated by s. 184(15).

In *Bowen v. City of Edmonton* (1977), 75 D.L.R. (3d) 131, 2 Alta. L.R. (2d) 112, 3 A.R. 63, Clement, J.A., sitting as a trial Judge, held communication to be implicit in the term "render its decision" in s. 128 of the *Planning Act*. Similarly in *Re United Ass'n of Journeymen & Apprentices, etc. and Board of Industrial Relations* (1975), 49 D.L.R. (3d) 708, [1975] 2 W.W.R. 470, Prowse, J.A., held that the word "issuance" in s. 71(4) of the Alberta Labour Act includes the element of communication to the parties affected; he concluded that to hold otherwise would be to nullify or curtail the relief afforded by the section. In my view s. 184(16) must be interpreted as permitting the action within 20 days after the shareholder becomes aware that the corporation had not commenced an action within the 50 days allowed to it.

Since the issues on this application are merely points of law preliminary to the action, I leave costs for determination by the trial Judge.

NOTES AND QUESTIONS

What is the legislative policy that produced "this procedural morass"?

In *Re Domglas Inc.* (1980), 13 B.L.R. 135 (Que. S.C.); affd 22 B.L.R. 21 (Que. C.A.), those shareholders who failed to make the C.B.C.A. s. 187(7) demand for payment were held not to be "dissenting shareholders". What is the effect of such a finding? Contrast the ruling in *Manning v. Harris Steel Group Inc.*, [1985] 2 W.W.R. 230 (B.C.C.A.), a case involving a demand for "fair value" in a squeeze-out situation [see *infra*]. It was held that if one dissenting shareholder has filed an application within the time limits, all other dissenters are protected by C.B.C.A., s. 190(13), which requires that they be made parties to the application. "On that view of the matter the issue of whether the time limit provided in the statute had been met is determined by looking at the date upon which the first application by a dissenting shareholder is brought". It will be noted from these two rulings that some fine points of statutory interpretation will be coming before the courts under these sections. Are the two cases distinguishable?

Once the preliminary exchange of documents takes place and the corporation makes its offer for the shares, one of three things can happen. The shareholder and the corporation can agree on a price; this would end the matter. If there is no agreement, the corporation has a limited amount of time to apply to the court to have "fair value" assessed (C.B.C.A., s. 190(15)). If the corporation does not do so, the shareholder may (C.B.C.A., s. 190(16)). This raises a complex issue: what does "fair value" mean?

RE MONTGOMERY AND SHELL CANADA LTD.

[1980] S.J. No. 196, 111 D.L.R. (3d) 116 (Q.B.)

[Dissenting shareholders in a "class veto" situation sought a valuation of their shares under then-C.B.C.A., s. 184 [now s. 190]. It was clear from s. 184(3) that the date for which the value was to be fixed was the day before the class voted to adopt the resolution. The shares had traded on the Toronto Stock Exchange on that day at $16.50 per share. The dissentients sought a valuation of $28.50 per share, based on "asset value."]

Estey J.: — The fact is not disputed that the applicants have followed the proper procedure in order to become dissenting shareholders under the Act and, therefore, the sole question to be determined by the Court is a fair value for the shares held by the applicants. Pursuant to s. 184(3) [rep. & sub., *idem*, s. 60(2)], the Court is to determine the fair value of the applicants' shareholdings as of the close of business on December 12, 1978, being the day before the shareholders of Shell adopted the resolution with which we are concerned.

The facts are that in December, 1978, the applicant, John Montgomery, was the owner of 550 class A common shares of Shell, while the applicant, Mary Montgomery, was the owner of 150 class A common shares. A special meeting of the shareholders of the said class A shares was held December 18, 1978. The purpose of the said meeting was to approve of the creation of a new class of preferred shares which shares would rank in priority to the class A common shares. The resolution approving and creating the said preferred shares was adopted at the said meeting. The applicants deemed these preferred shares to adversely affect the position of the class A common shares, and did become dissenting shareholders.

I do not think the Court is concerned about whether the applicants were right or wrong in their decision to become dissenting shareholders. Nor do I believe the Court is concerned with the reasons for Shell creating the said preferred shares.

Shell says the fair value of a class A common share as of December 12, 1978, was $16.50 per share, while the applicants say a fair value on the said date was $28.50 per share. The position of the applicants is that a fair value is the asset value of the shares, while the respondent takes the position that the best method of ascertaining a fair value is to take the market value as of December 12, 1978.

According to the affidavit of Mr. T.P.O. McKeag, general counsel for Shell, the issued shares of Shell consisted of 63,840,147 class A common shares, 9,087,039 class B Commons shares, and 100 5% cumulative redeemable preferred shares. The difference between the class A and class B common shares is that holders of the latter are entitled to four times the dividend paid on the class A shares. There are, therefore, slightly in excess of 100,000,000 common shares for the purpose of calculating the asset value per share. Some of the class A common shares are listed in Canada on the Toronto, Vancouver and Montreal stock exchanges. As of the date with which we are concerned, 66.7% of the class A common shares were owned by Shell Investments Limited, and 33.3% were held by the investing public. The class B common shares were all owned by Shell Investments Limited, as were the 4% cumulative redeemable preferred shares. Mr. McKeag, when examined on his affidavit, stated that "to the best of my knowledge", Shell Investments Limited had not engaged in trading the shares held by it in Shell since 1963.

For the purpose of this application, I propose to deal with the application of the shareholder, John Montgomery (hereinafter referred to as the "applicant"), for the facts of each application are very similar. The applicant bases his price of $28.50 primarily on reports concerning Shell prepared by well-known investment firms. The report of Pitfield MacKay Ross Limited, dated May 10, 1978, places an "appraised worth" of Shell to be approximately 2.7 billion dollars, and after dividing the said amount by the issued common shares, the "appraised worth" per share of Shell, according to the report, is $27.17. A report on Shell as of July 28, 1978, was prepared by F. Deacon Hodgson Inc. which places a "worth per common share" of $26.44. The Applicant further filed a report on Shell prepared by Wood Gundy Limited dated April 11, 1978, which fixes the "net asset value" per share at $27.50. The applicant's position, from a reading of his affidavit and his examination on that affidavit, is simply that the "fair value" is the asset value per common share and not the market price. The applicant, is referring to the Wood Gundy appraisal, in Q. 158 of his examination states:

> 158. ... the basis of this report is if all of the assets were sold and liabilities were paid off, each shareholder would get $27.50.

In support of the applicant, there was filed the affidavit of Russell Martel, a stockbroker and a minority shareholder in St. Lawrence Securities Limited. He was examined on his affidavits. Mr. Martel has had 13 years' experience with member firms of the Toronto Stock Exchange. In para. 5 of his affidavit, he defines "fair value" as:

> the price at which all or most of the shareholders would sell their shares to a buyer or the value obtained upon the hypothetical liquidation of the assets of a company when an arm's length sale of all or most of the shares is not possible.

As there was not evidence that Shell Investments Limited, the majority holder of the common shares in Shell, was prepared to sell any of its shareholdings, it would appear that Mr. Martel takes the view that a fair value per share is an asset value. During his examination on his affidavit, he stated that St. Lawrence Securities Limited was in December, 1978, the owner of 10,500 common shares in Shell, and as the company did not want to get involved in a prolonged struggle to determine a fair value per share, it accepted the price of $16.50 for each of its common shares. He favoured calculating the fair value on the basis of a hypothetical liquidation which, in my view, is an asset value per share, and admitted that in order to determine such a valuation, the services of an appraiser or appraisers would be required. He expressed the belief that the market price for a common share of Shell would not correctly reflect the value of Shell's oil and gas reserves, i.e., that the value of such reserves as expressed by the market price is lower than the actual value of such reserves. He admitted he did not know the extent of such undervaluation, but stated that such could be determined by a qualified appraiser. His knowledge of the matter of reserves was obtained to some extent from literature received from other investment house. Mr. Martel, in the answer to Q. 569 of his examination, when referring to the cost of such appraisal for a company as large as Shell stated:

569. A detailed appraisal certainly would be in the ... I would say in the millions to be quite honest.

Section 184(12) appears on the facts of this case to give Shell seven days from the date on which it received the notice referred to therein to calculate the fair value, to advise a dissenting shareholder of such fair value and offer to the shareholder the fair value as calculated. Mr. Martel, in his examination, admits that to do an appraisal such as he suggest of a company the size of Shell is just not possible in seven days.

Mr. McKeag, in his affidavit, stated that originally 21 shareholders representing 22,459 class A shares commenced the procedure to become dissenting shareholders, but two of these shareholders did not file demands for payment pursuant to the Act. The situation is, according to Mr. McKeag, of the 19 dissenting shareholders, 17 accepted the fair value figure of $16.50. The applicants were therefore the only dissenting shareholders who did not accept the fair value figure of $16.50 per common share as offered by the respondent. Mr. McKeag pointed out that the board of directors of Shell appointed Wood Gundy Limited to prepare a report on the fair value of a class A common share, and the said report is ex. F to the affidavit of Mr. McKeag. This report will be referred to later in this judgment. Suffice it to say at this time that fair values so determined were $16.12 per common share or $16.50 per common share, The former value was the closing price of Shell's class A common shares on the Toronto Stock Exchange on December 12, 1978, and latter value a weighted average for the closing prices during the period November 13, 1978 to December 12, 1978. The board of directors accepted as a fair value per share the figure of $16.50.

The respondent filed the affidavit of Mr. G.E. King, a vice-president and director of Wood Gundy Limited, who was responsible for the report given on the fair value of the shares by Wood Gundy Limited. In para. 7 of his affidavit, he states:

> That I am of the opinion that the fair value of a Class "A" Common Share of Shell Canada Limited as of the close of business on December 12, 1978 in these circumstances would most appropriately be the price which could be realized through the sale of each share on a recognized stock exchange.

In para. 9 of his affidavit, he sets out further reasons for relying on the market price taken from the Toronto Stock Exchange when he states:

> THAT the market price is the best and most convincing test of the fair value of a Class "A" Common Share of Shell Canada Limited as of the close of business on December 12, 1978 because, in these circumstances as of that time;
>
> (*a*) the Class "A" Common Shares of Shell Canada Limited were widely-traded;
>
> (*b*) the Class "A" Common Shares of Shell Canada Limited were actively-traded;
>
> (*c*) information as to the operation of Shell Canada Limited's business was widely disseminated; and
>
> (*d*) there had been no material changes in Shell Canada Limited's financial position, business or assets other than as disclosed on a timely basis.

The above reasons are also set out in para. 4 of the letter of Mr. King to Shell's board of directors dated December 13, 1978.

Counsel for the applicant, during her examinations on the various affidavits filed by the respondent, and in her argument, sought to discredit the valuation of Mr. King and associates due to the fact that Wood Gundy Limited was in a conflict of interest position so far as Shell was concerned. The company was the underwriter under the preferred share issue approved at the meeting of December 13, 1978, and was likewise retained to supply a fair value per common share. I do not think there was evidence before the Court to establish a conflict of interest position. As underwriter, Wood Gundy Limited was to market the preferred shares, which I deem to be entirely separate from preparing a valuation. As I understand Mr. King's evidence, to determine the fair value of a common share, you must look at the "nature of the transaction" to determine the method to be allowed to obtain the fair value. One can, for instance, receive very little assistance in the determination of a fair value from the Act, for such phrase is not defined therein. There may be situations where shares in the company are not actively traded on a stock exchange and, therefore, one should use the asset value or some other method, rather than the market value to determine the fair value. Mr. King, when examined on his affidavit, pointed out that in 1978, the value of the Shell class A common shares traded on the three main stock exchanges in Canada was $67,000,000. Such a figure suggests that the class A common shares held other than by Shell Investments Limited were actively traded in Canada. Mr. King acknowledged that the "net asset value" of Shell's commons shares on December 13, 1978, was in the area of $27.50.

The applicant says that the fair value should be the net asset value, because the latter represents what a common shareholder would receive per share if the company were liquidated and the assets sold. As to the availability of the net asset value per share to a shareholder in the event of liquidation, Mr. King at p. 25 of his examination, in answer to Q. 141 states:

> 141. ... that that resulting net asset value is not a figure which, in the event of a liquidation, would be available to the shareholder or any shareholder because it does not take into account the fact that if the company was liquidated, the enormous amount of tax that would have to be paid by the company upon the liquidation both of such fixed assets as refineries, and other assets such as reserves, before any funds would be available to shareholders. So that an assumption that a net asset amount as calculated by appraised value calculations, or net asset value calculations would be available to a shareholder, is an unwarranted assumption.

He further pointed out that in the case of oil companies, in some cases the market value is less than the net asset value, and in others the market value is higher than the net asset value.

There appears to be little law in Canada on the concept of a dissenting shareholder so far as fair value is concerned. It appears that the concept of fair value in connection with a dissenting shareholder was borrowed from certain jurisdictions in the United States.

The case of *Endicott Johnson Corp. v. Bade et al.* (1975), 376 N.Y.S. (2d) 103, illustrates the attitude of the Court of Appeal of New York on the question of ascertaining the fair value of shares when concerned with a dissenting shareholder. This was the case of a merger of two companies where certain shareholders dissented, and an appraiser was called in to ascertain the fair value of a share. The attitude of the New York Court is set out in the judgment of Fuchsberg, J., at pp. 106-7 when he writes:

> Although the statute itself is silent as to how fair value is to be determined, it is well established by case law that, in our State, the elements which are to enter into such an appraisal are net asset value, investment value and market value. ... While, in order to provide the elasticity deemed necessary to reach a just result, all three factors are to be considered, the weight to be accorded to each varies with the facts and circumstances in a particular case.
>
> ...
>
> It follows that all three elements do not have to influence the result in every valuation proceeding. It suffices if they are all considered. ... No estimation of net asset value was attempted by the parties or the appraiser. Since the corporation was not being liquidated, but was to continue to operate as part of the surviving parent McDonough Corporation, that made business and legal sense. ...
>
> Indeed, in this case investment value, for all practical purposes, became the sole determinant of fair value when the appraiser eliminated market value as a meaningful factor by reporting as follows:
>
>> My opinion is that little weight should be given to the past history of market value prior to 1969 because I believe that there was a radical enough change in the management of the company so that it had "turned around", and that the pre-1969 market is not particularly helpful.
>
> ...
>
> Subsequent to 1969 I believe the market became so thin because of the control of McDonough and the subsequent delisting that it is fairly meaningless.

The *Endicott Johnson* case, illustrates facts in which the market price should not be the dominant consideration in ascertaining the fair value. In that case, the Court upheld the appraiser when he eliminated market value "as a meaningful factor". The appraiser relied in the main upon investment value, in determining the fair value. One of the main reasons for disregarding the market value appears to be the fact that for a period prior to the merger, the company's shares were delisted from the New York Stock Exchange. Moreover, it appears from the report that there was not extensive trading in the company shares prior to the merger, which, of course, would create a situation where the market price might not reflect a fair value. It is interesting to note that Shell's class A common shares were actively traded during 1978. The Court approved of this appraiser's reasoning that the asset value method should not be used due to the fact the company was not being wound up or liquidated. This, in my view, is a very cogent reason in the present case to examine very carefully the applicability of the asset value concept.

From the *Endicott Johnson* case, and the Canadian cases which will be referred to, it appears no general rule can be laid down as to whether the market value or the asset value should be the dominating factor in ascertaining the fair value. The method to be used in ascertaining the fair value depends on the facts of each case.

The question of a dissenting shareholder and the fair value of a share was dealt with in a judgment of Macfarlane, J., of the British Columbia Supreme Court, in *Re Wall & Redekop Corp. et al.* (1974), 50 D.L.R. (3d) 733, [1975] 1 W.W.R. 621. This case dealt with the British Columbia Companies Act. It involved a resolution by Wall & Redekop to amalgamate with certain of its subsidiaries. The majority of the shares were held by three individuals and by two holding companies controlled by those individuals. From a reading of the report, it appears that there had not been active trading in the shares of the company. The Judge was not prepared to accept the per share value obtained from the stock exchange, and requested an appraised value.

Macfarlane, J. refers to *American General Corp. v. Camp et al.* (1937), 190 A. 225, and writes at p. 736 D.L.R. pp. 624-5 W.W.R.:

> Although the Court would appear to be saying that the corporation's assets should be valued on a liquidation basis, it should be kept in mind that in the American General case the assets of the corporation were primarily bonds and other marketable securities so that a hypothetical liquidation was an appropriate method to use.

I certainly agree with Macfarlane, J., that in the case of a corporation where the vast majority of assets are securities or real property, that the asset value may be the proper method of ascertaining the fair value. Current values of such assets can usually be obtained without difficulty.

The Court was referred to *Re VCS Holdings Ltd. et al. and Kerby*, [1978] 5 W.W.R. 559, 5 B.L.R. 265, where the Court approved of a special referee's finding as to the fair value of a share. The method of valuation was based on the "asset basis approach" and "earning basis". The company involved had a total of 12,500 issued shares. There is nothing to indicate that the shares were listed on a stock exchange or that recent transactions had taken place from which a market value could be obtained.

The Court was also referred to the case of *Neonex Int'l Ltd. v. Kolasa et al.* (1978), 84 D.L.R. (3d) 446, [1978] 2 W.W.R. 593, 3 B.L.R. 1. This is a case where two companies amalgamated to form a third company under the provisions of the Canada Business Corporation Act. The amalgamating companies were Neonex International Ltd. (hereinafter referred to as "the old company") and Jim Pattison (British Columbia) Ltd. (hereinafter referred to as "J.P.L."). The company arising out of the amalgamation was Neonex International Ltd. An application was made to ascertain the fair value of a share as certain shareholders dissented. J.P.L. was wholly owned by one J.A. Pattison through a holding company, and the said Pattison, in his personal capacity, or through associated companies, owned 46.5% of the issued shares of the old company. According to the report, the resolution dealing with amalgamation had to be carried by two-thirds of the votes cast by shareholders at each of the company meetings. Mr. Pattison's 46.5% interest in the old company represented 62.3% of the shares present at the meeting to approve the amalgamation, and as pointed out by Bouck, J., in his judgment, it would not be difficult for Mr. Pattison to obtain another 4% or 5% of the shares voted. In so far as J.P.L. is concerned, of course, Mr. Pattison, by voting the shares, could approve the amalgamation. The directors sought to have the Court approve a fair value of $3 per share. There was evidence that from January, 1975 to July, 1977, 2,155,373 shares of the old company were traded on a stock exchange and of these, 494,223 shares were sales or purchases by insiders. Bouck, J., directed that the petition presented to the Court be converted into an action for determining fair value. It appears to me that the Neonex action was an example of a situation where the market value should not have been taken as the fair value, due to the extensive shareholdings of Mr. Pattison, the activity of insiders on the stock exchange and as pointed out by Bouck, J. [at p. 453 D.L.R., p. 601 W.W.R.], that Mr. Pattison "... derived substantial benefits because of the amalgamation".

In the present case, Shell Investments Limited, the holder of two-thirds of the class A common shares has not traded these shares for years. The market value has been determined by trading in the remaining one-third or a portion thereof. There was no evidence to suggest that the actions of Shell Investments Limited or of Shell in December, 1978, or prior thereto, in any way affected the price of class A common shares on the Canadian stock exchanges.

The facts in the present case differ from those in the Neonex case. In the latter case there was an amalgamation where one party actually controlled 100% of the shares in one company and for all practical purposes controlled the other company. Indeed, from a reading of the report, the same party controlled the new company. As pointed out by the Judge, it was in that party's interest to keep the fair value at the lowest possible figure. Indeed, 20% to 25% of the shares traded in one of the amalgamated companies in the two years prior to the amalgamation were traded by "insiders". It was, in my view, a case where on the facts, great care should have been exercised by the Court, as indeed it was prior to determining a "fair value".

The sole question before the Court is whether the Court should adopt the market value or the asset value as a "fair value". Neither counsel seriously suggested that such value should be determined from book value or an investment value, although it may be difficult at times to eliminate entirely the concepts of book value and investment value in determining the "fair value".

It appears from the authorities, especially *Endicott Johnson, supra,* that the "fair value" should not be ascertained by the asset value method when a corporation is to continue as a going concern. The three reports filed, placing the fair net asset value per share at around $27, do not suggest that such a figure could be obtained on liquidation or even on a hypothetical liquidation. I agree with Mr. King at p. 26 of his examination that the net asset value does not take into consideration "the enormous amount of tax that would have to be paid by the company upon liquidation, both of such fixed assets as refineries, and other assets before any funds would be available to shareholders". So far as tax liability is concerned, the reports simply refer to Shell's deferred income tax and not to any tax arising in the event of liquidation.

The said reports were not, in my view, prepared on the basis that the per share value or the net worth per share was a figure which one share would attract in the event of the liquidation of Shell or in the event of what the applicant refers to as a hypothetical liquidation. For example, the last paragraph of the Pitfield Mackay report reads in part:

> At $14-5/8, Shell is trading at 9.3x estimated 1978 earnings and at 47 percent discount from our $27.17 per share appraised worth estimate — this estimate incorporating an eventual return of profits in refining and a restoration of natural gas markets.

The figure of $27.17 per share is therefore based on "eventual return of profits" to Shell and should not be taken as a figure in which to base a "fair value" per share as of December 12, 1978. In the F.H. Deacon, Hodgsen Inc. report, the paragraph immediately preceding the calculation of $26.44 as the net worth per share reads in part:

> In the following appraisal, the estimated value of oil and gas reserves is based on the discounted present value (12 percent discount factor) of the estimated future annual

revenues from the reported proven reserves, on the basis of future royalties, income taxes, and well head prices which may be reasonably expected.

Again, the calculations are based on future estimates of such things as future royalties and taxes. I do not think this report can form the basis of a fair value per share as of December 12, 1978.

The report of K.L. Slater, C.F.A. of Wood Gundy Limited, dated April 11, 1978, appears to be a comparison between Gulf Oil Canada and Shell with a recommendation that investors in Shell switch to Gulf Oil Canada. The net asset value of $27.50 in this report appears to be calculated to some extent on an estimate of the future performance of Shell.

The said reports appear to be published for the benefit of the author's clients. They indicate what may happen if the company's future performances are as indicated by the authors. The calculations may turn out to be right or may turn out to be wrong. They do not represent, as set out in s. 184(3), the fair value of a common share "determined as of the close of business on the day before the resolution was adopted", namely, December 12, 1978.

Counsel for the applicant stressed the fact that a "fair value" is the value attached to one common share on a hypothetical winding-up of Shell. We are dealing with a very large corporation of which the board has no intention of winding-up. The expenses of winding-up and the taxes incurred by a winding-up, hypothetical or otherwise, really cannot be determined with any degree of certainty until a winding-up takes place.

On the facts placed before the Court, it appears that the best method of ascertaining the fair value of a common share is to take the market value. The applicant's position appears to be that such is not a "fair value" due to the fact that two-thirds of the class A common shares were held by a holding company and only one-third traded on the leading Canadian stock exchanges. Such reasoning, in my view, overlooks two important facts: firstly, the holding company had not for years traded any of its holdings in Shell; secondly, that approximately 21 million class A common shares were held by the public and were widely and actively traded in 1978. I believe that such facts substantially prevent a situation arising where the shares held by the holding company would depress the market value to an extent that such would not be a "fair value" for the purposes of the Act. The market value, when there is no indication of a majority shareholder trading, is certainly some evidence of the price at which small and comparatively large shareholders are prepared to sell and are prepared to buy the class A common shares. It is not an estimate but an actual price.

I therefore find $16.50 to be the "fair value" of a class A common share of Shell as of December 12, 1978. It is obvious I see no need of appointing an appraiser to assist the Court in determining a "fair value". An appraisal of a company the size of Shell would take a considerable length of time and according to the evidence, cost millions of dollars.

Section 184(23) of the Act provides that the Court may:

> 184.(23) ... allow a reasonable rate of interest on the amount payable to each dissenting shareholder from the date the action approved by the resolution is effective until the date of payment.

In my view, a "reasonable rate of interest" would be 12% and I so order. If the parties cannot agree to the date on which interest commences to run, either party may apply to the Court on three days' notice to determine such date.

NOTES AND QUESTIONS

Do you agree? Do "fair value" and "market value" bear any relationship to one another at all? If yes, what is it? If no, what does "fair" mean? What do you think the appropriate standard ought to be?

In *Belman v. Belman*, [1995] O.J. No. 3155, 26 B.L.R. (2d) 52 (Gen. Div.), it was said that "fair value," for the purposes of an oppression remedy under s. 248(3)(*f*) of the O.B.C.A. (requiring a corporation to purchase the shares of a shareholder) was to be determined by ascertaining the fair value to the shareholder. Such "fair value" was said in *Belman* to be properly calculated on the basis of fair market value unless the selling shareholder could demonstrate why such valuation would be improper under the circumstances.

In *SevenWay Capital Corp. v. Alberta Treasury Branches*, [2000] A.J. No. 502, 5 B.L.R. (3d) 190 (Q.B.), Hart J. said that where the shares of the corporation in question had been suspended from the Toronto Stock Exchange, "fair value" was to be determined by regarding the corporation on a going concern basis rather than a liquidation.

RE CYPRUS ANVIL MINING CORP. AND DICKSON

[1986] B.C.J. No. 1204, 33 D.L.R. (4th) 641 (C.A.)

[The shares of dissenting shareholders were being compulsorily acquired pursuant to a takeover offer. Apart from the takeover bid there was no market for the shares and no history of revenue. The takeover offer was $1.75 per share, but at trial Chief Justice McEachern adopted a "discount cash flow" basis and found a share value of $19.04. His judgment was varied on appeal and fair value set at $8.]

Lambert J.A. (for the majority at pp. 651-55): — In this Part I propose to comment on the general process of judicial determination of fair value under s. 199 of the *Canada Business Corporations Act* and under similar legislation.

Perhaps the best starting point, though not the chronological beginning, is this passage from the reasons of Mr. Justice Bouck in *Neonex Int'l Ltd. v. Kolasa et al.* (1978), 84 D.L.R. (3d) 446 at p. 453, [1978] 2 W.W.R. 593 at p. 601, 3 B.L.R. 1:

2. There are at least four ways of valuing shares in a company:

    (a) Market Value: this method uses quotes from the stock exchange.

    (b) Net Asset Value: this takes into account the current value of the company's assets and not just the book value.

    (c) Investment Value: this method relates to the earning capacity of the company.

    (d) *A combination of the preceding three.*

(Emphasis added.)

See also, to the same effect, *Domglas Inc. v. Jarislowsky, Fraser & Co. Ltd. et al.*, [1980] Que. S.C. 925 at p. 950, 13 B.L.R. at p. 192; affirmed 138 D.L.R. (3d) 521 at p. 526, 22 B.L.R. 121 at p. 128 (Que. C.A.).

From there I would pass on to *Re Wall & Redekop Corp. et al.* (1974), 50 D.L.R. (3d) 733, [1975] 1 W.W.R. 621 (B.C.S.C.) (affirmed by an unreported decision of this court dated April 29, 1975, C.A. 712/74). In that case, Mr. Justice

Macfarlane, then sitting as a judge of the Supreme Court of British Columbia, reviewed a number of United States authorities on determining the value or fair value or fair market value of the shares of dissenting shareholders whose shares were being compulsorily acquired. In particular, he considered *American General Corp. v. Camp et al.* (1937), 190 A. 225; *Warren v. Baltimore Transit Co.* (1959), 154 A. 2d 796; *Roessler et al. v. Security Savings & Loan Co.* (1947), 72 N.E. 2d 259; *Phelps et al. v. Watson-Stillman Co.* (1956), 293 S.W. 2d 429; *Martignette et al. v. Sagamore Manufacturing Co. et al.* (1959), 163 N.E. 2d 9; *Woodward et al. v. Quigley* (1965), 133 N.W. 2d 38, and *Southdown, Inc. v. McGinnis et al.* (1973), 510 P. 2d 636. It is not necessary for me to analyze those cases or to quote from them. The point that they emphasize is that the problem of finding fair value of stock is a special problem in every particular instance. It defies being reduced to a set of rules for selecting a method of valuation, or to a formula or equation which will produce an answer with the illusion of mathematical certainty. Each case must be examined on its own facts, and each presents its own difficulties. Factors which may be critically important in one case may be meaningless in another. Calculations which may be accurate guides for one stock may be entirely flawed when applied to another stock.

The one true rule is to consider all the evidence that might be helpful, and to consider the particular factors in the particular case, and to exercise the best judgment that can be brought to bear on all the evidence and all the factors. I emphasize: it is a question of judgment. No apology need be offered for that. Parliament has decreed that fair value be determined by the courts and not by a formula that can be stated in the legislation.

Where Parliament has called for judgment, and where judgment is being exercised, the scope of the judgment should not be obscured. If the judgment is about which formula to adopt, then that should be made clear; if the judgment is about the assumptions to which the formula is to be applied, then that also should be made clear; and if the judgment is about the final result, with the formula being treated only as an aid, then that should be apparent.

Suppose, in a hypothetical case, method A produced a value of $1,000, method B a value of $800 and method C a value of $1,200. A simple average would produce $1,000. But maybe the judge who is determining the value thinks that method C is the most accurate method in the circumstances, but that all methods have some value, and that fair value is $1,100. It adds nothing to that reasoning process to say that method C should have a 60% weight, method A a 30% weight, and method B a 10% weight (giving the same answer of $1,100 ($720 plus $320 plus $80), but now buttressed by mathematics), unless the assignment of weights to the different methods of reaching value is a true aid to the judgment process through assessing the worth of the methods, and not merely a way of dressing up the judgment process to make it fancier than it is, or, even worse, working back from the final answer to make the premises come out right (as I have just done in this example). (For comments on the "Delaware Block" approach as exemplified in *Swanton v. State Guaranty Corp.* (1965), 215 A. 2d 242, see *Weinberger v. UOP, Inc.* (1983), 457 A. 2d 701.)

In summary, it is my opinion that no method of determining value which might provide guidance should be rejected. Each formula that might prove useful should be worked out, using evidence, mathematics, assessment, judgment or whatever is required. But when all that has been done, the judge is still left only with a mixture of raw material and processed material on which he must exercise his judgment to determine fair value.

There is nothing in the cases to which we were referred which is contrary to the approach that I have set out. In particular, the carefully considered decisions of the Manitoba Court of Appeal in *Re LoCicero et al. and BACM Industries Ltd.* (1986), 25 D.L.R. (4th) 269, [1986] 2 W.W.R. 152, 38 Man. R. (2d) 134, and of Mr. Justice Greenberg and the Quebec Court of Appeal in *Re Domglas Inc.*, are wholly consistent with the approach I have set out, though they dealt with somewhat different problems.

…

It follows from the general approach that I have discussed in Part IV that I think the approach adopted by Chief Justice McEachern was in error and led to a wrong result.

In the context of the decisions on this court's powers of review, I think that the result is "wholly erroneous": I think that the approach that was adopted was "clearly and palpably wrong", with respect to matters of fact, in that relevant evidence of the negotiated deal between Cyprus Anvil and Kerr Addison was entirely set aside and given no weight; and I think that the error arose through a misapplication of the law as to the approach that ought to be adopted to a determination of fair value under s. 199 of the Act. For each of those three reasons, any one of which would be sufficient, I consider that this court is required to set aside the fair value arrived at by the Chief Justice, and either to substitute its own fair value, if the evidence is sufficient, or to direct a new determination in accordance with the correct approach.

In particular, when the Chief Justice said that "one becomes a captive of a method of valuation. When one starts down the discounted cash flow path [one] cannot easily get off" (54 B.C.L.R. at p. 228); and when he said; "Having made these difficult choices, I feel constrained, as was said of General Grant, to let the chips fall where they may, even though the result seems very generous to the respondents", I think that he fell into the error of letting adherence to a mathematical formula usurp the exercise of judgment called for by the statutory powers granted to the court by s. 199.

It is true that the discounted net cash flow method of indicating value cannot be tinkered with, in the sense that it loses utility unless it is applied in accordance with ascertained facts and neutral judgment, uncoloured by the result that intuition might appear to favour. But having got the result by that method, the next step must be to consider whether the method itself may be something less than entirely reliable. If so, the result should be given weight in proportion to its reliability, and regarded as only one among the considerations from which the court, acting on all the evidence, should derive fair value. It was that next step that was omitted in this case. …

NOTES AND QUESTIONS

Do you agree with this analysis? Is such leeway necessary to perfect fairness or is certainty being unduly sacrificed?

A first course in corporate law is not the place to absorb complex details concerning discretionary remedies to be applied in widely divergent circumstances. Two lengthy Canadian articles on the appraisal remedy — Magnet, "Shareholders' Appraisal Rights in Canada" (1979), 11 Ottawa L. Rev. 100 and Chertkow, "Compulsory Acquisition of Shares under Section 199 of the Canada Business Corporations Act and Re Whitehorse Copper Mines Ltd: An Offer You Can Refuse" (1982-83), 7 Can. Bus. L.J. 154 — and a wealth of American experience ought to be consulted should a particular problem arise.

The appraisal remedy may also be triggered in a "squeeze-out" situation following a successful corporate takeover. Typically, one who acquires 90 per cent or more of shares she did not previously hold is statutorily authorized to force the transfer to her of the remaining shares: see, for example, C.B.C.A., s. 206(3)(*a*). Note also the definitions of "associate" and "affiliate" which are included to plug rather obvious loopholes. What is the date for assessment of "fair value" under C.B.C.A., s. 206?

It has been suggested that an appraisal of "fair value" in a squeeze-out situation includes a premium to compensate the shareholder as a victim of expropriation: see *Re Domglas Inc.* (1981), 13 B.L.R. 135 at 222; aff'd 22 B.L.R. 121 (Que. C.A.). The idea was applied, though somewhat quizzically, in *Investissements Mon-Soleil Inc. v. National Drug Ltd.* (1982), 22 B.L.R. 139 (Que. S.C.).

LoCICERO v. B.A.C.M. INDUSTRIES LTD.

[1986] N.J. No. 44, 38 Man. R. (2d) 134 (C.A.)

[The majority shareholder announced an intention to cause a merger and offered to purchase the minority's interest. The minority shareholders rejected the offered price and caused an evaluation by the court. The trial judge determined the market value (the offered price) was the fair value. The Manitoba Court of Appeal disagreed.]

O'Sullivan J.A. (at 137-39): — ... The learned judge in this case quotes with apparent approval a statement from *Roessler et al. v. Security Savings & Loan Co.*, 72 N.E. (2d) 259, at p. 260:

"Fair cash value" of the shares of a dissenting shareholder in a corporation means the intrinsic value of such shares determined from the assets and liabilities of such corporation, considered in the light of every factor bearing on value.

The learned trial judge goes on to say, however, that one of the established and recognized methods of valuation is "market value or the quoted market price of a stock in the stock exchange". He also refers to net asset value in the liquidation approach and capitalization of maintainable earnings, or a combination.

In my opinion, this is error. What is to be valued is not the market value of shares or liquidation value of shares, but the overall fair value of the corporation and the attribution to the shares of an aliquot part of the overall value.

In Canada at one time there was a dispute among some judges as to the fair test to be applied in valuation in the absence of express statutory direction.

In *The King v. Thomas Lawson & Sons Limited*, [1948] Ex. C.R. 44, Thorson, P., reaffirmed that the test to be applied for valuing expropriated property is market value. He said indeed that this was one of the cardinal principles of expropriation law. He firmly rejected the idea that value should be value to the owner and demonstrated to his own satisfaction that statements to the contrary in judgments of the Supreme Court of Canada were wrong, and should not be allowed.

But in *Diggon-Hibben, Limited v. The Queen*, [1949] S.C.R. 712, the Supreme Court judges agreed that market value is not the criterion, although compensation can never be less. Rather, it is value to owner, recognizing this value does not include merely sentimental value.

As Estey, J., said at p. 717: It is the value to the owner and not the market value or value to the purchaser that must be determined.

In *R. v. Woods Manufacturing Company Limited*, [1949] Ex. C.R. 9, Thorson, P., returned to a consideration of the principles of compensation and again persuaded himself that the Supreme Court was wrong. He said there was no difference between the concept of value to owner and market value. At p. 41 he gave his version of fair value, or value to owner:

> It is the loss of the value of the land that is to be replaced by its equivalent in money, so that the total value of the owner's property remains the same. It is only the form of the property that is changed; instead of the land, the owner has its money equivalent. It is also clear that the money equivalent referred to is the market value of the land, that is to say, the amount of money the owner could turn it into if he offered it for sale. Its worth to him in money is not what he thinks it is worth but what he could get for it. This statement is not affected by the requirement that the money equivalent of the land is estimated on its value to the owner and not on its value to the purchaser. This does not mean, as has been frequently contended, that the value of the land to its owner is something more or other than its market value.

Although he did not say who were the frequent contenders whose view he rejected, most people knew that among them were some eminent Supreme Court judges.

Incidentally, the judgment of Thorson, P., is useful in its discussion of American law with quotations from *Nichols* (op. cit.), which provide a timely warning against over-reliance in Canada on American precedent.

The decision of Thorson, P. was reversed by a unanimous seven man Supreme Court, ([1951] S.C.R. 505). The court expressly adopted the view expressed by Duff, J. (as he then was), in *Lake Erie & Northern R. Co. v. Brantford Golf and Country Club* (1917) 32 D.L.R. 219, at p. 229:

> It does not follow, of course, that the owner whose land is compulsorily taken is entitled only to compensation measured by the scale of the selling price of the land in the open market. He is entitled to that in any event … .

The Supreme Court expressly disagreed with the statement by Thorson, P., that "value to the owner is essentially the same as that of fair market value".

It was in this case that Rinfret, C.J., expressed a famous admonition to lower court judges to accept the interpretation of the law as laid down by higher courts.

In my opinion, in Canada, the principle must be accepted that, where legislatures provide for the taking of property, it must be presumed it is intended that fair value should be value to owner, and not market value.

After all, market value presumes a willing seller, whereas in expropriation the expropriated one is an unwilling seller.

In many jurisdictions, some appraisers and lawyers felt uncomfortable with Woods, (*supra*), and persuaded legislatures to adopt the rules from the United States with which they were familiar, so many statutes now provide for market value plus compensation for special factors, but this is not the case in the appeal now before us.

The statement from *Roessler* (above) sets out the test that should be applied, recognizing that what is being valued is not minority shares but an aliquot share of the stock equity of the corporation taken as a whole, at its value to the corporation. I further adopt what was said in *Re Wall & Redekopp*, [1975] 1 W.W.R. 621, quoting *American General Corp. v. Camp* (1937), 190 A 225, at p. 228:

> The problem of finding the fair value of stock is a special problem in every particular instance. … The owner of shares of stock in a corporation whose legal

existence is at an end would be entitled to receive the aliquot proportion which the number of shares held would be entitled to receive in the distribution of the amount of the corporate funds in which his particular kind of stock would be entitled to share. Thus, by an ascertainment of all the assets and liabilities of the corporation, the intrinsic value of the stock, and not merely its market value, when traded in by the public, would be determined. If the dissenting owner received this amount, so ascertained, he would receive the fair value of his stock.

It must be appreciated further that stock markets are places for the exchange of marginal shares offered by willing shareholders, and while fair value can never be less than the free market, value is not limited to that. It is common that a takeover bid almost always will be more than the market quotations.

NOTES AND QUESTIONS

The Supreme Court of Canada reversed the decision of the Manitoba Court of Appeal ([1988] S.C.J. No. 25, [1988] 1 S.C.R. 399) and restored the valuation of the trial judge ([1984] M.J. No. 55, 31 Man R. (2d) 208).

If the payment of a premium is appropriate when a minority shareholder is being squeezed out, is such a premium appropriate when a shareholder dissents and seeks a "buy-out" under C.B.C.A., s. 190? See *Brant Investments Ltd. v. KeepRite Inc.*, [1991] O.J. No. 683, 1 B.L.R. (2d) 225 (C.A.).

It has been decided that "fair value" should be defined as the *pro rata* portion of the "en bloc fair market value" of the company with no minority discount applied to the dissenter's shares. (*Baniuk v. Carpenter*, [1990] N.B.J. No. 1109, 1 B.L.R. (2d) 300 (Q.B.)). Would the market apply such a discount?

Who bears the onus of establishing fair value? The shareholder? The corporation? Neither? If the latter, does anyone bear any evidentiary onus? See *Smeenk v. Dexleigh Corp.*, [1993] O.J. No. 2020, 15 O.R. (3d) 608 (C.A.).

At what date does one appraise the value of the shares when the appraisal remedy is sought? See C.B.C.A., s. 190(3). When appraisal occurs under a "squeeze out"? See C.B.C.A., s. 206(9) and (10). When the court orders a buy out under s. 241(3)? See *Westfair Foods Ltd. v. Watt (No. 2)*, [1992] A.J. No. 708, 5 B.L.R. (2d) 179 (C.A.).

G. INVESTIGATIONS, AUDITS AND THE "BIG D" DIRECTOR

Lack of information can seriously inhibit minority shareholder protection. The reformed Canadian statutes address this problem in three ways:

(1) court-ordered investigations (see, *e.g.*, C.B.C.A., s. 229), under which an inspector may be appointed with extensive powers to look into and report upon the affairs of the corporation;

(2) elected (*e.g.*, C.B.C.A., ss. 104(1)(*e*), 162) or judicially appointed (*e.g.*, C.B.C.A., s. 167) auditors, whose job it is to report to the shareholders on the corporation's financial state;

(3) a "Director," who is the civil servant responsible for the administration of the Act, but who is given power to intervene in some situations (see, *e.g.*, C.B.C.A., s. 238(*c*), where the Director is included as a "complainant," and *Sparling v. Royal Trustco Ltd.* (1984), 1 O.A.C. 279 (C.A.)).

A survey of the applicable statute will give some indication of the substantial degree to which the possibility of judicially supervised intervention has changed from the *Burland v. Earle* ([1902] A.C. 83 (Ont. J.C.P.C.)) position.

H. CAPITAL PUNISHMENT

Finally, and generally only if all else fails, a minority shareholder might be able to have the corporation killed. See, for example, C.B.C.A., s. 214.

214(1) A court may order the liquidation and dissolution of a corporation or any of its affiliated corporations upon the application of a shareholder,

    (*a*)   if the court is satisfied that in respect of a corporation or any of its affiliates

        (i)   any act or omission of the corporation or any of its affiliates effects a result,

        (ii)   the business or affairs of the corporation or any of its affiliates are or have been carried on or conducted in a manner, or

        (iii) the powers of the directors of the corporation or any of its affiliates are or have been exercised in a manner

        that is oppressive or unfairly prejudicial to or that unfairly disregards the interests of any security holder, creditor, director or officer; or

    (*b*)   if the court is satisfied that

        (i)   a unanimous shareholder agreement entitles a complaining shareholder to demand dissolution of the corporation after the occurrence of a specified event and that event has occurred, or

        (ii)   it is just and equitable that the corporation should be dissolved.

    (2) On an application under this section, a court may make such order under this section or Section 241 as it thinks fit.

    (3) Section 242 applies to an application under this section.

Is s. 214 redundant? Why is it in the statute? Why, particularly, is subsection (2) included?

CHAPTER 10

THE CORPORATE CAPITAL STRUCTURE

A. DEBT AND SHARES CONTRASTED

There are two principal ways corporations can raise capital. They can convince other people to give them money in exchange for "equity securities" (corporate shares) or "debt securities". When a corporation issues securities to another person, that person (the security holder) will acquire rights in relation to the corporation. The rights acquired depend on the nature of the security and can vary widely. This chapter will focus on the typical rights of equity securities and how they are acquired.

WELLING, CORPORATE LAW IN CANADA: THE GOVERNING PRINCIPLES

(3rd ed., 2006), Ch. 9, "A. Shares and Non-Shares", pp. 639-41

Corporate shares ... are simply a subcategory of property. They are called "equity securities" in business-speak. I have no idea why. The adjective has nothing to do with the Equity evolved in the Chancellor's court. At any rate, business jargon divides the corporate capital structure into two types — "equity securities" and "debt securities" — and shares are the "equity" portion.

The distinction is slippery in economics. In legal theory the contrast is stark. The holder of debt securities is simply a creditor of the corporation — a lender whose relationship with the corporation will terminate once the loan is repaid. A holder of equity securities (shares) normally expects the corporation–shareholder relationship to continue indefinitely.

Debt securities fall broadly into three categories: notes, bonds, and debentures. These are not terms of legal art and are best avoided when talking law. The three tend to be similar in that they represent advances to the corporation in anticipation of periodic interest payments for a fixed term, followed by a repayment of the capital. They differ in practical ways in business usage.

The label "note" is usually reserved for relatively short term debt advanced by a single lender. Typical examples are short term bank loans to cover cash flow crises and one or two year loans with scheduled repayments of interest and capital. They are usually, though not necessarily, secured by accounts receivable or inventories. Notes may also be issued for loans from individuals, but this is usually done only by small, closely held corporations.

"Bonds" are usually issued in units to raise a collective sum from many lenders. Bonds normally have a longer redemption period than notes and normally do not call for any payments of principal until the term expires. They are secured against property of the corporation and will most often be issued through a trustee, usually one of the major trust companies. They compete with other stable investments like Canada savings bonds.

"Debentures" are usually issued through a trustee to raise a large sum from many independent lenders. Debentures are ordinarily secured by a floating charge over the corporate assets. The term debenture is frequently used by lawyers, though no precise legal meaning can be found. Rather, a debt instrument is labelled a debenture if it displays certain characteristics: these, however, are notoriously vague.

B. DEBT CAPITAL

About the only basic corporate law question that arises in debt capital involves the corporate power to borrow. This need not pose substantial problems. A company incorporated in English model registration jurisdictions requires authorization to borrow in its memorandum of association, usually implied if not explicit. "If the company is a 'trading company', the power to accept and issue bills and notes, or to borrow, is implied on the broad ground of convenience. In every case in which the power is not expressly given, it can only be implied where, upon a reasonable construction of the memorandum, it appears that it was intended to be conferred". *Kerr v. University Press Ltd.*, [1923] 2 W.W.R. 187, 17 Sask. L.R. 136, [1923] 2 D.L.R. 948 (C.A.); *Peruvian Railways Co. v. Thames & Mersey Marine Insurance Co.* (1867), 2 Ch. App. 617, at 623; *Re General Estates Co.; Ex p. City Bank* (1868), 3 Ch. App. 758.

In the reformed Canadian jurisdictions, such problems no longer exist. Sections like C.B.C.A., s. 15(1) give corporations "the capacity ... of a natural person" and individuals come without constitutional restrictions on their borrowing capacity. This position is made clearer by the extensive statutory protection innocent lenders can claim when relying on corporate agents (see Chapter 5).

Corporate debt capital can involve intricate banking and accounting problems, and often requires intricate legal analysis under statutes regulating the public issue of securities, personal property security, mortgages, bankruptcy, and any number of other areas. But few of the issues raised are unique to corporate law as such, and their study is better left to other books and courses.

C. SHARE CAPITAL

1. Shares as Property

Share capital is distinctly corporate in nature. A corporate share cannot be understood by either the practical analogy of friends sharing a bottle of wine or by the legal notion of joint tenants sharing residential housing. A corporate share is property. As such, its analogs are ownership, a patent, an estate in fee tail, an easement. A share is a "chose in action", but that is just legalese and not particularly helpful. It is more insightful to think of a share as one thinks of any form of property: it consists of rights exercisable to the exclusion of other people.

What are these rights? Some of them were canvassed (in Chapters 8 and 9), but that analysis was organized around the political relationships between shareholders and management, and within an existing shareholder group. Now we take a more basic approach.

2. Creation of Shares

Corporate shares begin their existence when issued by a corporation. They cease to exist upon cancellation by that corporation. Terminology like "unissued shares" is, therefore, self-contradictory and unnecessarily complicates the analysis of the corporate capital structure. Beginning with the statute, rather than with judicial commentary based on earlier statutes, keeps both the analysis and the terminology simple. Again, the C.B.C.A. can be viewed as a model of most Canadian jurisdictions.

6(1) Articles of incorporation shall … set out …

(*c*) … any maximum number of shares that the corporation is authorized to issue …

(*d*) if the issue, transfer or ownership of shares of the corporation is to be restricted, a statement to that effect and a statement as to the nature of such restrictions;

25(1) Subject to the articles, the by-laws and any unanimous shareholder agreement and to section 28, shares may be issued at such times and to such persons and for such consideration as the directors may determine.

…

(3) A share shall not be issued until the consideration for the share is fully paid in money or in property or past services that are not less in value than the fair equivalent of the money that the corporation would have received if the share had been issued for money.

…

(5) For the purposes of this section, "property" does not include a promissory note or a promise to pay … .

28(1) If the articles so provide, no shares of a class shall be issued unless the shares have first been offered to the shareholders holding shares of that class, and those shareholders have a pre-emptive right to acquire the offered shares in proportion to their holdings of the shares of that class, at such price and on such terms as those shares are to be offered to others.

(2) Notwithstanding that the articles provide the pre-emptive right referred to in subsection (1), shareholders have no pre-emptive right in respect of shares to be issued.

(*a*)   for a consideration other than money;

(*b*)   as a share dividend; or

(*c*)   pursuant to the exercise of conversion privileges, options or rights previously granted by the corporation.

It will be noted from s. 6(1)(*c*) that it is not compulsory to specify in the articles a maximum number of shares that the corporation may issue. Under previous statutes the "authorized capital" of a corporation was either the maximum number of shares the corporation could issue or money that could be raised through share issues. The C.B.C.A. does not incorporators from imposing such limits; nor does it outlaw the label. However, there is no point in keeping the term alive, as it no longer has universal application and would cause more confusion than clarity. Is there a statutory basis for the assumption that the articles can still specify a maximum number of shares issued? What about a maximum amount that can be raised by share issues?

"Issued capital" used to describe that portion of the authorized capital that had been issued. It too is no longer relevant.

Section 25(1) gives the directors power to cause the issue of shares but this is restricted in at least two ways. The more obvious one is the statutory requirement (C.B.C.A., s. 122(1)) that the directors act "with a view to the best interests of the corporation" in exercising any of their powers. The second restriction is set out in C.B.C.A., s. 25(3). What happens if no consideration is received by the corporation, yet the directors resolve that a share be issued?

The basic legal rules concerning how corporations must account for share capital are simple and straightforward, particularly under the C.B.C.A.

> 26(1) A corporation shall maintain a separate stated capital account for each class and series of shares it issues.

> (2) A corporation shall add to the appropriate stated capital account the full amount of any consideration for any shares it issues.

> ...

> (4) On the issue of a share a corporation shall not add to a stated capital account in respect of the share it issues an amount greater than the amount of the consideration' it received for the share.

> ...

> (10) A corporation shall not reduce its stated capital or any stated capital account except in the manner provided in this Act.

3. Minimum Requirements

Shares cannot exist without corporations. All corporations have constitutions. Corporate constitutions are generally regulated by the incorporating statute. The statute is therefore the starting point for share analysis.

C.B.C.A., s. 24 says:

> 24(1) Shares of a corporation shall be in registered form and shall be without nominal or par value.

The requirement that shares be in "registered form" is straightforward and traditional, if somewhat linguistically imprecise. This requirement is generally assumed to mean is that the corporation must keep a listing of what shares are held by whom. The detailed requirements are set out in C.B.C.A., s. 50. The share registration system was designed to allow both the corporation and anyone else who looked at the register to determine who was a shareholder at any time. Registration was, therefore, the key act in a share transfer. This is still technically true, but the law concerning share transfers has been greatly simplified under the reformed Canadian statutes.

The now prohibited "par value" was historically an arbitrary sum, prescribed in the corporate constitution, in exchange for which a share was to be issued. In small corporations, where political control matters most, it is the percentage of shares one holds that counts, whereas in large corporations whose shares trade on stock exchanges, it is today's market value that matters, and that has nothing whatever to do with a par value. For some reason there has been an ongoing debate in other countries (England and Australia, for example) over whether corporations ought to be allowed to issue no-par value shares. The Canadian position is accurately summarized in the *Dickerson Report*, which led to the enactment of the C.B.C.A. It noted, at Vol. I, para. 24: "The abolition of the utterly useless idea of par value removes all kinds of difficulties ...".

"Contributed surplus" was the sum of all amounts received on share issues in excess of par value. In corporate law, with the abolition of par value came the extinction of contributed surplus.

QUESTIONS

With some shares changing hands numerous times in a single day how are a corporation's records kept up-to-date? See C.B.C.A., s. 22(1), Part XX.1 and the *Canada Business Corporations Regulations, 2001*, SOR/2001-512, ss. 5-12.

A share must be in "registered form" according to C.B.C.A., s. 48(4). Recall the definition of a corporate share. Is it possible for a share to conform to that definition?

C.B.C.A., s. 24(4)(*a*) says that "the rights, privileges, restrictions and conditions in attaching to the shares shall be set out [in the articles]". This gives the corporation flexibility in determining what rights attach to a share. The corporation is constrained in the rights it can attach to a share by C.B.C.A., s. 24(3) which says that:

> Where a corporation has only one class of shares, the rights of the holders thereof are equal in all respects and include the rights
>
> (*a*) to vote at any meeting of shareholders of the corporation;
>
> (*b*) to receive any dividend declared by the corporation; and
>
> (*c*) to receive the remaining property of the corporation on dissolution.

4. Classes of Shares

(a) Defining the Classes

All systems of corporate law permit corporations to discriminate among their shareholders by dividing them into classes. Most corporate constitutions are set up with that capability. The applicable statute is the starting point. The C.B.C.A. is a useful model.

> 6(1) Articles of incorporation shall ... set out ...
>
> (*c*) the classes ... of shares that the corporation is authorized to issue, and
>
> (i) if there will be two or more classes of shares, the rights, privileges, restrictions and conditions attaching to each class of shares ...

When there are numerous classes of shares, the requirements listed in s. 24(3) for a single class of shares must still be met. However, C.B.C.A. s. 24(4)(*b*) allows each requirement to be met by attaching to different class of share. If all three listed rights attach to a single class of share the shares are traditionally referred to as "common shares".

M.R. GILLEN, SECURITIES REGULATION IN CANADA

(Toronto: Carswell, 1992), pp. 7-14 (Footnotes deleted.)

Preferred Shares

These shares are "preferred" because they are given preference with respect to the distribution of dividends and often also with respect to the distribution of the proceeds on liquidation. For instance, the shares may provide that they will receive a specified amount, say $10 per share, in any given year before any dividends will be distributed to subordinate shares. Preferred shares are usually non-voting.

Preferred shares may carry any of a wide variety of special features. The most common features of preferred shares are cumulative dividend rights, participation rights, conversion rights, call rights and retraction rights.

a. Cumulative (vs. Non-Cumulative)

Preferred shares usually have cumulative rights regarding dividends. This means that in any given year, dividends are either not declared or are not sufficient to pay the full amount of the annual preferred dividend on the preferred shares, then the amount unpaid carries over into the next year.

. . .

b. Participating (vs. Non-Participating)

Preferred shares may occasionally be participating shares. That is, they participate in dividends beyond the specified preferred amount they are to receive in any given year.

. . .

c. Redemption/Call Provision

Preferred shares may also be redeemable by the company. The company may want to facilitate a refinancing of the company by providing for a means of buying out the preferred shareholders. Consequently they may put in a redemption provision allowing them to buy back the shares from the shareholder at some future date for a specified price. The price is usually at a premium to the price for which the share is issued.

d. Retraction Rights

Preferred shares occasionally also have a retraction right. A retraction right permits the shareholder to tender the share to the company and the company has to buy it back at some price specified in advance.

4. Restricted Shares

"Restricted shares" (or sometimes called "uncommon common" shares) have become popular in Canada in recent years. A restricted share is like a common share in that it has a right to share pro rata in dividends and a right to share pro rata on a distribution of the proceeds of a liquidation of the assets of the company (subject, of course, to the preferred rights of any other classes of shares). However, the voting rights of such shares are restricted.

Restricted shares became popular because they allow a control group to raise capital with a sale of a share that is roughly equivalent to a common share, without losing control over the company. They can retain control because restricted shares normally do not allow voting over such important matters as the election of directors.

...

5. Rights

Often companies will raise funds through granting "rights" to existing shareholders to buy additional shares in the company. Holders of a specified number of rights will have the right, exercisable within a specified period of time, to buy a share in the company for a predetermined price.

...

6. Options

An option contract gives the holder of the option a right to buy or sell the item specified in the contract. An option contract may be entered into with respect to a particular security such as a share or debenture. The option contract would give the holder of the option the right to buy or sell a specified quantity of a specific security within a specified period of time at a stated price.

QUESTIONS

Must a corporation have any common shares? Can preferred, non-participating shares carrying the right to receive a $10 annual, cumulative dividend meet the minimum statutory requirements for a corporation's capital structure?

The following cases explore the important questions "what is a class?" and "how are classes differentiated?"

R. v. McCLURG

[1990] S.C.J. No. 134, [1990] 3 S.C.R. 1020, [1991] 2 W.W.R. 244

[The respondent and his partner were shareholders and directors of an S.B.C.A. corporation and the only other shareholders were their wives. The articles provided for three share classes: Class A (common, voting, and participating by right), Class B (common, non-voting, and participating by consent of the directors), and Class C (preferred, non-voting). The articles also contained a "discretionary dividend clause" that said the right of each class to receive dividends was exclusive of the other shares and at the directors' discretion. The husbands held 400 Class A shares each, and each of their wives held 100 Class B shares.

The corporation paid dividends to the Class B shareholders, and none to the Class A shareholders. The Minister of National Revenue took the position that the dividends were attributable to each husband in proportion to the common share holdings of the couple. The corporate law inspiration for the reassessment was the claim that dividends declared ought to be allocated equally to all common shares, regardless of class distinctions or the discretionary dividend clause.]

Dickson C.J.C.: — Having reviewed the legal basis for the payment of a dividend by a company, another fundamental principle of corporate law can be restated. The appellant ... argues, and it is conceded by the respondent, that the rights carried by all shares to receive a dividend declared by a company are equal unless otherwise provided in the Articles of Incorporation. This principle, like the managerial power to declare dividends, has been well accepted at common law. The principle, or, more accurately, the presumption, of equality, amongst shares and the prerequisites required to rebut that presumption are described in *Palmer's Company Law* [C.M. Schmitthoff (ed.)], 23rd ed., vol. 1, at p. 387, para. 33-06:

> Prima facie the rights carried by the shares rank *pari passu*, i.e. the shareholders participate in the benefits of membership equally. It is only when a company divides its share capital into different classes with different rights attached to them that the prima facie presumption of equality of shares may be displaced.

In my view, a precondition to the derogation from the presumption of equality, with respect to both entitlement to dividends and other shareholder entitlements, is the division of shares into different "classes". The rationale for this rule can be traced to the principle that shareholder rights attach to the shares themselves and not to shareholders. The division of shares into separate classes, then, is the means by which shares (as opposed to shareholders) are distinguished, and in turn allows for the derogation from the presumption of equality: *Bowater Can. Ltd. v. R.L. Crain Inc.* (1987), 62 O.R. (2d) 752 (C.A.) at p. 754 [39 B.L.R. 34, 46 D.L.R. (4th) 161, 26 O.A.C. 348] (*per* Houlden J.A.).

The concept of share "classes" is not technical in nature but rather is simply the accepted means by which differential treatment of shares is recognized in the Articles of Incorporation of a company. As Professor Welling, *supra*, succinctly explains, at p. 583, "a class is simply a sub-group of shares with rights and conditions in common which distinguish them from other shares". Indeed, the use of the share class is recognized in the *S.B.C.A.* as the means by which derogation from the principle of equality is to be achieved. The statute thus explicitly requires that "the rights, privileges, restrictions and conditions attaching to the shares of each class" must be expressly stated in the Articles of Incorporation: s. 24(4)(*a*).

Having outlined the underlying principles of corporate law relevant to the issues raised on this appeal, the application of those principles to the facts can be attempted. The appellant argues that the discretionary dividend clause in the Articles of Incorporation of Northland Trucks does not create discrete classes of shares with different rights to dividends. Furthermore, the Minister contends that the clause creates no right to dividends at all, and therefore does not comply with the statutory requirement in s. 24(4)(*a*). Consequently, the allocation of a dividend made pursuant to the discretionary dividend clause must be disregarded because of its failure to comply with the *S.B.C.A.* and with the principles of corporate and common law. As a result, the presumption of equality has not been rebutted and equality of distribution amongst the share classes prevails. As I have earlier noted, Desjardins J. in her dissenting reasons at the Court of Appeal accepted this argument, and held that the clause permits the directors to create differences in dividend allocation "at whim". She thus expressed doubts, at p. 369, as to whether:

such a discretion to be exercised by way of a resolution of the directors, can be equated with a derogation specific and substantive enough to discard the common law rule of equality of distribution since there is no rule by which the directors are to carry out their discretion.

The respondent argues, on the other hand, that the discretionary dividend clause is a valid exercise of contractual rights between the company and its shareholders in accordance with the common law and statute. Moreover, the right to receive dividends in potentially unique amounts gives each share class different rights. It is argued that this is a material distinction sufficient to create separate share classes with differentiated dividend entitlements, which, in turn, validly derogates from the principle of equality.

I agree with the arguments which the respondent has raised in this regard. In my opinion, the discretionary dividend clause is both a valid means of allocating declared dividends and is sufficient to rebut the presumption of equality amongst shares. I find this determination with respect to the presumption of equality to be a simple factual inquiry. In my view, the presence of a discretionary dividend clause can only be interpreted as creating differences between share classes, since that is the rationale for the clause. As far as the statutory requirements are concerned, the purpose of s. 24(4)(*a*) is to ensure that shareholders are fully aware of their entitlements and privileges to the extent that the presumption of equality is rendered inapplicable. To my mind, that purpose has been met, since the dividend entitlements are clearly set out in the description of the share classes.

INTERNATIONAL POWER CO. v. McMASTER UNIVERSITY AND MONTREAL TRUST CO.

[1946] S.C.R. 178, [1946] 2 D.L.R. 81, 27 C.B.R. 75

[Puerto Rico Power Co., Ltd. was incorporated by letters patent in 1906 under the provisions of the *Dominion Companies Act, 1902*. The original authorized capital was $3,000,000, in 30,000 common shares of par value $100. The corporation later created and issued $1,000,000 of preference stock divided into 10,000 shares of par value $100, the holders of which were entitled to 7 percent cumulative dividends prior to payment of dividends on the common stock, and "to priority on any division of the assets of the corporation to the extent of its repayment in full at par together with any dividends thereon then accrued due and remaining unpaid".

The main corporate holdings were the shares in a certain Puerto Rico subsidiary, the assets of which were expropriated by the Puerto Rican Government. The corporation went into voluntary liquidation in 1944, and was being wound up under the provisions of the *Dominion Winding-up Act*. The Montreal Trust Company was named as liquidator and had more than $6,000,000 available for distribution. It was authorized by the court to make a preliminary distribution of $100 per share to the preference shareholders plus unpaid dividends to date, and $150 per share to the holders of common stock. The liquidator reserved $500,000 against the eventuality that the preferred stockholders might claim greater rights. The liquidator then petitioned the court for authorization to distribute this sum to the common shareholders only.

International Power Co. Ltd., was a common shareholder in favour of the petition and contended that the rights of the preference shareholders were completely and exhaustively set out in the by-laws and supplementary letters patent, being cumulative dividends of 7 per cent per annum and $100 per share in the distribution of the assets.

McMaster University and the other preferred shareholders contended that they were entitled to equal treatment in all respects with the common shareholders, except to the extent to which the preference shares were given a priority by the supplementary letters patent and by-laws. They further alleged that no limitation was placed upon the rights of the preference shareholders, and that all the by-laws and supplementary letters patent provided was the extent of the priority given to the preference shareholders. They further claimed that the corporation had paid dividends to the common shareholders in excess of 7 percent received by the preference shareholders, and that the dividends paid constituted an advance and the preference shareholders were entitled to be placed on an equal basis.

Section 47 of the *Dominion Companies Act*, R.S.C. 1906, c. 79 said:

> The directors of the company may make by-laws for creating and issuing any part of the capital stock as preference stock, giving the same such preference and priority, as respects dividends and in any other respect, over ordinary stock as is by such by-laws declared.

Section 49 said:

> Holders of shares of such preference stock shall be shareholders within the meaning of this part, and shall in all respects possess the rights and be subject to the liabilities of shareholders within the meaning of this part provided that in respect of dividends, and in any other respect declared by by-law as authorized by this part, they shall, as against the ordinary shareholders, be entitled to the preferences and rights by such by-law.

Justice Boyer dismissed the contention of the preferred shareholders and directed that the remaining assets be distributed to the common shareholders only.

The Court of Appeal dismissed the claim of the preferred shareholders as to dividends, but ordered that the sum of $500,000 be distributed to the preferred shareholders and that the balance of the distributable assets be distributed amongst the preferred and ordinary shareholders in proportion to their holdings of shares without any distinction.

International Power Co. Ltd. appealed and McMaster University cross-appealed.]

Taschereau J.: — ... The decision of this case depends upon the true construction of the essential words of the supplementary letters patent and by laws already cited. It is clear, I think, that under the *Dominion Companies Act*, a preferred shareholder has all the rights and liabilities of a common shareholder. This proposition is found in section 49 of the *Companies Act*, R.S.C. 1906, chap. 79, which reads as follows: —

> Holders of shares of such preference stock shall be shareholders within the meaning of this part, and shall in all respects possess the rights and be subject to the liabilities of shareholders within the meaning of this part.

The preferred shareholders are however entitled to additional preferences and rights which are authorized by section 47 of the Act, which is to the effect that the directors of the company may make by-laws for creating and issuing any part of the capital stock as preference stock., giving the same such preference and priority, as respects dividend and in any other respect, over ordinary stock as is by such by-laws declared, and this is confirmed by subsection 49, which, after stating that holders of shares of preference stock are shareholders within the meaning of the Act, says that they are, as against the ordinary shareholders, entitled to the preferences and rights given by the by-laws.

Many judgments have been cited by both parties. As it will be seen the consensus of opinion appears to be that preference shareholders have all the rights and liabilities of common shareholders, and that the additional preferences and priorities, to which they may be entitled, must be found in the by-laws and supplementary letters patent of the company ... [Authorities extensively reviewed.]

From all these numerous judicial pronouncements, and from a careful reading of the *Companies Act*, I believe that one may rightly gather that the rights of all classes of shareholders are on a basis of equality, unless they have been modified by the by-laws or the letters patent of the company, and, that the right to the return of invested capital, and the right to share in surplus assets are quite different and distinct matters...

It is in the letters patent and the by-laws of the company that have to be found the priorities that may be attached to preference shares, and which are clearly authorized by section 47. It may of course happen that these priorities are exhaustive of the rights of the preference shareholders, and therefore negative any additional rights, or it may be also that they create additional rights which coexist with the original rights inherent to all classes of shareholders. But in order to determine the true meaning and the legal effect of these preferences and priority clauses, one must necessarily look at the creating clauses in order to find if there is or not an express or implied condition, which limits or adds to the ordinary rights of the shareholders. It is a mere question of construction of these clauses, which form part of the contract under which the shareholders hold their shares.

...

It is the contention of the cross-appellant that the stipulation for payment of cumulative dividends at the rate of 7 per cent, per annum for each and every year, in preference and priority to any payment of dividends on common stock, was not limitative in its terms and that in the event of the common shareholders receiving, in any year, a dividend exceeding the said rate of 7 per cent, per annum, then, the preferred shareholders were entitled to be paid on a basis of equality.

The preference shareholders have received each year the stipulated dividends of 7 per cent, until the winding-up of the company, and the common shareholders until 1931 have received dividends lower than 7 per cent per year. However, from 1931 to 1942, the directors have declared for the benefit of the common shareholders an annual dividend of 8 per cent, and in 1943 this dividend was 49-1/2 per cent. The preference shareholders ask for equal treatment in the matters of dividends. I cannot agree with this proposition, and it seems that the cases cited by the respondents on the main appeal defeat this very contention.

The question, I think, has been settled by the case of *Will v. United Lanket Plantation Company, Limited*, [1914] A.C. 11. In that case the Court of Appeal ([1912] 2 Ch. 571) decided that, in the distribution of profits, holders of the preference shares were not entitled to anything more than a 10 per cent dividend, and in the House of Lords Viscount Haldane said: —

> Moreover, I think that when you find — as you do find here — the word "dividend" used in the way in which the expression is used in the resolution and defined to be a "cumulative preferential dividend" you have something so definitely pointed to as to suggest that it contains the whole of what the shareholder is to look to from the company.

The right to dividend, while the company is a going concern and the right to capital and surplus assets in the winding-up, are quite distinct. In the present case, the right of preference shareholders is to be paid an annual dividend of 7 per cent and they have a priority for dividends accrued due and remaining unpaid. These dividends have been paid, and the preference shareholders, as to dividends, have therefore received all that they are legally entitled to.

The by-laws give priority to the preference shareholders to obtain reimbursement of their invested capital, in addition to their right to share in the division of assets, but a similar privilege as to dividends is not given. In the latter case, the privilege is only to assure the payment of a dividend of 7 per cent which has been declared, and which at the time of the winding-up accrued and remained unpaid. I should dismiss the cross-appeal.

[**Estey J.,** adopted the above reasons for judgment, **Rand** and **Kerwin JJ.** concurred separately, and **Rinfret C.J.C.** dissented in part on the point.]

NOTES

The essence of this case is perfectly clear: a statement of priority was judicially construed to impose a restriction.

The corporate constitution clearly established two classes of shares. For the moment, let's simply label them class X and class Y. The corporate constitution next said that class Y were "entitled out of any and all surplus net earnings whenever ascertained to cumulative dividends at the rate of seven per cent per annum for each and every year in preference and priority to any payment of dividends [on class X]". Everyone agreed that this meant that no dividends could be paid on the class X shares in any year until the 7 per cent dividend had been paid to all class Y shareholders (leaving aside the "cumulative" factor for the moment, as the complications it introduces are irrelevant to the point being made here). Everyone also agreed that a dividend of 7 per cent or less could next be paid on the class X shares.

What was to happen next was in dispute. Suppose, in a particular year, the corporation wished to pay further dividends. The priority clause set out above invited one of two interpretations:

(i)   class X were subordinated to class Y only so far as the first 7 per cent was concerned, and after that they ranked equally; or

(ii) class Y were entitled to a priority of 7 per cent which, by implication, also imposed an upper limit on the dividends they could be paid in any year.

The Supreme Court of Canada adopted interpretation (ii), ruling that any further dividends could be paid exclusively to class X shareholders. Would the priority clause be interpreted in the same way under C.B.C.A., s. 24(4)?

The Supreme Court of Canada in the *International Power* case was following a (garden?) path mapped out by English judges. You will have noted that the two classes were called "common" and "preferred" shares. These terms have an interesting past.

In *Birch v. Cropper* (1889), 14 App. Cas. 525 (Eng. H.L.), the articles of a company established two classes of shares. The two classes were referred to in the articles of association as "ordinary shares" and "new shares" [see the lower court decision (1888), 39 Ch. D., 2-4], but the latter seem to have been referred to as "preference shares" by the lawyers arguing the case and their terminology was picked up by the trial judge and in the subsequent appeals. The articles clearly and explicitly set out that the "new shares" had a 5 per cent priority dividend, but no further right to participate in dividend distributions. The articles were, however, silent as to what would happen on dissolution. When dissolution occurred, the argument of the "ordinary" shareholders was put as follows by Sir Horace, Davey Q.C. [see 14 A.C. 526]:

> repay the preference shareholders their capital and divide the rest among the ordinary shareholders. By the terms of their creation the preference shareholders are entitled to receive 5 per cent on their capital as long as the company is a going concern and is earning profits, and nothing more. They are in fact in the same position as debenture holders.

The English House of Lords rejected that argument. Lord Macnaughten attacked it directly [14 A.C. 546]:

> The ordinary shareholders say that the preference shareholders are entitled to a return of their capital, with 5 per cent interest up to the day of payment, and to nothing more. That is treating them as if they were debenture-holders, liable to be paid off at a moment's notice ... But they are not debenture-holders at all. For some reason or other the company invited them to come in as shareholders, and they must be treated as having all the rights of shareholders, except so far as they renounced those rights on their admission to the company. There was an express bargain made as to their rights in respect of profits arising from the business of the company. But there was no bargain — no provision of any sort — affecting their rights as shareholders in the capital of the company.

Do you agree? This straightforward approach didn't last long. In *Will v. United Lankat Plantations Co.*, [1914] A.C. 11 (Eng. H.L.), a company was set up with the power to create various classes of shares "on such terms and conditions, and ... with such preference or priority as regards dividends or in the distribution of assets, or as to voting or otherwise over other shares of any class ... as the company in general meeting may direct". The articles of association originally specified only one class of shares, which were referred to by the judges as "ordinary shares" though the articles set out in the reports did not label this original issue of shares in any way. Eventually, the articles were amended to authorize the issue of a second class of shares. The amending resolution stipulated that:

> the new shares be called preference shares and that the holders thereof be entitled to a cumulative preferential dividend at the rate of ten per cent per annum on the amount for the time being paid up on such shares; and that such preference shares rank, both as regards capital and dividend, in priority to the other shares.

A dispute arose when the company proposed to pay a substantial extra dividend. The trial judge issued a declaration

> that the preference shares were entitled to rank for dividend *pari passu* with the ordinary shares as against any profits of the company available for distribution as dividend after providing for a cumulative dividend of 10 per cent on the preference shares and a dividend of 10 per cent on the ordinary shares [see [1914] A.C. 14].

The English House of Lords this time came to a quite different conclusion! Viscount Haldane L.C. began sensibly (at 15):

[t]he point in dispute is one of construction, and construction must always depend on the terms of the particular instrument; it is only to a limited extent that other cases decided upon different documents afford any guidance ... .

However, he then proceeded to draw some remarkable conclusions from the documents before him (at 16-18).

Your Lordships will observe that the second resolution [the amendment set out above establishing the "preference" shares] gave the authority to make the bargain and defined the terms which the bargain was to contain. A shareholder comes to the company and says "I wish to contract with you for a share in your capital and so become a shareholder". He advances his money and the terms are contained in the bargain that is made between him and the company on the issue of the share to him, and that bargain is that he is to receive a cumulative preferential dividend at the rate of 10 per cent on the amount paid up on his share and that his preference share is to rank both as regards capital and dividend in priority to other shares.

My Lords, I should have thought that if we were dealing with an ordinary case of two individuals coming together, and if a document were produced saying "You are to have a cumulative preferential dividend of 10 per cent," or whatever might be the equivalent in the circumstances of the bargain, it would be naturally concluded that that was the whole of the bargain between the parties on that point. You do not look outside a document of this kind in order to see what the bargain is; you look for it as contained within the four corners of the document. And, although it is quite true that in article 115 the phrase is "Subject to any priorities that may be given upon the issue of any new shares, the profits of the company available for distribution (having regard to the provisions hereinbefore contained as to a reserve fund) shall be distributed as dividend among the members in accordance with the amounts paid on the shares held by them respectively," the real question is whether the documents have been silent as to the terms of distribution. If I am right the resolution was passed under the powers contained in article 43, and that defined the whole terms of the bargain between the shareholders and the company; and there is no room for saying that the general provisions of article 115 operate in a fashion in which they can only operate if the matter is not covered by express provision.

My Lords, I think that Farwell L.J. called attention to what is really a cardinal consideration in this matter. Shares are not issued in the abstract and priorities then attached to them; the issue of shares and the attachment of priorities proceed *uno flatu*; and when you turn to the terms on which the shares are issued you expect to find all the rights as regards dividends specified in the terms of the issue. And when you do find these things prescribed it certainly appears to me unnatural to go beyond them, and to look to the general provisions of an article which is only to apply if nothing different is said. Moreover I think that when you find — as you do find here — the word "dividend" used in the way in which the expression is used in the resolution and defined to be "a cumulative preferential dividend" you have something so definitely pointed to as to suggest that it contains the whole of what the shareholder is to look to from the company. And I think that is borne out by the concluding words of the resolution of July 13, 1891, to which I have just referred, namely, that the preference shares are to rank "both as regards capital and dividend in priority to the other shares." That is appropriate when the provision is for a cumulative preferential dividend at a fixed amount such as I have stated. It is not a natural expression if the rights are to be such as the appellant has asked us to infer.

My Lords, this case, as I have said, is a case of importance, and if I thought that by taking time I could have come to any other conclusion than the one at which I have arrived, I would have asked your Lordships to postpone the delivery of judgment. But my own mind is quite clear upon the subject.

What, if any, evidence did Haldane L.C. hear on the meaning of the terms used? If, prior to reading the above comments, you had been told "you are to have a cumulative preferential dividend of 10 per cent" would your reaction be:

(i)   "Oh swell";

(ii) "Let me see the specific terms and I'll consult my lawyer"; or

(iii) "Naturally I conclude that that is the whole of the bargain between us on that point"?

Somehow, over the years, the term "ordinary share" declined in favour and "common share" became the usual term. But both terms were essentially jargon; neither had any set meaning except as it was defined in any particular corporate constitution. Similarly, the term "preference share" (or "preferred share") acquired a judicially enhanced mystique despite its lack of specific meaning. The result was chaos, as is ever the case when the powerful speak in tongues.

The impact of the English judges' terminology and predisposition was felt in Canada as early as 1931 when Wegenast, in his influential book *Canadian Companies* (Burroughs & Co. Ltd., 1931) noted (p. 473):

> [p]referred stock ... may or may not be entitled to participate ... in further profits or dividends after their preferred dividends have been paid. Prima facie preferred stock is non-participating, but it is a matter of interpretation of the instrument establishing the preference.

This curious state of affairs seems accurately summed up in the following observation of Evershed M.R., in *In re the Isle of Thanet Electricity Supply Co.*, [1950] 1 Ch. 161 (Eng. C.A.) at 175.

> I think, for myself, that during the sixty years which have passed since *Birch v. Cropper* (1889), 14 App. Cas. 525, was before the House of Lords the view of the courts may have undergone some change in regard to the relative rights of preference and ordinary shareholders, and to the disadvantage of the preference shareholders, whose position has, in that interval of time, become somewhat more approximated to the role which Sir Horace Davey attempted to assign to them, but which Lord Macnaughten rejected in *Birch v. Cropper* (1889), 14 App. Cas. 525, namely, that of debenture holders.

In the same case Wynn-Parry J. made the following statement, at [1950] Ch. 161. It has come to be regarded by many as the standard rule for interpreting "preference" shareholders' rights.

> First, that in construing an article which deals with rights to share in profits, that is, dividend rights, and rights to share in the company's property in a liquidation, the same principle is applicable; and, second, that the principle is that, where the article sets out the rights attached to a class of shares to participate in profits while the company is a going concern, or to share in the property of the company in a liquidation, prima facie, the rights so set out are in each case exhaustive.

A couple of things seem perfectly clear after all this. One is that the rights in a particular area, dividends for example, are the same for all classes if the corporate constitution does not differentiate among them in that area. It is equally clear that if the corporate constitution explicitly and exhaustively sets out the rights of any particular class, that explicit and exhaustive statement of rights will be applied. Thus, no problems of interpretation should arise where the corporate constitution establishes "Class A shares with unrestricted dividend rights" and "Class B shares with the right to $5.00 in dividends each year before any dividends are paid on the Class A shares and to no further participation in dividend distributions whatever". What is less clear, and likely to invite litigation, is any clause which sacrifices clarity for brevity by leaving such matters unspecified.

What would be the outcome in the following case? A C.B.C.A. corporation has two classes of shares, Class A and Class B. So far as dividends are concerned, the articles state:

Class A shares are fully participating as to dividends.

Class B shares are entitled to be paid annual $5 dividends in priority to Class A.

Each class has 100 shares outstanding and the corporation wishes to distribute $10,000 by way of dividend. Do the Class B shareholders get $500 or $5,000?

The general theories advanced under this heading will apply whenever a corporate capital structure is divided into classes. What follows is a brief survey of four of the most common areas of class differentiation: voting, dividends, redemption, and participation on dissolution. This is followed by a note on issuing shares in series.

(b) Voting Rights

Several aspects of shareholders' voting rights have already been covered, in Chapters 7 and 8. It remains to explore the basic rules and re-emphasize some key points.

It has been traditional throughout the development of corporate law to entitle some or all shareholders to vote and to set out in the statute or corporate constitution the matters on which their votes will be determinative. The tradition is maintained under Canadian corporate law statutes: see *e.g.*, C.B.C.A., s. 24, in which subs. (3) says that all shareholders have equal voting rights if there is only one class and subs. (4) requires that at least one class carry a vote in all circumstances. The combined effect of ss. 6(1)(c)(i), 24(4) and 140(1) is that corporate designers who want to create a class of non-voting shares must be explicit on this point in the articles. Similarly, any limitations to the effect that voting rights are restricted to certain circumstances, or not applicable in others, are unlikely to be enforceable unless clearly set out in the corporate constitution.

Assume a corporate constitution clearly sets out that Class A shares carry one vote in all circumstances and Class B shares carry ten votes when held by Mr. X and one vote when held by anyone but Mr. X. Are the requirements under C.B.C.A., s. 24 met? Compare A.B.C.A., s. 26. Do historical corporate principles have any impact? See *Bowater Canadian Ltd. v. RL Crain Inc.*, [1987] O.J. No. 1157, 62 O.R. (2d) 752 (C.A.).

Assume a corporation that has 12 million shares, all of one class, has a provision in its constitution which clearly says that "no person shall be entitled to vote more than 1000 shares of the Defendant notwithstanding the number of shares actually held by that person". Does this arrangement contravene C.B.C.A.,

s. 24(3)? Is the limitation permitted under s. 24(4)? Is it necessary to refer to s. 140? This fact scenario was examined in *Jacobsen v. United Canso Oil & Gas Ltd.*, [1980] A.J. No. 513, 11 B.L.R. 313 (Q.B.)? Would this be permitted in an English-model corporation? See *Jacobsen v. United Canso Oil & Gas Ltd.*, [1980] N.S.J. No. 482, 12 B.L.R. 113 (S.C.).

The issue on non-voting shares is currently controversial among those involved in public securities regulation and stock exchanges. Some suggest that non-voting shares are yet another device for entrenching managements in large corporations. These observers suggest that laws, or stock exchange regulations, should not permit public trading in non-voting shares. What do you think is the reason, and do you agree with their conclusions?

Two other controversial issues in the area of voting rights are the concept of "ratification" and the rather vaguely developed notion that a shareholder's vote must sometimes be cast "in the best interests of the corporation", whatever that means. Both these issues were fully explored earlier in this book. On reflection, having now seen how the reformed Canadian statutes have re-designed the whole power balance between majority rule and minority protection, do you agree that these issues are red herrings?

Non-voting shares are given a statutory right to vote on certain issues. These are usually described as "fundamental changes" in the corporate constitution or the business activities. These circumstances are exhaustively listed in the statutes: see *e.g.*, C.B.C.A., ss. 176(1) and (3), 183(3), 189(6); M.C.A., S.B.C.A., A.B.C.A., ss. 176(1), 183(3), 189(3); O.B.C.A., ss. 170(1) and (3), 176(3), 184(6).

NOTE

Having the right to vote and being able to exercise that right may be two quite different things. Part XIII of the C.B.C.A., "Proxies", details the procedure for proxy voting. Any shareholder has the right to appoint a "proxy" to vote as agent at a shareholders' meeting (s. 148(1)). In addition, under the C.B.C.A., management of any corporation with more than 15 shareholders must send a proxy form (containing certain information with respect to the corporation's operations and the matters to be voted on) to all shareholders prior to the meeting. Parallel proxy voting requirements exist under provincial securities laws for corporations that have publicly traded shares.

CANADIAN EXPRESS LTD. v. BLAIR

(1989), 46 B.L.R. 92 (Ont. H.C.)

Holland J.: — This application succeeds with respect to the relief sought in paras. 87(a), (b) and (c) of the applicant's factum. An order shall issue declaring Price, not Blair, as a duly elected director of Enfield and naming Price to be the eleventh director of Enfield. All actions of the board of Enfield since July 20, 1989 are confirmed with the same force and effect as if the board had been fully constituted throughout, and the Enfield corporate records are to be amended accordingly. The issue of costs of these proceedings, at the request of all counsel, is reserved to be dealt with after counsel have made submissions thereon.

Reasons

This application, brought under s. 107 of the Ontario *Business Corporations Act, 1982*, S.O. 1982, c. 4, as amended, is, in essence, an appeal from the decisions of the Chairman, Blair, made at the shareholders' meeting of July 20, 1989 for the election of the directors of Enfield. While the section grants broad discretionary powers to the Court, it is only necessary in the disposition of this application to consider the true construction to be given to the proxies filed by Canadian Express and by Ravelston, the intention of the shareholders granting these proxies and the conduct of Blair immediately before and at the July 20 shareholder's meeting, including the reason given by Blair for disallowing votes cast under the disputed proxies for Price and counting these votes for the management slate. By this, Blair declared himself to have been elected, and that Price received no votes.

While many issues were raised during the argument, I did not consider them to be important in the ultimate resolution of the significant issues raised here. It is acceptable that Walt had completed one ballot for the total number of shares which he represented as proxyholder at the meeting. As well, it was argued here that there was some error in the authority granted by the scrutineers as to the number of shares which Walt and Boultbee were entitled to vote. However, no such dispute existed at the meeting and the tally of votes, when compiled, recognized the total number of votes cast pursuant to each of the disputed proxies.

I am satisfied that the true construction of the disputed proxies is that they conferred general discretion on Walt and Boultbee. These forms of proxy, before completion, could be said to be management forms. They were effectively converted to unsolicited shareholder proxies once the names of the proposed management proxyholders were deleted and the names of the shareholder designees were inserted. At that point, Note 3 on the back of the document ceased to apply as Note 3 was a condition of the management proxy contract only. Note 3 was central to the respondents' position.

In coming to this conclusion, I have accepted the evidence of Professor Crete, recognized by both sides as a leading authority in this country on proxies, which evidence dealt with the policies underlying the proxy solicitation process and particularly the importance of enabling shareholders to freely exercise their voting rights in accordance with their intentions. I have also accepted the evidence of King, DaCosta and Norris as establishing a generally accepted industry practice and, particularly, their evidence that shareholder designees who hold blank proxies as here submitted are recognized as having full discretion to vote as they see fit, just as the shareholders in person at the meeting could vote. I note as well that L. Keitch, one of the scrutineers provided by Montreal Trust for the meeting, in examination before trial, was of the same view. To that extent, this evidence was not convincingly or directly contradicted by either Summers or Stevens.

In considering the evidence on industry practice, I have rejected the respondents' submission that the evidence was being adduced to establish a legal usage, and that it failed to meet the requisite test of notoriety. The disputed proxies must be construed in light of surrounding circumstances and, where possible in a manner consistent with business common sense: *Prenn v. Simmonds*, [1971] 1 W.L.R. 1381, [1971] 3 All E.R. 237 (H.L.); *Antaios Cia Naviera S.A. v. Salen Rederierna A.B. (the Antaios)*, [1984] 3 All E.R. 229 (H.L.). To inquire into industry practice for the purpose of gaining assistance in properly construing a document is far different from receiving evidence as to a notorious trade usage for the purpose of implying a term into a contract: *Lac Minerals v. International Corona Resources Ltd.*, a judgment of the Supreme Court of Canada, released August 11, 1989 [now reported [1989] 2 S.C.R. 574, 69 O.R. (2d) 287, 44 B.L.R.

1, 35 E.T.R. 1, 6 R.P.R. (2d) 1, 61 D.L.R. (4th) 14, 101 N.R. 239, 36 O.A.C. 57, 26 C.P.R. (3d) 97].

With respect to the construction of the proxies, I find that *Re Langley's Ltd.*, [1938] O.R. 123, [1938] 3 D.L.R. 230(C.A.) is distinguishable on several grounds. It is, however, sufficient to note that, in that case, the disputed proxies were not completed in favour of a shareholder designee, but remained company proxies. The Note 3 equivalent, therefore, was considered in a different context.

As I am not disposed to go behind the scrutineer's attendance record as to the actual number of shares involved, I accept that ... the proxyholders intended to, and *did*, cast their votes for Price and not for Blair. It was conceded that, in the event that the ballots cast for Price were to be counted as validly cast, Price, not Blair, was the winner.

Section 160 of the Regulation made under the *Securities Act*, R.R.O. 1980, Reg. 910, as amended, must be read in its statutory context, including para. 35 of s. 139 of the *Securities Act*, R.S.O. 1980, c. 466, as amended, and therefore must be interpreted as governing only solicited proxies.

In any event, I find that Blair failed to meet the quasi-judicial standard of conduct demanded of a chairman: *Re Bomac Batten Ltd. and Pozhke* (1983), 43 O.R. (2d) 344, 23 B.L.R. 273, 1 D.L.R. (4th) 435 (*sub nom. Re Bomac Batten Ltd.*) B.C. Corps. L.G. 78,229 (H.C.). Based on the evidence as to the completion and filing of the disputed proxies and the events leading up to the July 20 meeting, which included the meeting on July 19 attended by Blair, the scrutineers and counsel for Enfield, the exchange at the directors' meeting on July 20 in the morning and the nomination of Price from the floor, it can be reasonably inferred that Blair was alerted to the fact that the election of the directors would be contentious and that he was likely to be in a position of conflict. It took approximately 1 1/2 hours after the balloting until Blair reconvened the meeting to announce the results of the balloting. At that time, reading from a statement prepared by his legal advisors, stated that Price had received no votes and that he, Blair, had been elected. This, *I am satisfied*, was in accordance with the plan conceived by Blair to protect his personal interests.

From the tally, it was clear that all the votes cast by Walt and Boultbee for Price had, by reason of the chairman's decision, been counted as votes resulting in his own election. He did not permit discussion at the meeting as to this decision. At the very least, he had an obligation to allow those affected by his ruling on the disputed ballots an opportunity to be heard. He chose to act as Judge in his own cause and it is properly inferred from the evidence that he had determined to act in this way, at least from the time of the July 19 meeting and until the announcement of the voting results. In view of Blair's conduct alone and quite apart from the true construction of the proxies, his ruling cannot stand.

It was Blair's decision and not that of the scrutineers to determine the ballots in this way. It is no excuse for Blair to say that in doing so he was relying upon legal advice. It was his responsibility to conduct himself quasi-judicially throughout the proceedings.

Counsel have undertaken that their clients will take no steps to undermine the holding of a further shareholders' meeting scheduled for October 31, 1989, which is to be presided over by an independent chairman and with independent scrutineers, for the purpose of electing a full slate of directors to the board of Enfield.

Order accordingly.

(c) Dividend Rights

Why do corporations pay dividends? They are under no legal obligation to do so.

R. v. McCLURG

[1990] S.C.J. No. 134, [1990] 3 S.C.R. 1020

[The facts of this case are set out above, at p. 567.]

Dickson C.J.C.: — I begin the analysis with a statement of the obvious. The decision to declare a dividend lies within the discretion of the directors of a company, subject to any restrictions which have been included in the Articles of Incorporation. This principle has long been accepted at common law and was explicitly recognized by Lord Davey, speaking for the Judicial Committee of the Privy Council, in *Burland v. Earle*, [1902] A.C. 83 at p. 95, wherein the principle was described in terms of the "internal management" of the company:

> Their Lordships are not aware of any principle which compels a joint stock company while a going concern to divide the whole of its profit amongst its shareholders. Whether the whole or any part should be divided, or what portion should be divided and what portion retained, are entirely questions of internal management which the shareholders must decide for themselves, and the Court has no jurisdiction to control or review their decision, or to say what is a "fair" or "reasonable" sum to retain undivided, or what reserve fund may be "properly" required.

With the advent of statutory regulation of corporations, the authority to pay dividends, recognized at common law as part of the internal management of the company, has been given statutory recognition. In the case at bar, the governing legislation is the Saskatchewan *Business Corporations Act* (hereafter "*S.B.C.A.*"). In my view, it cannot be disputed that the power to pay dividends is an integral component of the broad grant of managerial power for directors found in s. 97(1) of the Act, cited earlier. I take it, both from an observation of the workings of corporations, and from other provisions in the statute that the section embraces the common law power of directors. The power to declare dividends is expressly limited in the Act, in much the same way as it was at common law. For example, s. 40 of the *S.B.C.A.*, also cited earlier, prohibits the declaration of a dividend if there exist reasonable grounds to believe that to do so would leave the corporation unable to pay its debt, (s. 40(*a*)); or, if the payment of a dividend would render the realizable value of the assets of the corporation less than the aggregate of its liabilities and stated capital of all classes of shares (s. 40(*b*)). Although these restrictions are not brought into play by the declarations of dividends in issue in this appeal, the presence of those limitations in the Act suggests that the power to declare dividends is statutorily limited only by restrictions expressly stated.

Of course, the power to declare dividends is further qualified by the fact that the law has for many years recognized that the general managerial power which rests in the directors of a company is fiduciary in nature. The declaration of dividends, which is subsumed within that power, therefore is limited legally in that it must be exercised in good faith and in the best interests of the company. As Professor Bruce Welling recognized in his treatise *Corporate Law in Canada* (1984), at p. 614, this limitation exists when any disbursement is made by the directors of a company:

The directors' general managerial power is a fiduciary one, owed to the corporation. It must always be exercised in what the directors from time to time think is likely to serve the best interests of the corporation. It has been consistently urged throughout this book that "the corporation", as referred to in that context, means the legal and economic entity, not some vague aggregation of the shareholders' wants. This means that dividends should be seen as basically what they seem to be on a narrow, legalistic view: corporate gifts ... giving it is permissible only to the extent that the directors think that it will serve the corporate entity's best interest, as they then perceive those interests, beyond this, the declaration of any dividend, like any other unauthorized gift of corporate property, is a breach of directors' duty.

In my opinion, this is an accurate statement of the legal basis of the declaration of a dividend in the context of the modern corporation.

NOTE

If corporations are assumed to have the power to pay dividends, a perhaps questionable although unchallenged assumption, the question becomes who determines whether they will be paid. This will depend, of course, on the particular statute and corporate constitution. Absent some uncommon wording, the answer flows from the nature of dividend payments: no obligation to pay or right to receive dividends exists until the corporation decides to pay them; the decision, even if not specifically reserved to the directors, is probably included in the directors' powers to manage corporate affairs. The following case sets out the traditional judicial view of dividend payments.

BOND v. BARROW HAEMATITE STEEL CO.

[1902] 1 Ch. 353 (Eng. Ch.)

[This was an action by two classes of shareholders to compel the corporation to pay them dividends. The articles of association were not unusual. The key articles read as follows.

> Art. 95. The directors may, with the sanction of the company in general meeting, declare a dividend to be paid to the members in proportion to their shares or stock.

> Art. 97. The directors may, before recommending any dividend, set aside out of the profits of the company such sum as they think proper as a reserved fund to meet contingencies. ...

"The 8 per cent preference shares" were created under an article which authorized the directors "to issue preference shares to the amount of £37,700 bearing interest at 8 per cent per annum in perpetuity". "The 6 per cent preference shares" were created as "preference shares ... entitling the holder to a fixed dividend of 6 per centum per annum. ..." When the writ was issued on 30 May 1901, no dividends had been paid on the "8 per cent" shares for two years and one had been paid on the "6 per cent" shares for four years. The corporation had made profits in 1899 and 1900.]

Farwell J.: — The contention of the plaintiffs in this action is that they are entitled by contract to be paid a preferential dividend out of the balance to the credit of the profit and loss account in each year, and that the company cannot appropriate any part of that balance to reserve or carry over one shilling until they have been paid in full.

...

It is argued that the provisions as to the declaration of a dividend do not apply to shares on which a fixed preferential dividend is payable. In my opinion this is not so. The necessity for the declaration of a dividend as a condition precedent to an action to recover is stated in general terms in *Lindley on Companies*, 5th ed., p. 437, and, where the reserve fund article applies, it is obvious that such a declaration is essential, for the shareholder has no right to any payment until the corporate body has determined that the money can properly be paid away. It is urged that this puts the preference shareholders at the mercy of the company, but the preference shareholders came in on these terms, and this argument does not carry much weight in an action such as this, where bona fides is conceded. The opposite conclusion might enable the preference shareholders to ruin the company, and would certainly lead to great inconvenience in enabling them to compel the payment out of the last penny without carrying forward any balance. Granted that it is a hardship to go without dividends for a time, this hardship presses more heavily on the ordinary shareholders who have to wait until the preference shareholders have received all arrears before they can get anything. It was urged that art. 9 providing for the reserve fund cannot apply to preference shares, because one of its objects is to equalize dividends; but I cannot see that the mention of one object which is not applicable is any reason for excluding those objects which are applicable, and which are really for the benefit of all the shareholders. On the articles as they stand, I have no doubt that the true construction is that which I have stated.

But it is contended that the special resolutions have created larger rights.

Stress has been laid on the word "interest"; but in my opinion that word has slipped in per incuriam, and should be read as "dividend," as indeed is done when this resolution is referred to in the special resolutions of 1876, to which shall have to refer presently. Interest is not an apt word to express the return to which a shareholder is entitled in respect of shares paid up in due course and not by way of advance. Interest is compensation for delay in payment and is not accurately applied to the share of profits of trading, although it may be used as an inaccurate mode of expressing the measure of the share of those profits. It is impossible, in my opinion, to give to the word, used as it is in this case, so pregnant a meaning as the plaintiffs desire, reading it as equivalent to an alteration of the articles and as creating a right overriding the valuable and possibly essential article providing for reserve funds.

[A similar conclusion was reached on the "6 per cent" shares.]

There is no doubt as to the opinion of the witnesses in this case, and, further, the opinion of the directors cannot be altogether disregarded. The Courts have, no doubt, in many cases, overruled directors who proposed to pay dividends, but I am not aware of any case in which the Court has compelled them to pay when they have expressed their opinion that the state of the accounts did not admit of any such payment. In a matter depending on evidence and expert opinion, it would be a very strong measure for the Court to override the directors in such a manner.

NOTES

The position in letters patent jurisdictions was the same. *DeVall v. Wainwright Gas Co. Ltd.*, [1932] 1 W.W.R. 281 (Alta. C.A.) involved a corporation incorporated by letters patent under the *Canada Corporations Act*, R.S.C. 1906, c. 79. Section 108(b) of the statute gave the directors power regarding "the declaration and payment of dividends". The letters patent authorized the issue of "common shares" and "preferred shares" and went on to say: "The said preferred shares shall confer the right to receive out of the profits of each year a preferential dividend for each year at the rate of eight per centum (8%) per annum on the capital for the time being paid up …". The plaintiff, who held shares of both classes, sought a declaration that the corporation had earned profits and was bound to pay dividends. The plaintiff lost. McGillivray J.A. said (p. 290):

> Before attempting to construe the language of the part of the letters patent quoted, I may state that, in my opinion, in the absence of any statutory prohibition or any restriction to be found in the letters patent or by-laws, the directors are always entitled in the honest exercise of their powers to set up a reserve before declaring a dividend.

He continued, at pp. 293-94:

> In this case the respondent has not attempted to establish that the dividends withheld by the company are not required to be held to serve the best interests of the corporation. On the other hand, the appellant has established that it is highly important to the company that moneys should be available for the drilling of new wells… In these circumstances I think that it cannot be said that the directors in setting up a reserve exercised their discretion unwisely. I might add that I do not think it within the province of the Court to interfere in any event in the absence of fraud or illegality.

Canadian statutes must now be interpreted against that background. Consider the C.B.C.A. provisions in the following sections:

> 15(1) A corporation has the capacity and, subject to this Act, the rights, powers and privileges of a natural person.

> 24(3) Where a corporation has only one class of shares, the rights of the holders thereof are equal in all respects and include the rights …

>> (*b*) to receive any dividend declared by the corporation …

> (4) The articles may provide for more than one class of shares and, if they so provide, …

>> (*b*) The rights set out in subsection (3) shall be attached to at least one class of shares but all such rights are not required to be attached to one class.

> 43(1) A corporation may pay a dividend by issuing fully paid shares of the corporation and, subject to section 42, a corporation may pay a dividend in money or property.

> 102(1) Subject to any unanimous shareholder agreement, the directors shall manage the business and affairs of a corporation.

> 134(1) The directors may … fix in advance a date as the record date for the purpose of determining shareholders

>> (*a*) entitled to receive payment of a dividend; …

> (2) If no record date is fixed …

>> (*b*) the record date … shall be at the close of business on the day on which the directors pass the resolution. …

Contrast B.C.B.C.A., s. 70(1) and N.S.C.A., s. 26(4)(*h*): both explicitly say that companies may pay dividends. Is there any advantage to giving a corporation that statutory power?

Is it possible under the C.B.C.A. to have articles that give the majority of the shareholders power to "declare" dividends?

If the articles are silent, and if the directors' general managerial power is assumed to include the power to cause the corporation to pay dividends, s. 122(1) would seem to apply. On what basis can each individual director conclude that paying dividends is in "the best interests of the corporation"?

Suppose the articles state that "Class J" shares are entitled to a $5 dividend every year and that the dividend must be paid "whether declared or not". The share register says that Jones holds 100 class J shares. No dividend is declared by the directors. Does the corporation owe Jones $500?

They say the traditional rule is that a dividend, once "declared" becomes a debt payable to the shareholder. This would establish a debtor-creditor relationship between the parties until the dividend is paid. As to discharging the debt, a C.B.C.A. corporation is protected so long as the dividend is paid to the registered shareholder as of the record date: see s. 51(1). There may be more complex solutions under statutes with no equivalent sections.

The rule that a shareholder is not entitled to any dividend payment until a dividend is "declared" is difficult to reconcile with the notion of cumulative dividends. This term came up under the previous heading and it usually described dividend rights that carried over from one year to the next if no dividend was paid. The concept is easiest to explain in terms of classes with dividend priorities over other classes. Assume a corporation with two classes of shares. Class A have "unlimited" dividend rights. Class B have dividend rights of "$5.00 *per* year in priority to Class A". If the Class B dividends were specified as "cumulative", and there were no dividends in one year, the cumulation rule precludes the payment of any Class A dividends in the next year until $10 ($5 for each of the two years) had been paid on the Class B shares. In effect, it is the degree of priority that accumulates, not the amount that will eventually be paid as a cumulative dividend.

Where dividends are not specified as being cumulative, an interpretation problem arises. An oft-cited rule derived from the English cases is that "preference" dividends are presumed to be cumulative unless the corporate constitution states otherwise. This, as was pointed out earlier, assumes that the term "preference share" had a clear definition in law, which it did not. In the example set out above, would the Class B dividend be cumulative if the articles were silent on the point? Would the same dividends be cumulative if the articles didn't have the clause the dividend must be paid "whether declared or not".

R. v. McCLURG

[1990] S.C.J. No. 134, [1990] 3 S.C.R. 1020

[The facts of this case are set out above.]

Dickson C.J.C.: — I find the appellant's arguments, as they relate to the validity of a discretionary dividend clause in terms of general corporate law and the requirements of the *S.B.C.A.*, to be equally unpersuasive. Counsel for the appellant placed considerable emphasis in his arguments upon the nature of a shareholder "right", arguing that for the purposes of the statute and common law, a right to a dividend comprises a right to a portion of the total dividend declared, calculated according to the terms set out in the share description if and when the directors decide to make a distribution of the profits of the company. The appellant argues that the insertion of a discretionary dividend clause in the Articles of Incorporation is insufficient to confer a "right" since no corresponding duty is imposed on the company to pay dividends on the class once a dividend has been declared. Implicitly, Desjardins J. accepted this argument when she referred to the ability of the directors to allocate dividends "at whim". The appellant argues that this unconstrained discretion cannot be considered a "right" which is conferred by the shares.

I disagree with this analysis. In my opinion, the fact that dividend rights are contingent upon the exercise of the discretion of the directors to allocate the declared dividend between classes of shares does not render entitlement to a dividend any less a "right". Rather, it is the entitlement to be considered for a dividend which is more properly characterized in those terms. I agree with the respondent that the Class B common shareholders of the company have an entitlement comparable to that of a fixed dividend-holder to receive a dividend if the company's directors declare one. As well, the appellant's argument that there is no corresponding duty on directors as regards the "right" of shareholders is, in my view, specious. The directors are bound by their fiduciary *duty* to act in good faith for the best interests of the company in the declaration and allocation of any dividend. That duty is in no way circumvented by the presence of a discretionary dividend clause. Finally, I think that it should be borne in mind that many shareholder rights may be qualified and contingent (voting rights, the right to transfer shares, preferential rights to dividends, participation rights); yet the mere fact that these rights are fettered does not render them anything less than shareholder rights.

In a similar vein, I do not agree that the absence of a mathematical formula for the allocation of declared dividends in the Articles of Incorporation of the company is dispositive of the issue of the discretionary dividend clause. As the decision to declare a dividends and the determination of the funds available for a dividend are already within the discretion of the directors, it seems to me that a discretionary dividend clause is not a significant departure or extension of that discretion: *DeVall v. Wainwright Gas Co.*, [1932] 2 D.L.R. 145 (Alta. C.A.). If shares are divided into separate classes, one of which contains a preferred entitlement to dividends declared by the company, the directors effectively have the discretion to allocate dividends only to that preferred class. Thus, the respondent could have achieved precisely the same allocation of dividends by structuring the company so that Wilma McClurg and Suzanne Ellis constituted a preferred class of shareholders with first entitlement to dividends. Such a structure would be unimpeachable in terms of the principles of corporate law.

Furthermore, it cannot reasonably be maintained that the presence of a discretionary dividend clause inherently leads to a conflict of the duty of directors and their self-interest any more than does the discretion to declare a dividend in any company. Consequently, I cannot agree with those authors who take the position that the allocation of dividends by the directors, pursuant to a discretionary dividend clause, inherently cannot be exercised in the best interests of the company: see *Martel and Martel, La compagnie au Québec; Les aspects juridiques*, vol. I, at pp. 18-10 through 18-14C; Boivin, "Le Droit aux dividendes et le dividende 'discrétionnaire'" (1987), 47 R. du B. 73. I agree with the argument of the respondent that it is unrealistic to think that directors will not pay heed to the identity of shareholders and the contribution to the company of those shareholders any time a decision is made as to whether dividends of any sort should be declared. The fact that directors may consider the identity of shareholders does not necessarily render the declaration invalid on the basis of a conflict of duty and self-interest. For example, the discretion could be exercised for the purpose of rewarding a group of employees who comprise a preferred class of shareholders and who have been encouraged to invest in a company. Surely the fact that the identity of the holders of that class of shares was considered in the decision to declare a dividend and in the determination of the quantum of the dividend would not render the decision invalid. To reiterate, the limitation on the decision is purely a fiduciary one and the entitlement of a shareholder is "to share in the profits of the company when these are declared as dividends in respect of the shares of the class of which his share forms apart": Bryden, "The Law of Dividends", in Jacob S. Ziegel, ed., *Studies in Canadian Company Law*, at p. 270. That right is in no way undermined by the presence of a discretionary dividend clause.

In other words, the clause simply divides conceptually into two components — declaration and allocation — what has been, traditionally, one decision. In substance, though, the discretion which lies in the hands of the directors has always included both, subject to the provisions of the Articles of Incorporation. In this regard, the only other limitation upon the directors of which I am aware is that "if a dividend is declared by [a] corporation ... there must be some shares entitled to receive the dividend": *Welling, supra*, at pp. 588-89. The principle has been given statutory recognition in s. 24(4)(*b*) of the S.B.C.A. In my view, this rule is not defeated by the presence of the discretionary dividend clause because the identity of the class eligible for a dividend simply remains unknown until the allocation takes place. This conceptual division into declaration and allocation is not substantively different from any derogation from the presumption of equality in the payment of dividends. Consequently, for this Court to find that the use of a discretionary dividend clause on these facts was an invalid exercise of the discretion of the directors would be to defeat the substance of what was achieved solely on the basis of its form.

...

In conclusion, then, I find nothing untoward in the use of the discretionary dividend clause in the allocation of corporate dividends. There is nothing in the S.B.C.A. or at common law that prohibits this dividend allocation technique.

[**Wilson, La Forest** and **L'Heureux-Dubé JJ.** dissented.]

NOTES

The *dicta* in *McClurg* (at 1054 S.C.R.) confused many analysts because it said that a distinction could be made between "the exercise of a discretionary power to distribute dividends when the non-arm's length shareholder has made no contribution to the company ... and those cases in which a legitimate contribution has been made". In *Neuman v. M.N.R.*, [1998] S.C.J. No. 37, [1998] 1 S.C.R. 770 at paras. 60-64, Iacobucci J. clarified the law. He said that, even in the case of a closely held corporation, dividends are gifts and any contribution (of lack thereof) made to the corporation's success is a red herring. The only requisite consideration is that the shares that entitled the shareholder to receive the dividend were fully paid upon issue by the corporation.

The final issue concerning dividends is the description of circumstances in which no dividends may be paid. Under earlier statutory regimes this was covered under the code word "solvency". A rather complex and contradictory set of rules was developed on this subject. These rules are set out at great length in Bryden, "The Law of Dividends", found in Ziegel, *Canadian Company Law*, Vol. I (Toronto: Butterworths, 1967). These judicially developed rules have grown increasingly irrelevant in Canada as more jurisdictions adopt the C.B.C.A. approach found in these sections:

42. A corporation shall not declare or pay a dividend if there are reasonable grounds for believing that

(*a*) the corporation is, or would after the payment be, unable to pay its liabilities as they become due; or

(*b*) the realizable value of the corporation's assets would thereby be less than the aggregate of its liabilities and stated capital of all classes.

118(2) Directors of a corporation who vote for or consent to a resolution authorizing any of the following are jointly and severally ... liable to restore to the corporation any amounts so distributed or paid and not otherwise recovered by the corporation:

(*c*) a payment of a dividend contrary to section 42; ...

Note that s. 42 sets out two alternative tests. In the paragraph (*b*) test, with what degree of certainty would each of the three values be known at any time? Does this make the test difficult to apply? Now re-read the opening words of the section. Is the test quite different from what you initially thought it was? If not, state what facts you think would be required to prove a violation of s. 42(*b*).

Recall the general duty of care directors owe to the corporation under s. 122(1). Can you think of a situation where s. 42 is met but s. 122(1) is breached?

Recall your answer to "is it possible under the C.B.C.A. to have articles which give the majority of the shareholders power to 'declare' dividends?" Considering s. 118(2) and s. 45(1), is it wise policy for the C.B.C.A. to allow articles to give shareholders the ability to declare a dividend? Are there other subsections in s. 118 that address this problem?

(d) Redemption Rights

One technique used to market shares is to make them redeemable, usually within a specified time at a set price. In trade jargon, "redeemable" usually suggests that resale to the corporation is at the corporation's option, "retractable" suggests the option is the shareholder's, while "convertible" suggests that the shares, or bonds for that matter, may be transferred to the corporation in exchange for shares of another class. As with all jargon, the label cannot be relied on and the terms of the specific share issues must be consulted. Note the C.B.C.A. definition in s. 2(1).

If there is only one class of shares, can they be made redeemable?

What happens to "redeemed" shares? Judges traditionally said that a corporation could not hold its own shares: see *Trevor v. Whitworth* (1887), 12 App. Cas. 409 (Eng. H.L.). Why? What is the distinction between P. Inc. holding shares of Q. Inc. and Q. Inc. holding its own shares?

In the United States, the practice is for the corporation to hold redeemed shares "in treasury" for future re-issuance: hence the term "treasury shares". The C.B.C.A. and related statutes have generally made it difficult for a corporation to hold its own shares: see *e.g.*, C.B.C.A., ss. 30-34. Note particularly C.B.C.A., s. 34.

> 34(1) Subject to subsection (2) and to its articles, a corporation may purchase or otherwise acquire shares issued by it.
>
> (2) A corporation shall not make any payment to purchase or otherwise acquire shares issued by it if there are reasonable grounds for believing that
>
> (a) the corporation is, or would after the payment be, unable to pay its liabilities as they become due; or
>
> (b) the realizable value of the corporation's assets would after the payment be less than the aggregate of its liabilities and stated capital of all classes.

Most statutes require cancellation of redeemed share by sections like C.B.C.A., s. 36.

> 36(1) Notwithstanding subsection 34(2) or 35(3), but subject to subsection (2) and to its articles, a corporation may purchase or redeem any redeemable shares issued by it at prices not exceeding the redemption price thereof stated in the articles or calculated according to a formula stated in the articles.
>
> (2) A corporation shall not make any payment to purchase or redeem any redeemable shares issued by it if there are reasonable grounds for believing that
>
> (a) the corporation is, or would after the payment be, unable to pay its liabilities as they become due; or
>
> (b) the realizable value of the corporation's assets would after the payment be less than the aggregate of
>
> (i) its liabilities, and
>
> (ii) the amount that would be required to pay the holders of shares that have a right to be paid, on a redemption or in a liquidation, rateably with or prior to the holders of the shares to be purchased or redeemed.

When does s. 34 apply? When does s. 36 apply? Which has a more stringent test? The facts in *Nelson v. Rentown Enterprises Inc.*, [1992] A.J. No. 917, 7 B.L.R. (2d) 319 (Q.B.) illustrate the difference. The corporation was solvent at the time of the agreement to purchase the shares but insolvent when the shares were to be purchased. The court was asked when s. 34 applied: at the time the corporation agreed to purchase its own shares or at the agreed upon time of purchase; s. 36 wasn't considered.

When would a court refer to s. 36(2)? Would this provision primarily be used as a sword or a shield? See *Royal Bank v. Central Capital Corp.*, [1996] O.J. No. 359, 26 B.L.R. (2d) 88 (C.A.) and *684733 Alberta Ltd. v. Money's Mushrooms Ltd.*, [2003] B.C.J. No. 2475, 40 B.L.R. (3d) 270 (S.C.).

Remedies are also provided in case of an improper redemption:

> 118(2) Directors of a corporation who vote for or consent to a resolution authorizing any of the following are jointly and severally ... liable to restore to the corporation any amounts to distributed or paid and not otherwise recovered by the corporation:

(*a*) a purchase, redemption or other acquisition of shares contrary to section 34, 35 or 36; ...

This section allows s. 36(2) to be used as a sword.

(e) Participation on Dissolution

When corporations commit suicide the corporate constitution's final role is to act as a will, to distribute the corporation's property among its heirs once debts are paid. This is enshrined in C.B.C.A., s. 211(7):

(7) After issue of a certificate of intent to dissolve, the corporation shall ...

(*d*) after giving the notice required under paragraphs (*a*) and (*b*) and adequately providing for the payment or discharge of all its obligations, distribute its remaining property, either in money or in kind, among its shareholders according to their respective rights.

The shareholders' rights are, of course, set out in the corporate constitution as required by s. 24 of the C.B.C.A.:

24(3) Where a corporation has only one class of shares, the rights of the holders thereof are equal in all respects and include the rights ...

(*c*) to receive the remaining property of the corporation on dissolution.

(4) The articles may provide for more than one class of shares and if they so provide,

(*a*) the rights, privileges, restrictions and conditions attaching to the shares of each class shall be set out therein; and

(*b*) the right set out in subsection (3) shall be attached to at least one class of shares but all such rights are not required to be attached to one class.

The corporate constitution, like a will, can be either perfectly clear or vague as to who gets what. Where problems of interpretation arise, an interesting legal battle will likely be fought, based on two lines of reasoning of which the following two cases are the outstanding examples. Analyze to what extent the label "preference" shares affected the reasoning process.

INTERNATIONAL POWER CO. v. McMASTER UNIVERSITY AND MONTREAL TRUST CO.

[1946] S.C.R. 178, [1946] 2 D.L.R. 81, 27 C.B.R. 75

[The facts are set out earlier at p. 569 under the heading "Defining the Classes".]

Taschereau J.: — [I]n order to determine the true meaning and the legal effects of these preference and priority clauses, one must necessarily look at the creating clauses in order to find if there is or not an express or implied condition, which limits or adds to the ordinary rights of the shareholders. It is a mere question of construction of these clauses, which form part of the contract under which the shareholders hold their shares.

I entirely agree with the Court of Appeal that the provisions of the by-laws of the company do not expressly or by necessary implication, limit the rights of the holders of preference shares. They do create priorities, but these priorities are in addition to the existing rights, and are not a declaration of all the rights of this class of shareholders. These priorities consist in a right for the preference shareholders to be repaid of the invested capital at par, together with any dividends accrued and remaining unpaid, but do not affect their right to share in the profits. For the sharing in the profits which is the fundamental right of all shareholders, is a matter entirely different from the priority given to him.

In the present case the priority to repayment

> on any division of the assets of the company to the extent of its repayment in full at par together with any dividends thereon then accrued due and remaining unpaid ...

is a definition of the existing priority as to the sharing of assets, and cannot, I believe, be construed as a bar or a limitation to any further rights.

For these reasons, I come to the conclusion that the preference shareholders have a priority to be repaid at par, and that they are further entitled to share *pari passu* in the distribution of the assets of the company, with the common shareholders, after the latter have received payment at par.

The main appeal should therefore be dismissed.

IN RE THE ISLE OF THANET ELECTRICITY SUPPLY CO.

[1950] 1 Ch. 161 (Eng. C.A.)

Wynn-Parry J. (reviewed the facts and earlier authorities): — Having regard to the view which I take of the opinions of the majority of the House of Lords in the Scottish Insurance Corporation case it appears to me to be unnecessary to embark upon any review of the earlier authorities, all of which were considered in that case; and in my judgment the effect of the authorities as now in force is to establish the two principles for which Mr. Christie contended: first, that, in construing an article which deals with rights to share in profits, that is, dividend rights, and rights to share in the company's property in a liquidation, the same principle is applicable; and second, that that principle is that, where the article sets out the rights attached to a class of shares to participate in profits while the company is a going concern or to share in the property of the company in liquidation, prima facie, the rights so set out are exhaustive.

With those considerations in mind I turn back to art. 3 of the articles of association in this case. As regards the rights as to profits, the whole of the distributable profits are expressly dealt with. They are to be applied first in paying to the holders of the preference stock "a fixed cumulative preferential dividend at the rate of 6 per cent, per annum on the amounts for the time being paid up or credited as paid up thereon respectively in priority to the ordinary shares," and, secondly, in paying a non-cumulative dividend at the rate of 6 per cent a year calculated on the same basis to the holders of the ordinary shares; and the balance is then distributable between the two classes of shares *pari passu*. Nothing could be more plainly exhaustive than that language. Then as regards the rights in a winding-up, the holders of the preference shares are stated to be entitled to certain payments in priority to the ordinary shares. Those payments are, first of all, repayment of the capital paid up on the preference stock, and, second, any arrears of dividend whether earned or not. The question, then, is: is there anything to suggest that the language regarding the rights of the holders of the preference stock in a winding-up is not exhaustive? I can find nothing. The onus now, as I have said, is in my view on the holders of the preference stock to show that the provision is not exhaustive, and in my view they have failed to discharge that onus.

...

It was urged on us that in construing art. 3 we must have regard to the whole of the articles of association and to the surrounding circumstances. I accept that. It was urged on us that a relevant circumstance was that in this case the voting control rests in the hands of the preference stock; and from that it was sought to be argued that it is really impossible to conclude that the holders of the preference stock, the controllers of the company, should have contemplated that in a liquidation they would get no more than any arrears of dividend on their preference stock, together with the capital on it. I am unable to accept that argument. It involves speculation and therefore uncertainty. The bargain as regards rights of participation, whether in profits or assets, appears to me to be contained in art. 3. Nor can I find any context affecting the construction of that article to be derived from any other article in the articles of association.

Compare those reasons for judgment with the following excerpt from the Alberta Court of Appeal decision below *Westfair Foods Ltd. v. Watt*, [1997] A.J. No. 321, 79 D.L.R. (4th) 48, [1991] 4 W.W.R. 695 at 705 (C.A.):

Kerans J.A.: — [Background summarized. Westfair had class A shares with a right to a $2 per share preferred dividend per annum, non-cumulative, and the right to share equally, share for share, with the common shares, in the distribution of the assets of the corporation on liquidation, dissolution, or winding-up. The common shares had the rights to which all common shares are usually entitled and were held solely by Kelly Douglas. The corporation had adopted a dividend policy where all the previous year's earnings were paid as a dividend to Kelly Douglas and further expansion financed through loans from Kelly Douglas to Westfair. Justice Kerans noted that, typically, companies pay no more then 30 per cent of retained earnings as dividends and fund expansion through use of the remainder.

The trial court awarded the Class A shareholder a remedy under C.B.C.A., s. 241 on the basis that they were unfairly prejudiced. The unfair prejudice resulted from a decrease in the capital of Westfair caused by the large dividends. This decrease in capital affected the Class A shareholders because there would be less capital to distribute if Westfair were liquidated or wound up.]

My disagreement with the learned Chief Justice, while of great significance, can be simply stated. In the passage quoted, he said that the right to share in distribution of the assets on liquidation created an expectation by class A shareholders that they would share in the "success or failure" of the company. In my view, any expectation that they would share in the future *success* (as opposed to failure) of the company in a measure beyond the dividend promised them was not a reasonable expectation.

Conflict always exists between common shareholders as a class and the classification of those shareholders who have a right to claim a dividend in priority to the common shareholders. (I avoid the term "preferred" shares because the respondents seem to put some significance on the label.) The latter chose to purchase shares with a special form of access to earnings, the first claim on the dividend pool. Their advantage is to receive a dividend in lean years when there is nothing for the common shareholders. The price they pay is to give up any claim to share in larger profits in the years of plenty. From this point of view, undue emphasis on break-up rights gives the second class an indirect second dip in the dividend pool and an arguably unfair advantage over the common shareholders.

No doubt the bargain they struck gave them access to assets on liquidation. The traditional view of the right to share assets on liquidation is that it is a shield, not a sword. Its purpose is to offer some assurance of capital return if the company fails, not some assurance of profit if the company prospers. This is because liquidation for a business corporation ordinarily signifies failure, not success. ... Were this corporation created for a specific venture with the expectation of immediate liquidation, I might be of a different view. But this corporation by all accounts was created to carry on an ongoing business and prosper, and it was on that basis the shareholders invested. And it has survived and prospered just as the investors hoped. There never was nor is any expectation that it liquidate with a large surplus of assets over liabilities.

I accept that the propositions I have just made contain factual assumptions. In another social setting, people might see the right to share on break-up in a different light. But I am persuaded that I can fairly say, in the words of the House of Lords in the *United Lankat* case earlier cited, that the class A shareholders, in 1946, would have been "surprised, if gratified" to be told they had the expectation for which their counsel now contend.

In any event, nothing in the material before us persuades me that any act or omission of the company or its common shareholders, in 1946 or afterward, could reasonably be said to have encouraged a contrary hope.

I grant that the shareholders have a chance at a profit if for some reason this prosperous company liquidates. Their claim, and the root of the finding of the learned Chief Justice, is that they are to be assured, by a permanent policy of large retained earnings, of a boon if that chance ever realizes. In my view, that is an unwarranted extension of the claim to break-up assets that exists for precisely the opposite reason, that being to offer some chance of recovery of investment if the company fails.

Mr. Crawford, one of co-counsel for the shareholders, contended that a voluntary liquidation might be expected. Except for the shareholders, this company is now a wholly owned subsidiary of another company. I suppose in such an event one might hope for some sort of corporate reorganization. It has not happened, and no doubt will not happen while the class A shares remain outside the grasp of the holding corporation. I see nothing sinister in that. They have no duty to reorganize. It is contrary to their interests to do so because the class A shares would benefit from that at the expense of the holding corporation, and so they will not do it. So where is the reasonable expectation of a voluntary liquidation? It is, with respect, wishful thinking.

NOTES AND QUESTIONS

Do you agree with the reasoning of the trial judge or the Court of Appeal?

The liability to pay undeclared "cumulative" dividends on dissolution seems unclear. They do not appear to be corporate debts and it is not easy to formulate a general theory as to why they must be paid. Absent clear wording in the corporate constitution, what result is suggested by the C.B.C.A.?

(f) Series within a Class

Another way to complicate the corporate capital structure is to subdivide classes into series of shares. This permits groups of shareholders who have a common differentiation from other classes to be differentiated from one another on some other basis. Given your understanding of the term "class", could this be done without statutory authorization?

The C.B.C.A. permits series designations on the following terms contained in these sections:

> 2(1) In this Act,
>
> ... "series", in relation to shares, means a division of a class of shares;
>
> 27(1) The articles may authorize, subject to any limitations set out in them, the issue of any class of shares in one or more series and may ...
>
> > (*b*) authorize the directors to fix the number of shares in, and determine the designation, rights, privileges, restrictions and conditions attaching to the shares of, each series.
>
> > ...
>
> (3) No rights, privileges, restrictions or conditions attached to a series of shares authorized under this section shall confer upon a series a priority in respect of dividends or return of capital over any other series of shares of the same class that are then outstanding.

Note the degree of power these provisions give the directors to manipulate the corporate capital structure on an ongoing basis. Compare the lesser flexibility given to directors in issuing classes of shares. In what types of corporations would the creation of series of shares be advantageous, and to whom?

Subsections 27(2), (4), (5) and (6) impose further, detailed restrictions on the creation and use of series of shares. Review how the class veto provisions in Chapter 9 apply to series of shares: see, *e.g.*, C.B.C.A., ss. 173 and 176. Is a series veto triggered by directors' action under s. 27? What other circumstances would trigger a series veto? Do the losers in a series vote have an appraisal remedy?

5. Share Transfers

(a) The Basic Rules

Shares are property. Like most property, shares have long been assumed to be transferable unless specifically created otherwise. In *Weston's Case* (1868), 4 Ch. App. 20 (Eng. C.A.), Page Wood L.J. explained the then prevalent judicial view (p. 27):

> I have always understood that many persons enter these companies for the very reason that they are not like ordinary partnerships, but that they are partnerships from which members can retire at once, and free themselves from responsibility at any time they please by going into the market and disposing of and transferring their shares without the consent of the directors, or shareholders, or anybody ...

Shares are therefore usually transferable. Restrictions on transfer are covered under the next heading.

A share may be transferred by shareholder 1, who held the property at T1, to shareholder 2, who will hold the property at a subsequent time, T2. Just when between T1 and T2 the property transfer was effected is an interesting technical question. However, one of the significant benefits under the reformed Canadian statutes is that it is hard to imagine a situation in which one would care what the answer to the question was.

The reason is simple. Holding property gives one certain advantages over the rest of the world. These advantages take the form of legal obligations imposed on others. For practical purposes, someone who wants to become a shareholder by being a transferee of shares held by someone else will be interested in the obligations owed her by four types of other persons:

   (i)   the transferor;
   (ii) the corporation;
   (iii) subsequent transferees;
   (iv) anyone else in the world.

The fourth category is easiest to deal with. It is hard to conceive of a situation in which someone not in category (i), (ii), or (iii) will have directly interfered with a corporate share. Anyone who did might generate a property action, but unless a realistic problem exists, no solution is needed. Can you create such a problem? Clue: do not confuse shares (the property in question) with share certificates (the pieces of paper which evidence the existence of the shares and serve as transfer instruments).

The other three categories are more complex. However, the trend in Canada is to regulate the inter-personal obligations among these types of people through specific, statutory rules. Most transfers under the reformed Canadian statutes are probably fully regulated by these rules. Their function is to prescribe the types of transactions and formalities that a transferee must go through to become registered as a shareholder, which is, of course, the object of the game. The rules, if followed, will enable the transferee to achieve the status of shareholder. As to precisely when the property passes from transferor to transferee, only tax collectors are likely to care and, for tax purposes, the *Income Tax Act* can prescribe such rules. The corporate law question seems moot.

(b) Restricting Transfer

Share transfers may be restricted by the corporate constitution. There are two quite separate sub-issues involved in share transfer restrictions. The first is whether transfer is restricted at all. The second is whether an attempted transfer is caught by the restriction or outside its scope and thus effective.

Shares will be transferable unless made otherwise by the statute or corporate constitution. General incorporation statutes permit share transfers unless explicitly restricted by the corporate constitution: see, *e.g.*, C.B.C.A., s. 6(1)(*d*).

Several Canadian statutes have gone further and made all shares transferable unless the share certificate has a notation indicating "warning — transfer restrictions in effect", or something along those lines. See, *e.g.*, C.B.C.A., s. 49(8):

> (8) No restriction ... described in the following paragraphs is effective against a transferee of a security ... who has no actual knowledge of the restriction ... unless it or a reference to it is noted conspicuously on the security certificate:
>
> (*a*) a restriction on its transfer other than a constraint under section 174;

Compare M.C.A., S.B.C.A., s. 45(8); A.B.C.A., s. 48(8); O.B.C.A., s. 56(3).

In the past, share certificates were the primary instruments of transfer under these statutes. Anyone seeking registration as a shareholder by virtue of an alleged transfer from someone else who did not produce a certificate issued by the corporation to a previous transferor would thus likely be met by the corporate response "so you say". Practically speaking, every transferee seeking registration would have possession of a certificate and if a transfer restriction were noted conspicuously on that certificate, the transferee would be unlikely to succeed in becoming registered.

Share certificates may be a thing of the past, a relic of a "more leisurely era" (according to the New Zealand Law Commission). "Book-entry" or "uncertificated" securities are now the norm. An uncertificated security is one "not evidenced by a security certificate, the issue and any transfer of which is registered or recorded in records maintained for that purpose by or on behalf of the issuer" (O.B.C.A., s. 53(1)). Such records may now be computer generated, the evidence of who holds a share being reduced to just a few highly mobile electrons. In some European jurisdictions, only uncertificated securities are permitted for certain corporate entities. Article 8 of the United States *Uniform Commercial Code*, broadened by amendment to cover uncertificated securities in 1977, was an attempt to alleviate the "paper crunch" prompted by a rapid increase in volume of public trading in securities. It provides a regime for the transfer and the granting of securities interests in uncertificated securities, a modified version of which appears in the O.B.C.A. in part VI, "Investment Securities" in ss. 53(1) and 85(8)(*d*).

Where share transfer restrictions are in effect, the next issue becomes whether an attempted transfer has violated them. Most corporate constitutions will be explicit and clear. In such cases the answer is obvious, subject to arguments that could come up concerning the types of discriminatory provisions inhibited by human rights charters of various descriptions. However, one relatively common share transfer restriction warrants exposition. Share transfers are sometimes made subject to the approval of the board of directors. This type of restriction has been judicially reviewed in the past.

EDMONTON COUNTRY CLUB LTD. v. CASE

(1974), 44 D.L.R. (3d) 554 (S.C.C.)

[The articles of association said that "no shares in the company ... shall be transferred to any person without the consent of a majority of the Directors, who may refuse such consent ... in their unfettered discretion". The plaintiff claimed there was no such share transfer restriction.]

Dickson J.: — The question which must be answered is whether a company incorporated under the *Companies Act* of Alberta can give its directors such a power.

In *Canada National Fire Ins. Co. v. Hutchings* (1918), 39 D.L.R. 401... , the Privy Council held that a company incorporated by letters patent under the *Companies Act*, R.S.C. 1906, c.79, could not validly make a by-law giving the directors an unrestricted power to disapprove transfers, but Sir Walter Phillimore said in the course of the judgment, at p. 404:

There is ... for the present purposes no analogy between companies in the United Kingdom which are formed by contract ... and Canadian companies which are formed under the *Canadian Companies Act*, either by letters patent or by special Act.

and at p. 407, referring to the power of veto given the directors, he said:

> There are decided cases in the English courts which shew that such a power may be lawfully reserved on the occasion of the constitution of the company; and a sufficient number of such cases to shew that the power has been found convenient in use.

We find ... in Gower's *Modern Company Law*, 3rd ed. (1969), p. 392:

> These restrictions may take any form, but in practice they normally either give the existing members a right of pre-emption or first refusal, or confer a discretion on the directors to refuse to pass transfers.

I have concluded that art. 20A is not ultra vires the company. ... The power to refuse to consent to a transfer of shares was reserved to the directors upon incorporation of the company, by the contract contained in the articles, and is not something now sought to be imposed upon unwilling shareholders.

Laskin J. (dissenting on the point): I am of the opinion that the article should be struck out. The difference between us is whether this arbitrary power, not related to any standard for the exercise of an unfettered discretion, should be controlled only in the context of a particular case requiring its exercise (as [the majority] would have it), or whether it should be struck out simply because it is on its face utterly arbitrary (as I would have it).

...

It is said however, and certainly there is case law to support [the majority's] view that in memorandum and articles of association companies ... the contractual aspect of the memorandum and articles supports the power to include drastic restrictions on transfer. This has been also referred to as part of the general law governing such companies.

There are two comments that I would make on this submission. The first is that, although originating in contract, shares ... are a species of property and as such are entitled to the advantage of alienability free from unreasonable restrictions unless there is statutory warrant otherwise. The second comment concerns the so-called contractual aspect of memorandum of association companies. The memorandum of association is but a method of incorporation, under which its contractual aspect is submerged in a statutory regime subjecting the company to public regulation. I cannot, in such circumstances, and in the absence of express power in the memorandum, subscribe to the proposition that there is a contractual warrant for adopting an article of association which confers an unlimited discretion to refuse a transfer of shares.

My brother Dickson has referred to the judgment of the Judicial Committee in *Canada National Fire Ins. Co. v. Hutchings* ... where a distinction was drawn, in respect of the matter under consideration, between a letters patent company or one incorporated under a special Act and a memorandum of association company. I cannot be persuaded that the form of incorporation can have such a remarkable effect upon the permissible scope of a power to regulate or prescribe conditions for the transfer in a public company.

NOTES

With whom do you agree, and why? What do you think would be the result under the C.B.C.A. or any of the other reformed Canadian statutes?

The greatest significance of share transfer restrictions was in establishing a company as a "private company". Earlier corporate legislation in Canada, following older English legislation, had adopted the distinction between the "private" and the "public" company based on the number of shareholders, the existence of share transfer restrictions and a prohibition on the public offering of the company's securities. The C.B.C.A. eliminated the distinction: it contains no definition of private corporation. Under the C.B.C.A., functional distinctions are made on the basis of whether a corporation has made a "distribution to the public".

(c) The Corporation as Transferee

Is a corporation required to have any shareholders?

QUESTION 1: Corporation A is incorporated in your choice of Canadian jurisdictions. No shares are ever issued. Does this cause any insurmountable problems? What happens?

QUESTION 2: Corporation B is incorporated in your choice of Canadian jurisdictions. The corporate constitution authorizes two classes of shares. X shares are to have "unrestricted" rights. Y shares are to be redeemable, but their rights are otherwise unrestricted. Only Y shares are issued. One shareholders' meeting is held, after which all the Y shares are redeemed. Does this cause any insurmountable problems? What happens?

QUESTION 3: Corporation C is incorporated in your choice of Canadian jurisdictions. The corporate constitution authorizes only one class of shares. One hundred shares are issued, one to each of one hundred different persons. Three years later, all one hundred offer to transfer their shares to the corporation at twice the issue price. The directors vote to accept the offer, pay the agreed amount to each of the one hundred shareholders and receive possession of the share certificates, which are put in a desk drawer. Does this cause any insurmountable problems? What happens?

Check carefully all relevant sections of the applicable statute in answering these questions.

(d) Effecting Transfers: The Role of Share Certificates in Canada

Share certificates are "instruments". Any dictionary will confirm what this means: an instrument is a thing that is used to accomplish a particular purpose. The primary purpose of share certificates in Canada is to facilitate share transfers.

The share transfer system in most Canadian jurisdictions is conceptually simple. A shareholder who is the owner of a share certificate with his name on it endorses (affixes his signature, perhaps witnessed) the back of the certificate. He transfers possession of the certificate to his transferee. The transferee shows the endorsed certificate to the corporation that issued the shares (and the share certificate) and demands that the corporation enter her name on the share register. The corporation deletes the name of the transferor from the register, inserts the transferee's name, issues a new certificate in the transferee's name and destroys the old certificate. At some point during that process, the share was transferred.

The presence of stockbrokers as intermediaries need not obscure the simplicity of the above description. It is they who perform some of the delivery functions, but they do so as agents for the transferor and transferee. Their actions are, legally, those of the principals involved.

If all goes smoothly during the above process, there will be no legal problems. If however, one of the parties in the corporation — registered shareholder — transferee triangle fails to perform some detailed requirement, the system will temporarily break down. This will raise some legal issue. Solving the problem may be difficult in some Canadian jurisdictions, as some statutes direct limited attention to share transfers: common law rules of property and contracts may have to be researched.

The reformed Canadian jurisdictions have all enacted statutory codes to govern share transfers. It is important to note the extent to which both corporate and securities law simultaneously apply to the modern corporation. It is a common mistake to view a particular transaction as involving either corporate or securities law when, in reality, both apply. Corporate law is generally facilitative: it permits incorporators to incorporate a corporation that suits their needs. Securities law is restrictive: it restrains corporations from acting in ways that are perceived to be against the public interest. Securities law is a separate area of study from company law and highly regulated. It is best examined in other texts and courses.

The Uniform Law Conference of Canada (<http://www.ulcc.ca>) has promulgated a new Uniform Securities Transfer Act, modelled on Revised Article 8 of the U.S. Uniform Commercial Code. This statute will provide a legislative framework for the existing system of "indirect holding" of securities. In this system, the registered shareholder is usually an intermediary institution; the investor, who thinks he or she has acquired shares, never appears in the shareholder register but only in the records of the intermediary. The enactment of the Uniform Act is pending in Alberta, and other provinces are likely to follow suit in short order. What are the constitutional implications for C.B.C.A. corporations and other federal corporations?

INDEX